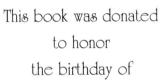

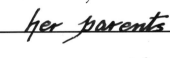

MOTHERS OF ACHIEVEMENT
IN
AMERICAN HISTORY
1776 - 1976

COMPILED BY

The American Mothers Committee, Inc.
Bi-Centennial Project   1974 - 1976

CHARLES E. TUTTLE COMPANY
RUTLAND, VERMONT

REPRESENTATIVES

For Continental Europe:
BOXERBOOKS, INC., Zurich

For the British Isles:
PRENTICE-HALL INTERNATIONAL, INC., London

For Canada:
HURTIG PUBLISHERS, Edmonton

For Australasia:
BOOK WISE (AUSTRALIA) PTY., LTD.
104 Sussex Street, Sydney

Published by The Charles E. Tuttle Company, Inc.
of Rutland, Vermont

Library of Congress Catalog Card No.: 76-461
International Standard Book No.: 0-8048-1201-2

First Printing 1976

Printed in USA

Table of Contents

FOREWORD

If ever there was evidence of the democratic process at work it has been in the assembling of data contained in this book. Over 500 people have given hours of time to research and in documenting information after conferences with librarians, genealogists and visits to Historical Societies and sites often involving hundreds of miles of travel—a labor of love. The work of the assigned State Chairmen and their Committees has been noteworthy. The hazard will be that there is such a wealth of material being uncovered that to choose a limited number of stories offers a severe challenge to the State juries. It is gratifying to report that 100% of those invited to serve on this assignment agreed. Their letters of appreciation are heartwarming— "I would not have missed this project—it has been exacting but exciting and rewarding. Little did we anticipate the drama that has unfolded."

Readers will be inspired by the hundreds of individual stories ranging from life begun in sod huts to the White House. They are heroic tales of mothers whose dreams and arduous efforts changed the tide of human events—involving education, politics, religion and the arts. It was Victor Hugo who is quoted as having said—"The most potent thing in the world is an idea whose time has come." Women have been both the dreamers and doers as these tales reveal. And the power of their ideas and their implementations have changed history.

Going back a few years when our nation became increasingly conscious of the significance of the Bicentennial—the American Mothers Committee Inc. pondered as to what it could contribute to this historic milestone year. A previous Conference theme was recalled that served as a springboard to their deliberations—"Our Heritage—the Past is Prologue." Like the god "Janus" they looked to the past to serve as inspiration for the future. During the last 35 years this small but distinguished organization, of which Sara Delano Roosevelt was first President, over 2000 Mothers of distinction have been elected by jury as mothers of their respective states, some achieving the honor of "National Mother of the Year." It was and is obvious that thousands more have been meritorious. This being true, what of the millions living since 1776 that have been unknown or unsung with but a few becoming famous. This realization inspired the current search for their stories that form a saga in American life. Certainly mothers played a strategic role over the centuries—in education, industry, religion, government and the professions. Mothers have given us some of our greatest leaders and in many cases themselves sparked necessary reforms and/or new concepts. Since earliest times women's role as mothers has demonstrated the fulfillment of the equal rights concept. The perusal of these stories is adequate proof.

Robert O'Brien, Senior Editor of the Readers Digest remarked at a dinner in 1974, "I think it's fitting and wonderful that you, the American Mothers, have chosen to key your Bi-Centennial contribution to the ideals and goals of the national heritage '76 program—to examine the vital role women have played in the history of your states, to collate your findings, and to publish them as a Bicentennial gift to the people of this country. It will be a truly monumental and priceless contribution. In our hearts, we all know that the home is the cornerstone of American democracy. It's well that you, who have done so much to keep our homes and families together and who have made these homes a haven of love and inspiration—it's well that you remind us of this heritage of American womanhood, and that the nation recognize and remember it, and engrave it upon the tablets of her history—I cannot imagine a more worthy and inspiring program, and I congratulate you and your officers— and wish you well."

Alistair Cooke, noted author and commentator, is quoted in the Wichita Beacon syndicated by the Knight Newspaper Service as saying before an audience of the Writers Guild of America, West, "And mostly I think—especially when I'm out in the middle of the country—of those numberless wives who, 100 years ago on the prairie, made a home against the Arctic winds and rancid summers and drunken husbands and disease and the steady winds and the ghastly loneliness. And I would like to think that we would write, without sentimentality, about these women, most of whom were deaf, and a great many of whom went mad from the wind . . . Now that is a subject mighty enough to warrant Bicentennial favor— the story of the women, past and present, who held the home front together while their husbands, or lovers, or brothers, or fathers went galloping off in pursuit of adventure, or fortune or glory, or whatever it was that motivated them, as to the prairies, it was the men who had the better part of the experience. And it is still that way in what we consider the age of enlightment. "Written history is grossly unfair simply because it does not record the monumental contribution of women to the winning of the Republic."

At first it was planned to publish the information in booklet form in each state, D.C. and Puerto Rico. But as time passed it became evident that many dramatic stories over-lapped borders and regions. Only a book could capture the tapestry of color and design of the varied lives of many of these storybook mothers—some brilliant—some monotone—some famous—some obscure—some who pioneered by oxcart across the plains—and some who jet-plane in our ultra modern society.

It must be recognized that most of the stories have been written by non-professionals, some in genealogical form—some in lyric style. Rarely has such a volume been participated in by hundreds of individuals, without benefit of rewriting of any kind. For the advice and participation of numerous persons representing Historical and Genealogical institutions we are deeply grateful and most of all to the hundreds of writers who have been contributors. Furthermore, we regret that complete uniformity could not be sustained because of lack of basic information. We express appreciation to Mr. John Warner, Administrator, ARBA—that we are accepted officially in the National Bicentennial Service Alliance. He writes "We welcome the humanitarian tradition and voluntary commitment of the American Mothers Committee, Inc. in our common effort to ensure a national commemoration touching the hearts and minds of all of our citizens."

In a stirring statement by John D. Rockefeller, 3rd, Chairman of the National Committee for the Bicentennial Era, he says in a Bicentennial Declaration "It strikes a dynamic note that a second American Revolution is called for—a revolution not of violence but of fulfillment of fresh purposes and of new directions."

So, in basic support of these inspired words, the American Mothers Committee Inc. gears itself to building a future society that can meet the high intelligence of today's youth and inspire them with a spiritual resolve to be worthy of their past inheritance, to be aware of God's grace and continuing blessing on our land bought through the faith and prayers of our forefathers. Let the clarion call of the New Hampshire farmer, General John Stark of Revolutionary fame, echo down the years ahead to the Triennial 2076 A.D., "Live Free or Die."

> Honorary Chairman—Mrs. Mamie Doud Eisenhower
> Mrs. Dorothy Lewis, National Chairman
> Mrs. Russell S. Marriott, Vice Chairman
> Mrs. Lynmar Brock, Consultant
> Mrs. Mary Filser Lohr, President Ex-Officio

April 1976—Waldorf Astoria, New York, N.Y.—The American Mothers Committee, Inc.

PREFACE

* * *

Ever since its inception the American Revolution Bicentennial Administration has stressed the importance of three themes in the observance of our nation's 200th birthday. These are Heritage, Festival, and Horizon. By Heritage is meant a re-examination of our national history and values; by Festival is implied the revival of the spirit of hospitality and cultural exchange which have made our country eminent; by Horizon is included the idea of priorities for the future. Thousands of communities and organizations are now at work on this three-fold objective.

I think that the present volume encompasses all three of these purposes. Certainly this listing of 500 notable mothers in the last two hundred years of American history is a worthy contribution to understanding our heritage as a nation. The pattern of their lives has cut across all boundaries of geography, class, race, and worldly circumstance, and has helped to make the United States into the great cultural entity that it is today. From their motivation we can glimpse what these women of achievement deemed worthy of the highest priority in living,—a challenge for us to do likewise in the days to come. That is why it has been given official recognition as a Bicentennial project by the Board of the A.R.B.A.

As a life-long student of history I can assure the readers of this remarkable volume that there is much to learn from its pages. Hundreds of devoted people from coast to coast have worked on it for several years. Mrs. Dorothy M. Lewis, who first conceived the idea of the book, and who has pushed it to completion, is deserving of our individual and collective thanks. The people who saw it through the complex processes of assembling the material, printing, and distributing it have done well.

From its narratives we can see again countless illustrations of what the poet, William Ross Wallace, once wrote:

> "They say that man is mighty,
> He governs land and sea,
> He wields a mighty scepter
> O'er lesser powers that be.
> But a mightier power and stronger
> Man from his throne has hurled,
> For the hand that rocks the cradle
> Is the hand that rules the world."
> —**J. Duane Squires, Vice Chairman**

**American Revolution
Bicentennial Administration**

This Volume is Dedicated
to
MRS. MAMIE DOUD EISENHOWER
One of America's Great Mothers, who was the Adored Wife
of
Dwight David Eisenhower
Military—Five Star General of the Army
Education—President—Columbia University, New York
Government—President of the United States
and who
With grace, dignity and charm set an example for the
world to admire in each of these exacting roles—and
later in semi-retirement at the farm, Gettysburg, Pennsylvania

MAMIE DOUD EISENHOWER
GREAT LADY OF THE LAND

In 1953, Mamie Doud Eisenhower stood next to her famous husband, Dwight D. Eisenhower, as he was inaugurated President of the United States.

Mamie Geneva Doud was born in Boone, Iowa on November 14, 1896. In 1906, she moved to Denver, Colorado with her parents, John Sheldon Doud and Elivera Mathilda Doud, and sisters Eleanor, Eda Mae (Buster) and Frances (Mike).

Mamie Doud's father retired at thirty-six from the John S. Doud and Company, a livestock commission business and devoted himself to handling his investments.

The Douds were a happy, united, religious family.

In 1915, Mamie, at her winter home in Texas, met Dwight D. Eisenhower, a second lieutenant just out of West Point. Eisenhower had always known a life of hard work and study. Mamie had always had security and luxury.

In July 1916, Mamie Doud and Lt. Eisenhower were married at 750 Lafayette Street, Denver, Colorado.

On September 23, 1917, Doud Dwight Eisenhower, "Icky" was born. He died in 1921. He was buried in Denver. August 8, 1922, a second son, John Sheldon Doud Eisenhower was born in Denver, Colorado. Like his father, he too graduated from West Point.

As an Army wife and mother-faithful Mamie—patiently marked time in Panama, and in the Phillipine Islands—and anxiously waited out the years of World War II. Charming, witty, Mamie readily accepted the responsibilities of Columbia University, Paris, and Washington, D. C. "I have lived in everything from shacks to castles", Mamie has often remarked.

By 1950 Dwight D. Eisenhower, a five star General, was appointed Supreme Commander of NATO forces. One year later Mamie's famous husband announced his candidacy for presidency and resigned from the Army.

Mamie Geneva Doud Eisenhower became First Lady of the Land and "First" in the hearts of all who came to know her.

Mamie Eisenhower returned to her "home" at 750 Lafayette Street in Denver, Colorado on many occasions.

In 1951, Mamie's father passed away.

In 1953, Mamie's Denver "home" became the Summer White House.

In 1957, Mamie Doud Eisenhower Park was dedicated in Denver, Colorado.

In 1958, Mamie's mother was named National Mother-in-Law of the year. She died in 1960.

In 1961, Mamie's home at 750 Lafayette Street, Denver, Colorado was sold. The furnishings were donated to the State Historical Society of Denver by Mamie and her sister, Frances Doud Moore.

In 1962, The Daughters of the American Revolution placed a historical plaque at 750 Lafayette Street, the girlhood home of Colorado's First Lady of the land, Mamie Geneva Doud Eisenhower.

After many years of travel and numerous headquarters and homes the famous Eisenhowers longed for a permanent home. So, with great joy they purchased "The Farm" in historic Gettysburg, Pennsylvania, overlooking the peaceful countryside, yet still near to our Nation's Capital. Here today, our beloved Mamie Doud Eisenhower entertains her friends and recalls glowing memories of public and private highlights of their distinguished life together.

Written by—Mrs. Jane Toth
Colorado Bi-centennial chairman
American Mothers Committee, Inc.

Alabama
1776-1976

Famous Mothers

Alabama

Nickname: The Cotton State

State Flower: Camellia

State Bird: Yellowhammer

Photos

1. "Gaineswood" Mansion, Demopolis
2. Oakleigh, A Southern Cottage
3. Governor's Mansion—Montgomery
4. Battleship Alabama—Mobile Bay
5. America's largest missile & Space exhibit, Huntsville
6. Ave Maria Grotto at St. Bernard
7. Bellingrath Home
8. Capitol Building

Committee Members

Chairman—Mrs. David W. Vess, Birmingham
Mrs. Edith Richardson, Jasper
Mrs. Tera Averett, Enterprise
Mrs. Sara R. Allen, Enterprise
Mrs. Mildred M. Son, Birmingham
Mrs. Frances C. Turner, Eastaboga
Mrs. Bruce B. Stewart, Fayette
Mrs. Lola L. Orr, Athens

Alabama

MARIE BANKHEAD OWEN
Born 1869

The magnificent ediface, which houses Alabama's worthwhile archives, is a worthy memorial to the life and work of one of the most remarkable women in the history of Alabama. Marie Bankhead Owen was a member of a most distinguished family—the Bankheads of Alabama. The father and one brother were senators in the U. S. Congress; another brother served in the House of Representatives, and a third one was a Congressional Medal of Honor winner. It has been said that they were equaled and surpassed in wisdom and public service by Mrs. Owen.

"Miss Marie" was the mother of two sons—Thomas McAdory Owen, Jr., and John Hollis, who died in infancy. Her husband was Thomas McAdory, Sr., a noted Birmingham lawyer. Discovering a valuable state document being used as a doorstop at the State Capitol building, Dr. Owen prepared a bill for the legislature which resulted in the establishment of the Archives and History Department in the state government. Dr. Owen was appointed director of the Department in 1901, the first of its kind in the Nation. With Mrs. Owen's assistance he began the monumental task of collecting and preserving priceless documents, records, curios and art objects. Upon his death in 1919, Mrs. Owen was appointed director, a post she held until her retirement in 1955.

History came to life in the mind and action of Mrs. Owen. She stirred the past and made it a part of the future. Her great interest was the preservation of Alabama history. Her leadership, driving force and persuasive power brought the Archives and History Department from cramped quarters in the basement of the Capitol to its present beautiful ediface on Washington Avenue—a building worthy of a great state and heroic people. It is the treasure house of the wisdom and courage of our ancestors and the hall of vision and inspiration of our posterity.

In 1920 Mrs. Owen completed Dr. Owen's History of Alabama, a work in four volumes. She

wrote several histories for Alabama's school children, as well as novels and plays. For five years she was on the staff of the Montgomery Advertiser, and was a contributing editor on the "Uncle Remus" magazine. She was one of few women writers officially given entree to the press galleries of both houses of Congress. She was a member of DAR, UDC, and American Legion Auxiliary, president of several civic clubs and farm organizations. She established a public library extension, providing a travelling library system which reached into small towns and rural communities. She made many literary and historical addresses, encouraging people to gather and preserve Alabama history.

A dynamic thinker, her sparkling vitality and eagerness for life, her untiring efforts, fortitude, great intelligence, wisdom and knowledge are only a few of the attributes possessed by this gracious Southern lady who shed the radiance of her extraordinary character on the lives of those around her, and gave to Alabama the fruit of her hands, brains and heart. An Alabama institution she is as much a part of the State as the Alabama River, the blue skies and the rugged mountains.

For her, as she lies wrapt in silence and peace, all hearts are full of love and praise and remembrance.

EMMA PAYNE FLOWERS
Ozark   Born 1892

Flowers, Emma Payne (Mrs. Grover), educator, Civil Defense Director-Co-ordinator, Ozark. Born in Ozark, Alabama, on January 29, 1892, she is the daughter of James Jackson and Minnie (Carroll) Payne. She is a graduate of Ozark City Schools, 1910; Troy State College, with a B.S. degree; Auburn University, M.S. degree in 1944; and had graduate work in Administration and Supervision at Columbia University, New York, New York; and special courses in Education. On June 11, 1912, she married Grover Flowers, oldest son of Mr. and Mrs. Edward Flowers of Ozark, Alabama. Before his death in 1955, he had served two terms as Mayor of Ozark. Mr. and Mrs. Flowers had two sons: Edward Erle of Ozark; and Ab Flowers of Fairfax Station, Va. Mrs. Flowers was engaged in elementary and secondary teaching and administration for thirty-seven years in Dale County Schools System. For twenty-five years, concurrently, she was employed as Ozark City Superintendent of Education, the first woman to hold that office in Alabama. She is now serving as Ozark-Dale County Civil Defense Director-Co-ordinator, a position she has held since 1960. Mrs. Flowers was first secretary of Alabama Civil Defense Association; member, National Civil Defense Association; and holds Administration Certification as Staff College Instructor for Civil Defense. She also holds Home Nursing Instructor's Certificate. Mrs. Flowers is a Life

Member of National Education Association; member of Alabama Education Association, former President of A.R.T. Al, 1961; member State and Area Superintendents Organization, State Health and Physical Teacher's Association for several terms; Chairman of local, State and National Education Committees. For four years, she served as a member of State Course of Study Committee, 1954-58; Chairman, South Alabama Study for Improvement and Accreditation of Elementary Schools, Southern Association of Cahaba Historical Commission by State Senator and State Representative, Alabama. Mrs. Flowers has published a book, "Ozark High School's March of Time", 1961 (Copyright) and "Short History of Alabama", 1974. She has written articles in the educational field for historical societies, and also has written poems. She is a member of Phi Kappa Phi, Honorary Education; Kappa Delta Phi; Delta Kappa Gamma, Honorary Women Teachers first President. She has received many honors from the schools in Ozark and Dale County. She was sponsor—Beta Sigma Phi Cultural and Social Sorority.

One of Ozark's elementary schools was named for her, The Emma P. Flowers School. She was Woman of the Year; 1953; "Outstanding Woman of the Year in 1954" and again in 1955; selected Alabama Mother of the Year 1965 and addressed the State Alabama Legislature, by invitation 1965; selected for the world's, "Who's Who of Women" 1975-76- Member of AAUW. Mrs. Flowers was featured in Auburn Alumnews; in 1955, and was named "Civil Defense Woman of the Year;" 1960-61 for Region III, Southeastern States of the United States. She is listed in "Who's Who" in American Education. For exceptional work in the March of Dimes campaigns, she received National and State Citations; and served as Dale County Women's Chairman of U. S. Savings Bonds Program and Educational work through Ozark and Dale County Schools. She was selected by GFWC as one of its First Ladies 1973.

Other memberships of Mrs. Flowers include: Dale County Historical Society; Daughters of the American Revolutions; Matron's Study Club, Charter Member, President for three terms; Ozark Woman's Guild, Ozark, organizer and honorary member; The Twentieth Century Club, Junior Club for Girls, organizer and counsellor; Advisory Board School of Nursing, Wallace State College, Napier Field, Alabama.

The Southern Star of Ozark, Alabama, published an article about Mrs. Flowers which reads in part, "Mrs. Flowers occupies a place in Ozark and Alabama that few women have ever achieved, a place unique in its way, because there are few feminine minds which have been clothed with the remarkable power of seeing things as they are; of grasping big situations and handling them in the way she does". A member of Ozark Baptist Church, Mrs. Flowers is a member of the Sunday School of which she has served as teacher, and is also a former choir member, pianist, and Y.W.A. Counsellor. With her busy life, she finds the time to enjoy sports, games, music, television shows, and travel.

In addition to her many achievements and the success of her Sons as college graduates and reaching heights in the business world–The Pilot Club of Ozark named Emma P. Flowers-Dale County Mother of the Year.

The Club had this to say to the State Mothers Committee–"Mrs. Flowers is charged with boundless energy and enthusiasm."

A New Orleans Business man had this to say of Mrs. Flowers; "It was you, Mrs. Flowers, who first kindled my interest, in the graphic arts, and that I now have my own printing and advertising firm, is due in a large measure to your early guidance. You have been a Mother to thousands of Alabama children. A dedication such as yours is rare and precious thing, and it is most fitting that it has been so appropriately recognized and rewarded."

CARRIE NEWTON WRIGHT
Fayette County   **Born 1893**

Carrie Newton Wright of Berry, Alabama, was born March 11, 1893 to Mr. and Mrs. Thomas Ezzard Newton in Fayette County, Alabama. While employed in her first teaching position, she met and married a handsome young physician, David Hudson Wright, an honor graduate from Vanderbilt University Medical School, who had established his office in Berry, Alabama.

During the depression years, the schools in Fayette County were forced to close due to lack of funds. They were unable to employ teachers and provide bus service to students. With the citizens joining together, school resumed but many farm parents were unable to provide transportation for their children to attend. Dr. and Mrs. Wright opened their home to house

numbers of these farm students, without reimbursement. Many of these students went on to great success, including a physician, business executive, two registered nurses and two school teachers.

The Wrights were blessed with a lovely daughter, Wimbreth Christine, who has achieved much success in art and music. She and her husband, William Grover Daniel reside in Tuscaloosa, Alabama. They have two children, Robert Edward, who has his PhD in cell Physiology and instructs at Murray State University in Kentucky. He was "Man of the Year in 1974; William Grover, II, has a Master's in Business Administration, a resident of Colorado and is a Captain in Medical Service Corporation. The Wright's son, William Thomas Wright, M.D., is a graduate of the University of Alabama Medical College and lives in Mobile, Alabama. He and his wife, the former Bivian Trussell of Crossville, Alabama, have four children, Jane, Ann, William Thomas, Jr. and David Hudson.

Mrs. Wright is a member of the Berry Methodist Church where she taught Sunday School for over fifty years. Following the death of her husband, she was elected to assume his position on the Official Board of the Church where she still serves. She served in the Medical Auxiliary, a former Vice President of the Southern Railway Surgeons Auxiliary, the Parent-Teachers Association and a Red Cross Volunteer. In 1955, she was chosen as one of "Alabama's Gracious Ladies". She is Regent of the Luxapallila Chapter of the Daughters of the American Revolution, the National Society of Colonial Dames XVII Century, and the Southern Dames of America.

Her hobbies include genealogy and is currently writing a history of the family. She studies china painting and has received awards for her creativity. Mrs. Wright is an avid traveller and photographer, and has visited every state in the United States and with one exception, every continent in our world.

Mrs. Wright's philosophy aptly describes this great Alabama Mother . . . "We have a past to honor and a future to mold".

MARY GEORGE JORDAN WAITE
Born 1918

Loving in abundance; living by enthusiasm; and lifting with dedication characterize Mary George Jordan Waite (Mrs. Dan, Jr.) since August 8, 1918. From pioneer Cherokee County families, her mother, Louise Smith Jordan, and her father, James Oleus Jordan (a soldier in France until her first birthday), gave Mary George a rich American heritage and set leadership examples.

Cherokee County High, Centre, Valedictorian, 1935; "Who's Who American Colleges", English and Sociology major, choir organist, tennis bug at Huntingdon College 1939; English teacher high school until she married Dan Waite, Jr. 1940 (University of Alabama graduate, engineer Southern Bell Telephone Co., presently church treasurer and civic leader, and her college roommate's brother!)

Betty (Dimple Elizabeth) born 1943 saw her South Pacific daddy soldier at one year. Betty, a University of Alabama cheerleader; a teacher; outstanding Jayceete; Outstanding Young Woman of America; clubwoman; Sunday School teacher; president First United Methodist Women; married Thomas S. Graves (Tommy), banker, in 1965. They have given Mary George and Dan Kim (8), Meg (5), Jake (3) for grandchildren.

Mary George's second daughter, Mary Diane, arrived in 1945 with a beautiful voice and a flair for design. Homemaker of tomorrow, student body president, cheerleader, one year college accomplishments were part of this 20 year leukemia victim.

Linda Gail, third daughter, born 1949 with a serious birth defect and lived three months. These sorrows tested Mary George and Dan's faith. This faith continues to grow as Mary George teaches the Pairs and Spares Methodist Sunday School class and serves as Chairman Council on Ministries. Chairman Board of Trustees Cherokee County High School 9 years (first woman); 1964 local and state BPW Woman of Achievement; 1965 Director Girls Nation; President Centre Chamber of Commerce (first woman); State President American Legion Auxiliary (1955); state President National Association Bankwomen (1961); state President Alabama Federation Women's Clubs (1968-70); state President Alabama Bankers Association (1971—first woman in U. S.); state Cancer Crusade Chairman 1973 (first woman); member State Banking Board 1969 (first woman); SME Chairman Choccolocco Council Boy Scouts 1975 (first woman); Honorary Doctor of Laws Huntington College 1973; Alabama Merit Mother 1964; Alumni Achievement Award Huntingdon 1972; Silver Fawn award 1974; Delta Kappa Gamma, and International Platform Association have combined with countless other activities in Mary George's life.

Currently Mary George holds directorships on Alabama Citizens for Transportation; Alabama Travel Council; Alabama Women's Hall of Fame; Alabama Law Center; Alabama Council on Humanities; Alabama 4-H Foundation; Alabama Cancer Association, and Peoples Telephone Company. She is Sequoyah District Chairman, Boy Scouts (first woman), Chairman International House Board Jacksonville State; Trustee National FFA Foundation (first woman); Director, American Bankers Association (first woman); Trustee Huntingdon College, Girls State Chairman; and Centre Bicentennial Finance Chairman.

Chairman of Board and President, Farmers and Merchants Bank, Centre, since January 1, 1957 when she left English classroom to succeed her daddy who died suddenly. She has seen her $5,000,000 bank reach $28,600,000. Listed in "Who's Who Among American Women"; "Who's Who in Finance"; she is a sought after speaker and an involved and dedicated American.

Loving, living, lifting every day is Mary George Jordan Waite.

DORIS ELLIOTT MAPLES

Born 1918

Mrs. William Mack Maples, the former Miss Doris Elliott before her marriage in 1936, was born on a farm in 1918 in Ardmore, Tenn. She was graduated from Athens High School, Athens, Ala., and attended Athens College for one year.

Mr. and Mrs. Maples moved to the Maples family farm—land which was a grant from President Andrew Jackson—after their marriage and the land has been farmed continuously by the Maples family. Mr. and Mrs. Maples are the seventh generation. They have five children, one son and four daughters. This is where they started a herd of registered Aberdeen Angus cattle for which the family is widely known.

Mrs. Maples has been active in her church, school and cultural, civic and political affairs through the years. She has served in every office in Limestone County Council of Home Demonstration Clubs and was twice president of the county council.

She was president of Limestone County Parents-Teachers Association Council from 1953-55 and elected vice president of District 8 PTA Council for two years.

While a member of Elkmont Methodist Church she was adviser for the Youth Fellowship and later joined Athens Presbyterian Church where she was elected to a two-year term as president of Athens United Presbyterian Women and was Youth adviser for Huntsville Presbytery.

She was instrumental in organizing Alabama Angus-cttcs and Alabama Cow-Belles and was president of the local Cow-Belle chapter. She was a member of American Angus Auxiliary and the Maples family was chosen Progressive Farmer Master Farm Family in 1963. Mrs. Maples was also featured in the Birmingham News series as one of Alabama's Gracious Ladies and received the Extension Service Leadership Award for Rural Improvement competition.

She was Limestone County chairman for "Hens for Henderson" during Bruce Henderson's campaign for Governor and chairman of Limestone County Women for Albert Brewer in his bid for Governor in 1969.

Mrs. Maples is a member of Three Arts Study Club, having recently served as president, area captain in the Cystic Fibrosis Fund drive, district chairman of Alabama Mothers' Committee, secretary of Limestone County Mental Health Association and a board member of the organization, chairman of "Operation Santa Claus" to collect gifts for Bryce and Partlow Mental Hospitals, member of Athens-Limestone Hospital Auxiliary while Mr. Maples was chairman of the hospital board, assisted with Mobile X-ray unit, Emphysema survey and other fund drives, and has been a substitute teacher in the county schools.

Through the years Mrs. Maples has assisted her husband with his cattle business as bookkeeper, hostess to untold number of visitors to the farm and attending state and national meetings. She was a member of Limestone

County Farm Bureau Board of Directors and directed the county's Maid of Cotton contest for two years.

Mrs. Maples says that she has engaged in these activities to help her husband, to aid her children and to grow and try to make a home, church and community a better place because she believes "service is the rent we pay for the space we occupy here on earth."

ANNIE ELSIE ZIMMERMAN GRAHAM

Born 1904

Annie Elsie Zimmerman, a devout Christian, member of United Methodist Church, Mother, Registered Nurse, Counsellor and Friend, was married to Ralph Emerson Graham, a teacher and later a Methodist minister of the Gospel, on December 24, 1927.

She was born March 13, 1904, near Florence, in Lauderdale County, Alabama, to Doctor Albert Sidney Zimmerman (M.D.) and his wife, the former Sydney Alice LeMay. She attended school in Florence, entering nurses' training at Eliza Coffee Memorial Hospital, September, 1922, graduating in September, 1925, becoming a Registered Nurse, after passing Nurses State Board examination. The proud mother of twelve children, four daughters, Sarah Alice, Joan Patricia, Phoebe Esther and Miriam Elsie and eight sons, Jack Zimmerman, Ronald Jonathan, Samuel Keith, Maurice Emerson, Patrick Edwin, William Ralph, Demetrius Benjamin Joseph and Marcellus Hebron, for whom she sacrificed to educate through college. They have gone into the world to labor and bless mankind as educators, welfare workers, scientists, mathematicians, and producers. She instilled in them love, honesty, morality, uprightness and a will to work. This Mother, who went to heaven, February 18, 1975, is praised for her faith in and fear of the Lord and she shall rejoice always!

Annie Elsie Zimmerman Graham, a great, good and noble person, has been a believer in Christ all of her life, attending Sunday School and Church from the time she was born. To make her Christian experience deeper in spirit and more pronounced, she walked the "Saw-dust Trail" to the Altar at an outstanding church revival in Florence, Alabama, conducted by Dr. Culpepper, a well-known Christian Evangelist. There, as a young lady, she openly and publicly confesesd Jesus Christ as her Lord and Savior. From this time on she trusted and obeyed and loved her Savior as she often expressed, "I love my Lord, Jesus." Her Christian spirit was shown to loved ones, friends, and neighbors as they attest, "She has earned her place in heaven," said a high school teacher. Another educator remarked, "I feel like I have been with an angel after being with Annie Graham." Two farmers in whose homes she nursed their very sick loved ones commented, "She is the best nurse and a good Christian."

Her skill as a registered nurse made her much in demand as one doctor, M.D., expressed about getting a nurse for his very, very sick patient, "If we can get Mrs. Annie Graham, she is the best I know." She nursed her neighbors in times of serious illnesses and most of the time without pay as they were poor and had no money. In the days of no wonder drugs, she would get on her knees in prayer at the bedside of the patient and arise to see the hand of the great physician at work. Miss Annie went where she was needed: school, homes, church, hospital or wherever the call. She was kind, patient, efficient, cheerful with never a selfish thought of herself.

MARY KATHARINE STONE

Mary Katharine Stone, educator; B.S. with honors in Elementary Education, Jacksonville State University, M.A. in School Administration, University of Alabama (all A); post graduate courses, University of Alabama and Jacksonville State University; married to Dr. Ernest Stone, President, Jacksonville State University; one son, Capt. William E. Stone, U.S. Army and two grandchildren. She has taught for thirty nine years beginning as an elementary teacher in 1933; principal and teacher in DeKalb and Fort Payne schools, a critic teacher in the School of Education at the University of Alabama; teacher and director of the Elementary Laboratory School of Jacksonville State University. Conducted workshops over state of Alabama, served on textbook committee, Alabama Title III Advisory Committee, Law Study Committee, as president of District VI Elementary Principals, on the Professional Standards Commission for State Department of Education. Associated with the American Association of University Women. She is a registered parliamentarian and member of all the honor societies in the field of professional education. Served on Executive Board of Alabama Federation of Women's Clubs for a quarter of a century. Member of the State Rehabilitation Association, Alabama Mother of the Year Association, National Platform Association. Was Alumnus of the year Jacksonville State University in 1962. "Kitty Stone Endowment Fund" a scholarship established by the Alabama Federation of Women's Clubs, for graduate study at Jacksonville State University, 1969.

"Human Resources of the U.S." award from the Library of Human Resources of the American Bicentennial Research Institute, in recognition of her professional and civic attainments; and her outstanding contributions to the growth and development of this American Republic, 1973.

Raised $25,000.00 from Alabama Federated Women's Clubs to establish a trust fund insuring a perpetual scholarship for a deserving young woman from another country, to attend Jacksonville State University and be a part of the International House Program.

Secured gift scholarships for hundreds of young women to attend college.

Worked fifteen years to secure accreditation of the Jacksonville State University Laboratory School with the Southern Association of Universities and Schools, 1970.

Planned and worked out "Open Classroom Teaching" in the Jacksonville State University Elementary Laboratory School which enabled her to conceive of the large six sided building complex for each grade level.

Developed and wrote curriculum for the Jacksonville State University Student Teacher Program.

Initiated and promoted Speech Pathology and Special Education at the Jacksonville State University Elementary Laboratory School. (Continual program of 25 years).

Promoted and developed a Speech Therapy Workshop for all children in Calhoun County.

Developed the Library Center at the Jacksonville State University Elementary Laboratory School. Over a half million dollars of audio-visual equipment is housed there.

Mary Katharine Stone is one of the best known women in Alabama. She is the kind of leader who can be aggressive, unrelenting, successful and still be kind, understanding and maintain an ever-growing coterie of friends. She is listed in *Who's Who in American Women, Who's Who in the South and Southeast, Personalities of the South, Who's Who in American Education,* and *Leaders in Education.*

Was granted the Honorary Doctor of Laws degree by trustees of Jacksonville State University. Truly a great Alabama Lady!

LOUISE SMITH MCCARTNEY

Louise Smith McCartney, born in Van Alstyne, Texas. Received her secondary education in Texas, Masters Degree, University of Oklahoma; graduate of Carver College and Southwestern Conservatory of Music, Fort Smith Arkansas; Graduate of Gregg College, Chicago. Married Franklin A. McCartney, has one daughter, Aida Louise McCartney Popp; six grandchildren. Louise McCartney has been active in First United Methodist Church for many years; Charter Member, Alabama Committee for Better Schools, Board Member, Alabama Society for Crippled Children and Adults; Member Alabama

Milk Control Board, twenty years on Anniston City Board of Education and was the first woman chairman; one of Alabama's Gracious Ladies, 1955; was given Citation for Christian Citizenship from National Council of United Church Women; Anniston Woman of the Year in 1960, received Citation from Salvation Army for twenty years service, selected as WHMA AM, FM, TV as Anniston's First Woman of the Year, 1972. Citation for service from Alabama State Council on the Arts and Humanitities, was appointed to original board by President John F. Kennedy. Youngest president, Alabama Federated Women's Clubs; President, South-

western Council General Federation of Womens Clubs; one of the founding members "Kennedy Center, Washington, D.C. She led the drive to establish the first sewing room for the Blind in Talladega. During World War II assisted Alabama State Chamber of Commerce to boost the lagging economy of Alabama by establishing the state wide project, "Know and Buy Alabama Products." Mrs. McCartney served as chairman Anniston Carnegie Library Board for a number of years, served as Vice President Anniston Business College and taught there thirteen years, member Alabama Association of Parliamentarians and National Association of Parliamentarians, member Sigma Chapter, the Delta Kappa Gamma Society. Mrs. McCartney has received the honor of speaking to high school graduating classes and during her office as president of Alabama Federation Women's Clubs was the guest of the Honorable John Bankhead and was presented to the Senate and asked to speak. Upon her retirement from the City Board of Education in Anniston she was presented with her portrait and inscription and educators from over the State of Alabama were there for her retirement and in recognition of her years of service to the field of education. Alabama is a better State because of the unselfish service to all humanity rendered by this gracious lady, Mrs. Louise Smith McCartney.

LURLEEN BURNS WALLACE
Born 1926

Lurleen Burns Wallace was born September 19, 1926, in the Fosters Community of Tuscaloosa County, the second child and only daughter of Janie Estelle Burroughs Burns and Henry Morgan Burns. From her humble background to the elevated position as Governor of Alabama, she remained the simple and sincere individual that charmed and captivated the hearts of family, friends and fellowmen.

Her childhood was spent in Tuscaloosa and at fifteen she was graduated from Tuscaloosa County High School in Northport, Alabama. Having decided to become a nurse, she was waiting to reach the minimum age for admittance to nurses' school when she met and fell in love with George Corley Wallace, a University of Alabama Law School student. They were married in May, 1943, and after World War II settled in Clayton, Alabama, where Lurleen be-

gan to make a home for her young lawyer-husband, and baby daughter Bobbi Jo. To George and Lurleen were also born, Peggy Sue, George Jr., and Janie Lee.

She was active in the civic and religious life of the community and enjoyed outdoor activities, including fishing, which was a favorite pastime. Lurleen also enjoyed handwork and became quite professional in knitting. This talent was used to benefit the residents of Alabama's nursing homes. Several Christmas Seasons she, with the help of a few friends, knitted foot warmers for them. This deed of love which was begun months ahead, and would be continued untiringly until completion, was only one evidence of her deep compassion for the less fortunate.

Indeed, her selfless devotion to her fellowman will stand out as a forceful characteristic of her nature.

At home in Clayton, Alabama, she looked to the needs of her household, bringing up the children to love and serve the Lord, to respect and honor their elders and to be upright, loyal citizens.

After following George in his campaigns for public office, it was natural for her to "stump the state" in her successful bid for election to Governor of Alabama. So solid was her support that from a field of ten candidates, she won a majority in the first primary, receiving nearly 75,000 more votes than her nine male opponents combined.

Lurleen Burns Wallace was inaugurated Governor of Alabama on January 16, 1967, which was a unique event. No other woman had ever obtained this honored place in the history of this state.

Her term as Governor of Alabama was short when measured by days, but it was marked with profound concern for the plight of the mentally infirm. Governor Lurleen Wallace was the first Governor of Alabama ever to personally visit the state mental institutions. Her determination to improve their situation resulted in increased financial support for existing mental institutions and the creation of additional facilities.

As a humanitarian, she will long be remembered for her many acts of kindness and thoughtfulness to others in need. Never one to seek praise or publicity, most of her deeds demonstrating her concern for others were done in secret. She was awarded an honorary Doctor of Humanities Degree from Judson College, Marion, Alabama, in 1967.

She endeavored to fulfill the duties of the Office of Governor of Alabama following the same philosophy as she practiced as a mother—a philosophy based on fairness, justice, independence, understanding, compassion and genuine love for each and for all.

ALASKA

Alaska

Nickname: The Last Frontier

State Flower: Forget-me-not

State Bird: Willow Ptarmigan

Photos

1. Arctic Dog Sled
2. Totem Poles
3. Alaska's Mt. McKinley
4. Midnight Sun
5. Icebergs
6. Flowers of the Arctic

ALASKA

AGNES POTTS HERING
Fairbanks   **Born 1874**

Hallybay, County Monoghan, Ireland was the birth place of Agnes Potts whose first baby cries August 7, 1874 gave no indication of the role she was to play in the pioneering of Alaska. Fifteen years were spent in her home village where her early schooling was acquired. At the age of fifteen she journeyed to Seattle, Washington, to visit a brother living in that city and to finish her schooling.

August 16, 1896 Agnes Potts became the bride of Edward Arthur Hering. The couple was married by Reverend Damon, beloved Seattle pastor of those early days.

The first of the couple's eleven children was born in Seattle. In 1899 the Herings left Seattle and from that date on their names have been associated with Alaskan history. The trip from Seattle to Dawson, Yukon Territory, took nineteen days by steamer and horsedrawn vehicles. The family was well known in Dawson and Dominion Creek where they lived seven years and where two of their children were born.

After mining on Dominion Creek for seven years, the family went to Fairbanks, traveling by six horse stage coach and steamer, arriving September 1, 1906. Mr. Hering was employed in the Fairbanks Post office for several years, later acquiring the Sourdough Express Co. in its horse and wagon days. He later converted it to motor vehicles before his death in 1927. The business is still operated by members of the family.

Eight children were born in Fairbanks. All surviving children are high school graduates and four college graduates. Twenty grandchildren and two great-grandchildren are in the Hering family. For forty-four years the Hering home has been a mecca for all the neighborhood children and is still regarded as such.

The many friends of Mrs. Hering, both old and new, recount many kindnesses shown them by this little lady who has seen the hardships of pioneering the Northland and has still retained her charm, courage, cheerfulness, patience, affection and kindness.

A beautiful large painting of "The Christ" was presented to Mrs. Hering in memory of her son who gave his life for his country. The painting has for several years hung in the Presbyterian Church of Fairbanks, of which Mrs. Hering has been a member for more than 43 years.

In 1949 the Soroptimist Club named Mrs. Hering "The Outstanding Woman of Fairbanks". She was the recipient of the honor on merits of "many little kindnesses" which endeared her to everyone since the earliest days of Fairbanks.

In 1950 she was chosen by the Fairbanks Women's Club as the most representative woman, mother, grandmother and great-grandmother, in the Territory. During that year she was honored as Alaska's Mother of the Year. Joining the Women's Club in honoring this gentle woman were many organizations, local and Territorial dignitaries, at a public reception and tea on Mother's Day, May 14, 1950.

ALYCE E. ANDERSON
Juneau

After a first trip to Juneau in 1897 to visit her husband who had been there for two or three years, in time Alyce Anderson hoped to give up her teaching in Western Washington and return to Alaska. In September 1901 the home in Kirkland, Washington, completely furnished, was outfitted with shutters and the family returned to Juneau. Here they stayed for seven years. The daughter in that same year, entered the University of Washington Civil Engineering School. Alyce Anderson was a great outdoor person—she climbed every peak in the Juneau area and in a rowboat, with small inboard engine, made it from Juneau to Warm Springs Bay on Baranof Island—Post Office now known as Baranof. Two summers were spent at this lovely spot.

While in Juneau, with the aid of an interpreter, a Carlyle graduate, she did research amongst Indians in that vicinity, accumulated many of their tribal myths and was held in great respect by those known as Takus as well as those living in Auk village.

In 1908 Governor Hoggatt asked if she would undertake establishment of the first Territorial school for white children outside of incorporated towns as Congress had just passed a bill creating funds for such schools. The first school was at Unga in the Shumagin Islands. After she taught there four years, a Territorial school was opened at Ninilchik. Again she was asked to undertake the task.

Much different than Unga where English was spoken, Ninilchik was an early Rursian settlement and even to this day the purity of Russian spoken there still remains. She arrived in November 1911, with neither housing for the teacher or a school, which presented quite a problem. Only transportation to Ninilchik then and for many years thereafter, was by means of boats in summer and dog team in winter. A two room log cabin in dilapidated condition finally housed the teacher and a small one-room log house used by the Russian priest, when he came from Kenai to teach the church membership the ritual of the Russian church, housed the school. Two years later a frame building was built on a hill overlooking Cook Inlet. It provided three small rooms for living quarters for the teacher and a large school room plus a well equipped manual training room. Alyce Anderson taught here for eight years before being re-

quested to take over responsibility of establishing a school at Chignik—upper lagoon. It had been a Bureau school as was the one at the lower cannery. Here she taught for four years. School started in April and continued until late November when many parents went trapping and took their children with them, leaving only three or four in the community.

Mrs. Anderson later taught at Naknek, a community where employment was provided by several canneries in the area. Here again a new school house had to be provided. Again, as it had assisted in bringing building materials for the Ninilchik school, the Northwest Cannery and canneries at Naknek gave much assistance.

While at Naknek, Mrs. Anderson made three attempts to get to the Valley of Ten Thousand Smokes. Crossing Lake Naknek in early April, the ice started to crack and the trip had to be terminated. The sled she was on, broke through the ice and she almost lost her life. Next spring, with a trapper, she made the trip across Lake Naknek then walked into the Valley of Ten Thousand Smokes. Here she gathered many little bags of colored sands from the fumeroles of the extinct steam escapements.

Following Naknek, she taught at False Pass, Sanak, and Port Lock. At Sanak were the ruins of the old "Sea Otter Church" where the Russians had built a chapel so sea otter hunters could come to worship. At that time Sanak was in the midst of the finest seal otter grounds. These places were remote and offered little companionship, but being a great reader and a student of many different things, no matter where she was, she found something of interest. She did not keep herself aloof from the community but made the schoolhouse the social center for both young and old. If she encountered hardships, they were never mentioned. She passed away at seventy-two years of age after a very short illness.

LOUISE FORSYTHE WALSH
Nome   **Born 1886**

Born August 28, 1886 in Lowell, Massachusetts, Louise Forsythe Walsh and her family headed West to Seattle, then to Nome in response to news of the Alaska Gold Rush. They were eager to seek a fortune and willing to take chances. Little did they realize that Nome would be their home for 72 years.

Louise completed high school in Nome, then returned to Boston where she enrolled in business college. After graduation she rejoined her family in Nome. For a time they lived at Sullivan City, East Fork in the Solomon River area and Nome where they engaged in mining and also operated boarding houses.

The family arrived on June 21, 1899 and due to a shortage of building materials, their first home was a tent on the Nome beach. Despite the severity of the winter and lack of conveniences, they never lost faith and determination to succeed.

In June 1906 an Irish immigrant, Michael Joseph Walsh arrived in Nome to join an older brother in seeking a fortune. Louise and Mike became acquainted and on August 1, 1909 were married. To this marriage ten children were born: four boys and six girls.

Economic conditions changed; mining came to a standstill and World War I called men from the community and the Flu epidemic of 1918 took its toll. Through all, the Walsh family continued to grow and work to combat these adversities. Reverses in mining made living a struggle but faith in God and man gave the family strength to meet the challenges.

Louise never worked outside the home. Without modern conveniences such as running water, central heating and automatic appliances, housekeeping was a full time job. Louise never lost her cheerful, calm disposition—she was never too busy to help a friend in need. A "pillar of strength" in the most serious, critical times, her faith in the Almighty never faltered.

Despite her many family responsibilities, she found time to participate in civic, religious and fraternal affairs. A member of the Catholic Church, she was active in the Altar Society, choir, Literary Guild and a staunch supporter of the Pilgram Springs Orphanage. Auxiliary #1, Pioneers of Alaska was an organization in which she had a life long dedication. She held various offices and continued to be active until physically unable to do so. She held offices in

the Women's Auxiliary, Loyal Order of the Moose and was active until the fire of 1934 dealt a death blow to the organization.

During World War II she served on the OPA Board; was an active member of the American Red Cross; did her share of knitting, writing letters and serving meals to soldiers away from home, trusting that her three sons who were in the service would receive similar care.

A stalwart helpmate to her husband, she was at his side sharing joys, disappointments, sorrow and successes. Never complaining, always smiling, expressing explicit faith in God, she accepted what came her way never flinching. She instilled in her children the concept that everyone is created equal and no matter the color of one's skin or his station in life, one must never ignore, mistreat, or refuse to assist his fellowman.

Louise Walsh served the Territory as Alaska Mother of the Year in 1951. She was an ardent supporter of Statehood for Alaska. The realization of this goal was the highlight of her life. Until her death June 28, 1971 she remained dedicated to the betterment of her fellowman and the growth of Alaska. She had no enemies, only friends!

RUTH ELIN HALL OST
Golovin   **Born 1886**

Born in Red Wing, Minnesota, January 18, 1886 Ruth Ost died in Nome, Alaska, April 9th, 1953. Through many years of physical hardship and suffering, she was dedicated to her missionary task and her influence is still being felt in many lives.

The Osts came to Golovin, Alaska in August of 1910 as missionaries for the Evangelical Covenant Church. Their first duty was to superintend the children's home with about forty orphaned Eskimo children, Mission teachers, a nurse, maintenance man and reindeer herders. Two floods and two fires added to the difficulties of pioneer life. Mrs. Ost was a midwife and did doctoring for many years even after she became so crippled with arthritis that she had to be carried.

After being confined to a wheel chair she wrote encouraging letters to hundreds and sent much good literature to others. Her ability to keep going was a constant source of amazement to those who knew her and a tribute to her Saviour. The Osts had five sons and three daughters and adopted a little orphaned Eskimo girl. The eldest son John became a wheel chair invalid but reflected much the same Christian spirit as his mother. Sons Nathan and Joe went to Africa as missionaries. Daughters Ruth, Betty and Lois raised their families in Alaska. Son Lincoln an Army Colonel, now retired and living in Alaska. Son Daniel is a missionary in Mexico. Mamie has helped in the church work. Several grandchildren are in full time Christian Service.

Mrs. Ost found untold encouragement from the scriptures. One of her favorite passages being "In everything give thanks" and with which she applied not only to the joys but also the disappointments of life. Her radiant smile was a benediction on many lives and will never be forgotten by those who knew her.

JUANITA ANDERSON

Born 1890

My first trip to Alaska was in 1897 when mother and I visited my father who had been in the Juneau area for several years. Making the trip on the Steamer Topeka from Seattle, we met the Duke of Abruzzie of Italy with his group of mountain climbers enroute to Lituja Bay to climb Mt. St. Elias. This was accomplished and St. Elias was climbed for the second time about four years ago (1971).

In 1901 our home in Kirkland, Washington was closed and remained so until some seven and a half years later when I entered the University of Washington School of Civil Engineering. Mother stayed on in Juneau.

During the years in Juneau every peak in that area was climbed and in a rowboat with small inboard motor, mother and I made the trip to Warm Springs on Baranof Island on numerous occasions, exploring points of interest along the way.

Traveling on the early day ships was quite an experience, oftentime with passengers sleeping both below and on top of dining room tables. In 1909 we were on the S.S. Portland that brought all of the members for the divided Third Division Court to be permanently stationed at Valdez. Previously the Central Alaska Coast from Cape Hichenbrook, west to Attue, to the Interior and well down the Yukon River—a huge area, was known as the Third Division. It was at this time it was divided and the Interior became the Fourth Division with headquarters in Fairbanks.

It was after leaving the S.S. Portland at Seward that mother and I boarded the old faithful S.S. Dora that carried mail from Seward to the Aleutian Islands. In 1911 on arrival at Ninilchik to teach, mother found only a dilapidated building for school use. I drew plans for a new school while attending the University of Alaska—figured all of the lumber, supplies and put in the order for everything. I then contacted Chris Buschman who was General Manager for all Northwestern Salmon Canneries in Alaska, to see if materials for the school could be shipped to Cook Inlet on the sailing vessel St. Paul which took cannery supplies and crews from Seattle to the cannery at Kenai. He not only offered to take all supplies needed for the new school building but when supplies were discharged on a scow, one of the cannery tenders towed it to Ninilchik and the crew assisted in unloading them on the beach along with the help of those who lived there. Such was the cooperation that the cannery people gave in the establishment of Territorial schools.

In 1912 Mrs. Stryker, mother of Enid McLane and Mrs. Jettie Peterson now of Kenai, my mother and I spent a most interesting summer. We became well acquainted with both the tides and Turnagain Arm winds as the small gas boat we were using was very temperamental. We visited Knik, stopped at Ship Creek where the railroad yards are now located in Anchorage. Later that same summer Mrs. Stryker, mother and I hiked from Sunrise to Moose Pass and on to Seward.

In 1915 Helen Matson of Ninilchik, age about 16, and I left Seldovia on the S.S. Admiral Evans enroute to Seward. It took five days (fare $10.00) before arriving at Seward as we made many stops on Kodiak Island and put ashore sheep, cattle and horses for a family that were locating near Uyak Bay. On arrival at Seward we prepared to hike to Sunrise. We had an interesting trip and met with wonderful hospitality. We went from Sunrise to Anchorage which was a tent city on the flat. There we ate at the Two Girls Waffle House—there was no place for us to sleep but one of the women offered us her bed. This lovely person later married Fred Parsons and they built the Parsons Hotel in Anchorage.

In 1916 Jettie Stryker Petterson, my mother and I hiked from Knik into the Willow Creek Mountain area where considerable quartz mining was going on. We were guests at the Free Gold Mine. We hiked to the Chickaloon area

where the Navy at one time hoped to extract anthracite coal and a spur of the Alaska Railroad was built into that area.

Just as my mother and I had explored the area around Juneau, as far as Sitka and Skagway, we also hiked over much of the Kenai Peninsula. We never carried a gun and never seemed conscious that both moose and brown bear might prove a hazard for us.

My thirty years in Seldovia, a beauty spot, acquainted me with many of the early stories of the area, also Russian customs that were carried on for many years. It has been a wonderful life, nothing too spectacular, but I feel that any early day teachers, brought not only an understanding of the English language but became a part of the social life and at all times, were good neighbors.

Much is being written about mothers having their children at home—both our sons were born at home in Seldovia—the first with my husband and midwife in attendance—the second attended by a doctor. The midwife was ill or would have been with us.

While now living in California, I will always be an Alaskan. I have returned north almost every year—traveled the Alaska Highway nine roundtrips—the first in 1948. Upon my more recent visits to Alaska by plane, I have been to Katmai and Valley of Ten Thousand Peaks; had a wonderful trip to Priblof Island; revisited Kodiak several times and about five years ago spent two days at Prudhoe Bay. Visited Pt. Barrow, Kotzebue and Nome. I will be 85 in September (1975).

JETRET STRYKER PETERSEN
Kenai   **Born 1895**

Jetret Stryker was born in Redmond, Washington March 24th, 1895 to James and Bertha W. Stryker. She came to Seldovia, Alaska for a visit in 1915 and began teaching there in 1918. In those days the only means of travel was by boat, dog or horse drawn team and by walking. On August 20th, 1920 she was married to Allan Petersen the other Seldovia teacher. Over the years the couple moved to Unga and Kenai— they had two children, James and Peggy. Mr. Petersen was Deputy U. S. Marshal at Unga for thirteen years and was later transferred to Kenai. Mrs. Petersen continued to teach until 1951.

"Jettie" is an outstanding lady of fine character and unusual ability. She was named in the 1968-1969 and 1970-1971 editions of Who's Who in America, also in the 1968 edition of "Outstanding Civic Leaders of America." She is a pioneer who has done much to make Alaska what it is today. She has covered much of the State located in the Anchorage and Kenai areas by foot; is never too busy to help in the village churches, the Methodist Mission and presently the Kenai Bible Church. She organized the first Cub Scout Den in Alaska and was its Den Mother.

While in Seldovia she was an active member of the Seldovia Women's Club and Alaska Federation of Women's Club. She is a member of Alpha Chi Omega and Rho Alumni. She has served as Foreign Relations Chairman of Alaska Federation of Women's Clubs; helped organize libraries in Seldovia, Unga and Kenai; is an active member of the Kenai Homemaker's club; the American Legion Auxiliary and Veterans of World War I auxiliary; active on the School Board she also organized the Alaska Retired Teachers Association. She is an active member of the American Association of Retired Persons; a Pioneer of Alaska; a member of the Kenai Garden Club and has worked with the Concert Association. She has worked with the Kenai Chamber of Commerce; the Alaska Crippled Children's Association; The Girl Scouts; American Cancer Society; American Red Cross and American Mothers Committee, Inc.; has served on the Governor's Council on Aging and was a delegate in 1971 to the White House Conference on Aging. She has worked hard in recent years to preserve Alaska's history through the Kenai Historical Society and the Kenai Bicentennial Committee.

In 1955 the Petersen's son James Dale, who was a World War II veteran and employed by the U. S. Fish and Wildlife was tragically lost in a boating accident. In 1969 Mr. Petersen succumbed to a long illness. Daughter Peggy May is married to James V. Arness and is secretary and manager of the Kenai Chamber of Commerce.

"Jettie" radiates kindness and concern and is never too busy to help when needed.

ENID STRYKER MCLANE
Kenai   Born 1896

Enid Stryker was born to James and Bertha Smith Stryker in Redmond, Washington, November 23rd, 1896. She has one sister, Mrs. Jettie Peterson of Kenai. Enid's parents had been in Alaska for some time.

Enid came to Ninilchik, Alaska in 1920 to teach in a one room, eight grade Territorial school. This was to have been a one year term before attending the Pratt Art Institute in New York. On the way to visit her sister in Seldovia, while crossing the bay, such a storm came up that she had to be tied to the mast to keep from being washed overboard. After an interesting year packed with excitement, it was easy to sign a contract for another year. While on a moose hunt at Tustemena she met her future husband, Archie McLane. With very meager means of transportation, it was difficult to get the wedding party together on Egg Island for the marriage ceremony a year later.

The McLane's homesteaded at Kasiloff and took up the then popular business of fox farming. The couple had a son and two daughters—Stanley, Jettiejeanne and Joan, all born on the homestead. Mrs. McLane helped with Sunday School and church services held in the different homes. The only means of travel was by dog or horse teams and by walking. The homesteaders built their own telephone lines to keep in touch. Mail came once a month by boat in summer and dogteam in winter. The McLane's popularity

with the mailman wained when the New York newspaper they sent for, accidently turned out to be a daily. The McLane's ran their fox farm for twenty-five years. Mr. McLane worked to improve the Alaska potato and was recognized by the State Legislature for his achievements.

With doctors days away in Anchorage, Mrs. McLane was often called on in emergencies and her strong faith in God upheld her. Getting supplies from Seattle was a tremendous yearly undertaking. It was necessary to order by case lot and some of her spices lasted for forty-five years. Salt packed eggs were "still" edible after a years storage. Finding a tagged egg in the box once, she knew it was eight or nine years old.

In true pioneer tradition the homesteaders helped each other with building, woodcutting, social times and many other needs.

When her children were older Mrs. McLane taught school in a bachelor's cabin in Kasiloff for six years. During spring breakup, with a plank which was moved along, and by tying the children to a rope, they were all safely transported. A few hours later the ice was gone. For high school, Mrs. McLane took her children and her niece and nephew to Seattle by Heinie Berger's small boat. This meant leaving Mr. McLane at home to tend the foxes. Over the years she managed to develop her skill in painting. Mrs. McLane was widowed in 1969. In 1974 the first building of the Peninsula Community College was named "The Enid McLane Building". She says "I'm most grateful to be in the category of a pioneer of Alaska, a homemaker, a teacher and thank God for his guidance, love and spiritual help."

MILDRED HOTCH SPARKS
Haines   **Born 1901**

Mildred was born November 16th, 1901 at Klukwan, Alaska to Dan and Maggie Hotch. Along with the other ten children in the family, she attended the Klukwan school. She enjoyed school and won several speech contests as well as prizes offered each year in competition with other students. At that time school was available only through the sixth grade, which Mildred completed. This did not satisfy her thirst for knowledge, so she continued her education as much as possible on her own. She was later helped in her education by Reverend Fred Falkoner, the minister at the Klukwan Presbyterian Church and his wife, who also taught her to cook and iron.

In 1914 Mildred was married to John H. Willard and had five children, the surviving three are living in Haines. Mildred worked for many years to help support her family by doing laundry, ironing and cleaning. In 1935 she married William Howard Sparks and had three children by this marriage. All of her children have taken an active part in the Chilkat Dancers as well as being active in school activities.

A devoted mother and grandmother (seventeen grandchildren), Mildred always had time and compassion for others. At present, she is caring for an elderly native lady who is living with her. All through the years she has taken in, housed and fed both children and adults of no relation to her. Her generosity and self-sacrifice have made her a revered mother and friend.

Mildred has held several offices in the Parent-Teacher organization; has been an active supporter of all school events, particularly the High School Letterman's Club of which she is an Honorary member. For ten years she served the Haines Health Council and was instrumental in bringing a doctor and dentist to the area; is a vital member of the Women's Club Museum Board which is setting up the Chilkat Museum (to include the Sheldon Collection). Served as Chaplain to the American Legion Auxiliary and in 1957 helped organize the Cannery workers at Haines Packing Co. under Merle Adlum, as the workers had been getting small seasonal pay and were not guaranteed a fair hourly rate.

In 1956 she was a representative to the National Republican Convention in San Francisco at which time she received a citation for her good work. In 1957 she helped in training a group of Boy Scouts who wished to form a Tlingit dance group (eventually became the Chilkat Dancers) and though the group has traveled in Europe and throughout the United States, it is still supported by Mildred.

Active in the Klukwan Church since childhood she joined the Haines Presbyterian Church in 1938. When the congregation was composed of mostly native folk, she translated services from English to Tlingit, taught Sunday School for many years; served as Elder since 1945; selected Deacon in 1963 and recently elected to the newly formed position of Elder-Deacon; held office of Social, Education and Action officer in Presbtery 1950 through 1953; Spiritual Life and Stewardship office 1955 through 1959; attended two Synods as representative from this Presbtery; was President of the United Presbyterian Women's Club in 1960 and has served as treasurer, a position she still holds. Time and space does not permit a record of all her accomplishments for her people, church and community.

Mrs. Sparks was elected as Alaska's Mother of the year in 1968.

LOUISE HENDERSON ARGETSINGER
Juneau   **Born 1904**

Louise Henderson was born in Quincy, Illinois 1904, received her early education in that area, later attending Antioch College, American University, University of Minnesota. She is a member of the Juneau Methodist Church in which she is very active. She was married to John Argetsinger, a Civil Engineer who died in February of 1967. Of this marriage four children were born.

Aside from her home activities, she found time to be an active Parent Teacher member in which organization she holds a life membership. For seventeen years she served in many capacities.

For fourteen years she worked with the Southeast Methodist camp, programs and physical facilities; spent most summer weekends taking children to camp, cooking, counseling and as a resource person.

She has held all offices in Juneau Women's Society of Christian Service and was chosen by the Juneau Rotary Club as Juneau's Woman of the year in 1962. She organized a group to investigate conditions in detention facilities throughout the State and which resulted in placing a bond issue before the voters for building a treatment center in the Anchorage area for Alaska's emotionally disturbed youth. Many hours of thought and physical energy went into making this project a success. She planned and created a supply of good used clothing for use of Child Welfare workers and Probation officers.

Louise served on the Alaska Committee for White House Conference; was on State Committee for Day Care Centers; was the moving spirit behind the drive for funds to create and put into operation the Juneau Receiving Home; was appointed by the Governor to serve on the first Status of Women's Commission. For seventeen years she served on the Official Board of Juneau Methodist Church. Mrs. Argetsinger is still active and a real pillar of strength in the church society.

ELISABETH SHELDON HAKKINEN
Haines   **Born 1914**

Elisabeth Sheldon Hakkinen was born at Skagway, Alaska, January 11th, 1914. Her father Stephen Beaumont Sheldon, English ancentry, was born in Columbus, Ohio in 1885, educated in England and America. He came to Haines in 1911 after seven trips to Nome as Commissary man in winter, during construction of Copper River Railroad, as a surveyor for Alaska Midland Railway, working under engineer H. P. M. Birkinbine. Her mother, Elisabeth Neidley Birkinbine, Pennsylvania Dutch ancestry; born in Philadelphia, Pennsylvania 1885. She was a graduate of Jefferson Medical School of Nursing; Deaconess in the Episcopal Church serving in the Philadelphia slums. She came to Haines in 1912 to visit her brother "for a month"; married Stephen Sheldon in 1913 and taught Government school for Indian children at Haines 1912-13.

Elisabeth Hakkinen graduated from grade and high school in Haines; attended Presbyterian Sunday School and choir as well as being active in all school activities. Later she attended colleges in California and Ohio. She taught school in Haines for five years and resigned to get married. She later worked for the Bureau of Indian Affairs in Juneau and in 1950, when her husband purchased her father's store in Haines, she too went to work in the store. Elisabeth was married July 11, 1940 to Felix Frederick Hak-

kinen of Finnish parentage. He came to Alaska in the Army in 1935 and was Supply Sergeant of Company F, Chilkoot Barracks, at the time of their marriage. It was here that their son and daughter were born.

Mrs. Hakkinen has rendered outstanding service to her church and community which has covered many fields of endeavor. For many years she worked with the Girl Scouts and spent endless hours with her children's choir known as The Church Cherubs of the Haines Presbyterian church. Before there was a bank in the community, many of the fishermen used to turn their money over to her for safe keeping. She also placed food in her freezer and locker so it would be handy to help the needy. During the years in Haines and other areas of the state, the family collected many Indian crafts and artifacts which she and her husband are now labeling and sorting and which will be on exhibit at the Sheldon Museum, Haines, Alaska.

ARIZONA

Arizona

Nickname: Grand Canyon State

State Flower: Saguaro Cactus

State Bird: Cactus wren

Photos

1. London Bridge (Lake Havasu City)
2. Indian Dwelling known as Montezuma Castle
3. View of Grand Canyon including the famous Indian trail
4. Governor's Mansion
5. San Xavier del Bac near Tucson
6. Grand Canyon view

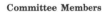

Arizona

JOSEPHINE BRAWLEY HUGHES
Tucson

Josephine Brawley Hughes, wife of ex-Governor L. C. Hughes, was born near Meadville, Pa. She married Hughes in July, 1868, and came to Tucson in 1872, having made the trip by rail to San Francisco, thence by steamer to San Diego, then by stage five hundred miles to Tucson, traveling with her little daughter in her arms, five days and five nights without halting save to change horses, and at a time when hostile Apaches were raiding that region, rendering the stage journey hazardous, strenuous, one requiring endurance, nerve and courage—the pronounced traits of character of Arizona pioneer women. Mrs. Hughes was the third American woman to locate permanently in Tucson. In 1873 Mrs. Hughes was appointed the first public woman school teacher in Arizona and established the first public school for girls in the Territory. In 1875 she was appointed Commissioner for Arizona to the Woman's Department of the Centennial Exposition, held in Philadelphia in 1876, and with her family journeyed back to Pennsylvania again running into the Apache gauntlet, to perform with patriotic pride the distinguished trust reposed in her by Arizona.

In 1877 with a small group of American ladies she raised money for the erection of the first Protestant Church in Arizona, under the auspices of the Presbyterian Board of Missions. Shortly thereafter she was the leading spirit in organizing the Methodist church in Tucson, having been a life long Methodist. She aided in constructing a brick church, which was her special pride for in this building were initiated most of the reforms of Arizona. Mrs. Hughes became President of the W.C.T.U. for the Territory and served for several years, during which she secured the passage of the Sunday Rest Bill by the Legislature in 1887. With the help of a National organizer she organized the suffrage sentiment—created by the Arizona Daily Star—into a Territorial Association of which Mrs. Hughes was elected President. Mrs. Hughes said: "Let us secure the vote for women first, then the victory for home and temperance will

soon follow." At the Constitutional Convention in 1891 a strong fight was made for incorporating and Equal Rights provision and was lead by General William Herring. Mrs. Hughes, then Territorial President, was invited to present the suffrage cause. As the record shows, the bill passed the Council in 1891, defeated in the Assembly; in 1893 it passed the House but was defeated by the Council, and met a similar fate in 1895 and 1897, 1899 and in 1901 passed both houses but was vetoed by Governor Brodie.

As one of the mother builders of the state for more than forty years, Arizona owes a vast debt of gratitude, not only for her energy of purpose or faithfulness of zeal in so arduous an undertaking for the general good, but because of the great unconscious influence of her strong and admirable personality.

The fruits of her marriage were three children: Gertrude, wife of Professor Sherman M. Woodward; John T. Hughes, State Senator and Josephine, deceased at the age of two years.

MARY ELIZABETH HERRING SEARGEANT
Phoenix   Born 1855

Mary Elizabeth Herring Seargeant (Mrs. W. F.) was born April 8, 1855 on a Missouri farm near Blackwater. Her father was Johnathan Herring of Maryland, and her mother Cordelia Harris, whose father operated a mill on Blackwater. The family later moved to Sweet Springs. She received the usual classical education of the day at a girl's seminary at Brunswick, Missouri. She married September 29, 1873 to William Fontaine Seargeant from Winchester, Tennessee and then established their home on his farm in Marshall township, Saline County, Missouri. Here four children were born: Johnathan William, second boy who died in infancy; Lawrence Herring and Elizabeth Cordelia.

In 1893, because of an ear infection contracted by John, she was advised to bring him to Arizona, and consequently established a home here for the rest of her life. Her husband later moved to Arizona. Mrs. Seargeant was a devoted member of the Central Christian Church and was partially responsible for the financial aid necessary to build the church, also the building of the YMCA.

She was keenly interested in the development of Roosevelt Dam and the water resources of our Salt River Valley and invested all the family spare resources in farm land here.

Lawrence Seargeant, her son was a close friend of the late U.S. Senator Carl Hayden of Arizona. They both attended Stanford University but were acquainted before they attended. Lawrence graduated as a mechanical engineer. He was the builder of the first automobile built in Phoenix. Lawrence and his wife May lived in an adobe ranch house at 27th Avenue and Grand Canel, where they could see the headgates from where the irrigation water was turned in to surrounding farms. Roosevelt Dam was being constructed, and river water was scarce. May Seargeant her daughter in law is now living at the home of the Beatitudes not too far from where their ranch house stood.

Mary Seargeant took great interest in Indians and Western life generally. Her collection of Indian baskets and relics became the nucleus for the Arizona Museum in 1923, after her death which occurred at her home, 649 North Third Avenue, February 21, 1921. She was buried in the family plot in Marshall, Missouri.

A memorial was established by her daughter Elizabeth S. Oldaker at the museum. Her granddaughter Mary Elizabeth Garretson is a staunch worker for the Arizona Museum.

Mrs. Seargeant had five grandchildren.

RACHEL E. ALLEN BERRY
St. Johns   Born 1859

Rachel E. Allen Berry was born in Ogden City, Utah, March 11, 1859. Her father was Rufus C. Allen from New York and her mother Mary Ann Yearsly who was born in Pennsylvania. When nearly twenty years old Rachel married William W. Berry January 22, 1879 in St. George Temple, Utah. About three years later they were called by the President of the Latter-day Saints Church, of which they were members, to locate in Arizona. On October 21, 1881, with genuine heartache and many misgivings, they bade farewell to their parents and friends and started for the land which they knew nothing about except what they had learned in school from geography and periodicals. In the former, it was "Arid Zona" and the latter the "Wild West." It was Christmas day, December 25, 1881, when they ferried across the Colorado River, at Lee's Ferry, and it was January 28, 1882, when they arrived at their destination in St. Johns, Apache County, Arizona. Other settlers had located there about three years earlier and were raising good field crops but had not yet made irrigation ditches for badly needed water on the town lots. They built the first brick house in Apache County, moved into it in March 1886.

Rachel Berry was the mother of seven children. One baby born April 3, 1887 lived only sixteen days, as Rachel and four of her children had diphtheria at the time of his birth and he contracted the disease. In 1903 the oldest son, William Wiley Berry, started for Phoenix with sheep, going over the mountains and while camped at Gisela, he was murdered, on the morning of December 22nd by John and Zack Booth. The Booths were tried at Globe, Arizona, John was freed because of being family man, Zack was hung. The other five children all obtained college educations and all became teachers. Mrs. Berry always contended that in the teaching profession one can find opportunities to be of great value to a community.

In 1914 Rachel Berry was elected a Representative to the Second State Legislature, taking office January 11, 1915. During a term of office she presented several bills, one that "No smoking be permitted on the floor of the house, during all sessions of the house; and that the Sargent at Arms, be instructed to enforce the same." This bill carried by a vote of twenty-five to ten. Another bill introduced was to allow the Bible to be read in public schools; this one passed the House; but the measure lost because, together with several others, which had been passed by other members was not carried over to the Senate and delivered, by the Clerk of the House. The Clerk was not re-appointed because of his negligence. One of the arguments in favor of the bill, was that one of the best educators of our country, had said; "One of the books of the Bible, is considered the best classic in Literature." Rachel Berry served one regular term, with three extra sessions—she claimed, "Lots of strange things were done during the old days in politics." One example was the qualification act, that is people had to be able to write their own names, before they were allowed to vote—this was discontinued soon. She was one of the first women to serve in the Legislation in Arizona.

Mrs. Berry was made Chairman of the County Child Welfare Board when it was first organized, in addition she served three years as School Trustee. Education had been her hobby and they spent more money in rearing their children on education, than any other one thing.

FANNIE MORTEN MARLAR
Phoenix   **Born 1863**

Fannie Caroline Morten was born in Salt Lake City, Utah, July 12, 1863, third child of immigrant Danish parents, Neils and Carrie Morten. At the age of thirteen, Fannie Morten left Utah with her parents and arrived in Mill City, Arizona (Phoenix, Arizona), December 24, 1876 after a three months wagon train journey. Fannie Morten lived with her parents on their homesteaded ranch west of Phoenix for three years after arriving in Arizona.

In 1879, she was married to James D. Marlar, the ceremony taking place in the then booming, mining town of Tombstone, Arizona. Twelve children were subsequently born of this union.

Mr. Marlar moved his wife back to Phoenix in the year 1881 to establish a 160 acre homestead ranch five miles west of Phoenix, on the Yuma Road which is now Van Buren Street. The young couple began a life destined to be of many facets. Community service and Arizona development was secondary only to survival.

James D. Marlar was a versatile and ambitious man. Fannie Marlar kept pace with her husband's activities and as Mr. Marlar's activities changed she found herself, in their lifetime together, a miner's wife, a farmer's wife, a grocerman's wife and, in 1903, a legislator's wife. Mr. Marlar died in April, 1912, with the responsibility of six unmarried children left to Mrs. Marlar. She accepted this without diminishing interest in either her family life or community activity. Always interested in community and religious affairs, Mrs. Marlar was an early and active member of the old Central Methodist Church. In 1932, she associated herself with the "First Families of Arizona" and became the first President of this organization, which office she held for six terms. Upon her retirement from active leadership, she was honored by the Society who gave her the lifetime title of President Emeritus.

Wife, Mother, Leader, Friend—Fannie C. Marlar died August 31, 1948 at the age of eighty-five years old. A great Arizona Pioneer woman was gone.

"A good woman is more precious than jewels. Her children rise up and call her Blessed."

BERTHA LOUISE SCHANTZ PALMER
Phoenix   Born 1881

What is more fascinating than glimpses of the city of Phoenix in its median years from one of its most beloved women, one of its most tireless workers for church, the arts and the community. Bertha Palmer, whose late husband, Dr. E. Payne Palmer, Sr., was a leading doctor and cancer pioneer of the Southwest.

She recalls—"When in 1907 I first came to Phoenix—it was a town of less than 10,000 inhabitants, no paved streets, no sidewalks—just all adobe mud. Hot sand storms arrived 'most every afternoon. There was no air-conditioning, and the summers could boast of temperatures as high as 118 degrees."

More than sixty-five years ago Phoenix had fine musicians and teachers. One musical event of the time was a moonlight picnic given in Echo Canyon by the DAR (Daughters of the Revolution). Bertha Palmer was a featured soloist for these events and performed dressed in Indian costume. Such musical programs as these marked the era of Phoenix in its half century years. In 1947 Mrs. Palmer was a great influence in the organization of the Phoenix Symphony—her dream came true. Like so many areas of city growth the beginning was one of struggles and heartaches, today Phoenix has one of the finest Symphony's in the country.

Milestones in Mrs. Palmer's life can almost parallel some in the life of Phoenix. Her first home at 1029 N. Central—"far at the edge of town." As the family grew with the arrival of six children they had to move further north into a larger home. Now she needs two "grandchild bracelets" to record the thirty eight grandchildren and the twenty-eight great grandchildren. Of all the fine churches, representing all denominations, and great hospitals, the St. Joseph's Hospital where her husband and two sons have done much medical work—is a proud part of the city. Mrs. Palmer was one of the workers that made this great hospital possible, after the old outmoded structure was ravished by flames in early days. The money for rebuilding the hospital was raised by concerts, cake sales and walking the streets selling tickets from door to door. St. Luke's is another incident of remarkable progress. The St. Luke's Ball, first one in 1915, was occasion for women in the community to bring food and raise money for the hospital. Mrs. Palmer always attends the

ball and always seems to have a grandchild as Flower Girl. The Symphony Ball, of course and the Cancer Ball are never missed by Mrs. Palmer—she will be 95 years old April 1, 1976.

In early days Mrs. Palmer would fix a lunch and go with her husband on calls—no roads so they made their own trails over desert and rocks. Barry Goldwater's mother was Dr. Palmer's first nurse in medical practice.

Due to the accomplishments of her children, and her outstanding work in community and church activities she was selected Arizona's first MOTHER OF THE YEAR in 1947.

Two sons Dr. E. Payne Palmer, Jr. and Dr. Paul J. Palmer are both medical doctors in Phoenix. Two sons own printing companies— James L. Palmer, Phoenix and E. Joseph Palmer, California. Mary Virginia Palmer Anderson married to a movie actor, (Herb Anderson) and Elaine Allen Banker Wright both women live in California.

Bertha Palmer still attends church every day at St. Francis Xavier Catholic Church.

Mrs. Palmer was born April 1, 1881 in Dayton, Ohio.

MARY LETTIE MOSSMAN JACK
Glendale   **Born 1875**

Lettie Jack paid a visit November 5, 1975 to a house she first called home in 1897. The house was transplanted this year from its original moorings at Grand Avenue and Camelback to Pioneer, a living history museum where it is un-dergoing restoration. The Santa Fe Railroad, current owners of the property, gave the house to Pioneer Museum to move from the site. Lettie's visit was a double celebration. It also commemorated her 100th birthday. Mrs. Jack was a young schoolmarm from Iowa when she first came to live in the house. She taught all grades in the old Jefferson School, her salary was $50 a month. She stated they had the only telephone in the early days and many people came to their house to use the phone.

After her marriage to E. E. Jack in 1901, she lived for a time on the Del Higo Ranch, but moved back about 1903 to the Grand Avenue house, she lived there another fifty years, raising her four daughters. The house contained an office for ranch operations, including cattle, alfalfa, pigs and a dairy. "I don't want to remember the dairy," said Mrs. Jack. When the milkers didn't show up I milked thirteen of the twenty-five cows. We rode horses or drove in a buggy, the roads were dusty and full of chuckholes. Before Cave Creek was dammed, flood waters would sometimes flow down the road along Lateral 16. The railroad embankment saved the Jack house from the water.

A hired girl helped with the housework but Lettie did the sewing for her daughters, and still found time for club work. She helped organize both the Glendale Woman's Club and the Alhambra Woman's Club, and was president of the Glendale Club its first ten years. During World War I she served in Red Cross sewing classes in Phoenix.

"Wherever I lived I couldn't help but get my fingers in the pot," she said. "I also carried petitions to get Camelback Road paved.

Mrs. Jack said she enjoyed the busy days in her house beside the road. The big thrill each day was to stand on the second story balcony and watch the train from Prescott go lumbering by to Phoenix.

Her interest in women's clubs was due to the fact she believed they were cultural institutions. She served in many capacities. Even in her 90th year she was a capable secretary for her Womans Club!

She befriended many people. One a graduate from Phoenix Indian School, Grace. A cousin of Lettie's taught her to cook and keep house. Grace worked for Lettie twenty six years, serving her until her own 70th birthday, when she wanted to return to the Reservation and help her people. Lettie supplied her with a refrigerator and other modern conveniences.

Mary Lettie Mossman Jack was born in Vinton, Iowa—November 15, 1875, Vinton is a small community about thirty miles from Cedar Rapids.

Her four daughters: Katherine Louise (in 1902, deceased 1953) who was Mrs. Llewellyn Bixby Smith; Elizabeth Niccolls (1904) now Mrs. Joseph H. Little; Margaret Mossman (1906) now Mrs. John A. Graye; and Josephine Burrell (1911) now Mrs. A. Maxon Smith. There are six grandchildren.

Mrs. Jack was responsible for the first ladies public rest room in downtown Phoenix. Because of her work the Korrick Department was forced to put one in.

Arizona did not become a state 'til after Mrs. Jack had lived here fifteen years and Roosevelt Dam was yet to be built.

NELLIE MILLER RITTER
Kirkland   **Born 1882**

Nellie Miller came to Arizona Territory in 1902, at the age of twenty. She left her home at Barracksville, West Virginia, to come to Prescott in Yavapai County—a little known part of Arizona Territory—to care for her sick brother, Curtis Miller. She did not anticipate spending her life here, becoming a ranch woman, and through her service, to win recognition which, at the age of seventy-three, Arizona women awarded her Mother of the Year 1955.

After her brother's health became so good that he had no real need of her care, a friend Lillie Morgan, persuaded her to go to Thompson Valley and live with her. Her days were busy keeping house, contributing service to the school and community, also she taught piano to private pupils.

The Ritter family were among the settlers there, homesteading and developing a large herd of cattle now the famous L brand, first recorded in Arizona Territory by Jake Ritter. Ed Ritter son of Jake Ritter and Nellie Miller fell in love and were married on June 5, 1907, by the Rev. R. H. Fields Pastor of the Methodist Episcopal Church.

Besides rearing her own three children, Edna—1908, Curtis—1916, and Alta—1920, she took a motherless boy Bill Kohnke, into her home and gave him attention, counsel and love along with her own youngsters.

She was active in school and community affairs in the Kirkland area from her earliest residence there, serving on the school board for eighteen years, being a charter member of Yavapai Cowbells since the first year of organization.

Nellie and Mrs. Joe Rudy began serving hot lunches for the school children during the early twenties, long before the school lunch program was started in Kirkland. The Kirkland Woman's Club financed the community activities for many years which Nellie took an active part in all phases of it.

Ed Ritter died in 1939 at only fifty-four years of age. Then Nellie had to assume full responsibility for the conduct of her ranch. It was in her favor that, at this trying time, she had the confidence of a good horsewoman and a woman competent with firearms.

In 1940, just a year after the death of her husband, her brother Curtis Miller, died. She accompanied her brother's remains to Barracksville, West Virginia. Although she could have stayed there, she knew that "Home is Where the Heart is," so came back knowing that Arizona and Kirkland and Ritter Ranch were truly home.

In the proclamation by Governor Ernest W. McFarland of State Mother's Week in 1955 he said, "The basic purpose of the American Mothers' Committee, established in 1933, is the encouragement of proper home life firmly built on a foundation of belief in God; with enthusiasms for the daily routine and responsibilities; and the will, the strength courage, and knowledge of better home making." In keeping with those views, aims and purposes it is the thought of Nellie's many friends and acquaintances that the State Selection Committee is to be congratulated upon having recognized how perfectly she fulfilled all the qualifications and so chose her Arizona Mother of the Year.

ZINA KARTCHNER PERKINS
Snowflake   **Born 1883**

Daughter of William Decatur Kartchner and Elizabeth Gale, who came to Snowflake, Arizona in 1878 where Zina was born December 7, 1883. Her father was the town's first Postmaster. Their first house was made of sawed timbers notched at the corners and layed up like a log cabin.

As a small girl, Zina worked for Mrs. Silver in her store. During her teen years, she served as chorister for the Primary department of her church, also taught a Primary class.

One night at a dance, Zina asked her girl friend, "Who is that young man at the organ? My he is attractive!" She answered, "That is Reuben Perkins."

This was the first time she saw her future husband. He danced with her during the evening. In the weeks that followed they began dating, soon were saving money to take the trip to Salt Lake, for both wanted a Temple Marriage. This became a reality October 11, 1904.

According to Mrs. Perkins they arrived back in Holbrook, hoping to buy supplies to start house-keeping, also needing a ride home. The Postmaster said, "Reuben we need a driver to take the mail, if you will drive the buckboard, you and your wife may have free passage." She says this gave us extra cash for the supplies we needed.

We lived in Taylor the next four years, here our first two little boys were born. In the spring of 1909, they took up a homestead with Reuben's father about twenty miles west of Snowflake. On March the 9th, they drove there in a small white topped buggy, set up a small tent just in time for a snow storm of eight inches. Reuben had walked and drove a cow and calf, so we would have milk. We had six hens for eggs. All through the spring and summer this was to be our home. I cooked over a camp fire, my only cupboard was a goods box nailed to a tree. Reuben cut cedar branches and stacked them for a wind break. When the north wind blew, I cooked, washed or did dishes on the south side. If the south wind blew I moved to the north side. With only an open fire I made bread, cakes and pies in a dutch oven."

Zina was the first woman in this area, and remembered how happy she was when others moved in. During these day's of handship and trials she had four more children.

As the settlement grew a meeting was held to choose a town name. Their first choice Mountain Dell, second Clay Springs. When the names were sent in for approval, Mountain Dell was rejected, so the town was named Clay Springs.

For two years Zina served on the school board.

Later they filed on a homestead, of their own two miles from Reuben's father's, they lived there until 1919, then moved to Chandler, where Reuben did carpenter work. Four more children blessed their home—ten in all. Eight are still living, honorable citizens, trying to help build their communities.

In 1924, they moved to Mesa where Reuben worked on the temple and Zina still resides there.

HARRIET EMELINE PHELPS MILLER
Mesa   **Born 1891**

Hyrum Smith Phelps and Mary Elizabeth Bingham Phelps, became discouraged with cold weather in Idaho and decided to move to a warmer climate. They arrived in 1880 and the next year their fifth child was born. Harriet Emeline Phelps was born March 12, 1891, and at the time of her death she was the oldest living person in Mesa to be native born.

The very earliest years of Harriet's life were spent in a three room house of adobe, which her father had built at the corner of First Avenue and Hibbert. At that time Mesa was a small community of large blocks and wide streets. Each block usually included a pasture of cows, horses, pigs, chickens and other farm animals that helped to make the families self sustaining. It was no easy matter to carve a home in the desert valley with its excessive heat and numerous summer dust storms.

A few years later eight acres were purchased east of Mesa, but the family still lived in town. Hattie, as she was known most of her life had the chore of driving the cows out to pasture in the morning and bringing them back at night. The milk was hauled to the creamery by Hattie and her brother Orson, where they would wait

for the milk to be separated. Butter was made from the cream but the skimmed milk was brought home to use. The $5 a month received for the cream was a boon to the frontier housewife.

Hattie had beautiful red hair, but the bane of her life was the freckles of her childhood which went with this complexion. She was a happy, spirited child with a keen sense of humor, which she never lost. Many a situation was saved by one of her wise cracks.

Education was limited to the children of early settlers. Hattie started her schooling in the one room school house on south Hibbert, where all classes met together. She finished the eighth grade at the new Irving School, this was the end of her formal education but she was full of wisdom gained from the experiences of pioneer life. Like the Phelps family she had an ear for music and a good alto voice.

When Hattie was 19 years old she met a young man by the name of Jim Miller. They were married May 1, 1901. After the birth of her first son, thirteen months later she and her sister Lucy started a millinery shop, but this business venture came to an end with the birth of her second son. Hattie was a wonderful wife and mother, and raised six sons and two daughters who became staunch members of society. Her husband died during the flu epidemic of 1918, and the next few years were not easy ones. Her children learned the virtue of hard work, with their mother leading the way. Her children Edwin, Carl, Gladys, Winton, Norman,

Wendell, Lorna and Lin. Her last two babies died soon after birth.

Hattie passed away on the 6th day of February, 1964, leaving a host of friends. She was 92 years old and was preceded in death by her husband and seven of her ten children.

ETHELINDA MURRAY OSBORN
Phoenix   **Born 1918**

In a case at the Arizona Museum (1002 West Van Buren Street, Phoenix) are dresses and uniforms from the past. Alongside the Governors' wives' inaugural ball gowns and elaborately lace trimmed silks, is a ruffled black grenadine dress with dainty blue accents.

The small black eyed, black haired beauty who was to wear it arrived in Arizona with her widowed father, William P. Murray, and her six sisters in a covered wagon in 1870. They rode from Texas in a spring wagon, carrying their belongings in ox-drawn carts and driving their two hundred head of cattle before them. Enroute to California, they stopped at Maricopa Well where they heard of the beauty of the Salt River Valley. When they drove north to see the valley they decided to stay and became the seventh family to settle there.

All of the pretty Murray girls created quite a stir in the community. Their mother had died and the oldest sister had taken on the task of rearing them. She soon had a husband to help her and her father but Ethelinda was a problem.

It was very soon after their arrival that William Louis Osborn lost his heart to this peppery fifteen year old, who stood no more than five feet in her size three shoes. He was the son of

John Preston and Perline Osborn, pioneers whose family name was to become well known. (Governor Sidney P. Osborn was his grandson) William was thirty at the time and her family considered Ethelinda too young for marriage. Her oldest sister and brother-in-law attempted to side track the romance by taking her to Redlands, California, to enroll her in school. But misfortune struck before they reached their destination. The brother-in-law was killed by a hold-up man and the plan was abandoned.

Some family members were sympathetic to the lovers and aided their plans. In those days a couple could be married and secure the license afterward. The pair eloped on horseback and one account says merely that they were married by Judge Griffin. June Osborn Cook, their only living child, says that the Justice of the Peace who married them was a friend who was celebrating the nuptials ahead of time and had to be sobered with coffee so he could perform the ceremony.

It was after their marriage that William Osborn bought the dress for Ethelinda. Twenty yards of goods were bought at Ochoa's store at $1 per yard and Mrs. Rush, wife of Judge Rush of Prescott, made the dress for $25.

Ethlinda and her husband first lived in Phoenix, then Prescott and Ash Creek for short periods before returning to Phoenix where they lived for many years on their ranch, where now stands Phoenix College.

Ethelinda bore and raised ten children, took an active part in the Southern Methodist Church (the John P. Osborns had been charter members and so was William), the Good Templars Lodge and most local affairs, taking her children with her wherever she went.

On their Golden Wedding Anniversary nine of their ten children were able to attend. Daughter June Osborn Cook wore the little black dress, reminding the guests how girls looked in the past days. Mrs. Cook, 87, still lives in the house where her mother spent several years of widowhood.

Osborn Road was named for her husband, (Osborn School was named for his father, who gave the property for it.

Ethelinda kept a pot of beans on the stove every day and kept bread and coffee in the house, ready to help anyone in need.

In the photograph she is shown holding her granddaughter, Frances Cook Rhodes, she now is 57 years old. She has two children, both teachers.

Arkansas

"Land of Opportunity"

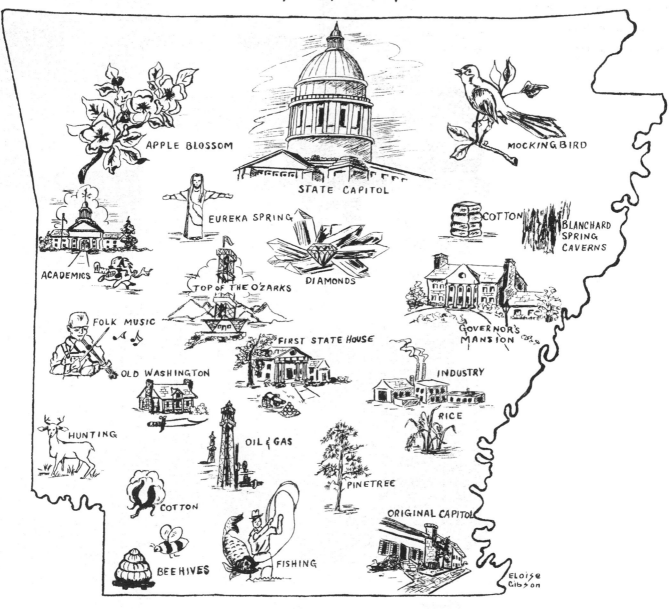

APPLE BLOSSOM

STATE CAPITOL

MOCKINGBIRD

EUREKA SPRING

COTTON

BLANCHARD SPRING CAVERNS

ACADEMICS

DIAMONDS

TOP OF THE O'ZARKS

FOLK MUSIC

GOVERNOR'S MANSION

FIRST STATE HOUSE

INDUSTRY

OLD WASHINGTON

RICE

HUNTING

OIL & GAS

PINETREE

COTTON

ORIGINAL CAPITOL

BEEHIVES

FISHING

Eloise Gibson

Arkansas

Nickname: The Land of Opportunity
State Flower: Apple Blossom
State Bird: Mocking bird

Committee Members

Chairman—Mrs. Mary K. Wyrick, Magnolia
Eloise Gibson—artist

Arkansas

ANN RECTOR CONWAY

Born 1770

Mrs. Thomas Conway, born in Fauquier County, Virginia, the daughter of Frederick and Elizabeth Wharton Rector, who had nine sons and four daughters. Like herself, nearly all of Ann's brothers and sisters achieved such distinction as has perpetuated their memory in the history of the West, to which the family moved soon after 1800. Ann Rector married Thomas Conway of Tennessee March 27, 1792; they moved to St. Louis in 1816 and to Arkansas in 1823, where they built the famous "Walnut Hills" plantation home on Red River.

Thomas and Ann Conway had seven sons: Henry W., Delegate to Congress from Arkansas Territory, 1821-1827; James S., first Governor of the state, 1836-1840; Elias N., Governor of Arkansas, 1852-1860; William B., Associate Justice of the Supreme Court, 1846-1852; Frederick R., many years U. S. Surveyor-General for Missouri-Illinois Land District; John R., distinguished as a physician and served as a U. S.

Commissioner in 1843 to establish the boundary between Texas and Arkansas. Thomas A. Conway died in his twenty-second year in Missouri.

She reared seven sons, six of whom lived to achieve distinction, and historians say she "bred more illustrious sons than any woman in all of American history."

She moved into Arkansas before it was a state and, through her sons and daughters, helped shape the territory into a state. During the War between the States, she furnished support for the leaders, overcame the hardships, and set an example as a perfect ideal of womankind—a mother extraordinary.

ELIZA BERTRAND CUNNINGHAM
Little Rock   Born 1788

The first woman resident of the new town, she arrived with her husband, Dr. Matthew Cunningham, from New York in 1817. It was wilderness, the site having been selected only a few weeks previously as the place on which it was proposed to build the capital city of the state, as it was to be.

She was born in Scotland and brought to America as a small child. She was first married to Pierre Bertrand, the scion of a distinguished French family. He lost his life soon after in Santo Domingo during a plantation uprising. His widow, only twenty at the time of her second marriage, was a woman bred to the best, culturally and otherwise. She was possessed of an impressive personality and displayed all the thrift synonymous with Scotch.

Dr. and Mrs. Cunningham built their house on the west side of Main Street, in the block between Third and Fourth streets.

She kept boarders to help with the expenses and for the accommodation of citizens and officials who came to the new seat of government. This put her in a position to influence the very formation of the state and its government.

When the doctor's practice of medicine grew with the population, Mrs. Cunningham no

longer needed to provide accommodations. Nevertheless, their home was the center of social and cultural activities.

There is no record of their children, their names or the number; yet, this lady—actually the First Lady of Little Rock—was said to have excelled as a wife, mother and friend.

MARY ELLIOTT ASHLEY
Little Rock   **Born 1798**

Honorable Chester Ashley, her husband, was possibly one of the greatest senators Arkansas has ever produced, and she was married in 1821 to this young lawyer who had helped name Little Rock and parcel out the territory. She graced his home in Washington as she had in the wilderness town.

The daughter of Benjamin Elliott of Ste. Genevieve, Missouri, she was buried in Mount Holly Cemetary, Little Rock.

A cousin of Stephen F. Austin, founder of Texas, and of John Pope, third governor of the Arkansas Territory, and also a U. S. Senator from Kentucky, she brought a touch of dignity, culture and refinement to this new territory. She reared her large family of prominent children and managed the domestic affairs of her large household of children and servants in such a way as to be acclaimed by historians. The Ashley mansion was famed throughout the state for its hospitality and refinements.

According to "The Arkansas Handbook," 1945-1946, "Mrs. Ashley, besides her accomplishments as a mother, a wife and the mistress of the mansion was a devout and generous patron of all the religious and social endeavors of her time, which had as their objective the social and civic improvement of the community for the betterment of all classes."

Mary Ashley takes her place in the history of our state by the side of—never in the shadow of—the great man she married. He was one of the first two lawyers to arrive in Little Rock having been in Arkansas Post from 1819 to 1820, but it was not until he had made an "estate" that he went to Missouri to marry lovely Mary.

CLARA ULALIA MORGAN DAVIES
Magnolia   **Born 1835**

A spirited little lady whose husband was the only Englishman in the area and who, at 92, was the oldest citizen in point of residence in Magnolia, then a city of 3,000 population, had left her family in Tuscubia, Alabama, to join the pioneers in this new state. Her family consisted of her father, James Morgan, a merchant, a stepmother, a brother who served in the State Legislature of Alabama, and her maternal grandfather, Rev. Joshua West (M.D.).

She and her new husband, Samuel Edward Davies, a tailor by trade, only recently from Liverpool, England, came by stage across Indian Trail and Military Road to The Travelers Inn in Washington, a little hamlet in Hempstead County, the first town in the territory. A population boom in this gateway to Texas sent the couple with their infant son south to the four year old town of Magnolia just a year later in 1857.

Their family came rapidly, 10 children (2 died in infancy). Even with the chores of caring for the family, gardening, serving, quilting, she found time for her neighbors. This couple who had never known hard physical labor forged a life in this undeveloped country.

Soon the war came and the young men marched off to battle in uniforms tailored by her husband who, at five feet, climbed on the table to do the cutting. She helped supply the homespun for these soldiers and watched them return ill, grotesquely maimed and starving. Unknown Confederate soldiers were buried in the graveyard only a short distance from their home and she joined her neighbors in saying

Among her great grandchildren, one served Magnolia as mayor, two grandsons were mayors of a small Louisiana town, and a great granddaughter is Chairman of this Arkansas chapter.

KATHERINE MALONEY HICKEY

At age 18, Katherine Hickey joined the American women of the Civil War period to nurse the casualties in the vicinity of the headquarters of General Ulysses S. Grant at Cairo, Illinois. She nursed on the United States gunboats up and down the Mississippi River and in the exchange of prisoners of war.

In 1864, she married her childhood sweetheart, farmboy turned soldier, Michael Hickey. In 1865, he was mustered out in Texas as a regimented officer. He joined his wife and, after a sad stay in Vicksburg, Mississippi, he transferred to the Commissary Department, which was located near the Army corrals in the eastern part of Little Rock.

Widowed in 1886, she was left with two daughters and a nine-year-old son. She carried

prayers at their graves. Her prayers were lifted regularly that war would never come again, yet she watched sadly as Magnolia's young men went off to World War I, including a grandson, Archie Merritt.

Widowed in 1880, at age 42, with four boys and four girls to rear, she decided to sell a part of her acreage, donate some for the fast-filling cemetary, and move nearer town (later 210 S. Washington)

During her husband's lifetime she was First Lady of Magnolia over a long period for her husband served three terms as mayor, having been the second mayor of the fast-growing little town. Later her third son served as mayor. With no relative to assist her, she maintained a good home, educated her family in local schools and sent three away to business school or careers.

Two young granddaughters came to live in her home when their mother died and there was always love and laughter, discipline and Bible reading.

Active in the Methodist Episcopal Church from 1857 until her last illness, she encouraged the formation of the first schools and even though women were not heard publicly, her influence was felt and she encouraged her sons to be active. One son, Sam, served the Treasury Department in Washington for 30 years—another was called "Squire" Will Davies; Goode was a successful businessman, and Archie served as mayor, Justice of Peace, and operated a real estate business. The daughters were: Mary (Merritt); Sally (McDonald); Ada (Goode) and Clara (Wade).

on the family business which had been established and acquired valuable property to be handed down to succeeding generations.

Her courage, too, was handed down to future generations. She drove spirited horses and had both arms broken by runaway accidents. Robbers didn't even faze her; she advanced on them one night when they blew the safe with only a lighted kerosene lamp as protection. The proceeds of the day's deposits were saved.

She made a large contribution to the building of the St. Andrews Catholic Cathedral, Seventh and Louisiana. Also, she contributed to the many charitable institutions and participated in all civic movements except "Suffragetts". She did vote, however, and discussed current issues and candidates at the family table with her husband and his friends.

Although a victim of cancer, she did not relinquish her fight until the last and lived to see her children educated through college and universities, two of her four married, and enjoyed her first two grandchildren, the children of her daughter, Margaret H. Letzig.

Her transmission of her early heritage to her family made her a vital force in their lives and in the community.

CARRY A. NATION
Eureka Springs   **Born 1846**

Her birth certificate reads: "Carry Moore", Garrard County, Kentucky, November 25, 1846. Her father was George Moore and her grandfather, Deacon James Campbell.

Carry, with her weapons, the Bible and the "Hatchet" and her fight to the end against "all evils" overshadowed her colorful parents. Oklahoma, Missouri, Texas and Kansas could each claim Carry but Arkansas is the State she loved.

Her background, with two unhappy marriages and a mother-in-law, a daughter sometimes called insane, step-children, she fought to make a living and a life for her household. Her second husband was a preacher and a lawyer but never made much money.

Her zeal against whiskey and crime began in Medicine Lodge, Kansas, and really made her famous when she arrived in Eureka Springs. She was "in jail" "out of jail" but her hatchet used on saloons attracted nation wide attention.

She sailed into the White House to protest and attempted to reform the students at Yale and Harvard.

Even though she hated whiskey she did not hate the drunkard and gave them food and money, sang to them and prayed with them.

She smashed many a saloon with her hatchet but as she grew older time softened her—but she was, until the end, a true crusader for the right.

Her last home was a 14 room boarding house named "Hatchet Hall". From here she gave a special course in cooking, Sunday School lessons, debates and parties for the young people she loved so dearly.

With the help of dynamite, Carrie discovered a spring that furnished water to her home below, she discovered a cave that she used and let neighbors use as a community refrigerator.

Old time citizens of Eureka Springs have said of Carry, "She demanded respect, and got it—even if she had to use the hatchet."

Carry left "foot prints" all over the world. These footprints can never be erased. She gave her money away and never had quite enough.

Stories are that when she became ill she went to Evergreen Hospital, in Leavenworth, Kansas,

1911, and died a few weeks later and was buried in the family cemetary in Belton, Missouri.

Out of her generosity she established in Kansas City, Kansas, a home for children of drunkards at a cost of $17,500.00. In 1891 she drove a horse and buggy a distance of 450 miles from her home, all but 150 miles of this she drove alone.

A statue of Carry may be standing in Seiling, Oklahoma, but her home in Eureka Springs stands as a curiosity for tourists.

Whether we agree with Carry's views she was one of the great characters of American history—and stood up to the courage of her convictions.

NETTIE HICKS KILLGORE
Magnolia   **Born 1867**

Columbia County's foremost historian, Mrs. Nettie Hicks Killgore, daughter of Jefferson and Julia Hicks, was born September 22, 1867, and died in 1961.

Her pioneer parents came from Alabama to Arkansas in 1857. She attended school locally before going to Blue Mountain College at Blue Mountain, Mississippi. After graduation Mrs. Killgore taught at Waldo, Magnolia and Camden.

During the "Gay Nineties", she married Albert Sydney Killgore in a beautiful church wedding, the first ever held in the First Methodist Church in Magnolia. He being a young lawyer it was natural that he became interested in politics and served in the state senate.

She loved writing and had two books published—*Golden Books of Dogs and Men* and *History of Columbia County*. Her feature stories were published in local and state papers and she collected historical articles throughout her long life. Her history was dedicated to the sturdy pioneers of Arkansas as a heritage to other generations.

Her stories of the years after the War between the States included seeing her father drive his horses and mules to the thick bottom lands to save them from the scavenging and looting Yankees. Burying the silver and cured hams was another of her reminices.

One of twenty charter members of the local Presbyterian Church in 1884, she was active almost to the end of her 94 years.

A charter member also of the United Daughters of the Confederacy, Sorosis Club, Authors and Composers Society and an honorary member of the Delta Kappa Gamma Society of Arkansas. Although never having children of her own they reared four, a niece and three nephews who were left homeless. (They were her heirs since she was widowed before they were grown.)

During her lifetime she loved to travel and met many famous people including Confederate Generals, William Jennings Bryan, Jane Adams, Dwight L. Moody, Sam Jones, entertainers and politicians.

Her collection and knowledge of antiques of old books, coins, stamps, early American Glass, and war relics caused her to be an authority in many fields.

She walked miles daily, calling on her friends, attending church activities and club functions, a small little lady beloved by everyone. Her home was always a Mecca for those searching for information, and was filled with the historically and sentimentally valuable memorabilia of the countries beginnings.

BERNIE SMADE BABCOCK

Born 1868

Bernie Babcock found life a thrilling challenge and throughout her 94 years her zest never lessened.

Daughter of Hiram Norton Smade and Charlotte Elizabeth Burnell Smade, Julia Burnelle (Bernie) was born April 28, 1868 at Unionville, Ohio.

When she was ten, her parents moved to Russellville, Arkansas. After attending old Little Rock University one year she married William Franklin Babcock and they made their home in Little Rock. They had five children: Lucille (Mrs. Samuel G. Boyce), Charlotte (Mrs. W. W. Shepherd), Frances (Mrs. Herwald Cutting), William F. II, and MacArthur.

Widowed at 29, she turned to writing in a serious way. She became a staff writer for *The Arkansas Democrat*. At the same time, she wrote many articles and stories published throughout the United States.

Her first writings to attract wide attention dealt with prohibition and woman suffrage. *The Daughter of a Republican* sold over 100,000 copies in six months.

Her lifelong pride in Arkansas was reflected in numerous early works, among them: *The Arkansas Sketch Book, Pictures and Poems of Arkansas*, and *The Man Who Lied on Arkansas and What Got Him*.

In 1919, the publication *The Soul of Ann Rutledge* made her internationally famous. This best seller went into 14 editions and was translated in several languages.

There followed: *The Soul of Abe Lincoln, Booth and the Spirit of Lincoln, Little Abe Lincoln, Lincoln's Mary and the Babies, Light Horse Harry's Boy, The Heart of George Washington, The Coming of The King, Little Dixie Devil*, and others.

Bernie Babcock considered one of her most important achievements founding The Arkansas Museum of Natural History. She almost single-handedly built the museum, which she established on the unfinished third floor of the City Hall until she was able to obtain a permanent home for it in the old Arsenal Building. As director and curator she gave unstintingly of her time, her money, and her labor for twenty-five years to further its development.

Retiring from the museum at age 83 to Petit Jean Mountain, she spent her last years painting, composing music, and writing. She died in 1962.

Among civic, cultural, and literary projects in which she played a prominent role were the National League of American Penwomen, Authors League of America, Arkansas Authors and Composers, Bookfellows, Poets Roundtable, and Arkansas Historical Society.

She was honored by the Psychical Research Society, London; Academie Latine des Sciences, Arts et Belles Lettres, Paris; International Academy of Lettres and Sciences, Italy. She is listed in *The International Blue Book* (four languages), *Who's Who in Arkansas*, and numerous similar publications. Signal among her honors was being the first woman to receive an honorary doctorate degree from the University of Arkansas. She was also the first woman from Arkansas to be in *Who's Who in America*.

A quote from *The Soul of Ann Ruthledge* expresses a way of life that was to her axiomatic," Any good thing we can do, let's do it. We won't be back this way you know."

MARCELLA MORGAN PEARCE
Magnolia   **Born 1868**

Many Ann Marcella Morgan, born at Fillmore near Shongaloo, Louisiana, May 7, 1868, had Scotch-Irish parents who pioneered to Arkansas and Louisiana from Fayette County, Georgia, before the War. Dr. T. J. Morgan, her father, a colonel in First Calvary Brigade was on duty at Washington, Arkansas Infirmary, while federal troops occupied Little Rock from 1863 to 1865.

Marcella, only 85 pounds, taught a new school after attending Magnolia Female Academy, and then rode off behind her stalwart groom, Levi Holcomb Pearce, to his farm. They lived for a time in a one-room log cabin during the building of a two-story white home on their property on Dudney Road which was to house their large family.

Despite her chores on the farm and caring for her many children (ten lived to be grown), she opened her home to orphans, students, even strangers. Education was very important in this family, and Marcella gave 38 years to Home Demonstration Clubs. She earned the Arkansas Merit Mother Award in 1952 and a daughter, Ola Davis, was later to become a State Mother.

After the 19th Amendment was passed in 1920, "Miss Marcy" was the first woman to vote locally.

They took their children to the Methodist Church, to Chatauquas and Lyceum programs, and all events of edification on foot, by buggy and wagon.

With thirty-two grandchildren and twelve great-grandchildren, at her death she had much to be proud of, for five of her children earned a college degree and all attended college. Honors came their way and she was a proud mother.

Diminutive Marcy Pearce "danced a jig and sang spirituals" at a club meeting as she neared 80, wearing the dress of the mother of Harvey Couch, a famous Arkansas son.

With sharp piercing eyes, this lively little lady had a keen sense of humor.

ROBERTA WAUGH FULBRIGHT
Fayetteville

The mother of one of Arkansas' most illustrious sons, J. William Fulbright, was the best known person in the Northwest section of the state.

Roberta Waugh Fulbright's family was of English origin from Virginia. She grew up in Missouri not far from Fayetteville where she moved with her husband, Jay Fulbright in 1906. She attended the University of Missouri which had the first School of Journalism in the world, but she did not finish, instead she returned home and began teaching in a country school outside Rothville, Jay's hometown. Married in 1893 his wedding present to her was a Bible, and for Christmas a copy of "Paradise Lost." She completed her college work and took a teacher's degree after her children were grown.

Her husband built a small town business empire in Fayetteville and died at 56, a wealthy man leaving his widow a major share in a bank, newspaper, bottling works with a Coca Cola franchise, creamery, produce house, lumber company, a wagon works and a small timber railroad and a large family, four girls and two boys. They were Anna, Lucille, the twins Helen and Roberta, Jack and J. William.

She took over the family enterprises not from choice for she loved homemaking and gardening and had the most beautiful garden in the area; but because it was thrust upon her and she did choose it in preference to going broke or dissipating her heritage or that of her children. She received no help; women were not accepted gracefully in the business world, and she was forced to fight to survive.

Miss Roberta became a persistant reformer in local politics, an active force in the community-she is credited with cleaning out a corrupt courthouse. The Fayetteville Library and a dormitory at the University of Arkansas are named for her. A small woman with a strong chin, and wonderfully alive eyes she loved to talk and even though she found her column in the local paper hard work her response to inquiries was always "I must." She spoke out forth rightly as she saw it. Commenting on her successes once, she is reported to have said "Let a woman do well and she is all but burned at the stake."

This dynamic woman was the second Arkansas Mother 1946. She took great pride in Bill's intellectual bent and allowed him time to read and study, and when he won a political race she wrote of his opponent, who was very derogatory, that "he has came and went" proving her sense of humor. In later years she spoke what was her epitaph: "I've lived long. I've loved working. I've loved fighting in the argumentative sense. I abhor war. I believe it must be abolished. I wish I could have done more for humanity."

A mother who did what had to be done for her family, her community in a time when this was unpopular in Arkansas.

HATTIE WYATT CARAWAY
Jonesboro   **Born 1878**

Hattie Caraway, the first woman elected to the U.S. Senate (1933-1939-1945), was a Methodist and a Democrat. She was also the first woman to preside over a Senate session. She supported prohibition, anti-lobbying bills, equal rights for women, and much of the New Deal legislation when this was not popular.

Named to the post by Governor Harvey Parnell to fill the unexpired term of her husband, Senator Thaddeus H. Caraway when he died, Mrs. Caraway liked politics. She came under the scrutiny of the late Huey P. Long, "the Kingfish", of Louisiana, who campaigned for her over Arkansas in barnstorming fashion.

Her husband, an attorney, served eleven years in the Senate. They met in Tennessee while she was attending Dixon, Tennessee Normal College.

After serving 13 years, she was defeated in 1944 at the age of 66 by J. William Fulbright.

The Caraways had three sons—Paul, Forrest, and Robert, who died in 1934.

A bronze marker has been installed on the Craig County Courthouse lawn in her honor.

Although she was not the first woman to serve in the Senate, she was the first one elected; and that election went down in the history of politics.

Born in Bakersville, Tennessee, she lived most of her life in Jonesboro.

ADOLPHINE FLETCHER TERRY
Little Rock   **Born 1881**

At 92 Mrs. Adolphine Fletcher Terry was honored at an autograph party to mark the introduction of her new book, a biography of Mrs. Charlotte Stephens, Little Rock's first black teacher.

Mrs. Terry had lived since childhood in the famous old Albert Pike home as a member of a distinguished Arkansas family. Her father, Col. John D. Fletcher, was an officer in the Confederate Army. Her husband, David D. Terry, was Representative from the Fifth District in Arkansas in the United States Congress from 1933-1942.

From the time of her graduation from Vassar College in 1902 Mrs. Terry has been in the forefront of nearly every move to improve educational, cultural, religious and political institutions in Little Rock and the entire State of Arkansas. For her public service, Vassar named her one of its one hundred most distinguished graduates.

She served as President of the Congressional Wives Club in Washington, D. C. and as a delegate to the Democratic Convention during the administration of Franklin D. Roosevelt. During one of his campaigns she toured Nebraska, speaking to many groups urging his reelection. She was chosen the second Arkansas Mother of the Year and was a Woman of the Year of Little Rock.

Active in Christ Episcopal Church, she served on the Paris Council and taught Sunday School.

Another book, "Courage", under the pseudonym of "Mary Lindsey", in 1938 was about her experiences in rearing a handicapped child, and "Cordelia", written affectionately about a negro girl her age who lived in her home showed a true feeling for all humanity.

She started the State Library Program and founded the Women's Emergency Committee to open our schools in the 1958 integration crisis, and the Phyllis Wheatley Branch of the YWCA for negroes and served on the first board.

Her suggestion resulted in a community chest and she served on the first board and organized the Pulaski County Juvenile Court in 1910, the first such court in Arkansas.

Mrs. Terry helped establish the Pulaski County Tuberculosis Association and served on the board. Active in American Legion Auxiliary, Federation of Women's Clubs, Family Service Agency and the Salvation Army, Civic Music Association and State Opera Association.

Her historic home has been deeded to the City and has for many years been open for tours on a scheduled day.

In 1971 the National Conference of Christians and Jews presented the National Brotherhood and Humanitarian Award which read in part:

"Who, endowed with a spirit of compassion and openness to the needs of men, has worked tirelessly throughout her life with deep personal commitment for better health, educational and cultural opportunities for all people . . .".

This emphasized her faith in the Brotherhood of Man under the Fatherhood of God.

DAISY RHEA ABBOTT
Magnolia   **Born 1891**

The oldest president of a Federated Womens Club in Arkansas, Daisy Rhea Abbott, serving Sorosis Club in Magnolia, Arkansas was born February 12, 1891 to Mr. & Mrs. Tom Hicks, operators of a small hotel in McNeil, Arkansas. As a child, she stood on a stool to register guests and listened to all their tales of other places, so it is no surprise that she married John W. Rhea, a young banker, on a train in 1909.

Mrs. Rhea became interested in politics in 1928 when she attended the Democratic National Convention at Houston, Texas. She campaigned that summer and, just prior to election, was called to New York where she was entertained by leaders of the party. Eleanor Roosevelt gave a reception for her in her home. Soon after she was made a member of the Democratic State Committee of Arkansas and served later as Vice-Chairman of the Committee. A delegate to five National Democratic Conventions, she had the honor at the 1932 convention of casting Arkansas' votes for Franklin Roosevelt. Only one other woman delegate has had this distinction.

The first woman in Arkansas to serve as an election judge and also the first woman in the state to be listed in "Who's Who in the Democratic Party".

During the Roosevelt administration, she held the position of Assistant Custodian of Securities in the U. S. Treasury at Washington, D. C., and was the first woman ever to hold this position.

She and Mr. Rhea had three sons and two daughters. Four of these were valedictorians of their classes. The youngest son, a West Pointer, won fame in the Battle of the Bulge during World War II. He later graduated number one in a class of 600 at the Army General Staff and Command School. Enroute to his West Point graduation, she broke her leg. Undaunted, she was put on a stretcher by a train window and arrived on the scene with full news coverage.

Named the first Arkansas Mother in 1945, she has also been listed in four editions of "Who's Who in American Women"; and in 1942 she won the National Safety Award at Atlantic City, New Jersey.

For 35 years a member of the Board of Directors of Arkansas Federation of Women's Clubs, she is presently serving as Chaplain of the State Federation and was a delegate to the International Convention of Women's Clubs held in Geneva, Switzerland in 1955.

Widowed in 1954, she married T. O. Abbott, an attorney of El Dorado in 1960; he lived only five years.

Her travels take her to faraway places and to see her eleven grandchildren and three great-grandchildren.

A teacher at 16, the former Daisy Hicks never stops learning, and is a driving force in Magnolia, Arkansas at 84 years.

California

California

Nickname: The Golden State

State Flower: Golden Poppy

State Bird: Calif. quail

Photos

1. San Francisco's Palace of Fine Arts
2. Red Rock Canyon
3. San Francisco's most charming mode of Transportation
4. Golden Gate
5. Disneyland
6. Amelia Earhart Putnam rededicated 1970, No. Hollywood

Committee Members

Chairman—Mrs. L. Dean Petty, Los Angeles (Woodland Hills)

California

SUSAN TOLMAN MILLS

Born 1825

Susan Tolman Mills (1821-1912), missionary, teacher, and college president, was born in Enosburg, Vermont. Susan was a teacher at Mount Holyoke when she met and married Cyrus Mills, who had just completed his studies at Williams College and Union Theological Seminary. They set sail for Batticotta Mission in Ceylon where they spent six years before going to Hawaii to head the staff of Punahou School.

A New England heritage of Puritanism and practicality, seasoned with idealism, and given scope are the elements that led Cyrus and Susan Mills to found the first women's college west of the Mississippi. While still in Hawaii, they decided to found Mills College in California to carry out their educational idea that "in no way could more be accomplished for the good of this Coast . . . than by the proper education of young women."

Mills College was founded by these two old-fashioned teachers, Cyrus and Susan Mills, who had caught from their own small alma maters a burning faith in education. Most large colleges and universities, starting from humble beginnings, have outgrown the faith of their founders. These teachers, however, had what it takes to start an ongoing institution. With Mills as head of the seminary, Mrs. Mills held the title of lady principal, taking turns sharing all the teaching and administrative duties.

With the death of Cyrus in 1884 and the diminishing need for a seminary as public high schools were established in California, it was decided by the trustees to develop the school into a college. Susan continued as lady principal, household manager, and comptroller. Internal dissension wracked the institution during these years, and in 1890, Mrs. Mills, who had doubted her ability to run a college, was elected president. It was she who carried through the shift to college status begun by President Stratton. Mistrustful of higher admission standards and faculty specialization, and reluctant to drop the profitable preparatory department, she was nevertheless determined to see her college accred-

ited. A very large part of the accomplishment of her goals was her wonderful gift for selecting teachers and winning and keeping their loyalty.

A science building, an auditorium, a library, and a gymnasium were added to the campus before Susan Mills retired from the presidency in 1909, at the age of eighty-four. She died three years later and was buried beside her husband on the college campus. Mills remains today the oldest women's college on the Pacific Coast.

PHOEBE APPERSON HEARST

Born 1842

Phoebe Apperson Hearst (December 3, 1842-April 13, 1919), philanthropist, was born in Franklin County, Missouri. She was the oldest of three children. After attending the local school, Phoebe studied for an additional year at St. James, Missouri, and began teaching when she was seventeen.

She met George Hearst, twenty-two years her senior, when he returned to Franklin County after a dozen years of mining gold and silver in California and Nevada. Phoebe married Hearst on June 15, 1862, and accompanied him by sea to San Francisco where their only child, William Randolph Hearst, was born on April 29, 1863.

Mrs. Hearst became noted for her interest in talented people and her serious study of architecture, music and French. She loved traveling and used her trips to complete her education.

Back in San Francisco once more, Mrs. Hearst embarked upon the educational and charitable ventures to which she devoted the balance of her life. She contributed to local hospitals and nurseries, sent young people abroad for study, and aided artists and composers. She also endowed libraries, nurseries, and kindergartens in towns where her husband's mining interests were centered.

When George Hearst was appointed to the United States Senate in 1886, Mrs. Hearst shifted to Washington for a time, while keeping up her interest in kindergartens.

In 1897, Mrs. Hearst worked to found the National Congress of Mothers, largely financing the early years of that organization. In the early 1890's, her greatest interest was the University of California at Berkeley.

Of particular interest are her contributions to aid archaeology and anthropology. She helped finance archaeological digs and specified that artifacts were to be sent to the University of California at Berkeley. By 1901, enough artifacts were gathered to open the University Museum, paid for by Mrs. Hearst.

Mrs. Hearst was an indulgent parent who promoted the education of her son, giving him encouragement as needed.

In 1919, at the age of seventy-six, Mrs. Hearst died of influenza.

CHARLOTTE AMANDA BLAKE-BROWN

Born 1846

Charlotte Amanda Blake-Brown (December 22, 1846-April 19, 1904), was physician, surgeon, and founder of the San Francisco Children's Hospital. Her father was a graduate of Bowdoin College and a Presbyterian Minister, who moved to California with his family to become the editor of Pacific News when Amanda was five years old. Later, when he was called on a mission to Chile, the family moved back to the east again. Following her graduation from Elmira College, Amanda moved to Arizona, and it was there she married Henry Adams Brown. The couple moved to Napa, California, where Mrs. Brown became the mother of three children.

After the birth of her last child, and with the encouragement of her husband and her father, Mrs. Brown went back to the Women's Medical College in Philadelphia. Two years later she received her degree, and she and her family moved back to San Francisco. Mr. Brown worked with the Wells Fargo Bank, and Dr. Brown began her medical practice at the same time as they opened the Pacific Dispensary for Women and Children. After many tries and a few years later, Dr. Brown was admitted to the San Francisco Medical Society.

Naturally a keen observer of details, Dr. Brown published many articles and booklets on subjects she had researched. "Tumor Registry", "Obstetrics Among the Chinese", "The Health of Our Girls", "Importance of Sterilizing Milk", and many articles on "City Health Rules and Regulations" were among the subjects of her many medical treatises.

Dr. Brown remained very active in Children's Hospital when, with two of her sons (also physicians), she started the California Branch of the National Conference of Charities and Corrections.

In 1904, Dr. Brown died of intestinal paralysis. The Children's Hospital was wrecked in the earthquake of 1906, but was rebuilt to continue Dr. Brown's inspired work.

MARION MILLER

Born 1862

Although having been born in New York City, and having spent her earliest years in Detroit, Michigan, she can declare herself a Floridian from the age of four until twenty-five. Attending Florida schools, she majored in music and education (as a scholarship student) at the University of Miami (Coral Gables, Florida), graduating cum laude in 1941. Moving with her parents from Miami to Jacksonville, Florida, she taught school there during the war years, and participated in volunteer war efforts in the radar centers and hospitals. She met her husband, Paul, who was an officer in the United States Maritime Service, at a USO party, where she was entertaining for the servicemen by playing the piano, and they were married a year later. After the war ended, they moved with her parents to Los Angeles, settling down in business and raising her family.

They had two children, Paul, Jr. and Betsy Lou, when in 1950 she was approached by the Federal Bureau of Investigation to serve our country by acting as a volunteer undercover agent within the Communist Party. It was necessary, at that time, to investigate a certain suspected Communist front group which had invited her to join because of her affiliations with prominent women's organizations. At the request of the FBI, she did follow through, and joined not only this Communist Front group, but the Communist Party itself for the explicit purpose of furnishing valuable information to our Government. This activity terminated with her hospitalization for ulcers. In 1955, the Justice Department called her to Washington, D.C., to testify regarding her knowledge of the link between this communist front group and the Communist Party, USA.

Despite this extra-curricular activity, she and her husband made every effort to raise their children in religious faith teaching them to love God and their country. Their daughter, Betsy, was confirmed, and their two sons had their Bar Mitzvahs in the Jewish Temple. They are long-time members of the Wilshire Boulevard Temple, under the spiritual guidance of Rabbi Edgar Magnin.

Their older son, Paul, Jr., attended Whittier College, where he was a music scholarship student (he is a fine pianist), and he now works for the Tax Assessor's Office of Los Angeles County. Betsy Lou, their only daughter, studied art at Chouinard and has been affiliated with the Bank of America for several years. She is happily married. Robert, their youngest, is studying medicine at San Francisco State University as a scholarship student, having made the Dean's List continuously since he entered. Their children are devoted to their family and to each other, independent, self-sustaining, and responsible citizens.

Her mother, now 93 years old, has lived in their home for the past ten years and is an integral part of the family. Marion and her mother have always been extremely devoted to one another, especially since Marion was an only child. They are blessed to have her with them as a grandmother, mother, and close advisor. She joins them in all their social activities and enjoys life with the family.

As a "joiner", Marion has worked with almost every prominent national health organization, local charitable groups, PTA, local youth groups, such as the Boy Scouts and Girl Scouts, served as Executive Director of CHRISTIANS AND JEWS FOR LAW AND MORALITY, ran for public office as member of the Los Angeles School Board, was elected several times as member of the Republican Central Committee in Los Angeles County, was appointed by Governor Reagan to the Advisory Board of Metropolitan State Hospital where she served as Chairman for two terms, worked with youth in anti-drug programs, served on Mayor Yorty's Youth Advisory Committee, District Attorney's Youth Advisory Council, and was Senior Citizens Chair-

man for Los Angeles County Republican Central Committee. In addition, she had her own daily radio program, which she wrote and directed for almost four years, has written articles, and continues to lecture for schools, religious and civic organizations. Her book, "I Was A Spy", became a best seller, and inspired Ronald Reagan to produce her life story for television on the "General Electric Theater".

At present, she is Executive Sales Administrator of DISC/3 COMPANY, which deals in computers. She is one of America's most decorated and honored woman and mother.

LOU HENRY HOOVER

Born 1874

Mrs. Hoover's life was one of continuous service, along with her illustrious husband, President Hoover. Their interests and activities were legion, taking them to many foreign countries, and covering world-wide interests and activities in humanitarian, philanthropic, and patriotic areas. The welfare of all races, creeds, and colors from California to China, Australia, India, Italy, France, Germany, Belgium, Poland, Finland, Russia, Siberia, and England were among their concerns:

Lou's special interest centered around Youth, and every activity of the Girl Scout movement in America. She became National Chairman, and she provided a permanent headquarters for them in the "Lou Henry Memorial Institute" at Palo Alto, so that programs to benefit women and girls would always continue.

Hundreds of millions of men, women, and children, families of war-torn countries, love, bless, and revere Lou Henry and her husband, who worked without pay, spending their own private fortune to succor sick and hungry, maimed humanity, without regard to race, color, or creed.

Lou Henry was born in Waterloo, Iowa, March 29, 1874, where her father built a bank. After eight years, he was asked to start a bank at Whittier, California; and when the banks all over the country were folding, he brought his through without a single loss to any stockholder. From there, Charles Henry was asked to come to Monterey to start a second bank, and he moved his family there. It was here that Lou Henry acquired her love of geology and nature.

Lou Henry was the only girl to matriculate in geology at Stanford University, and it was there she met the brilliant young senior, Herbert Hoover, who was assistant in the Geology and Engineering Department and a student of mining engineering. After getting her B.A. at Stanford, followed by other training at San Jose Normal, she and Herbert Hoover were married and off to China. This proved to be a perfect marriage.

She was plunged into the Boxer Rebellion in Tienstsen where they were living in the Foreign Compound. Amid shots and shells, she did relief work, gathering food and materials for bandages and dressings, along with first aid and hospital work.

It would be next to impossible to find an equal to Lou Henry Hoover as a complete person, fitted by nature, education, and environment, to meet and master any and every situation with which she was confronted. Wherever they went, Lou made a home for her husband and two sons, Herbert, Jr., and Allan; no matter how long or short the stay. In the White House, she graced the Executive Mansion with dignity and simplicity.

No family in public life ever took less or gave more to the world and to the United States than this magnificent couple, Lou and Herbert Hoover. They donated their privately-owned headquarters in London to the British Government during both world wars. They also donated to the United States Government an extensive park area near Washington, which they landscaped, building fifteen homes and a recreation area, to be used by future Presidents, and their magnificent Palo Alto estate, their home, to Stanford University as the official residence of Presidents.

In recognition of the magnificent work of these dedicated patriots, King Leopold of Belgium, with Queen Elizabeth and the Crown Prince, came to the White House to personally express the love and gratitude of the Crown and people of Belgium. The King also conferred upon Lou "The Cross of the Chevalier" Order of Leopold.

The great Paderewiski also came as a guest of the White House, offering his services by giving a series of concerts to help the needy in America, this to repay the great debt of gratitude the Polish people felt for the help they had received through the American War Relief, administered by the Hoovers.

While still in the midst of relief work, Lou Hoover had a massive heart attack and died within a few minutes. She was buried in Palo Alto, with no eulogy, at her request, but merchants closed their doors during the services.

ADELA ROGERS ST. JOHNS
Born 1894

Adela Rogers St. Johns was born in 1894, author and America's first woman sportswriter, one of the most celebrated newspaperwomen of this century and author of hundreds of short stories and novelettes, was the daughter of famed defense attorney, Earl Rogers. At the age of eight, Adela became her father's full-time companion and grew up in his law office, where her playmates were the clerks, cops, bodyguards, acquitted murderers, and denizens of the underworld who peopled her father's life.

Mrs. St. Johns became the highest paid woman reporter of her day with the San Francisco Examiner (1913), Los Angeles Herald (1914), The Chicago American (1928), and The New York American (1929). Her star journalism covered four decades of features from the Hauptmann "Trial of the Century" to the abdication of Edward VIII to the long-count Dempsey-Tunney fight in Chicago to the assassination of Huey Long; she wrote about everybody from Eleanor Roosevelt to the Duchess of Windsor, from Ma Barker to Jean Harlow, from Babe Ruth to Rudolph Valentino, from Wyatt Earp to Bobby Kennedy.

Mrs. St. Johns' books include *Final Verdict*, a best-selling biography of her late father, published in 1962. In it, she not only recounted his brilliant court cases, but told of her running duel with his alcoholic urge, which culminated in her signing a court order to have him put away for his own good. Earl Rogers asked permission to cross-examine the witness, and took on his beloved daughter. He won—and died free and far too soon.

Mrs. St. Johns' writings echo the great truth taught her by her father: that truth always has the power to make itself believed. In her compelling and candid autobiography, *The Honeycomb* (1969), she details with heart, vitality, wit, and wisdom the progress of both an honest pilgrim and a genuine pioneer. Closely woven is the double thread of her professional life and her personal pilgrimage. Of the latter, she writes, "As a female member of the human race I was an involuntary pioneer . . . not by my consent or choice or conviction, but by sheer accident of birth: The circumstances of being Earl Rogers' daughter for the first 18 years of my life." Again, referring to her father, she says, "Far ahead of his time Earl Rogers believed in careers for women". The daughter he raised to be "a free soul" became "A primary prototype of the Modern Woman . . . during the Roaring Twenties and Fabulous Thirties when the experiment of the Modern Woman was so new and all."

Not very religious, still Mrs. St. Johns could observe, "more than with every man, the story of every woman is naught but her relationship to the Spirit" . . . and . . . "If she chooses, woman can use the wings of her spirit . . . without the winged spirit, the word *woman* is a mockery . . . without her wings she is as dangerous as a forest fire."

LAURA MILDRED TANNER PETTIT

Born 1895

Laura Mildred Tanner Pettit was born of godly parents in Payson, Utah on August 9, 1895. She was the third child in a family of ten. Her father, Henry Smith Tanner, was the first city judge in Salt Lake City; her mother, Laura Lauretta Woodland, was the first woman to serve in the Utah State Legislature and the first State President of the PTA. Mildred's four grandparents were pioneers on the famed Mormon trek.

Mildred was endowed with many talents. She played the piano by ear and could play for the family to sing hymns for morning devotional when she was eleven. Her musical career began with piano lessons when she was twelve, and at age fourteen her name was on the church roll as organist. She studied for ten years with Tracy Y. Cannon, a Salt Lake Tabernacle organist, and he taught her harmony, composition, and teaching methods. She started teaching piano when she was a senior in high school, and from then on her after-school classes paid for her education at the University of Utah.

On the twentieth of April, nineteen hundred and twenty one, Laura Mildred Tanner and Dr. William Alfred Pettit were married in the Latter Day Saint Temple in Salt Lake City, Utah.

From this union have come four sons and one daughter, twenty-five grandchildren, and three great-grandchildren. The sons are: Dr. William A. Pettit, Jr., ophthalmologist, Pasadena, California, Dr. John T. Pettit, Corporate Director of Summa Corporation, Dr. Thomas H. Pettit, Professor of Ophthalmology and Associate Director of the Jules Stein Eye Institute at UCLA Medical Center, Edwin Ray Pettit, Elder in his church and temple worker in the Los Angeles Temple. Their daughter, Dorothy Ann Pettit Maxfield, holds a Bachelor of Science degree and three teaching credentials. She mirrors her mother's ability and sense of responsibility in rearing eleven children.

Mildred's opportunities have been great. She was called to be a member of the General Board of the Primary in 1932. This board is comprised of women who are called to write teaching materials and music for use in the Mormon church throughout the world. Music has run as a golden thread through her life. At the age of eighteen, her first composition, "The Butterfly Dance", was published and enjoyed by children in many lands. It was also danced in the final program of the famed Salt Lake Theater. Through the years fifty of her songs and four operettas have been published and used to teach children all over the world. Countless lives have been influenced by her music. Her best known and most beloved song is "I Am a Child of God" for which she composed the music. *Printed* in every language where the Mormon church exists, it has been used in many programs and sung by many choirs. It was a featured song of "Christmas with the King Family" on their television special in December, 1974.

She moved to South Pasadena in 1936, and with all the tasks a mother does for her family, she was a leader in the local and district Parent Teacher Association for fourteen years. In 1942, she was asked to write the fiftieth anniversary pagent, "Golden Jubilee", for the PTA. It was produced in the San Gabriel Valley Mission Playhouse, and twelve hundred school children performed in this memorable event, for which she received national recognition. Today, many schools and parents are grateful for her foresight in creating the "Back-to-School-Night" program, whereby parents have an opportunity to learn first-hand about their children's school activities.

In 1940, Mildred's husband was made President of the Pasadena Stake with ten churches or Wards over which to preside, and Mildred was the official mother and hostess for many social gatherings in their home. For ten years, the great and the small came through her doors and her table was always "spread with the bounties of the earth and no one was ever turned away from her door hungry".

When Mildred was made President of the Relief Society in South Pasadena, she made a survey of homes and found there were children sleeping on the floor in sleeping bags because they had no beds. It was then she started her famous quilting project. She fashioned her own style "tie-tie" quilt that has been copied in many lands. When a new chapel near her home was built, she made and sold over three hundred quilts to support the project.

Other community service includes:
> Los Angeles County Coordinating Council—two years,
> Member South Pasadena Recreation Commission—five years,
> Red Cross, Community Chest and Rationing Board Committee, (World War II).

She has been the recipient of many awards and honors, including:
> 1938—honors presented in Kingsbury Hall, University of Utah for the music to the operetta "Land of Happy Hearts" performed for over 1,000 teachers of music and recreation representing many nations of the earth,
> April 1954—In the Salt Lake Tabernacle, when two of her new songs were introduced by a chorus of 220 California teachers, and accompanied on the organ by Alexander Schreiner,
> 1957—35 year pin for service to the Primary organization,
> 1958—Honorary member of the Delta Kappa Gamma Society International,
> 1961—Heritage Award of the California-Utah Women's Organization,
> 1966—Runner-up Award for the California Mother of the Year given by the American Mothers Committee.

Her life has been one of service to her family, her church, and her community, and she has developed special talents through her courage and ability. Of these she has freely given, and to such a successful extent that she has earned a place of honor in our choicest halls of fame.

Now, at the age of eighty, she is an organist in the Los Angeles Temple and meets the duties of each day with poise and grace, and her life has been that of one of the most noble and saintly of women. She has been a widow for five years and has a deep and abiding faith in eternal life and the joyful reunion with loved ones in the kingdom of our Father in Heaven.

One of her poems is as follows:
"My regrets
> Are not for things I've done
But for the little things I meant to do.
The violets I picked and failed to send;
Words of love I did not give a friend.
The call I should have made at sorrow's door;
Comforts that I could have sent the poor.
The letter that somehow I did not pen.
Chances lost will never come again.
> These are my regrets . . ."

HARRIETT BULPITT RANDALL
Born 1904

Harriett Bulpitt Randall, M.D. (Mrs. Paul Omar Campbell), born in Bishop, California, on August 11, 1904, now resides in Glendale, California. Her parents were Fred and Ella Bulpitt. She is well known because of her outstanding service in the public health and preventive medicine fields.

Her numerous contributions lie largely in the field of child health, particularly in administrative leadership and in school health programs and child psychiatry. She was Administrator, Health and Medical Services, Los Angeles City Schools from 1960-70, and Child Psychiatrist, Pasadena Child Guidance Clinic, from 1970 to the present.

She has had published over 100 articles and reports in professional and lay journals. She was the recipient of the coveted Howe Award from the American School Health Association in 1970, and the Anderson Award in recognition of the quality and excellence of her contributions to school health.

Dr. Randall is a past president of the American School Health Association, and has received its Distinguished Service Award. She received her Doctor of Medicine degree from Loma Linda University, is a Diplomate of the National Board of Medical Examiners, a member of the American Board of Preventive Medicine and the California Medical Association, and a Lecturer in the University of California at Los Angeles School of Public Health in the field of Preventive Medicine.

Dr. Randall has served with great distinction in the field of school health education. She has given a lifetime of service to local, state, national, and international committees and commissions relating to the field of child health. She has been a member of the Board of Directors of the Los Angeles Child Guidance Clinic, the Los Angeles City Schools' Drug Abuse Committee, the Southern California Psychiatric Society, the American Psychiatric Association and is a Fellow of the American Public Health Association.

In her personal life, Harriett Randall Campbell is a loving mother and wife of Paul Omar Campbell, Professor of Speech at Loma Linda University. He is on the ministerial staff of Glendale Seventh-Day Adventist Church, where his wife is superintendent of the Sabbath School.

Dr. Randall has three outstanding children: Dwight T. Randall, Jr., Doctor of Jurisprudence, a Los Angeles attorney; Eleanor Fanselau, M.D., a pediatrician in a mission hospital in Argentina, and Elizabeth Adams Randall, M.D., working in the field of public health after graduate work at Loma Linda University.

In 1972 Dr. Randall was one of the California Merit Mothers and in 1974 the California Mother of the Year, selected by the American Mothers Committee, Inc. She competed with the other 50 State Mothers in New York for the 1974 National Mother of the Year, who is recognized on Mother's Day.

The prayers of Harriett Randall Campbell would be for wisdom, strength, and the opportunity to serve and accomplish more, because she realizes that the best one can do is still very small compared with the need and the challenge of what is yet to be attained.

PEARL BAILEY

Born 1918

Pearlie Mae Bailey was born March 29, 1918, in Newport News, Virginia. A young child of four, she moved with her family to Washington, D.C. In her autobiography, published in 1968, she describes her Reverend father as the "salt" in her life, and her charming mother as the "sugar". Her parents were separated when she was quite young and Pearl stayed with her mother until the divorce, after which she moved with her brother Bill (Willie), and sisters, Virgie and Eura, to live with their father. Not long afterwards, however, she returned to live with her mother, who had remarried in Philadelphia.

At age fifteen, Pearl had ambitions to be a school teacher. It was during this time her brother Willie was becoming an established and reputable tap dancer in show business. Her first debut occurred one evening after she'd skipped over to the Pearl Theatre to deliver a message to Bill. It was Amateur Night and her songs, "The Talk of the Town" and "Poor Butterfly" in addition to a "fast buck dance" won her the contest. An award of five dollars and a week's work at $30 initiated her career as an entertainer. Enchanted with the theatre, Pearl lost interest in high school and began her education on the outside.

During a visit to her brother's home in New York she again entered an Amateur Hour and won for her own arrangement of "In My Solitude". Recognition backstage as "Bill's little sister" exposed her to many celebrities and the life of the theatre. She landed a job in a song and dance routine for three weeks, and, from there, the producer gave her a job in the chorus, making $22 a week. From there, she became involved in the coal circuit of Pennsylvania. It was during this time that she married a drummer which marriage lasted only about eighteen months.

When she moved back to Washington, D.C. and while she was working at the Republican Gardens, the bandleader offered her a job as a vocalist with his orchestra. After the band dispersed she got bookings in various clubs, and while performing at the Apollo Theatre in New York she was asked to accompany the Sunset Royal Band to Baltimore and Washington.

World War II took her on a USO tour across the country and to the West Coast. Finally, she obtained some management and did a wide Variety of arrangements. In 1944, she had a trial engagement at the Blue Angel in New York, and her name quickly infiltrated the theatre circles.

In 1948 she married a man she had met in Arizona while doing the USO tour. At the dissolution of the marriage, Pearl married a wealthy Washington playboy who had sold her old house. This third marriage ended unhappily after approximately two years. But even as her personal life was suffering, her career flourished. Her recordings include "Tired", "15 Years", and "That's Good Enough for Me". Having moved from vaudeville to clubs, she now did legitimate theatre. Her first stage play was *St. Louis Woman* in 1946, for which she received the Donaldson Award. Her second theatre performance along this line was in *Arms & the Girl* which opened on Broadway.

Pearl's first starring role on Broadway was in the *House of Flowers*, in which she played the madam. Her first Hollywood film was *Variety Girl. Isn't it Romantic* came next followed by *That Certain Feeling, St. Louis Blues, Fine Young Cannibals, Porgy & Bess*, and *Carmen Jones*. She worked with, and for, many important people, from performers to government officials.

In 1952 Pearl Bailey married Louis Bellson. Before their marriage, while performing in London and awaiting the arrival of her fiance, she received a telegram from her prospective father-in-law. It read, "my son is marrying out of the race" to which her well-known reply was "there is only one race, the human race".

When they returned to the States, Pearl and Louis bought a ranch in Apple Valley, California. Soon thereafter, they adopted their first child, a son named Tony. A few years later, they adopted a three-month-old girl they named Dee Dee after Louis' sister.

Pearl Bailey's most highly acclaimed performance is the smash "Hello Dolly". She's written two books which portray a character of unlimited warmth, love, and generosity.

IVY BAKER PRIEST

Ivy Baker Priest was born in Kimberly, Utah, the daughter of Orange Decatur Baker and Clara Fernley. She was educated in public schools, U.S.A.; she received Honorable Doctorates in Human Letters Elmira, New York College Science of Business Administration, Bryant College, Providence, Rhode Island; honorable, LLD, Doctor of Laws, Rider College, Trenton, New Jersey.

She married Roy Priest, who died in June of 1959. She married Sidney W. Stevens, in 1961. He died March 24, 1972. She had daughters, Mrs. Pierce A. (Patricia Ann Priest) Jensen, Jr.; Mrs. J. A. (Nancy Priest) Valenzuela, born June 5, 1941; a son Roy Baker Priest, born Oct 22,

1942, and died June 1971. Mrs. Priest's career included: Treasurer of the United States, 1953 to 1960, Treasurer of the State of California, 1967, to the time of her death in 1973.

Mrs. Priest was the author of the book, "Green Grows Ivy". Among the awards she received, she was nominated one of 20 outstanding women of this century by Women's Newspaper Editors and Publishers association; She received the achievement award for outstanding accomplishment in politics, the Women's National Press club award.

Mrs. Priest was a member trustee, National Society for Crippled Children. She served as director of California Easter Seal Society. She served as Director of Greater Los Angeles Safety Council. She was a member of International Soroptimist Club; a member of Business and Professional Women's Club. She was given an honorary life membership in Women's Advertising Club of Washington D.C. She was a member of the International Beta Sigma Phi. She was Vice Chairman of the Republican National Committee in 1952-1953. She served as Vice President of the Republican Association of Eleven Western States:

Mrs. Priest was a member of Delta Zeta, (Church of Jesus Christ of Latter Day Saints). She resided, until her death, at 1500 7th Street, Sacramento, California. As California State Treasurer, she occupied Room 128, State Capitol, Sacramento, California.

SHIRLEY TEMPLE BLACK
Born 1928

The famed child star of the '30's, characterized by her dimpled cheeks and blond curls, was born the youngest of three children in Santa Monica, California. She entered dancing school at three-and-a-half years, and soon was discovered by a talent scout.

By 1932, Shirley Temple was appearing in one-reel films. Soon thereafter, Fox Film Corporation—now known as 20th Century Fox—found her and cast her in "Stand Up and Cheer" (1934) which established her stardom. She continued performing in the movie industry and was awarded an Oscar in 1934 as the "outstanding personality of '34". It has been said that her early popularity was due to her bubbling enthusiasm and energy, which had a wide appeal to the grim spirit of the depression era.

By 1940, the film industry was suffering as a result of the loss of the foreign market in World War II. Shirley then did a radio series, but still continued filming, in nonstarring roles.

In June of '45, she graduated from Westlake School for Girls in Los Angeles. This was also the year of the publication of her autobiography *My Young life*. In September, '45, she was married to Sergeant John Agar Jr., of the Army Air Force. They performed together briefly, but were divorced two years after the birth of their daughter, Linda Susan.

On December 16, 1950, Shirley Temple married Charles A. Black, a wealthy San Francisco business executive. She gave birth to two more children by him. During the Korean War, he served as a lieutenant commander at the Pentagon. It was during this time, while living in the Washington area, that Shirley Black became interested in politics. She was soon to become a leader in civic and political affairs.

In the late '50's, they moved back to California. Shirley made a comeback in show business, on television, and became active in civic and community affairs. She was involved in the development of the San Francisco International Film Festival. However, she resigned from the executive committee in October '66, protesting the inclusion of a Swedish film titled *Night Games*. Her controversial position won her the 1967 Kiwanis International Award for her firm stand on decency in the motion picture industry.

It was in August of 1967 that Shirley Temple Black announced her candidacy for Congress, for the seat in the House of Representatives which had been vacated by the death of J.A.

Younger. Running Republican, and as the only woman candidate, Shirley T. Black ran close, but was defeated by McClowsky.

Continuing in community affairs, she led an active fight against the disease of Multiple Sclerosis, with which her brother is afflicted. She is the co-founder of the International Federation of M.S. Societies.

In 1969, Richard Nixon named her to the five-member United States delegation to the 24th Session of the United Nations General Assembly, as a "public member".

In 1972, she publicized her mastectomy operation to spur other women in detecting breast cancer and having it treated without delay.

She was named Ambassador to Ghana in August of '74. She said she had "no problem being taken seriously as a woman and a diplomat". Ghana is a matriarchal society where the men are the laborers and the women leaders. "My only problems," she said, "have been with Americans who, in the beginning, refused to believe I had grown up since my movies."

As a political figure, Shirley has participated in numerous Republican finance and campaign committees, at all levels from community to national. In 1968 she served on the Women's Advisory Committee for Nixon, campaigning for him while she was traveling in Europe. She served as a member on the California Republican State Committee, the California Council on Crime and Justice. She was chairman for the Youth Week in Golden Gate Center, San Francisco: and the list goes on.

She graduated from Notre Dame in 1972, and, though an avid contributor to society, she is very devoted to her family and holds firm views on the attention and discipline required by children.

COLORADO

Colorado

Nickname: The Centennial State

State Flower: Blue Colorado Columbine

State Tree: Blue Spruce

State Bird: Lark Bunting

Photos

1. Red Rocks Park and Theater
2. Air Force Academy Chapel
3. Garden of the Gods,
4. Chipeta, in Ute Indian Museum
5. State Capitol
6. "Buffalo Bill"

Committee Members

Chairman—Mrs. Coleman Toth Jr.
   Westminister
Mr. James Blue
Mr. Robert Petteys
Mr. James Woodruff
Mrs. Dorothy Smith
Ms. Pat Jorgenson
Mr. Ralph Taylor, Historian and author*
Mr. Mark McFeely
Mrs. Arthur Cordova
Mrs. Mary L. Taylor, Denver
Mrs. Sharon Rouse, Crested Butte,
Mr. Theodore C. Kahn Pueblo
Mrs. C.J. Corwin, Aurora
Mrs. Amy Thompson, Delores
Mrs. Elizabeth Oliveto, Denver
Miss Deby Wilson, Fleming
Mrs. Leo Kirk, Denver
Mrs. Nancy Penfold, Fort Lupton
Family of Josephine Olivia Falsetto Cuzzetto
Mrs. Janine Lutrey Solano, Artist

Colorado

CHIPETA—

Born 1843

The famous Eugene Field, one time Colorado editor once wrote—
"Give her a page in history too,
Though she is rotting in humble shrouds,
And write on the whitest of God's white clouds
Chipeta's name in eternal blue."

Chipeta was the wife of Ouray, great chief of all the Ute tribes, respected by her own people and admired by the Whites.

Chipeta and Ouray advocated peace more than a century ago, when there existed open and continual warfare between those whose skins were red and the Caucasian settlers of the West. Their fight for peaceful co-existence was credited with averting many bloody confrontations. They influenced treaties which finally saw the Western Colorado lands of the Utes opened to white gold seekers and ranchers, and the Utes removed to reservations in Southern Colorado and Utah.

In 1859, the Taberguache Ute girl became Ouray's wife. She never was a squaw. Because of her intelligence, dignity and opinions, she was queen to Ouray and to all of the Utes. Chipeta's

intelligence matched that of her highly-respected spouse.

Chipeta was the only woman ever allowed to participate in the councils of the Utes, and the only woman who accompanied the Indian leaders to Washington, D. C. to make treaty talks with the Great White Father.

Chipeta made historical decisions long before white men allowed their women to vote, to own land, or to have personal liberation.

Chipeta's cry was "Peace, peace". She sensed the futility of clashes between the races that eventually could only be resolved by understanding.

In 1868, Governor A. Comeron Hunt negotiated a treaty, giving the Utes reserved lands, but troubles persisted with the Whites.

Again and again, after much negotiation, the hope for peace was again destroyed because of the Whites and the defiance of Chipeta's race.

After the Meeker Massacre, in 1878 there was little hope to even hold the lands of the Utes. Nathan Meeker, one-time agricultural editor of Horace Greeley's New York Tribune, and Indian agent at Meeker, was killed by the Utes. Chipeta and Ouray were enraged with their people. Chipeta and Ouray sought and found three female captives. They had been horribly abused. Chipeta returned them to relatives. The kidnapers were sent to prison.

Chipeta, had a son, Cotoan. While a small child, Cotoan was kidnaped by a band of Sioux. Ouray and Chipeta spent many years trying to trace the child. Many moons later, after the tribes had agreed upon peace among themselves, Cotoan realized that he was the son of Ouray and Chipeta. Cotoan rode over the horizon for a reunion with his parents, Ouray and Chipeta, but he died before he reached them.

Chief Ouray died August 24, 1880.

Chipeta died in 1924 at the age of 81, exiled and forgotten, in a reservation, by the white people she loved. Chipeta's remains were buried on Ouray homestead near Montrose.

Montrose citizens and the State Historical Society of Colorado erected a concrete tepee and the monument to Ouray and Chipeta in a memorial park.

FRANCES JACOBS

Born 1843

In the rotunda of the gold-domed Colorado capitol building in Denver, portraits of 16 Empire builders in stained glass fill honored niches. In 1958, in this significant circle, the state's Hall of Fame, there was one woman, Mrs. Frances Jacobs.

Mrs. Jacobs' contribution was love for her fellow man expressed in unselfish service. Frances Jacobs was fairly wealthy, but she was keenly aware of the extreme poverty that existed. She wore the plainest of clothes and devoted her time and energy to the unfortunate.

Newspaper files of the late 1880's reveal little of this remarkable woman. "Aunt Frank", as she was called, was a rare combination of dreamer and doer. She not only dreamed of free kindergartens and orphanages, a home for the aged and a hospital, but with good business sense, she brought them to reality.

Mrs. Jacobs wore a severe hair-do piled atop her head, a hint of a pompadour accentuating her generous ears. Her jaw showed energy and determination and here eyes were gentle. Her full lips and wide mouth suggested a sense of humor.

"Aunt Frank" never hesitated to approach the well-do-do business man or church leader of any denomination with her pleas for aid. Business, religious, and social leaders who heard Frances Jacobs never forgot the appeal she made for a free kindergarten at the Denver Charities annual meeting in 1890. And soon afterward Colorado established its first free kindergarten.

Mrs. Jacobs always carried several bars of "Granpa Tar Soap" in her voluminous purse. People held their noses and giggled whenever she opened her bag.

Mrs. Jacobs played such a part in the founding of the *National Jewish Hospital* in Denver for consumptives that when the building was completed in 1880, her name was placed in gold letters above the entrance. Later, under her guidance, this institution became the first in America to "treat without charge and without distinction of creed," and "none may enter who can pay and none can pay who enter," became the institution's motto, displayed on a large sign.

In 1880 Mrs. Jacobs reorganized many private charity agencies into a federation. Because of this organization, forerunner of the present Community Chest and United Fund, Mrs. Frances Jacobs was called "Mother of the Charities."

In 1892, Frances Jacobs caught a severe cold—becoming drenched in a cold rain as she carried medicine and supplies to sick children on Lawrence Street, in one of the most run-down sections of Denver. Two days later she developed pneumonia. "The Mother of Charities" died that October 1892, at age 49.

ADELIA RIVERA DE VALDEZ
Born 1874

"The triumvirate of God, Motherhood, and Country controls the destiny of America—Man's very existence depends on Motherhood."

Adelia Rivera de Valdez, La Jara, Colorado graduated from the "University of Life", with GL (Guiding Light) and MA (Motherhood Achievement) degrees.

Adelia Rivera de Valdez was born in the vicinity of Conejos, Colorado in 1874 and died in La Jara, Colorado in 1957.

Adelia possessed the strong and admirable qualities of her historical ancestors and pioneering women.

Mrs. Valdez had the adventurous spirit of her ancestor Ortiz, who got a grant from Charles V. of Spain. Hers was the deep religious zeal of Juan Onate's people who, in 1598 established Santa Fe, the oldest existing settlement in the United States. Hers was her grandparents' and parents' pioneering ruggedness when founding Conejos and San Luis in 1851—the oldest settlements in Colorado.

Francisco Valdez, Adelia's husband, and she operated a communal flour mill and undertook farming and stock raising at the Alamosa Canyon homestead. Here the children began to get her guidance in clearing land, irrigating, raising good livestock, preparing food and equipment for her husband who spent his summers at the cattle and sheep camps.

Mrs. Valdez was aware that her children would encounter many challenges under a new government with a new language, strange laws, and customs. Because of this she challenged her children to greater accomplishments, thus she had hundreds of activities for the almost self-sufficient family of thirteen.

In later years she encouraged and inspired her grand-children and others into the professions and businesses.

In 1912 the family left Esequiel and Joe P. with the Alamosa Canyon holdings and moved to La Jara where Mr. and Mrs. Valdez trained by twos Felix and Ernest, Esequiel and Joe P., Tony and Bonnie, Louis the youngest joined in later years, to become experimenting and enterprising farmers. They started with sage brush lands and transformed them into flourishing and productive farms.

There was time also for college training in electricity, mechanics and bookkeeping to operate the farm efficiently. Whatever knowledge

they acquired in their experimentation they shared with college researchers.

Mr. Valdez died when much needed, but Adelia, more than ever before, counseled for togetherness, compassion, and learning among all.

The daughters took instruction in music and Rebecca (the oldest of the girls), Estefanita, and Maria prepared to teach in elementary, junior and senior high and college. Carlota, separated from her husband, received much respect, love, and help. Emilia died at an early age and Cidelia, the handicapped child was loved as God's special gift.

Adelia was most active in the religious and social life. Fun activities were undertaken after her giving instructions in wool carding, spinning, making blankets, processing foods, nightly reading of the Bible, etc.

Adelia Rivera de Valdez was beautiful, gentle, humble, strong, and optimistic. Her love for God, country, family, and all cultures was unquestionable. By her guidance her children acquired big land-holdings, wealth, and respectability.

Adelia represents nearly perfect womanhood and motherhood. Her descendants call her "The Guiding Light".

PORTIA LUBCHENCO, M.D.
Born 1887

Named Colorado Mother of the Year for 1954, Dr. Portia Lubchenco, known to friends and patients as Doctor Portia, and to her 5 children, 21 grandchildren and 9 great grandchildren as "Mom" continues to exemplify those qualities which prompted that honor 21 years ago.

One of 9 children born to Peter and Lula McKnight, Doctor Portia was attracted early in life to the practice of medicine as she saw it practiced in rural South Carolina because she thought it afforded a valuable service to people.

The first woman admitted to and graduated from the North Carolina Medical College, Doctor Portia graduated second in the class of 1912. She was wed shortly thereafter to Alexis Lubchenco whom she had met while he was studying cotton culture on her parents' farm. He was an agronomist sent to the United States by Czar Nicholas II. Portia returned with him to Russia to start a family and practice medicine.

Forced to flee her new home because of the Russian revolution of 1917 she, Alexis and their 3 young children returned to the United States.

After several years of general practice in South Carolina, they moved to Haxtun, Colorado. Alexis utilized his chemical training to set up a clinical laboratory while Portia practiced medicine with her brother, James McKnight.

For the next 50 years Doctor Portia lived and practiced medicine in the Sterling-Haxtun, Colorado Area winning the love and admiration of the community with her gentle and quiet manner, lively sense of humor and her dedication to the people she served. Although her medical talents were constantly in demand, Doctor Portia's family remained of prime importance. She has instilled her strong feelings about community service and love of medicine in her 5 children, as well as in her grandchildren. Many of her children and grandchildren, exposed to her love of medicine, have also chosen to make it their life's work.

In 1967, at the age of 80, she "retired" and moved to Denver. Feeling too young and too vital to sit idly, and understanding first-hand the problems of those more than 60 years young, Doctor Portia began a second career, bringing good medicine and a greater understanding to those confined to nursing homes in the Denver area. Five years later Doctor Portia was forced to give up the active practice of medicine because of the problems she had been treating in others. Today, at 88 and still vital and blessed with her marvelous sense of humor, her counsel and company is still prized by her children and grandchildren and those many persons met socially and professionally who love and respect Doctor Portia.

A book "Doctor Portia" a warm intimate story of Colorado's Dr. Portia Lubchenco, her first fifty years in medicine, was written by Anna C. Petteys. It was dedicated to the Lubchenco children and grandchildren.

In 1972, the Denver Clinic honored Dr. Portia as she reitred a second time from active practice.

Dr. Portia, the sharp and quick witted mother with a good sense of humor, will long be remembered in Colorado.

HAZEL RHOADS GATES, SR.
Born 1891

"Mommie G." was the pet name for Mrs. Charles C. Gates Sr. of Denver, Colorado. If it were not for Mrs. Charles C. Gates, there would be no Gates Rubber Company of Denver, the world's sixth largest manufacturer of rubber products, no 17,000 employees, and no 12 plants spread throughout eight states and five countries.

In 1910, Hazel La Dora Rhoads met Charles Cassius Gates, 32, a mining engineer in Denver. Six weeks after they met, on April 4, 1910, they were married. Mrs. Gates was born March 28, 1891 and was just 19 years old. She, by her own admission, was a "social butterfly".

It was because Hazel Gates wanted her husband to stay home instead of traveling to various mines that the Gates Rubber Company was born. She persuaded him to buy a business in Denver.

They found three likely manufacturing concerns for sale—one made toilet paper, another soap and the third, tire covers. So it was the tire covers they chose. Her patchwork quilt, out of scraps of elk hide, provided the idea for the first business success. The stitched elk hide, provided the idea for the first business success. The stitched elk leather scraps were extremely strong and Gates decided to use them for "never break horse halters."

Mrs. considered her "greatest achievement", was the production of a son, after four daughters, during those early years of company progress.

Mrs. Gates, "Mommie G" was known for her successful way as a mother of five living children, 15 grandchildren, and one great grandchild. "Mommie G." was also loved by the more than 10,000 children of Gates employees in the United States and Canada.

The immediate family of Charles and Hazel Gates is known all over the world, for their strength of character and prestige.

"Mommie G's" "baby" was the Gates Rubber Company Christmas Party, a tradition since 1922, for the children of her employees. She previewed the gifts, and they had to be very nice. She was generous with her talents, generous with her time, and generous with her gifts.

"Mommie G." had a beautiful philosophy of life, "you can be anything, do anything, have anything you really want—if you try hard enough and hurt no one in trying, and to re-

member to value things by what they mean and not by what they cost."

The dynamic Mrs. Charles Gates Sr. the "Mommie G." long to be remembered, died September 19, 1973.

ANNA C. PETTEYS

Mrs. Anna C. Petteys was born in Bryant, Iowa. She was a graduate of Grinnell College in 1912. She met her husband Alonzo Petteys while attending Grinnell. They were married in 1914 and came to Colorado in 1920. Mr. Petteys, who became a widely known financier and banker in Northwestern Colorado died in 1968.

Mrs. Petteys taught school one year at George, Iowa following her graduation. She then spent one at home, "learning to cook" before her marriage.

Following the rearing of four children, Mrs. Petteys in 1942, decided to continue her education and enrolled at Colorado State College of Education in Greeley, Colorado. She received her master of arts degree there in 1943, and also received an honorary doctorate from the same college. She was a member of Phi Beta Kappa, Pi Lambda Theta, Alpha Delta Kappa and Delta Kappa Gamma.

Mr. and Mrs. Petteys assisted in the education of a Chinese girl who had come to the United States but was unable to continue her education because of wartime conditions. Mrs. Petteys and the girl, Ellison Jee enrolled together at the University of Chicago.

Mrs. Petteys was a Gold Star Mother. Her oldest son, Jack was killed during flight training in Arizona while serving with the U. S. Army Air Corps. Following his death the Petteys family established a Jack Petteys Memorial Scholarship to be awarded annually to outstanding boy graduates in Colorado.

Following the end of World War II Mrs. Petteys took an active interest in the United Nations and toured Colorado lecturing on the objectives of the organization. In 1948 she went to Parish to attend a general assembly meeting of the United Nations. From her tours of the United States and trips abroad, Mrs. Petteys became noted for her lecturing ability.

In 1950 Mrs. Petteys was elected to the newly created Colorado Board of Education. She served continously for 18 years. She also served 10 years as a member of the Board of Trustees for the State Colleges beginning in 1945.

Mrs. Petteys and her son Robert, a graduate of Pomona College in California began joint publication of the Fort Morgan Herald, a weekly newspaper. Later the family acquired the Sterling Farm Journal. In 1953 they bought the Sterling Advocate and combined the news-papers into the Sterling Journal Advocate. In 1970 Mrs. Petteys sold the Journal-Advocate but continued to write a daily column.

"Dr. Portia", the warm intimate story of Colorado's Dr. Portia Lubchenco, was written by Anna C. Petteys and published in 1964.

Anna C. Petteys is listed in Who's Who in Education, Who's Who in Colorado History.

Anna C. Petteys was the mother of Robert Petteys, Colorado, Mrs. W. M. Watrous of Colorado and Mrs. Lyle Pattee of Canada.

Anna C. Petteys died in 1970 in a auto-truck collison in Colorado.

MARIE CHANDLER GREENWOOD
Born 1901

The Postmaster retired after 29 years of service. The retired Postmaster of Stratton, Colorado wrote a letter that "set the state of Colorado on fire". Retired or not, this tiny, white haired mother, slightly bent by the winds that rake the plains, so vigorously promoted her town, that the Denver Post, Colorado's largest newspaper, met her challenge of ignoring mid-eastern Colorado, by featuring the City of Stratton and its citizens in a story befitting a King, Queen, or President.

Marie Chandler Greenwood, the eldest of the five children of Charles Chandler and Meta Loep Chandler, was born November 11, 1901, on a farm near Wagner, South Dakota. The English and German lineage of her parents and the rigorous experiences of her early childhood gave Marie the heritage and environment for a staunch personality which has characterized her life as pioneer child, student, school teacher, wife, mother, small town postmaster, community and county leader.

On a blizzardly March, 1909, day the Chandlers came by train to live 7½ miles north of Stratton, Colorado, on a homestead relinquishment they had purchased from a Mr. Gill, who had built a three-roomed sod house on it. A house nicer than most because of its wood floors, native lime-plastered walls and deep-silled windows, where in violent snow and hail-storms, fenceless prairies, miles of open range as a little girl on a saddleless horse she hunted for the cattle. She walked by lantern light in the dark night to "fetch" the neighbor lady the

night her youngest sister was born. She learned phonics, reading, writing, spelling, and cried over multiplication tables as she received her early years of education from her schoolteacher mother prior to entering public school at age eight as a 6th grader . . . these are a few of Marie Greenwood's memories of childhood.

Times were hard, but gradually as machinery and horses were acquired farming began to supplement the milk cows as the source of family income. Marie recalls dropping the kernels of corn in the furrow behind her father as he rolled the sod with his plow. At the end of a harvest season a clothing inventory was made, catalogs were studied, clothes were ordered from Montgomery Ward and their arrival in a big wooden box was quite an event. In good years there was enough money for a winter supply of apples and fifty pounds of honey!

Marie Greenwood attended three years of high school, (1914-1917). She attended the University of Colorado (1918-1920). At age 18, she began teaching school.

She met Harry H. Greenwood, son of early Colorado settlers, and they were married in 1923, and she continued to teach school.

From 1925 to 1936 Marie devoted her full time to husband, Harry, Laura, Thelma, and Allen. In 1936 Mrs. Greenwood started to teach again and would take her three children with her each day.

In 1943, Marie Greenwood was appointed Postmaster of Stratton, Colorado. She served in this capacity for 29 years until she retired in 1971, at 70 years *young*.

In spite of retirement, Marie Chandler Greenwood continues to play a dynamic and vital role in her corner of Colorado.

IDA GREENBERG

"All that I am," said Abraham Lincoln, "or hope to be, I owe to my angel mother."

From the conception of her child until her love follows him to her last breath, the true mother encourages, inspires and prays that her offspring shall attain and fulfill the greatest potentials within himself, and for betterment of all mankind.

This narration begins in Russia more than a century ago when a girl named Ida first heard about a far-off country called America where those of lowly birth could rise to pinnacles of achievement in the service of the multitudes.

Ida fell in love with an ambitious fellow named Samuel Greenberg. He shared her dreams. Samuel and Ida and their three children came to America and settled in Pueblo, Colorado. The three children born in Russia, eventually had four brothers.

The six Greenberg sons and one daughter remember that while growing up in Pueblo they were just a bunch of kids. Money was scarce, but they conceived their own forms of enjoyment in the relatively little time they had be-

tween studying, doing odd jobs, and helping maintain the home and grocery store. Their mother never let them lose sight of the high goals she hoped they would reach.

Ida saw instances of American achievement. She cared so much that her sons should distinguish themselves that the stress was made on education. As the children expanded their knowledge, Ida also went to school to learn to read and write. Ida's offspring made his imprint upon the community and the profession of which he became a part. Many thousands of American families have produced one or two outstanding achievers. Comparatively few match the mass attainments of the Greenberg brothers. One such example, of course, is that of the Eisenhower brothers. Here, the mother had saved and encouraged the childredn.

In 1940 Ida Greenberg died. So thoroughly had she ingrained her love and her concern about achievement that five of her sons became nationally famous, and one internationally distinguished.

Jessie Greenberg Speken, married a successful businessman and lives in Pueblo, Colorado.

William Greenberg, now retired, became a very successful businessman, in Pueblo, Colorado.

Dr. David Greenberg spent his entire professional career at the University of California. Ida lived to see him become one of the top scientists of the nation in biochemistry, noted for his study of cancer and the discovery of a new treatment for hemophilia. Retired, he now lives in California.

Louis Greenberg became a biochemist and a professor at the University of California.

Roy Greenberg, an electrical engineer, was always fascinated with business, and he operated a jewelry and sports store in Texas until his death in 1964.

Milton (Mendel) Greenberg is a physicist and lecturer in Connecticut.

Dr. Max Greenberg practiced medicine in Louisiana until his retirement recently.

Each has made history. Someone might suggest they would have made their marks without the encouragement and dreams of their mother. Even the master egoist, Napoleon Bonaparte, said, "The future destiny of the child is always the work of the mother."

RUTH FLOWERS

At a time when a great deal of publicity is given to women who find themselves bearing the twin responsibilities of a career and motherhood, it is necessary to remind ourselves that throughout our country's history, and long before the days of "Women's Lib," American women have been successfully combining the two.

A Colorado mother who can be proud of both her careers is Dr. Ruth Cave Flowers of Boulder. Ruth Flowers has no biological children, but at the age of 43 when she was asked to become a foster mother to a three month old boy who desperately needed mothering, there could be only one answer for Ruth.

Even though she was at that time a practicing attorney and attending classes toward her doctorate in foreign languages, there was no hesitation or wondering about how she would fit a child into her life. For Ruth knew from the recollections of her own childhood that anything is possible if one tries hard enough, and that time and space can always be made in your life for others if you're willing to give enough.

Ruth didn't have to attend any workshops or encounter groups to learn these lessons of life; they were a part of the heritage left to her by her own mother and grandmother, and the

other women of the Black community in which she grew up.

The sacrifices made by Ruth's mother and grandmother were not in vain, as Ruth maintained high academic standards from her elementary school days at Colorado Springs and Cripple Creek to that proud day in 1924 when she became the first Negro woman to graduate from the University of Colorado.

Ruth went on to receive a Master's degree at Colorado, a law degree from Robert F. Terrel Law School in Washington, D. C., and her Ph.D. from the Catholic University of America.

Ruth has devoted more than 30 years of her life to teaching at both the high school and college level. The love and respect she felt for her students was reciprocated in 1969 when one of her former students nominated her to receive Harvard University's 'Teacher of the Year' award. She was one of four secondary teachers in the nation so honored that year.

In 1961 she was listed in "Who's Who in American Women."

After 30 years on the east coast, Ruth's love for her native state brought her back to Boulder in 1959. She and her son Harold took up residence in the modest home that she and her grandmother had built themselves in 1921.

Ruth ended her teaching career with seven years of service at Boulder's Fairview High School, while her son Harold attended Boulder High School and the University of Colorado, receiving his law degree from C.U. in 1971.

Although racial prejudice was one of the many obstacles on the road to her success, Ruth Flowers has not allowed bitterness to taint her thoughts. She attained her academic and career goals long before the civil rights legislation of the 1960's, and she became a single-parent mother before it was fashionable to do so. The fact that she has been successful at both has made her a credit to her race—the human race.

VIRGINIA NEAL BLUE

Born 1910

Virginia Neal Blue—a native of Colorado—born February 4, 1910, in Meeker was the first woman in Colorado history to be elected to state executive office, State Treasurer (1967-1970).

Mrs. Blue's life and death were stories of unprecedented achievement and magnificent courage. She was electioneering in Rocky Ford on the day before she was admitted to the hospital, a victim of cancer to which she succumbed September 16, 1970. She left behind her husband, James E. Blue, and two sons, James Neal and Linden.

Virginia Neal Blue's career reflected the pioneer spirit of her father, a Colorado rancher and banker, Joseph N. Neal. Without benefit of needing "liberation" she entered business in fields natural to her, but normally restricted to men: banking, real estate and politics. She went about her business calmly, quietly, and efficiently and rose to prominence through sheer competency, vision, valor, and strength of persuasive diplomatic personality. She was a shining example as well as a staunch advocate of greater responsibility and a more active voice for women.

Mrs. Blue chaired the first Colorado Commission on the Status of Women, established by Executive Order in 1964. One of the results of the 1966 report of the Commission has been the establishment of a Colorado Resource Center for Women. Virginia Neal Blue Resource Centers for Women are now in Denver, Pueblo, Arapahoe County, the San Luis Valley, Grand Junction, and Colorado Springs: with a seventh planned for Fort Collins.

Virginia Neal Blue was a devoted wife and mother and a partner in the family real estate firm: Mrs. Blue was elected to a six-year term as Regent of her Alma Mater, the University of Colorado 1952 to 1958: She served as president and executive director of the Association of Governing Boards of State Universities and Allied Institutions from 1957 to 1964.

President Eisenhower appointed her to his Advisory Council on Youth Fitness. She served as vice-chairman of the Golden Anniversary White House Conference on Children and Youth 1958 to 1960—she served the American Association of University Women as president of the Denver branch from 1950 to 1952. She received the University of Colorado's highest accolade to one of its alumni: The Norlin Award in 1970.

Mrs. Blue was active in her church and political groups; Child research Council; Denver Society for Crippled Children; Colorado Society for Crippled Children (trustee); Alpha Delta Pi (grand secretary-treasurer in 1955-1963); Denver City Panhellenic (president, 1951); Colorado Association of Real Estate Boards; Denver Board of Realtors (director); Downtown Business and Professional Women's Club of Denver.

Mrs. Blue was "first" woman president of the University of Colorado Associated Alumni. Mrs. Blue was "first" woman to be acclaimed Denver Realtor of the Year (1962).

Mrs. Blue was listed in *Who's Who of American Women, Who's Who in Education, Who's Who in the West, and Who's Who in Colorado.*

Virginia Neal Blue was a dedicated Coloradoan who gave extraordinarily of herself in service to her church, community, and state. She was described by a former Colorado Chief Executive as "A Great Person".

Connecticut

AMERICAN ROBIN

MOUNTAIN LAUREL

THE CHARTER OAK

SIGILLUM REIPUBLICÆ CONNECTICUTENSIS
QUI TRANSTULIT SUSTINET

Connecticut

Nickname: The Constitution State

State Flower: Mountain laurel

State Tree: White Oak

State Bird: Robin

Photos

1. P.T. Barnum Monument, Seaside Park, Bridgeport
2. The Conn. Turnpike
3. Harkness Memorial Tower, Yale University, New Haven
4. American Shakespeare Festival Theatre, Stratford
5. Covered Bridge spanning Housatonic River

Committee Members

Chairman—Mrs. William H. Conley
Mrs. Peter Crawford
Mrs. George Turrell
Mrs. Saul Rosenberg
Mrs. Philip Hutt
Mrs. Frederick Isleib
Mrs. Fred M. Coleman
Mrs. Robert Weinerman
Mr. Chris Wesche—Artist

Connecticut

FAITH ROBINSON TRUMBULL
Lebanon   **Born 1718**

Of the many patriotic mothers in Connecticut during the Revolution, one of the most outstanding was Faith Robinson Trumbull, wife of Connecticut's War Governor. Born December 15, 1718, she was a direct descendent of the celebrated John and Priscilla Alden through her mother, Hannah Wiswall Robinson.

Faith was only five years old when her mother was lost in a tragic accident at sea, and she was educated under the direct guidance of her father, the Reverend John Robinson.

At the age of seventeen Faith was married to Jonanthan, who was to become the Governor of Connecticut, and the young couple made their home in Lebanon, later the scene of events which are now famous. Six children were born to them between the years of 1737 and 1756, each of whom had a notable career, and all of whom were directly interested in the Revolution.

In middle life, with her children grown, Faith Trumbull gave herself, with her husband, to the struggle of the Revolutionary cause, in which she strongly believed, and for which she worked selflessly. Jonathan Trumbull became the adviser of George Washington, and their home became the meeting place for numerous dignitaries of the time. The importance and secrecy of the meetings placed a great danger upon the Trumbulls, and the bronze plaque now in the famous War Office of Governor Trumbull lists "more than eleven hundred meetings" which took place there. Throughout all this danger Faith Trumbull sponsored the necessary collections for the suffering soldiers, organizing societies of women to send them clothing and consoling messages, giving herself in every possible way to the cause in which she devoutly believed. On one occasion, it is said, she contributed a scarlet cloak which was cut into strips and used as red trimmings for the uniforms of the soldiers.

The four sons of Faith and Jonathan Trumbull, and the husbands of their two daughters also distinguished themselves for zeal and effort during the Revolutionary War. The eldest son, Joseph, died as a result of exhaustion brought on by his enormous responsibilities in the army of Washington, where he held the post of Commissary-General. The second son, Jonathan Trumbull, Jr., held many positions of responsibility during and after the War, in the Congress, the Senate, the Supreme Court of the State of Connecticut, and for eleven consecutive terms as Governor.

For forty-five years Faith Trumbull was a faithful and helpful companion to her husband. She did not live to see the end of the struggle, but after years of service and sacrifice, including the deaths of two of her children, she died in 1880.

Every school child in Connecticut knows the inspiring story of Faith Robinson Trumbull, one of the great ladies of this state.

FREELOVE BALDWIN STOW
Milford   **Born 1728**

Perhaps one of the most poignant stories of patriotism and sacrifice of women of achievement in the early history of Connecticut is that of Freelove Baldwin Stow, who was called upon to endure the anguish of relinquishing her husband to an almost certain death.

Freelove Baldwin was born in 1728 on December 5, daughter of Phineas and Rebecca Baldwin. Her ancestry was distinguished, being traceable to English aristocracy, and her great grandfather John Baldwin to whom she was related through both parents had been one of the first settlers in Milford in 1640. She was married to Captain Stephen Stow, three of whose connections were Presidents of Yale College, dating back to its earliest existence. Four sons were born to this marriage and this mother gave all four sons to the cause in which the family so devoutly believed.

The great moment of renunciation came to the family in December of 1776, when a British vessel cast ashore on the beach two hundred or more half-starved, sick or dying soldiers who had been transferred from a prison ship. The residents of the area were horrified to hear wierd cries outside the homes during that night, and when Captain Stow opened his doors to investigate, these pitiful creatures streamed into his home in the most desperate conditions of illness and agony.

The family gave care to these poor men, but realized that there was little they could do for most of them, so advanced was their sickness and disease. In fact, they were stricken with small pox, acquired in the horror of the prison ship from which they had been brought, and about which little was known as to treatment.

The Milford townhouse was made into a sort of hospital, and the men were taken there, but the need for nurses was desperate. It was then that Captain Stephen Stow must have made his decision of renunciation of self and family for his fellow men.

First he made his will, then offered himself as nurse to the prisoners, and cared for them day and night until he too was stricken by the disease, and died. The burying ground at Milford was the resting place of nearly fifty of the dead, and with them was buried the man who had sacrificed himself for them.

While this appears to be the story of Stephen Stow, only the most callous reader of the tragic tale could fail to comprehend what this event required of Stephen's wife. Freelove Baldwin Stow could not even be allowed to claim the body of her husband, but had to live on after this hideous experience, consoled only by the knowledge of the magnificence of his heroism. When she died it was in the same Milford area that her happier early married years had been spent. No wonder the people of the town of Milford honor her memory.

MARY FISH SILLIMAN
North Stonington   **Born 1736**

Every mother on the rolls of the Revolutionary period was a heroine, bravely attempting to carry on the day to day business of family life in the midst of uncertainty and sometimes terror. Among those whose stories have come down through the generations as unique, the name of Mary Silliman is prominent.

Mary Fish Silliman was born in 1736 in North Stonington, the eldest daughter of the Reverend Joseph Fish, pastor of the church in North Stonington for nearly fifty years. She was carefully educated, and especially prepared by example and teaching for the responsible role which the later years would thrust upon her. She, too, was a fifth generation descendant of John and Priscilla Alden, tracing her ancestry through her mother, Rebecca Peabody.

At the age of twenty-two Mary was married to Reverend Noyes, who died in 1767, leaving his young widow with three sons. Mary and her children remained in New Haven for several years before returning to Stonington to her father's home. In 1775, at the age of thirty-nine, Mary Fish Noyes married Colonel Gold Selleck Silliman, a widower with one son. She moved into the Silliman home near Fairfield, on a beautiful height overlooking Long Island Sound, an area still known as Holland Hill.

The superb education and womanly charm of Mary Silliman invited the interest and friendship of the leading families of Fairfield, and her home was a gathering spot for persons whose family names are still prominent in the Fairfield area.

As the ferment of the Revolution intensified, Fairfield soon became a center of military activity. Throughout this time Mary Silliman kept a detailed and fascinating journal of the events of these ominous days, which has been an invaluable aid to researchers of the period. In May of 1775 her husband was put in charge of superintending the defense of the southwestern frontier of Connecticut, a key area because of its proximity to the Sound. This entailed months of separation from his family, at a time when Mary was carrying his child, Gold Selleck, who was born October 26, 1777. In May of 1779, in a midnight attack upon her home, and into her very bedroom, General Silliman and his son William were kidnapped by a British party sent out from New York. Fearing an invasion of Fairfield, Mary and her children moved their most cherished belongings to the home of a friend in Trumbull, a distance from the Sound, and began at once to plan for his exchange. She masterminded the capture of a prominent Judge of the Supreme Court of New York, and with her usual composure, offered him the courtesy of her home and the choicest foods she could procure while an exchange was arranged. During this time another son was born to her, whom her husband did not see until May of 1780, when he was returned home in exchange for the Judge.

Mary outlived her husband, and in 1804 married again, being widowed a third time in 1811. She died in 1818, an incredible woman, model of poise and serene strength.

EMMA HART WILLARD
Berlin   **Born 1787**

One of the most distinguished women of the early days of the state was Emma Hart Willard, born in Berlin on February 23, 1787 to Samuel Hart and his wife Lydia Hinsdale Hart. Emma was the sixteenth child of her father and the ninth of her mother.

The early education of Emma was carefully supervised by her father, and by the age of fifteen she had a well-rounded reading and had learned all that the local schools could teach her. She attended a private school where she developed an ability in composition which was to serve her in her productive literary life.

After further education in Hartford, Emma began her teaching career, first in Berlin and later in Vermont and Massachusetts. In 1799, at the age of twenty-two she married Dr. John Willard, and for a time devoted herself to family responsibilities. In 1814 she opened her first school in Middlebury, where she showed herself to be a teacher of great competence. She was impressed with the great need for better and more education for the women of her time, and had the opportunity to address the New York assembly to urge that the state appropriate funds for a seminary for women, an unheard of idea to many of the citizens. Although she did not manage to secure the appropriation, she was offered assistance by the people, and even by the official corporation of Troy, and through these sources she was able to open the Troy Female Seminary, for which the women of America shall always be in her debt.

At a moment in history when higher education for women was not an accepted idea, Emma Hart Willard pointed out the need for further study in the basic branches of knowledge. She herself wrote some of the texts which were used in her seminary.

Emma continued the conduct of this fine school for women until 1854, at which time she retired and gave over the goverance to her son John H. Willard and his wife.

A traveler to Europe on two occasions, Emma Willard acquired the friendship of many notables, who recognized the signal contribution she had made to higher education for women. In addition, she was a fine writer, published several text-books, composed hymns and poems, of which "Rocked in the Cradle of the Deep" is known to everyone.

Emma Willard died on April 15, 1870, and her place in the annals of American education is assured. Spanning the period between the Revolutionary and the War between the States, she represents the finest attributes of family devotion, scholarship and patriotism.

HARRIET BEECHER STOWE
Litchfield   **Born 1811**

Among the Connecticut women whose fame has spread far beyond the boundaries of the state is the authoress Harriet Beecher Stowe.

Harriet was born June 14, 1811, in the town of Litchfield, to the Reverend Lyman Beecher and his first wife, Roxanna Foote Beecher. Five children had been born to this marriage before the birth of Harriet, and later two other sons, Henry Ward and Charles. At the age of four Harriet's life was saddened by the death of her mother, and some of the most touching writings of Harriet referred to her recollections of this pious and gracious woman whom she had known for such a short time.

After the mother's death, Harriet's oldest sister Catherine assumed the responsibility of her care, still in the Litchfield area, and later in Hartford, where a most serious and deeply religious method of instruction was adopted for this small child, a practice which had an enormous influence on her personality and her later writings. Her sharp perception and amazing memory as shown in her memoirs of this period have afforded her biographers graphic material for study.

When Harriet was six her father married again, and the birth of a daughter to that marriage matured Harriet even more. By the age of twelve she was composing veritable treatises on the immortality of the soul. Shortly thereafter she was sent to Hartford to a school operated by her sister Catherine, apparently a remarkable woman whose personality and character were of the greatest influence upon Harriet. In 1832, when Harriet was twenty-one years of age, the father accepted a call to a church in Cincinnati, and in 1836 Harriet met and married a professor at the seminary where her father was President—Lane Theological. It was then that Harriet encountered for the first time the reality of slavery, which was an accepted matter in Kentucky. In 1850 the Stowes moved to Maine where Calvin Stowe joined the faculty of Bowdoin College, and here in the midst of her responsibilities to her six children Harriet began the writing which was to afford her immortality in the literary world. *Uncle Tom's Cabin* first appeared in serial form in an abolitionist periodical in 1851. When it appeared in book form in 1852 it created a sensation and sold 300,000 copies within a year. By 1900 the book had been translated into twenty languages.

It was this book which really grasped at the conscience of the people in the north, and the abolitionist movement was immeasureably advanced. A second volume furnished the documentation which fortified the argument of the first.

Although this remarkable woman wrote many other works, many of which were published in religious journals by her brother Henry Ward, it was "Uncle Tom's Cabin" which affords her a place of honor among the women of achievement.

EDITH KERMIT CAROW ROOSEVELT
Norwich   **Born 1861**

Edith Kermit Carow Roosevelt, born in 1861 in the town of Norwich, was the only Connecticut woman to marry a President of the United States. She was the second wife of Theodore Roosevelt. The devotion between Theodore Roosevelt and Edith Carow dated from their childhood, when Edith had been a close friend of Theodore's sister Corinne, and as children they had played together. Doubtless there was surprise, therefore, when early in 1880 Theodore became engaged to Alice Lee of Chestnut Hill, Massachusetts. The wedding occurred on October 27, 1880, and two of the very few New Yorkers not related to the family whom the Lees invited to stay with them for the event were Edith Carow and Fanny Smith. Thus on this occasion in Theodore's career which took him out of her own life, Edith was present. Early in 1884 Alice Lee Roosevelt died. In October, 1886, Theodore became engaged to Edith Carow, a surprise even to those who knew them well.

That Edith appreciated Theodore's aims, entered into every plan, and loved him, was evident to all who knew this devoted couple. James Amos, their butler for many years, wrote that he had not heard either of them say an impatient word to the other.

Five children were born of this marriage—Theodore, Jr., Kermit, Ethel, Archie and Quentin—and Alice from his first marriage. In the running of the household and the disciplining of the children Theodore gladly yielded to Edith's leadership, ably abetted by a warmhearted Irishwoman, "Mame" Ledwith, who had been Edith's own nurse. It must have been a stormy, hilarious nursery as the children, Alice among them, developed the Roosevelt traits of being not only self-absorbed but highly independent. Fortunately the parents understood.

Edith was a fifth generation descendant of Jonathan Edwards, the stern and dominant New Englad revivalist preacher, and she might well have derived from him her strength, her deep sense of right and wrong, and of duty. Having received an excellent schooling, she read avidly, loved music and the arts, spoke and read French fluently. She fulfilled the responsibilities imposed by her husband's positions as long as she had the strength to do so. As hostess at the White House her dignity and distinction of appearance were matched by a combination of friendliness and formality.

Edith Carow Roosevelt died in 1948. A recent biographer expressed the opinion that "Roosevelt would not have been Roosevelt without Edith Carow".

SARA SHERMAN LEVINSON
Bridgeport   **Born 1886**

Sara Rachel Sherman Levinson was born on August 18, 1886 in Yasse, Romania, the eldest of nine children, seven sisters and two brothers. At the age of sixteen she was the family pioneer to brave the new world, working as a sewing machine operator in a New York sweat shop, which was the custom of many immigrants at the time. This work enabled her to start her family coming to America in a sort of chain fashion, each helping the other until they were all reunited.

In March, 1907, Sara married another Romanian immigrant, Jacob Levinson, and bore him four sons—Louis, Isadore, Allen and Max. Encouraged by a cousin in Connecticut, Jacob and Sara left New York and went into business in Bridgeport. A daughter was born to them, and eventually they were able to purchase the home in which they lived for over fifty years. Throughout the years they underwent business losses and financial difficulties, but they managed to raise their family and overcome the reverses.

When she was not helping in her husband's store Sara assumed various community responsibilities, sewing for the Hebrew Orphan Home and serving many hours a week at the Old Age home. She was responsible for starting a Jewish book department in the Bridgeport Public Library, spending hundreds of hours collecting books for this purpose.

Sara gave over 5000 hours to the Red Cross, making garments which were distributed around the world. She was made a member of the Gallon Club of blood donors of Red Cross, although she actually gave only seven pints. When she offered the eighth pint she was refused, being over sixty years of age, but it was felt she had earned the honor.

The effort in which Sara attained national prominence was the Red Mogen Duvid, the American Red Cross activity for Israel. From the establishment of the state of Israel in 1948 she devoted six days a week, with a day off on Saturday for the Sabbath, to raising funds for the Middle Eastern country. Through her efforts an iron lung was sent to that country, and later on a fully equipped ambulance, on the door of which was painted: "presented to the people of Israel by the Bridgeport community through the devoted efforts of Mrs. Sara Levinson".

In 1968 the Bridgeport papers reported that in working for the Israeli Red Cross effort for fourteen years Sara Levinson, then 81, had raised enough money from community individuals and firms to send drugs, equipment for a first aid station and a medical research library, a bloodbank. The report further stated that in terms of ambulances her collections had provided the equivalent of thirty vehicles, and she was still actively collecting from her room at the Jewish Home for the Elderly.

Thus did this incredible woman give to her children, her grandchildren and great grandchildren an example of devotion to her adopted country, and steadfast concern for the people of Israel. Now nearly ninety, she continues to be an inspiration to all who know the story of her single-handed campaign of love.

JULIA KOTEL VARGA
Fairfield   **Born 1889**

Born in Fenyes Like, Szabolcs County, Hungary, in the year 1889, Julia Kotel Varga came to the United States at the age of sixteen, in November, 1905. Upon arrival in Bridgeport, Connecticut she lived with friends and worked in a shirt factory for two years. She met John Varga at the Magyar Reformed Church on Pine Street, and they were married there on August 24, 1907. For a while they remained at a friend's home until they could set up housekeeping for themselves. They were blessed with five children: Elizabeth, John, Zoltan, Helen and Ethel. All but John are living today. There are eleven grandchildren and eighteen great-grandchildren.

Julia Kotel Varga's door was always open to relatives and friends, and indeed, to anyone who had no place to go upon arrival in this country, or who were destitute because of other circumstances. Her home became a veritable center of material and spiritual support to immigrants in need.

In 1915, the Varga family moved to Fairfield, where they had bought a house for the growing family. Soon the house became too small since there were always other families living with them. They decided to build their own home, where they lived for fifty-two years among the people they loved, at 855 Old Stratfield Road in Fairfield.

Church going was a problem, since the closest church was in the old neighborhood on Pine Street, three miles away. Julia and her husband persuaded a few other Hungarian families that the time was ripe to establish a Hungarian Reformed Church in Fairfield. At their urging the pastor of the Magyar Reformed Church of Bridgeport established a Sunday School in Fairfield. The first worship service in Fairfield was held at 901 King's Highway, in a house donated to the congregation by Mrs. Maroness Fiske.

Mrs. Varga and her husband were instrumental in laying down the foundations of the new church, toward which they devoted all their energy and effort. Mrs. Varga became the first President of the Ladies Aid Society, in which capacity she served ten years. To this day she is honorary President and an active member whose experience and support are sought after by younger members.

In 1956, during and after the ill-fated Revolution in Hungary Julia Varga sponsored many refugees to the United States, and gave them loving welcome and a start in finding home and opportunity in their new land.

This brave and kind woman, in her unassuming way, has indeed merited a place among the mothers of achievement in Connecticut. She has been an inspiration to all who have come in contact with her, and has been responsible for the loyal citizenship of untold numbers of newcomers to her beloved community. All members of her church, now known as the Calvin United Church of Christ, as well as members of the greater community, hold her in highest esteem.

MARGARET CONNORS DRISCOLL
Bridgeport   **Born 1915**

In a country where, even today, the percentage of women in the legal profession is small, and of women Judges infinitesimal, this native of Bridgeport has practiced the profession successfully for over thirty-five years, and has achieved a position of national distinction in her area of specialization.

Margaret Connors Driscoll was born in Bridgeport in 1915, the eldest daughter of James W. and Theresa Kelley Connors. With her sisters Geraldine and Jane, Margaret attended the Bridgeport schools, and went on for further studies to Wellesley College and to Yale Law School, where she earned the degree of Juris Doctor in 1938. She was admitted to practice before the Bar of Connecticut in that same year. She began at once to practice law in her native Bridgeport, becoming interested in the field of Labor law.

In 1946 she married John J. Driscoll, a graduate of Wesleyan College, and also interested in Labor relations. Mr. Driscoll is now President of the Connecticut State Labor Council AFL-CIO. Their son, David J. Driscoll, a graduate of Wesleyan as is his father, lives in Virginia Beach, Virginia, where he is a professional photographer.

From 1945-1958 Margaret served as Counsel and Legislative Agent of the Connecticut State Labor Council CIO, and as legislative counsel from 1958-60. She has been admitted to practice before State and Federal Courts, including the United States Supreme Court, United States Court of Claims, and the Immigration and Naturalization Service. She is a member of the American, Connecticut and Bridgeport Bar Associations.

In 1960 Margaret Driscoll was appointed Judge of Connecticut Juvenile Court—First District, a post which she has occupied with distinction for fifteen years. She has at the same time reached the peak of honor in the area of Juvenile Court service, having served as Treasurer and Vice-President of the National Council of Juvenile Court Judges, and having been chosen President-elect of that august body at the recent conference in Hawaii.

This remarkable woman, in spite of all the burdens attendant upon her responsible position, has shown herself to be a person filled with compassion and concern for the people of her community. She never turned away from civic activities where her expertise was needed.

She serves as a member of the Board of the Bishop's Commission on Human Rights, the advisory Council of the Youth Services Bureau, the Board of Directors of United Way of Eastern Fairfield County, and the President's Advisory Council of Fairfield University.

In 1966 she received the Papal Medal "Pro Ecclesia et Pontifice" which is the highest honor which the Roman Catholic church can confer upon a woman.

The accomplishments of Margaret Driscoll have brought honor to the legal profession, and inspiration and example to women lawyers who are entering the field. Her court is a model of decorum, efficiency and above all of personal concern for the youth of the community whom she serves so well.

HONORABLE ELLA TAMBUSSI GRASSO

Windsor Locks   **Born 1919**

Ella Tambussi Grasso was born in Windsor Locks May 10, 1919 to James and Maria Oliva Tambussi. By her high grades at St. Mary's school she earned a Rockefeller scholarship to the Chaffee School near Hartford, from which she proceeded to Mt. Holyoke College. Elected to Phi Beta Kappa in her Junior year, she received a B.A. with honors in 1940 and an M.A. in economics and sociology in 1942. During World War II she served as Assistant Director of Research for the War Manpower Commission of Connecticut.

Ella Tambussi married Thomas Grasso, an educator. They are the parents of two children, Susane and James.

Mrs. Grasso was elected to the General Assembly in 1952 and 1954 and served as a floor leader in the State Legislature in 1955. From 1959 to 1970 she was Secretary of the State of Connecticut, a post she served with great distinction. She was also vice chairman of the Executive Committee on Human Rights and Opportunities and chairman of the Planning Committee for the Governor's Commission on the status of women. She served as chairman of the Bipartisan Commission to Prepare for the Connecticut Constitutional Convention, and in 1965 she was elected a delegate to the Convention and served as Democratic floor leader.

During two terms in the Congress as Representative from the sixth district of Connecticut, Mrs. Grasso served as a member of the Veterans' Affairs Committee and the Education and Labor Committee. Her work led to the drafting of the Emergency Employment Act, as well as essential legislative proposals for Older Americans.

Mrs. Grasso was chairman of the Democratic State Platform Committee from 1956 to 1968, a member of the National Platform Committee in 1960 and co-chairman of the Resolutions Committee of the Democratic National Convention in 1964 and 1968. She has been active in many civic, church, educational, cultural and service organizations. For ten years she was general chairman of the Connecticut Children's Cystic Fibrosis Association of Connecticut. She represented Governor John Dempsey in the Board of Education for the Blind, and served on the Board of Directors of Project Cause, a children to children program of the State Department of Health's Office of Mental Retardation.

Recognition has been accorded Mrs. Grasso for her work in many areas, and she has received honorary Doctorates from several universities and colleges.

In November, 1974, she was awarded the greatest honor of her career—election to the high office of Governor of Connecticut. In this signal achievement she has the distinction of being the first woman in the history of the United States to win election to the post of Governor in her own behalf. The people of Connecticut are justly proud of this remarkable woman.

DELAWARE

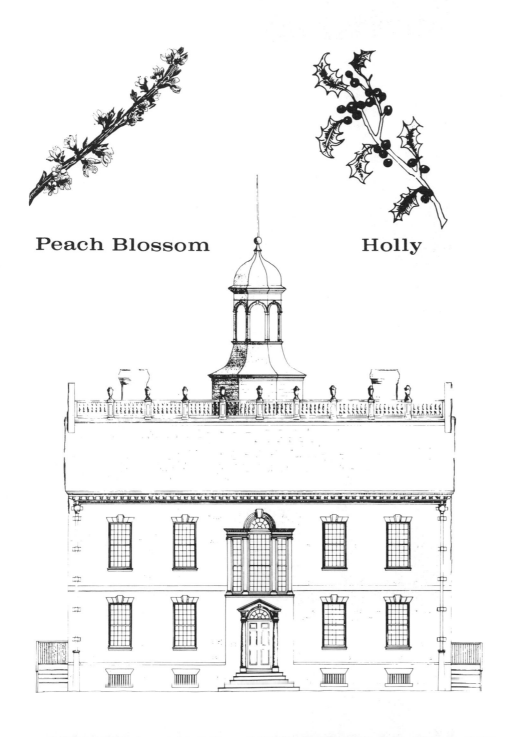

Peach Blossom   Holly

LIBERTY AND INDEPENDENCE

Delaware

Nickname: Diamond State

State Flower: Peach blossom

State Tree: American Holly

State Bird: Blue hen chicken

Photos

1. Quaker Meeting House
2. Christ Church—Dover
3. Rehoboth Beach
4. Museum Bldg.
5. Governor's House
6. Alee House
7. Dickinson Mansion

Committee Members

Chairman—Mrs. William N. Cann, Sr.
Mrs. William B. Mitten, Sr.
Mrs. J. Edwin Lewis

Delaware

MABEL LLOYD FISHER RIDGELY
Born 1872

Mrs. Mabel Lloyd Ridgely, the daughter of Charles Fisher and Philippa Lloyd, was born in 1872 in Washington, D.C. She was educated in private schools in Baltimore and New York; later she attended the art school of the Metropolitan Museum of Art and studied architecture under Arthur Lyman Tuckerman of the Beaux Arts, Paris.

She married Henry Ridgely of Dover in 1893. He was later to become one of the prominent citizens of Delaware—lawyer, civic leader, and president of the Farmer's Bank of Delaware.

Mrs. Ridgely belonged to many prestigious societies including: The Colonial Dames, the Wilmington Society of the Fine Arts, The Friends of the John Dickinson Mansion, the National Trust for Historical Preservation, the Dover Century Club and the Friends of Old Dover, of which she was a founder and an officer for a long time.

As one of the founders and presidents of the former State Archives Commission she was responsible for saving thousands of public documents.

She worked for women's suffrage and was president of the Delaware Women's Suffrage Association when women won the right to vote in 1920. In 1921 she became the first president of the Delaware League of Women Voters. She was one of the first supporters of the public library movement in southern Delaware. During World War I Mrs. Ridgely was chairman of the Women's Liberty Loan Committee of Delaware. She succeeded her husband as a member of the Board of Trustees of the University of Delaware in 1941 and received an honorary degree of humane letters in 1957.

In 1949 she wrote a book *What Them Befell*, letters from 1751 to 1890, a chronicle of life in colonial and federal times from archives of the Ridgely family.

She is survived by a daughter, two grandchildren and eight great-grandchildren.

MARY CAULK LEWIS
Born 1880

Mary Caulk Lewis was born on March 27, 1880 near Dover, Delaware. She attended a country school until she was 12, then attended Wilmington schools, graduating from Wilmington High School in June 1898.

Mary Caulk married Robert Edwin Lewis, a flour and grain dealer on December 18, 1902. They had two sons, John Edwin, and Robert Francis and 5 grandchildren and 20 great-grandchildren. Both sons graduated from Dover High School and attended the University of Delaware.

Mrs. Lewis was a bookkeeper for her husband in the Dover Flour Mill (1906-1922), Secretary in the R.E. Lewis Insurance Agency (1928-1947), President of P.T.A. in Dover (1908-1920), State President of P.T.A. (1924-1928), President of Dover Century Club (1921-1924) and (1932-1934), President of Kent County of State Federation of Clubs, President of Dover Woman's Christian Temperance Union (1940-1970). She was a member of Peoples Congregational Christian Church of Dover, Superintendent of the Children's Divi-

sion of Peoples Church Sunday School from 1924-1948, President of Women's Fellowship in Peoples Church (1948-1949), Deaconess of Peoples Church and a member of the choir for 35 years. She was also a member of the Board of Managers of the Detention Home for Juveniles for 25 years and President of the Board for 18 years. She was a member of the Board of Managers of Woods Haven School for Girls, Claymont, until the state took it over. She was elected a Pioneer of the Delaware P.T.A. in 1932 and a Pioneer of the Dover Century Club in 1940. She was also a corresponding secretary of the Delaware Woman's Christian Temperance Union (1950-1952).

BESSIE BRUCE ELLEGOOD MAYER

Born 1880

Mrs. Harry Mayer, age 95, recipient of the Delaware Mother of the Year Award in 1960.

Prior to entering the Methodist Country House, Wilmington, in 1961, Mrs. Mayer lived in Dover on King's Highway, one of the oldest streets in Delaware. Her late husband, a former Dover mayor and civic leader was Secretary-Treasurer of Richardson & Robbins.

Mrs. Mayer is probably best known for her work in Kent General Hospital. She was a Charter Member and President for many years of the Hospital Auxiliary. She was instrumental in organizing the Hospital Junior Board and be-

came a life-time Honorary member, having been the first President of the Kent General Hospital.

Mrs. Mayer organized the Community Concert Association of Dover and served as its President for seven years. She also assisted in organizing the Theatre Guild in Wilmington and the Shakespearean Living Theatre in Stratford, Connecticut.

Her religious activities included active membership for fifty-six years in the Wesley Methodist Church of Dover. She is an Honorary member of the Dover Century Club, where she was an active member for fifty-six years.

In 1937 she served a two-year term as a member of the State Board of Charities. In 1958 she was presented the first Honorary membership as an Alumnae of Wesley College.

Mrs. Mayer's other affiliations included "The Friends of Old Dover" "Dover Days" "Friends of the John Dickinson Mansion", Dover Y M C A, Dover U S O. Unbeknown to her children, at the age of 78 she became The Society Editor for the Delaware State News under the title "Dover Doings".

Her Son, Harry Mayer, Jr., who has been with the Continental American Life Insurance Company in Wilmington since his graduation from Yale University in 1935, was chosen "Young Man of the Year" in 1945 by the Wilmington Junior Chamber of Commerce.

Elizabeth E. Mayer, a daughter, deceased in 1974, was a Librarian at Enoch Pratt in Baltimore for thirty years, following graduation from Mt. Holyoke College and Library School.

Mrs. Mary Louise Tilghman, a daughter, resides in Dover. She was a Foreign Exchange Student at the Sorbonne, Paris, France, before her graduation from the University of Delaware. She pursued an active career of twenty-five years in volunteer work before retiring.

Mrs. Mayer has three grand-children and six great-grandchildren.

LETTIE VAUGHN BOGGS
Kent County   **Born 1885**

We find Mrs. Edgar J. Boggs located in Cheswold, in the State of Delaware.

Her 1954 "Mother of the Year" citation said, "The Boggs home is truly an American home, and in the community, Mrs. Boggs gives freely and in full measure of her time and resources to civic, religious and other worthy activities. She enjoys and possesses the love and highest admiration of her family, friends and acquaintances of the community and state."

She was cited for her contribution of blood during World War II. Her physician said that Mrs. Boggs often made blood donations even against his advice and at one time had to be hospitalized after a donation.

Among Mrs. Boggs' many community activities throughout the years were the American Red Cross, the American Cancer Society of which she was a very active and longtime volunteer worker, the Official Board of the Cheswold United Methodist Church, at onetime she conducted the largest Sunday School class at the Church and was cited by the Pastor for "teaching by example"; the Auxiliary of the Cheswold Volunteer Fire Company, the Cheswold Board of Education, the Smyrna Century Club, and was Chaplain of the Federation of Republican Women's Clubs of Delaware. In 1952, she was an alternate delegate and attended the Republican National Convention in Chicago.

Mrs. Boggs was a lifelong resident of Delaware. She was the former Lettie Vaughn and graduated from Wesley College in Dover, Delaware.

Mr. Boggs conducted a wholesale tomato and pepperseed business from the family farm near Cheswold. Mr. and Mrs. Boggs celebrated their 50th Wedding Anniversary on December 5, 1956 before Mr. Boggs' death in 1958.

She was praised for her exemplary community life for the way she conducted her home and reared four sons and for her continued interest in community, State and national affairs.

Mrs. Boggs lost two of her four sons. One son, Capt. Edgar C. Boggs, a West Point graduate, United States Army Silver Star recipient, was killed in action in the Pacific during World War II. Another son, Austin, died at the age of 16 from stomach injuries from athletics.

The two surviving sons are Calvin Boggs, a prominent businessman, seedsman and farmer. He is a 6 Campaign Star veteran, 1st United States Marine Corps Division of World War II in the Pacific Theatre, he is Treasurer and lay leader in the Cheswold United Methodist Church, he is a former Kent County Chairman of the Republican Party, he is active in Church, civic, business and political affairs.

Her other surviving son, J. Caleb Boggs, is a lawyer, a former Representative in the U.S. Congress '47-'53; a former Governor of the State of Delaware '53-'60; a former U.S. Senator from Delaware '61-'73; a veteran of 6th Armored Division, World War II, with 5 Campaign Stars in the European Theatre.

She was very proud and fond of her grandchildren and great-grandchildren. One granddaughter, Marilu Boggs, and three grandsons, J. Caleb Boggs, Jr., Edgar Clayton Boggs, and Calvin Jefferson Boggs. The two great-grandchildren are great-granddaughter, Erin Jeanne Boggs, and the great-grandson, J. Caleb Boggs, III.

Mrs. Boggs passed away in March of 1971 at the age of 86. She had lived a long, active, meaningful and full life. At the time of her death, the Delaware State Legislature adopted a most kind and thoughtful Resolution of sympathy honoring her memory.

MARJORIE WILLOUGHBY JOSEPHS SPEAKMAN

Born 1890

Marjorie Willoughby Josephs Speakman has been an accomplished leader in the Delaware community. Not only did she raise a family of three children, she was also active in business and politics, and some 35 service organizations.

Mrs. Speakman is especially noted for having founded Bird-Speakman, a popular Delaware ladies' apparel store with branches in Easton and Rehoboth, Delaware.

Active in Republican politics, Mrs. Speakman was elected to the National Council of Republican Women. Her business talents led her to be appointed the only woman member of the National Council of Consultants to the Small Business Administration.

Marjorie Speakman worked tirelessly in the educational field, serving on numerous college boards and committees. She chaired the steering committee for the restoration of Loockerman Hall at Delaware State College and was founder of the Duck Creek Historical Society. It was through her efforts that the Gambrel Roof House at Duck Creek was preserved.

Mrs. Speakman originated and co-chaired the Wesley College Annie Jumb Cannon Centennial honoring outstanding working women. Honored at the first Centennial were Helen Hayes, Marian Anderson, and Jacqueline Cochran. While she was a member of the Board of Directors of Wesley College, Dover, Mrs. Speakman was awarded a Wesley Award Citation for Outstanding Accomplishments in Business, the Arts, Education, Citizenship, and the Preservation of History.

Born in Philadelphia on July 10, 1889, Mrs. Speakman is the mother of three children, eight grandchildren, and three great-grandchildren.

ALINE ELIZABETH NOREN EHINGER

Born 1891

Born in Humbolt, Kansas, August 27, 1891, Aline Noren Ehinger moved to Portland, Oregon in 1903 where she and her family were active in the Hawthorn Presbyterian Church. A graduate of Washington High School, she earned her B A Degree in English at the University of Oregon in 1914, and taught English and Latin in the Oregon Public School System from 1914 to 1918. She returned to teach at Washington High School in 1917. In the summers, she worked as a City Playground Director in Portland, and, during World War I, served in France as a YMCA canteen worker at Besancon. While in Chamonix, she climbed to the summit of Mount Blanc on June 11, 1919.

In 1920, she went to New Zealand and Australia as a Program Director for a touring Chautauqua Company. In Sydney, Australia, she participated in the demonstrations which led to the city's first supervised playground program.

Returning to the University of Oregon in 1922 to do graduate work in the School of Social Work, she met George Ehinger, her husband, who was Executive Secretary of the State Child Welfare Commission and also a professor in the School of Social Work. It was during this period that a devastating fire swept the town of Astoria, Oregon and Aline Noren was among those who assisted in the disaster relief and rehabilitation of this community. From 1924 to 1927 she was a Field Social Worker for the Oregon State Child Welfare Commission.

The Ehingers were married in Portland, Oregon, and moved to Dover, Delaware, in 1927 where Mr. Ehinger served as the Superintendent of the Elizabeth W. Murphey School until his death in 1970. In Dover, the Ehinger family became very much a part of the Presbyterian Church as well as being active in a wide range of community interests.

In 1928, Mrs. Ehinger supervised the first organized playground program in this community, sponsored by the Dover Century Club. During World War II, she was one of the founders of the Dover USO, and a member of the Rent Con-

trol Board, as well as organizing volunteers for the Aircraft Warning Service.

She also invested considerable energies in community service through leadership roles in the American Field Service, The Easter Seal Society for Crippled Children, The Fresh Air Fund, The Child Welfare Commission of the American Legion Auxiliary, as well as other civic groups.

Mrs. Ehinger taught English at Dover High School from 1943 until 1966. She was named Delaware Mother of the Year in 1958, and Dover Woman of the Year for 1969. Mrs. Ehinger's recently published book entitled *Bridge Across The Years* is a history of the Presbyterian Church of Dover and also the history of City of Dover from the time it was directed to be laid out by William Penn to the present time. She has a family of four sons and fifteen grandchildren.

VERA GILBRIDE DAVIS

Born 1894

Vera Gilbride Davis was born July 22, 1894, in Wilmington, Delaware. Her parents were Mary E. Crumlish and John J. Gilbride. Vera's childhood was spent in Wilmington where she attended Ursiline Academy. In addition, she studied voice in Wilmington and in New York City. During her early life, she devoted much of her time to singing in Wilmington, as well as other parts of the state.

On September 8, 1915, she married Frank H. Davis, an attorney in Dover, Delaware.

During World War I she began her lifetime of volunteer work by singing at "Bond Drives" assisting the Government raise funds for the War effort.

Political life began for Vera in 1919 when she worked for Women's Suffrage. Her record over more than forty years of public service reveals a number of "Firsts":

First Woman Bill Clerk, House of Representatives, 1927.

First Woman Secretary of the Senate, 1941.

First Woman elected to the State Senate, 1946.

First Woman elected President Pro-Tem of the Senate, 1949.

First Woman elected House Majority Leader, 1952.

First Woman elected to a State-wide Office, State Treasurer of Delaware, 1956.

In addition, she was also a Kent County Republican Committeewoman, as well as a member of the Executive Committee of the Kent County Republican Party.

Her public service was not limited to her political life. She was an active parishioner of Holy Cross Roman Catholic Church, Dover, and served as the Church Choir Directress for many years. She served as President of the Delaware Society for Crippled Children and Adults; served longer than any other member of the Board of

Directors of Kent General Hospital in Dover; was a member of the State Board of Charities; The Boys and Girls State Projects and a member of the Auxiliaries of the American Legion and Veterans of Foreign Wars. In 1915 she joined the Dover Century Club. Finally, she was a member of the Capital City Business and Professional Womens Club of Dover.

Although she was pleased with her many political and civic accomplishments, she was probably proudest of having raised a family and relished telling of her two sons, three grandchildren and one great-grandson.

MARGARET MOFFETT O'NEILL
Born 1900

Anna Margaret Moffett was born November 14, 1900, in Kenton, Delaware. She attended grade school in Kenton, and high school at Smyrna. In 1922, she graduated from Women's College, University of Delaware and began her teaching career in the Wilmington School System and later in the Smyrna School System.

She was married to Francis J. O'Neill of Clayton, Delaware, an employee of the Pennsylvania Railroad. She had a son, Francis J. Jr., who attended Symrna Schools, University of Delaware and graduated from Villanova College. She also had a daughter, Jane, who attended Smyrna Schools, Ursuline Academy and graduated from the University of Delaware. She had four grandchildren and one great-grandchild.

Mrs. O'Neill was always active in her church affairs. As a member of St. Joseph's Church in Clayton, she served as Prefect of the Sodality, Co-chairman of the Annual Bazaars, organized a Sunday Nursery School, taught Sunday School, was a member of the Inter-Racial Council, and represented the Parish at the Religion and Race Conference in 1963.

Margaret O'Neill's activities in her community and state affairs were many and varied. In 1937, she was Organization Chairman for the first Girl Scout Troop in Smyrna, served on the Troop Committee, and until her death was active in the Chesapeake Bay Council of Girl Scouts. She was President of the Twentieth Century Club of Smyrna, President of the Smyrna Homemakers Club, President of the American Legion Auxiliary, serving as Chairman of Girls' State.

In 1950, she was the first woman elected to the Town Council of Smyrna, and in 1951 she

received the Lions' Club Outstanding Citizen Award. From 1951 until 1960 Mrs. O'Neill was active in many educational activities: member of the P.T.A., First woman Principal of Smyrna High School, and President of the Smyrna School Board. On the state level she served as Treasurer of the State School Board Association and later served as President of the Delaware School Board Association.

Other activities include Chairman of the Smyrna Cancer Crusade, member of the Kent County Cancer Society Board of Directors, President of Stockley Home Auxiliary for the retarded, charter member and a member of the Board of Directors of the American Field Service, and represented the State of Delaware at "White House Conference for Children and Youth". She was also on the executive board of the Delaware Society for Crippled Children and Adults. She was President of the Duck Creek Historical Society and a member of the "People to People" organization. In 1964, she was appointed by Governor Carvel to serve on the Human Relations Commission, and later served on the Kent County Regional Planning Commission.

Mrs. O'Neill became Delaware's 1964 Mother of the Year, continuing to be active in that organization until her death. In 1968, she was a candidate for State Representative from her district. She also served on the Board of Directors of Bryn Zion Cemetery, was President of the Confraternity of Christian Doctrine, an original member of the Board of Directors of the Catholic Press of Wilmington, served on the Board of Directors of the Catholic Social Services, was Vice-President of the Old Bohemia Historical Society, and was President of the Bicentennial Program at St. Polycarp's Church of Smyrna at the time of her death. She received a citation from the veterans of Foreign Wars for her participation in the Voice of Democracy Program, was included and recorded in Who's Who of American Women, and was appointed by Governor Sherman Tribbitt to the State Comprehension Health Planning Council just one month before her death on September 20, 1975.

Her many accomplishments throughout the years proved her to be an outstanding citizen.

MARY MADALINE ELLIOTT BUCHANAN

Born 1908

Mrs. Mary Madaline Elliott Buchanan, church woman, club woman and active participant in cultural and educational affairs, was born in Edenton, North Carolina, the daughter of Mr. and Mrs. John M. Elliott, and was named Mary Madaline. She graduated from Edenton High School and Meredith College, where she received the Bachelor of Arts degree. She returned to Meredith as director of religious activities for a period of three years. During the last year, also served as assistant dean of women.

In 1931, she married Edgar W. Buchanan whose connection with The Firestone Tire and Rubber Co. brought them to Delaware to live. Mr. Buchanan (Buck) died in 1969 after having given thirty-eight years of devoted service to his community and state. They had one daughter, Mrs. Joseph Gates (Becky) and four grandchildren who live in Dover. Becky is National Democratic Committeewoman for Delaware.

Madaline Buchanan has been an active member of First Baptist Church of Dover since 1931. At the present time, she is teacher of the Adult Women's Bible Class, a member of the Church Library Committee, and a member of the Board of Deacons.

She has been active in all areas of the Women's Society, serving four years as president. At present, is Chairman of the Spiritual Growth Committee.

In 1965, Madaline was elected Church Moderator, the first and only woman to hold this office in the history of the church. In addition, she served as a trustee of the Delaware Baptist Convention and as president of the American Baptist Women of Delaware.

On the national level of her denomination, Madaline served for nine years as a member of the Board of Education and Publication of the American Baptist Convention. She represented that board on the Board of Managers of American Baptist Women and on the General Council. In 1967 she was elected Second Vice President of the national organization and served as a member of the Program Committee for the 1968 national convention.

Having served as president of the Dover Council of Church Women United, she was elected President of Church Women United of Delaware.

As a member of the Women's Committee for the Japan International Christian University, she served as Chairwoman in 1974 for the state of Delaware's observance of the twenty-fifth anniversary of the founding of J.I.C.U.

In addition to church-related activities, Madaline has been a committed clubwoman. After three separate terms as president of the Dover Century Club, she was elected President of the Delaware State Federation of Women's Clubs. Other offices held in the state organization include those of Director, Trustee, Historian, Editor of the Federation Magazine and President of the Past State Presidents' Club. Departments she has chaired are: Public Affairs, Communications, Environmental Responsibility. At present, is Dean of Department Chairmen for the Federation and Bicentennial Celebration Chairman for the Dover Century Club.

In the educational field, Madaline has the honor of having been the first woman to serve on the Delaware State Board of Education. She served for six years, during which time she was elected Chairman, the only woman to have served in this capacity. During her term on the Board, the members complied with the Supreme Court's decision concerning segregation in the public schools and set up guidelines for integrating the Delaware school system. Later, Madaline became a member of the Scholarship Advisory Council of the State Board of Education.

For six years, Madaline was a member of the Board of Trustees of Delaware State College, serving as secretary.

Since 1971, has been a member of the Board of Trustees of Wesley College, where she is a member of the Faculty and Curriculum Committee and of the Nominating Committee of the Board.

She is a member of the Sprig and Twig Garden Club, serving as president 1971-73; an honorary Board member of the Delaware Regional Ballet Company; member of the Governor's Committee to select the Mother-of-the-Year for Delaware, as well as a member of the Dover Chamber of Commerce Committee to select their Man-of-the-Year.

Her hobbies are collecting antiques (glass and china); growing roses; flower arranging; making inspirational scrapbooks; and working with other people on worthwhile projects.

ESTHER VIOLA SCHAUER FREAR
Born 1909

Mrs. J. Allen Frear, Jr., wife of Delaware's United States Senator, 1949-61, was born in Hartford, Wisconsin. She is a graduate of Lawrence University, Appleton, Wisconsin where she received a Bachelor of Arts Degree. The Frears have two children, Fred and Mrs. Richard M. Baylis, and three granddaughters, Leanne, Marla and Allison Frear.

Mrs. Frear has been the first and only woman member elected to Dover City Council, serving from 1947-1949. She was sponsored by the women's clubs of Dover.

Mrs. Frear sponsored Beta Sigma Phi sorority in Dover. Mu chapter was started in 1949 and followed by Xi Theta, Upsilon, and Perceptor Gamma. She was made an International Honorary member of Beta Sigma Phi in 1960. While in college, Mrs. Frear was preshdent of her sorority, Kappa Delta, and later became National Vice President, 1955-57; National Panhellenic Conference Delegate, 1963-75, supervising the Panhellenic programs on 115 college campuses for her sorority. She also served as Alpha and Alumnae President, Chairman of Evaluation and Constitution By Laws Committees, and member of the Endowment Fund Committee, totally twenty-five years of National Officer work.

While in Washington, Mrs. Frear was active in many congressional groups, and served as President of the Woman's National Democratic Club for 1957-58. She is a Life Member of the Congressional Club of which she served as Vice President, 1954-56. She was organizer and first President, 1953-56, of International Group II; a Vice President and member of the Board of Directors of Ladies of the Senate; a member of Former Members of Congress Auxiliary: the 81st Congressional Club Group, and the American Newspaper Women's Club. In Delaware,

Mrs. Frear has been active in the Dover Century Club, a 42-year member, and Vice President and Secretary of the Delaware State Federation of Women's Clubs, presently serving as State Historian. Her other D.S.F.W.C. chairmanships include: Legislative, Economic Security, Pan 'merican, and International Affairs Committees.

Mrs. Frear holds membership in the following National Civic Organizations: American Legion Auxiliary, Unit 2; Ladies Auxiliary of Foreign Wars, #9962; Order of the Eastern Star, Hartford, WI; The Needlework Guild; The American Red Cross; The American Cancer Society; and Delaware Committee member of PROJECT HOPE.

In Delaware, Mrs. Frear is a member of "The Friends of John Dickinson" Mansion; having served on the renovation committee of the Mansion and Director, 1963-66; a Charter Member of the Junior Board, Kent General Hospital; Delaware Association for Retarded Children; Delaware Special Olympics, Inc., Honorary Committee; Dover Century Club; Honorary President, Community Concert Association; Rehoboth Art League, Life Member; Palmer Home Friends; Kent County Democratic Club; Friends of Wesley College; Restoration Committee for Loockerman Hall; Kent General Hospital, Life Member; Sponsor of Golden Opportunity Center, Inc., 1962; Trustee of Delaware Foundation for Retarded Children, Inc. and only woman member 1958-1968; organizer of International Order of Job's Daughters, Dover; member of People's Church, being President of Woman's Fellowship 1947-48.

The Board of Trustees of the Department of Mental Health recognized Mrs. Frear with a Resolution for her chairmanship of a fund drive to raise $130,000 to build an All Faith Chapel at Stockley, Delaware which was dedicated in 1969.

Mrs. Delaware continues yearly participation in the All Star Football Game Committee which benefits Delaware Retarded Children and has been part of the Gold Team which has raised over $240,000 toward the Annual Game. Over the years, the Frears have travelled extensively abroad and shared their trips with many civic groups.

Both children majored in banking. Fred is manager of Lewes, Rehoboth, Seaford Delaware Trust Company Banks while Mrs. Louise Frear Baylis has been associated with Wilmington Trust Company, Wilmington; Bankers Trust Co., London and accountant for Mae Hall McCabe Realty Firm, Rehoboth Beach, Delaware.

District Of Columbia

Photos

1. White House
2. Jefferson Memorial
3. Smithsonian Institution
4. Lincoln Statue
5. U.S. Marine Monument
6. Kennedy Theatre
7. Ford's Theatre
8. Washington Monument
9. Spirit of St. Louis

3   SMITHSONIAN INSTITUTION.

Committee Members

Chairman—Helen Chittick Elsen
Mrs. Genevieve Johnson
Mrs. Russell S. Marriott
Mrs. J. Willard Marriott
Mrs. Casper Nannes
Mrs. John A. Patterson, Jr.
Mrs. Barton Richwine
Mrs. Merritt L. Smith
Mrs. Walter Washington

5

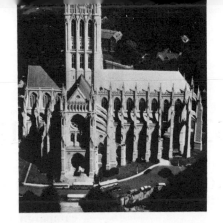

District of Columbia

HUBBARD-BELL-GROSVENOR
A THREE-GENERATION TRILOGY*   1829

One family of unique achievers produced three distinguished women whose careers belong to the world. Of Scottish-American heritage, Washington was their home, Nova Scotia their family retreat and center of creative invention.

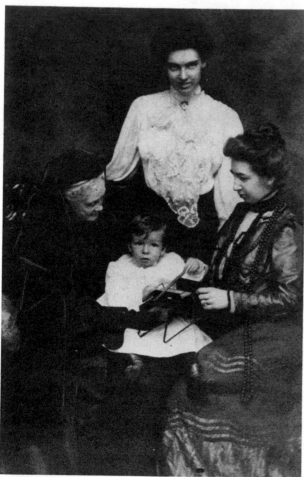

GERTRUDE McCURDY HUBBARD
Born 1829

Gertrude Mercer McCurdy, daughter of a prominent New York merchant, married Gardiner Greene Hubbard, son of a Justice of the Supreme Court of Massachusetts. Five daughters were born to them. When scarlet fever struck, their five-year-old daughter, Mabel, was left to-

tally and permanently deaf and seemingly speechless. Then began Gertrude's indomitable campaign to keep alive her child's latent speech and teach her lip reading. Every night Mabel had said her prayers to her mother. When she was suddenly afflicted, these became her lifeline to speech and the hearing world.

Gertrude would place Mabel where she could watch her mother's lips, then repeat over and over The Lord's Prayer, the 23rd Psalm and other prayers with which Mabel was familiar. Imagine the mother's joy when Mabel smiled and in a husky voice repeated the words, "and goodness and mercy shall follow me all the days of my life."

When Mabel's lip-reading and speech became better a teacher was brought into the home where Mabel, with her sisters, had more formal lessons. Later she spent a winter in school in Germany, learned to speak the language fluently, and acquired an excellent education.

The Hubbards discovered Alexander Graham Bell, a youthful professor of speech with new techniques for teaching the deaf to speak clearly, and who was already at work on his studies, which led to the invention of the telephone.

To their surprise this brilliant young Scot fell deeply in love with his fifteen and one-half year old pupil. Gertrude understood and supported his courtship. Mabel and Alex were married on July 11, 1877. Soon after the Hubbards moved to Washington where Gertrude's leadership in charitable affairs and her administrative skills were immediately recognized. She became the first woman Board member of the Washington Home for Incurables, a founding member of the Church of the Covenant (later to become the National Presbyterian Church), and she also supervised the building of their Victorian home "Twin Oaks" now occupied by the Chinese Ambassador to Washington. In her later years, Gertrude Hubbard was a familiar sight going about her duties in her shiny black automobile. Her death in 1909 was the first automobile fatality in the capital city, causing widespread shock over the danger of this new form of vehicle that was replacing the horse and carriage.

MABEL HUBBARD BELL
Born 1857

Although engaged to Alexander Graham Bell on her eighteenth birthday, Mabel refused to marry him until he exhibited his telephone at the Centennial Exhibition in Philadelphia in 1876. There a distinguished British observer, Judge Sir William Thompson, declared it "the most wonderful thing I have seen in America."

After living in England, the Bells moved to Washington, D.C. in 1881. It was Mabel who always handled their finances, managed their homes, superintended the laboratories and workshops. When fire broke out in the middle of a January night, and Alec was out of town, Mabel first saw that the children were carried to safety and then returned to Alec's third floor study to instruct the firemen to "Go after my husband's manuscripts and books. If we lose everything else, they must be saved."

In 1891 Mabel organized the Young Ladies Club of Baddeck, Nova Scotia, the first women's club in Canada. Out of the activities of this club came the formation of the Parent-Teacher Association, the pioneer in all of Canada of the present Canadian Home and School Association.

Mabel sponsored Bell's human flight experiments, and suggested and financed an organization for the purpose of building aircraft and getting a man in the air. Thus was born the Aerial Experiment Association and Mabel Bell became the first woman patron of aviation. On February 23, 1909, J. A. D. McCurdy, one of the young men in this association built and flew his Silver Dart over Baddeck Bay beside the Bell home, the first flight by a British subject in the British Empire.

Without this remarkable deaf partner who had a talent for "creative listening", scientific understanding, and managerial skills, the world might well have been denied the inventions of Alec Bell.

ELSIE MAY BELL GROSVENOR
Born 1878

Few women of her day traveled so far, saw so much and knew so many persons on all levels of life as Elsie May Bell. She was born in London in 1878 where her father, Alexander Graham Bell, was demonstrating his telephone to Queen Victoria. Elsie's eighty-six years of life were ones of high adventure in an age when men conquered space and gave new dimension to old concepts of the universe.

Elsie was a seasoned traveler at the time of her marriage to Gilbert Grosvenor, young editor of the newly organized *National Geographic* Magazine. She had studied in France and Italy and traveled to England, Norway and Japan where she was presented to the Empress. As a young girl she survived a shipwreck on Newfoundland's barren cliffs.

Affectionately known as "Mr. and Mrs. Geography", Gilbert and Elsie traveled by mule, camel, elephant, ship and plane through jungles, deserts, mountains and seas for more than half a century, often accompanied by one or more of their six children. As a team they traveled to both Czarist and Soviet Russia, China Japan, North Africa during the Berber War, Peru and Alaska. Several years after their fiftieth anniversary they traveled thirty thousand miles on an African safari and Elsie told the story in two beautifully written articles for National Geographic. Her seventy-six-year-old husband made the remarkable color illustrations.

Avid sailors on their yawls ALEXANDER, and later ELSIE, they passed on their seamanship and their love of the sea to their children: Melville, Gertrude, Mabel, Lilian, Carol and Gloria. Today the ELSIE still sails with Grosvenor children, grandchildren and great-grandchildren as skipper and crew.

Elsie's community interests were as varied as her world travels. President of several women's clubs, organizer of others, associated with the Society of Women Geographers and the National League of American Pen Women, she was proudest perhaps of her role as a woman activist, parading down Pennsylvania Avenue in 1913 in the Suffragette Parade on the eve of President Wilson's inauguration. She also enthusiastically supported and furthered the work of the Alexander Graham Bell Association for the Deaf in Georgetown, Washington, D.C., continuing the life work of her parents.

Elsie Grosvenor once wrote: "I can hardly remember being in a place where there were not things that a woman, rather than a man, would notice about the lives and ways of people. American women who live and travel abroad could do much to help break down the barriers which all too often separate us from the people whose guests we are."

Together Elsie and Gilbert broke down barriers of separation across the world through written word and magnificent photography in a magazine unrivaled in its field, and motion pictures still shown across the television screens and theatres in areas farther afield than even the Grosvenors were able to travel.

Worthy candidates for Washington's hall of fame, this daughter-mother-grandmother combination, busy with the affairs of the world, nevertheless made their primary calling that of home building. Guiding their children in direct and indirect ways, they gave them enough freedom to become mature individuals. By special permission, their stories are submitted as a family unit.

VINNIE REAM HOXIE

Born 1847

At the age of 19, Vinnie Ream became the first woman to be given a commission from the United States Government for a sculpture. Thus began a modern-day Cinderella story, complete with fame, honors and acclaim.

Vinnie Ream was born in Madison, Wisconsin on September 25, 1847, the daughter of Lavinia McDonald and Robert Lee Ream. She spent her early childhood in Washington, D.C. where her father had found employment. Within a few years her family returned to the West, and Vinnie attended Christian College in Missouri.

During the Civil War, Vinnie, her sister and her parents moved back to Washington. Following a visit one day to the studio of a well-known sculptor, Clark Mills, she became interested in exacting likenesses from clay. Under the guidance and tutorage of Mills, she devoted herself to the full-time study of sculpture.

In less than a year she gained favorable criticism from many friends who approached President Lincoln and asked if he would consider sitting for this young, gifted artist. As Vinnie later recounted, "Lincoln had been painted and modeled before, and when friends of mine first asked him to sit for me he dismissed them wea-

rily until he was told that I was but an ambitious girl, poor and obscure. He granted me sittings for no other reason than that I was in need. Had I been the greatest sculptor in the world I am quite sure I would have been refused."

The sittings lasted one half hour every day for six months. The degree to which she grew to know Lincoln is attested to by the quality of the clay bust which she completed a few days before his assassination. Three years later she was commissioned by the government to execute Lincoln's statue. The fact that she was a woman and an unknown artist caused criticism from other artists. Some went to great lengths to infer falsely that her family was involved with the assassination plot. She was given a room in the Capitol to execute her clay model of Lincoln, but social and political persecution caused her to leave rather abruptly.

Her parents accompanied her to Italy to have the clay model executed in marble. While in Europe Vinnie Ream moved in sophisticated circles where she became known and respected by leading artists. She made busts of literary, religious and political figures including Franz Listz, Cardinal Antonelli, and Gustave Dore. Following completion of the marble statue of Lincoln, she returned to Washington where it was unveiled in the Rotunda of the Capitol. Four years later she signed a twenty-thousand dollar contract with the Government for a bronze statue of Admiral Farragut, now standing in Farragut Square in Washington.

While working on the Farragut memorial, Miss Ream was introduced to Lt. Richard Le-

veridge Hoxie of the United States Army. On May 28, 1878 they were married. Vinnie Ream Hoxie casily adapted to her role of Washington hostess; at her husband's request she abandoned her career for eighteen years to raise their son, Richard Ream Hoxie.

Mrs. Hoxie led a most interesting social life in their "K" Street home. Her personality was one of great warmth and kindness and she was much loved by all who knew her, including young people. A love for music was expressed in her playing of the piano and harp, and many evenings were spent in the company of friends, playing and singing the music of her childhood.

In later life, Vinnie Ream Hoxie was commissioned by the legislature of Oklahoma to execute a statue of Sequoya to be presented to the U.S. Congress for Statuary Hall. The model was finished shortly before her death on November 20, 1914 and shows a more established technique than her earlier works. This remarkable wife and mother left lasting memorials indicative of the talent and abilities seldom attributed to women of her era.

KATE WALLER BARRETT
Born 1857

Kate Waller Barrett was born in antebellum times, but she was far ahead of them, overtaking the post-bellum periods of both the Civil War and World War I. With less educational and social opportunity than some of her contemporaries, she became more resourceful and eminent, soaring above them, while lifting many sho were helplessly floundering.

Born January 24, 1857 in Falmouth on the Rappahannock River, she lived at "Clifton" on the Potomac. Pleasant scenes of childhood gave way to grim ones with the "War," and the stand of her kinsman, Robert E. Lee, who challenged his people to like dedication. Her father joincd Lee's staff and Kate delighted in the wartime hustle and bustle. Men in blue walking the streets caused no more fear in her stout young heart than men in gray.

Kate grew up, became engaged to Robert S. Barrett, an Alexandria ministerial graduate then filling the pulpit at Aquia Church, and was married with her six sisters as bridesmaids. Her husband accepted a church in Richmond in a slum area. Each day they plunged deeper into the pit of human misery, hoping to help those less fortunate than themselves. Helping an outcast young girl with two fatherless children Kate realized that society was closing every door to the girl and her children. Now she and her husband set up stations to aid victims of the seamy side of life and found more satisfaction in their work with them than with conventional church members.

When Kate was twenty-nine, her husband became Dean of St. Luke's Cathedral in Atlanta and Kate became President of the Auxiliary of the Y.M.C.A. and of the Women's Cooperative Club. She wanted to help "fallen" women and began a battle against the double standard that condoned the man while condemning the prostitute. Kate decided to study the medical aspect, enrolled at the Women's Medical College of Georgia and received her medical degree in 1892. When a church opposed a house of prostitution being turned into a rescue house, the newspapers came to her aid. Opposed, undaunted Kate Barrett appeared before the City Council and forced the issue, and grudgingly they gave her four acres beyond city limits. She implored Charles Nelson Crittenton, who had established such homes in other cities, to help out in Atlanta and he supplied the funds necessary

to proceed. She worked diligently in Mission work until the summer of 1894, when Dean Barrett became ill with typhoid fever in London and Kate decided to take a postgraduate course in nursing at St. Thomas Hospital. When they came to Washington, where they made their home, her many contacts in social and political circles stood her in good stead.

Kate was left a widow at thirty-nine with six children between nine and seventeen years old to support and educate. She took the position as General Superintendent of the recently founded National Florence Crittenton Mission. After giving two-thirds of her life to the cause, she would become the leading world authority on her branch of sociology. Her cardinal principle was to keep mother and child together, a concept which she initiated in welfare work, and her paper *The Care of the Unmarried Mother* is a sociological classic. Kate Barrett became a national mother image, often called "Mother of Girls." She had known, and had ar guests, President Benjamin Harrison and President Grover Cleveland, but it was President William McKinley who signed the charter which established the National Florence Crittenton Mission, and Kate Barrett became its motivating force.

She made as many as two hundred addresses in a few months before Womens' Clubs, legislatures, and other important bodies. She foresaw the need of women acquiring the vote; she was a member of the Board of Trustees of William and Mary College. Theodore Roosevelt encouraged her social projects; William Howard Taft wrote words of praise; and Woodrow Wilson wrote that the Crittenton Mission "should command the sympathetic interest of every good citizen."

Dr. Barrett testified before Congress on all bills involving unwed mothers; and on prostitutes, and what would happen to them when they were ousted from houses closed by Law; helped train unwed mothers for jobs; and worked for the Kenyon Red Light Bill that ordered the abolishment of disorderly houses.

Dr. Barrett was the first woman to cross the Atlantic on a battleship, she was appointed by President Wilson as one of ten women to attend the Versailles Conference; and was one of five women delegates to the Zurich Peace Conference of 1919.

In establishing nearly a hundred Florence Crittenton Homes in 50 States, she and Mr. Crittenton brought hope to thousands, and had the satisfaction of knowing that many of "her girls" turned to respectable and useful lives.

FRANCES FOLSOM CLEVELAND
Born 1864

"I'm only waiting for my wife to grow up." This was the answer Grover Cleveland gave when his sister asked the forty-eight-year-old bachelor President if he ever intended to marry.

Frances Folsom Cleveland was the first and only President's wife to be married in the White House. She was still almost two months short of her 22nd birthday when she married Grover Cleveland in a flower-bedecked Blue Room on June 21, 1886.

She was an immediate success as First Lady. "After Cleveland's marriage, both he and the White House underwent a striking change," wrote one journalist. "His friends observed that he was happier, brighter, and more companionable."

"I have seen many women of various types through all the long years of my service in the White House," said Col. W. H. Crook. "But neither there nor elsewhere have I seen anyone providing the same downright *loveliness* which was as much a part of Mrs. Cleveland as her voice, her marvelous eyes, or her warm smile of welcome."

Grover Cleveland was Governor of New York when he was elected to the Presidency in 1884. As a student at Wells College in Buffalo, Frances was the envy of her classmates because she received frequent letters and occasional gifts from the Governor.

Frances' father, Oscar Folsom, had been Cleveland's law partner. He was killed in a

102

tragic accident when Frances was 11, and she had become Cleveland's ward when he was appointed executor of her father's estate.

Upon her graduation shortly after Cleveland entered the White House she and her mother left for a year's trip to Europe. Rumors of their engagement began to leak out a few months later and it was officially announced by the President when the Folsoms returned to the States in the spring of 1886.

President Cleveland was narrowly defeated for re-election in 1888 by Benjamin Harrison. As she bade farewell to the White House staff, Mrs. Cleveland told them to "take good care of all the furniture and ornaments, for I want to find everything just as it is now when we come back again . . . four years from today."

They did come back. Cleveland defeated Harrison in 1892 and is the only President to serve two non-consecutive terms.

During the campaign of 1892, political opponents circulated vicious, untrue stories about Cleveland and his young wife. She answered them effectively in a letter to a woman who had written requesting the "true facts" about their marriage.

"I can only say in answer to your letter," replied Mrs. Cleveland, "that I wish our country no greater blessing than their homes and lives may be as happy and their husbands as kind, attentive, considerate, and affectionate as mine."

Between terms, the Clevelands lived in New York where he practiced law. Their first child,

Ruth, was born there in 1891. The second daughter, Esther, who was born in 1893, is the only child of a president to be born in the White House. They had three more children, Marion, Richard, and Francis. Ruth Cleveland died in 1904 when she was 13 years old.

After the second term, the family lived in Princeton, New Jersey, where Cleveland died in 1908. Five years later Frances married Thomas J. Preston, a professor at Princeton University, who had been a teacher at Wells College when she was a student there.

For some years prior to her death, she was one of the outstanding leaders in the work of the Needlework Guild of America, supplying garments for the needy through its many branches in the United States. She served several terms as national president of that organization. She died at 83 on October 29, 1947.

When the Clevelands left after his second term, a contemporary historian wrote:

"It is not amiss to say that in popular estimation Mrs. Cleveland, next to Dolly Madison, holds a preeminent place among those who have filled this exacting post. And she possessed two qualities that the vivacious Dolly lacked—youth and beauty. Yet she had two other qualities which Dolly had—self forgetfulness and a desire to make people happy."

Frances Folsom Cleveland expressed her deep feeling of love of her husband in a note she wrote to him on his seventieth birthday: "My heart is full of gratitude for what the years of your life have meant to me. You know how dearly I love you. I repeat it and repeat it and ask God's blessing on you . . . Your loving wife."

DR. ANITA NEWCOMB McGEE
Born 1864

Washington has known a succession of First Ladies, born in other parts of the country and residing briefly in the White House. However, Washington has also produced its own first ladies. Anita Newcomb McGee is one of these notable firsts: First acting woman surgeon of the United States Army, First Superintendent of the Army Nurse Corps, First American woman to be decorated by the Emperor of Japan, First President of the Society of Spanish War Nurses, and the only woman eligible for membership in the United Spanish War Veterans.

Born in 1864 in the shadow of the Naval Ob-

servatory, Anita was the daughter of the famous astronomer, Qimon Newcomb. Shortly before his daughter's birth, Newcomb was named professor of mathematics by the United States Navy and assigned to Washington to supervise the construction of a 26-inch equatorial telescope to track the orbits of the Moon, Venus, Mars, Uranus, Neptune, and Saturn. Perhaps it was his later experiments to determine the velocity of light by means of fixed and revolving mirrors along opposite banks of the Potomac River that inspired Anita to undertake advanced scientific studies.

Certainly her father and her mother, Mary Caroline Hassler Newcomb, made possible for Anita an education unusual for a young woman of that day. She studied in Switzerland at the Osborne Seminary High School and at the Universtiy of Geneva, then crossed the channel to Cambridge University, completing her studies in the United States at the University of California and Johns Hopkins University in Baltimore. In 1892, at twenty-eight, she had become Mrs. Anita Newcomb McGee and a graduate of George Washington University Medical School in Washington.

Anita's husband, Dr. W. J. McGee, was head of the United States Geological Survey. She practiced medicine in the District of Columbia from 1892 to 1896, and still found time to raise two children, daughter Klotho and son Eric, who later took for his surname his mother's maiden name and was known as Eric McGee Newcomb.

Anita McGee was thirty-four years old when she was named Acting Assistant Surgeon attached to the Surgeon General's Office of the United States Army. This was the year 1898, not yet the beginning of the twentieth century with opening doors of opportunity for women. During this military assignment, Anita organized the Army Nurse Corps, and served as its Superintendent until 1900, when the Corps was taken over by the military services.

Four years later, in 1904, while serving with distinction with the Japanese Army in the Russo-Japanese War, she was honored by the Emperor of Japan and his Empress with the Order of the Sacred Crown and the War Medal of Japan.

Anita McGee's talents found other outlets than the practice of medicine. She was an organizer, a writer, journalist, and collector of genealogical records for scientific purposes. She made significant contributions also to such varied fields as public health education, parliamentary law, and biography.

Her seventy-six years of active service spanned eventful periods in the history of her country. Born during the last year of the Civil War, she died on October 5, 1940, just before America's entrance into World War II and too early for the era to follow of exploration into the outer space pioneered by her father.

MARY McLEOD BETHUNE

Born 1875

Mary McLeod Bethune was a legend in her own time; a symbol of black heritage; a forerunner for equality between races and sexes. As her life drew to a close, America's outstanding lady of the land prepared a legacy: "I leave you Love. I leave you Hope. I leave you the challenge of developing confidence in one another. I leave you a thirst for education. I leave you respect for the use of power. I leave you faith. I leave you racial dignity. I leave you a desire to live harmoniously with your fellow man. I leave you, finally, a responsibility for our young people."

Mary Bethune was born July 10, 1875, the fifteenth of seventeen children, to Samuel and Patsy McLeod. At her birth her mother called her "A gift from God." She stood out from the other children; she always pursued an extraordinary quest for knowledge. In 1882 she attended the Presbyterian Mission School in Mayesville, South Carolina, then Scotia Seminary in North Carolina, and Moody Bible Institute in Chicago in 1894. Although she married Albert Bethune in 1897, and they had one son, Albert, she continued her studies. She began winning academic degrees in 1910 with a Master of Science from South Carolina State College; Master of Arts from both Wilberforce University and Tuskegee Institute in 1915 and 1937. She went on to receive Honorary Doctor of Letters degrees between 1935 and 1943 from Lincoln University, Howard University, Atlanta University, and Wiley College in Texas. She also received honorary Doctor of Humanities degrees from Bennett College, West Virginia State College, Rollins College and Benedict College.

She founded the Daytona Normal and Industrial School for Girls, now Bethune-Cookman College, Daytona Beach, Florida, serving as President from 1932 to 1942 and again in 1946 and 1947. Afterwards she served as President Emeritus and Trustee and Chairman of the Advisory Board of the College.

She was founder and President of the National Council of Negro Women and a close friend and advisor to five Presidents of the United States, Theodore Roosevelt, Calvin Coolidge, Herbert Hoover, Franklin D. Roosevelt, and Harry S. Truman.

During the Administration of Franklin D. Roosevelt she was Director of the Office of Negro Affairs and special assistant to the Secretary of War for selecting candidates to the first Women's Army Corps Officers Candidate School. Standing in the presence of the President of the United States she felt there was no barrier to prevent a black man or woman from achieving that office. She said, "Faith in God is the greatest power, but great too is faith in oneself. To know God is to have a profound sense of security in the midst of insecurity." And she had

this sense of security as she stressed the need for education for people of all races, and built her college with love as a shrine.

Her list of honors is too lengthy to give in detail, but included awards from the National Association for the Advancement of Colored People, the Southern Conference Award for Human Welfare, and the Star of Africa from the Republic of Liberia. She served the Federal Government on President Calvin Coolidge's National Child Welfare Commission and President Hoover's National Commission on Home Building and Home Ownership. She was Director of the Florida Chapter of the American Red Cross. For President Franklin D. Roosevelt she was Special Advisor on Minority Affairs and Director of the Division of Negro Affairs, National Youth Administration. She also served as a member of the Board of Directors of American Women Volunteer Services, worked with the Women's Army Corps for National Defense and with hospitals advising on rehabilitation of veterans. Most important, she was chosen as consultant to the Conference to draft the United Nations' Charter in San Francisco in April of 1945, and appointed by President Truman to the Committee of Twelve for National Defense in 1951. She also represented President Truman at the two Inaugurals of President Tubman of Liberia.

The first American Memorial to a Black American or to a woman in a public park in Washington, D.C., our Nation's Capital, was erected to Mary McLeod Bethune on July 10, 1974. This monument will serve as a lasting tribute to a great woman who walked among so many, black and white, and left her mark on many hearts as she served her Nation and her people.

FRANCES PERKINS

Born 1882

Frances Perkins, the first woman ever to achieve Cabinet rank, was appointed Secretary of Labor by President Franklin D. Roosevelt in March, 1933. She served in that post until 1945.

Born in Boston, Massachusetts, April 10, 1882, Miss Perkins was educated in private and public schools in Massachusetts. In 1902 she was graduated from Mount Holyoke College, where she had majored in chemistry and biology. A teaching position at a girls' school near Chicago, with residence at Hull House, led her to an interest

in social work. In 1910, she received a Master's Degree in Sociology and economics from Columbia University.

Following her graduation she became executive secretary of the Consumer's League of New York City, and was instrumental in achieving passage by the New York State Legislature of the Jackson-McManus Bill, 1912, commonly known as the Fifty-Four Hour Bill, which limited the hours of labor of women in mercantile establishments in New York to 54 hours a week or 9 hours a day.

As an eyewitness of the fire at the Triangle Shirtwaist factory in New York, in which 146 girls lost their lives, many by jumping from 9th story windows, Miss Perkins beaame acutely aware of the necessity of safety standards. She became secretary of the Committee on Safety in New York and director of investigations of the New York State Factory Commission. She helped draft new Labor Law provisions relating to the prevention of hazards-to-life from fire and accidents.

During her 4 years as Industrial Commissioner of New York, Miss Perkins paid particular attention to unemployment problems, issuing a monthly statement on employment trends in 1,800 New York factories. She continually stressed the importance to the general economic welfare of maintaining the wage earner's purchasing power. She was also instrumental in having passed the 48-hour law limiting the labor of women and young people in factories to 8 hours a day or 48 hours a week.

As Secretary of Labor, Frances Perkins launched a program of history-making social reform. She considered her chief accomplishment,

as a major architect of the New Deal, the passage of the Social Security Act—providing for unemployment compensation, old-age pensions and old-age insurance, mothers' pensions, aid to crippled children and to the blind. During the depression years, she took an active part in shaping the policies of the National Recovery Act and the Civilian Conservation Corps, and was instrumental in bringing to public approval much of the New Deal legislation of the early and mid-1930's, including the Walsh-Healy Act and the Fair Labor Standards Act.

In a reorganization of the Department of Labor, she established the United States Employment Service and the Wage and Hour and Public Contracts Divisions. She overhauled the Immigration Service, and expanded and improved the Bureau of Labor Statistics. She held regular regional and national conferences on Labor legislation. Her one daughter, Suzanne, was not interested in her mother's reforms.

In the International field, she personally influenced the participation of the US Government in the International Labor Organization, and the close relationship between the ILO and the US Department of Labor. In 1941 she served as President of the Conference of the International Labor Organization.

During World War II, she acted as a member of the War Manpower Commission and the Office of Economic Stabilization. Under her Administration, the Department of labor focused its attention on mobilization for defense industries and war production, and later, the preparation for reconversion to peace-time activities.

Frances Perkins served as Secretary of Labor longer than any person in history. Shortly after her resignation in June, 1945, she accepted an appointment by President Truman as Chairman of the Civil Service Commission. She remained in this post until January, 1953, when she retired to private life. In retirement she continued her writing, and acted as visiting lecturer at the New York State School of Industrial and Labor Relations at Cornell University.

Her service to the United States, and to the world as chairman of the United States delegation to the International Labor Organization in 1915, was rewarded a number of times. Yet, perhaps, no tribute captured better the esteem in which she was held than the Elizabeth Blackwell Award by Hobard and William Smith Colleges in 1962. It was presented to Miss Perkins for "outstanding service to mankind."

REBECCA BURGESS BULLOCK
Born 1886

The life of Rebecca Burgess Bullock was devoted to the enrichment of the lives and minds of all whom she encountered. She had a miraculous gift for communicating the force of her own dreams not only to her children, but to countless young people and students who benefited from her life long work to alleviate social ills and educational inadequacies. This great and strong, yet gentle woman, was one of the most prominent religious and civic leaders and dedicated mothers in the Washington community.

Rebecca Burgess Bullock was born in Warrenton, North Carolina, on January 25, 1886, to William and Emma Frances Burgess. She attended public schools and Shilo Normal Industrial Institute in Warrenton, and Shaw University in Raleigh, North Carolina, where she met her future husband, the Reverend George O. Bullock.

Following graduation, Rebecca taught elementary school for three years prior to her marriage. Of the Bullocks eight children, three, including the wife of the Mayor of the District of Columbia, are educators. One is a Social Welfare Administrator. Three entered the field of medicine and one is an attorney. Their commitment is indicative of her love for her family and her unique ability to light the fire of inspiration. In 1950, Mrs. Bullock was the first black woman to be honored as Washington's Mother of the Year.

A spirited and intellectual companion to her husband, Rebecca Bullock contributed to the life and develnpment of communities in which she lived and to the church, which was a prime focal point in her life. This compassionate woman

was a leader in helping the underprivileged who were suffering from economic, social and religious deprivation. During her husband's pastorates in Charlotte and Winston Salem, North Carolina, and in Washington, D.C. at the Third Baptist Church, where The Reverend Bullock served for forty years, she was an indispensable helpmate, organizer, a talented musician and a persuasive public speaker.

Mrs. Bullock held offices in a number of women's groups besides her membership on the Deaconess Board, Christian Endeavor Society, Sunday School Faculty and Missionary Circle of her church. She was active in the Y.W.C.A., Council of Churches, and served as President of the Baptist Wives and the Interdenominational Wives in the Washington area.

Rebecca believed in extending the benefits of education to all, and was a life-long supporter of her alma mater, Shaw University, where her husband became the first black chairman of the Board of Trustees. An outstanding fund raiser even during her advanced years, she received the Shaw University Distinguished Service Award in 1950.

Rebecca Bullock's commitment to humanity extended beyond her own community and nation to the world. This was reflected in her long and faithful service as treasurer of the Lott Carey Foreign Missionary Society and as President of the District of Columbia Branch of the Convention.

This generous woman shared fully her talents and abilities with the world. A passionate believer in the unique value of every human being, she consciously used her energies and talents to illuminate life. Among the good things in life, Rebecca gave priority to prayer, music, and education which she believed should be accessible to all. Her heart and her home were always open to those in need and she remained active throughout her life even when confined to her home in her advanced years.

Rebecca Burgess Bullock lived to see the day when educational, social and economic justice were beginning to become a reality for many to whom they had been traditionally denied. She lived to see her children make distinguished contributions to the intellectual and social life of an ever widening community where diversity was sought and uniqueness was honored. Her children and others whose lives she touched have drawn strength from her determination and resourcefulness in their efforts to create a better society. This is her legacy.

AGNES E. MEYER

Born 1887

On a biographical questionnaire prepared for her publisher, Agnes Elizabeth Meyer once listed her occupation simply as "housewife." Later she was to use a phrase that better sums up a life of family and public responsibility: "practicing American citizen."

When her autobiographical memoir, "Out of These Roots," was published, Mrs. Meyer said it was her hope "to encourage American women to realize that it is not necessary to hold political office to serve the common good in their community and country."

Her life was a testimony to this thesis. While raising a family of one son and four daughters—"boisterous" was her word for them—Mrs. Meyer found time, energy, and concern for public causes. She was a driving force—writing trenchantly, speaking forcefully, working unflaggingly on committees and commissions, ceaselessly prodding citizen apathy and official indifference—for better public schools and health care, decent housing, equal opportunity, and human welfare and rights.

Once urged to run for Congress, Mrs. Meyer declined because of the demands of "steady responsibility" of political office. The explanation must have been viewed with a touch of wry humor by those who worked with her for summer lunch programs, elementary school libraries, the Westchester Recreation Commission, a District Urban Service Corps, a cultural center for the Nation's Capital, social and psychological services in the schools, and the numerous other projects that have bettered and brightened the lives of residents of the District of Columbia and its suburbs.

In her life of public service, Mrs. Meyer was guided by passionate belief in public education and the family as central institutions of a free, democratic society. She fought fearlessly and tirelessly for Federal aid to public schools and was an early advocate of a Federal department of health, education, and welfare. At the age of 75, she organized the National Committee for the Support of the Public Schools, a national grass-roots organization to upgrade public education. Although she was confined to a wheelchair in her later years before her death in 1970 at the age of 83, her crusading zeal never waned nor did her righteous indignation at social injustices.

Mrs. Meyer was born Agnes Elizabeth Ernst on January 2, 1887, in New York City, the daughter of an attorney. After studying at Barnard College and the Sorbonne and moving in the intellectual and artistic circles of Paris, she married Eugene Meyer, a young banker, who later was to come to Washington as a Government official and subsequently owner of The Washington Post newspaper. Both strong individuals, Mr. and Mrs. Meyer, as husband and wife, supported and sustained each other in their family and public life.

A woman of wealth, position, intellectual attainment, singular energy, and lively social conscience, Mrs. Meyer could be a formidable force in pursuit of a cause. Her range of interests was remarkable. She wrote a scholarly book on Chinese painting, translated Thomas Mann from German, and collected French Impressionists in the early days before their critical recognition. Her parties, with artists, writers, politicians, and intellectuals as guests, were an intellectual adornment to Washington social life. In appearances before Congressional committees and on the lecture platform, she was a forceful lobbyist for public education and human welfare. She wrote influential articles on social problems for newspapers and magazines, combining a reporter's fact-finding with a constructive critic's evaluation and recommendations for reform.

In the District of Columbia, there is an elementary school named in honor of Eugene and Agnes Meyer. There is a foundation, bearing the names of husband and wife, that has provided millions in grants to support education, community service, health, and the humanities. Visitors to the Freer Gallery of Art can delight in the glories of Oriental art in a collection given in both names. But perhaps the most enduring legacy of Agnes E. Meyer is the example of her life as a "practicing American citizen" fulfilling both family and public responsibilities.

AGNES INGLIS O'NEIL

Born 1897

Agnes Inglis O'Neil was born in 1897 and died in 1975, and the years between span a life based on caring and doing for all children everywhere. She was the mother of five boys, whom she adopted as a single parent. She founded and directed two distinguished schools, and she aided in the rescue of many thousands of children during World War II.

Her acceptance of children was total. No matter how unrealized their lives, she found a way to hold up a standard of excellence for them. Other teachers and parents found in her teaching an example and an inspiration for the nurture of their own young. Everyone called her

"Ag", or "Aggie", and in return she saw things the way children see them. As a result she could explain concepts—in mathematics, for instance— so vividly that her students remember them and the way they learned them a lifetime later. Young people then, productive adults now, remember their years in her schools, or summers on her Western trips, as the one experience that got them through the time when they most needed to grow and learn.

Ag always lived in such a way that stray children could be housed, fed, cared-for, and recharged. To her various homes—in the Catskills and in Washington, D.C.—children came to stay and go to school, or to attend camp, when things were tough at home. They were the waifs of the middle class, tattered and messy long before it was the fashion, too much for their parents to cope with; disappointing to their expectations; caught by family fragmentation. Her substitute motherhood was extraordinarily effective; today they live in a wide variety of productive styles.

Ag herself left Vassar in the middle of her first year following an injury in a riding accident. She worked at the Spring Street Settlement House in New York and later taught at a missionary school in India. About 1920, she returned to the United States to help start Windward School, a home for the children of separated parents in White Plains, New York.

Ag left Windward in 1933. Always venturesome, always a teacher, she made a return visit to India, but took with her a group of children and kept school on shipboard. She returned soon to the United States to join the Rural Resettlement Administration and design school systems for the new communities created to combat the Great Depression. Her insight into childrens' problems was bringing her into contact with concerned national leaders. In 1940, when the Field Foundation was created to improve the life of children and better race relations, Marshall Field asked Ag to become a founding member, and she remained on the Board of that Foundation all her life.

With the advent of World War II, Ag O'Neil became Executive Secretary of the Non-Sectarian Committee for German Refugee Children. After the United States entered the war, she became a Director of the United States Committee for the Care of European Children. This Committee brought hundreds of children to this country from war-torn Europe.

Ag's interest in and concern for children during war was not limited to Europe, she developed a national program to care for the children of working mothers which was the predecessor of today's Day-Care Centers.

In 1945 Ag formed Georgetown Day School, the first racially integrated school in the Nation's Capital. This school, which she directed until her retirement in 1961, grew characteristically out of the need for a better educational environment for her own boys and her desire to share the meeting of that need with others. The educational design of that school was pure "Ag": it was parent-owned, relied heavily on parent-trustees for financial and moral support, and entered into Washington's inter-racial community, where it gave and received a warm welcome.

Ag's love for children was all-encompassing and their response to her delight in them was magical. Two educational institutions stand as her monument, but there are thousands of children whose lives have been touched by hers, who are able to love others more easily because she loved them. They are her real monument.

Florida

Florida

Nickname: Sunshine State

State Flower: Orange blossom

State Tree: Sabal Palm

State Bird: Mocking bird

Photos

1. Miami Beach
2. Kennedy Space Center
3. Everglades
4. Ft. Walton
5. Sabal Palm

Florida

MARY McLEOD BETHUNE
Humanitarian   **Born 1876**

Mary McLeod Bethune was a remarkable negro girl who wanted desperately to learn to read and to share that learning with others of her race. She made the trek from a barefoot cotton picker to a world-acclaimed college president and civic leader in Daytona Beach, Florida.

Upon her graduation from high school, her spirits were low because there was no money available to continue her education. Soon she received a letter from a Colorado dressmaker, Mary Chrissman, who was anxious to educate a worthy negro. Mary had been recommended to her for this honor and assistance.

A friend gave Mary McLeod a railroad ticket to visit Miss Chrissman for an interview. As Mary McLeod fell on her knees in thankfulness, her friends were making dresses and knitting stockings for her. Everyone helped to get her ready for her appointment at Scotia University, with Miss Chrissman.

There were many questions in Mary's mind:
—Where did negroes really come from? Why were they in America where most people were white? Why had they been slaves? Why did Lincoln free them? These questions with answers caused Mary McLeod to stay in College long and work hard to educate her people. Her plans were fulfilled to go to Moody Institute. She was the only negro at Moody Institute but in her heart she felt no difference between the white man or the black man. She was a member of the Gospel Choir and sang and talked in towns where many children had never seen a negro. Her voice was beautiful.

Her studies continued at several other institutes, but it was at Kendall Institute in Sumter, South Carolina, that she met and married Albertus Bethune who was teaching there. They had one son, Albert. Having a child of her own made Mary more anxious than ever to make the America she loved a better place for negroes. Mary Bethune and her husband settled in Palatka, Florida, where he had a new teaching position. Mary had a dream of building a school for negroes in nearby Daytona Beach. In 1904

she and little Albert visited friends in Daytona where she rented a small dilapidated building for eleven dollars a month. Donations were made and friends helped clean and paint the building. Her school began with five girls as students. The school grew and received large donations from wealthy winter visitors. In 1916 a big assembly hall had been built and named "White Hall". Another addition followed with "Faith Hall".

In the year 1923, Mrs. Bethune decided that her school should be open to both girls and boys. She liked the boys' school in Jacksonville called "Cookman Institute", owned by the Methodist Church. Soon the church and Mrs. Bethune merged the two schools into one large Institute for both boys and girls. It was called the Bethune-Cookman Institute and Mary Bethune became its first President.

Widowed in 1919, Mary traveled extensively to London, Paris, and Rome where she was given a blessing by the Pope. Upon returning home, Mrs. Eleanor Roosevelt met and entertained her at luncheon. Her assistance helped Mary to organize the National Council of Colored Women. President Roosevelt set up another organization for negroes, called the National Youth Administration. The President asked Mary Bethune to serve on its Advisory Board.

This was the beginning of her work for equal rights for negroes. Her honors never ceased. In 1945 the trustees of Rollins College in Winter Park, Florida, asked Mary to accept an honorary degree. She accepted the honor which became the first honorary degree ever given to a negro by a white southern college. She was also awarded the Doctor of Humanities Degree by President Holt of Rollins College in Winter Park, Florida.

Just before her death in 1954, at the age of seventy-nine, she was happy when the Supreme Court of the United States announced the decision that all schools must be open to every child of every color. Congress erected a stone monument to Mary Bethune, in Washington, D.C., the first ever erected for a negro woman. It is called Mary Bethune's living monument.

Florida and Rollins college are honored to have Mary Bethune's beloved Bethune-Cookman College for Negroes as a living memmorial to Mary Bethune.

MARY ALICE PRITCHARD MYERS MUGGE
Florida Poet and Writer   **Born 1895**

Mary Alice Mugge, born in 1895 during the Victorian Age, now lives in her native Florida and watches with continued fascination the progress of the world in the Space Age.

With a great capacity for responding to people and situations, she is still active at the age of eighty in her Lutheran church, community and civic work, group singing, and giving illustrated talks on foreign trips. She makes the lives of others brighter with her consistent helpful ideas.

She has written prose and poetry for many years, and still reads her poems and verse for

groups. In 1975 she published a book of her poems entitled *Scattered Showers*. She is now compiling a book of poems for children.

Mary Alice, the second of three daughters of Annie Shelley (a decendent of the poet Shelley) and George Olin Pritchard, was born in Jacksonville, Florida. She lived there until her elopement at the age of fifteen with Burns Legrand Myers, favorite son of an indulgent father. They were married at the railway station on the way to the Myers family home in Meldin, Georgia. Her trousseau, seven yards of baby blue ribbon acquired when she was pressed to name her fondest wish, laced the eyelet trim on her white nightgown, was "snatched on the run from the sewing basket."

Burns Myers was the son of Mattie Cooper Myers and William Myers, a wealth landowner who was at one time a turpentine woods rider in southern Georgia and northern Florida. Mary Alice successfully adapted to life in the alien household of her husband's family, crowded with sisters- and brothers-in-law. As an example of her ingenuity, she and a favorite sister-in-law, Mattie, developed a method of communication— a kind of talking backwards, i.e., Alice became "Eckila" and Mattie, "Eyetam." As the years passed and their need to share secrets grew, they structured grammar and perfected rules to disguise those back-words too easily identified by listeners.

114

When babies came, as they did to all the women in the big house, Alice's were happily breast-fed. During the nursing months of her second child, Margaret, Alice also nursed to health Holbrook, tiny son of a black servant.

After the births of three children (Olin, the first-born died), Alice, Burns, Margaret and Shelley moved to Tampa, where Anne was born. Alice was then twenty-four. When Burns became a semi-invalid, she doubled her parental role and multiplied other efforts. Their home continued to be warm and filled with the benefits of mutual love—the best of friends, music, books, and foods (with specialties for certain friends). Outdoor activities—the year-round boating and beaching, picnicing, and fishing—rounded out an ideal childhood for the children.

Throughout the years, with courage, kindness, wit, and wisdom, Alice coped with the trouble and tragedy and the sometimes ludicrous aspects of events that often challenge the strongest in large, close-woven families. After the death of her husband in 1946, Alice Myers devoted herself to making a home for her son and encouraging and assisting her daughters, friends and grandchildren in varying situations. In 1949 she married an old friend, August Bremmer Mugge, thereby acquiring another family—his four grown children and their growing children.

Following several years of intermittent travel to Europe and the Middle East, Alice and August Mugge now live in Melbourne, Florida. In 1974, Alice celebrated her second Silver Wedding Anniversary.

The liveliness of her personality and her mind continues undiminished, as does her zest and her love of life.

MRS. MARJORIE KENNAN RAWLINGS
Writer   **Born 1896**

Mrs. Marjorie Kennan Rawlings had a fascinating and absorbing literary life. An extensive study of her life and works, shows the warmth of her love affair with Florida. The primitive natives with whom she chose to live in a small country settlement called Cross Creek near Gainesville, Florida, was the basis for many of her writings.

She wrote many books while living in her little home at Cross Creek. Some of her best

were *South Moon Under, Cross Creek, Golden Apples, The Yearling* and *The Sojourner*.

Mrs. Rawlings explained her love for Florida Crackers by saying they are a people without a history, as Florida is a state with gaps in its genealogy. The Crackers have a background of rice, tobacco and cotton plantings, of fishing and hunting, living mostly in the Florida hammocks. Marjorie truly loved the deep woods that she lived in and used for the setting of her writings.

Born in 1896 in Washington, D.C., she attended the University of Wisconsin in 1914 as an English major. She graduated from the University of Wisconsin in 1918 after becoming a Phi Beta Kappa during her junior year.

Her marriage to Charles A. Rawlings in 1919 took her to Rochester, where she soon became a feature writer for the "Courier-Journal" and the "Journal-American". She worked continually on short fiction but was unable to publish any of these works.

Her life really began in March, 1928, when she bought the Cross Creek grove property and moved to Florida. It was only two years later, in 1930, that Marjorie Kennan Rawlings achieved sudden literary fame and her writings began to sell. She liked to tell the story of how she was down to a box of crackers and a can of tomato soup in 1933, when she received unexpectedly a five hundred dollar check from the O. Henry Memorial Award. She had just received a final divorce decree from Charles Rawlings. During the following year Marjorie fell from a horse and broke her neck. Many adversities accompanied the successful completion of her book *Golden Apples*. Her brother, Arthur Kenneth, gave her a beautiful trip to visit him in Seattle with a boat trip on the Inland Waterway to Alaska. The research she found to help with her writings was invaluable. On her return to her home in Central Florida swamp land, *The Yearling* was published and Metro-Goldwyn-Mayer bought the film rights to the book for thirty thousand dollars. The book not only became a major best-seller but Marjorie Kennan Rawlings began to be a national celebrity.

Her heart was broken when in 1943 her friend, Zelma Cason, sued Marjorie for one hundred thousand dollars, for "invasion of privacy". Marjorie had used Zelma's name in one of her books, *The Sojourner*. The trial was held in nearby Gainesville, Florida, but the Florida Supreme Court directed Mrs. Rawlings to pay Zelma one dollar and cost. Marjorie Rawlings was alone in her swamp land home in Cross Creek in 1952 when she suffered a coronary heart attack. She recovered from the attack and returned to her writings for a short time. She suffered a cerebral hemorrhage in January 1953 at Crescent Beach, Florida, which took her life. Marjorie K. Rawlings was buried at Antioch Cemetary near her home in Island Grove, Florida. She may not have reached the height of literary fame for which she hoped, but the mark she made was deep and will last forever, especially among Floridians.

DEACONESS HARRIETT BEDELL
Missionary

Deaconess Harriett Bedell, missionary to the Everglades Indians, is one of the best known Florida missionary figures in the United States. Her work among the Indians has won her a lasting place in the hearts of Christian people everywhere.

Many years of labor with the Indians—teaching, guiding, inspiring, came to an abrupt halt when Hurricane Donna wiped out her mission in 1960.

A beautifully written book on the life of Deaconess Bedell was written by her friends, William and Ellen Hartley of Miami, entitled *A Woman Set Apart*.

Harriett's life was a steady dedication to the Indians and their welfare. She taught about fifty Indian pupils each day, teaching them to read and write and telling them stories from the Bible. In 1911 much had happened in the little mission school house. Their horse had died and there were many other deaths. In desperation Harriett had told of her needs to a wealthy woman visitor. She gave her a five hundred dollar donation. Then an anonymous contributor sent her two thousand dollars to build a new chapel.

Things began to get better and another young deaconess came to assist Harriett in her mission work. But Harriett, very tired, decided on a vacation. When she visited a doctor, they found that she had an active case of tuberculosis. Harriett cried bitterly at this. If she really had tuberculosis, could she ever return to her Indian Welfare work that she loved so much?

She kept her faith, remembering that "all things work together for good, for those who love God".

Tuberculosis was prevalent among the Indians, and there was constant work to be done. Harriett and her deaconess friend were sent to Denver's high altitude for a rest and cure. Shortly after their arrival there, Deaconess Harriett attended a quiet service of healing in St. Mark's Church. The spiritual depth of this service was almost overwhelming. She came away from it, feeling a great exultation. Two days later the doctor pronounced her well and in perfect condition. They were all deeply puzzled when they heard the news. This experience was tremendous. She had to force from her mind the word "miracle". She felt unworthy of such a blessing from God but was grateful.

She returned to her Mission and the Indians, especially the children who swarmed around her. She kept one thought in mind: "Lord, I do give thanks to Thee for the abundance that is mine". As Bishops came to visit the little mission, they all affirmed that Harriett had done a remarkable job within the Indian Reservation. She received a flood of visits and invitations for speaking engagements. Eventually her speaking took her to Canada's Yukon Territory, Tanana, Dawson City in the Klondike and many faraway places. Harriett's greatest problem, however, was with the Indians themselves. Many of them now understood the significance of Christianity, many believed; but they would not accept the rites of the church. The medicine man influenced the Council; and the Council held back the people. The resistance was polite but firm. In essence, the Indians said, we believe in your Holy Spirit and the message of Jesus, but we are Seminole Indians. We refuse to engage in a White Ceremony. We accept your teaching but not your rites.

Work with the Seminoles never ceased, even as the severe Hurricane hit the Everglades in September, 1960. Deaconess Bedell was taken to the home of friends in Ochopee, Florida. When it finally passed over, the lovable deaconess was carried to Davenport, Florida, to enter the Bishop Gray Inn for elderly people. This is an Episcopalian retirement home. The Mission had been washed away and the beloved Deaconess Harriett Bedell was sick from shock. Her Glade-Cross Mission in the Indian Reservation was demolished. She soon passed away. The Diocese of South Florida rebuilt Glade-Cross Mission which is now a memory to her honor, Deaconess Harriett Bedell.

MRS. MYRTIS HAWTHORNE MILLER
Civic   **Born 1906**

Myrtis Rosalie Hawthorne, daughter of Alexander Miller Hawthorne and Myrtis Alethia Farmer, was born December 21, 1906, in Columbia County, Florida, near Lake City. She is one of five children—all girls.

Rosalie attended the Mt. Tabor Consolidated School, graduated from Columbia High with honors, and attended Florida State University. In college she studied sociology, psychology and philosophy. She had planned to be a social case worker, in order to help people. July 4, 1933, at Mikesville, Columbia County, Florida, she married Albert Hiers Miller, also a native Floridian, born February 17, 1904, at Crescent City, Florida.

To this union were born four children, a son, Charles, and three daughters.

Mr. and Mrs. Miller owned and operated the Miller Well Drilling Company of Gainesville. After his death on June 24, 1973, their son, Charles, became the manager. Charles had been in the business with his father over a long period of time. Mrs. Miller had given much of her time and service in assisting her husband in his duties as a past president as well as secretary-treasurer of the Florida Water Well Association. In July 1975 she was honored by Florida Water Well Association with an Honorary Life Membership and a Certificate of Appreciation. She is a member of the Florida Water Well Association Ladies Division.

Mrs. Miller enjoys her association with people, especially through the church and patriotic and historical organizations.

She joined the methodist church with her husband and is a member of the First United

Methodist Church of Gainesville, also, a member of the Wesley Fidelis Sunday School Class, the Miriam Spottswood Circle, and the United Methodist Women. Mrs. Miller served as historian for several rural churches with which she has been associated and has spent much time in making scrapbooks and photographs. Mr. and Mrs. Miller were regular attendees for annual homecoming in five or six of these churches.

In 1950 she became a member of the Gainesville Chapter Daughters of the American Revolution and has served the chapter well in many capacities. She was a compiler of three volumes of Alachua County Cemetery Records and is presently Lineage-Research Chairman. Mrs. Miller, an Honorary Senior State President of the Florida Society, Children of the American Revolution served as Senior State President 1958-1960. She is also a past senior president of the Jacob Roberts Brown Society C.A.R. in Gainesville.

Becoming a member of the United Daughters of the Confederacy in 1954, Mrs. Miller has been President of the Kirby-Smith Chapter #202, Gainesville, since 1964. On the state level, she was Florida Division Treasurer 1968-1970 and is currently serving as Second Vice President, and Press Relations of the Florida UDC.

Among other organizations in which she holds valued memberships are: Order of the Eastern Star (Past Matron of Lake Butler #40), Lula Tomkies Club—OES Auxiliary, and Scimitar Circle of the Gainesville Shrine Club; Gainesville Woman's Club; American Association of University Women; Florida Mu Chapter of Phi Sigma Alpha, International Sorority (Charter member and past president); The Retired Officers Association—Ladies Division; an honorary member of the Colonial Dames of the XVII Century. Also, she has been a former member of Begonia Circle of the Gainesville Garden Club, in which her special interest was Conservation. She made many slides of Florida wildflowers, which were used for programs, and also, a state award winning wildflower scrapbook. She has been much involved with horticulture. Her husband, Albert, was a World War II Major, Corps of Army Engineers.

From her interest in government, she has been a member of the Alachua County Democratic Executive Committee some twelve years, presently serving on the Steering Committee.

There are several other groups in which she is an active member: the English Speaking Union (Jacksonville Branch); Southern Dames of America (Jacksonville Society—serving as Vice President); The American Security Council (National) Advisory Board; and the Spirit of '76 Society. Interested in history, Rosalie Miller is a member of the Historical Society of Gainesville, the Florida Historical Society and the South Carolina Historical Society.

She finds genealogy a fascinating hobby and has assisted many people in genealogical research. Rosalie is a charter member of the Gainesville, Florida, Genealogical Society, and belongs to the Jacksonville Genealogical Society. As a member of the Hiers Research Committee, she was co-ordinator of the Florida—Georgia Hiers, for the recently published book—The Hiers Family Genealogy. For the Lastinger Family Association, she has served as secretary-treasurer some thirteen or fourteen years.

Rosalie Hawthorne Miller is listed in *Who's Who of American Women* by Marquis—1964 edition, and in the Bi-Centennial Edition of *Personalities of the South*, (1975-1976 edition).

Mrs. Miller was always available to drive her elderly friends and neighbors to the grocery store, doctor's office or other appointments. In this way she learned patience and understanding in dealing with people with problems.

In working in collaboration with Mrs. Jack Silber, President of Florida Mother's Program, Mrs. Miller served as an area representative several years.

MY PRAYER

Guide each moment of my day
    Let me not waste the time away
Because Thou didst so much for me
    May my aim be always pleasing Thee.
To aid all others in their needs
    And share Thy love through thoughts and deeds

               Amen

MRS. ALICE GULLEN SMITH
Tampa

Miss Alice Gullen received her B.A. degree from Wayne State University in 1932 with work in English, Speech, French, and Latin. She later added work in Library Science at the University of Michigan and served as a school librarian for several years. Immediately after receiving her degree she began a long period of association with Wayne State University as an Adjunct-professor in Library Science. In 1939 she was married in Detroit, Michigan to Norman Victor Smith by her father, Reverend George Gullen, and Bishop Allen of the Methodist Church who had baptized her as a child.

Norman Smith graduated with the B.A. and M.A. degrees (1926 and 1927) in Chemical Engineering and Metallurgy, having the highest academic honors in the class. By 1939 he was rising to preeminence in the Bohn Aluminum, Brass, and Bronze Company and in time became the chief metallurgist in charge of operations and plant design. This company went into receivership in 1958 and he turned to the academic field, teaching in various technical schools while at the same time preparing himself for teaching in higher education. In 1965 Mr. Smith became a charter member of the faculty of the College of Engineering at the University of South Florida. At his recent retirement he was honored as the engineer who had done the most for Florida in the last ten years.

Three children were born to Alice and Norman: Susan Marguerite, Dean Lance, and Martha Kathleen.

Susan is married to Mr. Roger Simpkin, M.D., Ph.D. (Biology), and has two children, aged five and seven. She obtained the Ph.D. degree in Astrophysics from the University of Wisconsin in 1966 and is now Assistant Professor of Astronomy in Michigan State University. She is the author of more than sixty published research papers in astronomy and is a widely-travelled lecturer and professional consultant.

Dean Lance Smith is married to Patricka (nee Cote) Smith, Ph.D. in Pharmacy. He obtained the Ph.D. degree in Electrical Engineering at the University of Michigan in 1971. He is presently Assistant Professor of Electrical Engineering at Louisiana Institute of Technology at Ruston, Louisiana. He has published approximately fifteen technical articles in his field and one definitive textbook for graduate studies.

Martha Kathleen, an excellent flutist, won a music scholarship to the University of Michigan but stayed to major in mathematics in the Honors College. She received her Ph.D. degree in Mathematics at the University of Chicago. Miss Smith is presently Assistant Professor of Mathematics at the University of Texas. She has published seventeen research papers in the Mathematical Theory of Rings.

The importance of motherhood was first impressed upon young Alice at the age of twelve when her mother died. Her father's deep faith

was a source of inspiration in this great loss and deepened the awareness of God in her life. The twenty year period as an Adjunct-professor at Wayne State University provided her with the flexibility of schedule to meet the needs of her growing children. In the next five years with the maturing of her children she increased her professional involvement in Library Science and received the Ed.D. degree in 1965 from Wayne State University. That Fall she was appointed Assistant Professor and Chairman of the Department of Library Science in the University of South Florida. She was made Professor and Chairman of the department in 1970; and now the Department of Library Science has received full accreditation for its Library Science Program. Having achieved the goal she set out to attain, she has now resigned the chairmanship of the department in order to spend more time with her husband who has just retired.

RUTH BURR SAWYER
Educator   **Born 1912**

Ruth Burr Sawyer, youthful and active pre-World War II classroom teacher of Cocoa, Florida, became an after-War leader in the development of public school counseling and exceptional child education in Florida and the Southeast. She was born Ruth Elizabeth Burr in the Cumberland Valley of Pennsylvania and raised and educated among the simple but culturally rich ways of the old prosperous Pennsylvania Dutch who moved west of the Susquehanna River to liberate their youth from Amish ways. After graduating with honors in Latin, Math, and 4-H activities from one of the early large vocational high schools, she entered Dickinson College in Carlisle, Pennsylvania. While in college she tasted her first teaching experiences among under-privileged children of the Harrisburg industrial areas, where she instructed in language and also acted as home visitor and counselor while majoring as a senior in biology, language, and educational psychology.

After she received her A.B. in 1935, she moved to Florida where she had previously visited relatives and attended two terms at John B. Stetson University. She taught in Cocoa High School, Cocoa, Florida, from 1936 to 1943 when she married her fellow teacher, U.S. Navy Lt. Earl M. Sawyer. While teaching at Cocoa she helped start the local branch of the National Honor Society for high school students. Also while in Cocoa she actively worked with the Florida Secondary Education Curriculum Committee and the Florida Education Association

Committees for development of the Florida Teachers' Retirement System. As World War II closed in and Cocoa became a huge United States Naval Base, Ruth Sawyer became one of the first full time teenage counselors, working after hours a full eight hour shift, counseling through many crisis months of 1942 and 1943. She says it was during these months that she resolved to equip herself and take leadership in seeing that future teenagers of Florida have counselors in their schools. While her husband served in the Pacific she further added to her experiences in counseling by doing war relief work in the Pasadena area of California where family services and school counseling systems had already started to develop under educational leadership.

Ruth returned with her husband to Florida and in 1946 entered the graduate school at the University of Florida, Gainesville, Florida, where Earl majored and graduated in Physics and she majored in Counseling and Exceptional Child Education while acting at the same time as the newly appointed Visiting Teacher and Counselor for the Alachua County Public School System. She received her M.A. and Rank 1 in 1950 and 1952, and upon her second completion of special studies in counseling she was appointed the first Supervisor for Guidance and Exceptional Child Education for Alachua County. She organized the department and started each branch of her supervision with one unit each. However in the sixteen years to follow the services in Guidance and Exceptional Child Education developed in Alachua County at a pace which was noted throughout the Southeast.

Ruth Sawyer became a member of the Florida State Department of Education's Committee for evaluation of similar Guidance and Exceptional Child Education programs in many parts of the state as calls for setting up new programs came through the period of 1953 to 1967. She received appointment in 1953 to the Florida Children's Commission and served three terms as President of the Alachua County Branch of that Commission. As early as 1947 she had been a charter member of the Alachua County Community Services Association and served twice as its president. This association was, and is, notable because some twenty of the Florida counties developed almost exact copies of the same type of all-agency informational association to aid community workers and educators to know each other and intercooperate effectively.

She acted as the organizational chairman of the Alachua County Mental Health Association in 1957 and continued to serve on its board for eight years.

In 1968 she stepped up from the wide and somewhat scattered field of general supervision and became a director of clinical counseling doing intensive study on the current problems of teenagers, especially those of her own county surrounding the huge University of Florida. She notably helped bring members of the various fields of psychiatry into direct contact with high school counselors and teachers, as well as with high school teenagers prior to their involvement with drugs and crime.

Her services to teaching, counseling and community civic efforts have been honored repeatedly by the school system which she has served and by civic organizations, and in 1971 and 1973 the Women's Clubs of Gainesville and Cocoa, Florida, nominated her their "Teacher of the year" respectively for those years. Since then she has retired from public school service and entered private practice in clinical counseling for educational and family problems and has served as the local President of the Gainesville Altrusa Club, and Altrusa International (a very active group of professional women dedicated to community service and educational scholarships).

BEVERLY FISHER DOZIER

Born 1933

Beverly Fisher Dozier became the first woman in Florida history to run for the office of Secretary of State and only the second to run for a Cabinet level position in 1974 when she finished a close second in the Democratic primary run-off.

Presently serving as Manpower Management Planning Supervisor in the Florida Department of Community Affairs, Mrs. Dozier has served as the Director of the Division of Cultural Affairs for the State of Florida. She has also worked as a recruitment specialist for the Florida State Personnel Board, Coordinator of the Florida Cultural Arts Program, a teacher, and was also employed by Naval Intelligence in Washington, D.C.

A native of Branford, Florida, the 42-year-old Mrs. Dozier holds a B.A. in political science and

an M.A. in Educational Administration from Florida State University in Tallahassee.

She is chairman of the board of the proposed First Women's Bank of Florida and holds memberships in the Tallahassee Fine Arts Council Board, Tallahassee Junior League, National Women's Political Caucus, Florida Motion Picture and TV Association, Springtime Tallahassee, Asolo Angels, Capital Tiger Bay Club, Capital Medical Society Auxiliary and Trinity Methodist Church in Tallahassee; is a former board member of the Florida Heart Association and chaired the Tallahassee area Heart Fund drive for two years.

She is listed in several publications, including: *Who's Who in the South and Southwest; Personalities of the South; Who's Who in Florida for 1973; Directory of International Biography; Who's Who in American Women; Who's Who in Government;* and *Who's Who in America.*

Mrs. Dozier resides in Tallahassee with her husband, Dr. L. L. Dozier, Jr. and sons Tom, 17, and David, 14.

GEORGIA

Georgia

Nickname: Empire State for the South

State Flower: Cherokee Rose

State Bird: Brown Thrasher

Photos

1. The Illges House in Columbus
2. The Tybee Light on Tybee Island
3. Little White House near Warm Springs
4. Mill wheel on the grounds of Berry College
5. Historic Christ Church
6. Curved forms of modern sculpture— Atlanta
7. Davenport House—Savannah
8. Ocmulgee National Monument

Committee Members

Chairman—Mrs. J. Mac Barber, Commerce
Mrs. Emmet O. Cabaniss, Maxeys
Mrs. Sherman Drawdy, Augusta
Miss Daisy Elzey, Atlanta
Mrs. Joe J. Hewell, Atlanta
Mrs. Charles B. McGarity, Dallas
Mrs. E.D. Ricketson, Warrenton
Mrs. William A. Selman, Palmetto
Mrs. R. Stevens Tumlin, (Ex-Officio), Marietta
Emory Univer.
Mrs. Julia Voorhees Emmons, Atlanta
Students
Angie Cook
Joyce Crookall
Ellen Dierlein
Susan Foote
Mary Evelyn Gilbert
Roger Hux
Judy Keating
Michael Lynch
Linda Matthews
Marilyn Mollenkamp
Deborah Raemer
Kathy Sharp
Cerise Soroka
Magda Sossa
Thomas Wooten
Kay Youles
Deborah Zeiler

GEORGIA

REBECCA ANN LATIMER FELTON
Born 1835

Rebecca Ann Latimer Felton, writer, reformer and first woman seated in the United States Senate, was born near Decatur, Georgia, in DeKalb County. Descended from a long line of women of great vitality and longevity, Rebecca was the oldest child of Charles and Eleanor (Swift) Latimer. She received her early education in private schools in Oxford, Ga. and in Decatur. Entering the Madison (Ga.) Female College at the age of 15, she graduated two years later at the head of her class. A year after graduation, on October 11, 1853, Rebecca married her commencement speaker, Dr. William Harrell Felton, a physician and Methodist clergyman.

Surviving the turbulent, destructive years of the Civil War, Mrs. Felton taught in a school she and her husband established in Cartersville. In an attempt to rebuild the community life shattered by the war, Mrs. Felton participated in local temperance meetings and became president of the Confederate ladies aid society. Her first contact with politics came in 1874 when she served as her husband's campaign manager and press secretary in his successful bid for Congress on the Independent ticket. When Dr. Felton was victorious again in 1876, a newspaper headline read "Mrs. Felton and Her Husband Returned." Mrs. Felton's political involvement became increasingly intense during her husband's three terms in the U.S. Congress (1875-1881), and his three terms in the Georgia state legislature (1884-1890).

From her days as a school girl, Mrs. Felton had been interested in writing and journalism. In 1885, she and her husband started their Cartersville newspaper, the *Courant*, which she managed almost single-handedly as her husband's time was taken up with legislative affairs. In 1899, in order to increase its circulation in rural areas, the publisher of the semi-weekly edition of the Atlanta *Journal* asked Mrs. Felton to write a column, which she continued to contribute for over twenty years. Mrs. Felton's literary ambition was not confined to journal-

ism. She was the author of three books: *My Memoirs of Georgia Politics* (1911), which shows her to be a master of political debate; *Country Life in Georgia in the Days of My Youth* (1919), a disconnected autobiography; and *The Romantic Story of Georgia's Women* (1930), which contains many scenes from her own life.

Throughout most of her long life, Mrs. Felton was active in a series of reform movements, including prohibition, women's rights, public education and prison reform. She joined the Women's Christian Temperance Union in 1886, and made her first public speech on the horrors of the convict lease system at its annual convention. She saw her efforts at reform rewarded in 1908 with the passage of legislation which outlawed liquor and the convict lease system. Becoming active in the suffrage movement relatively late, Mrs. Felton debated the issue before a committee of the state legislature in 1914 and again in 1915. Her interest in education and women's rights found a common ground in her agitation for the admission of women to the state university, and the creation in 1915 of the Georgia Training School for Girls in Atlanta, a goal she had long sought.

The ultimate reward for Rebecca Felton's long devotion to public affairs came in 1922, when upon the death of Senator Thomas E. Watson, she was appointed to fill his unexpired term. Although Walter George was selected to succeed Watson before Congress convened, Mrs. Felton was allowed to present her credentials on November 21, 1922, and thus became the first woman seated in the United States Senate. The following day she made a brief, witty speech and relinquished her seat to George.

Rebecca Felton was the mother of five children, only one of whom survived to maturity. Mrs. Felton died in Atlanta of bronchial pneumonia at the age of 94, and was buried in Cartersville near the grave of her husband.

NELLIE PETERS BLACK

Born 1851

Nellie Peters Black, Georgia agriculturalist and church and civic leader, helped establish many of Georgia's first welfare organizations, and was a prime force behind social and educational reform in the state, especially as it related to women and children. Her most extensive work was accomplished through the Georgia Federation of Women's Clubs, of which she was president from 1916 until her death.

Christened Mary Ellen, Nellie was born in Atlanta, Georgia, February 9, 1851, the second of seven children of Richard and Mary Jane Thompson Peters. Her father, a pioneer in Georgia railroads, was an outstanding agriculturalist, land promoter, and financier. Her mother's family were Atlanta pioneers. Nellie grew up in a close, religious family, and a home filled with constant social activity. As a child, she witnessed the chaos and suffering following Atlanta's destruction in the Civil War. Having previously attended day school in Atlanta, she spent the years 1865-66 at Miss Maria Eastman's Brooke Hall, in Media, Pennsylvania. As a graduation present from her father, instead of a diamond ring, she chose a black horse, upon which she made frequent visits to Atlanta's poor. At this time she was instrumental in founding Atlanta's first mission, the Holy Innocents Mission.

In April, 1877, Nellie Peters married George Robison Black, a lawyer, planter, and politician from Screven County, Georgia. While a representative to Congress, Black suffered a paralytic stroke in 1882, and the family returned to Screven County, where he died in 1886. The Blacks

were the parents of three children, Nita Hughes, Louise King, and Ralph Peters, and also raised the four children of his first marriage.

Moving her family back to Atlanta in 1888, Mrs. Black resumed her involvement in civic affairs. She was a prime organizer, in 1892, of King's Daughters Hospital, Atlanta's first free hospital. In 1894, she was elected president of the Free Kindergarten Association, a post she held until 1914.

From the late 1890's to her death, Mrs. Black managed her father's farm in Gordon County.

Feeling that women had a responsibility to accomplish educational and social reforms, she helped found the Georgia Federation of Women's Clubs in 1896. As president, she led the Federation in wartime agricultural work, and organized and addressed a series of agricultural rallies throughout the state. Owning a strong mind and persuasive personality, Mrs. Black was a wonderful speaker, and in 1915, appeared at schools and colleges, campaigning against illiteracy. Two years later, the Department of Conservation in Washington, under Hoover, asked her to be speaker.

In these years she appeared frequently before the state legislature in behalf of compulsory education, admitting women to law practice and to the University of Georgia, and numerous other causes.

Among many awards, she was appointed "Dollar a Year" Woman by President Wilson.

After a sudden illness, Mrs. Black died in Atlanta, August 4, 1919, and was buried in Oakland Cemetery, Atlanta.

KATE WALLER BARRETT

Born 1857

Kate Waller Barrett was an early social welfare reformer. Fighting against the contemporary theory that prostitution was an evil necessity, Kate Barrett focused much of her attention on the plight of the unwed mother. Her deep social and moral commitment to this problem resulted in the solidification and organization of the National Florence Crittenton Missions for unwed mothers. Kate Barrett's interests, however, were not limited by her personal crusade: throughout her life she held numerous posts in various organizations, serving as Vice-President of the Virginia Equal Suffrage League, delegate to the National Democratic Convention of 1924, President of the National Women's Auxiliary of the American Legion, and Virginia Regent of the Daughters of the American Revolution.

Born in Falmouth, Virginia to Wither Waller and Ann Eliza (Stribling) Waller, Kate was the eldest of ten children. She spent her childhood on the 1000-acre Potomac estate of Clifton, which had been deeded to a Waller ancestor by Charles II. Although Kate attended the Arlington Institute for Girls in Alexandria for two years, she received most of her education at home.

On July 19, 1876, at the age of nineteen, Kate married Rev. Robert South Barrett, an Episcopal rector from Milton, North Carolina. They spent the first four years of their married life

in Richmond, Virginia where their eldest son was born. During their residence in a Richmond slum called "Butchertown," a young unwed mother knocked at the door one December night in search of food and shelter for herself and her child. Sensing that it was only by a quirk of fate that this destitute pair was not she and her own son, Kate immediately took them in. This experience led to a strong conviction that unwed girls should be treated with justice and decency; Kate made a convenant with God: ". . . as long as I live my voice should always be lifted in behalf of this outcast class, and my hand always held out to aid them." (Wilson, *Fifty Years*, p. 156)

Kate immediately began establishing stations for unwed girls in "Butchertown". She carried her work to Henderson, Kentucky when her husband was transferred there. In 1886 the Barretts moved to Atlanta when Rev. Barrett received the Deanship of St. Luke's Cathedral. Shortly after their arrival, Kate enrolled in the Women's Medical College of Georgia on the premise that this training would better qualify her for her work. In 1893, one year after receiving her M.D. degree, Kate opened a home for unwed mothers in Atlanta. Although she initially got little public support for the establishment, she eventually convinced the city council to donate both money and land for the home.

In an effort to build a home suited for her needs, Kate wrote to Charles N. Crittenton, a fellow social crusader who had already established several homes to rehabilitate prostitutes. Crittenton was impressed with Kate's work and contributed $5000 with the stipulation that the home be called a Florence Crittenton Home, after his deceased daughter; Kate accepted. As a result, the Atlanta Mission, a thirty-five room house completed in 1893, became the fifth Florence Crittenton Mission in the country.

Rev. Barrett died in 1896 in Washington, D.C. where the Barretts had moved two years earlier. Kate, left with six children, became more devoted than ever to the National Florence Crittenton Missions. Serving as vice-president and supervisor of over fifty missions across the country Dr. Barrett clarified her philosophy on rescue work in two publications: *Fourteen Years' Work Among "Erring Girls'* (1897), and *Some Practical Suggestions on the Conduct of a Rescue Home* (1903). Upon the death of Charles Crittenton in 1909, Dr. Barrett succeeded him as president, a post she held until her own death. Her work with unwed mothers and prostitues brought the National Florence Crittenton Missions national recognition.

Dr. Barrett died in 1925 at her home in Alexandria, Virginia. The legacy of Kate Waller Barrett, however, lives on in the present day Florence Crittenton Association of America.

ALICE MCLELLAN BIRNEY
Born 1858

In the eighteen-nineties Alice McLellan Birney conceived the idea of a national organization of mothers which would improve conditions for children in home, school and workplace. Her determination and organizing abilities were responsible in 1897 for the National Congress of Mothers, which met in Washington, D.C. The enthusiastic response to the first Congress revealed the vast energies of America's middle class women, waiting to be tapped at the beginning of the Progressive Era. Congresses were held each year thereafter; membership expanded with great speed: to 50,000 in 1899, and to 1,300,000 in 1927. In 1925, to reflect its changing membership, the organization title was changed to the National Congress of Parents and Teachers—the P.T.A.

Alice McLellan Birney was born in Marietta, Georgia near Atlanta, on October 19, 1858. Her father, Leander C. McLellan, was a cotton planter and broker who had come to Georgia from his birthplace in North Carolina. Her mother was Harriet Tatem McLellan, the daughter of English parents who had established their home in the Caribbean island of St. Croix. As a girl Alice enjoyed a warm secure home life, despite the upheavals of the Civil War and Reconstruction. To her own fortunate upbringing she later attributed her concern for the well-being of children.

Her earliest formal education was at a private school in Atlanta, followed by high school in Marietta. After high school, Alice attended the Marietta Female Academy and also studied for a year at Mount Holyoke College in Massachusetts.

On February 26, 1879, she married Alonzo White, a young lawyer from Charleston, South Carolina. The young couple moved to Charleston, but after little more than a year of marriage, and while they were expecting their first

child, Alonzo was taken ill and died. Mrs. White returned to her family and home where her daughter Alonzita was born.

Alice was determined to study medicine, but after the death of her father, in 1883, financial necessity forced her to pursue a business career. For some time she was able to earn her living as a representative of a woman's apparel manufacturer, while working for a social reform in which she was interested, the acceptance of less constrictive clothing for women. For a short while she lived in New York City and sold advertising but she soon returned to Atlanta where she and her mother had moved after her father's death. Her business career did not prevent her having an active social life in Atlanta. A scrapbook she kept at the time, preserved at the Atlanta Public Library, is filled with programs from theatrical and musical performances and newspaper accounts of lectures and social gatherings in which Mrs. Alice White is often mentioned. For active recreation she rode a horse and played tennis. Her skill at the piano and her lovely voice led her to take part in private musical entertainments.

During this time she met Theodore W. Birney, a lawyer from Washington, D.C., the grandson of James G. Birney who had been a prominent abolitionist, founder and twice presidential candidate of the Liberty party. They were married on December 6, 1892, and moved to Chevy Chase, Maryland where two daughters, Catherine and Lillian were born in 1894 and 1895. At this time Mrs. Birney's great idea began to take form. Her wide reading, especially of the psychologist G. Stanley Hall, kindergarten innovator Freidrich Froebel, and the philosopher Herbert Spencer, convinced her that the lives of many children were warped through the ignorance of well-meaning parents. Her idea was of a great meeting of mothers which would encourage the wide dispersal of the most advanced knowledge about childhood, and which could enlist the support of others like herself, willing to work to improve the lives of children.

She won the support of educational and civic leaders, including most notably, Mrs. Phoebe Apperson Hearst, a wealthy lady known for her philanthropy and her interest in children. With Mrs. Hearst's generous financial support, plans were made for the Congress. When all plans were made and the appointed day approached, the organizers assured themselves that if 50 persons attended they would have a successful beginning. Instead, they were overwhelmed by 2,000 from all over the country and a larger meeting-place had to be obtained. The meeting was widely reported and delegates were received at a White House reception. At the meeting a national organization was formed with Mrs. Birney as the first president.

Mr. Birney had been in poor health for some time, and after the Congress his condition deteriorated further; he died in July of 1897.

After his death Mrs. Birney devoted herself to the work of the Congress travelling widely and encouraging the formation of local associations of mothers. In 1902, her own health forced her to resign from the office of president. She then turned to writing and produced a series of essays on child rearing for the *Delineator* magazine. In 1905, these essays were collected in a book, *Childhood,* with an introduction by G. Stanley Hall. Her health continued to fail, however, and in December of 1907 she died of cancer at the age of forty-nine. She was buried in Washington.

In 1972 the United States Post Office Department issued a Commemorative Stamp in recognition of the founding of the PTA and a ceremony was held in Atlanta on the day following issuance, with special tributes to Mrs. Birney.

MARY HARRIS ARMOR

Born 1863

Mrs. Mary Harris Armor is perhaps best known for the fact that Georgia went "dry" in 1907 while she was President of the Georgia Woman's Christian Temperance Union. Her intensive campaigning, devotion, and inspiring leadership to the cause of temperance made her largely instrumental in the adoption of Georgia statewide prohibition. The fact that Georgia was one of the first three states in the union to go dry was a result of Mrs. Armor's extensive efforts in conjunction with the Georgia White Ribboners and the Protestant pastors. The "Georgia Cyclone", as she was known, was asked to speak to groups throughout the United States and in various foreign countries. She addressed legislatures, city councils, congressional committees, military groups, college and university groups, and church groups in forty-six states, New Zealand, Cuba, Scotland, England and Switzerland.

Mrs. Armor, born in Penfield, Georgia, March 9, 1863, was the daughter of Dr. William Lindsay Manning and Sarah Johnson Harris. She was educated in private schools in Greensboro, Georgia, and in 1918, was awarded an honorary

LL.D. by Wesleyan College in Macon, Georgia. In 1883, she married Walter Florence Armor. They had five children: Fannie Lou Armor Smith, Mattie Armor Hale, William Nelson, Holcombe Harris, and Ella Florence.

Mrs. Armor served two terms as President of the Georgia Woman's Christian Temperance Union (1905-1909 and 1924-1926), and was Evangelistic Director and Organizer of the National WCTU. She addressed the World's WCTU Conventions in Boston (1906), Glasgow (1910), Brooklyn (1913), London (1920), Lausanne (1928), and Toronto (1931). Her appeal for temperance was so effective that she inspired an audience at one of the National WCTU conventions to donate three thousand dollars to the cause, an unheard of sum at that time. Her nickname of the "Georgia Cyclone" came after a reporter sent to cover one of her speeches found it impossible to keep pace with her enthusiasm. He uttered in frustration that he had been sent to cover a speech, not a cyclone.

Mrs. Armor's activities and honors reflect her varied interests and efforts: appointed by Woodrow Wilson to represent the United States at the World Congress on Alcoholism in Milan, Italy (1913); named a member of the Speakers' Bureau of the U. S. Food Administration during World War I (1917); Delegate-at-large to the Democratic National Conventions in 1924 and 1928; Southern Visitor to the Quintennial of International Council of Women in Washington (1925); only woman member of the Methodist (church-wide) Board of Temperance and Social Service (1926); Trustee of Asbury College in Kentucky; member, Macon Writers' Club, Woman's Club, Daughters of the American Revolution, United Daughters of the Confederacy, Business and Professional Women's Club, Woman's Missionary Society, Parent-Teachers' Association, Pi Gamma Mu; Chairman, Department of International Cooperation for Prevention of War, Georgia League of Women Voters; and member Georgia Committee Sponsoring League of Nations. Mrs. Armor is listed in *Women Torchbearers* (1924), *Georgia Women of 1926* (1926), *Who's Who in the South* (1927), *Who's Who in America* (vol. 18, 1934-1935 and vol. 19, 1936-1937), *American Women. The Standard Biographical Dictionary of Notable Women* (1935-1936 and vol. III, 1939-1940), and *Who Was Who in America* (vol. IV, 1961-1968).

Mrs. Armor lectured until 1936, when she retired. She died on November 6, 1950, in Eastman, Georgia, while visiting a daughter.

JULIA HARRIS

Born 1875

Julia Florida Collier Harris author and journalist, shared in the first Pulitzer Prize awarded to a newspaper in Georgia when the Columbus *Enquirer-Sun*, of which she was associate editor and joint owner, received the gold medal in 1926 for meritorious public service. In addition to her career as a newspaperwoman, Mrs. Harris was the author of three books, one a biography of her father-in-law, Joel Chandler Harris.

Julia Collier was born in Atlanta, the daughter of Charles Augustus and Susie (Rawson) Collier. Her father was mayor of Atlanta, 1867-1898, and President of the Cotton States and International Exposition of 1895. After graduating from Washington Seminary in Atlanta, she studied art in Boston at Miss Chamberlayne's School and Cowles Art School, and intended to pursue art as a career. The death of her mother in 1897 and of her father in 1900 left Julia as guardian for her younger brothers and sisters and forced her to abandon her earlier plans. On October 26, 1897, Julia Collier was married to Julian LeRose Harris, eldest son of Joel Chandler Harris and, at that time, managing editor of the Atlanta *Constitution*. The Harrises had two children, Charles Collier Harris, who died in 1903 at the age of 4 years, and Pierre LaRose Harris who died in 1904, four months later, at the age of 2½ years.

Mrs. Harris's career in journalism began in 1911 when she wrote articles on literary subjects and the arts and handled the club news for the Atlanta *Constitution,* serving for two years as a state editor for the Georgia Federation of Women's Clubs. In 1914, when her husband became Sunday editor for James Gordon Bennett's *New York Herald,* Julia began to contribute articles for the Herald Syndicate under the pseudonym of Constance Bine. She wrote a series of feature articles for the *Herald* from Paris, 1915-1916, and again in 1919-1920, when she was one of the few women to witness the signing of the Treaty of Versailles.

In 1920 she invested most of her savings in her husband's purchase of half ownership of the Columbus, *Enquirer-Sun,* and in 1922, when the Harrises secured complete ownership, Julia Harris became vice-president of the company. Her articles and editorials on art, music, current literature, education, evolution, and on other social and educational topics won wide acclaim. She wrote a series of articles in 1924-25 opposing the anti-evolution bill in the Georgia legislature, which was defeated, a highly praised feature series on the Scopes trial in Dayton, Tenn. (1925), and contributed editorially to the newspaper's outspoken campaign against the Ku Klux Klan. The Pulitzer committee cited the newspaper's "brave and energetic fight against the Ku Klux Klan, and against the enactment of the law barring the teaching of evolution" in awarding the *Enquirer-Sun* the prize.

Although the Harrises lost their newspaper during the beginning months of the Great Depression in 1929, Julia Harris pursued an active career in journalism until the late 1930's. She continued to publish articles in the Atlanta *Constitution* and in literary and popular periodicals. She served as contributing editor for the Chattanooga (Tenn.) *Times,* 1935-1938. In 1938 she retired from newspaper work due to poor health, and spent the rest of her years in Atlanta, encouraging young people and fledgling writers, and keeping a critical eye on government. Throughout her newspaper career she supported, through her editorials and feature articles, advancements in education and expansion of libraries and other facilities for public enjoyment of books and the arts. She also actively encouraged the participation of women in the professions and in public life, and strongly opposed racial injustice, the convict lease system, lynching and violence in all forms. Forceful of personality, confident of her abilities, and secure in her convictions, Julia Harris was determined that the South should be rid of the brutality and backwardness which had marred its recent past.

Besides her newspaper work, Mrs. Harris was active in the Association of Southern Women for the Prevention of Lynching and in the League of Women Voters. She also published three books: *Life and Letters of Joel Chandler Harris* (1919), *The Foundling Prince* (1917), and *Joel Chandler Harris, Editor and Essayist* (1931).

DOROTHY TILLY

Born 1883

Dorothy Gugeria Rogers Tilly will long be remembered as one of the most active and noteworthy humanitarians in the history of Georgia. Both as a private citizen and as a member of the Methodist Church, this tiny sparrow-like woman, with her unlimited energy and undaunted determination, was able to initiate many far-reaching and permanent contributions in the field of human-civil rights.

Mrs. Tilly was born in Hampton, Georgia on June 30, 1883 to Methodist minister Richard Wade and Francis (Eubank) Rogers. She was educated locally, receiving an AB from Wesleyan College (Macon, Georgia) in 1901. On November 24, 1903 she married Milton Eben Tilly, a chemical manufacturer, with whom she had one child, a son Eben Fletcher Tilly. Throughout her life Mrs. Tilly received much encouragement and support in her work from her husband. In fact, according to Dorothy Tilly, it was he who first exposed her to the plight of poor people during the Depression when they would take Sunday drives around Atlanta. On these excursions Mrs. Tilly would see things she could not bear to look at such as black children eating out of a downtown Atlantan hotel's garbage cans. Mrs. Tilly complained that she didn't want to see anymore because she couldn't do anything about it; to which Mr. Tilly had retorted that if it was painful she could but tell others and with them do something constructive. She followed the suggestion.

At an early age she began her lifelong commitment to Methodist churchwork. Initially she served as a teacher and gradually expanded her role. She was a delegate in 1938, 1940 and 1944

to the General Conference of the Methodist Episcopal church and, in 1939, to the Uniting Conference. From 1940-1948 she acted as the secretary of the Department of Relations, Woman's Society of Christian Services. In 1944 she became permanently associated with the Southern Regional Council and for twenty years acted as its director.

In addition to her churchwork, Mrs. Tilly was also active in the Georgia Conference of Social Work, the Urban League, the American Civil Liberties Union, and the Americans for Democratic Action. In 1946 she was appointed to the National Commission on Children and Youth. The following year she became the only southern woman appointed to serve on President Truman's Civil Rights Commission. In 1949 under her leadership the Fellowship of the Concerned was established as an organization that monitored the courtrooms and polls in the South to make sure there were no irregularities in the voting process and that, in general, justice was done. Besides all of this, Mrs. Tilly also successfully supported the passage of legislation funding the Georgia Training School for Delinquent Negro Girls, though it had previously been denied state funds, by gathering 28,000 supporting churchwomens' signatures.

Not surprisingly Mrs. Tilly's achievements and contributions have received wide recognition. Among the numerous awards she got from local, regional, and national organizations were those from the Methodist church commending her for her contribution to the church. (e.g. Life Patron Woman's Society of Christian Science 1950; Outstanding Methodist Woman of the first twenty-five years of the Woman's Society of Christian Service in the Methodist Church's Southeast Jurisdiction, 1965) and to others (e.g. citation for long time service in the field of human rights, 1963). Her work was also acknowledged by many honorary and civic associations: in 1948 she was chosen the "Woman of the South in Social Welfare" by the *Atlanta Constitution* and the Atlanta Woman's Chamber of Commerce; in 1950, she was honored by the National Council of Negro Women, the National Phi Mu and the Emory University Chapter of Phi Sigma Alpha; in 1956, the Philadelphia Fellowship Commission cited her for her lifetime of dedication to the advancement of human dignity and the Frontier Club of America honored her for her leadership in the freedom of race relations; and, in 1963, she was awarded one of the greater Atlanta Good Neighbor of the Year awards from the National Council of Christians and Jews.

Mrs. Tilly died in Atlanta, Georgia on March 16, 1970 at the age of 86, a much loved and revered woman.

VIRGINIA HAND CALLAWAY
Born 1900

Virginia Hand Callaway (Mrs. Cason Sr.) is recognized for her accomplishments in conservation. Throughout her life, she has worked to preserve the natural beauty of Georgia and to educate others in this cause.

Born in Pelham, Georgia, to Judson L. and Florence Hollis Hand, Virginia grew up in the woodlands of southern Georgia, where she nurtured a growing appreciation for her natural surroundings. At the age of twenty, shortly after her debut in Atlanta, Virginia met and married Cason J. Callaway on April 3, 1920. Their first child, Virginia Hand, was born August 21, 1921. They later had two sons, Cason Jr., and Howard (Bo) Hollis.

A favorite picnic spot of this growing family was the land around Pine Mountain, next to the clear water of Blue Springs. It was here that Cason Sr. picked a rare flower to bring home to his wife. Virginia, already a knowledgeable horticulturalist, identified this unusual blossom as a prunifolia azalea. Later, Virginia fought for the protection of this rare shrub, which can only be found within a 100 mile radius of Blue Springs.

Cason purchased the Blue Springs property and 3,000 acres of land surrounding it in 1930. From the very start, Mrs. Callaway supervised the gardening on the estate, thus acquiring an expert knowledge of the trees and wildflowers of Pine Mountain. During the 1940's, the Callaways decided to share the natural beauty of their land with others and began work on the estate to create what is now Callaway Gardens. They designed tree-shaded roads, dammed streams to form lakes for fishing and swimming, and developed stunning displays of local flora.

Under the trust of the Ida Carson Callaway Foundation, the Callaway Gardens opened in 1952 for the purpose of preserving the natural surroundings of that area and for providing a recreational and serene setting for all families to share. After the death of her husband in

1961, Mrs. Callaway continued the development of the estate; as chairman and life trustee of the Ida Cason Callaway Foundation, she has worked for the expansion of educational and recreational facilities in the Gardens.

Mrs. Callaway's conservation efforts have not been confined to the Gardens. In 1971, after plans had been made public for a highway which would disrupt the ecology of Pine Mountain and uproot the rare azalea, Mrs. Callaway began the fight to "save the mountain". Through her efforts in educating the public of the necessity to maintain the natural balance in the environment, and her efforts in gathering their support in the fight against the potentially corrosive effects of the road, she succeeded in having the highway rerouted. The Cason J. Callaway Memorial Forest was established in 1970 and was declared a National Landmark on April 23, 1973. This undisturbed forest, in the transitional zone where the Eastern and Southern plant forms meet, has been preserved for the educational and aesthetic study of all.

As committee chairman for the Birds and Wildflowers section of the Garden Club of Georgia, Inc., Mrs. Callaway has been instrumental in the campaign to bring the bluebird back to Georgia. She has endorsed, through example, the stationing of bluebird houses to replace the natural nesting grounds destroyed by development. She has also initiated a program, in cooperation with the State Highway Department, to propagate Georgia's native wildflowers along the highways.

Virginia Callaway's efforts in conserving Georgia's natural resources have not gone unnoticed: she was made an honorary member of Phi Theta Kappa for her work to preserve the natural resources of the State; she won WSB Radio Beaver Award for "doing good deeds for the benefit and betterment of mankind"; and, in 1974, she was elected Conservation Educator of the Year by the Georgia Wildlife Federation. All who visit Callaway Gardens can be grateful for her talent and interest in preserving the natural beauty of Georgia.

BERNICE BROWN McCULLAR
Born 1905

Bernice Brown McCullar was a noted Georgia educator, journalist, historian, author, and lecturer. As a young woman, Mrs. McCullar taught at the college level, practiced law, and edited a newspaper. In later life, she was appointed Director of Information for the Georgia Department of Education, a position which she held from 1951 until 1966. She also lectured throughout the United States and wrote a daily newspaper column. Mrs. McCullar was the author of *This Is Your Georgia*, a history textbook used in the public schools of the state. The recipient of many awards for her varied professional activities, Mrs. McCullar was named Atlanta's Woman of the Year in 1965.

Bernice Louise Brown was born in Richland, Stewart County, Georgia on March 9, 1905. She was the daughter of the Reverend M. B. Brown and Carrie Wright Brown. Her father was a Baptist minister, newspaper owner and editor, and a mayor of Richland. On June 28, 1924, Bernice Brown married Claudius Benjamin McCullar. Mr. McCullar, a lawyer from Milledgeville, Georgia, held a law degree from National University, and was a former editor of the *Law Review*. He and his wife Bernice McCullar (who was also a member of the Georgia Bar) practiced law together in Milledgeville as McCullar and McCullar. C. B. McCullar served as judge of the County Court of Baldwin County from 1941 until his death on May 7, 1942. He was also a former editor and publisher of the *Milledgeville Times* and the *Milledgeville News*. C. B. and Bernice McCullar were the parents of two children, Eleanor (Mrs. J. L. Sibley Jennings) and C. B. McCullar, Jr.

Bernice McCullar received her bachelor's degree from Georgia State College for Women in 1924. She went on to earn a master's degree at Mercer University, where she eventually served as a trustee. Mrs. McCullar did additional graduate work at Columbia University, and later returned to the Georgia State College for Women, where she taught as an associate professor of English, and acted as director of public relations for a period of twelve years.

Mrs. McCullar was an active figure in the fields of journalism and communications in Georgia. She was a former editor of the *Milledgeville Times* and the *Alumnae Journal* of the Georgia State College for Women. During the 1960's, Mrs. McCullar wrote a daily column

on Georgia history, "Georgia Notebook," for the *Atlanta Journal*. While serving as Director of Information for the State Department of Education, Mrs. McCullar had her own television program, "Minds in Motion." She also taught a television course on Georgia history, which provided the basis for her textbook, *This Is Your Georgia*, published in 1967.

In addition to *This Is Your Georgia*, Mrs. McCullar co-authored a textbook on home economics, *Building Your Home Life*. In 1972, she wrote a pamphlet, "Georgia and Its Gold-Domed Capitol," which is used as a guide for visitors to Georgia's State Capitol. Mrs. McCullar also contributed articles to various magazines, including *The Atlanta Journal-Constitution Sunday Magazine*, *The Christian Science Monitor*, *McCall's*, *Coronet*, *Farm Journal* and *The New York Times Magazine*.

In addition to being honored as Atlanta's Woman of the Year, Bernice McCullar was selected Georgia's Woman of the Year in Education by the Georgia Federation of Women's Clubs. She was one of four people and the only woman chosen by WSB, an Atlanta radio station, and Atlanta banks as a "Great Georgian." Other awards received by Mrs. McCullar include the M. D. Collins trophy from the Future Teachers of America; the Quill award from the Atlanta Chapter of Sigma Delata Chi journalism society; an achievement award from Theta Sigma Phi women journalists; an award for outstanding service in education from Chi Omega; and the Alumni Achievement award from Mercer University. The Georgia College Alumni Association recently established a scholarship in her honor. The Georgia Professional Chapter, Women in Communications presented Mrs. McCullar with its Award for Communications Excellence in 1975 in the form of a cash donation to the scholarship fund. The Georgia State Senate and House of Representatives honored Mrs. McCullar by adopting resolutions commending her service to the state. Governor Jimmy Carter declared March 9, 1974, Mrs. McCullar's 69th birthday, "Bernice McCullar Day" in Georgia.

Bernice McCullar died on May 31, 1975 of cancer in Decatur, Georgia.

GRACE HAMILTON

Born 1907

Grace Towns Hamilton, the first black woman to be elected to the Georgia House of Representatives, has displayed a singular spirit of dedication to public service throughout her professional career. Her tireless dedication, together with a deep concern for the individual, has brought her national as well as statewide recognition and esteem.

Grace Towns was born in Atlanta, Georgia on February 10, 1907. The daughter of George Alexander and Nellie McNair Towns, both Atlanta University professors, she grew up in a somewhat isolated environment on the Atlanta University campus. Grace professes not to have known that black discrimination existed until she had graduated from college and became a part of the outside world. This fact is highly significant in the development of her ability to sustain good working relationships with both blacks and whites. When asked if any childhood experiences became a dominating influence in her life, she will respond affirmatively: she grew up without the burden of hating white people.

In 1927, Grace Towns graduated with an A. A. B. from Atlanta University and went on to earn her A.M. from Ohio State University in 1929. The following year, she married Henry Cooke Hamilton, a noted black educator. Their daughter, Eleanor Towns Hamilton, was born on

March 5, 1931. Mrs. Hamilton's work experience prior to the Second World War included work with the YWCA in Columbus, Ohio and two teaching positions in Psychology, first at Clark College, Atlanta (1929-1930) and later at LeMoyne College, Memphis (1930-1934). During 1935-1936 she worked as Director of the Survey of White Collar and Skilled Negro Workers in Memphis.

From 1943-1960 Mrs. Hamilton served as Executive Director of the Atlanta Urban League and it is at this point in her career that her distinguished role in public service really began. Her accomplishments of obtaining better park, school and hospital facilities for Negroes came at a time when equal rights was nothing more than an empty phrase. Her most significant single achievement with the Urban League was in acquiring the Hughes Spalding Pavilion of Grady Hospital which serves to provide many job opportunities for Blacks and has even begun a graduate medical training program for Black doctors.

In 1966, Grace Hamilton was elected to the Georgia General Assembly. Reelected three times, here her career continues to be distinguished. She was called to Washington by President Kennedy to confer over civil rights issues and in 1966 was appointed by President Johnson to his eleven member Citizens Advisory Committee on Recreation and Natural Beauty. Legislation she has introduced and supported includes aid to those displaced by highway construction, providing aid beyond the arbitrary price normally set, tax relief to slum property owners who make improvements in hopes of encouraging such urban renewal, and a bill to enable cities to move against owners of substandard property to enforce demolition. Though her duties in the House are very demanding, she also serves in many volunteer positions: as Trustee of Atlanta University, Trustee of McHarry Medical College, Nashville, Tennessee, on the Advisory Board of the Fulton County Democratic Party, on the Executive Committee of the Citizens Advisory Committee for Urban Renewal, Atlanta, as a member on the Governor's Committee on the Status of Women. In addition, she still continues the close association she has held throughout the years with the National YWCA.

In 1971 Grace Hamilton was honored as Atlanta's Professional Woman of the Year.

Hawaii

Hawaii

Nickname: Paradise of the Pacific

State Flower: Hibiscus

State Tree: Coconut Palm

State Bird: Nene

Photos

1. Opaekaa Falls, Kauai
2. Nuuanu Pali
3. A quiet moment beside a pool

Committee Members

Chairman—Mrs. Moses Moepono
Dr. Hubert V. Everly
Mr. William A. Amona
Mrs. Eleanor A. Judd
Mr. Hirotoshi Yamamoto
Mr. John Dominis Holt IV, Author
Mr. Abraham Piianaio
Rev. Charles M.C. Kwock

Hawaii

ELIZABETA KAAHUMANU

Born 1772

Elizabeta Kaahumanu was probably born a few years before the arrival of Captain Cook. She was one of the children of the High Chiefs Keeaumoku and Namahana, who were from the island of Maui and members of the great Piilani clan who ruled that island.

Kaahumanu was King Kamehameha's favorite wife. This marriage did not produce heirs, however, Kamehameha before his death created a special position for Kaahumanu, should he die first. In this position Kaahumanu was to serve as joint ruler of Hawaii with respect to the succession of the three children born to Kamehameha by the highest ranking of his wives, Keopuolani. Kaahumanu assumed this role titled Kuhina Nui at Kamehameha's death. Along with Kamehameha II, she ruled Hawaii. Within a year she influenced Kamehameha II or Liholiho to end the ancient system of law, known as *ai kapu*. In her view these "laws" were overly restrictive and not compatible with the new order which had come so rapidly into existence with the coming of foreigners, who visited or settled in the paradise so long hidden from the rest of the world.

After the death of Kamehameha II and his wife, Kamamalu, in London in 1824, Kaahumanu with the help of American missionary Hiram Bingham, succeeded in bringing about the first laws of the Hawaiian Kingdom affecting both natives and foreigners alike. They were patterned closely after Old Testament style injunctions and read like the Ten Commandments.

Kaahumanu was virtually ruler of Hawaii from the death of Kamehameha II in 1824 until her own death in 1832. Officially she performed as Regent to Kamehameha III, who was ten years old when his brother died in London. Kaahumanu seemed to understand the needs of the new society shaping itself upon the ruins of the old order better than most chiefs of her time. She took a realistic view of the drastic results change had brought upon her people. In her last years she was determined to make the matchlessly beautiful islands of her birth a better place for both native and foreigner alike. In her desire to rule with judicious objectivity and fairness to all, she urged upon her people the desire to accept foreign laws, education and religion.

HIGH CHIEFESS KEKUIAPOIWA II

This remarkable lady, mother of the great Paiea or Kamehameha I, was born sometime in the early decades of the eighteenth century. There are no written records concerning her life as writing was not practiced by Hawaiians before the coming of Americans and Europeans. Enough has come down to us from oral traditions to provide a scanty biography of Kekuiapoiwa II. She was the daughter of the High Chiefess Kekelaokalani and the High Chief Haae-a-Mahi, both of whom were the grandchildren of the ranking alii (royal person) of her day. Kekealani Kekuiapoiwa II's high rank linked her to the kings and queens of Oahu, Maui and Hawaii.

Perhaps her outstanding act as a royal personage is found in an unusual act recorded by Gertrude MacKinnon Damon from lore given her by Hawaiians in the nineteen thirties. The story was told to Mrs. Damon from reliable sources that Kekuiapoiwa II came to Oahu from Molokai with a retinue to confer with her nephew, King Kalanikupule, conqueror of Oahu,

during the wars of conquest. Sometime before the battle of Nuuanu Kekuiapoiwa arrived at Waikiki uninvited to explain to Kalanikupule that in terms of succession Kamehameha had a higher claim to rulership of Oahu. This is born out in careful study of the genealogies. It was the intention of this remarkable woman in doing this to end the wars of conquest of the islands which had extended over more than a ten-year period.

She was not successful in influencing Kalanikupule to the point of relinquishing control of Oahu, but the High Chiefess Kekuiapoiwa II was granted honors of high priests for her daring act. She became also a figure greatly beloved by the common people for her daring imaginative attempt to bring the destruction and misery of war to an end.

LAURA FISH JUDD

Born 1804

On September 20, 1827, Laura Fish became the bride of Doctor Gerrit P. Judd. Shortly after this, Doctor and Mrs. Judd sailed from Boston to the Sandwich Islands where doctor Judd was to work as medical missionary.

Laura Judd was born at Plainfield Township, Otsego County, New York, the sixth child of Elias Fish and Sybil Williams Fish.

From the earliest years of Mrs. Judd's residence in Hawaii, she was a favorite of the highest ranking chiefs. She encouraged education, motivated in this by her own experiences as a teacher before coming to the Sandwich Islands. Mrs. Judd and her husband were influential in creating the School for Royal Children where in time more than twenty young chiefs, five of whom became rulers of Hawaii, were educated.

Mrs. Judd gave valuable assistance to her husband in his role as missionary doctor and became equally effective in providing him support after he left the Mission to become an official of government. He was in time Minister of Finance, Minister of Foreign Affairs, Minister of the Interior, and for one session he was a member of the Legislature of the Hawaiian Kingdom.

In 1861 Mrs. Judd published in Honolulu, a work called "Sketches of Life: Social, Political and Religious, in the Hawaiian Islands from 1828 to 1860". In this book, Mrs. Judd wrote

personal memoirs describing people, important political events and general descriptions of places which caught her fancy. She wrote with clarity and humor, and undeniable fairness. It has become a classic of recent Hawaiian literature used widely by student, scholar and general reader alike. It remains a work that reflects with charm and grace, aspects of life in Hawaii written from the standpoint of someone who came from the stern climate and moral atmosphere of New England who found the islands she came to call home a place of great beauty where enjoyment, hard work and sorrow could be shared in fairly equal amounts without grimness predominating.

Mrs. Judd found Hawaii to be for all of its problems, a joyous place—the great family which she helped to establish has provided the islands with many of its leaders to this very day.

HIGH CHIEFESS KINAU

Born 1805

The High Chiefess Kinau was born in the early years of the nineteenth Century. She was the daughter of the Chief Kekuanaoa and the High Chiefess Pauahi, a daughter of King Kamehameha and his wife, Pauahi.

Kinau, whose mother died soon after the child's birth, grew up under the care of the great Kaahumanu. Because of her high rank she was prepared carefully by Kaahumanu to assume in time the position of Kuhina Nui. Kinau was perhaps the first of the chiefs to become thoroughly converted to Christianity. She was instructed in all branches of foreign knowledge by members of the American Congregational Mission.

When she became Kuhina Nui in 1832, a serious dispute arose between her half-brother, Kamehameha III, and herself concerning areas of power over which each would predominate. Kinau wished to assume all the authority held by Kaahumanu. This meant virtually having total control of Hawaiian Government. Kamehameha III had relinquished political authority to Kaahumanu in the years of his youth. When his sister Kinau assumed Kaahumanu's office, Kamehameha III was eighteen years old. Encouraged by a circle of friends including the powerful chiefess of very high rank, Kuini Liliha, he immediately declared his intention to assume powers of the Kuhina Nui which in his thinking were now rightfully his to exercise.

Kinau, a zealous convert of the Congregational Mission stressed interest in enforcing devotion to religion and to reform. She refused to relinquish her authority as Kuhina Nui. She strongly advocated strengthening of the existing laws no matter the consequences to native culture or the spirit of her people. Her strong support of the Congregational Mission led to suppression of any other Christian group from establishing itself in the Hawaiian Kingdom. From her succession to office of Kuhina Nui until her death in 1839, Kinau was relentless in her efforts to keep a Catholic Mission from settling in Hawaii. This caused much trouble with France for a period of twenty years. The Catholic priests, who from the first, were determined to work as Christians among the Hawaiians, were of French origin.

Kinau was successful in strengthening the laws governing the tiny kingdom in which a burgeoning social order far different from the one of her father's time was struggling for growth. Kinau made valuable suggestions toward revising the general plan for the city of Honolulu. Her suggestions gave Honolulu the shape it assumed over one hundred twenty five years ago and which to this day, in the old section of the city, remains intact.

The High Chiefess Kinau was the mother of King Kamehameha IV, King Kamehameha V and the Princess Victoria Kamamalu.

PRINCESS BERNICE PAUAHI
(Mrs. Charles R. Bishop)

Born 1831

The largest and most meaningful of Hawaiian royal legacies was the one created by the Princess Bernice Pauahi, Mrs. Charles R. Bishop.

Princess Pauahi was the only child of High Chief Paki and his wife, the High Chiefess Konia. Konia was of the royal strain from the island of Hawaii; Paki, a Chief of very high rank was a member of the royal family of Maui.

Princess Pauahi was educated at the School for Royal Children, which she attended for nine years. She was considered by the Co-founder and Director, Mrs. Juliette Montague Cooke, to be the outstanding student among the royal pupils of the School.

At the end of her studies, Princess Pauahi was married in a ceremony held at the school to

a young American businessman, Charles R. Bishop. This union was not approved by Pauahi's parents, who had hoped that their daughter would marry one of the native princes, a fellow student at the school.

Shortly after her marriage to Charles Bishop, the Princess Pauahi's father, Abner Paki, died. At this time Mr. and Mrs. Bishop went to live with her mother in the imposing mansion "Haleakala". The house and its lush gardens sat close to the center of old Honolulu. Here Mrs. Bishop skilfully performed the duties of one of the leading citizens of the Hawaiian Kingdom. Her husband in turn founded the first bank in Hawaii and before long became a man of wide influence in community affairs.

Princess Pauahi was the last officially recognized heir to the Great Kamehameha. Because of this, all the lands of the Kamehameha family came to her following the deaths of several cousins.

She left in trust these vast estates, stipulating in her Will that the income earned from these lands be used toward creation of schools to provide education for children of Hawaiian ancestry.

Herself childless, she and her husband had adopted six children from various of the chiefly families, all of whom unfortunately died very young. In creating the Kamehameha Schools, however, the Princess Bernice Pauahi has become the symbolic mother of all the students who have attended them.

The Kamehameha Schools grow ever more into a lasting tribute to this woman of outstanding intelligence, foresight and heart.

HIGH CHIEFESS HANAKAULANI-O-KAMAMALU
(Mrs. Owen Jones Holt)
Born 1843

This part-Hawaiian woman of royal rank was the child of a young chiefess Kamalo-o-Leleiohoku and George, Lord Paulet, 14th Marquess of Winchester. She was the grandchild of Kamehameha III. The identity of her grandmother remains hidden.

Hanakaulani grew up in the household of the Chief Kekuananoa and his daughter, Princess Victoria Kamamalu. She received her education from her cousin the princess and various tutors. Princess Kamamalu had also attended the School for Royal Children and was accomplished in music and well read in English literature. She was a witty, gracious hostess as the mistress of her father's household where many distinguished foreign visitors were entertained. Some of Victoria Kamamalu's accomplishments were passed on to the young Hanakaulani.

The High Chiefess Hanakaulani was first married to Owen Jones Holt in 1859, in a ceremony performed by the Catholic Bishop of Hawaii. Their vows were pledged for a second time after the Episcopal mission was established in Hawaii. This took place on March 15, 1862, officiated by the Very Reverend, Mr. E. W. Clarke, Dean of St. Andrews Cathedral.

Owen Holt and his brothers, John and James, were heirs to large landed estates used principally for ranching. Hanakaulani, an expert horsewoman gave constant and valuable assistance to her husband in the management of the Holt ranches. Imported breeds of cattle and horses were bred and produced for commercial use. Coffee and rice plantations and fruit orchards were cultivated on the Holt estates, all of which were held under family management until shortly after her death. Hanakaulani, as the ward of Princess Kamamalu and her father, Kekuanaoa, received excellent preparation for the role she came to assume as the wife of Owen Holt. Together they created Makaha Valley into a highly productive and profitable ranch. They built a gingerbread mansion in that remote place, surrounded it with lawns and gardens over which flocks of peacocks and other rare birds roamed and reproduced.

In its heyday Makaha was visited by hordes of people from all levels of society. European royalty of varying rank, American writers and businessmen, artists, musicians and members of

the leading Hawaiian families were constant visitors to the Makaha establishment. Over two-hundred people were employed to keep all aspects of the ranch in operation. The hospitality of Hanakaulani and Owen Holt remains a legend to this day.

The High Chiefess Hanakaulani while offering constant assistance to her husband in furthering ranch development on Oahu, and being the celebrated mistress of the Makaha estate, gave birth to 16 children. Nine survived to produce large families of their own. Eight of Hanakaulani's children married into other distinguished Hawaiian families to become progenitors of the great Holt clan of today's Hawaii.

MRS. MARY HAPPER DAMON

Mother Damon as she had been affectionately called in Hawaii was born near Pittsburgh, Pennsylvania on September 23, 1858. As an infant, she was taken to South China by her missionary parents, Mr. and Mrs. Andrew P. Happer and there she lived till the time she was a young lady.

Her parents were founders of the Chinese University in Canton now called Lingham University, probably the largest and best known educational institution in south China. Raised

and educated in this compound from infancy, Mrs. Damon developed a great understanding and a profound knowledge of the Chinese as a people. This understanding caused her to love them and worked with them with a high degree of effectiveness. She spoke Chinese so beautifully without a trace of foreign accent that if one were to listen to her speak through the telephone one would think she was a native born Chinese of culture and fine upbringing.

It was in Canton that she first met her husband Francis Williams Damon while each was paddling a canoe on one of the beautiful lakes in south China. It was love at first sight, because she was such a beautiful and genteel woman. After a brief courtship in 1883, Mr. Damon returned home to Hawaii after a tour of duty as the Chargé D'Affaires at the Imperial Court of Germany where he was secretary and interpreter to the Hawaiian minister, Henry P. Carter. His parents were the Reverend and Mrs. Samuel Chenery Damon, who came to the islands as pioneer missionaries. As the minister of the Bethel Church in Honolulu, it was he who first befriended the Chinese Christian immigrants who came to Hawaii to make their homes here. They were converted by the Swiss Basel missionaries in south China.

In 1884, Mr. Damon returned to Canton and the marriage took place on May 1st. Soon after, they sailed to Honolulu where both devoted their lives to church, missionary and educational work.

Together they worked toward the founding of the First Chinese Church of Christ which is now one of the largest and most influential churches in Hawaii.

The Damon home on Chaplain Lane in 1892 was opened as a school in which Chinese boys were taught English. It later became the Mills School. Eventually it was united with the Kawaiahao Girls' Seminary and the Okumura School to become what is now known as Mid-Pacific Institute.

Also it was the Damons who inspired the founding of the Free Kindergarten Association in Hawaii.

In spite of her active life as a missionary, she was a good and faithful mother who raised up a family of five children, two sons and three daughters. Although they have all died, her five grandchildren are still active in church work and have remained outstanding citizens of their community.

From 1900 until December 7, 1941, when the government took over the site during the war years, her home in Mokumoa, near Moanalua Gardens was virtually a little of China transplanted to Hawaii, with a Chinese sedan chair or palanquin, teakwood furnitures and various other artifacts; for she was a lover of things Chinese. The door of her home was always open to all who came to visit because she was such a friendly and hospitable soul.

KATSU OKUMURA

Katsu Ogawa, daughter of an Osaka rice dealer, married Takie Okumura on January 15, 1887, when she was 21 and he was 22. Her husband, brought up as a samurai, was not adept at business and after several ventures before and after his marriage found that his entire fortune was gone.

Losing confidence in himself, he left everything in his wife's hands and spent his time praying and reading. His wife, mother and grandmother had to take in washing and sewing to keep the home going.

He decided to go into the ministry. He entered Doshisha Divinity School* and was graduated in 1894. He immediately left by himself for Hawaii to become assistant pastor of Nuuanu Congregational Church in Honolulu. Two years later, he brought his wife and three children to Hawaii.

At the outset, he told her that she was not to inject even one word into church matters and in return he would not interfere in matters concerning the home.

Katsu saw that her husband had already begun taking care of two little boys of friends in his home. And now that there was a house mother, more and more children came to live in this Christian home. That was the beginning of the labors of Katsu. She raised her own children and she had a hand in rearing 1,400 other boys and girls. Of her children, three died young and three died just as they reached maturity. Two were Yale graduates, one entered the ministry and one became an agricultural extension agent; another son became a physician and still another an attorney at law. All three daughters married New Yorkers and went to live in New York.

Of the boys and girls who received Katsu Okumura's living Christian care, one, Spark M. Matsunaga, became a Congressman from Hawaii. Others became a Supreme Court Justice, school teachers, school principals, businessmen, physicians, clergymen, nurses, attorneys, legislators—people in every walk of life—who influenced profoundly the communities in which they chose to live.

In the early days, the boys ranged in age from eight to twelve. Room and board for a boy was $3.50 a month. This was raised from time to time but even with generous help from good friends it was only by the strictest economy that the home could be operated as a home.

The Rev. Takie Okumura served at Nuuanu for eight years, then struck out for himself in virgin territory and founded Makiki Christian Church in 1904, served as its pastor for 33 years, then as emeritus pastor until he died in 1951.

The number of boarders at the home continued to increase, reaching an average of 70 per year, and the home was moved from one place to another until it finally settled at 1230 South King Street.

Boarders at the home began to come from the neighbor islands and even Japan to attend high school, business school or the University of Hawaii. A separate home for girls was started in the early 1920's near the church.

For 45 years, Katsu Okumura labored, toiling from morning till night, marketing, cooking, cleaning, washing. She was a housemaid, a waitress, a nurse. She was able to do all she did only because she loved each boy and girl and worried about them as she did for her own children.

When war came on December 7, 1941, it was too much for her. Worry over her children in New York and all the boys and girls under her care weakened her. On March 15, 1942, Katsu Okumura passed on from her earthly labors to her eternal rest.

*Kyoto, Japan

MARY ATHERTON RICHARDS
Born 1869

"Between friends, there may be differences of opinion, but always sympathy, differences of station but always courtesy, differences of temperament but always kindliness, differences of creed but always charity," Mary Atherton Richards so described the precepts she learned from her Congregational missionary family.

Carrying on the educational traditions of her grandparents who brought up and educated the fourteen young princes and princesses of Hawaiian Royalty (five of whom grew up to become monarchs) Mary, with her husband Theodore Richards, organized and led many Christian educational enterprises.

She trained hundreds of future Sunday School teachers at the Honolulu Bible Training School. Together they founded the Friend Peace Scholarships, the first privately endowed international student exchange program for young adults of Hawaii, Japan, and China.

She was a fine executive and was elected President of a number of organizations, including the Hawaiian Mission Children's Society, the Morning Music Club, and Women's Board of Missions for the Pacific Islands. This latter organization serves to train women for community service throughout the Hawaiian Is-

lands and in Micronesia. She served as President for 26 years.

She was a President of the Free Kindergarten and Children's Aid Association. A history of this organization contains this tribute to Mrs. Richards: "Her contribution far exceeded mere service on the board, for she has, in addition to the broad vision of an educator, the deep sympathy and understanding that motivates all her work for the poorer children of the community. Quietly and unobtrusively, she has exerted a powerful influence on affairs of the association. Not only has she eagerly accepted the sweeping changes of modern progressive methods in kindergarten curriculum, but she has also aided materially in their adoption."

Her four adult children were great products of her wise and loving training. Ruth Midkiff, her oldest daughter, followed her in many community service organizations, but particularly in the Young Women's Christian Association. Her son, Atherton, became President of the Hawaiian Pineapple Company and a Trustee of the Bernice P. Bishop Estate, the foundation for the Kamehameha Schools. Herbert was, for most of his life, successor to his father as Treasurer and Business Manager of the Hawaiian Evangelical Association, (later, the United Church of Christ). Polly, the youngest, is a distinguished musician and worker in religious causes.

There are many beautiful educational buildings and chapels named in her honor in modern Hawaii. But greater memorial than these landmarks are the men and women in Hawaii, and in Oceania, Asia, and Africa, whose lives were enriched and fulfilled through contact with this loving woman and her innovative husband.

Idaho

Nickname: Gem State

State Flower: Syringa

State Tree: Western White Pine

State Bird: Mountain Bluebird

Photos

1. Idaho's State Capital
2. Neg Perce matriarch (Talmaks)
3. A pack trip into Idaho's unspoiled primitive areas
4. Spatter and cinder cone chain at Crater of the Moon National Monument near Arco
5. One of Idaho's alpine mountain lakes
6. Hells Canyon, deepest gorge in U.S.
7. The Pioneer Range of the Sawtooth mountains
8. Cataldo's Sacred Heart Mission

Committee Members

Chairman—Mrs. C.H. Higer, Emmett

Idaho

SACAJAWEA
Lemhi County   **Born-1786**

The history of Idaho mothers begins with this remarkable Shoshone woman. Born in the Lemhi Valley, of the Lemhi Tribe, in what would be Idaho, in 1786. Captured as a child, taken to a Mandan Village in North Dakota, she married Toussaint Charbonneau, a French-Canadian trapper, and with him and their baby son, Baptiste, accompanied Captains Lewis and Clark on their long journey to the West Coast.

Her native wisdom in discovering edible plants and other sources of food along the way was surpassed only by her coolness in emergencies, such as rescuing from a capsizing canoe articles "indispensable to the success of the enterprise."

As a guide she recognized landmarks, helped locate caches, chose the best of alternate paths, and decided on the site for Fort Clatsop. (Oregon coast)

As an interpreter (she spoke Shoshone and Minnetaree) her services were invaluable. And by her presence she made a successful expedition possible. Indians, suspicious of white strangers, were reassured since no Indian woman with a child, would join a war party. "Had she not accompanied the expedition, no doubt it would never have been heard of again."

Perhaps her greatest service to the enterprise came when the party reached her people, the Shoshone. Lewis wrote that it was "all important to meet these people who have horses—without which we cannot carry all the supplies necessary for the completion of the journey." Between rivers and over the Continental Divide, transportation other than boat was essential.

As the group entered Shoshone country Lewis went ahead to negotiate with Chief Cameahwait of the Lemhis. Unable to communicate adequately, the plan could not be carried out until Sacajawea came to act as interpreter, recognized Chief Cameahwait as her brother, and thus secured his promise to furnish the needed animals and a guide. And again, before the horses were actually theirs, Sacajawea forestalled a call by Cameahwait for a Lemhi buf-

falo-hunting party. If the Indians heard this before the horses were delivered, every horse and brave would be gone. Through her influence with her brother the contract was completed, and the expedition proceeded as planned.

As an interpreter in her later years she continued to use her abilities. She spoke in Councils—an unthinkable thing—ordinarily, but she represented the white as well as the red man. Through a common ancestor, Chief Tendoy, Sacajawea was related to a later-day Chief Washakie, who sought her counsel on matters of importance. She spoke in his Councils, and she did speak at the signing of the treaty with the United States Government at Fort Bridger, Wyoming, in 1868. Her understanding of languages,—which now included English, French, and several Indian tongues,—her understanding of the intents and purposes of the two races enabled her to act as a go-between for the white man and the red.

The name Sacajawea, mis-translated "Bird Woman" by Charbonneau, actually was a Shoshone word meaning "Canoe Launcher". Her burial spot in the Shoshone Windriver reservation is marked and reads: "Died April 9, 1884.

A lasting tribute from her own people is the sun-dance performed each summer on the Fort Hall reservation, near Pocatello, Idaho, brought by Sacajawea from the plains Indians to the Shoshone.

One son, Baptiste, baby of the Expedition, was educated in Germany, served as an interpreter, and was with the Mormon Battalion on its March to California. Bazil, son of her dead sister, was very close to his foster mother. He held an important and dignified position on the councils of his tribe and was a popular after-dinner speaker.

"The influence of Sacajawea and Bazil and to a lesser extent of Baptiste in interpreting the white man to their fellow-tribesmen and in urging them to adopt his methods of agriculture was of greatest service to the Shoshone ('our children were often hungry; now they can get bread and vegetables when we are not fortunate in hunting meat' [Bazil]) and to the government agents and those sent to teach the Shoshone and Bannock how to farm."

References and authorities: *Sacajawea* by Grace Raymond Hebard, University of Wyoming; Lewis and Clark Journals; "Idaho Yesterdays": Vol2,No.2,1958 *The Idaho Story* Vol. 2 by Poets and Writer's Guild

MRS. REBECCA MITCHELL
Idaho Falls   **Born 1834**

Mrs. Rebecca Mitchell was born in Macoupin county, Illinois, January 23, 1834. Not much is known of her parents, but it is but natural to suppose that they were honest, God-fearing people. She attended the district schools in her home town, but most of her education was received after she became a widow, when she attended school with her children. She attended the Baptist Missionary Training School in Chicago, and here she was fitted for her life work before coming west.

Mrs. Mitchell came here as a self-supporting missionary and church worker from Hoopston, Illinois, June 6, 1882. She seemed to realize at once the need of the little western settlement, for the very first Sunday after her arrival she set to work to organize the Baptist Sunday school. This was organized in the little board shanty in which she lived June 11, 1882. This first Sunday school met a long felt need, but no one before Mrs. Mitchell had had the courage to attempt such work. It was attended by quite a

number of faithful ones, and members were rapidly added as people came from the east to settle in the new country. The day after the Sunday school was organized, this courageous woman organized the first day school and so became the first school teacher in Idaho Falls. The trouble and hardships endured by Mrs. Mitchell in those days no one can realize. There were very few people at that time who cared for this kind of work Mrs. Mitchell was trying to do. She had to be a real missionary to win people to help her. There was no suitable building for the Sunday school and day school, so part of her own home was used as a school room and fitted up with wooden boxes to serve as desks. All the time Mrs. Mitchell was struggling to build a church. As she set out to work to raise money for this purpose. She received considerable help from benevolent Baptists in the New England states, to whom she had written, stating the needs of the new country. The church was organized with the help of Rev. Lamb and Rev. Spencer, August, 1884, just two years after Mrs. Mitchell's arrival here. To her was given the honor of throwing the first shovelful of dirt for the foundation. Three persons were on that day baptized in Snake river. Work was begun at once, and though it is almost impossible to realize, the church building was finished three months from the time of organization and was dedicated in November, 1884. The building was the first church edifice erected between Ogden and Butte, and the only church building in eastern Idaho.

Mrs. Mitchell continued her public school work, but when the railroad shops were moved away she gave this up and all her time and efforts were given to her church, club and temperance work.

It seems that Mrs. Mitchell is identified with every good and noble work done in the city. She organized the local W. C. T. U., and this society accomplished much good in Idaho Falls. Mrs. Mitchell was also the state W.C.T.U. organizer and traveled over every part of the state, organizing societies and endangering her health by long, cold stage drives in out-of-the-way places. In 1892 she was the state president of the W. C. T. U., as well as its organizer, and in that capacity she lectured in every town and hamlet in Idaho. Mrs. Mitchell was a very able public speaker. She had a strong, beautiful voice and was very witty and entertaining. She was sent as a delegate to the national W. C. T. U. conventions held in St. Louis, Buffalo, Toronto and Chicago.

She was the superintendent of legislation for the state W. C. T. U. and spent one winter in Boise during the session of the state legislature. Here her most important work for the state as a whole was done. During the session she secured the passage of numerous reform laws and was responsible for getting the equal suffrage bill before the people. She was unceasing in her efforts to secure the passage of this bill, and we realize now that fully nine-tenths of the credit for equal suffrage in Idaho is due directly to the efforts of this untiring worker. During the sessions of the general assembly in Boise in 1896-7 and 9, Mrs. Mitchell was Chaplain of the House of Representatives, and was the only woman in the world who ever held such a position.

While Mrs. Mitchell's whole heart was in her W. C. T. U. work, she was a prominent member of the Village Improvement Society and the Round Table Club, and was one of the most faithful workers, ever ready to respond when her health would permit her to do so, and even when unable she would write articles and have them read by others. One of her last pieces was written for the Woman's Federation of Clubs at Blackfoot.

At her death in Idaho Falls, September 30, 1908, memorial services were held in a number of towns of the state and resolutions adopted. Interment was made in the beautiful Rose Hill cemetery, and her grave has a handsome marker erected by the club women of the city. Idaho Falls has been greatly honored to number Mrs. Mitchell among its citizens, and are proud to think that she lived and labored among us.

DR. MINNIE FRANCES HOWARD
Pocatello   **Born 1872**

This pioneer mother was once chosen by the Idaho Federation of Business and Professional Women as one of the ten women who have contributed most to Idaho communities.

Minnie Frances Hayden, born in Memphis, Missouri, on August 23, 1872, came from a long line of distinguished ancestors. Her father, Jacob J. and her mother, Carrie Jane (Woods) Hayden were both descended from among the oldest families in America, including Quakers who came as early as 1636 to find religious freedom and tolerance. Her grandfather invented the first automatic corn planter, built the first threshing machine used west of the Alleghenies, and ante-dated McCormick in the construction of the reaper; but as a Quaker he felt he could not take out a patent.

Educated in the public schools of Missouri and Kansas, Minnie Hayden began her teaching career at 17 years of age, without ever attending high school. Studying nights she passed the Kansas state teacher examinations and completed her high school work.

On August 23, 1894, her twenty-second birthday, she was married to William F. Howard in Larned, Kansas. Both she and her husband finished school, then entered separate medical colleges, he at the University of Kansas and she at the Hospital for Women and Children in Kansas City, Missouri where she also interned. She took further study in the Post-Graduate Medical School and Hospital in New York City and finished her studies in the University of Chicago in 1906-08.

Her medical practice continued with excellent success for eight years until the cares of her home and her activities required her time. However, she was always ready to serve any need in her community, often without pay to save the health or eye-sight of some child.

Moving to Pocatello, Idaho, in 1902, she again worked for the best good of the community. Dr. Howard helped to organize The Civic Club of Pocatello—"the most potent organization active in the general affairs in this city." As chairman of the library committee of the Civic Club, she raised money for the site, corresponded with the Carnegie administration, and managed the work of founding the Carnegie Public Library. Once before she had been one of the founders of a county library in Kansas.

The two Drs. Howard spent a year abroad in study, he in diagnosis and surgery with especial attention to diseases of women. His private practice followed these lines. Dr. Minnie studied in Italy and Vienna, Austria, specializing in art as a civic force. Then in Idaho she created a wide interest in art throughout the state. The State Federation of Women's Clubs was the medium by which she pioneered in bringing art exhibits into the western states, with appropriate lectures. The latter she often paid for herself. She was a member of the various state art organizations.

"It may be said that Dr. Howard is one of the most energetic, active and influential women in Idaho,—without being in public life, for she is essentially a homemaker, and her influence is strong and far-reaching."

All four sons, Nelson Jacob, Richard Phillip, Forrest Hayden, and Francis became successful doctors of medicine.

NELLIE IRETON MILLS
Boise   **Born 1880**

Nellie Ireton Millr was born April 23, 1880, at the Marsh-Mitchell-Ireton Ranch on the Payette River, now the site of Montour, to John and Josephine Ireton, Idaho pioneers.

She was educated in Emmett, Idaho, at Portland University, Portland, Oregon and at the University of Idaho. At the University of Idaho she served as editor of the Argonaut, the student annual.

She graduated from University of Idaho in 1903 and came to Boise with her family and lived there until her marriage to J. C. Mills, Jr., of Garden Valley on January 20, 1914. They lived here until 1940 when they moved to Boise. While in Garden Valley she helped to establish Garden Valley High School and was a member of the Garden Valley School Board for twenty (20) years.

In Boise she helped to establish the Boise Young Womens Christian Association and the Boise chapter of the American Association of University Women. She also served as a clerk for the Idaho Legislature.

During her lifetime, she authored numerous publications, among them a book entitled "All along the River,"; the "Idaho Reader," "Scenic Idaho," numerous pioneer stories and sketches and many other works.

She was the mother of four sons, Warner C. Mills, at one time Idaho Commissioner of Law Enforcement, James C. Mills, Paul J. Mills and Buckley E. Mills who died in 1940.

Mrs. Mills was 87 at the time of her death in 1967.

ALICE BUTTERWORTH PITTINGER
Boise

Alice Butterworth Pittinger was born in Chicago.

She was a doctor of medicine and practiced for two years before her marriage. For a year and a half she studied voice at the Boston Conservatory of Music. Her grasp of parliamentary law was amazing, she was an outstanding horsewoman, she loved the out-of-doors and was a good camper. A woman of social attainments, she was also a quick and deft seamstress, an excellent cook and homemaker.

She married Dr. F. A. Pittinger in 1902 and came to Boise in 1905. She had a deep compassion for pets, children and their adopted daughter's death was a loss from which she never recovered. Because of this loss she became deeply involved in the work of the Girl Scouts. She presented to them a permanent campsite at Payette Lakes, McCall, which was named Camp Alice Pittinger. She was one of the founders of the Boise Children's Home and served on its Executive Committee for many years. She was state president of the Women's Auxiliary of the American Legion and on several occasions was a delegate to various world organizations meeting in countries abroad.

She served as state president of the Idaho Federation of Women's Clubs 1912-14. During her administration progress was made in obtaining funds for the Home Economics Department at the University of Idaho through the Smith-Lever bill. Much effort was put forward, for women, in the fields of uniform divorce laws, civil service reform, civic clean-up and since Idaho was a new state a project was started to collect its historical data.

ANNA HANSEN HAYES
Twin Falls   **Born 1886**

Anna Hansen Hayes was born at Rock Creek, Idaho, July 23, 1886 the daughter of John Frederich and Anna Elizabeth Peterson Hayes.

She was educated in schools in Albion and Shoshone and graduated from Idaho Normal College, Albion in 1901.

She married John E. Hayes, a civil engineer in 1906 and lived in Twin Falls where they lived with their four children. In 1910 they moved to Denver where she produced her first book of po-

etry "The Lure of the Trail." In Denver she also became involved in Parent Teacher Association which led to the presidency of the National PTA in 1949-52.

The family returned to Twin Falls in 1929. She was assistant editor for child welfare, magazine of the PTA and later for the Parent Teacher Magazine. For a number of years she was assistant editor for the standard publications. Since 1965 she has been advisory member for Highlights for Children, Honesdale, Pennsylvania.

As president of the National Congress of Parents and Teachers, she lectured throughout the United States and in many foreign countries. Under the direction of General Douglas MacArthur she helped develop the "Ways & Spirit of Democracy" through PTA work in Japan. She is the author of Idaho historical books "Adventures of Hedvig & Lollie", "Buckskin & Smoke", and has also had widely published articles and her poetry included in ten anthologies. She is listed in numerous biographical directories including "Who's Who in America" and "International Poets."

She has been awarded honorary degrees in literature by the University of Idaho and in Humanities by the College of Idaho.

Her son is a chemical engineer, two daughters are homemakers and teachers. One son was deceased in 1920.

Her many activities include the following:

Chairman Twin Falls County Territorial Centennial Committee—1960-66

National Federation President Women, 1952-60

DACONWITS National Advisory Committee On Women in the Service, 1953-57

Executive Committee White House Conference on Children & Youth, 1950

U. S. Commission of UNESCO 1949-52

State Representative National Foundation for Infantile Paralysis, 1945-49

Regional Director Eugene Field Society; National Federation Press Women

Idaho Chairman Women's Division, War Finance Committee, 1942-45

She is an active Episcopalian and served for many years as chairman of Church Periodical Club promoting Christian reading material within Idaho and overseas and only recently has resigned this position.

She is an honorary member of numerous groups including Idaho Public Health Association; Delta Kappa, Gamma, American Association of University Women, Beta Sigma Phi.

EMMA EDWARDS GREEN
Boise   **Born 1890**

Women's Lib appeared in Boise, in the person of Emma Edwards, shortly after Idaho had become a State on July 3, 1890.

Miss Emma was the daughter of the aristocratic John C. Edwards, former governor of Missouri, who later moved to Stockton, California and acquired large land holdings, became Mayor of the City, and married Emma Catherine Richards.

Emma Edwards Green was the first born of eight children and was exceptionally well educated for a woman of her time.

She arrived in Boise from New York where she had been attending art school, to live with her uncle, Major George W. Brumm and his two daughters. Among new friends she met were Margaret and Caroline Roberts, daughters of Idaho's first attorney general, George H. Roberts.

One of the first actions of the first session of the Idaho State Legislature was to be the selection of a great State seal. General Roberts and others suggested Miss Emma design a seal for the competition to be held for its selection.

She had previously obtained permission from her parents to open art classes in Boise and moved to a new home and started work on a design.

She decided a state seal must embody the resources, principally mining—so a miner was put on the seal; woman's suffrage was coming so a woman was put on the seal opposite the miner to signify the equality between sexes. The Legislature Committee wanted the submitted drawing to be exactly the size of the seal as it would be used, so she finished her design in this manner. A bill was introduced and her design was accepted over all others. She received $100 for her work and she became the only woman in the country to create an official State seal.

Later the Great Seal of the State of Idaho was designed to center the State flag and all this was done under Miss Emma's direction.

She taught school in several of the wilder outposts of Idaho, including the Hells Canyon country.

She met James G. Green, an Idaho mining man, and their marriage was an idyll of the Old West where she accompanied him on all of his exploratory journeys, painting happily from the log cabin porch or under the shelter of a tent flap. Their mountain home was five miles above Lowman.

Her life was not entirely of the mountains—she often lived in Boise at their home beside a slowly turning water wheel. In Boise she went with a quiet, determined smile to work for the cause of women and to edit the society page of the Capital Evening News.

She raised and made a home for a nephew, Darrel B. Edwards, an attorney in Oakland and is also the aunt of Ralph Edwards of "This Is Your Life" fame.

She died in Boise January 6, 1942 and was buried in Oakland beside her husband, Jim.

ANNA MARIE OSLUND
Coeur d' Alene   **Born 1891**

Anna Marie Oslund was born in Forssa, Helsingland, Sweden on September 14, 1891. Her parents, Anna Marie and Gabriel Anderson, brought their four daughters to America in 1904. Her father had come to the Troy area in 1892, and had homesteaded a 160 acre farm and built a home for his family.

Anna Marie and her sisters helped their father clear land and farm. The girls performed tasks such as dynamiting stumps and other extremely difficult work. They walked to a school which was three miles away.

Mrs. Oslund acquired her teaching certificate five years after arriving in the United States and began her teaching career in Helmer in a one-room school. She also taught in Gilbert, Stanford, Sandpoint and Troy, the latter for 40 years.

In 1917 she proved-up on her own homestead lots on the Colville Reservation in Washington and with the aid of a girlfriend she helped build her own house and dug her own well. This optimistic young woman was awarded the title of "Idaho Ann" by a newspaper journalist who was impressed by her enthusiasm and vigor.

On March 29, 1920 she married a neighbor, Alex H. Oslund, who had just returned from overseas duty of World War I. They settled in Troy and raised four children. The daughters are Mrs. Marie Chaney of Gilroy, California, Mrs. Liviah Olin of Coeur d' Alene, and Mrs. Cynthia Cox of Moscow. The son, Alex, resides in Burley.

Life for Mrs. Oslund was hard—but it never got her down. She has always had a strong conviction that God would see her through whatever difficulty she had to face. One of the most trying periods of her life was when her husband died on Christmas Eve 1929. She was then three months pregnant with her last baby, the son her husband never saw. The nation's economy was at a very low tide, but as she struggled to meet mortgage payments, clothe, feed and educate her children alone, she never complained. She was used to hard work and she taught her children to work together and to enjoy the accomplishments of their own hands. Those children have never forgotten the lessons they learned, and have in turn, taught their own children to never be afraid of work.

She never wanted her children to be deprived of things other children had, just because she couldn't afford them. Somehow she did manage to see them receive college degrees. She raised cattle, and huge gardens every year. She sold strawberries, cream and eggs. She canned, preserved, pickled and dried food for family consumption.

She was instrumental in securing electricity, a mail route, and graveled roads to the North Troy area. She pastured the University of Idaho Cavalry horses every summer for years so that her children could learn to ride. She held a summer school for children on the ranch—long known as Ancestral Acres—to help teach her own children the need to help others.

She always was for the under-dog and gave of herself, seemingly beyond endurance, to anyone who needed help. She was especially partial to boys—giving them jobs on the ranch, sometimes room and board also. Elderly people have long been a target of concern and love. Two of them lived in her home until they died of the infirmities of age. She raised two orphan boys, along with her own children, from the time they were twelve and thirteen until they were grown.

She has been a member of the Troy Lutheran Church since she was Confirmed as a child and is a state honorary member of Delta Kappa Gamma.

This is only a small fraction of her accomplishments during fifty-five years of teaching children—45 years in the classrooms and ten years as Troy librarian. She worked until she was 80 years old. In all those years she was absent from school, because of illness, only 22 days.

She has 13 grandchildren and 5 great grandchildren—all her beloved babies. In failing health, her home now is with her daughter, Liviah, in Coeur d' Alene, Idaho.

GRACE EDGINGTON JORDAN
Boise

Grace Edgington Jordan grew up in a small town in Eastern Oregon, the daughter of a country doctor, Dr. Jesse Edgington and Martha Ann Hartley Edgington, a school teacher. She graduated in journalism at the University of Oregon, did a year's reporting on a Eugene daily, then taught short story and newswriting at the university level. In 1924 she married Len Jordan, a World War I veteran, who had graduated in Business Administration and done graduate work at the University of Oregon. They lived briefly in Portland where Jordan was office manager for the Thurlow Glove Company. They then moved to Wallowa county to begin sheep and cattle ranching.

In 1932 with three small children they moved to Kirkwood Bar, a sheep ranch on the Idaho side of the Snake, 20 miles below Hell's Canyon. With no access roads and only a weekly mail boat when the river was at sufficient stage, they learned how to live with the depression. To her cooking for ranch hands and travelers from the trail, plus gardening and canning, Grace Jordan added teaching her children.

In 1941 Len Jordan built a stone house in Grangeville, the nearest town with a high school. He bought farm land, raised registered cattle and certified grass seed, and took on in succession a real estate and insurance business,

management of grain elevators, and a Ford dealership. At the Grangeville Free Press, where war had reduced the working staff, Grace Jordan filled in. Later she taught in the high school and worked on community drives.

In 1946 Len Jordan was elected to the Idaho legislature, and in 1950 he became Governor. He had no political machine; his was "a fresh face" and a business approach to state problems.

The Governor's house became a meeting place for many kinds of organizations—"the house belongs to the state," Mrs. Jordan said. At this time at the request of a New York Publisher, Grace Jordan wrote "Home Below Hell's Canyon", which was put into Braille by the Library of Congress, was serialized, then translated into six foreign languages. Out of print in hard cover and very expensive, it is available in paperback in many bookstores.

Three later books were Idaho based. The fifth, a sequel to Home Below Hell's Canyon, takes the Jordans to Washington, D.C., for two terms in the U. S. Senate. Jordan retired "to make room for younger men". With his three years in Washington with President Dwight D. Eisenhower he had given a total of twenty years to political life.

Between 1959 and 1962, Grace Jordan taught short story again, two years for the Young Womens Christian Association and a year at Boise Junior College.

The three Jordan children each paid half of their college expenses. Pat has worked as a home economist and in realty. Joe, a West Pointer, is an engineer, as is Steve. There are 10 Jordan grandchildren, two of them Steve's Asian adoptees.

In Boise Grace Jordan monitors a women's discussion group, now in its third year. She makes frequent talks to social and professional groups and as a former political wife has a heavy correspondence to maintain. She is listed in Who's Who of World Women, a British publication, and in Who's Who of American Women.

MARY T. BROOKS
Gooding

Mrs. Mary T. Brooks was appointed by President Nixon in March, 1969 to be the twenty-eighth Director of the United States Bureau of the Mint. She was reappointed by President Nixon and took the oath of office on August 8, 1974. Mrs. Brooks is the third woman to fill this important position.

Mrs. Brooks assumed her duties as Director of the Mint on September 1, 1969. She had been Assistant Chairman of the Republican National Committee, a position she had held since May of 1965. She was elected as the only woman to the Idaho State Senate in 1964 and re-elected in 1966 and 1968. She resigned in 1969 when President Nixon appointed her to be Director of the Mint. During her tenure in the Idaho Legislature, Mrs. Brooks was chairman of the Republican Caucus as well as the State Affairs Committee and the Agriculture Committee. She also served as a member of the Fish, Game and Recreation Committee and the Transportation and Defense Committee.

Mrs. Brooks was born in Colby, Kansas and reared in Gooding, Idaho. She attended Mills College in California and received her Bachelor of Arts degree from the University of Idaho. She is the daughter of the former United States Senator John Thomas of Idaho and served as his Administrative Assistant prior to his death in 1945. Mrs. Brooks also worked in the family

banking chain over the years before the chain was sold to the First Security Corporation. She has managed and developed a large sheep and cattle ranch in southern Idaho, the Flat Top Livestock Company in Muldoon, Idaho.

Married in 1939 to Arthur J. Peavey, Jr., who died in a hunting accident in 1941, Mrs. Brooks has a son, Idaho State Senator, John Thomas Peavey, who manages the family sheep and cattle ranch. Her daughter, Mrs. Gordon Eccles, lives in Picabo, Idaho. There are six grandchildren.

Mrs. Brooks was married in 1945 to United States Senator C. Wayland Brooks from Illinois who later served as a member of the Republican National Committee. She was elected Vice Chairman of the Committee on July 29, 1960 and was Official Hostess to the Republican National Convention in Chicago in 1960. She served as Vice Chairman of the Committee on Big City Politics under the chairmanship of Ray Bliss in 1961. After her resignation from the Republican National Committee in 1963, she returned to Idaho to manage the ranch until her election to the Idaho Senate.

During 1971-72 Mrs. Brooks served as a member of the President's Commission on School Finance. She is also a member of the Coins and Medal Advisory Panel, American Revolution Bicentennial Commission.

Her present and past memberships in civic, social and political organizations include: Kappa Kappa Gamma, American Association of University Women, American Legion Auxiliary, Board of the Idaho Youth Ranch, Advisory Committee on Women in the Services, Vice Chairman of her Red Cross District, Mental Health Board, Immigrant Service League, Illinois Children's Home and Aid, Light House for the Blind, Arden Shore Association, and Board of Illinois Federation of Republican Women, Board Member of the American Newspaper Women's Club and the Advisory Council of the International Eye Foundation.

Since taking office in September of 1969, Mrs. Brooks has received the following awards:

1969 Elected New York Women's National Republican Club's Woman of the Year;

1970 Voted Idaho's Woman of the Year;

1970 Elected to University of Idaho's Hall of Fame;

1972 Presented the Exceptional Service Award from the Treasury Department;

1972 Presented the "I left My Heart in San Francisco" award from the San Francisco Convention & Visitors Bureau for her efforts in the restoration and preservation of the Old Mint Building;

1973 Awarded the Certificate of Merit from the California Historical Society;

1974 Received the Laura Bride Powers award from the Laura Bride Powers Award Committee and the San Francisco Birthday Celebration Committee;

1974 Received the Kappa Kappa Gamma Fraternity Achievement Award.

Mary Brooks has one of the most fascinating, large ranches in Idaho. She inherited the original ranch holdings from her father, Sen. John Thomas, who came to Idaho from Kansas in the early days. Sen. Thomas got off the train where Gooding (where Mrs. Brooks was reared) was an alfalfa field. He helped settle the little town beginning with a telephone office and bank. Ending up in the Senate of the U.S. for two different terms, he brought water to the thirsty desert of South Idaho—and served as Chairman of Irrigation and Reclamation, Banking & Currency and Committee on Committees. He was later appointed for the second time to the Senate when William E. Borah died and served on Finance, Military Affairs and Committees on Committees.

Since her father's death, Mrs. Brooks and her people have reclaimed thousands of acres from the original sage brush to useful grasses and alfalfa. She has added thousands of acres to the original sheep ranch. It runs the length of the Little Wood River a few miles north of Carey.

The home ranch is real old west. The original ranch house is a series of very old log cabins joined with the rooms opening onto the porch which runs the length of the house.

There was no electricity until a few years ago. Mrs. Brooks' men also built a modern telephone line over 23 miles in a mountain pass, using her cow pony to pull the wire off the spindle by tying it to the saddle horn! Then the Mountain States Telephone Company bought the line for a dollar—but will maintain it at their expense forever. Four other ranches now hook into it. The original telephone line was built in 1906 and only worked occasionally. It was made of barbed wire and beer bottles in places.

Mrs. Brooks cooks for the hands at times in the big cook house. Several times this happened in the winter when all were snowed in and the only heat was from wood burning stoves. She went to the desert and cooked in the chuckwagon when the annual cow exodus took place in the late fall—750 cows walked 120 miles south—and the cowboys had to be fed.

Her son, John Peavey, who is a State Senator, now manages the cattle operation and an old-time manager, Dennis Burks, reputed to be the best sheepman in Idaho, manages the sheep—as he has for 30 years.

The ranch is a haven for wild life—although heavy hunting is reducing the sage grouse, elk and deer to Mrs. Brooks' great sorrow. She has a meadow where as many as 75 sandhill cranes have been counted at one time.

Mrs. Brooks ran for the State Senate from a Democratic County and claims to be the original walker. She decided to call on every one in her county (5500 at the time) and almost made it by election time. She lost the sole on one shoe but still keeps her lucky shoes with an occasional trip to the shoemaker for a resole job. She also won the election—1964 and was re-elected in 1966 and 1968.

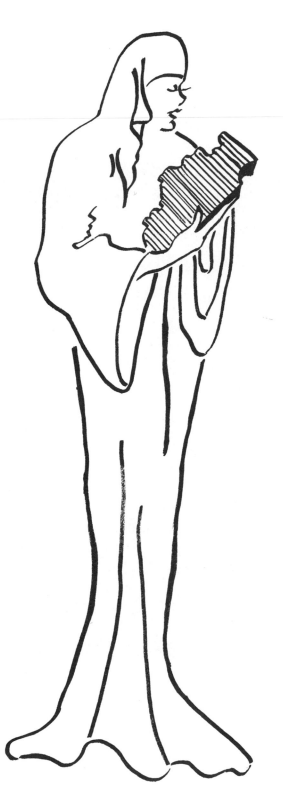

Illinois

Illinois

Nickname: Prairie State

State Flower: Violet

State Tree: Oak

State Bird: Cardinal

Committee Members

Chairman—Dr. Felicia Dorothy Koch,
  Granite City
Mrs. Charles H. Woods, Lincoln
Mrs. Francis C. Tucker, Freeport
Mrs. Barney C. Browning, Benton
Mrs. Homer W. Alvey, Lincoln
Mrs. William G. Gollmer, Urbana
Mrs. Guy W. Akerly, Milford
Paul Bacon
Miss Minnie Delhass
Miss Garreta Busey
Mrs. Norma H. Woods
Mrs. Eva Jane Follmer
Willa Dean Brown

Illinois

MARY ANN BALL BICKERDYKE
Galesburg   **Born 1817**

Mary Ann was born in 1817 to Hiram and Anna (Rodgers) Ball in Knox County, Ohio. She attended Oberlin College and became a nurse. She married a widowed musician and had three children, James, Hiram and Martha who died at two. In 1859 the family moved from Cinncinati to Galesburg. Mr. Bickerdyke died in 1859 leaving Mary to support the children by practicing botanic medicine.

At the outbreak of the Civil War in 1861, the Congregational Church Minister pleaded for help in alleviating the appalling neglect of the Illinois volunteers in Cairo, Illinois. Mrs. Bickerdyke volunteered and found conditions worse than described. She fearlessly made trips to battlefields, helping evacuate wounded to the hospital. She joined forces with Grant's Army, moving constantly wherever she was needed. Her midnight visits to battlefields, searching for wounded men among the dead were heroic.

When asked by a surgeon on whose authority she acted, she retorted "On the authority of Lord God Almighty—have you anything that outranks that?"

In 1863 she became matron of the Gayoso Military Hospital. Indignant over inadequate food, she returned to Illinois on a whirlwind tour to solicit contributions of chickens, milk, eggs, etc. which she transported to Memphis.

She was the only woman on the scene at nineteen battles including Vicksburg and Chattanooga. She worked in mud and freezing rain to care for the wounded Union soldiers, assisted at amputations and brewed barrels of coffee. The soldiers named her "Mother Bickerdyke".

In 1865, with no war to serve, she obtained donations and a personal loan to establish a home in Salina, Kansas for disabled Veterans. The president of the Chicago, Burlington and Quincy Railroad, Charles Hammond granted her free passage for fifty veterans. Since she did not charge her "guests", she was unable to pay off the mortgage and eventually the Railroad took over the establishment.

She attempted, in 1870 to clean up the slums in New York with a co-worker, Mary Stafford. After four years, she returned to Kansas.

Her health failing, Mother Bickerdyke settled in the warm climate of California for eleven years hoping to alleviate arthritis of her hardworking hands. Undaunted, she continued to serve her "boys", visiting Soldier's Homes, etc. She sought pensions for Veterans, even journeying to Washington to plead for them. Congress granted her a pension of $25 a month in 1886.

In 1901 at the age of 84, she died in her son's home in Salina.

A statue of Mother Bickerdyke, kneeling beside a wounded soldier, holding a cup to his lips, stands on the Knox County Courthouse lawn in Galesburg where she is buried.

During World War II, a ship was christened the "S.S. Mary A. Bickerdyke". It was a "workhorse" of the sea and like Mother Bickerdyke, it took no part in battle but carried food and medical supplies.

"A ministering Angel"
Shakespeare, Hamlet V.

MARY TODD LINCOLN
Springfield

Born 1818

Mary Ann Todd was born in Lexington, Kentucky in 1818, the year of Illinois Statehood and nine years after her future President husband who was born in a humble log cabin in the rugged hills of Kentucky.

Her parents Robert Smith and Eliza (Parker) Todd were of successful families in business and cultural circles. Mary remembered Henry Clay discussing current events with her father in the Todd living room.

When she was seven, Mary's mother died. A year later, her father remarried. The new Mrs. Todd brought her niece with her, providing Mary with a devoted friend with whom she attended Dr. Ward's Academy. Later Mary continued her formal education at Madame Victoria Mentelle's select boarding school.

The pressures of the growing Todd family compelled Mary to leave the Todd residence. She made her home with her sister Elizabeth, wife of Ninian Edwards. The Edwards family was one of Springfield's most prominent. Ninian's father had been Illinois Governor and Ninian served in the State Legislature. Their home was the scene of gatherings for outstanding frontier Illinois personalities.

Mary first met the man who one day would be an American giant at one of these functions. Abraham Lincoln was but a struggling lawyer in Springfield. Mary's interest in him was discouraged by her family, for others, more educated, refined and successful, especially Stephen Douglas, were encouraged as more suitable prospects for marriage.

In spite of disapproval, Mary and Abraham were married November 4, 1842. Her wedding ring carried these engraved words "Love is Eternal".

For nearly twenty years the Lincolns lived in Springfield. Four sons were born. Edward died at four. Robert, William and Thomas saw their father elected President. Her husband was elected to Congress for a term and then lost the race for U.S. Senate seat twice, the final time to Stephen Douglas in 1858. Finally in 1860, Mary's husband announced—"Well, mother, we are elected"—to the Presidency.

The Washington years were troubled and lonely for the "First Lady". Civil War was raging, her own half-brothers were fighting for the Confederacy. The South despised her and the North doubted her loyalty. Tragedy struck again, first with the death of son Willie and finally with the assasination of her husband in 1865.

Mrs. Lincoln's son Todd died in 1872. On the petition of her son, Robert, she was judged insane and committed to a private sanatorium in Batavia, Illinois in 1873 for one year.

Humiliated, Mary traveled in Europe for four years. Upon returning to Springfield, she died in Elizabeth's home and was buried beside her husband in 1882. "When I again rest by his side, I will be comforted".

So passed one of the outstanding women in Illinois history. Who can really measure all that Mary contributed in helping to shape the man unmatched in the history of Illinois or even perhaps that of the Nation!

"The hand of the Lord hath strengthened thee and therefore thou shalt be blessed".
Judith 15:11

ANN ARMSTRONG KEYS
Beason   **Born 1845**

Ann Armstrong Keys is better known in the Beason Community as "Aunt Ann Keys". In the year 1856, Aunt Ann's mother, Sarah Armstrong, a widow from County Fermanagh, Ireland, undertook a voyage to America with her eight children. Ann, who was eleven years old at the time, has often spoken of the Atlantic trip in a sailing vessel which was a fifteen weeks journey. She recalls that at this time the ship was in quarantine off the coast of New Orleans and when it finally landed, the family journeyed to Logan County, Illinois.

In 1868 Ann married Francis Keys, whose parents also came from Ireland. Ann and her husband moved to a farm near Beason. Francis Keys built the house in 1875 which still exists. The original bill for the construction, dated September 25, 1874 reads: "Received of Francis Keys $476.45 in full for his dwelling house, signed—O. Crandale". In 1927 the "Centennial Family Award" certificate by the State Department of Agriculture was awarded to the family.

The Keys had five children and farmed three hundred-twenty acres of land. When the young-est child Harold, was four years old, his father died, leaving the widow to carry on the burden of supervising the farm and rearing her five children. While the task seemed insurmountable, Mrs. Keys, with great courage, faith and stamina conquered all difficulties, helping all who knew her.

She not only was a woman of faith and kindness, but a great financier. After her husband's death, by shrewd business ability, she purchased two other farms of one hundred-sixty acres each and also a timber tract of about seventeen acres which was never cultivated. Because of her supervision and proper care of the trees, the tract has been accepted as "Tree Farm"—the only one in Logan County.

Often she took sickly and malnourished children into her home caring for them until they were restored to health.

After her husband's mother Mary Keys was widowed, she lived with Aunt Ann who gave her the best room in the house. Her old spinning wheel, wool reel and trundle bed are still in existence.

Aunt Ann was very religious and along with her family was dedicated in the support of the Beason Methodist Church. She taught a Sunday School class of little ones in her advanced age. A framed certificate of her life membership of the Methodist Missionary Society, signed by Peter Cartwright a noted circuit rider of the early Methodist Church, remains in the family possession.

Aunt Ann died in 1910 at the age of 65. The day of the funeral, out of respect and in honor of her memory, seven schools were closed. A good woman called "Home"—Aunt Ann Keys.

"Mighty is the force of motherhood!
It transforms all things by its vital heat".
George Eliot

KATE BAKER BUSEY
Urbana   Born 1855

Kate Baker Busey (1855-1934) was a woman of unusual talents and varied interests. Her social conscience reflected her background. She was born in Ripon, Wisconsin, the daughter of Garrett Hyer and Frances Elmina Clapp Baker. The family lived in the domain of Wisconsin Phalanx, a commune, made up of a group of social reformers, seeking to put into practice the philosophy of Charles Fourier of France. Mr. Baker operated a nursery, but soon after Kate's birth, moved to Cobden, Illinois, where he became a large fruit and vegetable grower, who shipped tons of produce to the Chicago market. Here the Bakers, ardent Abolitionists frequently came into conflict with the Southern sympathizers of Southern Illinois.

In the 1880's Kate travelled to Virginia where she taught wood carving to the Blacks at Hampton Institute. Later she became a teacher to the Indians at the Colorado River Indian Reservation in Arizona. Here she met George W. Busey of Urbana, Illinois, who was spending two years as the Indian Agent at the Reservation. On May 14, 1890, they were married at Cobden and set-

tled in Urbana where Mr. Busey resumed his banking interests. They became parents of a son and two daughters.

In 1904 Mrs. Busey was the organizing regent of the Alliance Chapter of D.A.R. She entertained, frequently and lavishly, the ladies of the Chapter in her home at 503 Elm Street. In 1914, a talk by Judge J. C. Cunningham to the Chapter on the subject of the "Real Lincoln Highway", inspired her to organize the nearby Chapters and convinced the Illinois State Organization to mark the Circuit of the Old Eighth Judicial District which Cunningham had traveled with Lincoln.

Mrs. Busey served as County Director for Champaign County. The marker in front of the Court House is the result of her efforts. Mrs. Busey organized the first P.T.A. and frequently entertained the teachers and parents in her home in an effort to create better understanding between them. She involved herself in the work of the building of good country roads for the sake of making better education more accessible to the children. The first kindergarten in Urbana, with a hired teacher, was held in her home. Woman's suffrage was close to her heart and she spent endless hours promoting the movement.

Kate Baker Busey was indeed an enlightened feminist, working tirelessly for better education for children and for the advancement of womankind in general.

"Good works do not make a good woman but a good woman does good work".
                                          Anonymous

FLORENCE FIFER BOHRER
Bloomington   **Born 1877**

The same spirit which sent the twelve year old Florence zooming down the curved banister in the Governor's Mansion on the occasion of her father's inauguration as Governor of Illinois in 1889 sent her into State politics as the first woman Senator in 1924. Florence, daughter of Joseph W. and Gertrude (Lewis) Fifer was born January 24, 1877 in Bloomington.

Florence enjoyed outdoor sports, and with her brother frequently outdid Tom Sawyer's adventures. Florence attended the Unitarian Hillside Home School.

In 1898 she married Attorney Jacob Bohrer. For the next several years she devoted her time to her two sons and husband who died in 1928.

"While woman's first duty is to care for her children and home, intelligent woman accepted long since, the fact that to be a good mother and homemaker, she must push out the walls of her home to include the community".

Florence began by initiating the Mother's Club, a forerunner of the P.T.A., establishing the Lucy Orme Morgan Home for dependent girls and assisting the Booker T. Washington home for Negro children.

Acutely aware of the tuberculosis plague, she worked in the organization of the McLean County Tuberculosis Association. Her first successful experience in lobbying was a tax levy for a sanatorium. In 1919 the Fairview Sanatorium was dedicated.

Once women achieved the right to vote, they should aim for political office. In 1924 Florence was urged to run for State Senate. On the Republican ticket, her platform called for "Law enforcement, Christian citizenship and reduction of taxes".

A controversial figure in the Senate, she was more concerned with issues rather than party politics. She won a second term.

The Illinois constituents were pleased with Senator Bohrer's bills which were passed. These were: Real Estate tax payments in two installments; Foster homes for Welfare children; Act requiring registration and qualifications for public health nurses; Regulation of dance halls by County Supervisors; Control of State Parks by Department of Public Works and Buildings; Adoption of the State song "Illinois".

The Governor appointed Mrs. Bohrer to a commission for legal changes concerning the care of dependent, delinquent and handicapped children.

The Unitarian Church was an important facet of her life wherein she served as choir member, President of the Board, and Director of the American Unitarian Association.

A persistent lobbyist, as President of the State League of Women Voters, she influenced permanent voter registration, the act for Aid to Dependent Children and revision of the adoption law.

The Bloomington Community Service Award in 1934, Illinois Welfare Association Citation in 1945 and Distinguished Service Award from Southern Illinois University in 1956 were only a few of the honors bestowed upon her.

At age 83, she died and was buried in Bloomington, in 1960. To the very end she remained active mentally and physically.

A newly organized Chapter of the Questers Club has been named in her honor in 1972.

"And every excellent work shall be justified and the worker thereof shall be honoured therein".
Ecclesiasticus 14:21

GERTRUDE BAGGETT PRESLEY
Paris   Born 1880

Mrs. Gertrude Baggett Presley was born in Paris, Texas in 1880. After the Civil War, circumstances found Gertrude, a Rebel orphan, abandoned in a Yankee settlement near Cobden. A Rebel soldier, Jerry Sisk and his wife reared her on their small farm.

As Gertie grew into a lovely young woman, she became aware of the bitterness, which existed between Northerners and Southerners. Being alert to their many needs and with great sympathy, she endeavored to bring about understanding, thus helping to heal the wounds of war.

She married James Presley, a Scotchman, and they settled on the Sisk farm. In true pioneer fashion, she farmed, carried water, helped saw trees, and with shotgun in hand, guarded her chickens from foxes and hawks, assisting her husband in every way. In addition, she found time to administer to the sick and needy of the community.

The Presleys had seven children, two of whom were polio victims. Ralph died at the age of 38, and Mrs. Dorothea Davis, "Dottie Dee" of WCIL radio fame, is still on crutches. She remains active, and her latest role is "Granny and the Aggervatin' Youngin." She has written short stories, autobiographies, and T.V. shows. The Presley sons Wayman, Herbert, and Alfred reside in Illinois. Owen and Ernest are deceased.

A film, "Shawnee Hills, Water Valley and Cross of Peace," produced by Hollywood Films stars the eldest son Wayman, and portrays the beauty of Illinois. The biography of Wayman is included in the Royal Blue Book of London, and International Register of Who's Who. He was "Man of the Year in Illinois," "2000 Men of Achievement in the World" and also appeared on "This is Your Life" T.V. Show. He received no degrees, never held high office nor moved from Makanda, Illinois.

As a rural mailman, he discovered a little girl with an incurable disease. Being compassionate, he drove her 120 miles over almost impassable roads to Barnes Hospital, St. Louis and offered to pay for her medical treatments. After five years and twenty-two trips, the child was cured of elephantiasis, a disease considered incurable at that time.

Another accomplishment was the unification of 116 ununited Christian denominations, after a twenty-five year struggle to unify them. This unity resulted in the construction of the largest Cross of Peace which stands on Bald Knob Mountain with the inscription, "Faith, Hope, Charity and Love," his mother's favorite words.

Every Sunday, Mrs. Presley drove her five sons, in the farm wagon, to the Walter Valley Christian Church, leaving Jim, her husband, at home to care for the two invalids. She taught her family about God and the brotherhood of man.

Uncomplaining, cheerful, working long hours without bitterness, caring for her afflicted as well as healthy children and helping her neighbors, she truly was "a friend as described in the Bible."

Mrs. Presley died in 1933 at the age of 53 and was buried in Makanda, Illinois.

Gertie's spirit is perpetuated through her surviving children who cherish her memory and emulate her virtues.

"Her children rise up and call her blessed".
Proverbs 31:28

BEULAH FRAZIER BELL
Mount Vernon   **Born 1886**

Beulah Bell's maternal grandfather Henry "Lucky", a Louisiana slave, bought his freedom and married an Indian woman to insure freedom for his children.

Two generations later on August 21, 1886, Beulah Frazier was born in Cape Girardeau, Missouri on a farm near Lucky's home, formerly an Indian outpost. She recalls livestock, poultry and merchandise being transported on the wagon roads.

The Fraziers, Burrel Morgan and Elizabeth (Lucky), had eight children, many of whom were talented musicians. Beulah's brother Ira has his own concert band in Chicago.

Being the only Negroes in the community, they were accepted as neighbors but the children walked four miles to attend the Negro school. Beulah enjoyed school, reading and studying far beyond the requirements. She treasures her official, beribboned grade school diploma which she received in 1905. Her oration was the best of all the graduates in her class.

Aspiring to be a teacher, she passed the State examination and taught in a country school at

$30 a month. To reach the school, she either got a "lift" in a buggy or rode in the caboose of a freight train. Wolves and wild hogs in the wooded country made walking treacherous.

Beulah married Damon Giboney and had two sons. In 1918 she came to Mount Vernon with her sons and second husband, William Bell, a chef on the C. & E. I. Railroad.

Here she organized the forerunner of the P.T.A., raised funds for the Washington School playground, assisted World War I rehabilitation, visited imprisoned youths and wrote scripts for the Methodist Church pageants. Throughout the years, Mrs. Bell has been active in efforts to elevate the socio-economic status of Blacks in Mount Vernon.

Her son, LeRoy organized the American Legion Post 952 where his mother promoted memorial services for World War I Veterans at the Zion Methodist Church. At these dinners, one table was set, bearing place cards of deceased Veterans. In appreciation, Mrs. Bell was named "Mammy of the American Legion".

Beulah Bell wrote her first poem "Negro Soldier's Blues" in 1928. Unlike most war protest compositions, this was for fighting—after the Army refused her brother for World War I. It was a time, the poem notes, for setting people free. Beulah continued to write poetry in spite of failing health and cancer treatments.

After her husband and son Felix died, she was forced to receive State Aid. A welfare case worker noticed a stack of her poems on a table and encouraged Beulah to publish them.

In 1975, at the age of 89, her anthology of favorite poems and prose "Two Roads" was published. It is divided into sections titled "Sacred", "Young Love", "Family" and "Patriotic".

Her poetry reflects her rural heritage with homespun language, simple rhythm and often a touch of earthy humor.

She is in the process of writing a book on her family history. It is representative of Black history, especially the Black struggle.

Her philosophy is "Give to live and live to give".

VIOLET SIMPSON SCULLY
Lincoln   Born 1902

Few immigrated to America and made their adopted country the recipient of so much effort and many gifts toward its betterment and the welfare of others as Violet Scully who was born in Penn, Buckinghamshire, England in 1902. She was educated in England and took postgraduate art work in Paris, France where she married Thomas A. Scully in 1924. They lived in London until coming to the United States in 1925. They finally settled in Lincoln in the red sandstone Scully Building, built in 1909 as an office and living quarters.

Mrs. Scully's father, Sir William Simpson, an eminent tropical and preventive medical physician was knighted by Queen Victoria. Her mother, Mary Jane (Jamison) came from Scotland and her grandfather was Chief Presbyterian Minister of Old Aberdeen Cathedral for forty years.

Mr. Scully's father William, came to the United States in 1850 from Ireland, purchased extensive tracts of swamp land thought worthless by the pioneers, ditched, drained and put them into production. He and Thomas started permanent soil rotation fertility in 1927 and soil conservation in 1954.

The Scullys have two sons. Michael is a graduate of Harvard and Peter of Princeton. Both are married and engaged in agricultural projects in connection with their land. Mr. Thomas Scully died in 1961.

Mrs. Scully's community activities include many catagories. She organized the American Red Cross sewing production for World War I, also served as Regional Chairman for Girl Scouts and located suitable sites for camping. She was a member of the local Board of Governors of the Salvation Army, making generous contributions. She was the first president of the Civic Recreation Center which developed into the present Park District with a $600,000 Recreation Complex. She belongs to the Zonta Club and is a generous supporter of the Episcopalian Church. She was active in the Home Extension Service of the Farm Bureau and in obtaining a new garden at the Governor's Mansion in Springfield. She contributed $50,000 toward the Scully Natatorium at Lincoln College.

Her main interest at present is the creation of a foundation to preserve natural areas in the County for recreation and nature study, "A Green Belt around Lincoln". She generously donated 450 acres to this project which is being improved for fishing, riding and hiking.

The landscaping of the Courthouse grounds, Washington Park and the Railroad Station is financed by Mrs. Scully. The Post Office grounds were completed by federal funds and received a special award from Lady Bird Johnson.

In 1942 Mr. Scully completed a residence on his property adjacent to Lincoln, surrounded by extensive lawns, flower and vegetable gardens. Mrs. Scully designed the landscaping and now spends many hours working with her gardener to care for them. She is most gracious in inviting local organizations to her home and annually entertains at an outdoor dinner for her tenants on the estate.

Mrs. Scully's policy is to support projects in Logan County and to encourage outdoor activities for health and appreciation of nature.

"Give her of the fruit of her hands and let her works praise her in the gates."
Proverbs 31:31

JESSIE BORRER MORGAN
Monticello   Born 1907

A newspaperwomaan for the past 55 years, starting as a part-time reporter at the age of thirteen, Mrs. Birch E. Morgan is a noted authority on her state and community's historical heritage.

Mrs. Morgan was born on a farm near Potomac, Vermillion County, Illinois in 1907. Her parents were William M. and Martha Ellen (Neff). She is a 1925 graduate of Rossville High School. She received a Bachelor of Arts degree in history from Indiana University in 1930 and continued study in political science as a graduate student there.

Her career began as a part time reporter on the Rossville Press. She became editor of the Indiana Daily Student, the campus newspaper in 1930 and was a reporter for the Commercial News and Decatur Herald Review in Decatur, Illinois.

At the present time she is feature writer and Piatt County reporter for the Urbana Courier.

She is the author of various publications, including "The Good Life in Piatt County"; Piatt County History (1968); Monticello Centennial Program (1937); History of Monticello Methodist Church (1953); and editor of Centennial edition of Piatt County Journal (1956).

Mrs. Morgan has completed extensive research on the Allerton family in preparation for publishing the life and times of both Samuel and Robert Allerton, prominent in Illinois politics. She makes frequent appearances before women's groups, speaking on historical subjects, current topics and the importance of women today.

Mrs. Morgan served as Piatt County chairman for the Illinois Sesquicentennial observance (1968) and is now Piatt County chairman for the Bicentennial celebration. She was chosen as a member of the "Committee of 150" by former Illinois Governor Otto Kerner in 1968 in recognition of her work in promoting interest in Illinois History.

She is among the organizers, and serving at present as assistant Curator of the Illinois Pioneer Heritage Museum in Monticello; a former Vice-Chairman and current Director of the Illinois State Historical Society, charter member of the Illinois State Genealogical Society; past president (for 7 years) of Piatt County Historical Society; Alpha Sigma Phi, professional journalism Society and is active with the Monticello Federated Woman's Club, Business and Professional Women's Club, John and Mary Kirby Hospital Auxiliary and Monticello United Methodist Church.

In 1974-75 she assisted University of Illinois students in an environmental planning workshop in the study and publication of "Historic Preservation—Pride and Progress for Monticello". At the present she serves as resource adviser in the Monticello Schools.

Jessie married Birch E. Morgan (1936), Sixth Judicial Circuit and presiding circuit Judge of Champaign County. He has been a member of the State Judiciary for the past 33 years. The couple are parents of a son Jerry, executive vice-president of Lake River Terminal Division of Kinark Corporation and a daughter Emily Birch, a teacher in the Hammond, Indiana School System. They have three grandchildren.

"Her discipline is a gift from God"
Ecclesiasticus 14:21

CAROL KARRAKER KIMMEL
Rock Island   **Born 1917**

Carol, daughter of Grace (Kerr) and Clyde Karraker, was born in Dangola, Illinois in 1917. She is a graduate of Bethel College, Hopkinsville, Kentucky and Southern Illinois University. Carol married Walter Kimmel in 1938 in Rock Island. The Kimmels are parents of three children, Walter, Carol Allison and Ralph.

As a public school music teacher, she perceived the need for improvement of educational systems and broader legislation for the schools in Illinois. She is a careful researcher of background material for any causes she espouses.

Her leadership and participation was soon recognized by local, state and national legislative and educational authorities.

Mrs. Kimmel was elected President of the National P.T.A. in June, 1975. Her theme as national leader is "P.T.A.–Today". One of the projects she will be urging is a revamping of school health programs using a $140,706 H.E.W. grant.

Her membership on the National P.T.A. Executive Committee began with her election as Chairman of the National Chairmen's Confer-

ence, and has continued with her election as the National P.T.A.'s first coordinator of legislative activity. Formerly a member of the National P.T.A. Board of Managers as Chairman of the Committee on Founder's Day, and as President of the Illinois P.T.A., she has served on a number of special committees of the National P.T.A. and was chairman of the special committees on administration continuity and the legislative program. She was also a member of the budget and Endowment Fund committees.

Mrs. Kimmel is a member of the Illinois Board of Higher Education's Task Force on the education of teachers; the National Task Force on responsible decisions about alcohol; and the Illinois Advisory Council, having been appointed by the State Superintendent of Public Instruction.

She is a former member of the Illinois Commission on the Status of Women, the Illinois Master Plan for higher education and the Illinois Task Force on education.

Mrs. Kimmel is a past president of the Rock Island Board of Education, served as a delegate to the 1970 White House Conference on Children, and is a former chairman and charter member of the Illinois Citizens Education Committee. She is an honorary member of Alpha Delta Kappa and Delta Kappa Gamma, education societies.

Always active in community and Church, she has done choir work all her life. She served as Trustee, Deaconess and member of the Christian Education Committee.

"Mrs. P.T.A." as she is fondly called, is in constant demand to speak to groups on citizenship, education and legislation.

"By their fruits ye shall know them".
Matthew 7:20

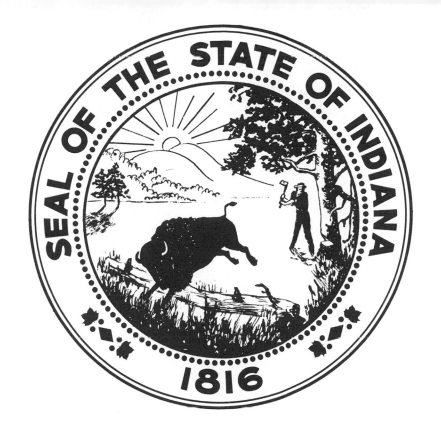

Indiana

Nickname: Hoosier State

State Flower: Ainnia

State Tree: Tulip Tree

State Bird: Cardinal

Photos

1. Indianapolis 500 mile race (Racing Capital of the World)
2. Krannert Pavilion, The Indianapolis Museum of Art
3. The roofless church in New Harmony
4. Soldiers & Sailors Monument, Monument Circle
5. Clowes Hall, Culbural Center, Indianapolis, on Butler University Campus
6. Old Indiana Capital at Corydon
7. The Governor's Mansion, Indianapolis
8. Pres. Benjamin Harrison Memorial Home, Indianapolis

Committee Members

Chairman—Mrs. Margaret Post—Indianapolis

Indiana

FRANCES SLOCUM

Born 1773

The capture of Fort Sackville at Vincennes, Indiana, and the holding of the Northwest Territory, form the historical setting for the life of Frances Slocum, kidnapped by the Indians in Pennsylvania and brought over land and water to soil which became Indiana.

The British in 1778 were providing guns and ammunition for Indians in the Allegheny Mountains, and were paying a bonus for scalps.

Jonathan Slocum, a Quaker, his wife and children lived on the north fork of the Susquehanna River (where Wilkes-Barre now stands) in 1778 when Tories and Indians moved through the area, plundering, burning and scalping. The Slocums, who had made friends with Indians, remained in the area.

The men were not at home when the Indians began their plunder. Mrs. Slocum ran to the woods with most of the children, but five-year old Frances and a lame brother hid under the stairs. The lad was released, but Frances, crying for her mother, was carried on the shoulder of an Indian who disappeared into the forest.

She lived as a youth with the Delawares in Ohio, and then was adopted by the Miami Indians in Indiana.

Many braves sought her hand, and she married Chief She-po-can-ah. She was christened by the Miamis as Ma-con-a-quah, and the couple had two daughters, Ke-ke-mok-esh-wa and O-zah-shin-quah.

Years later, one of Frances Slocum's brothers read a story in a Lancaster, Pennsylvania newspaper which told of an overnight meeting of Colonel George W. Ewing, officer of U.S. Indian service, with a family at Peru, Ind., in which a proud Indian matriarch presided over the household.

Her name was Ma-con-a-quah, and her complexion was lighter than other members of the family, and the end of her index finger was missing. That night, according to the story, Colonel Ewing talked with Ma-con-a-quah in the language of her tribe. She confided that she had been stolen as a child, that her parents

were Quakers, and that she lived in the valley of the Susquehanna. Her husband had died, and she was living quietly with her two daughters and a son-in-law.

Frances Slocum's two brothers and a sister set out on the long journey to Peru, Ind. A meeting was arranged; they saw a woman with leathery face, sitting quietly before them. Links of a 60-year story were pieced together. They saw the hand which had been injured so long ago.

"Come home with us?" they pleaded.

"These are my people," she answered. "I will stay with my children."

Ma-con-a-quah returned to her home on the Mississenewa River, and there on March 2, 1847, she died at the age of 74.

Today a state forest commemorates the memory of the little girl who became the "White Rose of the Miamis," and who earned the respect and love of her fellow American Indians. The Frances Slocum Trail follows the Wabash River, and the Mississinewa, and the name of the woman who left an imprint on Hoosier history carries with it the saga of early civilization in the Northwest Territory.

NANCY HANKS LINCOLN

Born 1784

"You are facing the wooded knoll on which sleeps Nancy Hanks Lincoln, Mother of the President, who lived in this Hoosier environment during the formative years of his life from 1816 to 1830.

"Beyond, to the north, is marked the site of the humble log cabin where she led him for a little while along the path to greatness."

These words are on the stone which points the way at Lincoln City, Indiana, to the grave of Nancy Hanks Lincoln, and to two spacious halls of Indiana limestone and Spencer County timber, one dedicated to Abraham Lincoln's memory, and the other to the memory of his mother. In 1962 Lincoln State Park, Indiana, became a unit of the national park system.

What of youthful Nancy Hanks Lincoln, who died when 34 years old, a pioneer sacrifice, with memories of endless days of chores, mystic Bible verses read over and over for their promises of blue, wistful hills and a summer when crab apple blossoms flamed pink-white and she carried a boy child into the world?

Nancy Hanks Lincoln was born Feb. 5, 1784, as recorded in the family Bible by her son, Abraham Lincoln. Born in Virginia, the daughter of Lucy Shipley Hanks and James Hanks, she moved to Kentucky with her mother when her father died. Her mother married Henry Sparrow, and Nancy Hanks spent several years in the pleasant home of her uncle and aunt, Richard and Rachel Berry.

A mile and a half from the Berry Settlement was the home of Thomas Lincoln and his widowed mother. The Lincolns and Berrys had been neighbors for 17 years.

It was on June 12, 1806 that the Berry home at Beechland was the setting of the wedding of 28-year old Thomas Lincoln and 22-year old Nancy Hanks. Guests came on horseback, and the Reverend Jesse Head arrived on his gray mare. After the infare, the new husband put his bride on a horse, and they rode away on the red clay road along the timber trails to Elizabethtown to make a home in a cabin close to the country courthouse.

Tall, slender Nancy had happiness the following year. When they knew a baby was on the way, they rode to Little Mount Baptist Church and spoke prayers of hope for the child to come. On Feb. 10, 1807, little Sarah was born.

In the same town—Elizabethtown—Abraham Lincoln was born Feb. 12, 1809.

In the fall of 1816, the year that Indiana was admitted to the Union, the Lincoln family ferried over the Ohio to the soon-to-be new state. The journey to near Pigeon Creek in a jolting, crowded wagon with a borrowed team of shaggy-coated horses, was long and tedious.

On a square patch of land that Tom had acquired and partially cleared, the family erected a half-faced camp with three sides made of poles, twigs, dried weeds and moss plastered with mud. For the next 12 months, the Lincolns endured loneliness and griding hardships. Finally, Tom put up a doorframe and hung a cured skin of a huge black bear from the frame.

Nancy and her family were church-going folk, and she read the Bible during the long evenings. The region about the home was wild. There was nothing to excite ambition for education. "Nothing," Abraham Lincoln said, "Except a devoted mother." Nancy Lincoln also taught her son perseverance, industry and the impregnable honesty for which he became famous.

During an epidemic of the mysterious milk sickness in 1818, Nancy caught the dread sickness and died. When she knew death was near, she called her children to her bedside and asked them to be good to one another, to the world, and to live by love, reverence and to worship God. She was buried in a poplar thicket on a hillside.

Many times through the years Abraham Lincoln paid tribute to her with the words: "All that I am or shall ever hope to be, I owe to my loving angel mother, God bless her."

SARAH BARRETT BOLTON

Born 1814

Sarah T. Bolton, known widely as the author of "Paddle Your Own Canoe," was the first woman to receive votes in an election in Indiana.

Her husband, Nathaniel Bolton, was a candidate for state librarian in 1851, and was elected. However, she received two write-in votes, and it wasn't until 68 years later that women were allowed to vote or hold office in Indiana.

Mrs. Bolton, an Indianapolis Innkeeper who also helped her husband to publish the Indianapolis Gazette, first newspaper in the state capital, rallied public support for women's rights to own and control separate property while married. Mrs. Bolton was a devoted friend of Indiana's May Wright Sewall and her women's rights crusade.

Born in Newport, Kentucky, in 1814, the daughter of Jonathan B. and Esther Pendleton Barrett, her full name was Sarah Tittle Barrett.

The Pendletons were related to President James Madison. The family moved to Jennings County, Indiana, and then to Madison.

Sarah had her first poem published in a Madison newspaper when she was only 13, and she continued to write poems and prose.

Her literary efforts and contributions led to her acquaintance with Nathaniel Bolton, a Madison editor. They were married and moved to Indianapolis, making the trip by horseback.

The Gazette, which they founded, was unsuccessful financially, so they opened an inn on the farm they owned. The inn was the setting of many parties, especially during sessions of the Indiana legislature.

Sarah continued to write, and for 30 years she held a place as author of both poetry and prose. Her "Paddle Your Own Canoe" was translated into eight languages.

William Cullen Bryant considered her "Left on the Battlefield" one of the greatest war poems ever written, and included it in his collection of 50 greatest war poems of all times.

Robert Dale Owen, Hoosier social reformer, described her as "the first literary woman of the Mississippi Valley."

General Lew Wallace, author of "Ben Hur," characterized her as "the first singer of true note."

One account said no poem did more to rally and inspire friends of the Union at the time of the Civil War than her "The Union Forever," of 1861.

The Indiana Federation of Clubs adopted as its official slogan lines from the first stanza of her poem, "Indiana":

"The winds of Heaven never fanned,
The circling sunlight never spanned
The borders of a fairer land
Than our own Indiana."

The Boltons enjoyed entertaining, and among some of their guests were Stephen A. Douglas, General Lew Wallace, Rayard Taylor, Horace Greeley and Robert Dale Owen.

President Franklin D. Pierce named Bolton consul to Geneva, Switzerland, in 1855, and for two years Sarah and their son and daughter were hosts to the literati of the new world then living in Geneva.

Bolton became ill and the family returned to Indianapolis where he died in 1858. Their daughter died later, and this sadness was difficult for the usually courageous woman. She lived in Beech Grove, Indiana, until her death in 1893. A park is named for her in Beech Grove.

ZERALDA WALLACE

Born 1818

Zeralda Wallace, temperance champion, was just 19 years old in 1837 when she became the bride of Indiana's Lieutenant Governor David Wallace, a man 18 years her senior.

A few days later, she became Indiana's sixth First Lady when her husband took office as Governor following the death of Governor Noah Noble.

At the same time, she became the mother of David Wallace's three young sons by a former marriage. His first wife died when she was 27 years old. David and Zeralda Wallace had six children of their own, and they took in four children of a relative.

The story of Zeralda Wallace, who lived in a world beyond her time, began in 1817 in Bourbon County, Kentucky, in the blue grass country. She was one of five high-spirited, intelligent sisters whose ancestors helped to build America. One of her grandmothers was Eliza-beth Boone, sister of Daniel, and her mother was a member of the Singleton family of Virginia.

She taught herself to read by printing each letter of the alphabet on a shingle, and went to boarding school when she was 11 years old. She became so interested in the work of her father, a physician, that she went along on horseback when he called upon his patients and helped to care for them. She read his books and talked with his learned friends.

Years later, she was credited with being one of the best educated women in jurisprudence. She was deeply religious, and she believed that Christians should do everything within their power to correct injustices of any kind. Woman suffrage and temperance were the subjects on which she centered attention.

She was the first president of the Indiana Women's Christian Temperance Union (1874-1876) and was reelected for a four year period. In the national field, she was singled out for vice-president at the first national Women's Christian Temperance Union convention, and continued in this post several years. At the second national convention, she met with favor, even from anti-suffragists, when she introduced the first suffrage resolution:

"Resolved, that since women are the greatest sufferers of the liquor traffic, and realizing that it is to be ultimately suppressed by means of the ballot, we, the Christian women of this land, in convention assembled, do pray Almighty God, and all good and true men, that the question of prohibition of the liquor traffic should be submitted to all adult citizens, irrespective of race, color or sex."

However, when she sent her husband to plea for temperance signed by 10,000 women, his reply to the note since women had no vote was: "Madam, your plea might just as well have been signed by 10,000 mice."

Thereupon she became a worker for equal rights and a great feminist.

Mrs. Wallace helped to organize the National Christian Board of Missions (Disciples), and became its first president.

In private life, she often recalled her first meeting with the three Wallace boys when she and her father were married and went to their home in Crawfordville. William was a student at Wabash College, and the two younger boys, Edward and Lew, were boarding with a Covington family. Eight-year old Lew decided he didn't want to stay with his new mother, and after meeting her, he ran away to the woods for several days. When he came home with croup, Zeralda Wallace took care of him without a word of scolding. He became devoted to her, and she was a model for the mother in Lew Wallace's novel, "Ben Hur."

Following his term as Governor, David Wallace served one term in Congress, but was defeated for a second term, and the family lived in Indianapolis where he practiced law until his death. Because of poor investments, he left his widow only 50 cents. She took in boarders, and was successful in supporting the six Wallace children and four others whom they had taken in.

Mrs. Wallace became one of the most capable public speakers in Indiana, and she was in demand "on the platform" all over the United States until she was almost 80 years old.

VIRGINIA CLAYPOOL MEREDITH
Connersville   **Born 1848**

When Virginia Claypool Meredith's husband died in 1882, she assumed charge of a 400-acre Indiana farm; and thereby began a career of firsts in the field of agriculture.

In 1889 she was invited to speak on crops and livestock production before Farmers' Institutes, then innovated by the Indiana Board of Agriculture. The board, however, decided that no woman should be paid for such work. She gave her services for two years, and then the board paid her just as they did the men.

The daughter of Austin B. and Hannah Ann Petty Claypool, she was born in 1848 on a farm near Connersville, and died in 1936. She was graduated from Glendale College near Cincinnati, Ohio, in 1866.

She wrote for farm journals and other publications, was editor of the woman's page in the "Breeders Gazette" for many years, and addressed clubs, farm organizations and civic groups. One of her most famous talks was given at Memorial Day Exercises at Purdue University in 1933, which she called "Roads of Remembrance." Later the speech was published by the University.

She was the first woman trustee of Purdue University, serving from 1921 to 1936.

In 1897 the School of Agriculture of the University of Minnesota asked her to organize the women's work on the campus, and she served there from 1897 to 1902, teaching classes and supervising all activities of women.

She was designated as "Queen of American Agriculture" by citizens of Vicksburg, Miss., in 1895, and in 1931 was cited by the Christian Science Monitor as one of six women "High on Agriculture's Role of Honor." In 1930, the University of Wisconsin honored her with its "Award of Eminent Service."

Mrs. Meredith was chairman of the Board of Lady Managers at the Chicago Columbian Exposition. She was twice elected state president of the Indiana Union of Literary Clubs; honorary president of the Indiana Federation of Clubs; Indiana Home Economics Association, Indiana Historical Association; Indiana Society of Pioneers, Altrusa Club and the League of Women Voters.

The Merediths had no children of their own, but reared as "adopted" youths, two children of friends. They were Meredith and Mary Matthews became the internationally known dean of the School of Home Economics at Purdue University.

CAROLINE SCOTT HARRISON
Born 1832

Indiana's Mrs. Benjamin Harrison was the first president-general of the Daughters of the American Revolution while serving as the nation's First Lady. (1890)

The daughter of Professor and Mrs. John W. Scott of Miami University, Ohio, she and Benjamin Harrison were married in 1853. A musician, a painter, and an outgoing woman with high ideals, she is credited with helping her husband attain the highest office in the United States.

He attended Miami University and read law in Cincinnati. He then practiced law in Indianapolis and campaigned for the Republican Party. After the Civil War—he was a Colonel of the 70th Volunteer Infantry—he became a pillar of professional and civic stature in Indianapolis.

In the Presidential election, Harrison received 100,000 fewer popular votes than Cleveland, but carried the Electoral College 233 to 168.

President and Mrs. Harrison honored the fledgling Daughters of the American Revolution with two receptions in the White House, one in October, 1891, and the other on Washington's birthday the next year.

"We have within ourselves the only element of destruction; our foes are from within, not without," Mrs. Harrison told the Daughters of the American Revolution at its first congress. "It has been said that 'the men to make a country are made by self-denial'; and is it not true that this society, to live and grow and become what it would desire to be, must be composed of self-denying women?"

Mrs. Harrison enjoyed flowers on the White House lawn, in many bouquets and in her painting. Several pieces of her work hung in the White House during her husband's administration, with flowers painted on both canvas and porcelain.

She often used orchids as a subject for her china painting and water colors, and while she was First Lady, one of her white orchid water colors was lithographed and distributed "in dedication to the mothers, wives and daughters of America."

Many years later, in 1956, during the restoration of Mrs. Harrison's portrait, a curator noticed an orchid design woven into the fabric of her lustrous gray silk gown. Hence the link between Daughters of the American Revolution members' choice of orchid corsages. Mrs. Harrison's love of the orchid inspired the members' traditional badge.

In 1894, the first Daughters of the American Revolution chapter in Indiana was organized in Indianapolis and given the First Lady's name in her honor—the Caroline Scott Harrison chapter.

Mrs. Harrison (1832-1892) died at the White House during her husband's Presidency. Following services at the White House, her body was returned to Indianapolis for traditional Presbyterian services.

The Harrisons had two children, Russell B., a mining engineer and journalist (1854-1936), and Mary (Mrs. James R. McKee) (1858-1930).

After a year of extensive restoration and renovation, the Victorian Benjamin Harrison Home, 1230 North Delaware, was formally rededicated and opened to the public on October 6, 1974. The Daughters of the American Revolution, especially the Caroline Scott Harrison chapter, form the core of volunteer workers and docents for the museum.

LUELLA SMITH MCWHIRTER
Born 1859

Mrs. Felix T. McWhirter, the first woman bank director in Indiana, pioneer in legislation, temperance and suffrage, was the first woman for whose papers the Lilly Library of Collections at Indiana University, asked her heirs.

The papers were given to be kept in perpetuity. Luella Smith McWhirter was a director of the People's Bank and Trust Co., founded by her husband in Indianapolis in 1891, serving from that time until 1940.

Preceding the 1920 session of the Indiana General Assembly, Mrs. McWhirter organized the Legislative Council of Indiana Women, representing the eight leading state organizations of Women. Governor Samuel Ralston granted the council space for a small office in the Statehouse. The council, which represented 80,000 women, was credited with aiding significantly in getting the Prohibition and Woman's Suffrage amendments to the U.S. Constitution approved by the Indiana legislature.

Mrs. McWhirter's communications network between women of Indiana caught legislators by surprise. When she let it be known that it was time to voice their opinions on legislation pertaining to women and children, the women took action. One news issue brought in 9,000 letters at a moment's notice.

During Mrs. McWhirter's term as president of the Indiana Federation of Clubs, she founded (1912) the Woman's Department Club (Indianapolis), with 700 charter members, the first departmental club in the General Federation of Women's Clubs. Mrs. McWhirter's state slogan for the federation was "The Homes of Indiana."

By Governor's appointment, she represented Indiana in the Congress of Mothers, Washington, D.C., in 1908; was an organizer and vice-president of the Woman's Franchise League of Indiana (1911-16), and vice-president of the Indiana Dry Federation (1917).

She served on President Herbert Hoover's education and service committee for the Conference on Home Building and Home Ownership (1931-32) and was Indiana chairman for Better Homes in America. She founded "The Message," official monthly magazine of the Indiana Women's Christian Temperance Union, and was its editor for 45 years. She was a charter member of the Indiana branch, National League of American Pen Women, and the Woman's Press Club of Indiana.

One of her chief interests beyond her family was the Methodist Church.

Her daughter, Susan McWhirter Ostrom, distringuished journalist (columnist 50 years for The Indianapolis News), civic and church worker, said of her mother: "She loved others and seemed to have a God-given sixth sense to see potentials and abilities in other women whom she inspired to accomplish things they admittedly never thought they could—all this in an era when women were just beginning to emerge from the kitchen. But withal Mother's public career, she never lost her femininity or charm or exalted ideals of wifehood and motherhood."

Her other children: Luella S. (Mrs. Frank F. Hurchins) who died in 1966, high school teacher, world traveler, church missionary worker; Ethel T. (Mrs. Parker Wise), and after his death (Mrs. Thomas B. Scoggins, Nashville, Tennessee) died in 1967 (she had been a national Young Women's Christian Association secretary); Felix Marcus McWhirter, (who succeeded his father) founder of the now Peoples Bank & Trust Company, Indianapolis (now on board of directors).

GENE STRATTON PORTER

Born 1862

Gene Stratton Porter waded shallow rivers, fought the quicksand of lake shores, worked in slime of swamps and marshes and carried 40-pound cameras and 10-foot ladders across fields from the first dove of March to October's latest migrant. She gathered material for 23 novels and nature studies of the Limberlost which sold more than 10 million copies.

Today the Limberlost is an Indiana state memorial to the famous author.

When Gene Stratton Porter was a teen-ager, a gangling Hoosier trapper named "Limber Jim" Corbus wandered into a nameless swamp and was lost in quicksand. Word went out that "Limber-Jim's Lost," or "Limber Lost." In time, the wild, tangled area in northern Indiana became known as Limberlost.

Geneva Stratton, whose name as a child was shortened to Gene, was one of twelve children born to Mary Schallenberger and Mark Stratton, an ordained minister who conducted services at a little church on his farm. Her birth date was 1863.

During a summer holiday at Sylvan Lake in 1880, she met her husband-to-be, Charles Darwin Porter, a druggist who later became president of the Bank of Geneva, Indiana. The Porters lived first at Decatur, Indiana, where their daughter, Jeannette, was born. Then they built the now famous Limberlost cabin at the edge of a swamp in Geneva, and from the swamp's borders, wildlife and wild flowers literally tumbled into the literary life of the author.

Her first book was "The Song of the Cardinal," a haunting story in which the mating of brilliantly feathered birds brought realization of love into the lives of an aged farmer and his wife.

She studied all nature with the same intense absorption she put into her writing, and she had an acute sense of hearing sounds afield that an ordinary hiker left unnoticed. The discovery of a black vulture nest led to the writing of "Freckles," published in 1904. She wrote a series of bird articles for The Ladies Home Journal, and soon afterward wrote "At the Foot of the Rainbow," and "Birds of the Bible." In 1909, "A Girl of the Limberlost," received world-wide acclaim. It was translated into Arabic, and later seven other languages as well as braille.

The author turned to the life of her own father for the central character in "The Harvester."

At the second Limberlost Cabin in "Wildflower Woods," an area of 150 acres, the author set out 3,000 plants, trees, shrubs and vines in two years. "Michael O'Halloran," "Friends in Feathers," "A Daughter of the Land," and "Homing With the Birds," soon were published. A strict disciplinarian, the author devoted a certain number of hours daily to writing.

In 1920, Gene Stratton Porter moved to Catalina Island, California, where she wrote "The Keeper of the Bees," and "The Magic Garden." She had plans for many more volumes, but Mrs. Porter was fatally injured in 1924 in an automobile accident in Los Angeles.

Her daughter, Jeannette Porter Meehan, paid tribute to her mother in "The Lady of Limberlost." "I have seen her stop the horse, clamber down from the buggy and straighten a wild flower broken by some careless foot, pat the dirt around it, prop it up with a stick or stone, and give it a drink from her thermos bottle."

KATE MILNER RABB

Born 1866

Kate Milner Rabb born 1866, grew up in Rockport, Indiana, a town steeped in the lore of the Ohio River, proud of the fact that it was from there that Lincoln set forth on his famous flatboat trip.

Her father was the town's esteemed doctor, and readers of her books and columns credited much of the human element in her writing to the fact that as a little girl, red pigtails flying and nose bridged with freckles, she rode in the buggy with her father to make calls, and talked to patients.

At Indiana University, she was a classmate of William Lowe Bryan, later president and president-emeritus of the University. He commented that her "love of books helped her to grow in fine appreciation of what was best, to her masterly sense of what was fine and finest."

While at the University, she became engaged to Albert Rabb, and while he was studying law, she took a masters degree at Indiana, and then taught school in Jeffersonville and Rockport.

She sent stories to her hometown paper while in college, but Mrs. Rabb did not begin to write seriously until after her marriage in 1891 when the couple established their home in Indianapolis.

Her first book, "National Epics," was published in 1896, and it was followed in 1900 by "The Boer Boy," work of fiction translated from the German. In 1907 she edited a five-volume "Wit and Humor of America," published by Bobbs-Merrill Publishing Co., Indianapolis, for whom she read manuscripts many years. Her "Indiana Coverlet Weavers" was published by the Indiana Historical Society in 1928. In the 1890s she edited a weekly magazine, "Indiana Women."

Following the death of her husband in 1918, she began a weekly historical column in The Indianapolis Star, creating through research a mythical person one "John Parsons," who during the Harrison campaign used the stage coach, the canal boat, the steamboat, rode horseback and even ventured on the new fangled railroad. Many of Mrs. Rabb's close friends knew that the 1840 "tour" was fiction, and delighted in calling her attention to a daguerreotype when they were visitors in her home and asking, "Isn't that John Parsons?" The idea became so real that when the diary was put in book form, the same daguerreotype was used as the frontispiece.

Her next column was "The Old Town," which ran three times a week and traced the history of Indianapolis. She is remembered best, however, for her "The Hoosier Listening Post," which ran every day in The Indianapolis Star on the editorial page from 1920 until 1937. It provided good, earthy information, much of it in letters and diaries of pre-Civil War days. It touched on such varied subjects as feather beds, Hoosier wool picking, colonial literary societies, Jenny Lind's visit to Madison, covered bridges and old cemeteries. She received more than 3,000 letters per year and acknowledged them all. She knew every town in the state, and she made many pilgrimages to historical places.

Her children, both highly esteemed citizens, were Martha (Mrs. William Hobbs) and Albert Rabb Jr., attorney.

She was president of the Woman's Press Club of Indiana, active in the Daughters of the American Revolution, the Contemporary Club and was a member of Indiana Historical Commission.

She died in 1937.

Iowa

Nickname: The Hawkeye State

State Flower: Wild Rose

State Bird: American Goldfinch

Photos

1. Early covered bridge, Madison County
2. Old Capital
3. Milles sculpture at D.M. Art Center
4. The Shot Tower at Dubuque
5. The old meets the new at Amana
6. Little Brown Church at Nashua

Committee Members

Chairman—Mrs. W. W. Sackett, Spencer

Iowa

AMELIA JENKS BLOOMER
Born 1818

Three women became brides in 1840 who were destined to influence the world in contrasting ways; Queen Victoria married Prince Albert; Elizabeth Cady was wed to Henry Stanton and Amelia Jenks became Mrs. Dexter C. Bloomer. The last two weddings had one thing in common—the word obey was deliberately omitted from the women's vows.

Amelia Jenks Bloomer is the name of a valiant Iowa woman who pioneered many fronts in a struggle against prejudice. In April, 1855 she moved with her husband, an editor and a lawyer from Ohio to Council Bluffs, Iowa, at that time a city of 2,000 people. The beauty of the land and its promise caught her imagination. Then Iowa law in variance with laws in many other states held that women can hold and own property both real and personal. This appealed greatly to Amelia who in New York and Ohio had owned, edited and published *The Lily*, a widely read and quoted publication, which printed under its banner head the slogan—The Emancipation of Women from Intemperance, Injustice, Prejudice and Bigotry. Contributors to *The Lily*, published twenty five years before the enfranchisement of women in 1919, were her good friends—Elizabeth Cady Stanton, Lucretia Mott, Lucy Stone and Susan B. Anthony among others.

Upon moving to Council Bluffs she joined forces with Iowa's rights advocates becoming the first president of the Iowa Suffrage Movement in 1870. Carrie Chapman Catt of Mason City, Iowa, her co-worker and good friend and Amelia were in demand as speakers though limited in accepting engagements by the difficulty of travel. Amelia practically demonstrated women's rights to fill any place for which she had capacity. For half a century persistent, challenging, she spoke out for women's rights not only to the ballot, but to equal opportunity in educational and professional careers including the ministry, equal pay and dress reform. What a forerunner she was of the women's groups of today.

Her name became known the country over by an editorial sparring match with an opponent of women's suffrage, of a costume—short skirt and pantaloons gathered in below the knees, called bloomers. Amelia did not advocate men and women dressing alike but she inaugurated a radical reform in women's clothing so that they might be the free, healthy beings God made them instead of the corseted, crippled dragged down creatures of the costumes they had worn. Public lingo had given the costume her name—an embarrassment to her because it drew attention from what was of far greater importance—the question of women's right to better education, to a wider field of employment and better pay.

In Council Bluffs with her husband and sister, her son and daughter she set up a home with an open door for teachers, ministers, temperance speakers, nieces and nephews. She wrote back to New York—"we see Indians occasionally, but they are friendly and enjoy our hospitality."

She is buried in Fairview Cemetery in a grassy plot overlooking Council Bluffs, Iowa and Omaha, Nebraska. On her tombstone is printed *A Pioneer in Woman's Enfranchisement*. It is the grave of the true woman, the earnest reformer, the faithful Christian—one of Iowa's "greats."

ANN HARLAN

Born 1824

Ann Eliza Peck was born in Indiana in 1824. Orphaned before she was 5, Ann was raised by an uncle, Dr. Knight. In Greencastle at Asbury College, the forerunner of Indiana University, she met James Harlan, who on August 20, 1845 was one of 11 graduates to receive a BA degree. It is interesting that the total cash expenditures of his entire college course—from June 1, 1841 to August 20, 1845 totalled $266.72. On November 9, 1845 James and Ann were married and moved to the family farm to assist in making maple sugar. In mid March, 1846, Harlan accepted the principalship of Iowa College which had been incorporated by an act of the territorial legislature in 1843. It later became the State University of Iowa. Rather than take the expensive trip by stagecoach from Indiana to Iowa, the Harlans bought a sturdy horse and in an open buggy made the 12 day trip to their new home. In 1853 they moved from Iowa City to Mount Pleasant, where James Harlan became president of Iowa Wesleyan College. Their permanent residence was always there although for many years they also had a home in Washington. Harlan was a powerful force in Congress for 16 years, and in 1865 was appointed by Lincoln to his cabinet. He served as Secretary of the Interior under President Andrew Johnson. During those years, the Harlan home was the scene of many brilliant afternoon and evening receptions. The absence of dancing or liquor in any form apparently added to, instead of detracting from the pleasure with which these receptions were attended. Entertained were the Cabinet officers, members of foreign embassies, Senators, Representatives, military men and distinguished citizens, many of whom were accompanied by their wives and daughters.

In Washington the Harlans and Lincolns became close friends enjoying Sunday drives and family outings on the Potomac. Ann and James Harlan escorted Mrs. Lincoln to her husband's second inauguration and they were with her at his bedside following the assassination at Ford's Theater.

Through President Lincoln and Secretary of War Stanton, Ann was given a pass to cross the lines at Shiloh following a battle fought near the Tennessee River April 6, 7, 1862. Nearly 3500 men were killed, 20,000 wounded. Iowa regiments suffering the greatest casualties. At Shiloh General Halleck tried to turn her back but her pass signed by Stanton outranked him and she became one of the Florence Nightingales of the Civil War devoting all her time and energy and the money which the family exchequer would permit to visiting and caring for sick and wounded soldiers in the field and providing good clean food from the kitchens. Her first hand knowledge of conditions transmitted to the Government at Washington through her husband had much influence in awakening the nation to the crying need for proper care of its soldiers.

The Lincoln and Harlan families always close were united when Robert Todd Lincoln married Mary Harlan in 1868. They had 3 children—2 daughters and Abraham who was affectionately known as Jack. He was described as a handsome, gentle manly boy. When his father was appointed U.S. Minister to Great Britain and the family moved to London, Jack, preparing for Harvard went to Paris to study French. He became ill there and returned to London and died at the age of 16. A tennis enthusiast, he had left his net with a friend in Mount Pleasant until he returned. He never came back for it.

Robert Lincoln was president of the Pullman Co., in Chicago but returned after to Harlan House in Mt. Pleasant. The lovely home is now a historical museum.

Ann Harlan died at Old Point Comfort in Virginia on September 4, 1884 and was buried with military honors at Forest Home Cemetery in Mt. Pleasant.

ANNIE TURNER WHITTENMYER
Born 1827

One of the older children of a large family Annie Turner was born August 26, 1827 at Sandy Springs, Ohio. She spent some of her early years and had grade school education in Kentucky but graduated from a seminary in Ohio. In 1847 she was married to William Wittenmyer, an older man who was a wealthy merchant. The family moved in 1850 to Keokuk, Iowa where Mrs. Wittenmyer helped organize a Methodist church and established a free school for poor children. Shortly before the outbreak of the Civil War her husband died. The Wittenmyers had had 4 children losing 3 in infancy, Charles Albert surviving.

Since Keokuk was a point of embarkation for Civil War troops Annie was in a key position to observe their needs. She worked with the Western Sanitary Commission of St. Louis until the Iowa legislature in 1862 approved a bill for two Sanitary agents in the state and she received one of the appointments. Entrusting the care of her son to her mother and sister, she journeyed to the battles lines and with a surgeon and two nurses worked around the clock helping with the wounded at Vicksburg and distributing supplies to Union hospitals. General Grant assigned her a house to use as headquarters and there she organized diet kitchens, dispensing large sums of money entrusted to her by the legislature and loyal Iowans, who had heard her pleas for needed drugs and supplies. She recruited some one hundred gentlewomen who she stressed were not to be cooks or servants. The ladies supervised soldiers detailed for the physical work and made sure the food actually reached the patients. Ultimately her kitchens became an accepted part of the military hospital system.

In visiting hospitals she saw men die begging for care for the children they were leaving homeless. In October 1863 on a trip to Washington she persuaded the government to turn over to the Iowa Orphans Home Association some new barracks at Davenport and a large quantity of hospital supplies. And then the Annie Wittenmyer Home for Orphans came into being. In her era orphans of the Civil War were carried for at the cost of 33 cents a day. Through the years countless numbers of orphans have called the Annie Wittenmyer Home of Davenport home. Within the Methodist denomination she played a leading part in establishing in 1868 the

Ladies and Pastors Christian Union through which women under the guidance of their local pastors would visit and aid the sick and needy.

When the *Woman's Crusade* against alcohol swept the midwest in the winter of 1873-4 Annie Wittenmyer quickly joined the movement and was elected Woman's Crusade Temperance Union's first president. In 1878 she presented to Congress bulky petitions calling for investigation of the liquor traffic and enactment of a federal prohibition amendment. During her five year presidency of Woman's Crusade Temperance Union local unions, encompassing 26,000 members had been formed.

By this time the aging Mrs. Wittenmyer had returned to a cause associated with the Civil War. In 1889-90 she was president of the Woman's Relief Corps, the women's auxiliary of the Grand Army of the Republic. During her presidency she established in Ohio, a national Woman's Relief Corps Home for ex-nurses and for the widows and mothers of veterans. In 1892 her lobbying helped induce Congress to pass a bill to pension former war nurses.

After the late 1880's Annie Wittenmyer lived with her son in Pennsylvania. Her 70th birthday brought congratulations and gifts from all parts of the nation. Having inherited from her husband a substantial estate, Mrs. Wittenmyer experienced a degree of independence unusual for a woman of her day. Highly articulate and literate, she combined strong qualities of leadership with a persuasive approach which gained her many concessions. She died February 2, 1900 and is buried in Edgewood Cemetery, Sanatoga, Pa.

CORA BUSSEY HILLIS
Bloomfield   **Born 1858**

Cora Bussey Hillis, the daughter of Cyrus and Ellen Kiser Bussey was born in Bloomfield, Iowa on August 8, 1858. At the outbreak of the Civil War, her father resigned from the Iowa Senate to become Colonel of the Third Iowa Cavalry. He commanded Union forces at the important battle of Pea Ridge in Arkansas. At the close of the war with the rank of Brevet Major General he moved his family to New Orleans. There they were prominently identified with the business and civic activities of the city. The Bussey home on beautiful St. Charles Avenue was noted for its hospitality. General Bussey was a close friend of Ulysses S. Grant, later the President. In the Hillis home were many Grant mementos.

In 1875 Cora graduated from Sylvester Larned Institute and in 1880 was married to Isaac Lea Hillis, a graduate of the University of Michigan law school. They returned to Iowa in 1884 locating in Des Moines in a lovely home fascinating to their children's friends because it had an elevator. She joined the Des Moines Woman's Club serving as president and on the

board for many years. During her husband's term as Mayor of Des Moines, she established the first public bathing beach in Des Moines; established a Civic Center; obtained the first city plan (which the Secretary of the Greater Des Moines committee said advanced the development of the city by 50 years) and worked for the development of a juvenile court law in Iowa.

In the spring of 1899 the Congress of Mothers was holding its third annual meeting in Washington, D.C., and Mrs. Hillis attended carrying with her a letter of introduction from the Des Moines Woman's Club and one from the Women's Press Club. When she realized the group was considering having its next meeting outside of the Capitol she extended in the name of the Des Moines Woman's Club an invitation to meet in Iowa in 1900. Mrs. Birney, national president accepted. Hospitable Des Moines was ecstatic. This was the first national meeting the city had ever hosted.

One thousand delegates were to be entertained. Schools were to be closed for a week so teachers could attend the sessions, the reception was to be held in the state capitol. "Think of it ladies!" Mrs. Birney exclaimed, "We'll have the legislative halls all to ourselves!"

On May 21st, 1900 the fourth Congress of Mothers opened at the auditorium in Des Moines taxing to the utmost the capacity of that huge building. Interest was not confined to Des Moines, however, for papers all over the nation published detailed reports of the challenging meetings and outstanding speakers material (the success of that event prompted a drive for other national meetings and led the way to Des Moines becoming established as a convention city).

At the close of the meeting Mrs. Hillis organized the first branch of the Congress of Parents and Teachers in Iowa and for six years served as its president. Her last official act as a representative was a stirring speech delivered to thousands of men and women at Chautauqua, New York on July 27. She spoke of the educational value of cooperation between parents and teachers and of plans for the observance of American Education Week.

During the years from 1908-10, Cora Hillis served on President Roosevelt's Country Life Commission. In 1913 she fostered the *Save the Baby* campaign and was personally in charge of the fresh air camp for mothers and sick babies.

After years of preliminary work she organized in 1914 the Iowa Child Welfare Association. This group, made up of 30 different state organizations, with the Iowa Congress of Parents and Teachers in the foreground saw pass in 1917 an appropriation bill for the establishment of a Child Welfare Research Station at Iowa City, the first in the U.S. to be incorporated in a state university. A bill introduced in the legislature two years before asking for a $25,000 grant had failed and the money instead was appropriated to build a new sheep barn at the Iowa Fairgrounds. The Child Welfare Research Station became the roots of Iowa University's present complex for research and study of child development and behaviour. Children's Hospital at Iowa City is noted the world over. Past "greats" on its staff have been Dr. Albert Steindler, orthopedic surgeon, and Dr. Wendell Johnson, noted specialist in speech disorders.

Cora Hillis was killed in a tragic auto accident, August 12, 1924. Her name for newer generations of Des Moines children and parents is perpetuated in Hillis Elementary School. She was one of Iowa's great women of all time, recognized as such recently when the Iowa League of Women Voters officially placed her on the honor roll of Iowa's greatest women.

FLORENCE CALL COWLES
Algona   Born 1861

On August 28, 1861 Florence Call was born in Algona to Nancy Eliza and Ambrose Call, a pioneer of Northwest Iowa and one of the founding families of Algona. This was a time when the process of converting Iowa's prairie wilderness into the things of today had just begun. There was crudity of living conditions, deprivation, loneliness, peril but great opportunity. Caves in hillsides became schools and from them grew our modern colleges. Literary societies were created in villages and they were the beginnings of Iowa's vast contribution to the arts.

Florence was a member of the class of 1884 Northwestern University, Evanston, the earliest class to include women students. On December 4, 1884 she was married to Gardner Cowles the young man who was destined to be the builder of the *Des Moines Register and Tribune* newspaper empire. They moved to Des Moines in 1903 and immediately Florence Cowles became active in the Des Moines Woman's Club, D.A.R. P.E.O., Iowa Press & Authors Club and Conver-

sational Club. She was a leader in the literature department of the Iowa Federation of Women's Club, served the Des Moines club as president in 1917-18 and was a long term member of its board of directors.

Mrs. Cowles was the author of two books. The first was composed of letters written to members of her family while traveling abroad and is called *Foreign Skies Through Mother's Eyes.* The second book *Early Algona.* is an historical account of the settling of Kossuth County in northern Iowa. She had taught in the rural schools and Algona Academy so she had first hand information. Knowing and loving Iowa because she grew up with it—her story is not only factual but appreciative.

The Gardner Cowles had a large and interesting family. Gardner II was Editor and Publisher of the *Des Moines Register* and President of the company. He has also headed the Cowles Broadcasting Company, Cowles Publications (*Look Magazine* among others) and the Cowles Foundation.

John Cowles has been editor of the Minneapolis Star & Tribune Company; president of the Cowles Foundation; president of the Carnegie Endowment for International Peace; had an Eisenhower Exchange Fellowship and was given the Centennial Award by Northwestern University in 1951. His son John (grandson of Florence) is a director of the Walker Art Institute and headed the drive to bring the great Tyrone Guthrie Theater to Minneapolis. The Twin Cities has repeatedly recognized his contributions to life in Minnesota.

Russell Cowles is a painter of note. His works are in permanent collections of Dartmouth College, Swope Gallery, Des Moines Art Center, the Pennsylvania Academy of Fine Arts and other leading national exhibitions.

It was said of Helen Cowles Le Cron when she was editor of the Book Page of the *Des Moines Sunday Register* that she had done more to encourage literary output through the state than any other person. Her own stories appeared in *Life, Judge, Munsey's,* etc. Among her protegees were Phil Strong (author of *State Fair,*) Thomas Duncan (*Gus the Great*), MacKinlay Kanton *Best Years of Our Lives, Spirit Lake, Andersonville* and others. Literate Iowans avidly read Helen Le Cron's book page.

The son of Florence Cowles Kruidenier, David Kruidenier, is now managing editor of the *Des Moines Register & Tribune*.

The whole Cowles family has left an imprint upon Iowa and the nation. The long life Florence Call Cowles spent in Iowa—she died March 23, 1950 at the age of 88—invested in Iowa, and covered the span of her state's development. Her children and grandchildren are carrying on her traditions.

GRACE NOLL CROWELL
Inland   **Born 1877**

"I glittered it!" The glad cry rang through an old rambling farmhouse in Iowa and with it an absorbed little girl began to be a poet. She had been playing with a pewter tea set and after washing the teapot she had rubbed it until it glowed like silver in the sun. How marvelously Grace Noll Crowell by magazine, book, platform and radio has kept her promise. She has done more to "glitter" the everyday job of running a home than any other poet in all the world.

Grace Noll, one of 7 children, was born on a farm near Inland, Iowa, October 31, 1877. They were a family of staunch Methodists who never missed a prayer meeting or a Sunday service. After attending Norton Academy and German

College, she married Norman Crowell, a native of Dallas on September 4, 1901. They returned to Texas in 1919 and there Grace started writing vigorously sometimes turning out poems as frequently as one every 44 hours. In 1925 her first volume *White Fire* won the Poetry Society of Texas award and in 1936 in observance of the Texas Centennial the state senate elected her Poet Laureate of their state. Honors came in rapid succession. She became outstanding poet of the nation in 1938, joining among others, Edwin Arlington Robinson, Carl Sandburg and Robert Frost, former recipients of that distinguished award. In 1940 Baylor University conferred an honorary doctor of literature degree upon her. Her poems often set to music appeared regularly in Scribners, Good Housekeeping, Century, Hollands, New York Times, Christian Science Monitor, Chicago Herald, McCalls and others. "Poetry," she once said, "should do something to the heart." as witness

I have found such joy in simple things
A plain, clean room, a nut-brown loaf of bread
A cup of milk, a kettle as it sings
The shelter of a roof above my head
And in a leaf-faced square upon a floor
Where yellow sunlight glimmers through a door
Oh, I have found such joy! I wish I might
Tell every woman who goes seeking far
For some elusive, feverish delight

That very close to home the great joys are
These fundamental things—old as the race
Yet never, through the ages commonplace

By a unanimous vote of the National Mothers Day Commission, Grace Noll Crowell was named American Mother in 1938, the fourth woman to be so honored. Her husband Norman, their three fine sons and lovers of her poetry the world over applauded the selection and shared in the celebrations in her honor. Two sons Dean the banker and Reid the writer and artist continue to live in Dallas. The third, Dr. Norman Crowell is on the faculty of the University of New Mexico in Albuquerque.

Grace Crowell died at the age of 91 on March 31, 1969 in Dallas having written more than 5000 poems. She had published 40 volumes of verse in her lifetime. Indeed she "glittered" the commonplace for millions. Her poetry has been read over countless radio stations by request of people from all over America, Canada, Australia, the world. Letters begging for a particular poem came from tiny huts and great apartment buildings, from simple folk to royalty. Iowa proudly claims Grace Noll Crowell—her beginnings were in our sturdy midwestern culture, her relatives are our neighbors and good friends in Clay County.

JESSIE FIELD SHAMBAUGH
Page County   **Born 1881**

Of her mother, Jessie Field Shambaugh, Ruth Watkins wrote: "It seems the whole 4-H concept of quiet goals reached through careful nurturing and appreciation of individual aptitudes and achievements could only have been conceived by a woman for women have always been 'brightening the corners', discovering ways to work little everyday miracles to give life wider dimensions, deeper roots and shinier values."

Jessie Field was born June 26, 1881 in Page County, Iowa. She went to High School in Shenandoah and earned a B.A. degree from Tabor College in 1903. Doane College of Crete, Nebraska, conferred on her the honorary degree of Doctor of Humane Letters. After teaching in Wisconsin and Montana, she lived in New York for four years. There she was on the staff of the Y.W.C.A., as Secretary for work in the rural areas. In 1906 she returned to Iowa as Superintendent of Schools in Page County. A new chap-

ter began in the scholastic and agricultural history of the area. She correlated the practical arts of farming and of home making into the regular studies of reading, writing and arithmetic. Feeling it was necessary to find rainy day activities for students in the rural areas necessarily somewhat isolated from one another, she turned to the country's leading crop—corn—and started the boys in crop judging. The girls were encouraged in home making projects. She felt it was necessary for young people to learn to compete with one another in many ways to learn what each could do to make life in the country better. She entered her boy judging team in the corn judging contest held at Ames, Iowa's agricultural college. They took first place. Page County boys continued to win trophies. 4-H was born and Jessie Field became known as the Founder of 4-H, or the Corn Lady and was acclaimed "the world's greatest missionary for good."

Feeling that 10 day summer camps would provide more intensive training for the young competitors, she organized boys and girls camps. A forerunner of Boys State and Girls State of American Legion and Auxiliary many of the same principles were stressed. A senate was made of a boy representative from each tent with the camp director presiding—self government first hand.

At 4-H meetings and summer camps the young people experimented with new machinery—the Babcock milk tester and the seed corntester and grew varieties of corn in tin cans to observe growth and qualities. It was a different world then because of the slowness in travel, dirt roads, few cars, the difficulty in com-

munication, no t.v., few radios but parents learned from their children and strides were made.

The 3H pin, which Jessie Field awarded to those who achieved was accompanied by a leaflet entitled *Because you Tried*, the final stanza of which reads, "I wish for you eyes that can see how beautiful the open country is; minds that can understand how great a thing it is to be a good farmer or a good homemaker and hearts that can catch the vision of the things that can be done to make life in the country even better. . . ." To the 3H's, Head, Heart and Hands was eventually added the fourth H— Home. The movement spread from Page County, through all of Iowa and eventually the world.

The original Country Girl's Creed hangs in the Page County Lodge of the Iowa 4-H Foundation in Boone. Recited during each meeting by the millions of 4-H members, it starts:

"I am glad I live in the country. I love its beauty and its spirit. I rejoice in the things I can do as a country girl for my home and my neighborhood. . . ."

Jessie Field Shambaugh and Ira had two children: William H., a C.P.A. in Des Moines, who graduated from Cornell College in 1942. They have four children, and Phyllis Ruth Field Watkins, an Iowa University graduate who has had a career as an artist, photographer, writer and most important—the mother of 7 children. Heather, their youngest (11 years old) wrote recently "I am glad for all the things my grandmother did for her home, her community and her world—but even if she had done none of those, she still would have been a wonderful gramma."

Jessie Shambaugh died in December, 1971.

DOROTHY DEEMER HOUGHTON
Red Oak   **Born 1890**

Dorothy, the daughter of Judge and Mrs. Horace Deemer was born in Red Oak, Iowa March 11, 1890. Judge Deemer served for 23 years on the Iowa Supreme Court. She was graduated from Wellesley College in Massachusetts and holds honorary degrees from Coe College in Cedar Rapids, Iowa, Tarkio College in Missouri and American University of Washington, D.C. She served on the Iowa Board of Regents from

1939-1951; was an active member of the Board of Women's Medical College in Philadelphia and a board member of International Christian University in Tokyo.

Mrs. Houghton was national president of the General Federation of Women's Clubs with its more than 3 million members from 1950-52. During these years she led groups of U.S. clubwomen on world tours and entertained royal visitors and clubwomen dignitaries at General Federation Headquarters in Washington. In 1953 she was appointed by President Eisenhower to act as Director of the Office of Refugees, Migratory and Voluntary Assistance, a job involving hospitalization, integration or migration of 40,000,000 refugees. She served in this capacity until 1958 and during those years was decorated by four countries: the Netherlands, the Federal Republic of Germany, Greece and Italy.

Following the 1956 presidential election Mrs. Houghton was placed on the Electoral College Board and became president, the first women to be so honored. One of her prized possessions was a gavel given to her bearing the same inscription as those given to President Eisenhower and Vice President Nixon.

She was Iowa Mother of the Year in 1948 and often was the spokesman for the American Mothers Committee. In 1949 she was voted Iowa's most distinguished citizen. In 1964 the State University of Iowa conferred upon her their Distinguished Service Award, the citation saying in part . . . Dorothy Deemer Houghton has given her life to service, including a dozen years as a regent of the institutions of higher learning in Iowa. Drawing upon some infinite well of energy and zest and human affection, she has been organizer and inspirator to legions, and proud servant of presidents and monarchs.

... This University is proud to acknowledge the leadership of her example with this Distinguished Service Award.

In addition to P.E.O., Mrs. Houghton is a member of the Shakespeare Society at Wellesley College; D.A.R.; Zeta Phi Eta (National speech outs fraternity); Pi Beta Phi; Red Oak Club; New York Women's Republican Club and the Congregational Church. She was on the Board of UNICEF for 14 years; Unesco for 4 years; has served on the boards of CARE; the Tolstoy Foundation; the International Rescue Committee; the U.S. Committee for Refugees; the American Safety Council; Iowa Historical Society and was board chairman of the American Library Association.

The Houghtons had four fine children: Deemer of Red Oak, followed his father Hiram Cole Houghton into the family bank; Cole of Bethesda, Maryland; Clark, a graduate of University of Iowa Law School of the First National Bank of Iowa City and Joan, (Mrs. John Williams) of Washington, D.C.

An editorial in the *Des Moines Register* at the time of her death in 1972 regretted that she died four days before the Iowa legislature ratified the Equal Rights for Women Amendment, saying "Dorothy Houghton fought for equal rights for her sex even as she was establishing a worldwide reputation for herself in other areas of service. . . . She never took the view that everything ws better in the good old days. Always her thoughts seemed to be on the future and how to make this world a better one. Even though she hobnobbed at times with royalty, she never lost her common touch with the average citizen."

She died in 1972 at the age of 82, still not ready for a rocking chair.

RUTH BUXTON SAYRE
Indianola   **Born 1896**

Ruth Buxton was born January 25, 1896 in Indianola, Iowa. She earned her B.A. degree in Simpson College there and was subsequently awarded honorary degrees from Simpson in 1942 and 1955 and an honorary LLD from Iowa State University, Ames in 1952. Married to Raymond Sayre, her college classmate she made the 600 acre farm he operated her home for thirty-five years. As the only woman member ap-

pointed by President Eisenhower to his national agricultural advisory commission, she has received national recognition for her knowledge of agricultural problems and her many years of interest in and service to farm people.

As a bride Ruth persuaded the women of her township to become interested in rural welfare. She has been active in widening the horizons of farm people first as County, District and State chairman of the Farm Bureau Women's activities and then as regional director, vice-president and president of the Associated Women of the American Farm Bureau Federation. In 1936 Ruth Sayre was elected state and then national president of the Master Farmers Homemakers Guild. In 1939 she was sent to London as a delegate to the international meeting of the Associated Country Women of the World. In 1947 she attended their meeting in Amsterdam and was elected president of that great organization which numbers over six million members. She held this post until 1953 during which time she traveled all over the world and was the guest of many foreign governments. With an active interest in people and their problems, she brought back to America knowledge and a warm appreciation of the life and the thinking of people who live on farms the world over.

Mrs. Sayre has held important posts in Unesco of the United Nations and F.A.O., the Food and Agriculture Organization. She has represented the Associated Country Women of the World at the Geneva Conference of non-public consultative organizations to the United Nations. In 1949 she visited Germany at the in-

vitation of the Military government who were doing a survey of rural women's organizations.

All of her activities were not confined to farm related groups for she served on the advisory committee to the Secretary of Labor, became chairman of the Home and Family Life committee for Iowa P.T.A., and was appointed by President Roosevelt to the National Civilian Defense Committee. In 1955 she was a member of the National Safety Council.

To be selected Iowa Mother in 1950 was of special significance because the Sayres were parents of four outstanding children: William is Vice President of the Illinois Continental Bank of Chicago. He and his wife Ruth Ann have four children. John is an interior decorator in the J. C. Penney organization in Des Moines; Alice is with the U.S. Information Service and is stationed at Amman, Jordan. Helen who with her husband George Coolidge had two children, is deceased.

Ruth Sayre has had articles published in Womens Press (Y.W.C.A.), Farmers Magazine (Canada), American Home Economic Magazine and countless Farm Bureau and Country Women of the World publications. She won the Freedom Award in 1952 for an article in Farm Journal.

With dynamic energy and contagious enthusiasm she has generated tremendous interest in national and foreign relations and in the human side of international relations. With a singleness of purpose she has steadfastly and courageously cleared away prejudices and restraints to broaden the horizons of all who know her. Her philosophy may well be summed up in a paragraph from one of the reports she wrote shortly after a trip to the Far East.

"I believe that in all human beings there is a divinity that, if not thwarted, strives for a better life. . . . I feel that it is our role to call up from despair the spirit of those who have lost faith in human brotherhood. And backed by the spiritual credit of our own belief in progress and freedom, we can stop the run on the bank of faith and face the challenge of our time."

Ruth Sayre continues to live in Indianola.

MARY LOUISE SMITH
Eddyville   Born 1914

Mary Louise Epperson was born October 6, 1914 in Eddyville, Iowa. She attended the University of Iowa, graduating in 1935 with a B.A. degree in social work administration. While a student at the University, she met Elmer Smith, then a medical student. They were married in 1934.

In the 1940's Mary Louise Smith began her Republican Party work as a volunteer campaign worker and was elected precinct committeewoman and county vice chairman. She was also active in the Iowa Federation of Republican Women, serving in leadership positions on all levels of that organization. In 1964 she was Iowa Vice Chairman of the Presidential Campaign and in 1966 became a member of a special sub-committee of the Republican National Committee on Convention Reforms. She served as delegate-at-large and on the committee on Arrangements and Platform Committee for the 1968 and 1972 Republican National Conventions. In 1972 she was national co-chairman of the Physicians Committee for the Presidential campaign and co-chairman of the Iowa committee for the re-election of the President.

In her term as Republican National Committee co-chairman, Mrs. Smith was a member of the Executive Committee and the Republican Coordinating Committee and will retain her membership in both groups as chairman. Mrs. Smith also has served as one of two vice chairmen of the Rule 29 committee which was mandated by the 1972 National Convention to review and study party rules and procedures. She is a member of the Bipartisan Committee to Study Methods of Financing Quadrennial National Nominating Conventions.

Outside of her political activities, Mary Louise Smith has been active in a wide variety of civic and community affairs. In Eagle Grove where the Smith family resided for 18 years prior to 1963, she was active in the Community Chest, the Board of Education and the Mental Health Center of North Iowa. In 1961-63 she was a member of the Iowa Commission for the Blind, serving as chairman for the latter half of the term; she was also a member of the Governor's Commission on Aging. In 1969 Mrs. Smith was a member of the U.S. delegation to the 15th session of the Population Commission of the Economic and Social Council of the United Na-

tions in Geneva. In 1970-71 she was a member of the Presidents Commission for the 25th Anniversary of the United Nations. In 1973, she served on the U.S. delegation to the third extraordinary session of the general conference of Unesco in Paris.

Mrs. Smith is a member of the Congregational Church, P.E.O. Sisterhood; Kappa Alpha Theta social sorority and the National Women's Political Caucus. She was one of six co-convenors of the first Iowa Women's Political Caucus.

Dr. Elmer Smith, formerly in general practice and having served two tours of duty in Vietnam as a volunteer physician, is now consultant to the Medical Bureau of the Iowa State Department of Social Services. They are the parents of three children; Dr. Robert Smith of Des Moines, a graduate of Iowa University School of Medicine, is an internist affiliated with the Internal Medical Clinic in Des Moines. They have three children; James E. Smith, also a graduate of the University of Iowa, is a sales representative living in Denver. He and his wife Judy have 2 children. Their daughter Margaret, Mrs. Ron Byrne, who has her RN. and B.S. degrees from Iowa, is director of nursing services for the Children's Hospital, Oakland, California.

In November, 1975 an article in the *Wall Street Journal* said: "Mary Louise Smith is the best thing which has happened to the Republican Party recently." Her organizational qualities and her vision are consolidating party interests. The first woman ever to become Chairman of a great party is making political history.

KANSAS

Kansas

Nickname: Sunflower State

State Flower: Sunflower

State Tree: Cottonwood

State Bird: Western meadowlark

Committee Members

Chairman—Mrs. Lois Foreman, Valley Center

Writers

Joseph G. Gambone
Kittie Dale
Edna Sherman
William A. White
Esther Ebel
Rev. Roy F. Molander
Norma Jean Hamilton
Karen Butler Rohrer
Mrs. B. Horne
Zula Bennington Green
Mary D. Boyd
McDill Boyd

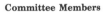

Kansas

CLARINA I. H. NICHOLS

Born 1810

In October, 1854, a quiet, motherly, soft-spoken 44-year-old woman's suffrage activist migrated to Kansas territory under auspices of the New England Emigrant Aid Company. Her arrival marked the beginning of the Kansas feminist movement that culminated, 27 years after her death, with passage of an equal suffrage amendment to the Kansas constitution in 1912.

Clarina Irene Howard Nichols helped sow the seeds of female equality and liberty from Vermont to California. Her greatest achievement was that the Kansas constitution included liberal property rights for women, equal guardianship of children and the right to vote in school district elections.

Born in West Townshend, Vt., January 25, 1810, to Chapin and Birsha Howard, Clarina was reared in the Baptist faith. She was educated at the district school in Townshend and in private school. At graduation in November, 1828, she delivered an original address, "Comparative of a Scientific and an Ornamental Education for Females."

Clarina taught in Vermont schools until her marriage to Justin Carpenter in 1830. They moved to western New York where she taught at Brockport Academy and founded a young ladies' seminary at Herkimer. A daughter, Birsha, and two sons, Chapin Howard and Aurelius Ormando, were born to this union.

By 1839 Clarina had returned to Vermont, rejoining the Second Baptist Church. She began writing for the Windham County *Democrat* of Brattleboro. On March 6, 1843, having divorced Carpenter the previous month, she married George W. Nichols, editor and publisher of the *Democrat*. A son, George Bainbridge, was born in 1844.

When Mr. Nichols became seriously ill, Clarina was forced to take editorial control of the paper. One of the most vocal woman's rights and temperance leaders in New England, she was in demand for lectures and debates. Her keen sense of humor and liberal use of Bible quotations won many ministers to her cause.

By 1854 she decided to move to the new territory of Kansas, believing more could be accomplished for women in a developing area. With sons A. O. and C. H., she left for Kansas in October. As they arrived in Lawrence she was asked to lecture in the newly built Methodist church.

She established a home for her sons and went back to Vermont, returning three months later with her husband and young son. The next summer she was invited to attend the Free-State constitutional convention in Topeka but her husband's fatal illness prevented her going. In December she returned to Vermont to settle her husband's small estate. While still in the East, open warfare broke out in Kansas and she took up the call of "bleeding Kansas."

At the request of Horace Greeley she was appointed by the Kansas National Aid Committee to canvass western New York and substantial provisions were sent the sufferers. She returned to Kansas in 1857, moved her family to Wyandotte County, and was associate editor of a Free-State journal.

During the Wyandotte constitutional convention she sat through each session quietly knitting. Although only an observer, she persuaded enough delegates that the elective franchise to women in school elections, equal protection for property rights and guardianship of children were adopted.

In 1863 she moved to Washington, D. C. to clerk in the army quartermaster department. Early in 1865 she was appointed matron of the Georgetown home operated by the National Association of Relief of Destitute Colored Women and Children. Her daughter Birsha assisted with care of the children.

Returning to Kansas in 1866 she saw the 1867 legislature approve a woman's suffrage amendment only to have it defeated by the electorate.

In December, 1871, she moved to Mendocina County, Calif., with her son George hoping a milder climate would improve her health. She continued her crusade through newspaper articles and correspondence with national leaders. She died January 11, 1886, at the Potter Valley home of her son.

MARTHA KERGAN SMITH
Logan County   **Born 1824**

In a decade of prominence of early Ellis, Kansas, brimming with frontier trouble, excitement and stunning grief, Martha Kergan Smith established an historic image of what a true pioneer mother could, and did endure.

President Theodore Roosevelt, on a campaign tour, arranged to stop and visit "this remarkable woman." Once when an Indian raid threatened, she held an all night vigil in her box-car home armed with a shotgun pointed at the door, her children huddled behind her.

Born in Logan County, Kentucky, May 11, 1824, Martha grew to womanhood with little education. At 18, she married W. H. Smith, Two years later the young family joined a colony moving to Cherokee County, Texas. Her husband died in 1858 leaving her with seven small children. Four had died in infancy.

At the outbreak of the Civil War, she felt it unwise to remain, fearing the country would be

devastated by armies. An aunt in Litchfield, Illinois, encouraged her to come there. By team and wagon they reached Alexandria, Louisiana, took a small boat to New Orleans and boarded the last Mississippi River boat to run the blockade. After six weeks they arrived in Alton. Relatives took them to Litchfield. After several years there she could see no future for her growing family. She was promised a position by the Kansas Pacific Railroad to manage a bunkhouse and cook for railroad workers at the new division point in Ellis.

In 1870, the family rode west on a chugging locomotive, through the great vacuum of the plains, the train stopping west of Fort Hays to let a herd of buffalo stampede across the tracks. Mid-morning, on October 10, she stepped down from the train, the first white woman to set foot on the buffalo sod in the small, lantern-lighted railroad camp.

In lonely despair and indecision she realized there was no bunkhouse awaiting her. As far as she could see, only a vast, desolate, treeless prairie met her eyes. Her weary children sat down on a pile of railroad ties and began to cry. The conductor gently suggested perhaps they should return to Kansas City.

Suddenly from the direction of the railroad shops, walking rapidly and shouting a welcome came the entire shop force to escort them to their improvised home—a box car on the tracks near Big Creek. She shook the dust from her petticoats and stepped inside.

Martha Smith mothered everyone, thus attaining the sobriquet of "Mother Smith." She nursed the homeless workmen when sick and counseled them through many problems. She gave bread to the hungry Indians who termed her their "heep good friend." For the immigrants living in dugouts along the creek, she taught culinary arts and methods of primitive living. The railroad built her bunkhouse.

Among the homesteaders came the Jordan family. Their son Richard married Martha's daughter Mary. He was a buffalo hunter, selling hides to an eastern market. Mary joined him on his next trip. Her mother begged her not to go. "Indian renegades are roaming the prairie," she pleaded.

Two weeks later a Scout rode in telling of a massacre on Hackberry Creek, Mother Smith knew that was where they planned to camp. The 7th Cavalry rode out from Fort Hays relaying back the message that all men in the party were killed. There was no sign of Mary, except her sunbonnet lying on the prairie. She was never seen again although soldiers searched for years and Mother Smith's Indian friends closely examined old trails.

This crowning tragedy grieved her deeply but did not deter her from continuing her kindly ministrations to others, indeed she was even more sensitive to their problems and needs. She died in Ellis, July 26, 1918.

MARY ANN HATTEN WHITE
Born 1830

She sat there on the box beside the stagecoach driver, a tiny Irish lass of about 90 pounds, five-foot-three, and size two and one-half shoes. Framed by dark red hair falling in long curls to her shoulders and a peaches and cream complexion, her hazel eyes gleamed in excitement as she looked upon the bright blue skies of 1865 Emporia, Kansas, where she planned to attend the new State Normal School.

Mary Ann Hatten had been born January 3, 1830 to Annie Kelly and Frank Hatten, natives of Longford, Ireland, who lived in the woods across Lake Ontario from Oswego, New York. Orphaned at 16, she cared for a younger brother and sister until they left home. She made her way to Galesburg, Illinois, with a Mr. and Mrs. Wright, Congregationalists interested in Knox College.

While in Galesburg, her alert, intelligent questing mind became fascinated with social and political problems of the time. She heard the famous fifth Lincoln-Douglas debate and idolized the great emancipator. She also listened to Henry Ward Beecher and other abolitionists of the period.

It took her ten years in Knox, off and on, to complete her sophomore year. Alternate years she earned money to go back to school, learning every respectable trade women in those days could know: seamstress, milliner, practical nurse and hired girl.

The Wright's had gone on west to Council Grove, Kansas, mail outfitting post on the Santa Fe Trail. News of the new normal school nearby was enough for Mary Hatten to come west also. When she could not find a room in Emporia, she went north to join her friends. She was hired to teach school.

Teaching a Sunday School class the day before school opened she invited the children to come to school. They did. One girl was a light skinned Negro. Southern sympathizers protested. Next morning she found the school padlocked and windows nailed shut. Her friend, Mr.

Wright, managed to open the school but attendance was light. Next year she taught in Cottonwood Falls, then left intending to complete her degree at Knox, but first went to Michigan to help her sister who was ill.

Those were not her last days in Kansas, however, for the two-year career did more than make her the heroine of abolitionists. One admirer became her husband.

During her first year in Kansas she had met Dr. Allen White at a dance in Emporia. An enterprising shopkeeper who also doubled as town physician, he was loved, respected and known for his kindness of heart which made bill collecting difficult. The courtship was conducted by correspondence. They were married in Lapeer, Michigan, April 15, 1867. Next February their son, William Allen, was born. Soon they moved to El Dorado where Dr. White ran a pharmacy and became happily involved in politics. They were to have another son who died in infancy.

Mary White was a perpetual hostess for her civic-minded husband who seemed to invite to their table everyone of import coming to town. Often she wished the station had not been just "up the street."

Her husband died in 1862 while mayor of the city. Soon after, she opened her home to roomers and later offered board. Her culinary talent was of renown. When her son entered the state university, she moved to Lawrence to make a home for him, and later to Topeka when he took a correspondent's job there.

Following her son's marriage and purchase of "The Gazette," she returned to Emporia and lived out her life as devoted mother, grandmother and neighbor to Kansas' most notable family of that day. She died there, May 6, 1924.

BETTY KOHN WOLLMAN

Born 1836

Betty Kohn was born in a small village near Pilsen, Bohemia in 1836, the daughter of Rabbi Herman Kohn. Foreseeing troubled times for his people after the ascent of Emperor Francis Joseph, her father came to the United States seeking a new home for his family. He settled in St. Louis, Missouri, then sent for his wife and children. Betty was 16 at the time.

Jonas Wollman had emigrated from Kempen, Prussia to Albany, New York, in 1850, where he

opened a clothing store. The pioneering urge brought him to St. Louis where he and Betty were married in 1855. Their honeymoon trip was a week-long journey by boat up the Missouri River. With them was merchandise for opening a store in Leavenworth, then a town of 150 people. Docking at Westport Landing, they made the last thirty miles of the trip by wagon.

They had settled in an area of heated factions of pro and anti-slavery conflict. With their personal backgrounds of oppression they had no trouble identifying with abolitionists. Jonas welcomed the Kansas Free Press that rented the loft over his store. When the newspaper was raided and its equipment thrown into the river, Jonas was closely guarded and Betty made her home elsewhere until the United States marshal completed his investigation and determined no crime had been committed. On three occasions the Wollman's were taken prisoner by pro-slavery forces. Once Betty and their first child, three-month-old Rose, took refuge from an approaching battle in a rowboat and found shelter eight miles downriver.

By 1858 the local civil war skirmishes had about subsided and the family business was prospering. Jonas took courage and built a handsome home and a new store building, the first brick and stone structure in Leavenworth.

Abraham Lincoln visited the Territory in 1859, hoping that it would be admitted as a state and its citizens enabled to vote in the 1860 election. He was a guest in the Wollman home. When he had gone, it was reported that Betty turned to her husband and said, "There is a great man, and some day he will be President."

Four daughters and four sons blessed the Wollman home. As the children grew and broadened their interests, the family moved to Kansas City. Business acumen of the sons eventually drew them to the investment world of New York City. Widowed in 1904, Betty moved there to be near her family. She died December 24, 1927.

There was no third generation, but the fruits of the family's labor carry on through extensive philanthropies. Scores of educational and charitable institutions have benefited from this stewardship—university and hospital buildings, family recreation facilities and social welfare organizations, with particular emphasis on those helping children.

Today, Kansans honor Betty Wollman for her vision and her charitable spirit which permeated the lives of her sons and daughters.

Enshrined in the halls of the Kansas State Historical Society in Topeka is an oil portrait of Betty, painted by Boris B. Gordon of Washington, D. C. in her 91st year. It shows her seated in a chair with a soft, knitted shawl around her shoulders. She is examining a picture of one of the models suggested for the statue of "The Pioneer Woman." Some art critics had objected to the sunbonnet of the selected model. Betty Wollman upheld the sculptor's interpretation, for she had known Kansas in sunbonnet days.

"Give her of the fruit of her
hands, and let her own works
praise her in the gates."
(Proverbs)

SARA BLOCK EITZEN

Born 1840

One hundred years ago Sara Block Eitzen was one of the pioneer Mennonite women, who with her husband and family left their native Russia to establish a new home in America, the land of the free. After a long and difficult journey the Abraham Eitzens arrived at Peabody, Kansas in mid July, 1876.

They purchased land along the Cottonwood River four and one half miles southeast of present day Hillsboro, Kansas. The enthusiastic young family of three sons and two daughters became kin to hard work. They broke the sod and planted Turkey Red Wheat seeds which they brought with them from the Ukraine. They

were a humble family who depended on their Creator to keep and prosper them.

The Eitzens did propser. Anna and Mary were born in the new country. During their second decade a three story house was completed and dedicated to be a haven for people in need. Two foster sons were reared from infancy to adulthood. A temporary home was provided for many immigrants.

Sara Block, born February 2, 1840 was the oldest of a large family. As a young woman she accepted Jesus Christ as her Savior and Lord. In her desire to serve God and man, she chose the healing arts and was apprenticed to a physician in South Russia.

Sara Block was twenty eight when widower Abraham Eitsen earnestly implored her to become his wife and the mother of his four children. Her gentle nature and deep abiding faith were outstanding. After prayerful consideration she gave up her medical career to become a wife and mother.

The joy of religious and political freedom in America gave courage and zeal to face the rigors of pioneer life. With medical aid almost unavailable the dreaded epidemics and childbirth complications took a heavy toll annually. The tremendous need for a midwife caused Sara Block Eitzen to put her early training into practice. This added a new dimension in the Eitzen family. They recognized the call to serve and cooperated in every way. She renewed her study

for practical midwifery and practiced homeopathy. Over eighteen hundred babies were delivered by her in those bygone horse and buggy days. When complications threatened the new mother, she stayed until it was safe to leave her. Sara Eitzen attributed her success to faith and prayer. Her monetary reward usually was $2.50 for a delivery.

In the fall of 1906 her best efforts could not restore the health of her husband. Abraham Eitzen died December 1. During her older years the midwifery tapered off. People in the community referred to her as Mother Eitzen. Rural conditions changed with the introduction of the telephone, automobile, and available medical help from doctors in Hillsboro.

When Tabor College was founded in Hillsboro in 1908 Sara Eitzen's active interests turned to education and missions. Here she attended the annual Bible conferences. She encouraged her grandchildren toward excellence in scholarship and example. Besides her church missionaries she supported a Christian Mission to the Jews in Brooklyn, N. Y.

Sara Eitzen's world expanded through travel to attend church conferences in Kansas, Nebraska and Oklahoma. Many remembered Mother Eitzen because of her midwifery. An extended visit to her sister in California in 1910 whetted her appetite to attend the 1915 World's Fair in San Francisco.

Until her last days she remained the Marvelous Mother and consultant to her families, including the grandchildren. She died unexpectedly on September 5, 1917.

Sara Eitzen's services were memorialized by furnishing the obstetric department in Salem Hospital which was built in 1918 in Hillsboro, Kansas.

ALMA CHRISTINA LIND SWENSSON

Born 1859

Writing of the renowned Lindsborg Messiah Festival in 1923, *The New York Times* stated: "Emerson tells us that every institution is the lengthened shadow of some towering personality. 'The Messiah' at Lindsborg, Kansas is the shadow of Alma Lind Swensson."

Alma Christina Lind was born in Bredaryd, Vastergotland, Sweden, December 11, 1859, the second of six children of the John Lind's. The family emigrated to the United States in 1864, living first in Andover, Illinois, an early Swedish settlement. Later they moved to nearby Moline.

At an early age, Alma showed great talent, especially in music. She became church organist at the age of twelve. On September 15, 1880 in Moline, she was united in marriage with Reverend Carl Aaron Swensson. They left immediately to establish their home in Lindsborg, Kansas, where her husband was minister of Bethany Lutheran Church.

This young couple were instrumental in establishing two significant institutions in Lindsborg during the next year: Bethany College and the Bethany College Oratorio Society, later known as the Lindsborg Messiah Chorus. Reverend Swensson served as the first president for the college and Alma conducted all rehearsals of the oratorio group the first year.

When the initial performance of Handel's "Messiah" took place on March 28, 1882, Alma Swensson sang the soprano solos. A conductor was brought to Lindsborg from Rock Island, Illinois, so she could carry the solo assignment.

Through the Swensson's influence Bethany College was founded as a co-educational institution. Mrs. Swensson was a strong supporter of the women's suffrage movement. She entertained national leaders on the Bethany campus. She was active in the civic life of the community and beyond. She supported the efforts of her husband who served in the Kansas House of Representatives and who was a member of the national speaker's bureau of the Republican Party.

Reverend Swensson died in 1904, at the age of 46, and his widow carried on her devotion to home, church and college. She served on Bethany's music faculty several years and was church organist forty years. She sang in "The Messiah" until the end of her life. Bethany conferred on her the honorary degree, Doctor of Humane Letters, in 1922, and a new women's dormitory was named Alma Swensson Hall in 1949.

Mrs. Swensson was nationally known in church circles. The national Women's Missonary Society of the Augustana Lutheran Church was founded in her home in June of 1892. She was the first corresponding secretary, became editor of "Mission Tidings," official publication of the society, and was a frequent contributor until her death, December 16, 1939.

Two daughters blessed the Swensson home. Both graduated from Bethany. A talented musician like her mother, Bertha was alto soloist several years for the oratorio. She also followed her mother in the role of college president's wife. Her husband, Dr. Axel Vestling, a Bethany alumnus, was president of Olivet College in Michigan.

The second daughter, Annie Theodora, pursued extensive graduate study and was a Bethany professor for many years. Part of this time she served as Dean of Women. She was founder and director of The Bethany Players drama group. Several generations of Bethany students held her in great esteem, as evidenced by a former student writing: "When I stood by Miss Swensson's grave, I felt I was on holy ground."

Holy Week of 1975 witnessed the 241st rendition of "The Messiah" in Lindsborg, a sacred tribute to the faith and vision of a talented young bride and her husband who cast their lot in service to their Lord and His people of the verdant plains of central Kansas in the autumn of 1880.

MARTHA GRIFFITH NEVINS
Born 1860

Martha Elizabeth Griffith was born in Winston-Salem, North Carolina, January 22, 1760, the daughter of Melvina Bodenheimer and Zenus Clark Griffith. She attended Winston-Salem schools. The family moved to Missouri in 1870. She attended the Girl's Seminary in Sarcoxie.

On September 4, 1881, Martha and Ozro Newton Nevins were married in Pierce City. They moved to Eureka Springs, Arkansas where there was an opportunity fn lumbering. Newt Nevins heard of the "free land" in Kansas. Being a pioneer by nature he wanted to tame the prairie and own his land. He homesteaded north of Dodge City with Martha and Eulalia, their three-year-old daughter.

Martha taught the school close to their claims for ten years, interspersed with raising four more babies. Following the tragic deaths of two children, a baby girl from measles complications, and a toddler son from an accident, the family moved to Ford, southeast of Dodge, where Martha resumed teaching. Three more children were born there.

By the close of Martha's last year of teaching at the Daisy Dell School in 1889, Eulalia was graduating from Normal School and started teaching there that fall. Mother and daughter were associated with Ford County schools for sixty years!

In order for the four younger children to attend high school, the family moved to Dodge City. The house they purchased was on Boot Hill, across from Third Ward School, now locale of the famous museum and cemetery.

Martha's first concern was quality education for her children. She had well-selected books in their library and they were read. Good paintings by recognized artists adorned the walls. Only the best of music was acceptable. She would say "A person seeing the sheet music on the piano could judge the type of family." Nothing shoddy was tolerated.

She struggled for women's rights in the 19th century and for women's liberation in the 20th, energetically supporting the 19th Amendment. She firmly believed in education and careers for her daughters. All three were college graduates, one earning two advanced degrees. All have been in "Who's Who of American Women." At an early age she joined the Methodist Church. She organized, then taught the Martha class of her Dodge City church. She was a woman who gave her all for family, church and community.

Among her descendents are listed business executives, college professor-department heads, county school superintendent, university dean, Rotary and Kiwanis club presidents, highest officers in Masonic bodies, state legislators, county attorney, Methodist minister, public relations director, Christian education director, Air Force pilot-instructor, church organist, school counselor, speech therapist, world recognized safety specialist, and may youth leaders. All are continuing to pioneer as did their mother/grandmother in an everchanging world.

Martha Nevins' life bridged from the wideopen prairie to cultured, law-abiding Dodge City, from backyard pump to city water tap, from no roads to paved highways, from human distress signal lantern on the windmill to the telephone.

At the time of Martha's death, October 29, 1923, she had not been ill. She had just worn out. Her husband was heard to say, "Mother was a luxury we all need very much!"

IDA STOVER EISENHOWER
Born 1862

The war in Europe was over. General Dwight D. Eisenhower was returning to a hero's welcome in his hometown. A reporter asked his mother if she wasn't proud of her son. "Which one?", she asked.

Ida Stover Eisenhower was proud of all her sons. All six who had reached maturity—the seventh son, Paul, died of diphtheria in infancy—were successful and respected in their chosen careers. This extraordinary family from the wrong side of the tracks in Abilene, Kansas, had produced a druggist, a banker, a lawyer, an engineer and journalist, a college president, and a famous soldier, soon to become President of the United States. But much of Ida Stover Eisenhower's life had been extraordinary.

She was born May 1, 1862, the only daughter of Elizabeth Ida Link and Simon P. Stover, at Mt. Sidney, Virginia, with the Civil War raging all around her. Her mother died when Ida was five. She and her brothers were sent to live with various relatives in the area. Ida's guardians felt that most of her time should be spent attending to baking and household chores. She did have time to memorize 1,365 verses of the Bible in six months in a competition and win the prize, a medal she always cherished. From that time on she had a ready scripture to quote in any situation.

After her father died in 1873, Ida and her brothers would take long horseback rides and stop in the woods to talk about their plans for using the inheritance they would each receive at age 21 to settle in Kansas. She wanted to go to college but her guardian did not feel that even high school was necessary for a girl. So at age 15 she ran away. She located a place to work for her room and board so she could go to school.

Ida finished high school at 19, taught for two years, collected her inheritance, and joined a Mennonite caravan to Kansas to meet her brothers who had gone on ahead and who assured her that the newly-founded Lane University in Lecompton would accept girls. At Lane Ida met David Eisenhower and on September 23, 1885, they were married in the college chapel. Both ended their college education at that point in order to begin their life together.

Because of their modest financial circumstances, and because the Eisenhower's had no daughters, each of the sons born to David and Ida was expected to contribute to the housework and cooking as well as more traditional boys' chores. Dwight attributed his and his brothers' character development in large part to the fact that they were needed, they each had responsible work to do. He said that their mother was the "greatest personal influence" in her sons' lives. She passed on to them her independence, desire for education, respect for hard work, her belief in self-discipline, and her good humor. She believed that each person should be free to choose his own way and never interfered with their choices, not even with Dwight's career as a professional soldier though she was a lifelong pacifist.

In 1945 she was named Kansas Mother of the Year and was also selected American Mother of the Year but deemed it unwise to travel to New York City to receive the award and allowed the honor to go to another.

Ida Stover Eisenhower died September 11, 1946, at age 84, having been a widow for four years. Of her, Dwight wrote: "Many such persons of her faith, selflessness, and boundless consideration of others have been called saintly. She was that—but above all she was a worker, an administrator, a teacher and guide, truly a wonderful woman."

FLORA KNISELY MENNINGER
Born 1863

Flora Vesta Knisely Menninger, was born of Pennsylvania Dutch parentage, April 23, 1863, the first of six children of Amanda Heikes and Samuel J. Knisely. As a child, Flo took care of her four brothers and one sister and when she was ten, her father died leaving his widow and young family without funds. The family was forced to move in with Flo's maternal grandparents, an unhappy solution.

In 1878, Flo's mother took her family and migrated to an eighty acre farm near Abilene, Kansas. Flo plowed, milked, built fences, dug storm cellars and traveled by horseback, often fighting off prairie wolves.

Late in 1878, Flo went to Abilene to high school and the following April began her first teaching job in a country school. When school closed, she went to Teacher's Institute in Abilene for one month. The following year, a new job paid her $25.00 a month, which she shared with her family.

In 1883, Flo taught in Clay Center, Kansas, and attended the summer term at Campbell College in Holton, where she met Professor

C. F. Menninger. In 1885, C. F. and Flo married.

Both had a voracious thirst for knowledge and while C. F. studied medicine in Chicago, Flo taught school and ran a boarding house in Holton. Following medical school, they moved to Topeka and C. F. set up his medical practice; Flo, always fearful of not having enough money, continued to teach for several years.

Flo Menninger believed that anyone who wanted to do anything strongly enough could. She was never quiet, she felt the only way to rest was to start another project. Her example and expectations made her a driving force to her three sons, Karl, Edwin and William, and her husband.

Practical Christian values were demonstrated as the Menninger house became home to a succession of people—people in need following a flood, people in need while attending school, people needing the love the Menningers had to offer.

The Menninger family made a real contribution to cultural activities in Topeka, not for social recognition, but out of a desire to share their knowledge. They often invited as many as 100 friends to their home for an evening of music and art education.

Education didn't stop in the home, as Flo Menninger began the Bible Study Classes which today are offered nationwide through the Topeka YWCA. Flo wrote her own four-volume study book and review books after attending classes herself to learn all she could.

In her book, *Days of My Life,* published in 1939, she wrote: "My aim in this Bible class work has always been to make the Bible characters live, to make the Book itself understandable and interesting to the reader." Annual enrollment in Menninger Bible classes has exceeded 4,000.

Her tremendous energy made her a compelling force within the family and inspired her husband and sons to be doers in the world. Flo did not take an active interest in the development of The Menninger Foundation. She did her part by making it possible for her husband and sons to be free to develop their dreams. Flo built a foundation from which C.F. and the boys could carry on with security. Their success, therefore, she took for granted. Her zeal for accomplishment may be simply stated—whatever she decided to do, she did thoroughly.

Flo Menninger died at her home in Topeka, February 9, 1945.

MAMIE ALEXANDER BOYD
Woodson County   **Born 1876**

Mamie Alexander was born in Woodson County, Kansas, December 3, 1876, third of thirteen children of Hester Ann Scott, who came to Kansas from Van Buren County, Iowa, and Joseph McDill Alexander, native of Brick Mills, Tennessee.

Mamie grew up sharing the family's work, both household and farm. She had little schooling until eight years old when her older sister conducted a classroom in their home. Later she worked for her room and board in Garnett to complete grade school.

There was no high school to attend so Mamie accompanied her sister to Teacher's Institute and earned a certificate. This accredited her for entering Kansas State Agricultural College. By writing the president of the college she found a job working in a boarding house. To pay her train fare to Manhattan, she sold her pet heifer, "Lovely," for $17.50 and had a few dollars left for future expenses.

Her roommate at the boarding home was a lovely girl of failing health to whom Mamie was devoted. When she became too weak to walk,

Mamie would carry her up and down stairs. At the end, she died in Mamie's arms, a victim of consumption.

For a year, Mamie sat in classes next to Frank W. Boyd, a young man from western Kansas on his way to being a newspaperman. They never spoke because they had not been introduced! During their sophomore year they both worked in the college printing office. They got acquainted!

Both graduated in 1902. Frank went to work on a paper in Phillipsburg. Mamie continued her print shop job and taught for the college. Three years later she had consumption. Her doctor advised "change of climate." She went to Colorado, earned her living with a part-time typing job and resigned herself to dying. Frank did not accept this.

Every weekend for ten months Frank used his newsman's railroad pass to visit Mamie. He realized she was losing ground fast. He convinced her that if she would come home and marry him he would cure her. They were married in Manhattan, August 17, 1905, and settled in Phillipsburg.

As Mamie improved, she started helping on the newspaper, which they were buying on credit. Two sons were born, both destined to be newspapermen. First son McDill, eventually took over the Phillipsburg paper and Frank Jr., a county weekly in Mankato. When Frank Volunteered in the Navy, Mamie moved to Mankato to run the paper.

Mamie was responsible for many firsts in her life, because, seeing a need, she went about meeting it. She believed in kindergarten, sent to Chicago for instruction and conducted one for her boys in her home. Her Presbyterian church boys wanted a basketball team. She organized, coached and scheduled inter-city competition for them and did the same for baseball. She organized a business and professional women's club and the City Library in her home town. She was charter member of the Kansas Tuberculosis Association and of the state Crippled Children's Commission. She was first woman president of Kansas State Alumni Association. A women's dormitory on the campus is named for her. She served on state boards for five governors.

Among her professional honors was the William Allen White Award for Journalistic Merit, "Woman of Achievement" by National Presswoman Association and the McKinney Award of National Newspaper Association. She was named Kansan of the Year in 1959 and was 1965 Kansas Mother.

Two grandsons are carrying on the family newspaper tradition. Of four granddaughters, three are devoted mothers and homemakers and the youngest is a university professor and specialist in mental health research.

To all her accolades Mamie Boyd would respond, "I have just been lucky and have lived longer than most people." She died October 15, 1973.

Kentucky

Kentucky State Mothers Association

Old Kentucky Home

Kentucky

Nickname: Bluegrass State

State Flower: Goldenrod

State Bird: Cardinal

Photos

1. Bluegrass Horse Farm
2. Old Fort Harrod
3. Churchill Downs (Kentucky Derby)
4. Kentucky State Capitol
5. Lincoln Memorial
6. Historic entrance to Mammoth Cave

Committee Members

Chairman—Mrs. Zelma Aton, Louisville

Kentucky

EMMA CLARISSA CLEMENT

Emma Clarissa Clement is a New Englander. Born in Providence, Rhode Island, she went to Salisbury, North Carolina to attend Livingstone College.

It was at Livingstone she met George Clinton Clement, a young theological student. As she explains it, he was her "teacher". "I wasn't very friendly," she admits, "I was raised in a town where you barely knew your next door neighbor."

She recalls the day she and Mr. Clement were walking down a street in Salisbury and suddenly he stopped and spoke to her.

"Emma", he said, "you've got to learn to speak to everybody. You can't go through life not being friendly, you've got to learn to speak to people."

George Clement's influence on his wife was all consuming. It was a good influence. Emma Clarissa Clement was aware of that, poignantly so. On the day of her reception in the Astor Gallery, Waldorf Astoria, her eyes filled with tears, but her voice did not falter. As she spoke of that great enduring emotion that she felt sure transcended even the boundaries of heaven.

"I know," she said simply, "that he sees this too. He wouldn't miss it. He'd be proud."

Aside from more personal ties, George Clinton's life was the church. Once when hard times hit them severely, Emma Clement with her back to her husband cried out that they had been completely forsaken by everyone, including the church.

There was silence for a long time after her outcry then slowly she turned about.

"He had pale, blue eyes," she recalls. "He stood there very straight and proud.

"Emma," he said quietly, "let's understand this now. Whatever I am the church made me."

George Clement's keen intelligence coupled with that vast deep spiritual understanding that characterized his life had found fulfillment in the church.

Emma Clarissa Clement's forebearers had known the bitter heritage of slavery. Her grandfather was a runaway slave who sought

refuge in Rhode Island and two generations of his descendents found security and freedom through his daring.

George Clinton Clement had been born, raised and educated within southern boundaries.

On the very day of their graduation from Livingstone College, Emma and George were married. The long years of hardship and struggle were before them. Their desires for their children were determined, coupled with their tenacious faith.

Dr. Rufus Clement, the president of Atlanta University, recalls his other's music pupils. They never had any great income, he remembers, only after the seventh child was born were they able to manage well. Yet, not withstanding their small income, George and Emma tithed faithfully even when the times were lean.

Emma Clarissa Clement's seven children weren't her only concern. She raised three others, saw that they were properly brought up and sent them to college. Mrs. Abbie Jackson, the eldest daughter, claims her role was that of guinea pig for the rest of the children.

The Clements have climbed far, but their approach to life is humble. They couple compassion with intelligence. They know man is not infallible. When they feel one of their number is in need of a reprimand they have no hesitancy in giving it. They are family proud! One is instantly aware of that sincere, heart warming pride as they speak of one another. It is in

Mrs. Clement's voice when she speaks of "my Children", when the brothers and sisters discuss one another or their mother and father.

Their father, George Clinton Clement's role is not forgotten. There were people, who meeting Mrs. Clement for the first time, were deeply impressed by that silent presence that seemed to guide her every move. George Clinton Clement has an eternal place among the members of his family. It is a normal natural recognition of a man whose inspiring influence was deeply felt. One feels an eager desire to have known this man who was truly "Grace under pressure".

The Clement children, raised in the South, are an outstanding credit to that relationship. "I raised my children without a color line", Mrs. Clement says firmly, "I raised them to be ladies and gentlemen. Parents should learn to keep an eye on their children." She is adamnant in her convictions that good home life and sincere faith are the bulwarks of family life.

Remarks: Born shortly after the Civil War. Belongs to a minority group and her success is all the more phenomenal because of that. Was National President of the Women's Society of the African Methodist Church, is a charter member of Southern Commission on Inter-racial Cooperation, Secretary (Negro Division) Kentucky Division of American Field Army Cancer Society; Statistician of Kentucky Federation of Women's Clubs. Has held offices in the society of her own church.

Mrs. Clement and her seven children are all graduates of Livingstone College in Salisbury, North Carolina.

Mother of Seven Children

Abbie, Church executive, exponent of faith that knows no frontiers.

Rufus, President of a college, moulder of tomorrow's leaders.

Frederick, Professor of physics, unfolding for young eyes an expanding universe.

Ruth, In Haiti with her husband, a messenger of good neighborship through education.

George, A Director of Red Cross overseas, cheering the lives of our fighters.

James, Professor of theology, Chaplain in the United States Army, the symbol of peace in a world at war.

Emma, Interpreting the precious heritage of English literature in historic Tuskegee Institute.

You have given to your children the example of godly living and high service. Alongside your husband, Bishop Clement, you have ministered to the spirit of your people, leading them nearer to God. You have taught diligently the members of your community elevating them to a more significant citizenship. You have helped the needy and given strength to the weak, setting them on the road to better living. This you have done as citizen, teacher, wife and mother.

The roots of your being have been set in hardship and lowliness. The Bell of Liberty rang late in the life of your people. It is the glory of America and yours, that you rose to the heights of its opportunities, that you acquired for yourself and gave to your children the fruits of freedom and democracy. Education, faith, service, have been the hallmarks of your life.

Thus in beauty of spirit, nobility of living and grace of example, you have in two short generations, repaid your country for its gift of freedom and transmuted the dark memories of a struggling past into the bright hope of mankind's nobler future.

Because of this, you have been selected as, *THE AMERICAN MOTHER OF 1946
*The first black woman to be so honored.

ABBIE CLEMENT JACKSON

Dr. Abbie Clement Jackson, President of the North American Area of the World Federation of Methodist Women, is ranked among America's most outstanding churchwomen.

She is the immediate past President of the Women's Home and Foreign Missionary Society of the African Methodist Episcopal Zion Church. In 1950, when the National Council of Churches of Christ in the U.S.A. was formed, Dr. Jackson served as one of it's Vice-Presidents. She was a delegate to the World Council of Churches at its first meeting in Amsterdam, and its second session in Evanston, Illinois.

Her whole life has been given in service both to the ecumenical church movement and her own denomination, which she has served faithfully for nearly forty years and in nearly every capacity where laymen serve. She was one of the women who met in 1941 to organize the United Church Women and has served on its National Board in many capacities.

Dr. Jackson is in demand as a speaker and has been honored by many organizations in her home city and state, Louisville, Kentucky and nationally.

She has served her city as a member of the following Boards:

Y.W.C.A., National Conference of Christians and Jews, the Mayors Committee on Public Accomodations, N.A.A.C.P., Urban League, the West-End Day Care Center and others.

Mrs. Jackson presently serves as President of the North American Area of the World Federation of Methodist Women; Second Vice-Chairman of the Division of Foreign Missions of the National Council of Churches of Christ in the U.S.A.; a member of the National Board of Directors for the Council of Negro Women, which organization she serves as Chaplain; the National Advisory Committee for the American Bible Society; the Women's Committee for the Japan Christian University; the National Religious Council of the Urban League; the Central Budget Board of the African Methodist Episcopal Zion Church; the Louisville Women's Council for Civil Rights; and the Mayor's Committee on Employment.

She has received numerous citations for her untiring efforts in religious and racial affairs from the following organizations:

The Louisville Council of Church Women.

The Louisville Defender—Central High School Kentucky Religion—National Council of Negro Women

The Christian Century—National Conference of Christians and Jews

National Women's Home and Foreign Missionary Society

African Methodist Episcopal Zion Church— The Artra Cosmetics Company.

In 1952, the Zeta Phi Beta National Sorority made Mrs. Jackson an honorary member. In 1961, Livingstone College, Salisbury, North Carolina, awarded Mrs. Jackson the Doctor of Humane Letters Degree.

Mrs. Jackson is listed in "Who's Who In America", "Who,'s Who Among American Women", and "Who's Who in Methodism".

Citations received:

1. 11972- Appreciation for Volunteer Service for Project V; Arthur S. Flemming, Chairman
2. Advisory member of The Marquis Biographical Library Society, a biography of Who's Who of American Women
3. Life Member of the American Bible Society- May 8, 1975

**She has spoken in every state of the United States except Alaska and have travelled in fifty different countries.

THELMA L. STOVALL

Thelma L. Stovall in 1976 is serving as Secretary of State of the Commonwealth of Kentucky.

Mrs. Stovall resides with her husband, Lonnie Raymond Stovall in Louisville, Kentucky. She is a Baptist and a Democrat, in that order and her business address is in the State Capitol, Frankfort, Kentucky.

She graduated from Louisville Girls High and Halleck Hall, and took a law course at LaSalle Extension University, Chicago, Illinois. She has worked at the University of Kentucky and at Eastern State University and took secretarial training at Mary Rose Kelly Secretarial School in Louisville.

She was employed at the Brown and Williamson Tobacco Company and was Secretary of Tobacco Workers International Union Local 185 for 11 years.

ELECTED OFFICES:

First woman to ever hold elective political office from Jefferson County, Louisville, Kentucky

Mrs. Stovall was State Representative from the 38th Legislative District for three terms: 1950-1955

Elected Secretary of State three terms: 1956-1960, 1964-1968, 1972- to present.

Elected State Treasurer two terms: 1960-1964, 1968-1972

She was elected the 1st woman to the Office of Lieutenant Governor in the November 4, 1975 General Election.

By virtue of her office, Mrs. Stovall serves as Chairman of the State Board of Election Commissioners, and is listed in Who's Who in American Politics

ACTIVITIES:

Mrs. Stovall is an active member of the Woman of the Moose, Eastern Star, Business and Professional Women's Club

She was a member of the Board of Directors of Education, Department of Kentucky State Federation of Labor for 8 years.

State Chairman, Muscular Dystrophy Association 1957-1973.

Vice President of Muscular Dystrophy Associations of America, Inc. 1970-71 and 1972-73.

National Committeewoman for Young Democrats of Kentucky 1956-58.

First woman to be elected president of the Young Democrats of Kentucky

Elected Recording Secretary of The National Association of Secretaries of State in 1967.

Secretary of The National Association of Secretaries of State in 1968. Served as Chairman of the Committee on Employment of the Governor's Commission on the Status of Women during the term of The Honorable Edward T. Breathitt.

Appointed as a member of the Kentucky Commission on Women by The Honorable Wendell H. Ford.

On December 9, 1975 Mrs. Stovall was inaugurated as the first woman Lieutenant Governor to serve the Commonwealth of Kentucky.

MABEL BRADBURY HITE
Seatonville   **Born 1909**

Mabel Bradbury Hite was born August 24, 1909, at Seatonville, Jefferson County, Kentucky, her parents were Frank and Anna Bradbury. Mabel married Minor C. Hite in April 1932. During the next eighteen years they had thirteen children, eight girls and five boys.

Mabel Hite attended Swamp College Grade School and Fren Creek High School, graduating in 1928. She then took a teacher's examination and attended Western Kentucky University during the summer session and was able to begin teaching elementary school the following year. During the next four years she attended Nazareth College on Saturdays while teaching.

Mable began her teaching profession during college. In 1953, she felt it necessary to seek work outside her home to supplement the income for her family. For four years she held jobs as a grocery clerk, nurses aide and worked in the Air Force Division at a factory. She began teaching again in 1957 and returned to college on a part-time basis, working toward a degree in Teaching Special Education. However, due to ill health in 1969, she was forced to retire from teaching and from her studies, just a few credits short of earning her degree.

Mabel Hite has been an active member of the First Baptist Church of Jeffersontown since 1923. She has been a member of the Kentucky Education Association, Jefferson County Teachers Education Association, National Education Association, as well as Classroom Teachers Association, School Representative for the Classroom Teachers Association.

She was a splendid leader of the "Handy Helpers" 4 H Group for Mentally Handicapped. Mabel Bradbury Hite received scholarships for her Special Education studies at the University of Louisville and Spaulding College. These scholarships came from Crusade for Children and Parents of Congress and Teachers Association.

Mabel Bradury Hite's greatest abilities and talents are accurately evaluated by her personal physician, Dr. E.B. Schoenbachler. "I have had

numerous occasions to see and to evaluate this very fine lady in her role as a patient, as a mother (and grandmother) and as a person with talents and ability as a teacher and professional woman. Her past occupation as a teacher in special education (Retardees) has benefited the community and in itself would cause her to deserve special recognition. Indeed, she was a pioneer in the area of special education. Although she has been forced to retire due to her health, her example and past performance serves on in the programs to help those children with special needs due to mental retardation. By special devotion to her family and her work, she has been able to contribute far more than she has ever received from this world."

* This was an excerpt from a letter of recommendation sent to the committee for the selection of "Kentucky Mother of the Year." Mabel Hite was a candidate and was then awarded the honor of being Kentucky Mother of the Year in 1973.

EDITH FOSTER
Glasgow   **Born 1914**

Edith (Mrs. Wendell) Foster has devoted her life to caring for other people's children. For twenty-nine years her name has been closely linked to cerebral palsied children in Owensboro, Kentucky.

Perhaps her own childhood helped shape her philosophy. Born in Glasgow, Kentucky, on October 14, 1914, her mother died when she was two. Her school teacher father remarried but her stepmother lived only six months, the victim of tuberculosis. She went to live with her grandparents where she had to work hard, helping with the farm chores.

She recalls; "Other children would get holidays and get to go on picnics but I was always working in the tobacco or chopping corn and I'd feel so sorry for myself. Now I'm glad I did have to work. I learned early that you can't have everything you want." After her grandparents died, she lived with aunts until she finished high school.

Married at nineteen to the boy who had bought her pie at a box supper when she was only eleven years old, the couple used their own misfortune to build a life of wide dimensions, creating a haven for handicapped children.

When their thirteen month old daughter, Louise, was diagnosed as being a "spastic", little was known about the care and treatment of this condition except that it resulted from a birth defect. When a son was stillborn to them four years after the birth of their daughter, their physician told them they could never have any more children. Denied a healthy, normal family of their own, the Fosters began a deliberate search for children afflicted with cerebral palsy. They were determined that someone must do something for these unfortunate children. From then on they dedicated their life to this goal.

In 1947, the Fosters opened their three room home to five cerebral palsied children. It has been a hard but steady upward climb. Under their dedicated efforts and with the support of the community, the school has steadily progressed. Today the Spastics' Home and School in Owensboro, Kentucky is housed in a modern brick and glass building and has an enrollment of 124 students. A well-trained staff and a corps of faithful volunteers work to give the children the best possible care and training.

Edith Foster is not one to seek the limelight. She prefers staying in the background, satisfied with her role as mother to the handicapped children entrusted to her care.

"Taking care of all these children just seems to come naturally," she says. "I have never been one to worry and as long as the Lord provides, why should we grumble? I just accepted my daughter's handicap and it has never bothered me to be around afflicted children."

LUCILE HICKS KIRKSEY
Hickman County   **Born 1904**

Lucile Hicks Kirksey, widow of John E. Kirksey and mother of two children, John David Kirksey, M.D., and Mrs. Maurelle Kirksey Holt, was born in Hickman County, Kentucky, December 2, 1904, daughter of a Cumberland Presbyterian Minister, Rev. E. Samuel Hicks and his wife, Eula McAlister Hicks. She has five grandchildren, Diane, John Samuel, and David Matthew Kirksey and John Lain and Kristen Noelle Holt.

Lucile Kirksey has given generously of her time and energy to historical, Civic, Educational and Religious Activities. Her education included Bethel College, McKenzie, Tennessee, 1922-23; Murray State University, Advanced Teacher's Certificate; Western State University, Special Courses; University of Kentucky, Special Courses in English & Latin; and Fuggazzi School of Business, Lexington, Kentucky, Bookkeeping Diploma.

Her activities have included: High School Teacher, English and Latin, 1924-27; bookkeeper Kentucky Court of Appeals State Law Library, 1928-30; District Director Jackson Purchase Area (eight counties) United States 1950 Census; Secretary Governor's Planning Committee 1950 Mid-Century White House Conference on Children and Youth and Chairman Sub-Com-

Many have echoed the sentiment expressed by one of the parents of a student. "Over the years we have seen her give tirelessly of her love, devotion and physical strength in caring for our children. She cares for each one as if it were her very own."

Not content to give all her time and energy to handicapped children, she has taught normal children in Sunday School at the First Baptist Church for many years.

Only four feet-eleven inches tall and weighing 102 pounds, her once coal-black hair is now a becoming gray. She has been the recipient of the community's recognition over the years. A banker called her "the biggest little woman in town." The right to be loved, the right to an education, the right to be accepted in the community . . . these are some of the things she has struggled to achieve for cerebral-palsied children.

In 1970 she was named a Merit Mother of the Year, has been given the Diana Award and also named Woman of Achievement by the Business & Professional Women's Club.

mittee on Education; Secretary 1960 Governor's Committee for White House Conference on Children & Youth and delegate to both Conferences; Vice-President Kentucky Council for Education, 1950-51; President, Kentucky Congress of Parents & Teachers, 1948-51; Board of Trustees, Rural Kentucky Medical Scholarship Fund since 1949; Secretary Paducah Centennial Committee, 1955-56; State Chairman, Women's Division, Harry Lee Waterfield Campaign for Governor, 1958-59; Women's Co-Ordinator Edward Breathitt Campaign for Governor, 1962-63; member Kentucky Mothers Association of the American Mothers Committee since 1955 Organization, Vice-President and Chairman of Young Mothers Council Service for six years, and President Kentucky Mothers Association 1965-69; President, Paducah-McCracken County Church Women United 1963, and State Chairman Christian Social Relations Church Women United, 1965-69; served on the following Kentucky State Boards and agencies: Citizens Health Committee; Advisory Committee on Maternal & Child Health; Library Advisory Commission, to promote the Bookmobile project; Committee for Kentucky; Committee on Public School Relations and Promising Practices in Elementary Education. Advisor and Sponsor for ten years for Junior Club Women of Reidland-Farley, Lone Oak and Paducah Clubs; Charter member, 1958, of Jackson Purchase Historical Society and first woman elected president, 1970-71, wrote two Historial Articles requiring much research published in Jackson Purchase Historical Journal 1974 and 1975; research made and papers presented on "Kentucky Under Two Flags", "Area Camps & Forts", "Smithland, Strategic Supply Base", "Kentucky's Historical Marker Program", and "Making Local History Live"; member Kentucky and National Historical Societies; Board Member, Young Historians of Paducah, the sponsor and operate the Alben W. Barkley Museum; Board member Mayor's Citizens Advisory Committee, Paducah, 1971-75; first woman elder in her church and first woman elected Commissioner from Mayfield Presbytery to General Assembly in 1976; she was elected Kentucky Mother of the Year 1962.

She is a Duchess of Paducah and a Kentucky Colonel and her service is listed in Outstanding Civic Leaders of America; Who's Who of American Women, Royal Blue Book, The Blue Book, The Two Thousand Women of Achievement, Personalities of the South, and The World Who's Who of Women.

GERTA BENDL

Gerta Bendl–Mrs. C. Richard is the mother of three children: Paula 20, Kurt 15, Erik 13. She was born in New Kensington, Pennsylvania, was educated at Pennsylvania College for Women, with fifteen years private tutoring in fine arts–fine languages.

Since 1967 Mrs. Bendl has been a moving force in abolishing underground mining in the City of Louisville. Gerta Bendl changed Public Works Statutes to create fairness in assessment processes. Mrs. Bendl has been instrumental in Flood Control and Water Management and has been the moving force behind creating the Public Transportation System.

She organized her neighbors and changed state law to create a vehicle for citizens role in logical change of school boundary lines. Gerta Bendl has served two terms as Alderman for Louisville's Third Ward. During her terms as Alderman she served on the following committees:

Public Transportation (Chairman)
Human Relations (Chairman)
Collective Bargaining (Chairman)
Collective Bargaining (Chairman)
Health, Sanitation, Pollution and Water Drainage (Chairman)

Planning, Zoning and Public Ways
Energy Crisis Committee
Emergency Medical Services
Finances and Appropriations
Street Lighting
Environmental Committee, National League of
    Cities
Legislative Committee, Kentucky Municipal
    League
IN COMMUNITY AFFAIRS
Mrs. Bendl has also served on the following
Boards and Committees:
    Highland Branch, Y.M.C.A.
March of Dimes, Walk Chairman, 1974-1975
March of Dimes (Ohio Valley Chapter)
Strategies for Environemental Control
Water Management Committee, Inc.
Bellarmine College Board of Overseers
Citizens' Advisory Council-Kentucky, State De-
    partment of Education
Transportation Advisory Committee, Kentucky-
    Indiana Planning and Development Agency
Chairman, Greater Louisville Fund for the Arts
Chairmen, Women's Awareness Week
Chamber of Commerce Transportation Com-
    mittee
Task Force, Inter-religious Council of Christians
    and Jews
State Chairman, Bethlehem Foundation, Inc.
Member, Business and Professional Women's
    Club
Water Quality Study Advisory Committee, Ken-
    tucky-Indiana
Planning and Development Agency
Gerta Bendl is recently serving her first term as
State Representative from the thirty-fourth
District of Louisville, Kentucky.

BEULAH MORGAN SMITH

The following list of activities of Beulah Morgan Smith of Bowling Green is ample evidence
of her outstanding contributions and broad vision.

Baptist-Choir, Soloist, Organ, Piano, Sunday
School Teacher, Music Director Summer Reviv-
als, Women's Missionary Society, Circle Leader,
Superintendent Intermediate Department Sun-
day School, Leader young people West Central
District, Certificate Study Courses, Women's
Missionary Society, Tither; Tuberculosis Associa-
tion Organizer (ten years), President (ten years)
Warren County Sanatorium Trustees, fifty-

seven years Volunteer Worker Tuberculosis
State Board Kentucky Tuberculosis Association
Constitution Bylaws, State National Workers
Conference, National Tuberculosis Association
Member, twelve years lobbyist legislature anti-
tuberculosis Member Construction of nine Tu-
berculculosis Sanatoriums, Kentucky Sanatorium
Commission; Salvation Army Board, Charter Or-
ganizer and Life Member, 65,000 chest Xrays
Elks Tuberculosis trailer; Charter and Local Or-
ganizer Altrusa International Club, Bowling
Green Womans Club, DAR, DAC, SDA, CAR,
Certificate of Honor American Genealogy
Society, Good Citizenship Pilgrimage DAR
Society, Hostess three years American Field
Service Students, Chairman five years Warren
County Crippled Children, Member Warren
County Historical Society, Postwar Advisory
Planning Commission of Kentucky State High-
way Safety Conference, Kentucky Federation
Music Clubs, League Women's Voters; Western
Normal School Certificate, Moody Bible Insti-
tute, Peabody College, Bowling Green Business
University; Teacher-Moon Light Schools, Pri-
mary Grades; two years Assistant Principal
Cuba High School, art, dramatics, music, coach
girls basketball; President Bowling Green City
Council PTA, Parliamentarian District PTA,
Secretary Western State College Faculty Wives
Club; "Mother" 1938 Western State College,
1963 Kentucky Mother; Western University Fac-
ulty Wife Emeriti, Peabody Dames and Faculty;
Councilor-Junior Music Club, Cooperative Concerts; Charter and Organizer Mothers Club, Secretary Garden Club; Volunteer Operator Blind

Concession Stand eleven months; Juror U.S. Federal Court, Circuit Court Disricts 1 and 2, Magistrate Police Courts, City Council, Precinct Officer, Judge, Sheriff, Secretary; Chaperone Lions Club Good Citizens Pilgrimage, DAR Good Citizens; Orchid-Loyalty KTB Award, Citizen of Week, Community Volunteer Worker; 10 years Service Board Member; Purple Rosette Bowling Green Garden Club; Safety Driving Award, Legion Safety Drivers; Co-worker Negro Health Education; Sponsor-Dihydrostreptomycin Medication for Children in TB Hospital-Seoul, Korea.

She was married to Bert Raldon Smith, Ph.D. of Bowling Greeen

Their sons are Raldon Morgan and Charles Burnette Smith

CLAUDIA SANDERS

Claudia Sanders, a native of Knox County, Kentucky, is known the world over as "The Colonel's Lady." One of fourteen children, she spent her early years on a farm in Laurel County. Little did she know that she was embarking on the road to fame and fortune when she joined her twin sister, Nell as employees of Colonel Sanders at his first restaurant in Corbin.

After waiting tables and minding the cash register for several years, Colonel Sanders sent her to Asheville, North Carolina in 1939 to run a restaurant he owned there. This was followed in 1945 by assignment in Miami as operator of a slenderizing salon in which the Colonel had an interest. When the business was sold, Claudia returned to Kentucky and in 1949 she and Colonel Sanders were married.

It was about this time that the Colonel was experimenting with his special combination of herbs and spices. His "finger lickin' good" fried chicken recipe was well received at the Corbin restaurant so he became interested in trying to

sell the idea elsewhere. In 1956, at the age of 66, the Colonel sold the Crobin restaurant, and he and Claudia went on the road franchising Kentucky Fried Chicken. When they were able to sell a franchise to a restaurant the Colonel would dress up in his white suit and fry the chicken while Claudia, dressed in an antebellum costume, would act as hostess.

Later it became Mrs. Sanders' job to remain at home in Corbin mixing the herbs and spices, packaging them and sending them to the various franchise restaurants, while the Colonel traveled the country selling more franchises. After a few years, the business prospered to the point where they moved to Shelbyville, Kentucky to be closer to shipping facilities in Louisville.

By 1963 the Colonel had 600 outlets that were providing gross income of $1000 per day. In 1964 the Colonel sold the business for $2 million and went on the payroll of the new corporation as a living trademark. Claudia Sanders settled into her role as the Colonel's Lady.

From their home in Shelbyville originated *Claudia Sanders Dinnerhouse*, a franchise restaurant featuring family-style service and her favorite Kentucky recipes.

RUTH FLOWERS BRYANT
Butler County   **Born 1917**

Ruth Flowers Bryant was born November 17, 1917, in Butler County, Kentucky, the only daughter and youngest of four children of Everette E. Flowers and Eva Lena Hocker Flowers. She attended a one-room school until the 8th grade. At fourteen she was the youngest graduate ever from Butler County High School. Ruth completed a course in business administration at Bowling Green Business University which prepared her for jobs as office manager, secretary, accounting clerk, corporate secretary and her work as a volunteer. From infancy she has been at church and Sunday school, serving in various chairmanships, teacher and pianist.

She was married in 1936 to Roy Simmons. Their daughter, Anita, was born in 1937, and Mr. Simmons passed away in 1938. She married Gilbert A. Bryant in 1950 and became the stepmother of Betty and Joyce. A son, Gilbert, Jr., was born in 1957. He won State Championship Shotput in 1975, and is now active in sports and

extracurricula actitivites at the University of Louisville. The girls are married . . . Betty, executive secretary, to Richard M. Folden, laboratory manager; Joyce, registered nurse, to Paxton S. Price (corporation board member and manager); Anita, vocal music teacher, to John H. Freer, psychiatrist. There are 5 grandchildren. All are active in their church as well as she and Mr. Bryant in the church which his family started in Eastwood. He is Vice-President of American Mutual Insurance Co., chairman of the county committee of the Agriculture Stabilization and Conservation Service, supervisor of Soil Conservation District and county member of the Farmers Home Administration Board, and they operate two farms (one of which is part of the original land grant to Abraham Linkhorn, grandfather of Abraham Lincoln.)

Her volunteer work includes membership since 1943 in Parent Teacher Association, serving in various chairmanships and elected offices of local, council, district and state. She served as juvenile protection chairman and director of "Judicial Concern for Children in Trouble," working with the National Council of Juvenile Court Judges, Kentucky Crime Commission, and Volunteers in Probation, a division of National Council on Crime and Delinquency. She established the first group of Volunteers in Juvenile Court in the state and conducted many conferences promoting the use of volunteers with juveniles, as such she was named 1973 Volunteer of the Year. She served as a charter member of the Drug Abuse Center, Drug Coordinating

Committee and Citizens Advisory Boards. She has served on the boards of Crusade vs Crime, the Eastwood Recreation Center and other civic, social and political clubs. She is now serving on a 12-member commission appointed to make a complete comprehensive study of and make recommendations for the juvenile justice system; which includes detention center planning, juvenile courtroom facilities and alternative programs. She was 1974 Kentucky Mother of the Year.

MISS ERCELL JANE EGBERT
Farmersville   **Born 1895**

Miss Ercell Jane Egbert's forty-one year career spanned the evolution of Western Kentucky University from its days as Western Kentucky State Normal School and Teachers College to shortly after it achieved university status. During those four decades, she instructed literally thousands of students.

Born October 22, 1895, at Farmersville, a small Kentucky community in Caldwell County, Miss Egbert attended grade school at Farmersville and in the spring of 1914 enrolled at Western Kentucky State Normal School in Bowling Green, where she completed her high school work. Her pursuit of a degree at Western was interrupted by teaching stints in Kentucky at the rural school at Liberty (1914-16), Farmersville High School, (where she was teacher and principal (1916-18), Burkesville High School (1920), special classes for World War I veterans at Western in the spring of 1922, and at Lakeland High School in Florida (1923).

Upon completion of her B.A. in 1925, Dr. A. M. Stickles employed Miss Egbert to join his small staff as a history teacher at Western. She completed her M.A. degree in 1930 from the University of Pennsylvania.

Miss Egbert's endeavors in research never ceased. She constantly worked to increase library holdings at Western, especially in English History, and she was a dedicated member of Western's first Faculty Research Committee. Her specific field was English History, but over the years, Miss Egbert taught a number of other courses with equal relish. She was a voracious reader of history and never ceased to be a learner. During her retirement years (1966-74), Miss Egbert visited for the first time the various geographical areas upon which she had spent an entire career of serious study. She died on Christmas morning, 1974.

Louisiana

SAN FRANCISCO, RESERVE, LA.

Louisiana

Nickname: Pelican State

State Flower: Magnolia

State Bird: Brown Pelican

Photos

1. Hodges Gardens
2. Gallier House, New Orleans
3. State Capital with Azaleas
4. Longue Vue Gardens, New Orleans
5. French Quarter Street, New Orleans
6. Old State Capital, Baton Rouge
7. Site of Revolutionary War Battle & Arsenal Museum
8. Oak Alley

Committee Members

Chairman—Mrs. Jack Sebastian, Monroe
Mary Alice Jackson, Epps
Loraine Blanks Turner, Shreveport
Noni G. O'Keefe, New Orleans
Marie Filhiol, Bosco
Mary Burkhalter, Ruston
Pat Garrett, Monroe
Eugene Benson Scott, New Orleans
Bobbye Clements, Baton Rouge
Alma Olsen, West Monroe
Grace Grimes, Tellulah
Vernon Sanders, Atlanta
Lucy A. Williamson, Epps
Mildred Spence, Shreveport
Pauline Smith, Monroe
Mrs. Dorothy King Scott, W. Monroe
Lois Pullig, Minden, Artist

Louisiana

MARY STAHL HERRING
Monroe   Born 1864

Mary Stahl Herring is revered in the Order of the Eastern Star for her dedication to the world's largest organization to which both men and women may belong. Her life's greatest achievements were accomplished through this Order which is dedicated to charity, truth and loving kindness.

She served as the first worthy matron of the Louise L. McGuire Chapter in Monroe, Louisiana, which is now one of the largest chapters in the state. It is definitely due to the capabilities and determined efforts of Mrs. Herring that it has enjoyed such growth and activity. This chapter was constituted October 12, 1892 and it was during this time that Mrs. Herring proved her ability as a great leader and organizer of women.

She inspired the Eastern Star members to call a convention in Alexandria for the purpose of organizing a Grand Chapter Order of the Eastern Star for Louisiana. There were eight chapters represented and Mrs. Herring was elected to serve as Worthy Grand Matron and would be the leader and chief officer of all the chapters in the state while in office. She knew that any active member in the Order who followed its principles would be an asset to the community in which she or he lived. This created a burning desire in her heart to get as many worthy people in the Order as possible. In visiting the nineteen chapters in the state she encountered much difficulty, having to travel a total of 2425 miles, 650 of which were by stage.

While her heart was in the work to help members in each chapter, Mrs. Herring's sole desire and ultimate goal was to build and establish an Eastern Star Home for the Aged in Louisiana. Even though her dream has not yet been realized, there are thousands who still work diligently for this project.

She served the Grand Chapter as Worthy Grand Matron so well that she was requested to serve a second term, an honor never bestowed upon any Worthy Grand Matron anywhere. Her humility and modesty caused her to decline the honor, but on a page of the proceedings of the Grand Session the resolution states in part: "Our thanks to Sister Mary Stahl Herring for her careful attention to every duty, her earnest efforts so intelligently acquired, her unwearied zeal and unswerving fidelity which accomplished so much for our Order as our first Worthy Grand Matron".

Her work did not stop with Grand Chapter. She continued to organize and institute many chapters over the state. In 1908 Grand Chapter gave her the endearing title of Mother Grand Matron, an unusual honor as it had never been used before and has never been used again. A page in the Grand Chapter proceedings dated 1921 is dedicated to her memory and reads: "IN MEMORIUM Dedicated to the memory of our beloved Sister Mary Stahl Herring, first Grand Matron and Mother of the Order of the Eastern Star in Louisiana, charter member of Louise L. McGuire Chapter #4 in Monroe, Louisiana, born January 18, 1864, Carondolot (now East St. Louis, Missouri), entered into rest May 11, 1920 at the home of her only child Mrs. W. J. Lockwood, Van Buren, Arkansas".

MARGARET GAFFNEY HAUGHERY
New Orleans   Born 1813

At Prytania and Camp Streets in New Orleans, on a plot of ground known as Margaret's Place, there stands the first statue erected to honor a woman in the United States. It honors Margaret Gaffney Haughery, born in 1813, daughter of William and Margaret O'Rourke Gaffney of County Caven, Ireland. The parents fled to Baltimore with their three youngest children in 1818 because of political and religious pressures.

In 1822, a yellow fever epidemic claimed both parents and one sister leaving nine year old Margaret and her brother. Margaret was taken into the home of a Mrs. Richards where she worked at household chores; but, being a devout Catholic, left when forbidden to attend church.

She married Charles Haughery October 10, 1835 and moved to New Orleans. To them was born one daughter, Frances. In poor health when they married, Mr. Haughery returned to Ireland for treatment. Shortly after, Margaret received word of his death. This was followed a few months later by the death of her infant daughter. Frustrated and resentful, uneducated, not even being able to read or write her name, she sought work in the laundry of the St. Charles Hotel. Across the street was the Poydras Orphan Asylum in which she became intensely interested and at age twenty-three found herself devoting her time to helping care for the homeless children.

In 1836 with the help of the Sisters of Charity, she opened the Catholic Orphans Asylum in Old Withers, a haunted house on the Mississippi River levee. With no money to sustain them, Margaret milked cows and sold the extra milk and butter from a pushcart to earn money for food. Her patient industry and high quality products were fruitful and with the generous donation of the building by its owner, the orphanage expanded.

Her charitable works included the establishing of the Baby House for infants to seven years and the Saint Elizabeth House for girls twelve to eighteen; the feeding of soldiers during the Civil War, even defying the Union blockade; the nursing care of the victims of the yellow fever epidemic of 1853 and other works too numerous to mention.

She owned and operated the first steam bakery in New Orleans, gaining ownership by giving financial aid to its owners who went into

default. It was first known as Margaret's Bakery and later as Klotz Cracker Company, being named for her foster son, Benjamin Klotz, who operated it.

Margaret Haughery died February 9, 1882, in the Hotel Dieu, leaving her estate to charities. She received the blessing and crucifix from Pope Pius IX. Her body now rests in St. Louis Cemetery #2; her funeral attended by thousands of all races, creeds and colors, both rich and poor. All stores, commercial places and city offices closed in respect to her.

A group known as the Margaret Haughery Club exists in New Orleans today to provide cheer for homeless children. Their motto: "We wanted children. God gave us none. So, we help orphans to whom God gave no parents". What a tribute to a great lady known by her simple dress and Quaker bonnett who gave her time, talent, energy and finances to the children of New Orleans.

KATE STONE HOLMES
Tallulah   Born 1841

Citizens in Tallulah, Louisiana celebrated Kate Stone Day, March 17, 1955, publication date of *Brokenburn, the Journal of Kate Stone, 1861-1868.* The diary notes were copied into two large ledger books in 1900. They were discovered in 1946 by Amy Holmes, Kate's daughter, who realized their worth. The journal covers the period when Kate Stone and her family journeyed from Brokenburn, their plantation home, to Texas and back during the Reconstruction Period.

Born to William and Amanda Stone in Mississippi Springs, Mississippi, January 8, 1841, Kate grew up on a typical southern plantation. She rode by her father's side over his vast acres or accompanied her mother through the slave quarters visiting the infirmary for the ill and helpless or the nursery where the babies were tended while their mothers worked. As Kate grew older, she assumed the supervision of housework and the looms in the spinning room and the allotment of clothes for the many dependents.

The Stone children were first taught by governesses and tutors who lived in the home. Kate later attended Dr. Elliott's finishing school in Nashville, Tennessee, where she excelled in literature and language.

Just prior to the Civil War, William Stone moved his family and possessions across the Mississippi River to Stonington Plantation near Delta, Louisiana. The family had now grown to nine children, with Kate, the eldest, faithful as advisor and companion to the others.

Tragedy hit in the midst of prosperity when William Stone received a slight wound that developed blood poisoning, proving fatal. Mrs. Stone sold Stonington and moved to Brokenburn in the southwest corner of Madison Parish. She set up a sawmill, built a spacious, comfortable home, slave quarters, a gin and other buildings. This was done midst constant threats of floods, bad crops, and slave uprisings along with the rumblings of war.

Kate, a young graduate, comforted and helped to enrich the lives of the household members with books, music and offering that gracious hospitality characteristic of many southern plantation homes. She started a diary, which depicts the long trek to Texas, the tragic news from the battle front, and the return to an impoverished farm and ruined home.

While the family was in voluntary exile in Texas, Kate met young Lieutenant Henry Holmes from Maryland. After the close of the Civil War, he sought her out and they were married December 8, 1869.

Henry Holmes farmed first in Ouachita Parish and later in Madison. He held offices of Clerk of Court and Sheriff of Madison Parish. They built the lovely home of Wayside on the banks of Brushy Bayou which runs through Tallulah. They had four children; two sons, Emmett, who died early, and William, who practiced law and served as District Attorney in Madison Parish; twin daughters, Kate, who died as an infant, and Amanda Julia.

Kate, a deeply religious woman, was a member of the Presbyterian Church. Her social and civic activities were many; she created the Madison Infantry Chapter of the United District Council; she was responsible for the young soldier that stands on the courthouse lawn in Tallulah; and she aided in the organization of the Tallulah Book Club.

Feeling a deep sense of loss at Kate's death, December 28, 1907, following a lengthy illness, all businesses closed in respect.

ELIZA JANE POITEVANT NICHOLSON

New Orleans   **Born 1849**

Eliza Jane Poitevant Nicholson was born March 11, 1849, at Pearlington, Mississippi, the daughter of Captain J. W. Poitevant, a wealthy lumberman and steamship builder. Due to the illness of her mother she was virtually adopted by a childless aunt, Mrs. Leonard Kimball, and was reared, the only white child, on an ante-bellum plantation where she enjoyed all the benefits and luxuries of plantation life. She received her early education at home and in rural grammar schools and was graduated at 18 from Amite Female Seminary of Louisiana. She was a curious, loving and humble child and began writing poetry at age of 14. She used as her pen name Pearl River for the river near the plantation.

While visiting her grandfather, Samuel Potter Russ, in New Orleans, she met Colonel Alva Morris Holbrook, owner of the Picayune. Col. Holbrook recognized her literary abilities and offered her a job on his newspaper. Against the wishes of her family she accepted, even though gentle-women were not at this time employed outside the home.

She married Col. Holbrook, who was 41 years her senior, in 1867 and divided her time between home and the Picayune. She instituted many things into the newspaper being credited with the origination of the society section as we know it today as well as sections on health aids, household hints, daily theatre news, a fashion column and articles for children. She was an ardent supporter of prevention of cruelty to animals and did her major public contributions in this field.

Col. Holbrook died in 1876 leaving her the newspaper and a debt of $80,000.00. Her family begged her to take bankruptcy and return home but she insisted that she must stay and clear the debt in order to keep both her name and that of the Picayune above reproach. With the help of George Nicholson, the business agent who bought an interest in the paper, she was successful. On June 27, 1878, they were married and again she divided her time between home and business. To them were born two sons, Leonard Kimball Nicholson and Yorke Poitevant Nicholson, who were her only survivors when she died February 15, 1896 in an influenza epidemic which had claimed her husband ten days earlier.

During the years Mrs. Nicholson had continued to write poems, fairy tales and children's stories. She published one book of poems titled "Lyrics". Even though she died at 47, she had done much in the literary field including serving as president of the Women's National Press Association in 1884. Dorothy Dix was her neighbor and it was through the encouragement of Mrs. Nicholson that she wrote her column which for many years was syndicated in the news.

Mrs. Nicholson was keen of mind, energetic and reflected her personality in everything she undertook to do. She was a tiny woman, her rings being too small for adult hands today. But, she accepted the challenge to combine the qualities of the gracious Southern lady she was with the steady businesslike woman she must be to be successful in the newspaper field. Even today women rarely find an opportunity to impress their life and ideas on as many people as did this great lady of the newspaper world. She was one of the charming and lovely women of her generation and a delightful daughter of the South.

LILY FAULKNER BLANKS
Columbia   Born 1856

Lily Faulkner Blanks was born December 8, 1856, in Caldwell Parish, Louisiana. Her mother was Louisiana Gilbert Higdon Faulkner whose parents had come to America from Holland to enjoy religious freedom. Her father was Anthony Wayne Faulkner, a Mississippi school teacher who came to Louisiana in 1851. He organized the Caldwell Guards in defense of the South and was a veteran of the Confederacy. He represented his district in the state legislature for twenty-six years and introduced the first bill providing for women's suffrage in the state. Her paternal grandfather had come to America from Ireland to fight for the colonies in the Revolutionary War.

In January 1881, Lily Faulkner was married to Henry Christopher Blanks of Columbia. Mr. Blanks was prominent in the agricultural and commercial development of the parish, serving as president of the Caldwell Bank & Trust Company, a member of the Bob Blanks Mercantile Company, and also engaged in the buying and selling of cotton and staves. He was an ardent leader in the Methodist Church, serving since age 18.

Mrs. Blanks was the mother of two children, Henry Wayne and Mary Martha Blanks. During the years of her husband's life, they enjoyed companionship and life to its fullest extent and together with their two children visited many parts of the world. Tragedy occurred in 1889 as Mrs. Blanks, Wayne and Mary were passengers on the steamboat, "Corona," on the Ouachita River near Plaquemine when its boiler exploded, killing forty-eight persons. A short time later a second tragedy struck when Mary drank in error carbolic acid and died.

In 1900 they made their first European journey, touring eleven countries. This trip was followed by three others in later years. The Blanks' home was in Columbia, its beauty reflecting the old Southern type architecture and holding many furnishings picked up on the trips abroad. In the large flower garden there were two of the largest sweet olive trees in the state.

Like her husband, Mrs. Blanks was always a leader and an ardent supporter of the Methodist Church, a strong force in the development of the moral and religious forces in the community and a promoter of the educational and social affairs of Caldwell Parish. She was an active member of the Woman's Christian Temperance Union and believed that liquor traffic was the greatest foe of human welfare and happiness.

A lovable character, possessing all the Christian graces of both mind and heart, she made many friends and enjoyed many years of excellent health, retaining her energy and industriousness until the age of eighty-six.

Her son, Henry Wayne, was educated at Centenary College and the University of Denver. He traveled extensively and was outstanding in his Christian endeavor. Once when he was in charge of industrial YMCA work in Concord, North Carolina, he worked with six hundred boys in Sunday School. They were known as the "Sunday Gang".

Lily Faulkner Blanks continues to be a sweet benediction in the lives of her great, great granddaughters, Lora and Michelle Goodman.

ELEANOR LONG FOSTER
Shreveport

Eleanor Long Foster was born in Natchitoches, Louisiana, the daughter of Dr. William Long, a native of Ireland and Emily Boggs Long, a native of Virginia. She was the descendant of Reverend John Boggs, a distinguished Presbyterian minister and Col. Ellis Cooke, a personal friend of George Washington. Her mother died when she was a child and she and her brother, John Long, were reared by an aunt who gave valuable aid to Dr. Long in his care of his motherless children. Eleanor graduated with honor from Mansfield College and soon married James M. Foster, a prominent Caddo Parish planter. They lived on the plantation until the birth of their third child and time came to think of education. Then they moved to Shreveport to the well known Foster home of "Curraghmuir".

Mrs. Foster was a devoted mother and spent much time in the upbringing of her children. However she was very talented in many ways and found herself sought in both social and civic gatherings. She was known as a peacemaker by members of the clubs she attended although she never seemed to be aggressive in her efforts.

She was active not only on a local level but also in state and national groups. As President for Louisiana, she addressed the George Washington Society at its national meeting. She was a distinguished guest at the Sorosis Club in New York and made an address while there.

She was first President of Hypatia Club, first President of the Federation of Womens Clubs of Louisiana, the first Regent of the Pelican Chapter, Daughters of the American Revolution of Shreveport, Vice State Regent of the Daughters of the American Revolution, a member of the Daughters of the Confederacy and for a number of years was President of the Home for the Homeless of Shreveport. One of her proudest works was founding the Old Ladies Home and realizing the success of her efforts in erecting the building which served as their home. She was closely connected with the literary, educational, civic and charitable efforts of Shreveport in every way. She attended only a few social functions because home work and various charities occupied all of her time. On the rare occasions she appeared, she was welcomed as an honor guest.

On her deathbed, November 16, 1910, she called her surviving children about her. Four had died as children, seven had reached adulthood but there were only five to gather about her bedside. All of them had attained prominent positions in life and they acknowledged the benefits of her teaching and example in reaching their goals.

Claiborne Lee Foster graduated at West Point in 1888 and died in 1890. John Gray Foster closely followed his father in death. William Long Foster was a cotton planter and railroad commissioner from his district. James M. Foster practiced law in Shreveport, served as a member of the Louisiana General Assembly, was district attorney and a delegate to the Democratic Convention. Of the three surviving daughters, Lucille was the wife of former Governor Benton McMillan of Tennessee who served in Congress for twenty years; M. E. Foster-Comegys, residing in New York, was the mother of three very talented daughters; and T. Olive Foster lived in Shreveport and managed the plantation which she had inherited.

Mrs. Foster led a full and fruitful life and met its demands with the courtesy and graciousness of a Christian gentlewoman of her generation.

FLORENCE MILLER FILHIOL
Logtown   Born 1878

America's ideal wife and mother is easily epitomized in the life and accomplishments of Mrs. Florence Miller Filhiol, a native of Monroe, Louisiana. This great lady, to whom the cliché "To know her is to love her" would readily apply on meeting her, was born on July 28, 1878, in her family's home which stood in the land area now occupied by Northeast Louisiana University. She was educated at St. Hyacinth's Academy, which her children were later to attend.

In 1905 she married John Baptiste Filhiol, great-great grandson of the founder of Monroe, Don Juan Filhiol. One son, now deceased, and two daughters were born to this happy couple who now lived in the Filhiol home at Logtown, south of Monroe. This home had been built in 1838 and had always been occupied by various Filhiols.

Despite the many duties incumbent on a mother and a plantation owner's wife, Mrs. Filhiol found time to organize the St. Matthews Altar Society in 1922 and became its first president—and she continued in this office for most of the remainder of her ninety-four years. She also founded the St. Matthews Mothers' Club and became a Catholic School Board Member. She raised much money through bazaars and

her ninetieth birthday KNOE Television Station gave an editorial tribute to this wonderful lady. Interviews and pictures also appeared in the local press.

Mrs. Filhiol was an active member of the Ft. Miro Chapter of the Daughters of the American Revolution, having ancestral lines back to the illustrious TUFTS lines of Massachusetts. She plainly adhered to the Daughters of the American Revolution objectives of support and service to GOD, FAMILY AND COUNTRY.

The ideals and morals this remarkable lady espoused will long live on in her two daughters, four grandchildren and eleven great-grandchildren even in this age of the erosion of traditions.

MARGARET HODGES JAMES
Ruston   **Born 1880**

To nurture children in youth and to relinquish them to adulthood demands that a mother express her noblest love. Margaret Hodges James, "Maggie" to those who knew her, gave to her husband and children profound resources issuing from the deep well of her faith. Her heirs mirror her convictions and their deeds bless the community in her honor.

Maggie was born in Cotton Valley, Louisiana, in 1880, graduated from Mansfield Female College in 1900, and married Thomas Lewis James in 1903. The foundation of their relationship was an abiding belief in the efficacy of conducting their lives with value priorities firmly established: the home, the children and the church came first. The practical demands of securing a livelihood never compromised the foundation of the home Maggie James so earnestly upheld.

She gave birth to six children, Lewis, Floyd, Bill, Helen, Mary and Frances. The family moved to Ruston in 1926 and established T. L. James and Company. With the firmness and gentle manner that so characterized her, Maggie James extended her influence beyond the home. She participated in the decision making which led to the extraordinary growth of the T. L. James Company. She served as a member of the Board of Directors until her death, 4 June, 1964. Today that company she helped found and nurture is the largest concrete paving concern in the United States. Holding fast to the in-

various means for St. Francis Hospital and St. Joseph's Home for the Aged. She also worked for orphans' homes and did catechistic work with the public school children. She was a charter member of the Catholic Daughters of America, and for her devotion and meritorious services to the Church and her personal achievements she received the accolade of "Pro Ecclesia et Pontifice" from Pope Pius XII in 1954.

In 1914 she founded and became the leader of the first Home Demonstration Club in this area. Her work in this field will be long remembered as she tried to ease the lot of farm women, teaching them sewing and canning and encouraging them in community events. She was nominated Woman of the Year in 1937 by the Home Demonstration Club, and received the Agricultural Service Award from the Farm Bureau in 1959. She was a Home Demonstration Club member for fifty years, being president of it for thirty-seven years, making sure knowledge and skills vital to farm life were known to members. She also served one term as President of the State Home Demonstration Council.

However, she was primarily a homemaker, wife and mother—and the priorities were orderly and inviolable with her. On the occasion of stincts for family unity, an idea to which Maggie and Tom James committed themselves at the beginning of the century, their children, grandchildren, and great-grandchildren have honored their forebears by their own achievements. To this day, ninety-three percent of the stock in the company is owned by the heirs of Maggie James. T. L. James & Company will mark its 50th year of operation in 1976, celebrating the nation's Bi-centennial with its own half-century birthday.

Her faithfulness to the Methodist Church was as singular as her love for her family. Her devotion to her church acknowledged its role in perpetuating that which would preserve the supernal essence of man. Her attention to spiritual matters manifested itself privately and publicly. It was not unusual to find her in the autumn of her life, alone in the evening in her upstairs bedroom, listening worshipfully to a recording of her favorite hymn, "How Great Thou Art". This influence of her faith reached beyond her immediate world. The company she helped found has given generously to Centenary College, Southern Methodist University, and the Methodist Hospital in New Orleans. In 1975 a chair of theology at Centenary was established

with a $400,000 endowment. The chair bears the James name.

Her years of support of the Louisiana Tech Concert Association and the Gottschalk Music Club attested her concern for all reaches of man's spirit.

The beauty of the earth always fascinated her. The family acquired a tract of land near Ruston that was once used for the famous Chautauquas of the 19th Century and converted it into a forest garden. It is preserved today as a natural memorial to the concept that man is steward of God's Earth.

One brother, the late A. J. Hodges, built Hodges Gardens, one of the nation's beauty spots. Another brother, Dr. John Hodges, was an authority in English literature at the University of Tennessee. Maggie herself was awarded an honorary Doctor's degree in home economics by John Brown University in 1938.

At a 1972 Hodges' family reunion in Cotton Valley, attended by a majority of her eight-six heirs, there was much in evidence that caused those in attendance to remember Maggie—good food, beautiful flowers, family pictures, and that which she would have enjoyed most, the closeness of loved ones delighting in each other's company.

ESTELLE SCHULZE SANDERS
Monroe   **Born 1905**

Estelle Schulze Sanders was born February 23, 1905 in Monroe, Louisiana, granddaughter of Thomas Nathaniel Conner, Civil War hero, and one of the few survivors of the Battle of Chickamauga, daughter of Judge Charles Schulze, prominent municipal judge for over thirty years, and Martha Henrietta Conner Schulze.

A 1923 graduate of the Monroe City High School, she was educated at the New England Conservatory of Music, 1923-1927. She studied voice with Clarence B. Shirley at Boston, 1923-1927, with Isaac Van Grove at Chicago Musical College in 1935 and with Paul Althouse at New York City, 1945.

While studying in Boston, she sang in the choir of the Copley Methodist Church and later was a member of the quartet of the Central Congregational Church. Director of the First Methodist Choir in Monroe from 1932-1950, and

Memorial Methodist Choir in Monroe from 1951-1970.

She has maintained her private voice studio since 1935.

She was married to Clyde Vernon Sanders September 1, 1928. Devoted to her family, she is the mother of one son, a physician, and grandmother of three growing teen-agers.

An active participant within the Methodist Church for over sixty years, giving unselfishly of her time and talent, she is always faithful to her Christian commitment and untiring in support of the Church's ministry. She participated in a lay witness mission in 1975, traveling to the Holy Land and to Ireland on a Peace Mission in word and song, hoping to bring Christ and peace to a troubled land.

Teacher of voice for over thirty-five years, she is more importantly a friend and counselor to hundreds of young people who come to her for advice and direction.

A member of *Who's Who in Music*, a Fellow in the National Association of Teachers of Singing (NATS), a member of the Louisiana Music Educators Association (LMEA), a member of the Music Educators National Conference (MENC), and the Monroe Musical Coterie.

Honored by her city for civic contributions over the years, she has been made an honorary citizen of West Monroe, recipient of Service to Mankind Award presented by Bayou Desiard Sertoma Club, the holder of two "Pace Setter" Awards given by the Mayor of Monroe for civic and cultural contributions, especially for the perennial musical production, "Spring Serenade" and its support of innumerable charities.

She has given generously through the years to her community and its people. Her influence for good has reached out and touched unnumbered lives. In return she has received the respect and devotion of her family, her friends, her peers, and particularly the young people with whom she has had such special rapport.

ELAINE SCHWARTZENBURG EDWARDS
Crowley   **Born 1929**

Elaine Schwartzenburg Edwards was born in 1929 at Marksville, Louisiana, the only daughter of Myrl Dupuy and Errol Schwartzenburg. At the age of nine, she contracted osteomyelitis in one leg and was an invalid for about five years. During that period she underwent surgery several times and was in almost constant pain; however, with courage and persistence, she managed to overcome this illness and today shows no outward effects. She graduated from Marksville High School, at the age of twenty married Edwin Edwards, Governor of the State of Louisiana and moved to Crowley, Louisiana.

She enjoyed being a homemaker, was active in Little Theatre, designed and made clothing for herself and their two daughters. She helped her husband in many political campaigns, helped plan inaugural activities, entertained a record number of guests and assisted his constituents with social security, military, welfare and other problems. She redecorated the Governor's Mansion without professional help and has received many compliments for her effort.

She served as United States Senator, completing the unexpired term of the deceased Senator Allen J. Ellender. During this time she served on the Senate Agriculture and Forestry Committee and the Committee on Public Works.

She has given many hours of time to Special Olympics for Retarded Children, Louisiana Association for Retarded Children, Louisiana Heart Association, American Cancer Society, Mental Health Association, Louisiana Educational TV Association, Youth Art, Grambling Foundation and the Alpha Delta Kappa and Beta Sigma Phi sororities.

She has helped Louisiana State Police obtain funds for a Boys Camp and serves on their Board of Directors, works with Operation Upgrade teaching reading to the illiterate and those with reading problems and served as Chairman of the Louisiana Disaster Fund for victims of Hurricane Fifi.

Certainly to be numbered among her more outstanding contributions to the state is her effort to raise one million dollars for the Crippled Children's Hospital of New Orleans, for their expansion and building program. The hospital serves children from all over the state, regardless of ability to pay. During the spring months of 1974, she coordinated several fund-raising activities for the hospital in different areas of the state, culminating in a "Day with the Stars" held at the Mansion, which coincided with the celebration of the Edwards twenty-fifth wedding anniversary—"I know of no better way to celebrate the occasion," she said. All of the fund-raising events were outstanding successes, and she continues to work toward the hospital goal of one million dollars. She has also been instrumental in helping comedian Marty Allen in his installation of a library at the hospital, continuing to donate books to this library from time to time.

Governor and Mrs. Edwards are the parents of four children—Anna, who is the mother of two young sons and yet finds time to attend law school; Vicki, who is an Louisiana State University major in advertising, an accomplished dancer, and holds a part-time modeling job; Stephen, a pre-law student interested in sports and especially racing; and David, who attends University High School and is working on a new concept in engines.

MAINE

Maine

Nickname: The Pine Tree State

State Flower: White Pine cone & tassel

State Tree: White Pine

State Bird: Chickadee

Photos

1. Ft. Western—Augusta (1754)
2. Fall Scenic
3. Pemaquid Lighthouse
4. Victory Chimes
5. Lobster, clams & gear
6. Duck Hunting
7. Wedding Cake House
8. Mt. Katahdin

Committee Members

Chairman—Mrs. Phyllis L. Gove, Augusta
Margaret Chase Smith, Honorary Chairman
Mrs. Beverly Pottle

Writers

Helen Cushman
Priscilla L. Gore
Ethel W. Gammon
Katy Perry
William C. Lewis Jr.
Nancy E. Brann
Lillian D. Poling
Harold C. Perham
Rosella A. Lovitt
Jaquelin Phillips

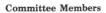

Maine

HANNAH CLOUGH WHITTIER

Before Revolutionary days, when Maine was a part of Massachusetts, Hannah Clough, as a child, was captured by Indians and brought, with other captives, to the Farmington area. They were put to work in corn fields in the great Intervale, where the Amasacontee Indians raised crops of corn, squash, pumpkins. Hannah was probably the first white female to penetrate the wilderness of the area. When she finally escaped and returned to Salem, she married Nathaniel Whittier and they had ten children.

After the close of the Revolution Hannah told her sons that she wished some of them would locate where she had been a captive.

Benjamin was the first to take his mother's advice. He built a fine house in Chesterville, and on his gravestone there is a note that he and his wife were the first couple to spend a winter in the Sandy River Valley.

Another son, Captain William Whittier, settled in Mount Vernon. He and his wife, Elizabeth, became renowned for their hospitality and kindness. Every night they left a light in the kitchen, with the door unlatched, and food on a table by the fire, so that any weary, hungry passerby might have a place for rest and refreshment. Their house still stands.

Nathaniel settled in Readfield, and with his son-in-law, bought most of what is now the Town of Vienna.

Hannah's children were ancestors of many generations. Her descendants have always been and are still prominent in the affairs of the towns in which they live.

JACATAQUA
Swan Island

Jacataqua and twelve of her warriors had been taken prisoner and were brought to Fort Western in Augusta to be questioned by Judge Howard. There were rumors that some French and English people were being held and tortured on Swan Island.

Jacataqua was the Sachem (chief) of Swan Island and also was known as the Queen of the Kennebec. She was tall, lithe, very beautiful, and fiercely proud of her Abernaquis background. Part Abnaki Indian and part French, she had been raised in a convent in Quebec. She spoke French, English and several Indian dialects fluently.

After a few days of questioning it was agreed that Jacataqua and her people were peace loving and an error had been made. The braves were sent home, two of them returning with clothes so that Jacataqua might attend a banquet to be held in her honor at the fort.

During the feasting Jacataqua heard about the problem they were having with bear in the cornfield. She insisted on taking care of it. Aaron Burr volunteered to help her. Jacataqua killed the bear, but one of the wounded ones hurt Burr. She dressed his wounds and mended his clothes.

Young Aaron Burr, just 19, had recently joined the Continental Army and was part of the group at the fort. He was quite taken with Jacataqua, as were all the others. He spent as much time as possible with her.

Benedict Arnold arrived at the fort with eleven hundred of his men on their way to Quebec. The year was 1775. When the march continued Jacataqua, her bloodhound, braves and Burr were part of the group. Strongwilled Jacataqua had insisted on going. She stayed well out of the way of Arnold as he had been much against her coming. However, Jacataqua and her party were invaluable, as they knew the area to be traveled. They guided, provided food and medicinal herbs when needed. Though this was one of the most tragic military marches in history, there would have been many more deaths without their aid.

Burr went on to Montreal, leaving Jacataqua at the same convent she grew up in. Their first child, Chestnutiana, was born there before he returned for her. He established a home for them on Long Island, visiting them when he could. Later a second daughter, Astoria, was born.

A mutual friend, a Scotsman named McPherson, looked after the girls while Jacataqua attended to her tribespeople at Swan Island. She later gave up being chief and appointed the most worthy warrior in her place.

Burr began to drink heavily and, after his duel with Hamilton, poured out all his troubles to Jacataqua, including a political marriage and another daughter, though this wife was now dead. In his drunken stupor he said he had never loved anyone but her and begged her forgiveness. Always proud and ever faithful, Jacataqua could not accept Burr's confession, and, feeling she would never see him again, walked into the East River and was drowned. About the same time Burr's daughter, Theodosia, was drowned at sea during a storm.

Aaron Burr had been Vice President of the United States during the height of his political career. He always seemed to lose those he loved. In his old age it was his daughter, Chestnutiana, who had been brought up by McPherson and married into a well-to-do New York family, that took him into her beautiful home and cared for him. He died a tragic old man at the age of eighty.

SALLY SAYWARD BERRELL KEATING WOOD
York—Wiscasset   **Born 1759**

The historic town of York was, on October 1, 1759, the birthplace of Sally Sayward Barrell Keating Wood, who, far in advance of her day and time, became the first writer of fiction in Maine. After she had acquired social prominence, she was known as Madam Wood. Member of a distinguished family in York County, which in her day comprised the entire District of Maine, her background was especially interesting. Some of her ancestors had been killed by Indians; her maternal grandfather, Judge Sayward, ranked, at one time, next to Sir William Pepperell as the richest man in Maine. Her father, Captain Nathaniel Barrell, a merchant and a descendant from one of Boston's oldest families, had, while serving under General Wolfe at Quebec, been promoted for gallantry.

Sally, one of eleven children, spent most of her early life at her grandfather's mansion in York, "imbibing the atmosphere of that unique

seaboard aristocracy, often loyalist in politics, moderately Anglican in religion, and rather gay and worldly in social tone." Her taste and literary outlook reflected her distinguished background, her philosophy, and to some extent, her personal experiences. Although her father and grandfather had manifested Tory sentiments, she approved the American Revolution.

Her long life of ninety-five years was not without sorrow; but blessed with a happy temperament, she exhibited stauch courage and a determination "to do good." She retained her mental faculties and in her nineties was characterized as "a delightful companion to her great-great grandchildren."

After the death of her first husband, Richard Keating, to whom she had borne two daughters and a son, she settled down at York to twenty-one years of widowhood. She resided in a lovely colonial home that her grandfather had given her as a wedding gift, reared her children, and launched her career as a novelist, especially utilizing the style of sentimental fiction. Her first four novels were "Julia," "Dorval or the Speculator," "Ferdinand and Elmira," a Russian story; and "Amelia or the Influence of Virtue." This fourth novel contained her central message: "female virtue is the key to personal fulfillment and social stability."

Her life changed in 1804 upon her marriage to General Abiel Wood, a well-to-do citizen of Wiscasset, at that time a leading commercial port. While living in that town, "surrounded by wealth and in the society of congenial companions," she continued her literary work. After the death of Mr. Wood, in 1811, she moved to Portland, and in this community, she was also socially prominent. It is interesting to note that her position concerning the role of women was definitely conservative.

Perhaps her best work, because it was based on her own knowledge of Maine, was "Tales of the Night," which was published in her sixty-eighth year. Her children, in the meantime, were attaining respectable positions in life. Her son, Richard, had become a sea captain and, in 1830, Madam Wood moved to New York City to be near him. After his untimely death, as the result of an accident in New York Harbor, she returned to Maine to live with a graddaughter in Kennebunk. She died on January 6, 1854.

This woman of distinction, who was always modest about her literary ability, certainly deserves a place of honor among Maine's outstanding mothers.

PATTY BENJAMIN WASHBURN
Livermore   **Born 1792**

Patty Benjamin Washburn is the only mother in the United States to have four sons elected to Congress. Though very little has been written about Patty her influence has been eloquently told in the lives of her seven sons who achieved political prominence during the Civil War era. Among her brood were two governors of two different states, four members of Congress from four different states, an army general, a navy captain, a secretary of state, a United States senator and two foreign ministers, as well as a banker, an inventor, a railroad president, three authors, and founders of two great flour companies.

Patty, whose given name was Martha, was born in 1792 in Livermore, Maine, the daughter of Tabitha Livermore and Lieutenant Samuel Benjamin. Her father had served in the Revolution from Lexington to Yorktown and Patty was proud of his record. So proud was she of her family name that she gave it as a middle name to four of her children.

Uneducated but intelligent, Patty possessed a greater than average interest in political affairs and the welfare of the infant republic. In 1812 she was married to Israel Washburn whose interests paralleled hers. Their farm home in Livermore was midway between two institutions which vastly influenced their lives and shaped the lives of their children. A few yards to the south stood the Universalist Church and to the north was the local district school.

Life in that remote region was primitive and Patty's life was not an easy one. She bore eleven children, losing one in infancy. Her hands were never idle for on the farm there was much to do, but always she found time to teach her children her own happy philosophy and fire them with ambition to rise above their present station in life. Early she taught them the dignity of hard work, the value of study, and the importance of sticking together. Both parents instilled in their children a love of learning, an active interest in politics, and a reverence for the teachings of the church.

Patty was a dreamer as well as a doer. She dreamed great dreams for her sons and when they grew to manhood they did not disappoint her. Illinois, Minnesota, Wisconsin and California, as well as Maine, were touched by their greatness. Wherever they went they carried out their duties with distinguished ability and untarnished records, extending Patty's influence far beyond the family fireside.

SYBIL JONES
South China   **Born 1808**

To rear five children and at the same time acquire distinction as a Quaker minister and foreign missionary, a person of great executive ability, and a persuasive and eloquent speaker, certainly entitles Sybil Jones to a place of merit among the leading mothers of Maine. In fact, she and her husband, Eli Jones, who was also a Quaker minister, travelled extensively, both in this country and abroad, and may be said to have inaugurated the foreign mission movement among American Friends.

Although she was born in Brunswick, Maine, on February 28, 1808, her childhood was spent in Augusta. Her father, Ephraim Jones, was a farmer and her mother, Susanna (Dudley) Jones, was a direct descendant of Governor Thomas Dudley of the Massachusetts Bay Colony. Described as a high-spirited young lady, Sybil manifested opposition to the humble Quaker garb that her mother insisted that she wear and, on occasions, asserted her independence. At the age of sixteen, she spent a year at the Friends Boarding School in Providence, Rhode Island, and then taught for eight years in schools in Maine.

After her marriage, she and her husband settled on a farm in South China; and, except for her travels, this was Sybil's home for the rest of her life. It was there that her five children were born. One of her sons, Richard, became headmaster of the William Penn Charter School in Philadelphia, a position that he held for many years.

Upon a visit to the South, Sybil became concerned with the plight of the Negro; and later, in 1851, since she "felt a call to preach the salvation of Christ to native Africans," she and Eli spent several months in Monrovia, Liberia. Apparently her influence became widespread and her preaching highly effective, as her visits to various parts of Europe and to the Holy Land would indicate. When she and her husband left for Palestine, two years after the Civil War, John G. Whittier, the renowned Quaker poet, had hoped to accompany them, but was unable to do so on account of ill health. With the aid of other members of their sect, the Joneses started in Palestine the Friends Girls' School, and later persuaded the New England Yearly Meeting to assume responsibility for this Ramallah Mission.

Helen Beedy, in her book, "Mothers of Maine," states that Sybil "developed into a devoted woman, her sweet face and persuasive words winning many hearts." Her warmth of character was clearly shown during the Civil War, at which time, in Philadelphia and Washington, she visited wounded and dying soldiers, including Confederate prisoners. The war years were especially distressing for her since her son, James, in spite of his Quaker tenets, volunteered for service in the Union Army and was killed in battle.

Her childhood contact with Methodism was probably responsible for the evangelical emphasis that she exhibited in her preaching and that "foreshadowed the growth of revivalism within the Society of Friends." The last few years of her life, except for frequent visits with Friends in New England, were spent at her home in South China. She died there at the age of sixty-five and was buried in the Dudley family graveyard adjoining the Friends cemetery. Whittier once wrote of her that her inspired eloquence and rare spirituality impressed all who knew her.

HANNAH LURVEY GILLEY
Bakers Island

Bakers Island, nearly round and about a half mile in diameter, lies four miles from Mount Desert Island and at low tide is connected with Cranberry Island. When William Gilley and his wife, Hannah, took possession of it in 1812, it was uninhabited, covered with trees and surrounded by a coastline of bare rock.

William was a large man, six feet tall, weighing over 200 pounds; Hannah was robust and strong. They built their first small shelter and moved all their worldly belongings and three small children to this remote area. Many times during the year it was impossible to either go to or leave the island.

Hannah was the daughter of Jacob and Hannah Lurvey (from German-Jewish Loewe and said to be descended from the Archangel in Russia). She lived in Newburyport and Byfield, Massachusetts until she was thirteen. During this time she received a good education and later was able to teach her own children as they grew up.

The Gilley family worked hard and prospered. Twelve children were born to them, six boys and six girls; all lived to grow up. This enterprising family got most of their living from their little island and the sea. They raised all of their vegetables, planted wheat and had it ground into flour. Fresh fish was available year round, except February and March. Lobsters could be picked up in shallow water. They kept cows, oxen, young cattle, sheep, hogs and poultry, slaughtering some depending on their needs. Butter and eggs were exchanged at the store for things they needed. Dried fish and feathers were shipped to Boston and smoked herring to New York.

The girls were a great help to their mother, as they spun wool into yarn and made linen from flax that they raised. The boys were in and out of boats from the age of ten. The eldest son made shoes for the whole family. In spite of the hard work they all had happy childhoods. The boys stayed home and contributed to the family until they were twenty-one; the girls left the island to go to work as they became old enough, or were married. William was able to give each son a small sum of money to get him started.

Hannah had an excellent mind and passed on her love of books. At night she read aloud to the children until they were old enough to take turns reading themselves.

In mild weather Hannah took the children to South West Harbor to the Congregational Church, going seven miles each way in an open boat. Bothered by the Hellfire and Damnation preached by the minister she bought books and, after considerable reading, changed to the more cheerful Universalist faith.

The government built a lighthouse on the island in 1828 and William was the lighthouse keeper for 21 years. He received $350 a year, free occupation of a house and all the sperm oil the family could use.

In 1837 he purchased Great Duck Island, five miles away, for $300 and raised livestock there. At the age of 63 he went there to live alone and remained there until he was nearly 80. From then until his death at 92 he lived with a son on Bakers Island.

Hannah, in poor health, visited William occasionally on Great Duck Island. She spent her last years with another son on Little Cranberry and died at the age of 69. This was the way families cared for their elderly when savings were small and only the able-bodied could earn a living.

LAURA ELIZABETH WARD RICHARDS
Gardiner   **Born 1850**

If any house in Maine could recount events that had transpired under its roof—no stories would be happier or more enticing than those told by the yellow house at the top of Vine Street in Gardiner.

Here Louise Elizabeth Richards lived with her husband, Henry, and their six children. Here the Richards family sang, played, laughed and grieved, welcomed the famous—(and none more famous than the brood's maternal grandmother, Julia Ward Howe)—and the near famous. Here there was a daily diet of reading (from the classics and in many languages) and writing. Yes, the writing. Laura Richards wrote daily.

Laura E. Ward was born in Boston on February 27, 1850. When, at 21, she married Henry Richards on June 17, 1871, her life style was dramatically changed. She left a life surrounded by family and friends in busy Boston and came to the veritable wilderness of Maine. Before too

many years had passed this sparkling wife and mother had attracted her own circle of friends and family and created an impressive literary circle in her community.

What of the writings? Laura Richards wrote for every age and every member of the family—biographies—"Florence Nightingale", "Joan of Arc", "The Life of Julia Ward Howe" (with her sister Maude Howe Elliott), nursery rhymes, children's stories, "nonsense rhymes"—reminiscences and chronicles of her life and times.

Laura Richards died at home in the yellow house after a three day bout with pneumonia in 1943. Her 93 years had been full and productive.

The youngest Richards child, Laura Elizabeth Richards II, Mrs. Charles Wiggins, sat in the book-lined parlor of the yellow house on a mild December Monday in 1975 and talked of her famous mother.

"Mother was extraordinary—She was a perfectly extraordinary person", she stated in an enthusiastic voice with more than a hint of her Boston years. "She came from a home visited by great literary figures, sheiks from Punjab—and famous actors—to this small Maine Village—and made a wonderful home for her family. Though she wrote every morning she gave her family her undivided attention—she *was* extraordinary!"

Mrs. Wiggins, a keen lady of 90 years, spoke adoringly of all her family. She chuckled happily (as one suspects her mother did), when she thought of some by-gone family incident. After one such outburst she explained, "I asked mother one time when I was home from college; 'Ma, do you believe in woman's suffrage?' Her prompt answer was, 'Yes of course, dear—Yes, I do!' But there was a long pause before she added with a chuckle, 'But I hope I'll be long dead before it ever comes.'

"You know mother wrote so easily. It just seemed no effort at all for her to create a story. She always wrote longhand, then typed her writing, edited it herself and re-typed it. Little wonder she seemed always to be at her desk. I guess she must have written 80 books!"

"I always marveled at her vitality and ability", she continued, "to find new and exciting things to write about— Once I said, Ma, how can you do it?'"

"Why child, it's perfectly simple. You just go down one step and say 'Tom', go down another step and say 'Tom'; on the third step you can say 'Tom, the Pig-Man'. Then you are off and away."

A brief Vignette that Betty Wiggins recounts could embody the uncluttered philosophy of Laura Richards. "Shortly after one of her babies was born, the family urged mother to go to Boston and enjoy a much-needed rest. When she left, the baby was completely happy and well. Within 24 hours the child was dead. Mother was home the next day for the funeral. Before the week was out—she started on a new book, "The Joyous Story of Toto", that does tell you something about mother, doesn't it?"

Laura Richards closes her interesting autobiography, "Stepping Westward", with this sentence.

"We have been young and have seen visions; we are old and have dreamed dreams, and the best of the dreams have come true."

CARRIE MATILDA MURRAY CHASE
Skowhegan   **Born 1876**

Carrie Matilda Murray Chase, the mother of the only woman ever elected to both the United States House of Representatives and the United States Senate, was never impressed by titles, rank, pomp and ceremony, or any other manifestations of prestige. She was truly her father's own daughter in spirit, attitudes and sense of values.

Instead she had a strong sense of family heritage and tradition. In an American society significantly characterized by migratory tendencies, she symbolized the sturdiness of those New Englanders whose roots grew deep and permanent. Born on May 10, 1876 in Skowhegan, Maine in the house built by her father, John L. Murray, for himself and his wife, Mary, several years earlier (except for short periods in Augusta and Shawmut), she never left this family house for the rest of her life prior to her terminal illness. And after she died, her funeral services were held in the family home. Her family house was the center for many activities in the interim, including being the 1948 campaign headquarters of the first woman ever elected to the U.S. Senate on her own.

Four Murray children were raised in this home. The oldest, Annie, became a well-known pianist. Carrie, who played the banjo, wished that she had been named Caroline Mae. A pretty and good student, her warm and friendly personality made her very popular in school. But she was impatient with school and intent on being on her own. Her eagerness to work made her regard school as a delaying barrier to her cherished desire of independence, significantly a dominant trait inherited by her daughter Margaret, who later was to have the same attitude toward school.

Encouraged by older girl friends and against the strong opposition of her father, she left school in her senior year to go to work. The great ambition of cabinetmaker John Murray was that all of his children obtain the best possible education and he dedicated himself to this goal. He stressed the value of a high school diploma to Carrie but her fierce independence made her deaf to his pleas and reasoning. But what he said was not completely in vain and without any lasting impact, for years later she insisted that her daughter Margaret complete high school when Margaret, in like-mother-like-daughter fashion, viewed high school as a frustrating delay and barrier to her own goal of independence.

Keenly disappointed by his daughter's decision, John Murray still exercised some discipline and a lesson to her when he notified her that, as a working girl, she would have to pay him a weekly board of five dollars while living in the family home. This did not deter her. Instead it pleased her sense of independence.

Two years later she married George Emery Chase, son of Reverend and Mrs. John Wesley Chase of Hinckley, Maine. Their wedding present from her thrifty father John was in the typical Murray tradition, for he presented her with a Skowhegan Savings Bank passbook with five hundred dollars credited to her account—the entire amount she thought she had been paying for her weekly board. In those days when the dollar was so much more valuable, this was a tremendous start for the young Chases.

Fourteen months later the first of six children, Margaret Madeline, was born in the Murray home as were subsequently Wilbur George, Roland Murray, Lawrence Franklin, Evelyn Mary and Laura Allison. Although in his work as a barber, George Chase had sufficient income to provide for the family, Carrie did not feel that it was enough to give the children all that she wanted them to have—full schooling, piano lessons, vacations and birthday parties. So she went to work to supplement the family income and to achieve her determination that her children do what she had failed to do—to complete high school. Her work through the years achieved this goal for her children.

A faithful wife, devoted mother and good housekeeper, she was also a thoughtful, helpful and delightful neighbor who dearly loved her telephone. Even after her husband George died in 1946, she continued living in the house her father built and in which she and all of her children had been born.

She dearly loved that little house, her family, her radio and her telephone. And she was particularly pleased when daughter Margaret sold the Clyde H. Smith big house and came back home to make the Murray house her campaign headquarters for her first Senate campaign in 1948. It was not the exciting campaign that pleased her so much as it was to have the little house vibrating again with occupants—Margaret and three members of her campaign staff whom Carrie mothered for those campaign months as her boarders.

On election night September 13, 1948, Carrie Murray Chase had mixed emotions. While she was happy that her daughter Margaret had been elected to the Senate, she was saddened by the thought that the end of the campaign meant the loss of her "campaign family".

In January 1949 Carrie went to Washington to see her daughter sworn in as the only woman in the United States Senate. She was pleased with the success, honor and admiration for her daughter—but as said at the outset, she was never impressed by titles, rank, pomp and ceremony, or any other manifestations of prestige. At a dinner given by Senator and Mrs. Owen Brewster honoring Margaret, Carrie's response to the compliments of Speaker Joseph W. Martin and Senate Majority Leader Kenneth Wherry, to Carrie on her daughter Margaret, was "You know that I have other children!" She never placed Margaret above the other children in her pride and affection.

In 1952 she underwent surgery for abdominal cancer at the Thayer Medical Center in Waterville, Maine. She remained there for two months with terminal diagnosis before being moved to the home of her daughter Evelyn and son-in-law Rexford St. Ledger, where she continued to receive round-the-clock care of fine nurses and doctors. A month later, she was moved to the home of Margaret, and a month later on election eve she passed away.

But in keeping with her wishes for her funeral services, she was taken back to her beloved little Murray home her father had built and her birthplace and that of her children where life had started not only for her but for hers.

MARTHA COBB BRANN
Lewiston   **Born 1882**

Martha Brann was born in Lewiston, Maine, January 22, 1882. She was educated in the Lewiston schools, employed by the telephone com-

pany, and on March 8, 1902, at the age of twenty, she married a young lawyer, Louis J. Brann. They had four children. Their first child, the only son, Donald L., lived but six years; this loss was a great blow. Three daughters followed, Marjorie Brann Doherty, Dorothy Brann Mac-Lennan, deceased, and Nancy E. Brann, who made her home with her mother. While her husband pursued his legal and political career she was busy caring for her family. She was not socially inclined but did belong to the Women's Literary Union and a bi-monthly sewing club.

In 1933 she went to Augusta to live as the wife of Maine's first Democratic Governor (Louis Jefferson Brann) to be elected since the Civil War. For four years she lived in the Blaine House where she established a reputation as one of the most gracious and admired hostesses ever to live in Blaine House. She travelled frequently with her husband and was always ready to assist in any way she could. Though the life in Augusta was a far cry from her usual way of life she adjusted immediately and thoroughly enjoyed her four years there. As a dinner guest at the White House she was seated next to President Roosevelt and found this a most enjoyable experience. Her husband was very proud of the wonderful job she did in Augusta. She and Margaret Chase Smith became close friends in Augusta, a friendship which endured over the years. The Senator was a regular visitor at Blaine House.

She was Christian Scientist and her religion was a source of great strength and comfort to her. A woman of high ideals but with a delightful sense of humor that could save the day with a warm smile. She was very fastidious in her dress, always perfectly groomed. She was noted for her lovely hats.

After her husband's tenure of office in Augusta she was glad to return to a more private life. They lived in Lewiston for five years, then at Falmouth Foreside. Her home was always open to her daughters and their families and they were frequent visitors, ever finding love and comfort there. When her husband passed on she moved to Portland and spent her remaining years quietly with a life centered around her three girls. Her daughter, Dorothy, passed on just five months after her mother. She was a truly lovely person of much strength and integrity. Her son-in-law, William H. Doherty, describes her as "the greatest", a lady in every way.

She passed on April 21, 1961.

Her two remaining daughters feel that they were greatly blessed by fine and loving parents.

TOY LEN GOON
Portland

Toy Len Chin, Brilliant Lotus, was born in Canton, China. She never attended school. When Toy Len was 19, Dogan Goon came to Canton from Portland, Maine to find a wife. Toy Len and Dogan left together for America and the laundry he established in Portland very soon after the wedding.

Portland had very few Chinese, but the Goons found a welcome among the sturdy New Englanders of the Maine city. They joined the First Baptist Church and there all the children participated in the activities. The Goons purchased war bonds and gave to civic causes even when money was scarce. They believed in America.

As each child grew old enough he was given small tasks in the laundry. Toy Len was careful to see that the children had time for sports and outdoor exercise, but study and work were done before play. She saw to it that they participated in civic activities and herself took over their share of the work in the laundry in order to release them. None of the children ever gave her

any serious concern—perhaps they were too busy to get into trouble. And they were popular in school—one son was elected vice president of his high school class, another was president.

As a result of his voluntary service in World War I, Dogan was an amputee and Toy Len shouldered a great share of the work. Dogan died in 1940, leaving Toy Len with eight children to raise, the youngest only three. Though she knew very little English she took over the business and made it successful. She made sure that the children would not have to give up their plans for schooling. As soon as she was able she purchased machinery which cut down the work time by a third. Eventually she purchased the three-story building which housed the laundry. This meant constant work and no luxuries. Toy Len made her own and her daughters' clothes. In the 12 years after her husband's death she had taken off only one week.

Toy Len's children include Carol, a medical doctor, Richard who studied at Rensselaer Polytechnic and later had his own television store, Edward, an MIT graduate with a PhD. from Rensselaer, Arthur who went on to Tufts after finishing his Navy hitch, Albert, a Law School graduate, and daughters Josephine and Doris, both married, and Janet who graduated from Simmons College.

According to Richard, his mother's favorite expression is "I'm glad." Perhaps this cheerful, persistent spirit is what has carried her through so many difficulties. She gives the credit to family solidarity, quoting a Chinese proverb: "If there is harmony in the family there is food in the larder and peace in the country." That gives us all something to think about.

Mothers of Achievement in American History   1776-1976

Sandra Morland

Maryland

Maryland

Nickname: Old Line State, Free State,
Oyster State

State Flower: Black-eyed Susan

State Bird: Baltimore Oriole

Committee Members

Chairman—Judge Allene L. Moreland,
Harewood

Writers

Vincent Godfrey Burns Poet Laureate of
Maryland
Colonel (Ret.) Allan Jackson Lamk
Mrs. Esta Fox
Mrs. Josephine Diefel
Mrs. Ethel Andrews
Mrs. Reed Dunn
Mrs. Anne Linder
Mrs. Bernice Carlton

Maryland

MARGARET BRENT

Born 1600

Colonial records reveal that Margaret Brent was a woman of "marked ability and great force of character." She was an extremely resourceful person in coping with the life situation in which she found herself. It has been suggested that her attitude was affected by her living in times when queens were ruling in many parts of the world.

The first patent of land recorded in Maryland is to two women, Margaret and Mary Brent. On October 7, 1639, they were granted land in St. Mary's County adjoining the land belonging to their brother, Colonel Giles Brent.

Margaret's sister Anne married Leonard Calvert. When he was the first governor of the colony, Calvert became critically ill. Some six hours before he died, he made a verbal will in the presence of Margaret Brent, Mistress Mary Brent and Thomas Greene (his successor). To Margaret Brent he said, "I make you sole executrix; tale all and pay all." Then he and Margaret held a private conference.

As executrix Margaret followed a strong course. She became lady of St. Gabriel's Manor. In 1648 as sole executrix of Calvert she demanded a seat in the General Assembly and a vote, in fact two votes: one for herself and one as the attorney for his Lordship. She was managing her own large plantation and also Leonard Calvert's. But her request astonished the gentlemen, and they turned her down. They thought only men should make the laws. It has been said that after the refusal, Margaret protested against every act of the Assembly.

Lord Baltimore was opposed to her participation in the Assembly. Margaret was vigilant in fighting to protect the estate for her sister's children. The question has been raised whether she realized that Leonard Calvert had a son and heir who was still in England. By 1650 she sold the Calvert great house and lot in the city of St. Mary's to Governor William Stone. (The heir's uncle Lord Baltimore recovered the property for him in 1658.)

When Lord Baltimore criticized Margaret's handling of the estate, the Assembly of 1649 defended her:

"As for Mistress Brent's undertaking and meddling with your estate, we do verily believe, and in conscience report, that it was better for the colony's safety at that time in her hands than in any man's else in the whole Province after your brother's death, for the soldiers would never have treated any other with that civility and respect, and though they were ever ready at several times to run into meeting, yet still she pacified them, till at last things were brought to that strait that she must be admitted and declared your Lordship's attorney by order of court."

Margaret Brent demonstrated the friendship of the Maryland colonists with the Indians by sponsoring the education of the young daughter of the Emperor of the Piscataway Indians. She and Leonard Calvert made her their ward.

When the colony of Maryland was first being planned, Margaret Brent and her sister Mary, who were close friends of the Calvert family, made careful plans to join the colony. On the first voyage Margaret sent five servants, so that land would be reserved for her and others of her family when they came a little later. In 1634 she, her sister, Mary, and Giles and Fulke, her two brothers arrived at St. Mary's, Maryland. The place of the Brent sisters, called Sisters Freehold, was just east of Leonard Calvert's. Margaret participated in the political and business discussions when Governor Calvert stopped by to talk with Giles Brent.

When political quarrels resulted in an attack on the town of St. Mary's and most of the townspeople took refuge in the fort, Margaret stayed defiantly in her own home. One attacker did take the hinges from her door, and made a fire with the door to roast some of her cattle for supper.

Although she lived in colonial times, Margaret Brent followed a way of thinking that was timeless.

DINAH NUTHEAD

The first seventeenth century business woman in Maryland and perhaps in America was Dinah Nuthead. Her husband had established a printing business.

Although Dinah could not write her own name, she supplied the capital and the brains to run her own business after her husband's death.

The General Assembly granted her a license on Feb. 7, 1694/5 to set up her printing press at Annapolis 'to print blanks, bills, bonds, writs, warrants of attorney, letters of administration and other necessary blanks useful for the public offices of this Province.'

The petition she presented to request the license promised that she would 'forfeit her license and her bond and go out of business if she should print anything other than specified.' She posted a bond of 100 pounds, lawful money of England.

Thus she became the public printer for the government, with employees operating the press.

MOLLY DARNALL CARROLL
Born 1749

America has heard the stories of Deborah Franklin, Abigail Adams and the young Martha Jefferson. Other women, less well known, stayed at home, burdened with children, aged parents, and hopes equal to those of the husbands they sent off to Philadelphia's Continental Congress. One of these was Molly Darnall Carroll.

Raised in the Carroll estate in Annapolis and distantly related to the family, Molly caught the attention of the promising son and heir on his return from sixteen years of studying and culturalization in Europe. She was sixteen when he returned, nineteen when she married him. About his future bride, Charles Carroll wrote a friend that Molly had "every quality to make me happy in the married state. Virtue, good sense, good temper . . . [She is] a sweet tempered, charming, neat girl." He might have added that she was intelligent and not without a fairly good education herself, and also that, as she would until her death, she adored him.

Like most colonial brides, Molly was doomed to bear many children (seven), bury several (three), and die before her thirty-fifth birthday. Her early years of marriage, however, were gay ones. Pretty, sociable, and adept at dancing and conversation, she helped her older and more serious husband enter fully into the society that had not readily hitherto admitted Catholic couples like the Carrolls. Even later, unwell herself and nursing several of her children through the effects of the new smallpox vacination, she entertained a distinguished guest, the Marquis de Lafayette with flair and enthusiasm.

Molly's avid interest in the birth of her new country was reflected in more than her expert social efforts. During the fourteen years of her marriage she was rarely in good health and had the heavy responsibilities of maintaining the welfare of a large estate; yet she encouraged her husband to give himself fully to such duties as those on the Continental Congress and the Board of War, duties which kept him far away most of the time. In all those years she and her husband had only one vacation trip together—to the health springs of Virginia. Once, in the winter of 1776, she apparently willed herself to recover from a grave illness sufficiently to allow her husband to make an inspection of General Washington's troops at Valley Forge. According to some, Molly's determination to allow her husband to make that visit was decisive in the future military fortunes of the struggling army as Charles Carroll was far more sympathetic to the plight of the General than others on the Board of War.

Concerned as she was about the momentous activities of the men in Valley Forge, Annapolis, and Philadelphia, Molly devoted herself fully to family matters. Her death in itself was a reflection of that devotion. Already ill herself, Molly watched her beloved father-in-law ("Papa") fall from a porch to his death. The shock killed her. Her husband never recovered from the double loss and lived his later years quietly with his daughter Mary. Doubtless Molly would have been proud of such accomplishments of his post war years as the freeing of his slaves and his efforts to help establish what later became the Republic of Liberia and of his laying of the first stone of the B and O Railroad. Surely she would have been proud of his soubriquet, "First Citizen" of Maryland.

NANCY HANKS LINCOLN
Born 1784

Abe Lincoln was born on February 12th, 1809, on a farm near Hodgenville, Kentucky. His mother was Nancy Hanks, who came from a family of humble and ordinary people in the area around Virginia and Maryland. She was the daughter of a fine woman named Lucy Hanks. In 1806 Nancy Hanks married Tom Lincoln, Abe's father. For the first months of their marriage Tom and Nancy lived in Elizabethtown, Kentucky. Their first child, Sarah, was born there. In 1808 Tom Lincoln bought a farm on the South Fork of Nolin River. Abe Lincoln was born there in a log cabin so rough and crude it looks more like a dog-house than a home. This log cabin may be seen exactly as it was when Abe Lincoln was born there, in a memorial building on the Lincoln farm near Hodgenville, Kentucky. Nancy must have been a very strong and courageous woman to bring up her family in that crude and primitive cabin.

The wind went howling that wintry day,
The snow was deep and the skies were gray,
Two neighbors met a crossroads store,
Seeking shelter from the blizzard's roar . . .

They huddled around a red-hot stove,
The cracker barrel their treasure-trove;
"Got any news out this-a-way, neighbor?"
The other coughed and groaned as if in labor
    . . .

"Heard tell Napoleon's on the march again—
This time, by cracky, I bet he'll win!
Madison's gone down to Washington
To get swore in for a four-years run—
Nuthin' ever happens out here I guess—
Here in this God-forsaken wilderness!" . . .

The storeman put a fresh log on the fire—
The dry pine crackled and the flames leaped
    higher—
"Down at Tom Lincoln's there's relief and joy,
The doc' jes' delivered them a ten-pound boy!"
    . . .

"Nuthin' ever happens"—and a mile away
In a log cabin shack on a cold winter's day
A baby was born who would some day be
A giant whose courage would set men free . . .

Little they knew on that cold wintry morn
What tremendous event in that place was born,
Nor to what heights that life would climb
In the seats of the mighty and the span of time
    . . .

In a smoke-filled cabin by a rough-hewn door
A cradle rocked on a bare earth floor—
A cradle containing the most precious freight—
The one whose hands would hold the nation's
    fate . . .

The wind went howling on that wintry day,
In a log cabin shack a baby lay
While a lonely woman with her face to the wall
Knew not that her son was the greatest of all!
    . . .

Vincent Godfrey Burns
Poet Laureate of Maryland

ANNIE CECELIA WIGGINS LAMB
Annapolis   **Born 1865**

Annie Cecelia Wiggins Lamb was born in the historic district of Annapolis, Maryland, on July 13, 1865. The little brick house of her family, which is still standing, was on East Street near State Circle and the colonial State House. She was the youngest of three daughters of Mr. and Mrs. William P. Wiggins. She was only six years old when her father died in 1871. Annie Cecelia was a dear Christian person. Widowed since 1935, she retired to her Heavenly Abode on Febuary 23, 1948, age 82, after a short illness. Three sons and one daughter still survive. At that time, she had four grandchildren. While she has no claim for greatness in public, she was great in her family's opinion "due to the *symplicity of her lifestyle*."—She was always at home when her children would return from school—which meant so much to them. She dressed them well, washed and mended their clothes, in fact, she would make the boys' shirts and her daughters' dresses. She was a wonderful cook too. She didn't demand her children do certain things (like being home by 10 pm), but she expected them to do what was right—and they respected her wishes. She saw that everyone went to Sunday School, and encouraged her family to go to church. She maintained a modest home, but a homey one. She didn't visit often (not having much free time)—but she loved to have company, both relatives and friends. This family has been so thankful, over the past 66 years, to have had a dear old-fashioned mother, who was a beacon guiding them to maturity. The family often thinks of the following phrase when recalling her passing on that cold-snowy morning on February 23, 1948:

"I am at home in my Father's house—in the mansion He prepared for me—in God's safe, quiet harbor".

Many miss her innate gentleness—her understanding of problems—her wisdom that helped lift the veil of depression, and her advice which put difficulties into a different perspective for so many people.

MAGGIE AUGUSTA BOONE

Born 1867

Maggie Augusta Boone was born in Broad Neck Hundred, Anne Arundel County, Maryland, on Thanksgiving Day, November 28, 1867. She was the daughter of Thomas Cross Boone and Mary Augusta Gambrill. Her parents lived at "Hollywood," a plantation which ran from Mill Creek to the main road.

On June 7, 1888, at St. Margaret's Episcopal Church, Broad Neck Hundred, Maggie Augusta Boone married Robert Moss, son of James Edward Moss and Adaline Melhorne. They were married by the Reverend Spencer.

Robert Moss practiced law in Annapolis, later becoming Judge of The Fifth Judicial Court of the Fifth District of Maryland. Judge and Mrs. Moss had four children, (Helen Louise (Mrs. Reynold Ronci) Robert Graham, James Ehlen and Mary Adelaide (Mrs. Benjamin Neilds Jackson) Major Graham Moss, USA, died in 1928.

Maggie Augusta Boone was educated at the Baltimore Female College Preparatory School 1880, the College proper in 1884, and the Maryland Normal School 1886. She was the Valedictorian of her class in 1884 and her thesis, "Heroic Women".

After graduation she entered the Maryland State Normal School, now State Teachers College, graduating in 1886. She was appointed teacher at the new school "Riverview", now known as Riva. Mrs. Moss was the first woman to serve on the board of school trustee of Anne Arundel County commencing in 1896.

On the 238th Anniversary of the convening of the first session of the General Assembly at the house of Major Edward Dorsey, Mrs. Moss was the official hostess to distinguished guests and visitors. This home of Mrs. Dorsey Gasway, later became the Public Library.

On May 7, 1934, she held her District Annual Meeting at St. Mary's Seminary to emphasize the Maryland Tercentenary being celebrated that year.

Mrs. Moss organized the first "Mothers' Circle", in Annapolis as it is now known throughout the years Parent-Teacher Associations. She was an ardent and faithful member of St. Anne's Episcopal Church. She was a woman of courage, vision and indomitable will.

1905-Organized Annapolis Civic League; its first president.

1914-Organized the Annapolis Branch of the Just Government League (Suffrage) President and member of advisory committee.

1915-Formed the Mothers' Circle (later Parent-Teacher Assn); with unbroken membership.

1916-Became first vice-president of the Maryland State Parent Teachers Association and remained on the Board in some capacity for 15 years.

1918-Chosen to plan the establishing of Young Women's Christian Association in Annapolis. President of Board of Directors and trustee.

1919-First President of Church Service League of Saint Anne's Parish- a merger of all the guilds and societies in the Parish.

1920-This was the year suffrage was granted and our Just Government League merged into Annapolis League of Women Voters. First President of that League.

1921-Appointed by Governor Ritchie as the Anne Arundel County Representative on his Advisory Committee for the consolidation of State Organizations.

Mrs. Moss died on April 28, 1942, she was active in community organizations until her death.

MARY ANN GRAHAM

Mary Ann Graham was born on a farm near Baltimore. Her mother was a professional singer and her father was a minister of the Gospel. As her parents were devoted Christians she had a heritage of love for God, man and nature. Mary loved to travel. She believed that understanding our own Nation was a very important and glorious part of human life. She travelled across the nation many times to the state of California. She went by bus and by car and several times by plane.

Mary Ann was a member of the American Farm Bureau. She was also a member of the Reisterstown Women's Club. She composed the words and music for twenty songs. She was a Sunday School teacher and also the Superintendent of the Sunday School. For nine years she also taught in the public schools. She loved fishing, crabbing, boating and swimming. She also was a horse-back rider and greatly enjoyed poetry, music and good literature, but most of all she loved the Bible.

Her patriotism was outstanding and she was a deeply dedicated disciple of the Lord Jesus Christ. She published a book of poems called "Do Not Want Too Much". Her poems are full of noble sentiments, very wise observations and uplifting thoughts. Her's was a life well-lived and in character and nobility she was one of America's great women. Mary was alive to things which are pure, lovely, kind, good and all of God's great creations. The knowledge that an everlasting Life awaited her made her very happy and very much alive!

Mary Ann Graham said: "The best preparation for a life to come is to live now, today right up to your highest and best. The life that God gives us is a great privilege and He allows us to use it exactly as we please. We are free when we can command ourselves!"

Mary Ann met a fine young man, a farmer, and they were married. She mothered four children. First a boy, then a girl, and then twin girls. The farm they owned was well-equipped and beautifully located, surrounded with natural beauty. There was always good food and there was plenty of healthy work for all. This was one happy family. She felt she had the riches of the whole world in her own hands, her children were her jewels.

Most of the time the family went about singing and working together, happy always to be in the home, on the farm, and at church together. Mary Ann was always a good example and an inspiration to all. Her life was rich and filled with joy, because she knew that she was safe in the hands of the Lord. Her life was a complete circle, it knew no end. We liken it to the inspiration of Springtime, the flowery growth of Summer, the beautiful harvests of Autumn, and the angelic contentment of the Winter. May God bless all mothers like Mary Ann Graham!

REBECCA LLOYD NICHOLSON

Early on a July morning in 1861 a group of young girls known as the Monument Street girls met, as they had become in the habit of doing, to sew garments for the use of Confederate soldiers. Many of their young friends and brothers would enlist shortly in the Confederate Army and leave. They met at the residence of Mr. James Carroll, 105 West Monument Street (now 225 West Monument Street) as guests of Mrs. Corwin, the daughter of Mr. Carroll, and her three daughters, Achsah, Ida, and Mary W., who also resided there. Among the friends who gathered daily to sew and exchange news was Rebecca Lloyd Nicholson. All in the group were in sympathy with the South.

A lawyer's son and a "handsome beau of the day", Mr. H. Rozier Dulany of Baltimore came by every day to bring news of the South to the ladies. One day he was very pleased with some verses that had been given to him by someone on Baltimore Street. When he read the verses, they were enthusiastically received. They were "Maryland! My Maryland!". James Ryder Randall, a Marylander teaching at Poydras College, Pointe Coupee, Louisana, had written the poem in indignation over hearing the news of the clash between Union soldiers and Baltimore civilians on Pratt Street on April 19, 1861. His call to Maryland to leave the Union and join the Confederacy was printed in the New Orleans *Delta*, reprinted in other papers through the South, including the Baltimore *The South*.

Mr. Dulany proposed that the words be set to music. Turning through the pages of a Yale book of songs on the piano, the young people tried some. Mr. Dulany proposed "Lauriger Horatius", a Yale college song. The Cary sisters, Jennie and Hettie, changed the second and fourth lines of each stanza to fit the music better. The one word "Maryland!" was changed to "Maryland! My Maryland!."

They decided the song should be published. "But those were the days when mothers even had to look for their babies, who wore red sashes and shoulder knots with their white dresses, at police stations, and Southern sympathizers were too often taken off to prison at Fort McHenry" so Mr. Dulany declined to take the song to a publisher. He felt Fort McHenry was too near for taking risks.

The girls accused him of being a coward, but he still refused. Rebecca Nicholson spoke up, with flashing eyes.

"I am not afraid. My father is a Union man, and if they put me in prison he will get me out."

Mrs. Norris copied the verses. Rebecca went to her home a few doors from Mr. Carroll's to get her music book, and copied the music. That same morning she took it in Miller and Beacham, a Baltimore music publishing firm. (Sometimes the music used is "Tannenbaum, O Tannenbaum.") The song was popular with the Confederate Army; it was sung as the unofficial state song of Maryland until it was made the official song in 1939.

Mr. Miller knew Rebecca. She told him if he would publish the song, she would give him the copyright. When he asked who should be credited with the music and the publishing, Rebecca remembered Mr. Dulany's concern. She replied any letters except R and D; her own initals were left out by this precaution. The initials C and E were used.

The publishers sent her six copies of the song, with their compliments. Afterwards the firm sent her copies of the different Southern songs they published, until they were arrested for publishing some.

Rebecca later married Edward Shippen. Her courageous and patriotic action did not lead her to prison.

CARRIE CAROLINE MILLIGAN REVELLE
Manokin   Born 1880

Carrie Caroline Milligan Revelle was born at Manokin, an Indian Reservation in the colonial days, Somerset County, on the Eastern Shore of Maryland, on April 15, 1880. Her original family home, which vanished many years ago, was a beautiful brick historic landmark on the banks of the Manokin River. It was interesting to hear her tell how the cooking was done in a very large fireplace, and that all the rooms were heated by the same method. Her mother was a seamstress and a nurse who in those days traveled near and far. Carrie Caroline used to accompany her on some of these visits. She reared her family by many hard days of work, having taught her children "to respect everyone and to give your best to whatever you undertook." Her father died very young, leaving her mother with fifteen children to care for. Mrs. Revelle's homey white clap-board house where she lived following her marriage, at age sixteen, still

stands at Upper Fairmount, Somerset County, near historic Princess Anne, Maryland. It is located in the vicinity of the country cemetery where her husband, Samuel, and her young son, Wendell, are buried. She retired to her Heavenly Abode on May 23, 1965, age eighty-five. At the time of her death, she had one grandchild and two great-grandchildren. She was a Christian mother who reared her children by the Bible, and inspired them to live by the Golden Rule. She worked hard and diligently in the home, with boarding facilities, to support her family. Later in life her daughters supported her in their lovely home in Eastport, Annapolis. She was traditional in that she said grace before each meal, "thanking the Lord for His blessings received and about to be received". She saw that her children went to Sunday School regularly as well as Sunday evening church services. Her three daughters still survive.

Mrs. Revelle was indeed a wonderful cook, specializing in Eastern Shore seafood cooking.

JULIA BOWIE TISDALE NORMAN
Born 1889

Julia Bowie Tisdale was born in Annapolis, Maryland on September 21, 1889, daughter of Lt. Ryland Dillard Tisdale and Julia Waring Merrick. Her father died when she was twelve and her mother moved from Prince George's County to Annapolis with six small children to support, which she did by running a boarding house.

Julia graduated from high school in 1906 and earned her Teaching Certificate from State Normal School in Towson, Maryland. She taught several years in a one-room school in Iglehart, Maryland. In 1911 she married John Hugh Norman, and went to New York to live. Her husband died in 1924 leaving her with very little money and five young children. She however, went on to Columbia University and received her Bachelor of science Degree and returned to teaching in order to support her family.

She went back to Annapolis in 1926 and taught school for the next 36 years in various schools. She purchased a home on Prince George Street where she has lived continuously for the past 49 years. During this time, through the depression years, when the State and County frequently had no money to pay their teachers, Mrs. Norman rented rooms to the Midshipmen's

Hop girls and took a few steady roomers to make ends meet. Although it was a tremendous struggle physically as well as financially, she managed to keep her family together and see that they all received their education. Four of her children graduated from Annapolis High School and one from Mount St. Joseph's in Baltimore. The oldest daughter went to business college and worked as a legal secretary. One son went into the Navy and one son went into the Army. One of the daughters married after high school graduation. Another child became a dental assistant. The five children are now scattered to the four corners of the Untied States. The oldest, Julia Waring Norman, married to Captain Donald F. Krick, USN Ret. lives in Seattle, Washington; John Hugh Norman, Jr. is retired and living in Hollywood, Florida; Eleanor Kirschner Norman is married to Colonel William D. Roberson, USMC Ret. and living in Coronado, California; Robert Ryland Tisdale Norman and his family live in Annapolis where he is a tax consultant; Katherine (Kathleen) Merrick Norman is married to Carl E. Johnson, a chemical engineer in Claremont, New Hampshire, where she is a service manager for W.T. Grant.

Mrs. Norman's interests have embraced history, government and art. While teaching history in high school, she also took courses at the Maryland Institute of Art, and as an extra curricular activity she sponsored an art club long before that subject was taught in the public schools.

After her retirement at the age of 70, she completed a correspondence course with the Famous Artists School and won many honors with her paintings. She is proud of her heritage and her country, believing in good government and citizen participation. She has kept up with world events as well as local by subscribing to current affairs and history publications. She is extremely interested in Maryland history as her ancestors settled here in the 1600's and have been prominent in government and law.

As a member of many patriotic organizations including DAR, UDC, Colonists, St. Mary's Association, Pen Women of America, Womens University Club etc. she has held various offices, including Historian. She is an accomplished public speaker and has spoken to various groups on history and current affairs.

As a devout Catholic she has raised her five children to be good Christians. The lives of her children reflect the influence exerted by her devotion to her family, her sheer determination and hard work that enabled her family to survive. Her acceptance of her responsibilities as a parent are a tremendous tribute to her strength, courage, and faith in God and herself. Her five children, twenty-six grandchildren and sixteen great grandchildren are lucky to share such a rich heritage.

EDNA RUBY LOUISE TROTT
Born 1920

Ruby Stevens was born in Shady Side, Maryland on March 3, 1920 to Richard Packard Trott and Elizabeth Sara Linton, one of two daughters born to them. She grew up in a small village of some 700 people. She attended the local elementary school and was graduated from high school to which she went by bus.

Ruby then went on to Fleet's Business School in Annapolis and this is where "destiny" stepped in. She met Raymond and married him in January 1940. They settled in Annapolis, the capital of the state. They became parents of three children, Raymond Russell, Jr., Robert Byron, and Mary Beth.

To watch Ruby's progress in life, while undergoing pregnancies intertwined with schooling and work, is an amazing picture. She must have excelled in English, Spelling, and Literature, for as you will note her positions deal with the need for these skills. She acted as secretary in many business firms before becoming an aide in a school for exceptional children. While doing this, Ruby matriculated at Maryland University in special education and became a teacher of exceptional children, teaching for seven years. From this work, she was called into the Board of Education in the county where she became secretary to the heads of several departments before becoming secretary to the Assistant Superintendent of Schools in Anne Arundel County. Finally, Ruby became "proof reader" in a new department "Word Processing" at the board. This work necessitated the proof reading of all materials dictated by the superintendents, supervisors, and others to secretaries before the material was sent to the parties intended. Each of these positions required special preparation and Ruby continued through night-schooling to meet the requirements. "As each type of work opened up to me, I felt challenged and immediately closed the gap in my education by dint of hard study".

All through this maze of new work and changes, Ruby Trott Stevens never wavered. She was a mother first and no amount of outside duty could swerve Ruby from the service to her family. Her children reveal this love and devotion. Steve is director of data processing at the local hospital having finished at the Baltimore Institute. Byron is a teacher of French in a local high school having graduated from Western Maryland College. Mary Beth is a dental assistant and attended Roanoke College. All of them are at mother's and dad's side on Sunday morning including Ruth Ann, a daughter-in-law

and two grandchildren. This means that their church is the center of their lives. Two teach Sunday school, while Ruby and Raymond sing in the choir.

As a mother, Ruby never seems to coerce, she performs by example. Her attitude shows tolerance, patience, understanding, determination and undergirding it all, a love of God and country. Her deep devotion permeates her ever-ready beautiful smile, her charming manner, her gracious act of listening and loyalty to her firm convictions.

Ruby with her family now lives in a comfortable home erected on acreage near Shady Side and has returned to her friends she knew in childhood, and to the church of her girlhood. She and Raymond are devoting themselves to the furtherance of beauty and brotherhood through the hours of labor in a "green house" and through their service to their community.

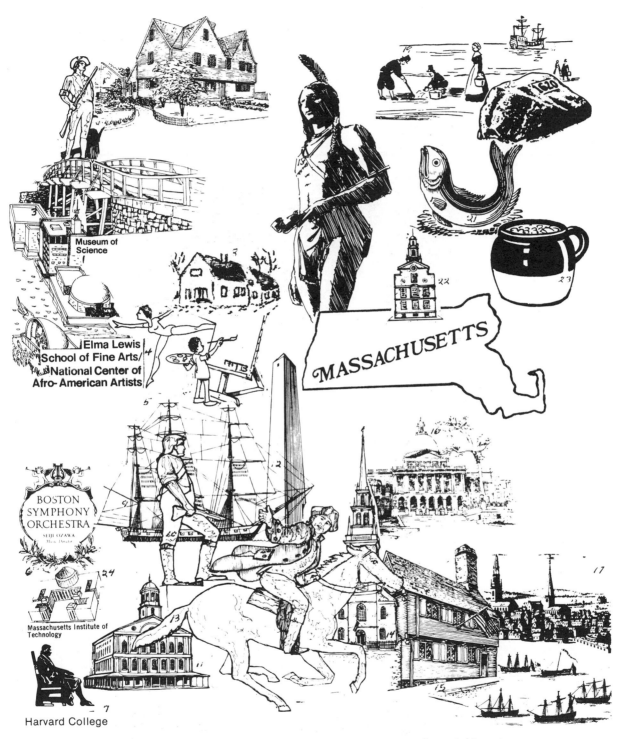

Museum of Science

Elma Lewis
School of Fine Arts/
National Center of
Afro-American Artists

MASSACHUSETTS

BOSTON
SYMPHONY
ORCHESTRA
SEIJI OZAWA
Music Director

Massachusetts Institute of
Technology

Harvard College

By the sword we seek peace, but peace only under liberty.

Sketch of Dorothy Quincy Hancock House

Massachusetts

. LET'S MAKE THE BI-CENTENNIAL A FAMILY CELEBRATION!

Massachusetts

SUSANNA BOYLSTON ADAMS
Muddy River   **Born 1709**

In the tiny village of Muddy River, Massachusetts, the residents all rejoiced with Mr. and Mrs. Peter Boylston when they welcomed the birth of their new daughter, Susanna, on March 5, 1709. The Boylston family began with Susanna's Grandfather Thomas Boylston's arrival in the new country in the 1600's. They had been major participants in the welfare of this little community which was to become the town of Brookline. Thomas's Son, Zabdiel, introduced the first method of smallpox inoculation into the Colonies, by inoculating the residents with the first smallpox serum used here. Susanna grew up in a fine house overlooking Boston Harbor, with its islands, woods, and fields bordering the water making a scenic panorama, providing an environment of abundance with beauty.

Susanna married the forty-three year old farmer, Deacon John Adams of Braintree, on October 31, 1734. Her sister was married to John's brother, a minister and graduate of Harvard. Deacon John, a descendant of the Pilgrims John and Priscilla Alden, was a farmer and a village Selectman. Each New England village had a town meeting form of Government with Selectmen to administer its affairs. Three sons were born to Susanna and John: John, Peter and Elihu. Susanna was well schooled in the basic skills of Reading, Writing, and Arithmetic as well as the art of homemaking.

Their first and most illustrious son, John, arrived on October 30, 1735. Peter and Elihu followed in quick succession. Since Susanna's ancestors were Harvard trained, it was decided that John would attend this famous school. Susanna and John were very proud of their firstborn, and it was felt that a Harvard education was his birthright as the eldest son. She nurtured and trained him to become a student and a minister. Although John found studying very difficult, he knew farm work to be much harder, so he applied himself diligently to his studies. As his studies progressed he chose not to become a minister, but apprenticed himself to understudy law in Worcester and became a member of the Massachusetts Bar of law. He was an avid reader and very interested in the current affairs of the times. He became one of New England's leading intellectuals, a patriot; and prior, during and after the Revolutionary War, a founding father of the new structure that changed America's history. He served as the first Vice-President of the new country under President George Washington and following their second Administration, John Adams became the second President of the United States but served only one term, losing his bid for a second term to Thomas Jefferson.

Susanna was widowed at age fifty-two. She remarried five years later, one Lieutenant John Hall. He was a good companion to her for the next fourteen years, but it was a match which her children never seemed to approve.

When Lieutenant Hall died, Susanna spent many lonely years, still a woman in her sixties. Peter and Elihu lived nearby, but John traveled extensively as he served America in many capacities. John's wife Abigail spent much time in the later years caring for his twice widowed mother. Both John's wife and mother missed his inaugural ceremonies held in New York City.

While Susanna was critically ill, in her last days, Abigail remained at her bedside lovingly attending her needs until her death, April 17, 1797, at eighty-eight years of age. Since her sons had refused to recognize her second marriage through the years, it is not surprising that at her death they continued to ignore it. They sadly mourned her passing—and her headstone bears their family name: SUSANNA ADAMS.

ABIGAIL SMITH ADAMS
Weymouth   **Born 1744**

Abigail Smith was born in Weymouth, Massachusetts on November 11, 1744. Though a frail child during the early growing years, this daughter of the Reverend William and Elizabeth Quincy Smith of Weymouth, Massachusetts, was encouraged by her Grandmother Smith, not only to master the skills of Reading, Writing and Arithmetic, but to also become a competent homemaker. This nurturing process gave her a balanced upbringing. It developed all the proficiency needed by the pioneer woman, while it strengthened her character and engendered a wholesome personality. These abilities coupled with her engaging wit attracted John Adams, an intellectual young lawyer in Braintree's tiny village, who had matriculated at Harvard College, 1755.

The Reverend Mr. Smith did not at first favor the idea of his daughter, Abigail, marrying John Adams. He considered the Adams family only farmers (and shoemakers when it rained) because the Smiths had aristocracy on their side. However, he succumbed to the pleadings of his young daughter and gave the young couple his blessing. So John and Abigail were married one evening at early candlelight in the church at Weymouth. While the reception was being held in the parsonage, John and Abigail slipped out the back gate, walked hand in hand down the road that passed through the woods, crossed a pasture lot and reached their small cottage in Braintree. The new home was all in order, for Abigail was well schooled in the homemaking arts. Their new life began with the glory of the rising sun.

As John became involved in the controversial issues of the day, he lost all of his old friends who remained loyal to the Crown. Abigail bolstered his courage as he wrote for the "Boston Gazette" and became an activist for the Revolutionary cause. Being well known for his Civil Rights stand, he was asked to defend the British soldiers, who were accused of murder in the Boston Massacre, and won their acquittal. This defense temporarily lost him the support of the Patriots, but that soon cleared as they saw that he meant fair trials and representation for all. Abigail's love, her trust, her common sense, and her skills coupled with her willingness to do hard work aided him as he served as Circuit Rider Judge, Representative to Massachusetts General Court, as well as a young lawyer who had a lucrative law practice.

During the first ten years of their marriage, five children were born: Abigail, 1765, John Quincy, 1767, Susannah, 1768, Charles, 1770, Thomas, 1772, (Elizabeth, their sixth, was born 1777 but still-born). Of these, Susannah died in infancy, and Charles in 1800. For years Abigail ran the farm and provided much of their food, such as dairy products and grain. Lovingly she wrote John in Boston of the children's doings and hers. In 1768 she and the children joined John in Boston for six years, but due to the Colonists' defiance in refusing to pay the tea tax at the time of the Boston Tea Party, 1773, Britain closed the Port, and the economy caused their move back to the tiny house on the farm with its increased acreage. After settling the family, her husband traveled overland to represent Massachusetts at the first Continental Congress in Philadelphia. Abigail operated the farm with prudence and provided well for her family and the help. Though she was supportive of John's activities, she missed him terribly the next ten years, until the Peace Accord was finally signed. After a brief time in France in 1777, John returned, but Congress soon sent him to Holland where he also took John Quincy and Charles in order to broaden their education.

In 1783 amid much rejoicing Abigail accepted John's invitation to join him in France. Leaving the younger boys with her sister and husband, she sailed with daughter Abigail, a courier and a maid, an ample supply of food and a cow. The Paris mansion near the park, Bois de Boulogne, was a real joy to this farm wife, and she basked in her new life. In 1785 John moved the family to Grosvenor Square, London, when he became the United States' first envoy to the

Court of St. James. Cooly and dutifully received according to the diplomatic protocol, they were then left alone. Those years, after having made their courtesy call on George III and plain Queen Charlotte, proved to be their happiest while in the political arena.

Abigail loved the social life of a Vice-President's wife for the eight years he served in that capacity, while he fumed and felt his minor duties as President of the Senate a waste of time. While he served his only term as President, 1798-1802, Abigail moved her family and furniture into the new White House. She found her new home damp and drafty. Her furnishings were sparse in the huge mansion, and she was glad to return to their new large home in Quincy which they had purchased on their return from Europe.

Due to her astute management in the early years, they enjoyed a prosperous old age. Abigail saw her son John Quincy become Secretary of State before she succumbed to typhoid in 1818. Her beloved husband outlived her by eight lonely years and witnessed his son John Quincy become the sixth President. He died on the Nation's fiftieth anniversary, July 4, 1826, having joined his Abigail again. Abigail Adams has been the only woman who was destined to be a wife and also the Mother of a President.

MARY ASHTON RICE LIVERMORE
Boston   **Born 1821**

Mary Ashton Rice Livermore, an American Reformer, was born in Boston, Massachusetts, December 19, 1821. She was educated in Boston and at fifteen entered the Charlestown Female Seminary. Before her first term ended one of the teachers died, and this intelligent, capable, alert young teenager (at this point of time she was considered a young lady) was asked to fill the vacancy. She earned enough money as a teacher to pay her costs, and through extra studies finished the four year course in two years.

After graduation she taught two years in a plantation school in Virginia. She returned to Massachusetts to assume charge of the Duxbury High School.

At the age of twenty-three, she married the Reverend D. P. Livermore. In 1857, with their three young daughters, they moved to Chicago where she aided her husband in editing THE NEW COVENANT, a religious paper.

In 1861 the nation found itself plunged into the Civil War. At this time, Mrs. Livermore was visiting in Boston where she witnessed the sons of Massachusetts depart for battle. Having been moved by the sad scenes of young men leaving for the war, she resolved to help them in every possible way. Returning to Chicago she became an associate member of the United States Sanitary Commission and became agent for the Northwest Branch. With a few other women she traveled to Washington to talk with President Lincoln. At this time there were barriers which kept women from serving soldiers in the war area. The women petitioned the President for the privilege of serving soldiers at war. The great heart of Lincoln was moved, and he nullified the barriers that existed. Now women could help the wounded, the sick and the dying soldiers in hospitals, behind the lines of battle or wherever there was a need.

Mrs. Livermore's first broad experience in war was after the battle of Fort Donelson, Dover, Tennessee, February 1862. There were no hospitals for the soldiers. The wounded and dying were hauled away on rough board Tennessee wagons, most of them dying before they reached St. Louis, Missouri. She saw the need of hospitals, of medical supplies for the injured and of hot soups, foods, etc. for the battle-weary soldiers. She directed that the Sanitary Commission send boatloads and wagon loads of needed supplies to the battle area. The women then joined in the work of the caring for and comforting of the soldiers of the North. They entered the army pits and the hospitals to bring comfort to the injured and peace to the dying.

To make money for the cause, Mary Livermore spoke to great throngs of people. She decided to try a Sanitary Commission Fair in Chicago. Farmers and merchants were solicited for their produce and merchandise. The Board of Trade in Chicago tried to discourage the project in which the women had invested $10,000.00 and hoped to clear $25,000.00. They realized over $100,000.00. Other large cities held like fairs, raising a total of over $2,000,000.00.

After the war Mrs. Livermore devoted her talents to promotion of woman's suffrage and to temperance reform. She founded the *Agitator* in Chicago in 1869, which in 1870 was merged into the *Woman's Journal* (Boston) of which she was the associate editor until 1872. She lectured in the United States, England and Scotland, contributed to magazines, authored several books, and with Frances E. Willard edited "Women of the Century" (Biographical Sketches of Leading American Women), in 1893. She was president of many of the women's organizations during that era. Her last years were spent in Melrose, Massachusetts, where she died May 23, 1905, at the age of 83 years.

MINNIE RYAN DWIGHT
North Hadley   **Born 1873**

Minnie Ryan Dwight was born June 22, 1873, the daughter of Patrick and Catherine Riley Ryan of North Hadley, Massachusetts. She graduated from Hopkins Academy, took special courses at Mount Holyoke College, and entered the teaching profession within her own community. In 1891 she left her teaching position in North Hadley to become a reporter for the "Holyoke Transcript" where she quickly displayed a remarkable talent for news gathering. Her success was largely due to one of her greatest assets—a warm and personal interest in people.

In 1896 Minnie Ryan married William G. Dwight, owner and publisher of the "Holyoke Transcript," whose first wife had died a few years earlier. Her influence became evident in a very short time as she joined her husband in revising the editorial policies of the paper.

Minnie Dwight was an early and enthusiastic champion of women's rights and committed the paper to a strong stand on women's suffrage and other social and political needs of the day, including child care and problems of the elderly.

Her countless community endeavors and involvements and honors bestowed upon her during her lifetime are far too numerous to list here. Her friends were legion and came from all walks of life, from the poor of Holyoke to Presidents of the United States. She was a gracious hostess as well as a shrewd businesswoman, and her home was often the focal point for community affairs.

Mrs. Dwight had three children: Helen Mary (Mrs. Oscar E. Schoeffler, Florida) and Laura Sluyter (Mrs. Richmond Lewis, Springfield) and one son, William. She also had a stepson, Henry, by her husband's first wife.

The Dwights built a second home in Fruitland Park, Florida, on an estate they called Pine Eden. Here they spent most of their winters, still working daily for the newspaper. Mr. Dwight died in 1930, and Minnie Dwight assumed the job as president-treasurer of the Transcript, which had by then merged with another paper and was called the "Holyoke Transcript-Telegram."

Mrs. Dwight was truly a legend in her own time. She was known as a woman who successfully incorporated into her life a profession, home, family, and community services. When she died July 31, 1957, after sixty-six years in newspaper work, she was known as the country's oldest woman newspaper publisher. After her death, William Dwight, Sr. carried on the family tradition and is still publisher of the "Holyoke Telegram." His son, William Dwight Jr., is the associate publisher and editor of the newspaper. Another son, Donald R. Dwight, distinguished himself and his family by being elected Lieutenant Governor of Massachusetts with Governor Francis W. Sargent, serving from 1971 to 1974.

Minnie Ryan Dwight's foremost desire was to make Holyoke a better place in which to live, and during her lifetime she never lost her concern for the people of her city. Her kindness and vigorous championships of myriad causes, particularly concerning women, and a brilliant journalistic career made her the soul and spirit of the paper she headed and the home she made for her family.

ROSE FITZGERALD KENNEDY
Boston   **Born 1890**

Rose Fitzgerald Kennedy has known the joys of the highest achievements of family members and the great sorrows of losing four adult children in tragic accidents. She has, along with other family members, devoted hundreds of hours to promote benefits for the 'special child'. There are children who, for reasons known only to God, go through this life physically and mentally handicapped. All of the Kennedys share this responsibility with her as they grieve over Rosemary's handicap. In 1946 they established the Kennedy Foundation in honor of Lt. Joe, Jr. who was lost in air combat in World War II. Since then they have continued to found and support over twenty hospitals and schools for research, education and care of these children.

Personally, Mrs. Kennedy has devoted much time and effort in giving lectures around the world to further many charitable causes. She has traveled extensively all of her life. In the early years she accompanied her father to Latin America and Europe. Following her marriage, she and Ambassador Kennedy and their family continued visiting and serving abroad.

Rose Elizabeth Fitzgerald, eldest child of John Francis Fitzgerald and Mary Josephine Hannon, was born in Boston's North End on July 22, 1890. Her father became affectionately known in Massachusetts politics as Honey-Fitz. His parents, Irish immigrants Thomas Fitzgerald and Rose Mary Murray, arrived in Boston from County Wexford in the 1840's and were married here. John Francis, a first generation American, served six years as a United States Representative and six years as Mayor of Boston. The Southeast Expressway in Boston is named in his

honor and memory. He was very proud of his beautiful daughter Rose and took her on his campaigning jaunts from an early age. With him she learned early to be a charming public speaker and has always been a great asset to her family in all of their services and campaigns. She graduated from Dorchester High School with honors at fifteen; then continuing her studies, she attended the Convent of the Sacred Heart in Boston and later the Sacred Heart Convent in Aachen, Germany, where she specialized in French, German, and Music. Mrs. Kennedy has always been interested in the French language and in French history. After graduating from college she belonged to the Alliance Francaise in Boston and the German Club. During the campaigns of her sons, the late U.S. President John Kennedy, the late Senator Bobby, and the present Senior Senator Teddy, she spoke French as well as English on many occasions. She is, along with daughters Jean Smith, Eunice Shriver, Patricia Lawford, and daughters-in-law Ethel, Jacqueline and Joan, a vivacious, and vibrant asset to the Kennedy men and in-laws in any campaign, business or government post in which they serve.

She married Joseph P. Kennedy, only son of another Irish immigrant family, Patrick Joseph Kennedy and Mary Hickey, of Boston in 1914. Joe and Rose had nine children. During his lifetime as a banker, businessman and government servant she was a gracious hostess in their homes in Boston, New York, Washington, D.C., or London. Their first home was in Brookline at 83 Beals Street and is now a part of the National Trust and open to the public. There, during the first five years of their marriage, they welcomed the births of their first four children, Joe, Jr., Jack, Rosemary, and Kathleen. They sold this house and moved to a larger one in the neighborhood on Naples Road in 1921, where Eunice, Pat and Bobby were born. Family enterprise business took the Kennedys to New York to live, but Mrs. Kennedy returned to St. Margaret's Hospital in Boston a couple of times for Jean's and then Teddy's birth.

While Ambassador Kennedy represented the United States at the Court of St. James, Mrs. Kennedy and the three eldest daughters were presented to the Royal Court.

Pope Pius XII conferred the title of Papal Countess in December, 1951, on Rose Elizabeth Fitzgerald Kennedy in recognition of her "exemplary motherhood and charitable works."

Mrs. Kennedy is still very active in public affairs, as her son Ted is Senior Senator from Massachusetts, and she has given of her vitality and vibrant health coupled with her wonderful personality to public activities, both political and charitable. The lessons taught by her father served her well through her husband's and sons' illustrious careers. Rose Kennedy has always set an admirable example for family, nation and the world. May she continue to serve in good health for many years.

JENNIE LOITMAN BARRON

Born 1891

To list, or even summarize the accomplishments of Jennie Loitman Barron, would be the compilation of a catalogue of "firsts." One of four daughters born of Jewish immigrants in Boston on October 12, 1891, she gained recognition early, chosen as the valedictorian of her high school class at the age of fifteen. When women's education stopped at the high school level, she worked her way not only through college, but law school, graduating from Boston University in 1911 and Boston University Law School in 1914. Marrying Samuel Barron, Jr. in June, 1918, she and her husband established the law firm of Barron and Barron. She was appointed the first female assistant attorney general of the Commonwealth of Massachusetts in 1934, the first female master of the Commonwealth in civil litigation, and a special justice of the Boston Municipal Court in 1934. Early in her career, she was admitted to practice before the United States Supreme Court. She attained another first with her appointment as a full-time justice of the Boston Municipal

Court in 1937, no other woman in the Commonwealth having accomplished that feat. She was elected president of the Massachusetts Association of Women Lawyers. She became the only United States female delegate to the first United Nations Congress on Crime held in Switzerland in 1955. Gaining further professional recognition, in 1959 she was appointed the first female justice of the Superior Court of the Commonwealth of Massachusetts. She was also the first and only female judge to sit with the judiciary of more than thirty foreign countries.

Jennie Loitman Barron had many interests in addition to her profession. She was an activist in women's lib decades before the phrase was coined, as she spoke widely in behalf of women's suffrage and jury rights, as well as drafting the bill allowing women to be notaries public. Also active in communal organizations, she became the founder, first president and honorary president of the New England women's division of the American Jewish Congress; a president of the Boston chapter of Hadassah; the first president of the Beth Israel Hospital women's auxiliary and subsequently its first honorary president, trustee and honorary trustee of the hospital, one of Harvard Medical School's outstanding teaching hospitals; and the first mother to serve on the Boston School Committee. Concerned with philanthropy, she was also a trustee and then an honorary trustee of the Combined Jewish Philanthropies. Vitally interested in her synagogue, she became the first woman trustee and later, the first female honorary trustee of Temple Israel in Boston.

Jennie Loitman Barron often remarked that of all her degrees, including the honorary degree awarded by Boston University Law School, the one most important to her was her MRS.

Her passionate devotion to her husband and family was unique. At her busiest, she always had time for her Sam and their three daughters, Erma, Deborah, and Joy, and took great pride in their achievements. Especially meaningful to her was her youngest daughter's graduation from Boston University Law School, and later, her oldest grandson's graduation, thus becoming the only family with three generations to graduate from Boston University Law School.

Her youngest daughter has said that her fondest memories are of the Friday nights when the sisters with their children and husbands gathered at the Barron house in Brookline for the traditional Sabbath meal and evening; the Passover Seders attended by the entire family including nieces, nephews and their children—never less than forty-five, sometimes as many as fifty-two people; the Chanukah parties hosted by Jennie and Samuel Barron, for the family. Exciting, too, were the festivities in 1959 when Jennie Barron was named Massachusetts Mother of the Year, and then American Mother of the Year. And when they observed their 50th wedding anniversary in June, 1968, a host of close friends, as well as the entire family, who knew them affectionately as Jennie and Sam, or Aunt Jennie and Uncle Sam, gathered to help celebrate the grand occasion. Sam died within a week after that party. Jennie, as active as ever, continued with all of her family, community, and professional activities, even presiding in court until six days before her death in March 1969. Her zest for life, vibrance and exuberance lasted until the very end of her lifetime, during which she was recognized as a unique human being, having accomplished more than any usual combination of people.

TESSIE LAWRENCE JASPER
Born 1893

Tessie Jasper, as she was affectionately called by all who knew her, spent her lifetime serving others.

When she was only four years old her family emigrated to New York City from Potenza, Italy. Tessie fondly recalled her first glimpse of the great Lady with the torch welcoming them to new freedoms and a new life. Her father published the first Italian language newspaper in this country and it was avidly read by the new residents from Italy then living in New

York, and sent to Italy to bring their families there the news. The family found New York exciting but challenging. Illness, hardships and finally her father's death, forced her mother to move the family to Rockland, Massachusetts, for a new start when Tessie was fifteen. Her mother, Tessie, her brothers and sister accepted the challenges that confronted them, and through industry and perseverance they prospered.

A Rockland contractor wooed and won Tessie's hand in marriage and they were blessed with four children. During those difficult depression years Teresa's intelligence, diligence and shrewd tenacity in making all things count made her an excellent helpmate to Lawrence Jasper. Together they prepared for their children's higher education. Rose graduated from Chandler and married Leo Caplice. Richard, a Worcester Technical College graduate, is an architect and an engineer. Josephine was elected to Who's Who at Simmons and became Harvard President James Conant's secretary. She married Ralph Lodi. Robert is a Harvard University graduate and an Air Force veteran. Her children have blessed the world with their own children.

A tireless worker, not only for her own family but for the many causes which touched her life, Tessie gave of her talents. She served in the Rockland Women's Club as a member and as President; The Massachusetts State Federation of Women's Clubs as a District Director; and as Chairman of its Junior Division; The American Red Cross Blood Bank as Chairman for many years; the South Shore Hospital Friends Assoc., as member and President; a Director of the Rockland Visiting Nurses Association, and as Area Chairman of Special Services for the Brockton Veterans Administration Hospital.

Feeling a great need for ethnic cultural continuation among the Italian Women of her community, she founded the Rockland Progressive Club. This led to a State Federation of Women's Italian Clubs with Tessie as their first State President.

As National chairman of the Young Mothers Council for American Mothers, she was lovingly revered by young Mothers all over the Nation. In 1966 she was honored with the William B. Jaffe Motherhood award.

Tessie was a charming hostess. She loved people and people loved her. A fascinating and interesting speaker, she was invited to speak at clubs and conferences. One of her favorite renditions was, "The Touch of the Master's Hand."

Some of the quotes made at the time of her selection as Massachusetts Mother of the Year in 1954 are: "I believe in a strong religious background on which to build family life"; "A congenial home atmosphere where adults and children alike can enjoy visiting with each other fosters family unity"; "Parents' most important life's work is to teach respect and understanding of all races and creeds to their children"; "Parents should often plan recreation with their own families—picnics, trips, dinners, etc.—to create a good understanding between the generations"; and finally, "Mothers, work together with your husbands and family, and you are bound to be successful."

Tessie Jasper is missed by all who knew her. The Master's Hand touched hers on a Sunday in July, 1973 at the end of a special celebration with her family.

ROSE DONABEDIAN ZULALIAN
Born 1895

Rose Donabedian, daughter of Hovagim and Maritza Donabedian, was born September 10, 1895, in Kikranagerd, Turkish Armenia. Her parents, Hovagim and Maritza Donabedian, immigrated to the United States in 1899 when Rose was only four years of age and settled in Boston, Massachusetts.

Rose attended the Boston Schools. Here also, she studied voice with Vincent Hubbard, Italian Opera with Maestro Peroni, and French Opera with Wilfred Pelletier. In 1916 she married Enofk Zulalian, an oriental rug dealer and art collector. They had three children: a son Forad, a daughter Zari, and son, Vaughn. Forad died at the age of twelve.

Rose was gifted with a dynamic and thrilling contralto voice. Critics and public alike acclaimed her one of America's foremost contraltos. She performed extensively in opera, concert and oratorio. With the San Carlo Opera she sang in "Carmen" and "Il Trovatore", and the role of Amneris in "Aida" with the Old Boston Opera House under the sponsorship of Mr. and Mrs. Arms Fisher. She also performed with the Handel and Haydn Society and the Scottish Festival in Boston. She was noted for singing Schubert's Lieder and the Japanese National Anthem. Her adaptability, diction and pronunciation were superb, whether she sang in Japanese, French, Armenian or any other language.

In Chicago, Illinois, 1932, Mrs. Zulalian opened the proceedings of the Democratic National Convention by singing "The Star-Spangled Banner." It was at this time that Franklin Delano Roosevelt was nominated Democratic Presidential candidate. For many years she was called upon to sing the National Anthem at both Republican and Democratic National Conventions. No public gathering in the greater Boston area could be classified as official without Madame Rose Zulalian opening the proceedings with "The Star-Spangled Banner." The late James Michael Curley, a former Mayor of Boston and Governor of Massachusetts, frequently called upon her to perform at major functions.

Philip Hale, Music Critic for the "Boston Evening Telegram," said of Rose Zulalian, "Her voice rose and fell in gentle modulation; her tones uttered with the greatest of ease penetrated to the farthest corner of the hall. Hers was technique forgotten, music outpouring, Schubert supreme."

The New York Telegram stated, "The Zulalian Contralto has wide range and power. She sings with a sense of song and intangible filament of genius so few concert musicians can ever snatch and hold."

In September, 1964, she was honored to receive a special invitation from His Holiness Vasken I, Supreme Patriarch and Catholicos of Armenians, to visit Etchmiazin and tour Armenia as his guest. She was well received and loved by her people.

A testimonial Jubilee Banquet given in her honor was held on May 18, 1969, at Holy Trinity Church in Cambridge, Mass. under the auspices of His Grace Archbishop Rorken Manoogian, Primate of the Armenian Church in America.

A purple velvet costume, weighing forty-four pounds, adorned with 24 karat gold threads embroidered on it, was worn by Madame Zulalian whenever she performed and was presented to the Armenian National Historical Museum in Erevan, Armenia by her children upon her death.

Rose Zulalian resided with her daughter Zari Zulalian, an advertising copywriter in Revere, after her husband's death in 1964. Vaughn, an electrical engineer, resided in Lynnfield with his wife and two children, nearby his mother and sister. Madame Zulalian's long and outstanding career in music ended on July 25, 1972 at her death.

Rose Zulalian was a gardening enthusiast and had a beautiful rose garden. She also was fond of animals, owning a number of pets which included a famous donkey.

NELLIE Y. Y. SHIH

Born 1903

Nellie Y. Y. Shih, 1975 Massachusetts Bicentennial Mother of the Year is beloved by many and epitomizes what every woman would like to achieve.

Her acceptance speech to the Massachusetts American Mothers Committee in Boston was so charming that we reprint some of it here in her own words along with excerpts from one made in New York City.

"Madame President, Blessed Mothers and Friends: First of all, I must thank you for your strong belief in the sacredness of motherhood. . . I feel I don't deserve the honors which you have showered on me . . . I accept your kindness with great humility . . .

"I am very proud to be the mother of a Christian minister . . . God had only one Son, and

He was a minister. Who am I to have this honor? Certainly it is by the grace of God that I was selected to be representative for all Massachusetts mothers. May all glory and praise be to Him, who is Lord of Lords and King of Kings.

"What a sacred and important privilege is ours to be a Mother! . . . Let me quote a few proverbs from different countries: 'I would rather have a mother who is a beggar than a father who is an emperor,' *Chinese* 'An ounce of mother is worth a ton of Priest.' *Spanish* 'God could not be everywhere, so He made mothers.' *Jewish* 'No man is poor who has had a Godly mother.' *U.S. Abraham Lincoln* 'The hand that rocks the cradle rules the World.' *British*

"For those having mothers who live with you, be sure you do something nice for them while they are living. Just like the Bible says, Honor thy father and mother, which is the first commandment with promise. My son, hear thy father's instruction and forsake not thy mother's law. Despise not thy mother when she is old. Remember a mother's love is just like God's love; He loves us not because we are lovable . . . but we are His . . .

"Sometimes when I go out speaking I am asked a familiar question. 'How do we solve the delinquent problems of children in this land?' My answer is: We have to go back to our great Grandmother's religion, and start our family altars again, teaching them to know, to love, and to serve Christ. Let us expand our mother's influence in the Community, the Nation and the World.

"As wives we must give much credit to our good husbands. I am very privileged that my

husband has been a Christian minister for forty-nine years. Our son, a Ph.D., and our daughter-in-law are both ordained ministers, as am I. My husband's father was a Christian minister in China for fifty-one years. We pray and hope that our grandchildren will be called by God to serve Him and His people."

The Chinese Christian Church is fortunate to have the Shihs minister unto them. Nellie Shih was born August 30, 1903 in Ningpo, Chekiang Province, China. She holds many *firsts* for girls in China. They are: First village girl to graduate from a Mission High School in a big city; to receive a B.S. in Sociology, Nanking University; two graduate degrees, M.S. Religious Ed. and B.D. from Nanking Theological Seminary. She married Dr. Peter Shih in 1929 and they shared their home with his parents until their deaths. She says: "We had three boys, but due to the Sino-Japanese war hardships, we lost our two older sons. We, with our aged parents and young children literally walked over a thousand miles from East to West China to escape the Japanese. We slept on the roadside or under trees and were often thirsty and hungry . . . We shared a strong faith in God, so we prayed and studied the Holy Bible together on our knees. We believe the only hope of this world is our Lord. Once my son and husband were critically ill so I prayed day and night, and God answered my prayer with their recovery. Now, my son and his wife have three lovely children, and I am a very proud grandmother. In China I served as principal of the Nanking Presbyterian High School; Dean of Women at Chungking Methodist college and at Union Theological Seminary in West China where my husband administered his office of Dean.

"Coming to the U.S. twenty-seven years ago, we worked as pastor and parish worker of the Chinese Christian Church of New England in Boston's Chinatown. We started the first Chinese Day Care Centers in 1948. I have served as a social worker in our community. Over seven hundred refugees and scores of students from Hong Kong and South East Asia call ours their home away from home and honor me as their Mother. We often speak on the Closeness of Chinese Family Life, The Sacredness of Marriage and Motherhood and other religious and cultural topics. Dr. Peter Shih has been honored as Chinese Missionary to America by many denominations across this country. In a word, we are very grateful to be co-workers with our Lord Jesus Christ."

LUCY MILLER MITCHELL

Lucy Miller was born in Daytona Beach, Florida. She attended the school established by Mary McLeod Bethune from kindergarten through high school.

Following high school graduation in 1918, and a brief visit to Boston, she entered Talladega College in Alabama. She received her BA Magna Cum Laude in 1923. She taught school for one year there and then moved to Boston. Here she met a young Harvard College graduate, who had just received his law degree from Boston University. They were married and made their home in Boston where Joseph S. Mitchell practiced law the next fifty years. Mr. Mitchell was active in Republican Party activities where he served as Executive Secretary to the Governor's Council when Leverett Saltonstall was Governor. For many years he was a member of the Parole Board and an Assistant District Attorney for the Commonwealth of Massachusetts.

In her early years of marriage Mrs. Mitchell gave lectures on race relations. The Mitchells have two children, a daughter, Laura, and a son, Joseph, Jr. Because of them she became a volunteer at the Ruggles Street Nursery Training School. This was a practice school to train teachers for the Nursery Training School of Boston, established by Dr. Abigail Adams Eliot, who served as its Director. Very impressed with Mrs. Mitchell's teaching, Dr. Eliot encouraged her to make a career of it.

In 1935 she earned her Ed.M. at Boston University School of Education. After becoming the

Director of the Robert Gould Shaw House Nursery School, which she helped found, she played an important role in its development and growth. For many years she pioneered in preschool education. She taught and held training workshops for teachers in this program and was much in demand as a lecturer on various phases of child development and management.

Mrs. Mitchell also has a distinguished background in other community services. Her participation in a social agency called the Associated Day Care Services of Metropolitan Boston resulted in the provision of day care services for Greater Boston children. This United Way Agency established eight area day nurseries. For fifteen years Lucy Mitchell served as Education Director and then as Acting Executive Director for two years. While thus engaged she was appointed to be a member of a Legislative Commission set up to study day care standards in Massachusetts.

When the National Head Start Program for pre-school children was inaugurated, Mrs. Mitchell was appointed to serve as one of the educational consultants for the Northeast region.

The two Mitchell children have followed the example set before them by their illustrious parents.

Laura Mitchell, like her mother, is a graduate of Talladega College. She did her graduate studies at Radcliffe. She has taught at Dillard University in New Orleans and at Fisk University in Nashville, Tennessee. A psychology professor, she taught after marriage on the faculty of Tennessee State University. She is married to Dr. Jerome Holland, who became President of Delaware State College and later Hampton Institute in Virginia.

President Richard Nixon appointed Dr. Holland to the post of United States Ambassador to Sweden, during the period of the Viet Nam conflict. With Mrs. Holland, he represented our country with dignity and success. He is now serving on the Board of the New York Stock Exchange and several corporate boards. The Hollands are the parents of Jerry, Lucy and Joseph.

Joseph S. Mitchell, Jr. graduated from Bates College in Maine and Boston University Law School. After practicing law a few years, he became a member of the legal staff for the Security Exchange. Later, he joined the law staff of Administration and Finance under Governor John A. Volpe, who appointed him a Justice of the Superior Court of Massachusetts, where he served for nine years. Judge Mitchell's wife, the former Doris Ganges, a Westchester State College, Pennsylvania, graduate, was Assistant Dean of Students at Radcliffe for five years. At present she is Director of Personnel at ABT Corporation. They have two sons, Joseph III, and Michael, and a daughter, Marcine.

Lucy Miller Mitchell continues to give much of herself to her family and her community.

Michigan

Michigan

Nickname: Wolverine State

State Flower: Apple Blossom

State Tree: White Pine

State Bird: Robin

Photos

1. Fort Michilimackinac, Mackinaw City
2. Mackinac Bridge between Mackinaw City and St. Ignace
3. City of Detroit
4. Miner's Castle
5. Tahquamenon Falls, near Newberry
6. Lake of the Clouds in Porcupine Mountains Wilderness State Park
7. Greenfield village, Dearborn

Committee Members

Chairman—Mrs. Jan S. Vander Heidi, Grand Rapids
Mrs. Vivian Boersma
Mrs. Harold Frier
Mrs. Julian Gromer
Mrs. Richard D. Kuhn
Mrs. T. Gordon Scupholm
Mrs. David B. Zuhlke
Mr. Charles F. Fox
Mrs. J.H. Heald
Mr. Adolf Lefler
Mrs. Olive McLeod
Mrs. N.L. Meredith
Michigan Dept. of Natural Resources—Tourist Council
Willard Library
Ford Archives
Miss Jennifer Jansma—Grand Rapids artist

Michigan

MRS. GERALD R. FORD
First Lady   **Born 1918**

Elizabeth Anne Bloomer was born in Chicago, Illinois on April 18, 1918, the youngest child and only daughter of Hortense and William Stephenson Bloomer. The Bloomers moved their three children to Grand Rapids, Michigan, when their daughter was three.

At the age of eight, Betty Bloomer began a lifelong enthusiasm by studying dance at the Calla Travis School. After graduation from Central High School in 1936, she attended two summer sessions of the Bennington School of Dance, where she first met Martha Graham. Her dance career continued in New York City, where she joined one of Miss Graham's troupes and modeled with the John Powers Agency.

Persuaded by her mother to return to Grand Rapids, Betty Bloomer became a fashion coordinator for a local department store. She also formed her own dance group and taught dance to handicapped children.

On October 15, 1948, Betty married Gerald R. Ford, who was elected to the U.S. House of Representatives from Michigan's Fifth District only weeks after their wedding.

The Fords settled in Alexandria, Virginia, and within seven years, had four children. Betty Ford's activities during the 1950s and 60s centered on her husband and children. Scouting, the PTA and keeping up with three sons Mike, Jack, Steve and daughter Susan left time for few other activities. Mrs. Ford chose to focus on the Episcopal Church and the Republican Party.

In 1973, with Susan the only child left in high school, Mrs. Ford seriously considered going back to work part-time. But her husband's confirmation as Vice-President in December, 1973, interrupted that thought. His new job brought new official responsibilities, which increased when he became President in August, 1974.

Official entertaining, a lively interest in the arts and concern about women's issues are part of her life now, but her most important duties remain those of a wife and mother.

One writer described Betty Ford this way: "Perhaps she is no different from a lot of good, strong, courageous women—that she represents the best of us—and that is what cheers us most—that we know there are a lot of Betty Fords in America who help to keep us together and give us strength as individuals, as families, as communities and as a Nation." That thought pleases Betty Ford very much.

SOJOURNER TRUTH
From Slave to Fame   Born 1797

Wife–Mother–Slave–Fighter for Human Rights–Public Speaker–All this in one woman? Yes. Born in 1797, Isabella (one of her many early names) was sold as a slave to the Van Wageners in New York who freed her and treated her as an employee. She said in 1856, "I have had five children and never could take one of them up and say 'My child or my children' unless it was when no one could see me."

Fifteen years after she was freed, after using many surnames, she gave herself a new name—"Sojourner" since as a sojourner on this earth she had a mission to perform. She started to travel and speak against slavery, for temperance, women's suffrage, and preached "the Lord's truth." Because slaves took the name of their masters and since God was her only master, she reasoned "God's name is Truth." Henceforth, I shall be "Sojourner Truth."

Having spoken only Dutch in her early years, she had acquired from her subsequent employers a large English vocabulary. Her forceful manner of speaking and her quick wit kept her

audiences spellbound. She even challenged God in a speech in the Quaker Meeting House in Battle Creek in 1856, ". . . When I was sold, I had a severe hard master, and I was up in the barn and whipped. Oh! 'till the blood ran down on the floor and I asked God, why don't you come and relieve me . . . if I was you, and you'se tied up so, I'd do it for you."

Sojourner Truth had interviews with Presidents Lincoln and Grant. Harriet Beecher Stowe wrote an article about her in a national magazine. Frederick Douglass, other intellectuals, religious leaders and politicians as well as the down-trodden, knew her. A jazz drama based on her life was presented in Carnegie Hall and a TV special was aired on a national network this year.

Pilgrimages to her grave-site in Oak Hill Cemetery, Battle Creek, where she was buried in 1883, are made by various groups every year. The Sojourner Truth Association, devoted to perpetuating her memory, placed a statue on her grave and purchased display cases for the Sojourner Truth room at the Kimball House Historical Museum. Hundreds of citizens and school children visit this each season. Mrs. Stanley (Berenice) Lowe has spent much time in research on this unusual woman and has supplied background material to other writers, historians and students, as well as to the Michigan Historical Collection at the University of Michigan.

In Boston, Frederick Douglass, a famous orator, was talking on the hopelessness of his fellow Negroes who were slaves. He became quite convinced, as he talked, that there was no future for them. Then a voice rang out which brought the entire audience to its feet, and changed the attitude of even Mr. Douglass. It was Sojourner Truth, and she had cried out, "Frederick, is God dead?"

On her simple marker there in Oak Hill Cemetery is her name, the dates of her life, and her famous question, "Is God Dead?"

MARY ANN LEASIA

Born 1822

Mary Ann Saranac was born in Detroit to Genevieve Campau and Francois Saranac. She came to live in the Saginaw Valley (bordering the Saginaw Bay of Lake Huron) with her widowed mother at the age of seven.

Her great grandfather was Jaques Campau who came to Detroit in 1707 as Secretary to Antoine De La Mothe Cadillac. Cadillac had been sent by the King of France to establish and command a fort on the Detroit River. Madame Cadillac had traveled over one thousand miles by canoe from Quebec to join her husband and set up housekeeping. She brought to Detroit the French life style and culture. Her fourth child, a daughter, was the first white child baptized in Michigan in a Catholic Mission Church. Because of the conquest by the English of the French in Montreal a few years later, the French leaders left Detroit and the English controlled Fort Detroit.

Mary Ann's grandfather was Henry Campau whose brother, Louis Campau, founded the settlement which later became Grand Rapids where a town square and street are named for him. Francois Saranac (after whom a mid-Michigan town is named), her father, was one of the members of a party which accompanied General Lewis Cass from Detroit on horseback through the old Indian Trail (the Dixie Highway) to negotiate a land treaty with the Indians in the Saginaw Valley. He had served in the War of 1812, earning special honors and recognition for his daring and bravery.

At the age of sixteen, Mary Ann married John B. Leasia, settled in Saginaw Valley in a log cabin, bore fifteen children, six of whom survived, and gained a reputation for her hospitality and courtesy to strangers and especially to the Indian Chiefs. She had completely mastered the Indian language and had a real career in carrying out the trading of furs and goods for both the white and Indian traders. The first Catholic Mass in the Saginaw Valley was celebrated in her home long before a mission had been established in this section.

In reports to the Peabody Museum of American Archeology, Lucian Carr points out that among the Huron Indians the clans were bound together by blood ties on the maternal side and presided over by a matriarch. The women owned the land and also helped decide when the tribe should hunt or go to war. When the Sachem died, the women had the right to nominate his successor. Mary Ann was so beloved of the Indians that she was often called upon to settle matters between members of their own tribe. This good relationship made for progress in settling the beautiful Saginaw Valley.

Mary Ann Leasia is typical of the woman who, besides doing all that is required of her to be a good wife, a mother par excellence to her children, and a faithful church member, can be of great value to her community and State. She was grandmother to seventy three and had fifteen great grandchildren, one of whom, Adolf B. Lefler, is still active in the city of Saginaw.

She died in Saginaw in 1910 after a full, happy, useful life.

SARA EMMA EDMONDS SEELYE
Born 1841

The story of Sara does not begin for us with her place of birth and names of parents. The first we know about her is that since she looked more like a boy at age 16, she hired out as a boy to sell books throughout the countryside. She sold more Bibles and books than many other salesmen did and was called in to visit her publishers in Connecticut. While there, the Civil War was declared. She returned to Flint and swept by patriotic emotion, volunteered to serve in the Army. No one questioned her sex and after one turn down, she was accepted as a soldier in Company F, Second Michigan Troops.

She trained in Fort Wayne, in Detroit and was sent to Washington, D.C. Just after her enlistment the physical examination rules were tightened and she would probably not have been able to enlist then. She was assigned to nursing duty as at this time recruitment for women nurses had not begun. President Lincoln soon called for nurses, putting Dorothea Dix in charge of this. Before this, States were responsible to provide matrons and nurses to cook, mend, and care for the sick and wounded. In 1864 General Grant ordered all women out of the Army.

Sara served as a nurse until after the battle of Manassas, when she was asked to train as a spy. To do this, she had to be a good marksman, show intelligence, have physical endurance, and swear allegiance. She was successful and served well until she became ill with malaria. She asked for a leave, was refused, and deserted, knowing that in a hospital her deception would be discovered. So, in 1863, after two years of service, she left the Army.

While recuperating from her illness, she wrote a book, "Nurse and Spy", which was her own true story. She decided to study at Oberlin College and was the first woman to be admitted there. After college she married, had three children, none of whom survived, and adopted two boys who gave her and her husband much happiness.

Many years later Congress recognized her service to the Army, wiped away her desertion record, and gave her an honorable discharge. They then adopted a bill which gave her a pension for the rest of her life. She moved to Texas and in 1897 she was accepted as a full member in the Grand Army of the Republic. She died there in 1901 and was buried in the D.A.R. Cemetery as Sara Emma Seelye, Army Nurse.

Colonel Frederick Schneider, in an address that year to the Second Michigan Troops, said, "None of the events recorded have surpassed the record of pure, unselfish patriotism as that of Sara Emma Edmonds, Frank Thompson, of Company F."

EMMA AUGUSTA FOX

Born 1847

"A generation of women will move to the measure of her step when she has long been gone," said Dr. Charles Haven Myers, minister of North Woodward Congregational Church, at the memorial service held February 12, 1945, for Mrs. Emma Augusta Fox, author, teacher, parliamentarian, and pioneer of women's rights.

Born Emma Augusta Stowell on March 29, 1847, Mrs. Fox was educated in public and private schools. She was teaching school in Chicago at the time of the great fire in 1871. It was while she was teaching later in Cambridge, Massachusetts, that she met Charles Edgar Fox, who in 1876 brought her to Detroit as his bride.

Mrs. Fox served on the Detroit Board of Education from 1893-95, the second woman so to serve. (Detroit's Emma A. Fox Primary School was dedicated in 1962 to honor her memory.) She involved herself in an intense study of parliamentary law and in 1899 founded the Detroit Parliamentary Law Club, an organization she was to direct for the next 45 years, instructing hundreds of women in the art of organizing clubs and conducting meetings. In 1898 she began writing a series of articles for the magazine of the General Federation of Women's Clubs. This series led to the publication in 1902 of her book entitled "Parliamentary Usage for Women's Clubs." (Recommended among 100 titles by the U. S. Occupation Forces in Japan following World War II, "Parliamentary Usage" was translated into Japanese and produced by a Japanese publisher.)

A highlight of her career took place at a mock Republican Convention in 1940, staged entirely by women but witnessed by industrialist Henry Ford and 100 other men in high places. After a deadlock on the first ballot, Mrs. Fox was nominated and unanimously chosen as candidate for President of the United States.

At age 95 she received an honorary Doctor of Letters from Wayne University, having earlier received an honorary Doctor of Humanics from Hillsdale College. At age 97 she flew to Nashville to serve for the twenty-eighth year as parliamentarian of the national convention of the Daughters of the Confederacy.

A bronze tablet erected to her memory is affixed to the west wall of the "Auto Club" building at 131 Bagley, Detroit, site of the early home of Mrs. Fox. Presented to the City of Detroit by the J. L. Hudson Company, the plaque was dedicated by the Detroit Federation of Women's Clubs.

During 1951 when Detroit observed its Sesquicentennial, twenty-five individuals were selected for their contributions to the city's 250-year history. Of the two women selected, one was Mme. Cadillac, wife of the City's founder. The other was Emma A. Fox.

Throughout a life of intense involvement in civic, church, and organizational affairs, Mrs. Fox placed family concerns above all others. Two sons, Maurice Winslow and Howard Stowell, and seven grandchildren were beneficiaries of her devotion and "private instruction."

CLARA BRYANT FORD

Born 1866

"We are grateful to God for life's task honorably discharged, for simplicity in the midst of fame, for humility when it would have been easy to be proud, for character that does not change in the midst of success and sorrow, for steadfastness in a changing world, for loneliness endured without defeat, for generosity." Thus the Bishop Richard Emerick prayed at the funeral of Clara Bryant Ford. Clara, eldest daughter of Martha Bench and Melvin Bryant, in 1888 married Henry Ford of Greenfield in the area that later became the setting for their beautiful estate "Fairlane". This is now a part of the Dearborn Campus of the University of Michigan—a lasting memorial to their love of gardens, books, architecture, and all beauty.

As she became financially able, she helped to establish with her beloved Episcopalian Church a resident home for working girls, supported several charities for children (her first love), the League of Women Voters, and aided Women Suffrage groups.

Clara—the Believer—had married Henry—the Dreamer. She believed that marriage must be a vital, live thing growing stronger with the passing years. She lovingly supported her husband in all his inventiveness and ambitions. Together they also shared their charities. She met Martha Berry through their friends, the Thomas Edisons, became interested in her school for the poor in Georgia and eventually gave over four million dollars to make it what it has become. When Henry moved Edison's Laboratory to Dearborn, which was the beginning of Greenfield Village, she asisted in every way and now it has over one hundred buildings, preserving the treasures of 200 years of United States History. After wintering in Florida with the Edison's for several years, they purchased 75,000 acres in Georgia where they built the "Hermitage", using bricks from an old mansion, started a reclamation program, built homes, schools, community centers, health clinics, planted fruit and other trees, and accomplished unbelievable results. This was wholly approved by their friend George Washington Carver.

She was devoted to her only son, Edsel, and later to his wife, Eleanor, and their four children. Christmas at Fairlane with them was always something special. At Edsel's death toward the end of World War II, the color went out of Clara's life. She and Henry went on, but it was never the same. They—who had met at a dancing party—never danced again.

Clara had always lived a "Waste not, Want not" life and hated extravagance. Not indulging in her grief, she devoted herself wholly to her husband and to her charities. Her most prized possessions were her ½ carat engagement ring and her wedding gift from Henry—her Prayer Book—which she willed for preservation to her Rector and Church.

After almost sixty years together, she lost her "Dreamer", her companion, friend, and confidante. She lived for three more years quietly, unaware how influential and wealthy she really was as Henry Ford's widow. Edsel had started the Ford Foundation with a $25,000 fund. Now the Foundation, one of the largest, is a legacy of Henry, Clara, Edsel, and Eleanor Ford to Michigan, the United States and to the world.

The Believer has now joined the Dreamer.

MATILDA RAUSCH WILSON
Born 1883

Mrs. Matilda Rausch Wilson, who devoted much of her life and fortune to many philanthropic causes, was perhaps best known as the benefactress of Oakland University in Rochester, Michigan. It was through her gift of land and cash in 1957 that the college was established as an affiliate of Michigan State University, on whose governing board she had served for six years.

Mrs. Wilson never attended college herself and was described as a "self-made woman." She had been a secretary to John F. Dodge, one of the early automotive pioneers, although two years out of his employment when they married in 1907. His first wife had died, leaving him with three children. Three children were born to this second marriage. After Dodge's death in 1920, his widow and their children moved from Detroit to the farm in Rochester, Michigan, which he had purchased several years before. She continued her activities in the First Presbyterian Church of Detroit, and it was there that she met Alfred G. Wilson in 1924. He was the son of a Presbyterian minister. They were married in 1925 and began planning Meadow Brook Hall. The mansion, built between 1926 and 1929, is now an Oakland University Cultural Center. Mr. amd Mrs. Wilson adopted two children. Mr. Wilson died in 1962.

Mrs. Wilson maintained an office and staff in Detroit. There she handled trust funds, kept a sharp eye on the stock market, and handled the business details of her continuing farm operation at Howell, Michigan. She was on a trip to Belgium to add to her stock of Belgium draft horses when fatally stricken by a heart attack a few weeks before her 84th birthday.

In the midst of her busy home and business life, Mrs. Wilson found time to serve in many capacities. She was president of the Woman's National Farm and Garden Association (1964-66); trustee of Beloit College, Wisconsin; Ruling Elder of the First Presbyterian Church of Detroit and Honorary President of the Woman's Association of that church; treasurer of the Michigan Synodical of the Presbyterian Church (1921-41); advisory board life member of The Salvation Army of Detroit and was awarded in 1947 the Distinguished Auxiliary Service Cross of The Salvation Army. She served as president of the Auxiliary to the Salvation Army for 26 years and became President Emeritus of that

organization. She also served as president of the Federation of Women's Clubs of Detroit and became Honorary President of the Federation; president of the Detroit Historic Memorials Society and president of the Village Woman's Club, Bloomfield Hills. She was also active in the USO during World War II and was a patron of the Detroit Historical Museum, Founders Society Detroit Institute of Arts, and Friends of the Detroit Public Library.

Mrs. Wilson had two honorary degrees bestowed upon her—Honorary Law Degree, Michigan State University in 1955 and Honorary Doctor of Humanities, Oakland University in 1963.

Mrs. Wilson left the bulk of her estate to the Matilda R. Wilson Fund to continue her generous support for widely varied educational and charitable purposes.

DOROTHY LEONARD JUDD
Born 1898

Born in Grand Rapids, September 14, 1898, daughter of Willie Stansbury and Harry Carr Leonard, she was educated in the public schools and received her AB Degree from Vassar College in 1920. She did graduate work in Political Science at the University of Michigan and taught American History and Government in Central High School. She married Siegel Wright Judd (lawyer), had two daughters and has five grandchildren.

In Grand Rapids she served on the Committee of 100 on Relief Administration, Citizen's Tax Committee, City Planning Commission, Committees of Capital Improvement, Parks and Recreation, and Study of the Future of Grand Rapids Junior College.

Governor Brucker appointed her to the Commission for Revision of Election Laws; Governor Fitzgerald to the Civil Service Study Commission; Governor Murphy to the Commission on Reform and Modernization of Government; Governor Williams to the Commission on Election Laws; and Governor Romney to the Civil Service Commission. She was a delegate to the Michigan Constitutional Convention, on its Local Government Committee, and Chairman of its County Government Sub-committee.

In 1963 Dr. John Hannah, U. S. Chairman of the Commission on Civil Rights appointed her Chairman of the State Advisory Committee.

She has been a member and president of the Grand Rapids and Michigan League of Women Voters, a director of the U. S. League and Chairman of its Department of Government and Operation. She authored "Budget Making and Administration with Special Reference to Cities" and "Constructive Economy in Local Government" for the U. S. League Publication in 1933. She was editor of "Our Metropolitan County" and "Our City Government", an official textbook used in the public schools of Grand Rapids.

She was a member of the Michigan Merit Systems Association Executive Committee which secured the adoption of the Civil Service Amendment to the State Constitution in 1940. She belongs to the Urban League and its Woman's Guild, and has been council member and vice-president of the National Municipal League. She was on the Revision of Model City Charter Committee, a member of the All American City Award Jury in 1952. She received the Distinguished Citizen Award in 1957.

She was active in the National Recreation Association until it joined the Michigan United Fund, a director of Grand Rapids Citizens Action which forced the resignation of the Mayor in 1954 and ended the city's political bossism. In 1958 she was a guest of the German Government for the Study of Government and Education.

She is a lifetime member of Fountain Street Church (Liberal Protestant), was chairman of its 1969 Centennial Celebration and Author of "Our Architectural Heritage: the Art and Architecture of Fountain Street Church."

She has Honorary Doctorates from Western Michigan University and the University of Michigan. In 1975 she received the Liberty Bell Award, Law Day USA, Grand Rapids Bar Association.

Truly the dedication of this gracious and capable lady has made the City of Grand Rapids and the State of Michigan better because of her great interest in good government.

LENORE LAFOUNT ROMNEY

Daughter of Alma Robinson and Harold Arundel Lafount, Lenore received an A.B. Degree from George Washington University in 1929, did post-graduate work at the American Laboratory School of the Theater in New York City obtaining a contract from Metro-Goldwyn-Mayer after winning a speech contest.

In 1931 she married George Wilcken Romney in the Salt Lake Temple of the Church of the Latter Day Saints. They moved to Washington, D. C., where two daughters, Lynne and Jane were born. Subsequently, they moved to Detroit, Michigan, where two sons, Scott and Willard Mitt were born. There Lenore was active in Theater Arts, Cub Scouts (Den Mother), leading the Women in the Relief Society and teaching Sunday School which she still does.

She became a director for the American Field Service, worked with the Youth for Understanding program, became an active campaigner for the new Michigan Constitution, worked vigorously for reforms throughout the State, and became involved in the Human Resources Council, homes for the emotionally disturbed, mentally ill, and the retarded. While her husband was Governor of Michigan and Secretary of Housing and Urban Development in Washington, D. C., she was deeply involved in all his activities.

Her own Senate Campaign in 1970 gave her an opportunity to express her ideas concerning reform in the National Welfare Program, the ADC program, prison reform, and better law enforcement.

Each of her children graduated from a University, married in the Temple, and is active in church and community. She has eighteen grandchildren.

She is currently on the Executive Committee for the National Center for Voluntary Action, Y.W.C.A., and Thomas Jefferson Research Center Advisory Boards, is a Woodrow Wilson Fellow, a lecturer, participant in WJR's Point of View Program on radio and a member of the American Association of University Women.

She has received Honorary Doctorates from Hillsdale, Hope, and Gwynedd-Mercy Colleges, Central, Eastern and Northern Michigan Universities, and the Detroit College of Business.

She has received awards from Religious Heritage of America, Associated Press, Lansing Community College Faculty Women's League, National Conference of Christians and Jews, Brigham Young University, Hadassah, National Women Newsmakers, the Marygrove College, and the Salvation Army.

She has received citations from the Michigan Association of Future Homemakers of America, Michigan Federation of Music Clubs, Business and Professional Women, International Platform Association, Michigan State University 37th College Week, and Glendale College (California).

She has served on many committees and boards willingly and efficiently—always striving to do the right thing at the right time to benefit the most people, truly a remarkable woman.

MARY STALLINGS COLEMAN
Justice, Supreme Court of Michigan
Born 1914

Beautiful, charming, capable Mary Stallings Coleman, daughter of Agnes Huther and Leslie C. Stallings, received her BA Degree from the University of Maryland and Juris Doctor Degree from George Washington University. In 1939 she married Creighton R. Coleman (Circuit Judge), became the mother of Leslie Coleman Gagan and Carol Coleman Salyer (both medical doctors) and has two grandchildren.

She is on the State Bar Committee on Juvenile Problems, the President's Commission on International Women's Year, and the first woman to be elected to the Michigan Supreme Court after 137 years of male domination. She is a member of the Bar in Michigan and the District of Columbia, of the National Advisory Council, Center for the Administration of Justice, Legislative Committee, the Committee to Revise Code of Judicial Ethics, and is a popular lecturer. She served as Probate and Juvenile Judge, is a member of the American Bar Association, the American Judicature Society, the Michigan and National Women's Lawyers Association, and a Fellow of the American Bar Foundation.

She served on the Governor's Commission of Law Enforcement, Youth, Crime and Delinquency; was President of the Michigan Probate and Juvenile Court Judges' Association; member of the State Bar Committee to Revise the Criminal Code; the Supreme Court Committee to draft Michigan Juvenile Court Rules of Procedure; Advisor to the Office of Youth Services to Western Michigan University on Court Services for Children; and Vice President of Children's Charter of the Courts of Michigan, Inc.

She received Honorary Doctorates from Nazareth, Alma, and Olivet Colleges, Eastern and Western Michigan Universities, and Detroit College of Law.

She is a trustee of Albion College, member of the American Legion Auxiliary, P.E.O., Business and Professional Women, and Honorary member of Beta Sigma Phi, Alpha Delta Kappa, Junior League, and Altrusa International. She is an accomplish pianist, an actress who cofounded with her husband the Marshall, Michigan Civic Theater, helped to start the Battle Creek Council of the Arts, and is a member and former director of Battle Creek Civic Theater. She is a Director of the Michigan Board of the American Association of University Women and was Marshall's first American Association of University Women President.

She has received awards from the Business and Professional Women's Association, Religious Heritage of America, Alpha Omicrom Phi, Probate and Juvenile Court Judges, and community groups.

With all her accomplishments she has never lost the common touch. A faithful wife, a good mother and grandmother, a meticulous housekeeper, a gourmet cook, a person who seldom misses church or a cultural event, yet who always looks band-box fresh, she performs every duty with grace and competence.

Minnesota

Minnesota

Nickname: North Star State

State Flower: Showy lady's-slipper

State Tree: Red Pine

State Bird: Loon

Photos

1. Kensington Runestone in Alexandria
2. Song of Hiawatha Pageant, Pipestone
3. Capital Building, St. Paul
4. Paul Bunyan and Babe
5. Duluth, Aerial Bridge and harbor
6. The Julius C. Wilkie Steamboat Museum in Winona
7. Sinclair Lewis' boyhood home, Saulk Centre

Committee Members

Chairman—Mrs. Adeline E. Ballenthin
Mrs. Hubert H. Humphrey—Honorary Chairman
Senator Clarence Purfeerst
Mrs. Walter Hauser
Ms. Kathleen Lentz
Ms. Mildred Marple
Gladys Kjeldahl Severson—artist
Northern States Power Co.
Northern State Bank
Chamber of Commerce
Mr. Mike Cooper, Editor, Faribault Daily News
Mrs. B.F. Fuller, Jr.
Virginia Holbert
Rolf W. Stageberg
Mary Ann Stickney
E.M. Szarte
Kathleen Tibbetts
Hazel H. Wahlberg
Nancy L. Woolworth

Minnesota

"AZA-YA-MAN-KA-WIN"
Mendota   **Born 1788**

Few mothers were propelled into public view in art, music, and literature on the early Minnesota frontier as was the Dakota mother "Berry Picker."

"The one-who-picks-blueberries-while-running" commonly known as "Old Bets" was thrust into the public eye in early Minnesota at the age of 75 years because of her kindness toward several hundred white captives at Camp Release in 1862. Few people, however, knew this grandmother-type person in her youth, when she was so adventuresome and so beautiful that Dakota warriors fought for her hand in marriage.

Before 1862, she lived the life of a typical Mdewakaton Dakota woman and mother, generous and acquisitive. She participated in scalp dances and wild racing parties at White Bear Lake.

Born in 1788 to two Dakota Indian parents, at the juncture of the Mississippi and Minnesota Rivers at Mendota, she lived an exciting, Native American female life. In childhood, she exhibited traits of daring, forecasting her future among white men and Indians. So beautiful was she that two warriors fought for her hand in marriage.

Eloping with her lover, "Chig-go-nia", she was followed by her brother and local shaman, "He-in-da-koo" who slew her lover. She returned to her village and married Iron Sword. At the time, Fort Snelling was being considered as a "Citadel in the Wilderness" by the United States Secretary of State.

Before Iron Sword died in 1840, she had borne at least four children, two boys and two girls. Most famous of these was "Taopi" or "Wounded Man", Chief of the Farmer Band of Dakota Indians in the 1860's.

In March, 1850, Lt. E.K. Thomas painted "Old Bets" as a vibrant Woodland Dakota Indian in front of her teepee at Mendota. After saving white captives at Camp Release, "Taopi" and "Betsy" were taken as prisoners in 1862 to Ft. Snelling.

After 1865, "Old Bets", her children, and other friendly Indians were moved to Faribault, Minnesota by Alexander Faribault, Bishop Henry B. Whipple, and Henry H. Sibley. Gradually she made her way back to Mendota and made her living in the streets of St. Paul, selling her photograph, moccasins, and fur skins.

A bust of her is displayed in the Minnesota Historical Society. Munger Brothers produced sheet music about a supposed centenarian called the "Old Bets March". Colonel Hankins wrote about her in 1868, first as an illusion of "Nokomis" in Longfellow's "Hiawatha" and then as an adventuress not unlike "Tom Sawyer" or "Huckleberry Finn". By March of 1868, "Ancient Elizabeth's" portraits had been published in half a dozen works and photographed by many artists. In 1872, a local artist painted her portrait, which hangs in the J.J. Hill Library in St. Paul.

Following a lengthy illness, she was baptized a Christian by Father Ravoux on Easter morning, 1873. She died April 30, 1873 at 85 years of age. The St. Paul Chamber of Commerce collected money for her burial at Mendota.

In 1893, Berry Picker's best biography, *Wa-Mda-ska*, was written by a member of "Taopi's" Band, in *The Literary Northwest Magazine*.

In 1904, the Hamline College Fortnightly Club recognized "Old Bets" as one of the few prominent women on the early Minnesota frontier.

CORNELIA WRIGHT WHIPPLE
Faribault   **Born 1816**

"The ruling passion of her life was caring for the poor and the suffering." Americans of three races have testified to this description of Cornelia Wright Whipple.

The eldest daughter of the Honorable Benjamin and Sarah Wright, Cornelia Wright Whipple was born in Adams, N.Y., November 10, 1816. After graduating from Emma Willard Female Seminary in Troy, (N.Y.), she was a teacher in South Carolina and helped finance her brother's education for the ministry.

She returned to Adams in 1842 to marry her childhood schoolmate, Henry Benjamin Whipple, then a merchant. She influenced him to forego tempting business offers and become an Episcopal priest. Following ordination, her husband served a parish in Rome, N.Y. for ten years, then took charge of a mission free church in Chicago in 1857. In her parish life, Mrs. Whipple

often went alone into lanes and alleys to minister to the sick.

Mr. Whipple was elected the first Episcopal Bishop of Minnesota in 1859 and the couple selected Faribault as their residence, where they lived for thirty years. From the beginning of her life in the West, Cornelia Whipple was a friend of the Indians. She took Indian girls into her home to care for and educate them. She often visited Sioux and Obijay missions to minister to the people. In tribute to her, the Indians at Birch Coulee (near Morton) named their church St. Cornelia's.

In 1866, the Whipples started Saint Mary's Hall, a boarding school for girls, in their home. In the history of Saint Mary's, Bishop Whipple is called the architect, and the two women, Mrs. Whipple and Sarah Darlington, the first principal, are called the builders of the school.

Saint Mary's has become a nationally known college preparatory school with 86 girls from all sections of the United States enrolled in 1975. Some 1500 living alumnae are scattered around the globe.

Just as she was admired for her commitment to helping others, Mrs. Whipple was respected in the Faribault community for her loving devotion to her husband and their six children, Cornelia, Frances, Jane, Sarah, John and Charles.

During the later years of her life, she spent several winters in Maitland, Florida. There she became the warm friend of black people, helping them personally and soliciting funds for them.

She was severely injured in a railroad accident on one of her trips south. When it became apparent that she would not recover, she wanted to return to Faribault. The night before she left for Minnesota, a crowd of her black friends gathered under her window to sing their farewell. She died in Faribault on July 16, 1890, six months after the accident.

Burial services were held in "The Cathedral of our Merciful Savior", the First Cathedral in the Episcopal Church of America, built three years after the Whipples came to Faribault and where Mrs. Whipple had given loving service for thirty years.

CHARLOTTE CLARK VAN CLEVE
Northwest Territory   **Born 1819**

Charlotte Ouisconsin Clark, reputedly the first white child born in the Northwest Territory, was born on July 1, 1819, at Prairie du Chien, a small trading settlement in what is now Wisconsin.

Her parents, Lieutenant Nathan and Charlotte Seymour Clark, their son, and the baby suffered many hardships as part of the small group of soldiers who had been sent to establish what was to become Fort Snelling, at the confluence of the Mississippi and Minnesota rivers.

Charlotte's childhood at the fort was happy, although the isolated community was occasionally disturbed by Indian wars.

In 1827, the family moved from the fort, living in Prairie du Chien, Kentucky, and Tennessee. Charlotte was educated at Mrs. Apthorpe's School for Young Ladies in New Haven, Connecticut. In 1836 she rejoined her family at Fort Winnebago (now in Wisconsin) where, at sixteen, she married Horatio Phillips Van Cleve, acceding to her father's dying wish.

A year later, Van Cleve resigned his military commission, and they moved to Ann Arbor, Long Prairie, Cincinnati and then to St. Anthony, now in Minnesota. While in Michigan, they operated a preparatory school for the newly-founded university.

In 1861, in response to a summons from Governor Alexander Ramsey, Van Cleve re-enlisted at Fort Snelling, and, by the end of the Civil War, had become a general. From 1862 they remained in Minneapolis and Van Cleve was appointed Adjutant General of Minnesota.

Charlotte was a true pioneer. She bore many hardships with resourcefulness, faith, and courage. She had twelve children, five of whom died young, and adopted nine others. Her spirit is illustrated by an episode in which she was forced to amputate a surveyor's frozen toes because no medical help was available.

She wrote voluminously, keeping personal correspondence and diaries, and writing much in connection with her charity work. Although somewhat burdened by the melodramatic and stylized literary fashion of the time, her autobiography, published in 1888, *Three Score Years and Ten*, offers a valuable picture of pioneer life in Minnesota. She recounted her reactions to the first steamboat to land at Fort Snelling, the first train to stop there, the first flour mill in the state, and to Andrew Jackson, whom she met in Nashville before he became President. Mrs. Van Cleve preserved an important historical reference by saving her papers when it had been common only for men to do so.

She actively promoted causes in which she believed, and travelled extensively in Minnesota to lecture for the Women's Foreign Missionary Auxiliary to the Presbyterian Society. In 1873, she helped found the Sisterhood of Bethany Home which gave shelter and aid to "fallen women" and other unfortunates. She regarded her work there as an evangelical mission that would prove her love for God.

Minneapolis was developing into a sizable city, and Mrs. Van Cleve saw a corresponding increase in the city's moral corruption. She said that the Devil had emissaries who infiltrated "our laundries, cigar shops, variety stores; our Intelligence offices, and other kinds of business where women and girls find employment and they are indefatigable in carrying out his base designs." She early recognized some of the economic and social factors contributing to prostitution.

Mrs. Van Cleve believed that women were responsible for the moral corruption in society because they have no "natural inclinations toward vice", but men do. Since men were naturally not as virtuous as women, women should be the moral pillars of society.

It is difficult to judge a person only from her writings and others' eulogies, but Mrs. Van Cleve's strong personality does come through her records. Sweet, and genuinely concerned with helping others, she apparently had a great wit and was an excellent story-teller. Her attitudes were fairly liberal; she was opposed to slavery, realized the white man's injustice to Indians, and favored woman suffrage.

Before her death at the age of eighty-eight on April 1, 1907, she had become almost totally blind and deaf. In her old age, she was sometimes in great pain but almost every day she began her diary with "A pleasant day."

She was a woman who made an important contribution to Minnesota's early history and who brought joy to those around her.

PHEBE SUTHERLAND FULLER
Born 1860

When Thomas Dewey was a candidate for the office of President of the United States, his picture appeared in the "St. Paul Dispatch" with a diminutive, bright-eyed lady in her eighties living at the Soldier's Home. He sought her out because he had been told, "Everybody knows Phebe".

Phebe's parents were of sturdy lineage. Her mother, Hannah Stephenson, was born in New Brunswick around 1820 and died in 1864. Her father, James Sutherland, was born in Scotland, came to America and settled in New Brunswick. Here he had a general merchandise business for a time and was a member of the General Assembly. Four years were then spent in the Australian gold mines and he returned to the

United States in the middle 1850's and farmed in Wisconsin.

Upon her mother's death, Phebe, the youngest of six children, was raised by her eldest sister, Hannah Rebekah Taylor. Hannah must have been a stimulating person since she acquired a reputation as a poet, reciting from memory her own long poems commemorating notable people and events.

Phebe was born in Belmont, Wisconsin, January 24, 1860. She attended Teachers' College at Mankato, Minnesota, graduating in 1880. Two years later she married Robert E. Fuller who was younger than she. He was ambitious and kindly, but not as well-educated. His letters reveal his respect for her keen mind and he valued her advice and judgment.

From his letters it is evident that he benefitted from her help. By 1895, he could say that their West Lawn Stock Farm in Mapleton, Minnesota was the best in the Northwest. Their horse, "Intrepid", won the Grand Sweepstakes at the American Horse Show in Chicago in 1890, the first of many triumphs for the horse, who was shown extensively at fairs and shows.

During those first years in the 1880's, two girls were born. One died at four and the other grew to maturity only to die in childbirth, leaving a daughter. Phebe felt it was her responsibility to raise this grandchild as her own. Three sons were born: Willard, who became a school superintendant; Benjamin, a dentist, and Robert, Jr. who farmed.

Because of the over-extension of Robert's partner in bank and railroad investment, the Fullers lost the farm, and creditors took over. They moved to Redwood Falls to begin anew. A new farm was built up, as successful as the first. Duroc hogs and quality short horn cattle were added to the stock of horses.

At Redwood Falls, Phebe plunged into patriotic, charitable and civic affairs with vigor. Her genius for organization left its imprint on many organizations in her area. She became active in Methodist groups, was a member of Eastern Star, Parent Teachers' Association (P.T.A.), Red Cross, League of Women Voters, American Legion Auxiliary, and Redwood Cemetery Association. Intense patriotism and a concern for the soldiers' welfare led her to seek various offices in the Grand Army of the Republic (G.A.R.), including president. She was a national aide for the National Patriotic Instructor's Association and worked diligently on the Soldiers' Home board with the Minnesota State Cemetery Association which developed Ft. Snelling cemetery.

Her leadership ability was recognized by the Women's Christian Temperance Union (WCTU). She was state superintendent of the legislation and law enforcement section. She was a delegate to the World's Convention in 1913 and received the prize for Christian Citizenship from the National WCTU. After becoming known as a speaker, she was chosen life member of the Matrons' Medal contest for oratory in 1918.

She organized the suffragettes in Redwood, and stumped the state for the women's vote. She served on the board of the Minnesota Crippled Children's Association. Governor Eberhart appointed her Minnesota delegate to the international Purity Congress in Indianapolis.

Robert died in 1917. The family lost the farm in the depth of the depression but nothing could suppress her buoyant spirit. She died in 1956, leaving a memory of her unflagging efforts to improve the quality of life in Minnesota.

MÖR JOHNSON HETTEEN
Roseau County   **Born 1861**

Betty, called Mör, was born October 8, 1861, to Tonte Cherstin and Tors Jonas Johnson, in Malung, Sweden.

She married Peter Hetteen, also of Malung, and the young couple, weary of eking out a living for their young family, took their three daughters, boarded the "Dominion of Canada" in 1890, and sailed to the "America" described to them in letters by Uncle Andrew Johnson.

Three weeks later, they landed in Canada and happily boarded the train for Warren, Minnesota.

They could have 160 acres of land in Roseau free, simply by living on it! So with their small cash reserve, they bought oxen and wagon and headed for the North Country.

On arrival, they found no tall buildings nor pretty shops as in Quebec, but only one small store and a post office. The store owner, Jacob Lindberg, insisted they stay with his family until they built a cabin on their homestead.

Finally the small house was ready, not with floor or furniture (lumber had to come from seven miles away), but green poles of Gilead trees created a ceiling which prompted Mör to write to her friends in Sweden, "now we have come to our beloved America where even the roof grows green leaves".

Mör beamed with pride when the settlers accepted her suggestion to name their location "Malung"—a link to their home "in the old country". She was proud, too, of her husband when he made beds (to get the children off the hay covered floor), a table, and chairs.

Soon she had a disturbing thought: Where would the children go to school? "We will not raise dunces," she said. She solved the problem. "We shall move to the loft, and the school shall be in our cabin," she announced. Per was aghast at the idea, but soon Anna Johnson, a teacher, slept in the school room on the bed he had made. The family moved upstairs.

While all this activity was going on, Indian eyes were daring to come closer to view this wonder. They carried moose meat on their shoulders, and soon a barter system was arranged, "Mör's good bread for moose meat". They became good friends.

Mör saw that there was spiritual education and Lars Hedin, "a minister of the Gospel" preached in different cabins. Mör had a good relationship with God. Once when the tamarack swamp was on fire and threatened their home she questioned, "God, do you intend to burn up everything?" His answer? The wind switched. The home was saved.

Another time she talked earnestly to God about the water situation; for Sucker Creek (later named Roseau River) had dried up. Again she pleaded: "God, you see we need water". The rains came that very night, she reported.

Children kept arriving at the Hetteen household. After the three little girls born in Sweden came Immanuel, John, Ida, Edward, Oscar, Albert and Elsie. Did such a large household, with conveniences unknown, deter Mör Hetteen from her rounds of mercy? Hardly so.

She was midwife, nurse, veterinarian, counselor, friend, and mother to anyone who needed her. Her two oldest daughters, Lena and Emma, could cook for railroad crews in Greenbush and Swift, or for single crews at the mills or at the Half-way House at Haycreek; for now Lydia was able to carry on in the home while Mör was away.

Education for the older children was continued in Roseau, weather and money permitting.

With fierce determination and a firm trust in God, Mör Hetteen believed the words from Philippians which read "Not that I complain of want; for I have learned, in whatever state I am, to be content . . . I can do all things in Him who strengthens me."

Of such pioneer spirit was Minnesota built!

SUSIE W. STAGEBERG
Red Wing   **Born 1877**

"Susie", as she was affectionately known throughout the state, was born January 30, 1877 on a farm at Badger, Iowa to Norwegian immigrant parents Ole Williamson and Kristi Sagaard.

She attended rural school, Tobin College (Fort Dodge), and taught rural school before she turned sixteen. She reported rural news for the "Fort Dodge Messenger," an activity to bear fruit in later life.

June, 1898, she married Olaf O. Stageberg, professor of mathematics and languages at Jewell College, Waldorf College, and Red Wing Seminary, successively. At Waldorf, she served as Dean of Women in 1907-1908.

She was active in church and community affairs whose goals were important to her in making a better world for her five sons and the people of the world. For over nineteen years she was president of the Red Wing chapter, Women's Christian Temperance Union; was a "pioneer feminist" and ardent advocate of Women's Suffrage; was an active member of the Prohibition Party. Her husband was that party's candidate for Governor of Minnesota in 1915.

When the Prohibition Party disbanded in 1920 she was already a member of the Nonpartisan League and friend of its founder, A.C. Townley. However, in March 1920 at the League's state convention in Minneapolis, she spoke challenging Mr. Townley's "Balance of

Power" plan and urged the formation of a third party. She, with a small group of associates, did not agree with Townley's plan to seek goals through existing parties.

We believe that it was she that made the motion which resulted in the establishment of the Farmer-Labor Party. She has often been referred to as the "Mother" of the Farmer-Labor Party.

She was the Farmer-Labor candidate for Secretary of State in 1922, 1924, 1928 and a candidate for Congress in 1932. She was the driving force behind the adoption of the Minnesota Mortgage Moratorium Act of the 30's, but she became disenchanted with the party after its merger with the Democrats and subsequently the DFL party. In 1950, during the campaign of Henry Wallace, she became candidate for Lieutenant Governor on the Progressive Party ticket.

In the 20's Susie took over a defunct liberal paper in Red Wing called "The Organized Farmer". She sold advertising, wrote editorials, increased circulation and finally put the paper in the black. However, she was replaced by a persuasive man who convinced the Board of Directors he could do a better job. The paper's demise soon followed.

Her work as newswoman included serving as a Farmer-Labor columnist under the heading "As a Woman See's It" published by the "Minnesota Leader," "Willmar Tribune," and others. Beginning in 1945 the "Norwegian Minnesota Posten" carried her column "This 'n That" for several years.

A life-long Lutheran and devoted member of the Hauge Synod until the 1918 merger of three Norwegian synods, she was a committed pietist. Her religious faith was the driving force in her life. Despite the absorption of her synod and the closing of the last Hauge Synod school (Red Wing Seminary) and the end of her husband's professorship, she still remained loyal to the new church, serving in the Sunday School as a teacher over fifty years.

A dedicated pioneer in the cause of Women's Suffrage, total abstinence, and populist political causes, Susie died in Red Wing, March 15, 1961 at the age of eighty-four.

IRENE LYONS TIBBETTS
Minneapolis • **Born 1883**

"I live for those who love me—
Whose hearts are good and true
For the God who smiles above me
And the good that I can do"

This summarizes the life of Irene Lyons Tibbetts. Born October 18, 1883 at Lyons Island, Minnesota, Irene was the ninth child of Thomas and Mary (Wallace) Lyons.

Her father, a teacher, was a school board member and "Master of the Grangers". Her mother taught public school and Sunday School and felt that the basic 3-R's were meaningless without the fourth "R", religion. This should come first, she felt.

Irene adopted her parents' philosophy, "make

the world happier and better because you have lived." Placing God first, she revealed her love through her treatment of family, friends, and anyone else who came her way seeking help. From her parents she acquired a zest for knowledge and a desire to help others.

After attending high school in Minneapolis, she graduated from Sinsinawa Finishing School, River Forest, Illinois, and taught school in Minnesota and North Dakota. Revered by her students, she comforted the discouraged with "It is by stumbling, my dear, that we learn to stand. We always grow stronger by trying."

October 25, 1904 she married Samuel Elgin Tibbetts, free lance artist and owner of the Tibbetts garages. They made their home in Minneapolis.

Early in marriage and while rearing her three children, she became active in Red Cross, and the St. Thomas and University of Minnesota Mothers' Clubs, the Heart Association, and the Election Board.

An educator, poet, dancer (Scottish and Irish dances), Irene never aspired to greatness for herself. She began writing poetry at the age of nine and later had poetry published in the "Ladies Home Journal"; "Devil's Lake Journal", North Dakota; "Novene Notes," Chicago, Illinois; "Queens Work," St. Louis, Missouri. She authored *What the Leaves Told Me*. Her watercolor landscapes mirrored her love of nature.

She strove to develop the full potential in others and in her children: Vincent, law enforcement; Kathleen, social work; and Laurene, author of stories, plays and the second official poet laureate in Minnesota's history.

Her courage and fearlessness, nourished by her faith in God, was demonstrated when she and her husband were inadvertently on the scene just after a "Piggly Wiggly" grocery store robbery: The robbers had taken refuge in a garage next to the store, and a gun battle with the police was threatened. Irene stationed herself in the line of fire between the two saying "There will be no shooting. I don't believe in shooting and I don't believe in stealing! Now you put your guns down!"

Both sides were speechless. Then one of the robbers called out "Don't shoot. The lady might get hurt," and they surrendered.

Irene, in accepting the reward money, gave it to the needy family of one of the robbers who, upon his prison release, became a law-abiding citizen and established his own small repair shop.

Inspiring, idealistic, unwavering in devotion to God and to her high principles, Irene taught, spoke and lived life beautifully.

She died in 1973 but her spirit and her philosophy of living will continue to influence for good the lives of every person who knew her.

MABEL OLSON WOLFF
Goodhue   Born 1895

"Wright County Bicentennial Lady", Mabel Olson Wolff was born March 29, 1895 to Peter C. and Regina Amundson Olson near Goodhue, Minnesota.

After attending school in Goodhue County, Red Wing and Winona Normal, she taught for three years and then worked in Washington, D.C. under Franklin Roosevelt, Under-secretary of State.

With the end of World War I, Mabel returned to Buffalo and married Henry Wolff, living in the same home for 55 years and raising two daughters; Mary, a teacher, and Ruth, a principal. Henry died in 1966.

Mabel's talent, kindness, and love have been shared unselfishly for over half a century in every conceivable community activity. She has touched the lives of thousands while fulfilling her role as homemaker, wife, mother, and grandmother.

She helped organize and became a charter member of the Buffalo American Legion Auxiliary; has been active for 55 years in the Woman's Club; is a member of "Friends of the Library", after having served 45 years on the Library Board, sixteen years as chairman. She even substituted in the absence of the librarian. Books are dear to her heart, for she is an avid reader.

World War II saw her taking charge in her area of surgical dressings, yarn, and knitted articles for servicemen.

Her deep compassion for the needy surfaced during her six years as a Welfare Board member and while serving on the Nursing Board.

Gifted musically, she was organist 30 years at St. John's Lutheran Church. Senior Citizens are regularly entertained by her.

Her interest in Red Cross began when her mother used their home as Red Cross Headquarters during World War I, and for 26 years Mabel has been Buffalo's Red Cross Blood Program chairman, helping the program to grow and de-

velop. A certificate from the Chapter Executive Director in 1974 recognized her contribution and loyalty to the program.

The Christmas Seal Program has had Mabel's volunteer services for over 50 years as she accompanies the X-Ray Unit over the entire county and works with units in schools, nursing homes, and even in the streets of Buffalo.

Another of her varied interests, in which she has been active for years, is the Cancer Detection Program, of which she is a local director of the Lung Organization.

Prior to elections, she conducts interviews for the "Minneapolis Tribune," "Northstar" and "Minnesota Polls."

Mabel was on the Planning Board for the Buffalo Memorial Hospital which opened in 1951, and served on the Hospital Board for 20 years, assisting in organizing the Hospital Auxiliary, in which she is still active.

In 1971, Buffalo selected her "Outstanding Citizen" for their "Buffalo Days" celebration, honoring her active leadership in so many organizations and community services.

Three years later, a "Certificate of Recognition" for "Outstanding Senior Citizen of Wright County" was signed by Governor Wendell R. Anderson, another testimony to her remarkable service to individuals and community through the years.

She still found time to collect post cards, coins, quilt and needlepoint, garden, play her organ, read and be loved by her two daughters and grandchildren who adore her.

Alert in mind, keen in wit, excessively modest—at 80 years of age Mabel Wolff has already left her imprint on the history of Wright County and of Minnesota!

LILLIAN BENDEKE PARSON
Elbow Lake   **Born 1896**

Dr. Lillian Bendeke Parson was reared in a family of Norwegian culture. Eldest of three sisters, she was born in 1896 in Grand Forks, North Dakota, to Josefin Olson and Halfdan Bendeke, Norwegian Consul, who became both mother and father to his daughters upon the early death of his wife.

Mature beyond her years, she was second mother to her sisters; a sustaining arm to her father. She bandaged the cuts; directed the shadow shows; helped organize Sunday School in the tent. Lill could do anything, it was thought!

Years passed. Lill left to spend one of her high school years in Switzerland. Degrees were obtained from North Dakota University and the Illinois University Medical School in Chicago, in 1922.

In 1920 she married medical classmate, Lester Parson. They were destined to become a "beloved" medical team.

Interning in Boston and Chicago, she had the signal honor of being "one of the first two interns" in the United States to work with the "newly-discovered insulin" under the direction of the Medical Chief, Presbyterian Hospital, Chicago.

She personally delivered nineteen babies in fourteen days without benefit of a hospital while working in Hull House in the Chicago ghetto.

Might she, an internist, with her husband, surgeon and urologist, decide to locate in Minneapolis, cultural center of art and music which was so much a part of her very being? No.

Instead, in 1923 they chose Elbow Lake, a village in Grant County, birthplace of "Dr. Les" as he became affectionately known.

"After three years, we go to the city," he promised. But three years stretched to over fifty. They built a clinic and reared their two off-spring while their practice spread across five counties.

In 1960 they moved their practice to their home and eight years later, Dr. "Les" died. As a team, they had delivered 6,400 babies through the span of their medical years.

Early in practice, "Dr. Lill" had to face head-on and overcome prejudice against women physicians.

No statistics record the many troubled homes kept intact because women, hesitant to confide in a male doctor, approached "Dr. Lill" for physical and mental assistance. She was not above cooking hot meals for mothers just home from hospitals nor washing dishes in kitchens while waiting for babies to be born. Patients were taken to her home to recuperate; she spent untold telephone hours dealing with personal problems of those who sought her guidance.

Only a selection of her activities follow:

Fifty years in Federated Women's Club

Fifty years in Eastern Star

Chairman, town's first Library Board

Member, Presbyterian Church and Choir

Medical Director, Grant County Cancer Society

Honored by Minnesota Medical Society

Her state of health? Five surgeries during her life; a new hip and still only semiretired, at age 79.

Recently in Minneapolis, instead of attending her beloved Minnesota Orchestra, she visited a University Hospital patient and stopped by a writer's home. Why?—To share two casserole recipes. Just like "Dr. Lill"; always loyal, thoughtful, and unchanging!

VERONA STUBBS DEVNEY
St. Paul   **Born 1916**

Verona Devney of Northfield, Minnesota, who wished to help serve her "neighbors," has motivated thousands all over the world to work for those in need. She has proved that a woman need not enter into the world, bodily, to become fulfilled.

Verona, daughter of Mr. and Mrs. Raymond (Schilling) Stubbs, was born in St. Paul, Minnesota, May 21, 1916. As a child she questioned herself, "Why was I so blessed when others are poor, sick, or infirm?" She has been seeking the answer since.

She attended Business College and St. Catherine's College in St. Paul, and the University of Minnesota in Minneapolis. She was a legal secretary for a St. Paul firm before marriage. Although she left the professional world, married and gave birth to four children, she was still searching for ways to help others.

Verona married Raymond Devney, a farmer, in November, 1951. Their four children are: twins, Mary and Joseph, born in 1954; Dorothy in 1956 and Thomas in 1960.

Her charity, her empathy with the poor are

traits that made for harmony in the family. An understanding husband has helped with Verona's projects; the children have grown through the parents' fine example and their sharing of this work for others.

As one article stated, "Verona has caught the spark of divine love . . . and is spreading it like holy contagion throughout America". Her most ambitious project, to date, "Operation Help Other People Everywhere (H.O.P.E.), crosses denominational, racial and cultural lines. Her efforts to help relieve the poor have helped tens of thousands of *receivers*. Once people become involved in working with Verona for Operation H.O.P.E. their lives assume new dimensions.

In 1965 she heard, and was much impressed by, a missionary's plea for clothing for the poor in the southern part of the United States. The words Mrs. Devney heard became "Feed my lambs". Soon she was directing an earth-girdling movement, bringing relief to thousands of destitute people. A recent count showed Verona that she now has many *thousands* of persons on her list—people who have the same "contagion", an excess of love and a desire to serve.

There is a drama in the story, how a Northfield housewife beseeched seven New York garment and textile manufacturers for scrap material, telling them how she planned to use it and enclosing five dollars for postage and cost of any scraps they might send. Who could resist this appeal for the world's forgotten? Not the businessmen in New York city! They returned her money and sent "mountains" of material to the Devney farm. Verona decided there were not enough women in her own parish to sew for the needy.

She invited women from all Northfield churches to join in sewing to make it a truly *ecumenical* work to help the poor. The project grew . . . today thousands are involved.

One of the first donors who had returned her five dollars sent back ten dollars and suggested that she discover the needs of the people in Vietnam. Women started sewing clothing for children. With the clothing, the first shipment included vitamins, canned and powdered milk, soap, baby bottles, and more than 700 pounds of school supplies.

Verona has received many impressive awards but she undoubtedly treasures most the *rewards* of working for others and the warmth and love she has found in return. Through Verona, others who have been waiting for a *call* have found a channel for their generosity.

MISSISSIPPI

Mississippi

Nickname: Magnolia State

State Flower: Southern Magnolia

State Tree: Southern Magnolia

State Bird: Mockingbird

Photos

1. Vicksburg Nat'l Military Park—Sunset over the Yazoo River
2. Picking Cotton
3. Mighty Mississippi
4. The "Showboat" Sprague, Vicksburg
5. Old Warren Country Courthouse, Vicksburg
6. King Cotton

Committee Members

Chairman—Mrs. Paul E. Ballard, Vicksburg

Mississippi

VARINA ANNE BANKS HOWELL DAVIS
Natchez   **Born 1826**

Varina Anne Banks Howell Davis, native Mississippian, filled many roles during her 80 years. She was Dixie Bell, wife, mother, politician, and silent bulwark to the Confederate President, Jefferson Davis. Born on May 7, 1826, Mrs. Davis was raised in Natchez, Mississippi. At 16, Varina met the aspiring young statesman, Jefferson Davis. They married in 1845, two years after they met.

Raised in the tradition of the Southern belle, Varina knew the importance of a social conversation and the method of handling servants, although still very young and unexperienced.

In 1845, Varina began aiding Jefferson as his personal and social secretary for the next fifteen years in Washington during Jefferson's terms of office as national Congressman and Senator from the state of Mississippi, excluding only 1846 when Jefferson served in the Mexican War.

Varina Davis was the mother of six children, the first being born on July 30, 1852, and named Samuel Emory Davis. The Davis' lost this child at the age of two, only to welcome the birth of Margaret Howell Davis on February 25, 1855. Waiting seven years to become a mother did not discourage Varina from having a large family. She joyfully received the next son, Jefferson Finis Davis, Jr. on January 16, 1857. In 1859 the Davises added yet another child to their family, Joseph Evan Davis. Joseph later died in 1864 from a fall from a balcony. The fifth child, William Howell Davis, entered the Davis family on December 16, 1861, during the Civil War. The sixth and last child, Varina Anne Davis (Winnie), was born on June 27, 1864. Margaret Davis alone survived as the remaining child following her mother's death.

Mrs. Davis followed her husband to Montgomery, Alabama, and Richmond, Virginia, to serve as part of the First Family of the Confederacy, in 1861. After the Civil War, Mrs. Davis successfully fought for the release of her husband from prison.

After a brief period in 1867, Jefferson and Varina Davis, along with their children, travelled to Canada, Cuba, and to the South while Mr. Davis recovered from his illness suffered in prison. From the South, they returned to Lennoxville, Quebec to live.

In 1868, the Davises went to London, England in hopes of job opportunities. None surfaced, and Jefferson returned to the United States in 1869. Mrs. Davis and the children remained in England until 1870.

In 1872 William Davis died of diphtheria, leaving a bereaved mother and family. The Davises continued to live in Memphis happily, until 1873 when Jefferson lost his job. Following this event, they fought for the possession of Brierfield and won in 1878. The Davises sailed for Europe once more in 1876, Jefferson returning in late 1876 to look for another job. Varina returned in 1878 after recovering from illness.

Soon they moved to Mississippi to live at Beauvoir together with their daughter, Winnie. Jefferson Davis died in 1889, leaving Beauvoir and Brierfield to Winnie and Varina. In 1890, Mrs. Davis published her biography of her husband: *Jefferson Davis: A Memoir By His Wife.* In 1890, Winnie returned from Europe and she and Varina lived both in New York and Beauvoir until 1892, when they permanently moved to New York for health reasons. Winnie died in 1898, leaving only Margaret, of the children alive. Varina Davis lived until October 10, 1906 in New York, where she died of pheumonia.

ELIZABETH ANN THOMPSON EAST

Copiah County   **Born 1849**

Elizabeth Ann was the oldest of five daughters of Dr. James Franklin Thompson (English ancestry) and Selina Smith Thompson (Dutch ancestry), who lived in Copiah County. They were devout Baptists. She was her father's constant companion and studied along with him from his library of literary, medical and law books. She accompanied him in his buggy, going day or night to minister to the sick. She helped him splint broken bones, deliver babies, and weigh calomel, ipecac, quinine, and other drugs. After the cyclone at Beauregard in 1883, she and Dr. Thompson spent a week there caring for the injured.

Elizabeth Ann realized there was a need for teachers. She attended the Catholic school in Hazlehurst to review academic subjects. She passed the State Teacher's examination and had her license. In 1867 she began her first pay school. People were poor from the ravages of the Civil War and very little tuition was charged. Her father built a school house, and she taught there for fourteen years.

During this time, she married Joel Walker East, a carpenter and cabinet maker. Five of her eight children lived. They were Julian, Clara, Elon, Clyde, and Selina. She kept a cradle in the schoolroom and older children helped care for the babies. When the family moved, she either taught at home, or Joel built a school house.

Miss Ann's school had the reputation of being better than the public school. She taught phonics and all basic subjects. Friday afternoon each child had to recite a poem or a speech. She was a strict disciplinarian. School books were handed down to relatives or friends. Some children had to walk four miles to school.

She was generous. One Christmas she had a large Christmas tree and invited the relatives and neighbors. Each received a gift and children scrambled for bags of candy and nuts. When her husband built a new home, she let a needy neighbor have the old one.

The great depression during McKinley's administration was being felt. Meat and cotton brought only four or five cents a pound. During vacation Elizabeth Ann helped grow vegetables and flowers to sell, driving into town on Saturday in a buggy with her wares.

She passed her last years trying to extend the education of her five children. In the fall of 1897, the family moved to Clinton, Mississippi. Julian and Elon entered Mississippi College, and Clara entered Hillman College. Until this time they had had no other teacher than their mother. Clyde and Selina attended a pay school.

After a lengthy illness her husband died in 1900. She died the next year. She had endowed her children with the desire for knowledge and the ambition to be "somebody." Julian became a lawyer, served as District Attorney, finished the unexpired term of a judgeship, and served in the Mississippi Legislature. Clara taught school and became a legal secretary. Elon taught singing, and farmed. Clyde and Selina each earned a Master's degree, and taught for thirty years.

Among Miss Ann's pupils are many well-known people of Copiah and Lincoln counties. She will be remembered as a courageous pioneer woman, who gave of herself through many channels.

ANNIE COLEMAN PEYTON
Madison County   **Born 1852**

Few Mississippi women realize the debt they owe Annie Coleman Peyton for the prominent role she played in initiating higher education for women in our state. Due to her efforts, Mississippi was the first state in the Union, if not the first organized government in the world, to establish a State-endowed college for the higher education of women.

Born in Madison County in 1852, she was the youngest child of Elias Hibben and Mary Gilchrist Coleman. Educated at home, in the country school and the Canton Female Seminary, she later entered Whitworth College and graduated from that institution in 1872. Married to Chancellor Ephraim Geoffrey Peyton of Gallatin, Mississippi, they had four children.

Her natural interest in the education of her own daughters, and her realization that many Mississippi girls were being deprived by poverty of any education beyond the most elementary, together with her abiding love for her native State and her keen perception of the problems facing the South as an aftermath of the Civil War and reconstruction, doubtless resulted in the idea of establishing a State-endowed college for women.

Though she lived in affluence, she sincerely desired that a higher education might be available to girls of meager means, thereby reducing poverty and illiteracy in Mississippi to a minimum.

With this goal in mind, she tirelessly campaigned in newspapers and by pamphlets, for passage of a Bill for a State-endowed college for women, modestly signing all her articles "A Mississippi Woman".

Undaunted by great opposition and many disappointments, Mrs. Peyton continued her efforts despite indifference and even hostility to the collegiate co-education of women. One of the fears expressed was that female education should be under the control of the church "so that the tender female character might not be exposed to the corrupting influence of State education". There was also to be overcome, the great financial difficulties of a state still suffering from the bankruptcy brought about by the mismanagement of the Carpet-bag government and the general poverty following the Civil War.

With the passage in 1884 of the long sought after Bill sponsored by John McCaleb Martin,

her dream became a reality. Her diligent efforts were finally rewarded when the Industrial Institute and College was formally opened on October 22, 1885 in Columbus, Mississippi.

In succeeding years, Peyton Hall would be dedicated to her at the Industrial Institute College (Mississippi State College for Women) and Mrs. Annie Coleman Peyton would be the first woman whose portrait was placed in the Mississippi Hall of Fame.

ELIZA GROVES HAMMETT
Fayette   **Born 1860**

Eliza Howard (Sammie) Groves was born January 8, 1860, in Fayette—all places mentioned are in Mississippi—to Malcolm Malachi Groves, a Virginian, and Avline Allen Groves, a New York Stater.

In the shadow of war, her spirit remained uncrushed.

1863 found Malachi in the Confederate Army—mother and daughter living in Port Gibson near besieged Vicksburg. Upon Avline's grave illness, they went by carriage and mulewagon to the home of her sister, Mrs. Wylie Burke of Hamburg, to stay for the duration. Letters tell of such episodes as the two making a 25-mile canoe trip in stormy weather and of

their fording a swollen stream riding double on a stallion with only his nose visible above the water.

When Sammie was fifteen, they were again in Fayette. Malachi, again a building contractor, suffered a fatal fall; mother and daughter again coped alone.

December 26, 1876, Sammie married Thomas Benton Hammett, 34, of Fayette, a Confederate veteran. Three children (Ona, Groves, Oscar) were born in Perth community, the writer many years later.

Soon they moved to three-storied, white-columned Poplar Hall. Here began her service of giving a home for years at a time to five persons not in the family. One was a humped-back British spinster. Two were boys brought home from their mother's funeral. One of these won his doctorate and became a college dean. The other, a successful pharmacist, wrote, "Your mother was like the shadow of a great rock in a weary land."

In 1913 a crushing blow fell, the death of her son, Groves, 34, in discharge of duty as Sheriff of Jefferson County. His father, 71, appointed to succeed him, found his first duty to calm an enraged group bent on lynching the mother of the two murderers. All this Sammie endured with fortitude.

The family occupied "Key Place,"—Main Street, Fayette—from 1915. Here she mothered the community. The first outdoor Christmas tree in town blossomed on the wide screened porch, celebrated by groups of singing friends. Amateur concerts on the porch by local musicians enlivened summers. When the church next door needed funds, ice-cream and cake appeared, and a fee was charged at the gate. She moved among the crowds on the lawn, loving and beloved.

She died suddenly February 2, 1927, her last act characteristically to rescue children in danger in construction work at the church.

Her home emanated public service. Besides Groves' service, her husband (1842-1960) was Sheriff and many years Assessor. Her daughter, Ona, born 1878, operated her Style Shop in Fayette; a remarkable 97, she resides in Cleveland. Her son, Oscar, (1882-1964) repeated his father's career. Her daughter, Evelyn, was long-time Professor of English at Delta State College and headed the department. Her story of a maternal colonial ancestor (I, Priscilla, Macmillan, 1960) appeared in German and in Braille and largeprint editions for the Xavier Society.

Sammie preferred her nickname, but "Eliza" (Consecrated to God) really described her.

BESSIE LACKEY STAPLETON
Crystal Springs   **Born 1861**

"I had a vision and like Banquo's Ghost 'it would not down.' The eyes of my own children and of all Mississippi children seemed to look into mine with a plea for help." These are the words of Bessie Lackey Stapleton, founder in Crystal Springs, Mississippi, of the Mississippi Congress of Parents and Teachers.

Mrs. Stapleton, wife of Dr. R. B. Stapleton of Hattiesburg and mother of four children, had the intellect, education, and character to succeed at a task even of the magnitude of the one she had set herself. Born in Crystal Springs, she was particularly fortunate in her parents and early training. Her mother, Elizabeth McRae Sumrall Stapleton, was a niece of Governor John J. McRae of Mississippi. Her father, Professor J. J. Lackey, was a brilliant and farseeing man. Though he was an orphan, he had

In 1914, Mrs. Stapleton, having served as president of the young organization since its first meeting in 1909, gave her final report as high-ranking officer and exultantly announced that there were more than one hundred PTA units in the state.

Because of the dream of this woman, inestimable good has been done in Mississippi through the years.

NELLIE NUGENT SOMERVILLE
Washington County   **Born 1863**

Nellie Nugent Somerville was a reformer in the early women's rights movement, a pioneer suffragist, and Mississippi's first female political leader. She was the mother of four outstanding Mississippians. Robert N. and Abram D. Somerville (both deceased now) were attorneys in

the good fortune to be educated by Henry Ward Beecher, the great American Congregational minister who was noted for his oratorical powers and for his championing of anti-slavery and of women's rights.

Besides the excellent examples and training of her early years, Mrs. Stapleton had the advantage of a college education at Lea in New Orleans, later a part of Sophie Newcomb; and at Hillman in Clinton, Mississippi.

It was during her busiest years in Hattiesburg that Bessie Lackey Stapleton made the first movement toward establishing the Mississippi PTA. Encouraged by Mrs. Frederic Schoff, then national president of the Congress of Mothers and PTA, she called a meeting for September 19, 1905, in her own home where the idea for the organization was discussed.

In October, 1909, a formal organization was made at Lake Chautauqua in Crystal Springs. Mrs. Stapleton became the first president. Some of the matters of vital concern that were brought up at the early meetings are today continuing to affect the state and its children. At Columbia the Industrial School for youth stands as one of the results of the early work of the organization, and "Better Babies" became much more important than "Better Hogs" and "Better Cows"!

Cleveland. Eleanor Somerville Shands, a prominent community leader, was the wife of a Cleveland attorney. Lucy Somerville Howorth is a distinguished personage in the fields of law, politics, and women's rights.

Born on a plantation near Greenville in Washington County, Mississippi, September 25, 1863, Mrs. Somerville lived most of her life in Jackson and Greenville, and she died in Cleveland in 1952. Her parents were William Lewis Nugent, a Confederate cavalry officer and lawyer; and Eleanor Smith Nugent, the daughter of pioneer settlers in Washington County.

After receiving her preparatory education at Whitworth College in Brookhaven, Mississippi, Mrs. Somerville graduated with a B.A. degree from Marth Washington College, Abingdon, Virginia, where she was valedictorian of the class of 1880. She married Robert Somerville, formerly of Virginia, and the couple settled in Greenville, where they raised their children.

Mrs. Somerville, a staunch patriot as well as a devoted wife and mother, believed that women were entitled to the same civil and political rights as men. She often expressed the fear that a "disfranchised motherhood (would mean) a lack of patriotic training" for American youth. She realized that women lacked influence in humanitarian reform without "the power of a consecrated ballot". Consequently, she became one of the first southern women to embrace the suffrage cause and she helped to launch the women's rights movement in Mississippi.

When the Mississippi Woman Suffrage Association was formed in 1897, Mrs. Somerville was chosen the first president and thereafter devoted much time to gaining political rights for women. She was the guiding light of the organization, serving as president from 1897 to 1899 and from 1908 to 1912. In 1914 as Legislative Chairman, she led the initial attempt to obtain a woman suffrage amendment to the state constitution. In 1915 she became second vice-president of the National American Woman Suffrage Association. During World War I she interrupted suffrage work to serve as Washington County Chairman, Woman's Committee, Council of National Defense.

After the Nineteenth Amendment granted women the right to vote and thereby qualifying them to hold office, Mrs. Somerville became the first woman ever elected to the Mississippi House of Representatives in 1923. She served a four-year term as chairman of the Committee on Eleemosynary Institutions. In 1924 she was a delegate from the state at large to the National Democratic Convention in New York City.

Mrs. Somerville did not confine her interests to political issues but vigorously supported social and humanitarian reforms, especially where a moral issue was involved. She was active in the Methodist Church, especially in Home Missions work. She was involved in several patriotic and service organizations: Daughters of the American Revolution, United Daughters of the Confederacy, Order of Eastern Star, and King's Daughters. She organized and for many years was president of the Greenville Civic Improvement Club. She served two terms as vice-president of the Mississippi Federation of Women's Clubs. She was president of the Mississippi Women's Christian Temperance Union from 1926 to 1930.

Mrs. Somerville was nominated by the American Sesqui-Centennial Committee in Philadelphia, Pennsylvania, as one of the four most outstanding women in Mississippi during the fifty years preceding 1926. Her name appeared in *Who's Who of American Women*, 1935. In her honor the "Nellie Nugent Somerville Lectures on Government and Public Affairs" were inaugurated in 1974 at Delta State University, Cleveland, Mississippi.

The Mississippi Woman's Day Annual "Woman of the Year Award" was renamed for her, and in 1975 the first recipient of the "Nellie Nugent Somerville Award" was her younger daughter, Lucy Somerville Howorth. Like her mother, Mrs. Howorth is recognized as a pioneer in politics and a champion of equal opportunities for women.

Both daughters attended Randolph-Macon Woman's College. Eleanor was the first student to study Physics there. Lucy received her law degree *magna cum laude* from the University of Mississippi. One of two women in the class, she graduated with first honors and was class orator.

With her husband, Joseph M. Howorth, Lucy practiced law in the Jackson firm of Howorth and Howorth. From 1927 through 1933 she was active in state government where, like her mother, she was elected to the Mississippi House of Representatives. Since then she has held appointed offices in federal agencies including General Counsel of the War Claims Commission and division director with the United States Commission of Government Security. Now retired, Mrs. Howorth resides with her husband in Cleveland, Mississippi.

302

MAUD CELESTE COLMER REEVES
Escatawpa   **Born 1886**

Mrs. Maud Celeste Reeves lead efforts to educate the people and create public sentiment in favor of setting up a branch of our State Government for forestry service and the conservation of our natural resources.

She followed the bill to establish a Forestry Commission through the legislature where it was passed on March 6, 1926. As recognition for her work she was appointed by Governor Henry Whitfield as a member of the first State Forestry Commission.

She served as Educational Director of the Commission from 1930 to 1934. She was at one time editor of the Forestry Commission's monthly publication. And, also, helped with the first forestry textbook adopted by the state.

She was Conservation Chairman of the Mississippi Federation of Women's Clubs for seventeen years and initiated "Mississippi Conservation Week" in the schools.

In 1936, Mrs. Reeves was a member of the Master Committee of Planning for the Mississippi Forest Service, representing the Mississippi Federation of Women's Clubs.

Mrs. Reeves was born in Escatawpa. She was married on May 10, 1911 to George Herman Reeves. The late Mr. Reeves was employed by the Gulf, Mobile and Ohio Railroad as commercial agent and later division freight agent. Magnolia tress were planted in Mr. Reeves' memory on the grounds of Riverside Park and St. Dominic's Hospital.

Mrs. Reeves had two daughters, the late Mrs. Anna Margaret (Dale W.) Read of Vancouver, Washington and Mrs. Dorothy (Roger) Martin, Jr. of Purvis, Mississippi. She had a brother, the Hon. William M. Colmer, and three sisters, Mrs. Posey N. Howell, Mrs. L. R. Weeks, and Mrs. R. L. Walton.

She attended Mississippi State College for Women and was a member of Galloway Memorial Methodist Church and later Riverside Independent Methodist Church.

Mrs. Reeves belonged to the Review Club, Belhaven Garden Club and the Cosmos Luncheon Club.

EVA WHITAKER DAVIS
Vicksburg   **Born 1892**

Mrs. Eva Whitaker Davis was born September 18, 1892 in the Redbone community of Warren County Mississippi the daughter of Tobias Adams Whitaker and Leila Bolls Whitaker. She died July 28, 1974 in Greenwood, Mississippi.

On February 18, 1917 she was married to Sherwood Davis and in the years following she gave birth to three daughters, Jean Carolyn (Mrs. Brown), Sybil Adiel (Mrs. Wright) and Betty Cecil (Mrs. Worley).

It was through the efforts of Mrs. Davis, affectionately known to many as "Miss Eva," that the old Warren County Court House was saved from probable destruction after it was abandoned in 1939 when the new building was erected across the street. She began a one-woman campaign to save the slave-built structure, which had been built in 1858. Through her efforts the Vicksburg and Warren County Historical Society was organized in 1946, and in 1948 she was elected president, a position she held until 1956.

Miss Eva secured permission from the Board of Supervisors to establish a museum in the Old Court House, and she opened the building to the public on June 3, 1947. Much of the preparation for the museum had been done by her personally, as she packed buckets of water up the high terraces to the old courthouse to clean the floors and walls.

Friends volunteered their labors, and when the Museum was opened, it consisted of one room. Donations were dropped in a fruit jar, and Miss Eva served as curator, guide, director, publicity agent, and janitor, working for a number of years without pay. Under her direction, the Museum has grown to nine rooms of displays, and the building houses the best collection of Confederate history in the South. In addition she fostered the McCardle Research Library housed also in the building.

For six years, from 1949 to 1955 she conducted a 30-minute daily radio program from the Museum, a program for which she wrote the script and sold the advertising. She also wrote a weekly column in the Vicksburg Sunday Post and edited a best-selling cookbook, "Mississippi Mixins".

With a love for preserving Vicksburg's history, Miss Eva organized the Mississippi Foundation for Historic Preservation, now known as the Vicksburg Foundation, and it was through her efforts that the home of Governor Alexander G. McNutt was saved from destruction and that the Balfour Home and Pemberton Headquarters were both placed on the National Register of Historic Places.

In 1966 the governing board of the Museum added her name to the building making it the Old Court House Museum—Eva W. Davis Memorial. The building was designated a National Historic Landmark, the first in Mississippi.

Mrs. Davis' efforts in Vicksburg sparked a statewide movement in historic interests which resulted in the revitalization of the state historical society.

After her retirement in July 1967 as Director of the Museum, she and Mr. Davis moved to Greenwood to be near one of their daughters. Miss Eva remained interested in Vicksburg. Her active mind continued to invision things to be done which she passed along to her successors back in Vicksburg. Her last suggestion was the erection of a historic marker at Antioch Cemetary, the site of the oldest Baptist Church in Warren County. The marker was erected the day before she died.

Mrs. Davis was instrumental in establishing Calvary Baptist Church in Warren County. She was a member of the Daughters of the American Revolution, United Daughters of the Confederacy, the Jersey Settlers, First Families of Mississippi, the John Forney Historical Society of Alabama, the Claiborne County Historical Society, the Mississippi Historical Society, Colonial Dames 17th Century, World War I Auxiliary, a life member of the Vicksburg and Warren County Historical Society, and Westminster Presbyterian Church.

MRS. ARNETT GILES
Pearlington   **Born 1901**

Born on August 8, 1901, seventy-five year old Mrs. Arnett Giles of Pearlington, Mississippi still has a houseful of adopted and foster children, and is carrying on a schedule a woman half her age would find difficult. She is the wife of Reverend Charles Giles. During the fifty-six years of their marriage, more than forty children found shelter in their home; many of them were retarded and handicapped.

For twenty-five years Mrs. Giles worked as a teacher's aide at the Clermont Harbor, Mississippi Retarded Children's School resigning in 1972. She accepted the position so she could get some education and training for her houseful of children as they were unacceptable for public school education. She also provided transportation for other housebound children.

Mrs. Giles' knowledge of retardation is not from formal education, but the result of a lifetime of experience, for no child who needed help was ever refused. She kept the large family well fed and cared for, while Reverend Giles and the children worked their small farm to provide a well stocked table.

Orphaned at an early age, Mrs. Giles was moved from relative to relative, never knowing what it was to be loved or wanted by anyone. Her one wish and prayer was to grow up and have a large house, so she could care for and love all children who needed help. Not many years following her marriage to Reverend Giles and the birth of their own four children, the couple began to take in needy and handicapped girls and boys, and at no time throughout their marriage did they not have a houseful of children.

Although Mrs. Giles was not permitted to attend school beyond the sixth grade, she availed herself of night school education, and passed her GED testing with flying colors at the age of sixty-eight. There is a lovely dignity about this woman, who excells as a public speaker. Her impressive extemporaneus talks bring tears to the eyes of many, as she pleads for help, education and training for the retarded and handicapped child.

In 1971 Mrs. Giles was selected as the Nation's Top Volunteer and honored by President Nixon and many of the nation's leaders. The five thousand dollar prize she received was spent for the children, first for a new car to provide them with better transportation, a fine television and other articles needed at the school. She insisted the money was given her, not for her use, but for the children.

The stories Mrs. Giles tells of "her children are forever inspirational, and although she and her family have never had much of the world's goods, they have always had an abundance of love, faith and joy of living. Mrs. Giles believes the retarded child can be helped with protection, love and continuous care. "Build up their self-confidence," she urges—"for they have so very little—make them feel important—they are, for they are God's Special Children."

MILDRED NUNGESTER WOLFE
Jackson   Born 1912

Mildred Nungester Wolfe, artist and teacher, has won acclaim in both her hometown of Jackson and the state of Mississippi for her many outstanding works of art and in particular her designs in stained glass.

Born August 23, 1912, in Celina, Ohio, she is the daughter of Cliff and Augusta Nungester. Her husband is Karl Wolfe a well-known Mississippi artist. Their daughter, Elizabeth Wolfe, is pursuing an art career in stained glass. Michael Wolfe, their son, is married to the former Elaine Lackey and they have two children, Lisa and Sarah.

In a quiet garden setting Mrs. Wolfe shares studio space with her husband and daughter. Here her talents combine with formal art education received from Athens College, Athens, Alabama, University of Montevallo, Alabama, where she was awarded the A. B. degree, Art Students League in New York, Chicago Art Institute, and Colorado Springs Fine Arts Center, Colorado, where she earned her M. A. degree. For five summers the artist attended the Dixie Art Colony at Wetumpka, Alabama, where she trained under J. Kelly Fitzpatrick.

Painting styles from realistic to semi-abstract are evident in her landscapes, still lifes, and portraits. She uses watercolor, oil, acrylic and pastels in her painting. Mrs. Wolfe's paintings are in many private collections and are included in the permanent collections of the Deposit Guaranty Bank, Jackson; The First National Bank, Jackson; Mississippi State College for Women; Mississippi Art Association, Laurel Museum, Laurel; Montgomery Museum of Fine Arts, Montgomery, Alabama; and the Library of Congress Artists for Victory collection.

Mrs. Wolfe uses other media as well, including woodcut, terra cotta, ceramics and mosaics. "I work in many mediums and with varying techniques, all dictated by a search for the means by which to better express my feeling for the subject."

Special commissions for work used in public buildings has given the artist a unique opportunity for communication. Her commissions have included the mosaic in stained glass, "Stations of the Cross" for St. Richards Catholic Church, Jackson, Mississippi, stained glass windows for the First Baptist Church in Hazlehurst, Mississippi, Old South mural, Jacksonian Highway Hotel, LeFleur's Restaurant, Jackson, mosaic "Orphesus" for the South Hills Branch Library, Jackson, mosaic "David" University Hospital, Jackson, mural panels "Four Freedoms", a logging mural, for Ben Stevens Store, Richton, Mississippi, nine windows for Riverside Methodist Church, Jackson, window for First Presbyterian Church, Columbia, Mississippi (in collaboration with Karl Wolfe), and a window for private chapel (concrete and glass) for Mr. and Mrs. Robert Parkes, Jackson.

In speaking of her work in mosaics, Mrs. Wolfe relates that "The Columbia window being in Karl's hometown, is the only one on which we both worked. It was the first window. Mr. Seavey, architect for the Hazlehurst church, had seen. The architect of Riverside had seen the Hazlehurst window. I have always been interested in stained glass because of the unparalleled color. Visiting the Chartres Cathedral in France deepened my interest. I hope the nine windows in the Riverside church are a unique re-statement, necessarily modern, of an old tradition. I had formed an association with Fenestra Studios, Louisville, Kentucky, during the making of the Hazlehurst window and all nine of the Riverside windows were faithfully executed from my designs by this studio."

In 1938 she won first prize in an exhibition of Southern painters at McDowell Galleries in New York, 1949, first prize in the National watercolor exhibition in Jackson. Also in that year she won third prize in the oils show. In 1952 she won first prize in the Delta Art Association Exhibition and an Award of Merit for Outstanding Contribution to the Arts in the Grumbacher International. In 1958 she was awarded second Purchase Prize in the National Oil Show in Jackson. She has won four Honorable Mentions in National Shows in Jackson, represented Alabama, where she resided until her marriage, in the New York World's Fair Exhibition of Paintings, and has had 30 prints of one outstanding lithograph shown simultaneously in 30 American Galleries. One of these prints is now in the collection of the Library of Congress.

An art history teacher at Millsaps College in Jackson, Mrs. Wolfe is listed in Who's Who in American Art and International Biographical Dictionary of the Art.

MISSOURI - THE "SHOW ME" STATE

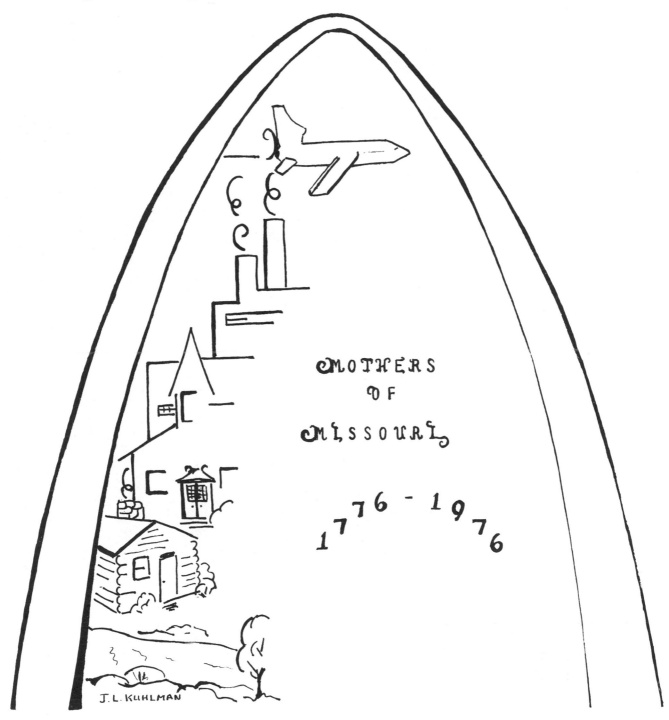

MOTHERS OF MISSOURI

1776 - 1976

J.L. KUHLMAN

GATEWAY TO THE WEST

Missouri

Nickname: Show Me State

State Flower: Hawthorn

State Tree: Dogwood

State Bird: Eastern bluebird

Photos

1. City Hall—Kansas City
2. The Pony Express
3. Harry S. Truman
4. **Mark Twain's** boyhood Home, Hannibal
5. Harry S. Truman Library
6. Float fishing the Big Springs country
7. St. Louis' famous Gateway Arch

Committee Members

Chairman—Mrs. C.M. Lederer Warrensburg
Mrs. Don Witt, Platte City
Mrs. Newton, R. Bradley, Lexington
Mrs. Charles L. Frevele, Kansas City
Mrs. Joe Ausmus, Centralia
Mrs. Valle, J. Nesslein, Perryville
Mrs. James Rodewald, Kansas City
Mrs. Harry C. Saunders, Shelbina
Mrs. Joe Volk, Florissant
Mrs. Vera J. Waltmire, Belton
Mrs. Wayne Kuhlman, Kansas City
Dr. William E. Foley, Warrensburg
Dr. Arthur F. McClure, Warrensburg,
  Consultants Missouri State Dept. of
  History

Missouri

HANNAH ALLISON COLE

In 1784 Hannah Allison married William Temple Cole in Wythe County, Virginia and they—with her sister Phoebe and her brother-in-law Stephen Cole—began to move westward. In 1807 the Cole families emigrated to Loutre Island in what is now Montgomery County, Missouri, becoming the first white settlers south of the Missouri River in Central Missouri. Hannah's husband, William Temple Cole, was brutally murdered in 1809 at Skull (Big Bone) Lick while pursuing Indians who had stolen horses from Loutre Island settlers. A month later, in January 1810, Hannah, with her nine children, and her brother-in-law and sister and their five children, began a perilous journey to what is now the present site of Boonville, Missouri. They crossed the Missouri River in a pirogue, swimming their horses alongside. Prevented by the ice-packed, swiftly flowing river from returning for provisions left on the opposite shore, for eleven days the party subsisted on acorns, slippery elm bark and one wild turkey.

Hannah built her cabin on the present site of St. Joseph's Hospital in Boonville, and her brother-in-law Stephen settled one and one-half miles farther east. The next year ten other families joined the Cole settlement. When troubles arose culminating in the War of 1812, the Coles and their neighbors built a fort at Stephen Cole's cabin. Seeking a more advantageous location after several Indian atrocities, a larger fort was built in 1814 at Hannah's cabin. Hannah's fort became a community center, and she was kept busy feeding the people who came there. Mrs. Cole helped make lead bullets and when anyone was wounded in the Indian fighting, she bandaged their wounds and took care of them. In 1815, Luke Williams, a Baptist minister, held services there. The territorial legislature selected her fort as the seat of justice for Cooper County, and the first court was held there, July 8, 1816.

Hannah was the original owner of the site of Boonville, preempting 160 acres which she later sold for $100 to establish the town. Daniel Boone, cousin of William Temple Cole, was re-

ported to have rested at Hannah's cabin on his last hunting trip through Missouri. In 1816, she, with her sons, operated a ferry over the Missouri River which earned for her the title of "Missouri's First Business Woman."

In 1825 Hannah built a cabin on preempted land located fifteen miles south of Boonville and there, with her faithful slave, Lucy, she lived until her death in 1843. Cole County was named for her husband. Monuments to her memory stand at her grave in Briscoe Cemetery, twelve miles south of Boonville, and on the grounds of the Boonville High School. The Boonville chapter of the Daughters of the American Revolution is named for her.

ANN HAWKINS GENTRY

Born 1791

Born January 21, 1791 in Madison County, Kentucky, Ann Hawkins became the bride of Richard Gentry at the age of nineteen. Son of a Kentucky Revolutionary War soldier, Gentry began his military career as a regimental Ensign under General William Henry Harrison in the War of 1812. Ann's first child was born while her husband was serving in the war.

When Richard returned home, the Gentrys packed their household goods in a covered wagon, drove some cattle before them and started for Missouri. Ann rode her thoroughbred mare, holding her infant daughter on her lap.

After settling first in St. Louis County, in 1818 they moved to Old Franklin. She knew a great anxiety when her husband was tried for the killing of Henry Carroll in a quarrel over slavery. He was twice acquitted by grand juries.

With others, the Gentrys founded the settlement of Smithton, forerunner of Columbia, Missouri, in 1820. There Ann set up housekeeping in a double log cabin which also served as the first tavern of the village. She assumed responsibility for the tavern and for her large family of thirteen children while her husband served as State Senator from 1826-1830; Marshal of a Santa Fe expedition, 1827; Major General of Missouri Militia in the Black Hawk War; helped to found Columbia College, 1831, and also Columbia Female Academy, 1833; and Columbia Postmaster, 1830-1837.

In 1831 the Gentry tavern, later known as the Columbia Hotel, was relocated in an L-shaped, two storied brick building on the northeast corner of Ninth Street and Broadway in Columbia. Mail was dispensed from one corner of the front room.

On October 6, 1837, Ann told her husband goodbye as he, with his regiment of mounted volunteers, left for the Florida War, waving a silk banner presented by students of the Columbia Female Academy. Proud to be the wife of a soldier, Ann said that she "would rather be a brave man's widow than a coward's wife." General Gentry was killed on Christmas day, 1837. The silk banner was returned to his widow and is now on display at the Missouri Resources Museum, Jefferson City, Missouri. Gentry County, Missouri, is named for the General.

After her husband's death, Ann Hawkins Gentry became the second woman in the nation to receive the official appointment of postmaster, and continued as postmistress of Columbia, Missouri from 1838 until 1865. It is thought she received her appointment through the influence of U.S. Senator Thomas Hart Benton, a friend of the family. Ann was noted for her courage and rare good judgment. She died on January 18, 1870 and was buried in Columbia Cemetary. In 1960 a roadside park in Gentry County was dedicated in her honor.

BERNICE MENARD CHOUTEAU
Born 1801

Known as the "Mother of Kansas City," Bernice Menard was born in 1801 in Kaskaskia, Illinois, the old French capital on the Mississippi River. Her father, Colonel Pierre Menard was the first territorial Governor of Illinois. Bernice married at eighteen and honeymooned on a boat trip up the Missouri River as far as St. Joseph, Missouri.

As the young bride of Francois Chouteau, Bernice was the wife of the first settler on the river front in what is now Kansas City. Their first home was built on the site of Westport Landing. They came by keel boat and although many trappers had come before 1821, there had been no women. Braving the hardships and dangers of the wilderness, she was a useful and much loved citizen for more than half a century.

At Westport Landing, the Chouteaus built a home and trading post. Everything about Bernice testifies to the force of her personality and character. She had a zest for living, and an ability to adapt herself to her surroundings. She was not afraid of hardships nor of death by violence, nor indeed, of much of anything in life.

In 1826 the Missouri River spring flood wiped out most of the log cabins, including the Chouteau home, so they next built in the vicinity of Troost Avenue. They came to know the Indians well and liked them. There were no doctors or clergy of any denomination and Mrs. Chouteau was a devout Catholic. When an epidemic struck among the Indians, Mrs. Chouteau turned nurse. She brewed medicines from herbs and cared for the dying Redskins. She did more than that—Indian babies, too small to have heard of Mrs. Chouteau's God, were dying. She persuaded mothers to have their babies baptized in the Christian faith. Between baptizing babies and caring for the ill, she found time to sew shrouds for her stricken neighbors. The Catholic Church named her the "Mother of the Diocese" and she maintained a chapel and an altar in her home and gave time and money to build the first Catholic Church in Kansas City.

Francois died in 1838, leaving his thirty-seven year old wife with ten children, nine sons and one daughter. Nevertheless, she found time to ride horseback to homes of the sick and to mother the entire community.

Madame Chouteau outlived her husband by fifty years and survived all her children. Always she remained vigorous and active, taking a vital part in the growth of the city. No picture is in existence (she was a tall, straight, grey-eyed woman) because she did not wish to leave one and saw to it, herself, before she died on November 19, 1888.

MARTHA ELLEN YOUNG TRUMAN
Born 1852

Martha Ellen Young Truman was the mother of Harry S. Truman, thirty-third President of the United States. She was born on November 25, 1852 and died on July 26, 1947. She was married to John Anderson Truman, whom she had known since childhood, and in 1881 they began their life together in Lamar, Missouri. They had two sons and a daughter; Harry was born on May 8, 1884; Vivian in 1886, and later, Mary Jane.

Martha attended the Baptist Female College in Lexington, Missouri. She loved horseback riding and dancing. Even in the 1870's and 1880's, Martha had a mind of her own on almost every subject from politics to plowing, spending most of her life on a farm. She was devoutly religious and a lifelong member of the Baptist church, as was her son, Harry. Martha Truman was what she called a "light-foot" Baptist, as opposed to the "hard-shell" variety. She did not believe in the restrictions laid on some congregations, but loved to dance and play cards. In her youth, rumor has it, she was quite a dancer.

There was an enormously strong intellectual and emotional bond between Harry and his mother. He was the son of a strong-minded woman. Besides giving her children moral fiber, she passed on to them her strong interest in books, music and art. Martha sustained Harry's years of studying the piano. Harry spent most of his time reading books that Martha carefully selected for him. She followed his career closely and never hesitated to give him advice.

President Truman sent the Presidential plane, The Sacred Cow, to Missouri for her on his first Mother's Day in the White House. Being met at the plane by the press corps and the photographers, her reaction was testy dismay. "Fiddlesticks," said Martha (her strongest oath). "If I'd known everybody was going to carry on like this, I wouldn't have come." She rode home on the train saying, "I'd rather stay on the ground. I can see more."

Her advice to Harry after he became President was, "Just belong to the key of B-natural—be good and be game, too." The President kept close contact with his mother both writing and telephoning her once or twice a week. When she died at the age of ninety-four, her son, Harry, proclaimed, "She's wonderful. They don't make them like that anymore."

SARAH BREEDLOVE WALKER
Born 1867

Sarah Breedlove Walker, pioneer Negro business woman and millionaire, better known as Madame C. J. Walker, was born in 1867 to ex-slave parents in Delta, Louisiana. Sarah Breedlove was orphaned at the age of seven, married at fourteen to Mr. McWilliams, bore a daughter, A'Lelia, and left a widow with a small child at the age of twenty.

Deciding to begin a new life, she traveled to St. Louis and worked as a laundress in order to send her daughter to school. In the late 1890's, Sarah Married Charles J. Walker and, under the name of Madame C. J. Walker, subsequently made famous her hair-styling formula.

In 1905 she developed—or, as she told it, dreamed—the formula for a preparation to improve the appearance of the hair of Negro women. Mixing her soaps and ointments in washtubs and kitchen utensils, and adapting and modifying hairdressing techniques already known, she arrived at what was to become known as "The Walker System." It included a shampoo, a pomade "hair grower," vigorous brushing and the application of heated iron combs to the hair. Lusterless hair was transformed into shining smoothness. She was encouraged by her success in St. Louis and later added a complete line of toiletries and cosmetics to her products. Sarah traveled extensively in the South and East, giving lecture-demonstra-

tions in Negro homes, clubs, and churches. She established a business and manufacturing headquarters in Denver, a second office in Pittsburgh, and later transferred both offices to Indianapolis.

The Madame C. J. Walker Manufacturing Company, of which she was president and sole owner, came to provide employment for some 3,000 persons. Her principal employees were the women known as "Walker Agents" who traveled throughout the United States and the Caribbean, dressed in characteristic white shirtwaists tucked into long black shirts and carrying black satchels containing the preparations and apparatus necessary for dressing hair.

Becoming the first Negro woman millionaire, Madame Walker moved to New York City in 1914 and in 1917 built Villa Lewaro, an Italianate country home at Irvington-on-Hudson, New York. She was well-known for her philanthropic activities, including large bequests to the NAACP, the YMCA of St. Louis, homes for the aged in St. Louis and Indianapolis, Tuskegee Institute, and Bethune-Cookman College.

Madame Walker became ill while in St. Louis and was removed to New York, where she died at Villa Lewaro in 1919. The bulk of her estate was left to her daughter with a trust fund providing for the establishment of an industrial and mission school in Africa, bequests to Negro orphans and old folks' homes and to private secondary and collegiate institutions.

LAURA INGALLS WILDER
Born 1867

Born February 7, 1867, near Pepin, Wisconsin, young Laura Ingalls moved with her family to Kansas, Minnesota, Iowa and South Dakota. She taught in rural schools in South Dakota and there at the age of eighteen was married to Almanzo Wilder. Their only daughter, Rose, was born in 1886. A series of misfortunes caused them to move from drought ridden South Dakota in 1894, after Laura had worked as a dressmaker from six in the morning to six in the evening for one dollar a day to save enough money to begin the move. At last she had $100, all in one bill, which she placed in a lap desk and they began their fifty-five day covered wagon journey which ended in the Missouri Ozarks at Mansfield. After they hunted for days

for land to buy, they found what they wanted. Laura excitedly prepared to go to the bank to sign the papers. She brought out the desk, lifted out the narrow tray that held the pen and inkwell—the $100 bill was gone. After a few agonizing days the bill, which had slipped into a crack in the desk, was recovered.

She and her husband bought forty uncleared acres, a log house and four hundred heeled-in apple trees. Within a year the Wilders moved from a log cabin on the farm to the two-room frame home built by Almanzo from native lumber. Gradually the home was enlarged and the farm expanded to two hundred acres.

After Laura's daughter, Rose Wilder Lane, won fame as an author, she urged her mother, then more than sixty years old, to write down the stories Laura had told her as a child. The resulting books, illustrated by Helen Sewell and Mildred Boyle and published by Harper and Brothers, gained worldwide popularity and she became famous as a writer of children's books. She portrayed the principles of democratic living so well that General Douglas MacArthur had her books translated into Japanese for use in the schools of that country.

Her eight "Little House" books have become children's classics and a successful television story "Little House on the Prairie." Her "Land of the Big Red Apple" is the story of their home on Rocky Ridge Farm. Four years after her death in 1957, the Laura Ingalls Wilder Home and Museum was opened to the public at Mansfield, Missouri.

MAUDE HALL JONES
Audrain County   Born 1872

Maude Hall Jones was born in 1872 north of Sturgeon in Audrain County, Missouri, where her parents, Mary Elizabeth Pickett and John Hall were pioneer settlers and among other achievements were founders of a church in the newly settled county.

After attending Centralia High School and Hardin College at Mexico, Missouri, Maude was married to Tarlton H. Jones, long a Moberly, Missouri druggist. They were parents of two children, Mary, and a son, Hall, who died when he was ten years old. The death of Maude's brother, Edward Hall, was followed shortly by the death of his widow and Maude became the mother to their orphaned children, two boys and a girl. She undertook the rearing or support of many youngsters, whether they were relatives, left homeless, or without a friend, sometimes at a risk to her own security and to her family's security. She became "Aunt Maude" to everyone in the community and in addition to rearing orphaned children she helped many boys and girls to get an education and start in business and professional life.

On the death of her husband in 1934, with the country still in the depths of the depression, "Aunt Maude" became a successful business

woman. She managed a farm, the drug store, and operated a restaurant specializing in fine foods.

Growing up in the day when women were to be totally in the background, Maude developed a feeling of the necessity of woman's part in the development of civic life and she participated actively in the business life of the community. As an officer in the U.S. Highway 24 Association, she represented the President of the Association at a bridge dedication when she was eighty-one years of age.

Maude Hall Jones died in 1954. In 1955 the late Judge Lue Lozier and his wife, Maude's daughter, Mrs. Mary Jones Lozier, dedicated as a memorial to Mrs. Jones, a roadside park on U.S. Highway 63. A monument in the park has the names of the mothers of Missouri recognized as State Mothers and each year the name of the current Missouri mother is added.

EDNA FISCHEL GELLHORN
St. Louis   **Born 1878**

Edna Fischel Gellhorn, one of the valiant women who formed the national League of Women Voters, was born December 18, 1878 in St. Louis. The daughter of Mr. and Mrs. Washington E. Fischel, she attended Mary Institute, St. Louis, and was graduated in 1900 from Bryn Mawr College. She served as lifetime president of her class and as an elected trustee of the college. In 1903 she married George Gellhorn, an internationally known gynecologist.

Elected chairman of the St. Louis Equal Suffrage League, she planned and directed the national American Woman Suffrage Convention in 1919 in St. Louis. An outgrowth of that convention was the organization of the National League of Women Voters and she was chosen the first vice-president. Mrs. Gellhorn served from 1919-1921 as the first president of the Missouri League of Women voters and again for the term of 1927-1929. She was active in the National League's drive against the spoils system in 1935, and in the 1940's she led the Missouri League's campaign in support of the 1945 Missouri Constitution.

In the early 1920's, after Missouri women were given the right to vote, the League began a program only by rut or by rail and Mrs. Gellhorn later recalled trips she often made, riding in the milk train caboose. "It wasn't ladylike to ride this way," she reminisced, "and one had to look ladylike so, although I didn't knit, I had my cook fix up some knitting and there I sat in the caboose, pretending to knit and look ladylike."

Mrs. Gellhorn pursued other civic interests. During World War I she served under Herbert Hoover as regional director of the Food Administration. In later years she was one of the organizers of the American Association of United Nations, the National Municipal League and the American Association of University Women, all of which honored her by awards. Washington University conferred the honorary LL.D. degree upon her in 1946, and she received the honorary degree of Humane Letters from Lindenwood College in 1956.

Mrs. Gellhorn was the mother of Walter Gellhorn, professor of law, Columbia University; Alfred Gellhorn, dean of the University of Pennsylvania Medical School; and a daughter, Martha Gellhorn, noted novelist and war correspondent. She died in St. Louis on September 24, 1970, three months before her ninety-second birthday.

CLARA MAE LEWIS STOVER
Born 1882

One of Missouri's most prominent and successful business women, Clara Mae Lewis Stover was born on a farm near Oxford, Iowa in 1882, the daughter of Lorinzo and Mary Ann (Jenkins) Lewis. She and her three sisters moved with their parents to Iowa City to complete preparatory studies and she was graduated from Iowa City Academy. She became a speech major at Iowa State University.

For three years, Clara Mae was a school teacher, teaching all eight grades in a one room school and driving a horse and buggy six miles each day. After marrying Russell Stover, they moved to Western Canada and rented a farm which failed financially. They moved to Winnipeg where she took a job in a dress factory. After four weeks of factory work, Clara Mae began selling magazines door to door and then began working in a drug store where she sold cigars, cigarettes and candy.

Russell was able to find a job with a confectionery firm, selling candy on the road. While working for this company, he learned a few good commercial confectionery recipes. They be-

gan experimenting in their own kitchen to make a better candy that would meet their high standards of excellence. From their home, they began to sell their product to neighborhood drug stores. Russell began to take their own candy with him on the road and soon was able to sell in one week all that they could make in their kitchen in three weeks. With the onset of World War I, came the shortage of sugar. Their venture was defeated and they returned to the United States.

Their next success was a new product, the Eskimo Pie, but because of so many imitators, it reaped little financial gain. Convinced of the superior quality of the candy they could produce and undaunted by their defeats, the Stovers began again. In 1922, Mrs. Stover's Bungalow Candies opened two stores in Kansas City, Missouri. In 1929, they expanded a factory and opened seven stores in Chicago. Again they met with discouragement, the depression closed the Chicago units. Able to continue the Kansas City stores until business began to prosper, they were on their road to success. In 1943 the name was changed to Russell Stover Candies and stores were opened in many areas of the United States. Russell died in 1954 and Clara Mae then headed the company.

The Stovers had a daughter, Mrs. Gloria Stover Fitz Townsend.

Clara Mae was a strong advocate of good health and walking and swimming. At 86 years of age, she said "I swim thirty times back and forth across my pool every morning at seven o'clock." Mrs. Russell Stover died June 9, 1975 leaving a tale of success in the American tradition.

EVELYN WEEKS DUNCAN
Kansas City   Born 1906

Born in Kansas City, Missouri on May 5, 1906, Evelyn Weeks Duncan was the daughter of C. B. and Maude Z. (Pearce) Weeks. After attending Kansas City Junior College, she was graduated from the former Kansas City Teachers College with a degree in education. In 1929 she was married to Herbert Ewing Duncan, a successful minister and architect. At that time, married women were not permitted to teach in the schools of Kansas City and Evelyn devoted

herself to volunteer services in her church and community.

As her children were growing up, Mrs. Duncan was active in Girl Scout work. While serving as Vice-President of the Girl Scout Area Council, she developed the God and Community Award for girl scouts. She felt such an award was needed because she was firmly convinced that once a young girl read the Bible daily and meditated, and once she had learned about the history of her religion and had given a year of service to her church, she would not stray far from the church as she grew into womanhood. The award has been adopted as a part of the program in most states and in several foreign countries.

After her three children were reared and at fifty-five years of age. Evelyn went back to college. Taking courses at the University of Kansas and at the University in Kansas City, she was graduated (again) with a degree in English language and literature and had earned a life certificate to teach English in Missouri schools. When the need for teachers grew acute, although she was busy in community and philanthropic activities, Evelyn became a reserve teacher at Barstow School for girls and Pembroke Country Day School for boys. During this time she also acted as a private tutor for students who needed extra help.

Feeling that some outside interests made a woman a better wife and mother ("but she shouldn't overdo it"), Evelyn served as president of many groups, including two terms as President of the Kansas City Council of Church Women and the United Church Women of Missouri. She is a charter member of an interdenominational prayer group devoted to the study of and prayers for the United Nations and world peace.

The Duncans were parents of three children: Herbert E. Duncan, Jr.; a member of the national board of the American Institute of Architects; Burris R. (Duke) Duncan, M.D., currently devoting two years as Director of Medical Services and the setting up of a pediatric residency program for Project Hope in Natal, Brazil; Carol Virginia Duncan Brient, a silversmith and wife of a medical doctor in Gainesville, Florida.

In demand as a book reviewer, active in many organizations, doing volunteer hospital work, Evelyn also organized a rapidly growing Young Mothers Council Service of the American Mothers Committee of New York in Kansas City and currently serves as its leader.

ORO Y PLATA

Montana

Montana

Nickname: Treasure State

State Flower: Bitterroot

State Tree: Ponderosa Pine

State Bird: Western Meadowlark

Photos

1. Pompey's Pillar
2. Montana State Capital building
3. Bannock, Montana's first Capital 1890
4. Clark Mansion in Butte
5. E.S. Paxson painting in Montana State Capital
6. Buffalo grazing in Flathead Valley

Committee Members

Chairman—Mrs. Lucille Middleton, Butte
Hulda M. Fields
Jack R. Olson—artist
Frank W. Wiley
Mrs. Chet (Tippy) Huntley
Katherine Lenington, Fort Benton
Seralda Nathe, Redstone
Mrs. J.S. McDede, Fort Benton
Betty Raymond, Butte
Mrs. Edwin G. Koch, Butte
Mrs. John Cromer, Butte
Mrs. George O'Connor, Butte
Mrs. Sam Chase, Butte
Mrs. Ned Staples, Butte
Mrs. Urban Roth, Butte

Honorary Committee

Governor Thomas L. Judge, Helena
Vivian Paladin, Helena
Harriet Meloy, Helena
Hal Stearns, Helena
John Willard, Billings
Clarence Kommers, Butte
E.E. (Boo) MacGilvra, Butte
Virginia Johnson, Missoula
Dorothy Johnson, Missoula
Belle Winestine, Helena
Elizabeth Lochrie, Ventura, Calif.

LEWIS AND CLARK AT THREE-FORKS

Montana

SACAJAWEA

Born 1787

Native American Sacajawea was only a girl of 17 when Capt. Meriweather Lewis and William Clark spent the winter in Fort Mandan of the Missouri River.

The men spent the entire time questioning about the route their expedition would launch upon in the spring.

They hired Touissant Charbonneau, a French-Canadian trapper, trader and interpreter for his knowledge, but maybe even more, for that of his wife, a Shoshone, who had been born on the Lemhi River in Idaho.

It was after she had been captured near Three Forks in Montana during a buffalo hunt and returned to the Mandan's village near Bismark, that she was acquired as a wife and slave by Charbonneau.

The expedition, Lewis and Clark, 28 other men, Charbonneau, Sacajawea and their two-month-old son, Jean Baptiste Charbonneau, later called Pomp, on the young Indian girl's back, left Fort Mandan April 7, 1805 and headed west on the Missouri River.

The little mother made herself invaluable to the expedition.

She taught the travelers which plants were edible. She taught and helped the men tan hides and make clothing, mitts and moccasins.

She gathered roots and barks that had medicinal qualities and demonstrated their use.

Probably the earliest incident of Women's Suffrage west of the Mississippi was when the party camped nine days at the mouth of the Marias River trying to determine which stream to follow. Sacajawea was allowed to vote when the decision was made.

Months later when they came upon the Three Forks of the Missouri, she recognized this to be the spot at which she had been captured a few years previously.

The party ascended the Jefferson River, passed up the Big Hole which they named the Wisdom River and chose the Beaverhead to follow.

Upon sighting the Beaverhead Rock, Sacajawea told Lewis and Clark, "Now I know we are on the road to the land of my people. We will find them at the head-waters of this stream or just over the divide where waters flow to the setting sun."

When the expedition reached the Shoshones, they secured horses from the Indians.

Until the expedition met the Shoshones, after 1400 miles and more than four and a half months, they hadn't seen an Indian but many had seen them. They had been safe along the route because the Indians had seen Sacajawea with her baby and their reasoning was it was a peaceful group: No war party has squaw and baby along.

Sacajawea had gone 4800 miles to the Pacific and back to Mandan, carrying a papoose.

She had made a contribution to her time that will live in history.

TISH NEVINS

Among the unsung heroines in the settling of the West is Tish Nevins, a mulatto and daughter of slavery who migrated from Missouri to Hamilton, Montana in 1899.

Aunt Tish—as she is fondly referred to by the oldtimers who knew her—became a legend in her time. Although Tish could neither read nor write, countless youngsters finished school under her care. Serving meals out of a former brothel in Hamilton, Tish became a cook of international reputation.

The saga of Aunt Tish began in Missouri in 1890 when Pete Smithey was five years old. Smithey's mother died after the birth of her tenth child and Tish, a 28-year-old housekeeper, took the five youngest children under her wing.

"She was the only mother we knew. When mother died, baby Mattie was 10 days old, Nell was three, Herb seven and Tom eight," Smithey said. Mattie died as a young woman, Tom died last spring at age 92. The "rest of the clique," as Pete calls it, is thriving into their 80's and

90's—which some say is a reflection of the loving care of Aunt Tish.

When Robert Smithey moved his family to Montana, Aunt Tish naturally went along. While raising her brood, Tish had a reputation as a fine cook but it wasn't until Mattie (whom she always referred to as "my baby") married in 1908 that Tish expanded her business.

Glenn Chaffin, widely-known writer and personal friend of Tish's, said Tish rented a large frame house in Hamilton which was originally a brothel and converted it into a dining room and boarding house. Chaffin said Tish had a great sense of humor and "the house" was the subject of some of her best stories.

"But Tish personally was a moral purist. She would have nothing to do with the only other Negro in Hamilton, a madam by the name of Mammy Smith," Chaffin said.

As a young scientist at the Rocky Mountain Lab in Hamilton, Bill Jellison boarded with Tish one summer.

"Tish had friends all over the world. When a friend died, she would mourn for days. Her boarders were like family to her. She would lecture us, give us advice," Jellison said.

Later, Jellison and his bride Gretchen lived with Tish for a short while. Tish could neither read nor write, but Gretchen said she had a profound respect for learning and requested that the young college graduate read Shakespeare to her.

"At that time she was cooking two meals a day for the public. A meal never included less than three kinds of meat, several vegetables, white and sweet potatoes, salads and desserts. She worked hard all day and when I'd read her Shakespeare after dinner she'd invariably fall asleep. But she insisted I read it," Gretchen said.

In her zeal for educational enlightenment, Tish supported the Chatauqua tours that brought cultural programs to small towns. She would buy tickets for the whole Smithey family and spend the whole week at the big tents.

During one tour William Jennings Bryan came to Hamilton and delivered his famous "Cross of Gold" speech in favor of sterling silver instead of gold for monetary use. He ate at Tish's table and later sent her a note saying it was one of the delights of his life. Chaffin said Tish kept the note pinned to the dining room wall.

Although statesmen and politician often ate at her table, Jellison said the talk never reverted to politics. Her table was a scene of merriment with talk of families and joys.

"Tish cared. She was interested in us, not in the problems of the world," Jellison said.

OLIVE PICKERING RANKIN

Born 1854

Born in Newington, New Hampshire, member of a family which in 1692 came to that state bearing a grant-in-land from the King of England, marked only in latitudes, and stated "as far West as you can go", Olive Pickering arrived by stage coach in Montana Territory in the 1870's, one of Missoula's earliest teachers, holding classes in a one room school, with Indians staring through the windows, astounded that a *woman* could teach *men!* (Some eighth grade pupils were bigger than she!)

Marrying John Rankin, a Scotch-Canadian lumberman and sawmill owner, she bore seven children, four at their Grant Creek Ranch, three in Missoula. Mr. Rankin died of tick (Rocky Mountain Spotted) fever, and one child died at age eight.

Resourceful and courageous she managed family and home efficiently, augmented by "paying guests" (children of ranch families who sent them into town to school) which often doubled her household during winter months. One of these "guests" recalls that Mrs. Rankin spoke with quiet, sometimes firm, but always gentle voice; dressed in white; rarely "went downtown", and, the only woman, served for many years on the Missoula School Board.

Her six children graduated from the University of Montana, which their father had helped found.

Daughters Harriet (Sedman), Mary (Bragg) and Edna (McKinnon) continued their education at Wellesley College; Grace (Kinney) at New England Conservatory of Music, and Jeannette at New York School of Philosophy. The only son, Wellington D., earned graduate and law degrees at Harvard and studied at Oxford. An attorney in Helena, he operated extensive land holdings, and was active in state and national politics.

Jeannette, the nations' first woman elected to Congress, (1916 and again in 1940) always an ardent pacifist and the only member of that body to vote against American involvement in the two World Wars, was a leader in pushing through the 19th Amendment to the Constitution, giving women the right to vote. In 1968 she lead the Jeannette Rankin Brigade's March on Washington to protest American involvement in the Vietnam War. Alert and involved at 92, one of her last public appearances in Montana was during the 1972 Constitutional Convention, declaring the present system of electing the chief executive ineffective and giving her ideas for a direct presidential preference election.

Edna McKinnon is a pioneer in the *Planned Parenthood Movement*, speaking and travelling throughout the world.

Harriet Sedman served as Dean of Women at the University of Montana.

Olive Rankin's nine grandchildren and fourteen great-grandchildren include professors, engineers, authors, teachers, lawyers, career foreign service officers, doctors, social workers, librarians, army captains, college trustees, and a Rhodes scholar!

Their heritage of a sense of responsibility in public service, scholarship and citizenship as set by their pioneer matriarch during an age which provided few privileges to women comes full circle in a century, into this era of Women's Lib, Anti-War and Ecology, as her values, activated by her progeny prove as relevant today as was her vision and faith in the 1870's.

NANNIE T. ALDERSON

Born 1860

Born in West Virginia in 1860, Nannie Tiffany Alderson grew up a Southern Belle, surrounded by silver, mahogony, dresses with fancy petticoats, servants, and leisure. She met Walter Alderson when he returned unexpectedly from Texas. The one thing that Walter said that Nannie always remembered throughout their life together was that he had never known pleasure in his home until she was in it. This strong feeling for home was the core of their marriage.

Nannie's relatives thought a Montana cattle ranch offered a fine opportunity, but they were concerned because of Walter's wild reputation. Nannie said, "It is not what a man has done before marriage that counts; it is what he does after."

Nannie arrived in Montana with unfrilled petticoats, practical dresses, and her Grandmother's silver candlesticks. She had one housekeeping accomplishment—how to make hot rolls. Her temporary log home had a door and window with a dirt roof and floor. A gray army blanket divided the bedroom and the kitchen. When Nannie sat down for dinner that first night, she ached for the Southern comforts. The cowboys, coatless, grizzled men in grimy-looking flannel shirts, cooked supper and it was the best she ever ate. Most of what Nannie learned those first years she learned from these men.

In looking back Nannie wondered if too much wasn't said about the grim aspects of frontier life. In 1883 the country was raw and challenging but the settlers were young and enthusiastic. They didn't mind the hard things because they didn't expect them to last. Montana was booming and a feverish optimism possessed them all.

Nannie thrilled to the new country and way of life. She had so many things to learn that she didn't languish on hardships and discomforts. She made pants for her husband and "foxed" them. Foxing was re-inforcing trousers by sewing a heart-shaped piece of buckskin to the seat and extending it down the inside seams of the leg. And always Nannie extended the hand of western hospitality to travelers, cowboys, drifters, Indians, and friends. No one was turned away from plain board and a clean bunk.

Nannie arrived in Montana six years after the Custer Massacre. Although the Indian wars were past, Nannie never felt completely at ease.

The Indians killed a young cattleman because he had unintentionally seen them butcher a range steer. Nannie worried about Walter being killed and scalped. Indians looted and burned her first four room home while she was in Miles City having her first baby. Nothing was saved—not even her Grandma's silver candlesticks.

Later an Indian uprising threatened because an Indian sicced his dogs on a cowboy and the cowboy shot and hit the Indian's arm. Suddenly the bluff across the river from their new lodgings thickened with black silhouettes of mounted Indians. All night fires burned and Indians chanted but when daylight came, they rode away.

In the fall of 1893 Nannie and Walter with their children, Mabel, Fay, Patty, and Walter, quit ranching and moved to Miles City where Mr. Alderson became deputy assessor. Times had been tough with low cattle prices and bank failures but finally their luck was turning. At last Nannie was free from the fear of Indians killing her husband. It was dreadful irony that Mr. Alderson died in Miles City, March, 1895 from the kicks of a stallion.

Nannie supported her children by running a boarding house, selling bread, catering, and operating a small store. Friends said she led a hard life, but Nannie said, "Perhaps—but I don't think an easy one is ever half so full."

MARY REA VALITON
Portrait of a Pioneer Mother   Born 1863

Mary Rea Valiton was a year old when her mother put her in the oven of a covered wagon stove to protect her against the fury of an Indian attack on the Bozeman Trail. Mary, a large lady, would jokingly tell years later, "It would take a big stove to hold me now."

Mary Rea was born in Portsville, New York in 1863. Her adventurous father, George, and family joined a wagon train headed West in 1864. When he died in 1902, a eulogy written in the Chicago Daily Tribune said, "George Rea was to Idaho and Montana what Daniel Boone was to Kentucky."

The Reas arrived at Virginia City, Montana in 1865; then to the Bozeman country; the Cedar Creek Mines; and on to Missoula, where Mary Rea attended the first school there.

In Butte, Mary met and married Henry Valiton. Her husband—a Democrat—was elected the second and tenth Mayor of Butte; and thus began her lifelong interest in politics.

But her loyalty was first to family—and then to a political party. Her son-in-law, Ernest T. Eaton of Billings was elected Montana's Lieutenant Governor—her son, Fred, Sheriff of Powell County at Deer Lodge—her grandson, Don, a State Senator. All were Republicans. All were inspired and helped by Mary Valiton. She worked hard for women's "right to vote"; and was the first woman to register to vote in her county.

Adversity was no stranger to this pioneer woman. She lost two children in their infant years. When her husband was invalided at their Deer Lodge home, Mary Valiton didn't hesitate. She "took in boarders". Many of these became prominent Montanans; and affectionately called her "Mother V". Somehow she managed a higher education for her son, Fred, and her daughter, Augusta. The 1918 flu epidemic took her daughter-in-law; and she "mothered" her four year old grandson to adulthood.

The Great Depression brought problems of "meeting the grocery bills". Mary sold some of her cherished jewelry for "old gold" values to help make ends meet. She'd send her small grandson to the creamery "to buy 10¢ worth of cream", because the 15¢ bottle was nearly full by the time the clerk would shut off the faucet. Another young cousin came to live with "Mother V", when he had no place to go.

Plagued with crippling rheumatism, it was difficult to remember that she had been a skilled horsewoman and a crack shot with a rifle.

Whenever possible, she went to her beloved Society of Montana Pioneers' conventions. Her proudest moment was when her fellow Pioneers elected her as the first woman president of that body.

As matron of the boys' dormitory at the old College of Montana in Deer Lodge; and as the first matron of the boys' dorm at the new Billings Polytechnic Institute—now Rocky Mountain College—she "mothered a lot of Montanans".

As church treasurer for thirty years, she would sit up late at night, counting the funds—with an old fashioned revolver at her side—just in case.

When "Mother V" passed away in 1946, many Montanans felt they had lost a Mother.

EDNA FAY KAISER

Born 1872

It astounded her friends but even more so Edna Fay Kaiser, when on Aug. 21, 1957, she was named on the charter of The Cowboy Hall of Fame.

The honor befitted the Illinois woman who, at 17, had come by train to Montana in 1889.

She was among those "who had made outstanding contributions to the development of the West." The founding group recognized the side-saddle riding Mrs. Kaiser as a devoted wife and a provident mother who had made high contribution to her community and nation through fine mothering.

The Hinckley, Illinois-born woman became Montana Park County's first school teacher.

She continued to teach the children of the

Potter and Blair families, who had accompanied her to the Treasure State, until she married in 1895.

The attractive "school marm" had caught the heart of William J. Kaiser, a young Meyersburg homesteader near Flathead Lake. He was a good musician, had played on the Helena baseball team and was a "nifty dresser and a graceful dancer."

The couple nestled down in the top end of the county in a spot, later called Potter Basin. They proved up on the homestead and lived 19 years before moving to Livingston and later Helena and Bozeman. The Kaisers reared 9 children. Another child died when 2.

Early day Montana tested a mother's self reliance, courage and patience.

Even horses and wagons mired down in impassable gumbo. insects battled for the family's table. medical crises were met by mother and God.

The daughter of a Dutch, New York mother, Mary Lanagan, and Ireland-born father, William Fay, Mother Kaiser, no doubt, inherited her strength of character and strong purpose.

Edna's father had walked two years, nine months and five days with the 105th Illinois Infantry during the Civil War.

Members of Mrs. Kaiser's flock volunteered for two world wars.

Two governors commended her for her sacrifice and the patriotism with which she instilled her brood.

During her late years in Bozeman, Mrs. Kaiser enjoyed retelling two stories.

Sitting Bull, the Sioux Indian leader who united the tribes that defeated Gen. Custer at the Battle of the Little Big Horn in 1776, had boarded her railway coach while her train was enroute to Montana.

She recalled her fright at the sight of the Indian but hastened to assure, Sitting Bull, did nothing to prompt her fear.

Sitting Bull's death is recorded Dec. 15, 1890, less than two years after the incident.

Mrs. Kaiser felt she was one of the first white women to take a camping trip with horses and wagons through Yellowstone Park.

The journey, in either 1890 or 91, was made with a number of people from Potter Basin. The party was in awe of the park's geyser. A highlight, she said, was "a colored cook who prepared such interesting and tasty meals."

Mrs. Kaiser died Jan. 12, 1962, 19 days short of a full 90-year life.

ELLA WHEELER TURPIN

Born 1876

Ellen Wheeler was born February 19, 1876, in Farmington, Minn., to Abbie and Edrick E. Wheeler. When she was about eight years old the family moved from Minnesota to Boudle, S. Dak., where they homesteaded on the South Dakota prairie. Ellen attended country schools and at the age of sixteen became a school teacher herself. It was the start of a life-long love affair and the ruling interest of her life has always been education.

She moved with her family to Kent, Minn., about 1895 where she continued teaching until she met and married Edward Turpin on February 10, 1897. She bore two sons and a daughter.

In 1910 the family moved to Malta, Montana and homesteaded 320 acres south of that pioneer railroad community.

After several years of disappointing crops and the advent of World War I, she returned to teaching at the gold mining camp of Ruby Gulch, near Zortman. Her oldest son, Nemyl, enlisted in the 15th Cavalry and went overseas in a few months, where he lost his life in July 1918. She is reputed to be the nation's oldest living Gold Star Mother, by the Veteran's of Foreign Wars. About this time she altered the spelling of her first name to "Ella" and henceforth has used that modification in her name.

After the war, she continued teaching and studying by correspondence and summer ses-

sions at the Normal School of Dillong and in 1925 received her diploma, Magna cum laude, with a life teaching certificate.

In 1928 she was elected Phillips County Superintendent of Schools, a position she held until the landslide of 1932 swept her out of office. Back to teaching again until retirement in 1939, to be better able to take care of her ailing husband. After his death in 1953 she returned to the familiar classroom and continued until past 80, when she decided to retire permanently. She assisted in organizing the Retired Teachers Association in the Kalispell area.

At age 88 she became interested in oil painting and in the next few years painted dozens of landscapes, mostly mountainous, to give to her friends and relatives. Her depth perception seemed uncanny and she took great pleasure in creating her scenes, until she could no longer see well enough.

She was always active in community affairs; an early and continuous member of the Federated Women's Clubs, American Legion Auxiliary, Order of Eastern Star and the Episcopal Church, she was always in the forefront of any activity. After her final retirement she became interested in studying her family tree and with the help of cousins succeeded in compiling a geneology of the Wheeler Family, tracing it back to Edward Fuller, a passenger on the voyage of the Mayflower in 1620. She is a member of the Montana Society of Mayflower Descendents and presented a copy of the Wheeler geneology with hundreds of entries, to the Montana Historical Society.

Her son, Leland Max Turpin, lives near Portland, Ore. and her daughter, Ruth Frisbee, lives in Cut Bank. She has been a resident of Immanuel Lutheran Home, Kalispell, for five years; she is nearly blind but keeps up with world affairs and remains keenly interested in her family. She has 5 living grand-children and 15 great grand-children and 1 great-great grand-child. Her son, L. M. Turpin, and his wife Estelle, make their home in Portland, Oregon, and daughter Ruth lives in Cut Bank.

IDA W. MYERS FEARNALL

Born 1877

My mother, Ida W. Fearnall, was born in 1877 in Mexico, New York, of Pennsylvania Dutch ancestry. Her maiden name was Myers. She grew up on a farm in northern New York, and in an environment which well prepared her for the rugged conditions of eastern Montana at the turn of the century.

As a teacher college graduate and at the age of twenty she accepted a teaching position with the school system of Miles City, Montana, in Custer County.

After teaching one year she married my father, Charles A. Wiley. He died, before I was two years old, in Colorado Springs, Colorado. Mother returned to Miles City, where she again taught school. In 1902 she was elected County Superintendent of Schools, a position she held for four years.

Miles City was a town of about 3,000 population, the county seat of Custer County, serving a trade area with a radius of over 100 miles in all directions. Some of the schools were over 100 miles away. All travel except by the railroad through Miles City was by ox team or by horses.

Mother visited the schools in the county, traveling by horse and buggy or by saddle horse. Stops were made at ranches, or at Road Ranches where board and lodging were available. The Road Ranches were designated postoffices served by horse-drawn mail stages, traveling on a biweekly schedule.

Most ranches carried a year's supply of food. Travelers stopped at any ranch when night overtook them; they were welcome guests of the lonely ranch people. If no one was home they stayed all night, washed up the dishes and filled the woodbox before they departed.

Mother took me along on many of her trips and at the age of four I had many adventures. She rescued me from a rough but playful antelope at one Road Ranch. This wild "goat" had been spoiled by the cowboys and butted me down every time I turned my back.

I remember an incident which happened many miles from the nearest ranch and on a hot day in a dry, arid country. One of the horses of the spirited team, fighting the swarm of noseflies, rubbed the bridle off on the neck yoke. Mother got out of the buggy, and when she tried to put the bridle on the horse he would rear up and strike at her with his front feet. After several hours two cowboys came along and they had to throw the horse to get the bridle on him! Seems the horse had never been bridled outside a barn.

Mother later became the principal of a grade school in Miles City. She was associated with

teaching for some 25 years, and contributed much to the economy and culture of the community. She was a Past Worthy Matron of Eastern Star, a member of the Methodist Church and a member of P.E.O., a women's fraternal organization. She was active in many social and civic affairs of our small Montana town, the economy of which was directly related to horses, cattle and sheep.

The State Industrial School for girls was located in Miles City. Mother took many of these underprivileged girls into her home, gave them wise counsel and employment. She had the satisfaction of seeing them become successful members of the communities in which they lived.

As a teenager I saw my first airplane, flown by Katherine Stinson at the State Fair in Helena, Montana. I confided in my mother my ambition to fly. She did not discourage me. In later life, with teenagers of my own, I realized the courage and foresight she must have had in giving me her moral support. The proudest day of my life was when I took her for her first airplane ride in a wood-and-fabric airplane of World War I vintage.

In the late twenties Mother moved to California with my stepfather who became a bridge engineer for the state. They lived in bridge camps along the Eel River in the Redwoods. Mother did much to help the Indian people in that area. After my stepfather's death in Carmel, she moved to southern California.

In later life and until her death in 1947 she was associated with a small hospital at the retirement home for P.E.O. women in Alhambra. Mother had charge of this hospital for eight years. She cared for and gave comfort to many of the elderly people there. She was loved by all and is remembered by a plaque on a small, round cherrywood table made by her father, a family heirloom, and given to this retirement home for P.E.O. women.

In her time, the family was the most important segment of our society. Mothers have shared equally with our fathers in the problems and trials which stimulated the efforts that have made this country great for 200 years.

MARY ROGERS DAVEY

Born 1877

MARY ROGERS DAVEY, Mrs. Frank S., of Deer Lodge, Montana, was my beloved mother, and the bravest, most versatile and most loving woman I have ever known.

Our 33 year old father was killed by a drunken man in 1903, leaving my mother a widow at age 26, with a family of four young children, a partly-paid-for home and little else. Mother was an accomplished musician and needle-woman but had no formal training and after a year of desperate struggle, found that she couldn't earn enough with her piano and needle to take care of us, so friends came to the rescue.

Senator W. A. Clark and others persuaded Dan Hennessey (of Butte's largest department store) to open an Art Department, making Mother the organizer and teacher, which proved so popular that the Butte School District persuaded her to establish similar classes, as well as cooking, in both the junior and senior high schools.

When the United States entered the first World War in 1913, my three teenage brothers enlisted. I was sent to Pratt Institute in New York for art training, and Mother also enlisted and was sent as Head Dietitian to Camp Lewis in Tacoma, Washington.

When the war ended in 1918, Mother was sent by the Y.M.C.A. to Honolulu, Hawaii to manage their large restaurant there; later, she also managed a similar one for the Y.W.C.A. and opened a small tea-room of her own, up town, then a second one at Waikiki beach, near Pearl Harbor. These were called, "Mrs. Davey's Kitchens," and were very successful. She was buying equipment to start a third Kitchen in San Francisco when she was stricken with pneumonia and died in 1926, leaving her children a sizable estate.

Mother always was active in community affairs, in the Episcopal church, in various Masonic orders, in all schools, and attended the University of Hawaii, getting her Master's degree in French, English and Dietetics, and later teaching these subjects at the University.

Mother visited us several times during these last twelve years, bringing each of us beautiful gifts, loving each and encouraging us in the ways of life we chose to follow.

Montana still refers to "Mar D.", as she was known, for her wisdom in advice pertaining to the schools and churches. Her family realize that Mother avoided re-marrying in order to spend more time with them, and we humbly attribute any successes we have gained to her constant love and encouragement.

ANNA BOE DAHL

Born 1892

Born August 13, 1892, just before the turn of the century, at Spooner, Wisconsin, Anna (Boe) Dahl was the daughter of Norwegian immigrant parents. She grew up on a farm in the sparce wooded country of northern Wisconsin, attended elementary school there and walked ten miles a day to attend high school.

In 1917 she came to Dagmar, Montana, where her brother and family lived on a homestead. Following a summer of teacher training at Malta, Montana, she spent two years teaching the neighborhood rural school at Dagmar.

Anna Boe and Andrew Dahl were married at Plentywood on September 17, 1919. They returned to his homestead where they farmed 640 acres of land, raised a family of four daughters and a son and lived together there for fifty years.

Lifelong members of the Immanuel Lutheran Congregation, the family attended church services regularly and the children attended and their mother taught Sunday School.

An avid reader herself, Mrs. Dahl encouraged her family to read good books and carefully screened the reading material the children were allowed to read. The battery radio was selectively tuned in for family entertainment so as to "save" the batteries for as much listening as possible. The children were taught to appreciate the beauty of the local bird-life, the trees planted on the farmsteads, and the occasional wild flowers that grew on the prairies during the drought stricken years.

The children of the family attended the same rural grade school that their mother had taught and all graduated from Plentywood High School.

High school attendance was accomplished at considerable sacrifice for the entire family. However, with much time and effort by their mother spent at the faithful Singer treadle sewing machine, attractive clothes were made for the four daughters who were all in high school at about the same time. Home-made baked things, meat, eggs, butter, milk, and garden vegetables all helped to provide food for the family at home and in the light housekeeping rooms during high school days.

The mother taught W.P.A. classes in Economics to help augment the family income during the high school years.

To provide electricity for farm families became increasingly urgent in the later 1930's and Mrs. Dahl was instrumental in organizing the rural electrification program in northeastern Montana. She was secretary of the board of directors at the time of incorporation and during the time the rural electrification dream came true. She served on the board of directors in various capacities until 1967 when she retired from the board.

Positions held by Mrs. Dahl during the years she was involved in rural energy programs included directorships on Northwest Public Power Association, Vancouver, Washington, Wisconsin Electric Cooperative, and Montana Associated Utilities.

She was the recipient of the Distinguished Service Award, Northwest Public Power Association in 1962 and the ACE (Ally of Cooperative Electrification) Award of the Wisconsin Electric Cooperative in 1967. She is listed in WHO'S WHO OF AMERICAN WOMEN, Fifth Edition, 1968-69.

Mrs. Dahl served as chairman of the Grenora, North Dakota, Cooperative Credit Union, is a member of the American Lutheran Church, the ALC Church Women, the Montana Farmers Union and the Democratic Party.

BLANCHE TATHAM HUNTLEY
A Spirited Montanan   **Born 1893**

The first time Blanche Tatham saw the Rocky Mountain West, she was seven years old, the year was 1900, and her father was taking the family from their home in Walkendaw, Missouri, to Colorado.

Now the year is 1975, and in 82 rich years, this spirited lady of the West enjoyed a long and rewarding marriage with Percy Adams ("Pat" or "Perce") Huntley, bore him four active children—Chet, Wadine, Marian, and Peggy—and contributed 72 of those marvelous years to the life and land of Montana.

"My father," recalls "Mom" Huntley from her living room at St. John's Lutheran Home in Billings, Montana, "was always interested in being someplace new. We left Colorado in a covered wagon, with 17 horses, mother, my little sister, my father and I. We even camped at Pike's Peak.

"After a year and a half we returned to Missouri, but then an uncle came to visit and talked about this wonderful place, Montana. Well, my dad had a notion to homestead in Montana, and off we went.

"Perce and I were married when I was 18; he was a telegrapher for the railroad, the Great Northern, and worked in towns all over the state. Then my dad found a good place to homestead outside of Saco, and together the two families farmed that land."

Mrs. Huntley, whose husband died in 1968, recalls the sense of neighborliness in Montana: "Oh yes, we visited and would have all sorts of dances from daylight 'til dark; and of course on Sunday, the minister would come, and everyone would go someplace in the afternoon, or have company.

It was also a hard life, but as her son, Chet Huntley, wrote in his autobiography of a young boy growing up in Montana, *The Generous Years*, life was full and it was generous.

The Huntley children grew up in an environment of appreciation of the land, of each other, of their friends and family . . . and of "schooling," a direct result of their mother's having been a school teacher prior to her marriage.

"School, through the eighth grade, was very important," said Mrs. Huntley, "but it was the four children themselves, really, who appreciated the idea of college. They were bound to get an education. And, they all did."

It's a fair assumption that the influence of Mom Huntley contributed greatly to her children's interest in education, however. There was a one-room school house even built on the homestead, where the Huntley children joined others from nearby ranches for their early reading and writing lessons.

The ranch life was beset by more catastrophes than one could imagine, in such a short time, however—hailstorms, fire, drought, locusts. All these, and the decision was made by Perce Huntley to return to railroading. The family lived for a time in Saco, and then had their first introduction to "real" mountains when they moved to Willow Creek in 1920.

For the next years, there were delightful times in towns everywhere in Montana: Logan, Big Timer, Norris, Whitehall, to name just a few. "Oh yes, we were just a roaming family," Mrs. Huntley remembers with delight. "It's a big state, and we saw all of it."

In 1938, the Huntleys arrived at Reedpoint, Montana, "and this was really our home then," said Mom Huntley. There, Mr. Huntley was agent with the Northern Pacific Railroad, and in 1964 he and Blanche moved to Billings. The highlight for the whole family was the celebration of Mr. and Mrs. Huntley's 50th wedding anniversary in 1960. Three hundred friends, old and young, from throughout the state, came to join the occasion, which was held in the Reedpoint High School Gymnasium. The honored couple also had the joy that day of meeting their first great grandchild, five weeks old. (There are now 21 children, grandchildren and great grandchildren.)

Mom Huntley smiles again, giving her marvelous warm laugh, and repeats, "I really don't know how we did it all . . . it almost sounds impossible now . . . but it's been a great life in Montana."

Nebraska

NEBRASKA

Mothers

GREAT SEAL OF THE STATE OF NEBRASKA
EQUALITY BEFORE THE LAW
MARCH 1ST 1867

Nebraska

Nickname: Cornhusker

State Flower: Goldenrod

State Tree: American Elm

State Bird: Western Meadowlark

Photos

1. Arbor Lodge, Nebraska City
2. Chimney Rock, Bayerd
3. State Capital Building, Lincoln
4. First Homestead in U.S.
5. Joslyn Art Museum, Omaha
6. Fairview, Lincoln

DANIEL FREEMAN'S HOME

Committee Members

Chairman—Mrs. Harold P. Stebbins, Lincoln
Dr. Anne Campbell, Lincoln
Mrs. Ed Cobb, Ogallala
Mrs. Richard Peck, Omaha
Mrs. Robert G. Simmons, Jr. Scottsbluff
Mrs. Ralph W. Hill, Lincoln
Mrs. Frederick E. Blumer, Lincoln
Mrs. C.R. Reinert, Lincoln
Mrs. William H. Hasbroock, Lincoln
Mrs. L.A. Enersen, Lincoln
Mrs. J. James Exon, Lincoln
Mrs. Nellie Snyder Yost, North Platte

Nebraska

MARY GALE LA FLESCHE

Born 1826

Mary Gale La Flesche was one of the first Omaha Indian women to try to bridge the gap between the culture of the Indians and that of the white man. She was born in 1826, the daughter of Nicomi, an Iowa-Omaha Indian girl married to Dr. John Gale, an army surgeon. When Dr. Gale's troop had to move, in 1827, Nicomi refused to go with him, not wanting the life of "a white woman." Before Dr. Gale died, shortly thereafter, he asked Indian trader Peter Sarpy to look after Nicomi and the little girl. Four years later—a time lapse decreed by Indian custom—Sarpy married the widow and provided for Mary's education in St. Louis.

When Mary returned to Nebraska, she met and married Sarpy's right-hand man, Joseph La Flesche, an energetic young man of integrity and good judgment. Succeeding his adoptive father, Joseph (known as "Iron-Eye") became the last tribal chief of the Omaha Indians. As a girl,

Mary and her mother had become involved with the activities of the trading post, where they had, in effect, interpreted the Indian point of view to the whites. As a wife, she was influential in her husband's efforts to teach his people the white man's skills in farming and in building houses and roads.

Mary La Flesche became the mother of four daughters, each remarkable for the distinction—unusual for those times—of having not only a career but a family as well. The oldest girl, Susette (known as "Bright Eyes") attended a girls' school in Elizabeth, New Jersey, taught school on the Omaha reservation, and traveled widely in America and Europe as a potent spokeswoman on the condition of the American Indians.

The second daughter, Rosalie, married to a local farmer, made their home a focal point for assistance and sympathy. She managed many of the Indians' financial affairs and served as a distributor and accountant of the funds sent by Eastern groups wanting to "help the poor Indians." Although she was the mother of nine children, she always found time to assist whoever came to her.

Marguerite, the third daughter, and Susan, the youngest, attended Susette's school in Elizabeth. On returning to the reservation in 1882, Marguerite taught school for a time. Then both girls went for further education to Hampton Institute. Marguerite returned and married but continued to teach.

Susan, however, went on to attend the Women's Medical College in Philadelphia. Being graduated at the head of her class in 1889, she was the first American Indian woman to become a Doctor of Medicine. Back on the reservation, Susan served as not only a doctor but also as nurse, interpreter, teacher, and social worker, always indefatigable and willing to help as she could.

Mary Gale La Flesche died February 28, 1909, at the age of eighty-three. Not only had her own life been one of vigor and inspiration, but her legacy—to her people—her diligent daughters was one of continuing and long-lasting value.

CAROLINE JOY FRENCH MORTON
Born 1833

Caroline Joy French Morton, wife of the founder of Arbor Day, deserves to be called a pioneer ecologist. She was born August 9, 1833, at Hallowell, Maine, to Hiram and Caroline Hayden ·Joy. Mrs. Joy died in 1835 in Detroit, and Hiram Joy left the baby to be cared for by family friends, Deacon David French and his wife Cynthia. Reared by these kind people, she added their surname to her own. She attended the Episcopal Girls' School in Detroit and later the Wesleyan Seminary at Albion, Michigan, where she met her future husband. At seventeen, she enrolled at the College for Women in Utica, New York. She was married to J. Sterling Morton in Detroit on October 30, 1854, and on the same day they began their journey to Nebraska by rail, riverboat, and stage.

Their first home, at Bellevue, Nebraska, was a two-room log cabin. Within a few months, they moved to Nebraska City, where Caroline selected the site for a four-room house, which over the years grew into the mansion of Arbor Lodge. Struck by the lack of trees in the new and unsettled country, one of their first acts was to import from the East a wide variety of shade and fruit trees, making the Arbor Lodge estate a veritable sylvan island on the prairie. As Mr. Morton was involved in politics and away from home a good deal, much of the tree-planting as well as the management of the farm and orchards fell to Caroline, aided by her sons.

Despite the initial hardships of pioneer home-making, Caroline Morton found time for the graces of life. She was an accomplished pianist, needleworker, and artist. She painted many of the pictures which adorned the walls, and tables and chairs displayed examples of her needle-craft. The house was described as a gay home, marked by parties for dancing and games, especially among the young friends of her four sons. One historian said of her that she "had one of the kindest hearts that ever beat in human bosom. . . . Her life was one continuous blessing and benediction upon the needy and the suffering. Her deeds of charity were constant among the humble and helpless poor."

The Mortons had four sons, all of whom became markedly successful. Joy and Mark Morton founded the Morton Salt Company. Paul Morton became a railway and business executive, Secretary of the Navy under President Theodore Roosevelt, and president of one of the largest life-insurance companies. Carl Morton founded the Argo Starch Company. Mark Morton once said of his mother, "Had it not been for her, none of us—including father—would have amounted to much."

Caroline Joy French Morton died at Arbor Lodge on June 29, 1881, at the age of forty-seven, after a lingering illness caused by a knee injury. Although a bronze statue of her husband graces the grounds of Arbor Lodge and he was elected in 1975 to the Nebraska Hall of Fame, she has no such monument. On the other hand, Arbor Lodge—now a National Historic Landmark—and Caroline Morton's influence on tree-planting in Nebraska and on the founding of Arbor Day may in themselves be a monument more memorable than bronze.

LAURA BIDDLECOMBE POUND
Born 1841

Laura Biddlecombe Pound, a pioneer citizen of Lincoln, was the mother of three children, all of whom had notable careers. She was born in Phelps, New York, May 15, 1841, to Joab Stafford and Olivia Mathewson Biddlecombe, both of whom were descended from Quaker families who had come to America in 1680. She attended school in Phelps and at the academy in Macedon, New York, and later went to Lombard College in Galesburg, Illinois. She married Judge Stephen Bosworth Pound on January 21, 1869, and in the same year they moved to Lincoln, Nebraska, then but a small cluster of houses spread over raw prairie.

Settled in Lincoln, Laura Pound took courses at the new state university (opened in 1870), particularly in German. She accumulated a substantial library in German and the English classics, which provided invaluable background for her children. From 1880 to 1890 she was a member of the city library board. In 1892, when the city fathers declined to appropriate funds for the library, she served as voluntary librarian to keep the institution alive. She and her husband were actively concerned with the university, and encouraged and aided several generations of college students, to whom she became known as "Mother Pound."

She was an early member of the State Historical Society, a charter member of a club which became the Nebraska Art Association, and of the Lincoln Woman's Club. She was also one of the founders of the Deborah Avery chapter of the Daughters of the American Revolution. She and her husband were members of the Religious Society of Friends.

Mrs. Pound spent a great deal of time with her children. She did not believe in applying pressure; instead, she let them develop and follow their own interests. In an interview late in life she said, "We never lectured our children," but "I always had my eye out and knew what they were doing. I was regular and painstaking with them and began early to teach them the wonderful advantage one has who is able to decide and not change his mind. I believe that the power to make a decision is most important to every person."

The children profited from her training. The son, Roscoe (1870-1964), became a lawyer and served as dean of the University of Nebraska Law School from 1903 to 1907 and of the Harvard Law School from 1916 to 1936. The elder daughter, Louise (1872-1958), became the first American woman to earn a Ph.D. degree at Heidelberg and taught at the University of Nebraska from 1900 to 1945. Widely known as a language scholar, she was the first woman president of the Modern Language Association of America. Olivia (1874-1961), a teacher, served as assistant principal of Lincoln High School from 1918 to 1943.

Laura Biddlecombe Pound died in Lincoln on December 10, 1928, at the age of eighty-seven.

ELIZABETH M. GRIFFIN ABBOTT
Born 1845

Elizabeth M. Griffin Abbott, a pioneer civic leader and women's rights advocate, devoted more than fifty years to worthy causes, besides rearing four successful children. She was born in De Kalb County, Illinois, January 20, 1845, to James and Emeline Gardner Griffin. Her parents, Quakers and early believers in women's rights, were also abolitionists and served as part of the "underground railroad" network which aided escaping slaves. She attended Lombard College at Galesburg, Illinois, and in 1868 was graduated from Rockford College (then Rockford Female Seminary). After teaching for some years in high schools, she married a young attorney, Othman Ali Abbott, at Sycamore, Illinois, on February 9, 1873, and moved to Grand Island, Nebraska, where he had established a law practice. Mr. Abbott served in the legislature and became the first lieutenant governor of the new state, later serving for a time as acting governor.

In 1882, Elizabeth Abbott became an officer of the Nebraska Woman Suffrage Association, and in the same year entertained Susan B. Anthony, who spoke for the cause in Grand Island. Instrumental in founding the city library in 1884, she was a member of the library board for forty-eight years. She was president of the board from 1905 to 1922 and later was named honorary president. In 1886, she was appointed by Governor James Dawes as a delegate to the thirteenth National Conference of Corrections and Charities at St. Paul, Minnesota (the early name of the present National Conference of Social Work). In 1887, she worked for the legislative act which in that year established the State Soldiers and Sailors Home (now the Nebraska Veterans Home) at Grand Island.

In the early 1900's, she organized the Women's Park Association, which raised some $9,000 for improving and landscaping the city park. She organized and was president of the first Grand Island Woman's Club, which lapsed during World War I. When the present Woman's Club was founded, in 1919, she was named honorary president. She was a member of the Unitarian Church.

The Abbotts had four children, all of whom followed the family tradition of civic involvement. Two sons, Othman A., Jr. (1874-1945) and Arthur (1880-1969), became attorneys. The two daughters, Edith (1876-1957) and Grace (1878-1939), both became well-known educators, social workers, and nationally known writers on social problems. In addition, Elizabeth Abbott, in the late 1880's, undertook the rearing of two young children of a deceased sister-in-law. Part of her legacy to her children was a love of literature and ideas, and a good share of her life-long interest in social progress, civic improvement, and the need for a constant search for truth. One historian has said, "Fortunate indeed for the four Abbott children . . . that Quaker mother who 'believed in gentle methods with the young,' but whose gentleness cloaked steadfast purpose."

Elizabeth M. Griffin Abbott died in Grand Island in 1941 at the age of ninety-six.

SARAH HANNAH SELLECK JOSLYN

Born 1851

Sarah Hannah Selleck Joslyn, art patron and philanthropist, born in Waterbury, Vermont, April 4, 1851, married George A. Joslyn in Montpelier on September 24, 1872. When the couple moved west, they arrived in Omaha in 1880 with only nine dollars. George Joslyn soon took over two small hotels, which, under Sarah's efficient New England hands, provided capital for other and larger ventures into business and real estate. The foundation of the substantial Joslyn fortune was the Western Newspaper Union, which supplied ready-printed inside pages for small-town newspapers. He died in 1916, leaving Sarah Joslyn, at her death in 1940, reportedly "Nebraska's richest woman."

Although the life style of the Joslyns was lavish—in a 32-room baronial stone mansion built in 1903, with a ballroom, a pipe organ, greenhouses, fine horses, and fine cars—Sarah Joslyn never lost her New England sense of thrift. She did her own shopping; and when friends protested that her hats were several years old, she would reply that she could not afford a new one. Although generous, she confined her gifts to objects and causes of permanent value. During the 1920's, her personal donations and fund-raising efforts made possible the then new quarters of the Nebraska Humane Society, with the first small-animal hospital in Nebraska and Iowa. Among other beneficiaries were the Omaha Women's Club, the Y.W.C.A., and the Child Saving Institute.

Her most notable contribution to the city was the Joslyn Memorial Art Museum, a $3,000,000 tribute to her husband. A graceful marble structure on a commanding height, it is unquestionably one of the state's most beautiful buildings as well as a focal point for Omaha's cultural life. When the building was completed in 1931, she provided an endowment of $1,700,000 and established the Joslyn Liberal Arts Society to own and operate the museum. Although she sat on the board of directors, she never influenced its decisions. When the directors set aside $5,000 for a portrait of her, she refused to sit for it, declaring that they did not need it; the artist had to settle for working from photographs.

Sarah Joslyn was the mother of two children, a son who died in infancy and an adopted daughter. Her tastes remained simple and practical. She loved animals and flowers, collected music boxes, and liked to work jigsaw puzzles. Asked why she did not move to California or some other less rigorous climate, she replied, in a phrase worthy of the Vermont Yankee tradition, "The money was made in Omaha, and it will be spent in Omaha." And anyone who has seen the Joslyn Museum is likely to concede that the money was well spent.

In 1928, Sarah Joslyn was named "Omaha's First Citizen" by the American Legion, and in 1937 she was awarded an honorary LL.D. degree by the University of Omaha. She died in Omaha on February 28, 1940, at the age of 88, leaving a great public memorial not only to her husband but to a gracious and philanthropic lady.

MARY ELIZABETH BAIRD BRYAN
Born 1861

Mary Elizabeth Baird Bryan, wife and life-long aide to American statesman William Jennings Bryan, was born in Perry, Illinois, June 17, 1861, the only child of John and Lovina Dexter Baird. She attended Monticello Seminary in Godfrey, Illinois, and the Jacksonville (Illinois) Female Academy, from which she was graduated with first honors in June 1881. While yet in college, she met handsome, brilliant, young W. J. Bryan; they were married October 1, 1884. He had started a law practice in Jacksonville, but in 1887 they moved to the small but promising town of Lincoln, Nebraska, their home for the next four decades.

In Jacksonville, Mary Bryan had begun to study law, and in Lincoln continued her studies. As the only female candidate, and pregnant at the time, she passed the Nebraska state bar examination on November 29, 1888, ranking third among the seventeen candidates. She also studied German, so as to keep her husband abreast of the German-language press, then quite influential in the Middle West. Although she never practiced law, her training made her an invaluable legal and literary assistant. Besides being a mother, a homemaker, and her husband's secretary, she also managed most of the family's finances—so well that starting from an annual income of $500 in Jacksonville, they were able by 1903 to build a substantial mansion, "Fairview," just outside of Lincoln. (This is now a Bryan museum, on the grounds of Bryan Memorial Hospital.)

The Bryans had three children, Ruth Baird, William Jennings, Jr., and Grace Dexter, whose early education was personally supervised by their mother.

Her oldest daughter, Ruth Bryan Owen (Rohde), became the first woman Representative from Florida (1929-1933), and, as Ambassador to Denmark (1933-1936), the first woman envoy from the United States to a foreign power.

Besides being a good mother, she was a dutiful daughter: her parents lived with the Bryans for many years. In his later years, Mr. Baird was blind, and Mary spent many hours reading to him from the Bible and the English classics. When in Lincoln, Mary taught Sunday School at the Methodist church in the near-by village of Normal. She was also active in civic organizations, including the Y.W.C.A. and the Woman's Club, and was one of the founders of the Lincoln Sorosis Club.

During her husband's long political career—twice a Representative from Nebraska (1891-1895), thrice Democratic candidate for U.S. President (1896, 1900, 1908), and for two years Secretary of State under Woodrow Wilson (1913-1915), Mary Bryan counseled and advised him on people and issues, and researched and wrote his speeches. With her husband, she campaigned for women's rights, the eight-hour day, currency reform, prohibition, the graduated income tax, international peace, and many other reforms. Although arthritis confined her to a wheelchair for the last twelve years of her life, she still accompanied her husband everywhere, as she had done on many of his campaigns. Mary Baird Bryan died January 21, 1930, at the age of sixty-eight.

LENORA DENNIS GRAY

Born 1873

Lenora Dennis Gray, black feminist leader, civic organizer, poet, and mother of eight children, was born in Atchison, Kansas, on November 8, 1873, and settled in Omaha, Nebraska, at the age of sixteen. In 1905, she was one of the organizers of the Nebraska Federation of Colored Women's Clubs (now the Nebraska Association of Colored Women's Clubs). She worked continuously with that organization for more than fifty years, during which she held, at one time or another, every office, and became chairman of the executive board; in 1943, she was

voted Trustee Emeritus of the organization. She also organized and worked with several other clubs: the Eureka Art Club, the South Side Civic Club, the Mary McLeod Bethune Club, and the Civic Matrons Club.

An earnest advocate of education for youth, Mrs. Gray worked with the Woodson Center in South Omaha in arts and crafts, rug braiding, needlework, and furniture refinishing. When Father Flanagan started his Boys' Home (later to become Boys' Town) with twelve boys in the old German-American Club on South 13th St., she catered for them from 1918 to 1921 free of charge. The Nebraska Association of Colored Women's Clubs established a scholarship bearing her name.

She was also concerned about the aged. Her hard work and leadership led to the purchase by the Nebraska Federation of Colored Women's Clubs of a house in Lincoln as a home for the aged. First called the Old Folks' Home, it was renamed the Federated Home in 1947.

A deeply religious woman, she was active in the Zion Baptist Church as a Sunday school teacher and member of the Mission Society and Welcome Circle. She was a charter member of the Colored Women's Church Council and served as its historian until the organization was dissolved in 1950-1951 and merged with the United

Church Women. She was also a member of the Ernest Evans Chapter No. 8 of the American War Mothers.

Early in the century, Lenora Gray wrote a poem entitled "Call to Women" which began, "Arise ye women! There is work for you to do." She gave the then new Nebraska Federation of Colored Women's Clubs its motto: "Sowing for others to reap." Her minister, in his eulogy, said, and said truly: "The deeds of Mrs. Lenora Gray will live on and on." She died in Omaha on November 30, 1957 at the age of eighty-four.

BESS STREETER ALDRICH

Born 1881

Bess Streeter Aldrich, novelist, short-story writer, and homemaker, was born in Cedar Falls, Iowa, on February 17, 1881. She was the eighth and last child of a pioneer couple, James Wareham Streeter and Mary W. Anderson Streeter. After being graduated from the Iowa State Teachers College at Cedar Falls, she taught school in Iowa and Utah for several years. On September 24, 1907, she married Charles Sweetzer Aldrich, and in 1909 the couple settled in Elmwood, Nebraska, a small town some twenty miles from Lincoln, where she reared a daughter and three sons. James be-

came an artist and illustrator in New York City; Charles became designing engineer and manufacturer in New York; Robert became a newspaper reporter, later a free-lance writer. The daughter, Mary Eleanor, married Milton Beechner, a Lincoln businessman, and still lives in Lincoln, on a street named for her mother.

Bess Aldrich had started writing at the age of fifteen, but her writing career dates from 1911, when she won a prize from the *Ladies' Home Journal* for a short story, "The Little House Next Door." In the early 1920's she became nationally known for stories about "Mother Mason" and "The Cutters," which appeared in the *American Magazine*, and which Rudyard Kipling praised as "typical American family stories." Her first novel, which she dedicated to her husband, took its title, *The Rim of the Prairie*, from his description of the view from her study window. Her best-known book, *A Lantern in Her Hand*, published in 1925, promptly became a best-seller and was translated into Braille and many foreign languages. This realistic but sympathetic account of pioneer life in the prairie country struck so popular a chord that it naturally called for a sequel. This, *A White Bird Flying*, published in 1931, also became a best-seller and was widely translated. *Miss Bishop*, a sympathetic novel about a female schoolteacher, was made into a movie, *Cheers for Miss Bishop*, in 1933. All told, she wrote fourteen novels and nearly two hundred short stories and had the satisfaction (somewhat rare among writers) of being able to say that she had sold everything that she had ever written.

After her husband's sudden death in 1925, she devoted herself entirely to writing and to the education of her children. Her family have described her as a mother first and an author second—always with time for her children. She continued to live in Elmwood until 1946, when she moved to Lincoln, where she completed two more books. She died at the age of 73 in Lincoln, Nebraska, on August 3, 1954.

She was a member of numerous writers' and women's organizations. In 1934 the University of Nebraska awarded her the honorary degree of Doctor of Letters, and in 1971 she was elected to the Nebraska Hall of Fame, the second of only two women thus far so honored, and the only mother. In 1973, the Nebraska Hall of Fame Commission placed her bust in the corridor of the unique and magnificent State House.

HAZEL HEMPEL ABEL

Born 1888

Hazel Hempel Abel, business executive, civic leader, educator, politician, and philanthropist, was the first woman from Nebraska and the third in history to be elected to the United States Senate. She was born in Plattsmouth, Nebraska, July 10, 1888, to Charles and Ella Beetison Hempel. Graduating at fifteen from the Omaha High School, she had to wait a year before entering the University of Nebraska, from which she was then graduated in three years, in 1908. After teaching English, Latin, and German in Nebraska high schools, on December 21, 1916, she married George Philip Abel, a self-made, hard-working, young man who had recently founded his own construction company, which rapidly became one of the largest in the state. Hazel Abel served as its secretary-treasurer until her husband's death in 1937, when she assumed the presidency; she retired in 1951 in favor of her son, George Philip Abel, Jr., remaining as chairman of the board.

During these busy years she bore and reared five children—Helen Louise, George Philip, Jr., Hazel Lenore, Alice Virginia, and Annette Lee—all of whom became successful in varied careers. Her contributions to higher education were lifelong. She served the University of Nebraska on many committees, and as a trustee of the University of Nebraska Foundation from 1937 until her death. She was also a trustee of Doane College (Crete, Nebraska), Hastings College (Hastings, Nebraska), and Nebraska Wesleyan University (Lincoln). Her interest in education and the problems of youth embraced all levels. She was instrumental in the formation of a statewide juvenile probation system, in improved courts for children, and in recodification of Nebraska children's laws.

Besides taking part in a multitude of civic organizations and functions in Lincoln and in her part-time second-home city of San Diego, she was influential in Republican politics, both locally and nationally, holding responsible party positions. In 1954, she won over fifteen men in the Republican senatorial primary and was elected U.S. Senator to fill a two-month interim vacancy caused by the death of Sen. Dwight Griswold. In 1960, at the age of seventy-one, she ran for governor and finished second in the Republican gubernatorial primary.

For her wide-ranging and numerous educational, civic, and social activities, Mrs. Abel re-

ceived a Distinguished Service Award from the University of Nebraska (1945) and an honorary D.H.L. degree from Doane College (1956). In 1963 she became the first woman to receive an honorary LL.D. degree from the University of Nebraska. She was a member of the American Association of University Women, the Nebraska State Teachers Association, and the Lincoln Woman's Club. Her distinguished record in both local and national works brought her the title, in 1957, of both Nebraska Mother and American Mother of the Year.

Hazel Abel died in Lincoln, Nebraska, July 30, 1966, at the age of seventy-eight. Nebraska Governor Frank Morrison paid a final tribute by saying, "She was a great lady and an outstanding mother."

MARGARET ELIZABETH McDONALD HASEBROOCK

Margaret Elizabeth Hasebroock of West Point, Nebraska, is one of the state's most active clubwomen as well as a wife and mother. The daughter of John and Sarah McDonald, she attended high school and Midland College in her home town, Fremont, Nebraska. She then earned an A.B. degree at Wayne (Nebraska) State College and later a Fine Arts degree at Grinnell College in Iowa. After college she had some three years of soprano coloratura concert experience, predominantly in the Midwest, and

has since taken various graduate courses at the University of Nebraska at Lincoln. She is married to the Hon. William H. Hasebroock, a senator in Nebraska's unique unicameral legislature. Their son Robert is a major executive of the Omaha National Bank.

Her memberships in and associations with educational, civic, and social organizations are wide-ranging. Among those of major relevance to her native state are these: past president of the Nebraska Federation of Women's Clubs and at present legislative chairman of the Nebraska Federation; trustee of Wayne State College and of Immanuel Hospital (Omaha); vice chairman of the Nebraska Educational Television Commission; president of the Omaha branch of the National League of American Pen Women (and first vice president of the National League, a post leading to the presidency); and past vice president of Nebraska's Founder's Day (the highest office granted a woman).

On the national scene, Margaret Hasebroock has been associated with the National Advisory Council for Laymen's National Bible Committee; the National Executive Council of the Lutheran Church in the U.S.A.; the American Association of University Women; the National Conference of Christians and Jews; and the Order of the Eastern Star. She is a past international president of the General Federation of Women's Clubs, and an executive of Freedom Foundation, Valley Forge, Pennsylvania. She was also the only woman on President Nixon's fifteen-member Task Force Committee on Crime and Law Observance.

Mrs. Hasebroock holds an honorary D.H.L. degree from Midland College. She has also received a Distinguished Service Award from Mississippi Women's College, two similar awards from Wayne State College, and a Good Neighbor Award from Ak-Sar-Ben (an Omaha-based civic group) for outstanding work with youth.

Margaret Hasebroock feels that success depends largely upon one's dedicated and disciplined efforts, and attributes her own to good health, understanding cooperation from husband and family, and close association with the church. "My parents," she says, "lovingly instilled in me self-confidence and a reliable standard of values. It has been my deliberate objective to live positively, defeating negative thoughts by giving full play to creative and constructive ideas." That background and philosophy are well reflected by her works.

AMERICAN MOTHER'S PRAYER

Thank you, God . . .

First and foremost that I'm a woman. What's more, an American woman—that luckiest of all possible beings, a female child of the U.S.A.

For nowhere else in the whole wide world could I be so respected, so cherished, so privileged (some people call it downright spoiled) and yet so free.

Thank you that I can vote or run for office (and win too). That I can marry or not, have children or not, work or not, and it's nobody's business but my own; there's nobody really to stop me but me.

Thank you that though prejudices persist and discrimination dies hard (men have run your world so long, God, and forgive me but you made men proud and slow to change) yet no doors are really closed to me. I can be a doctor—surgeon, dentist, vet. I can be a lawyer, I can be a judge. I can dance, swim, act—be an artist or an athlete, drive a truck if I prefer, be a jockey, umpire a baseball game. I can work in forests or harvest fields as well as offices if it suits me.

But, dear Lord, how I thank you that my government doesn't make me do any of these things.

I can stay home and "just be" a wife and mother if I please. I can be my own boss as I cook and sew and chase the kids and clean. "And while I'm at it, thank you for the marvelous staff of push-button servants that make keeping house in America easier than anyplace else on earth.) It's been said "Man's home is his castle." Chauvanistic? Maybe. But I don't mind a bit, God, as long as I can share his throne.

Thank you, God, for the prosperity and plenty of this incredible country. The abundance of our resources—coal and oil and water and grain; and human energy and skill.

For you know we've worked very hard to get where we are. Unlike the skeptical hireling of the parable, we didn't just bury the gifts you gave us, but plowed and sowed and sweat and made them bear fruit. And then, with arms

by MARJORIE HOLMES

Written expressly for the
American Mothers Committee, Inc.

and hearts overflowing, we rushed to the whole world's aid.

Thank you that we inherited not only our forefathers' and mothers' achievements, but their generosity, their willingness to share. That never in all our history have we turned our back on another nation in need.

Thank you, God, that my children were born in this remarkable land. Born free. *Daughters as well as sons, just as free as I am to do with their lives what they will. To do and think and be whatever they choose.*

Oh, help us truly to value that freedom, God, and guard it well. Don't let us take it for granted. Don't let us become weak, soft, vulnerable. So afraid of being considered old-fashioned, so eager to be sophisticated, modern, that we play into the hands of those who would take it away. Don't let us discount it, downgrade it. And, dear God, make us just as quick to praise our country's virtues and triumphs and blessings as we are to criticize. For who can do his best—man, woman, child or nation—if no credit is ever forthcoming, no appreciation—only blame?

Help us to stop criticizing ourselves *so much, God. Restrain our own breast beating. Help us to remember that no nation since the beginning of time has ever had even half the freedom and advantages we enjoy.*

Light in us fervent new fires of patriotism, Lord.

Patriotism. *A word of passionate honor in almost every country except the one that deserves it so much! Make us proud to be American patriots once again. Willing to shout our heritage from the housetops, wave the flag . . . That star-spangled banner. Let us thrill once more to the sight of it; may it fly from every flagpole, reappear in every schoolroom. Let us and our children pledge our allegiance to it wherever Americans gather, and sing the words of its anthem with joy and pride.*

Oh, Lord, dear Lord—as we celebrate the 200th birthday of this unique, this special land, remind us: We are so lucky to be Americans. And I'm so lucky to be an American woman!

Nevada

JERRY SCHUELER

Nevada

Nickname: Silver State or
                  Sagebrush State

State Flower: Sagebrush

State Tree: Pinon

State Bird: Mountain Bluebird

Photos

1. Nevada State Museum
2. Nevada State Museum
3. Nevada State Museum

Nevada

NELLIE VERRILL DAVIS

Born 1844

Nellie V. Davis was born in Greenwood, Maine, where her family lived. Her parents died within a few months of each other when she was about sixteen and she was left with the job of making a home and caring for the younger brothers and sisters. She had been prepared to enter Vassar and she always regretted that she was unable to carry out her educational plans.

When she was about twenty-two she was persuaded to marry a sweetheart of long standing H. R. Mighels, who had founded the Carson City Daily Appeal. He sent for Nellie and she came to Nevada from Maine via boat to the Isthmus of Panama, across the Isthmus on the little narrow railroad and then by boat to San Francisco. There they were married in 1866 and then they came to Carson City on the stage— long before the railroad was built. There were four children born to them.

Mr. Mighels became ill and Nellie learned to set type so that she could set his editorials in type at home and he could check them—since typographical mistakes annoyed him. She learned to set a very correct copy. When her husband died in 1879, Nellie immediately took over the management of the newspaper, handling it with great success. She had been engaged to act as a special reporter for two legislative sessions, so she bears the distinction of having been the first woman reporter in the West.

Sometime after Mr. Mighels' death, she engaged Sam P. Davis to act as her editor. Later, she married him in 1880 and he took over the entire duties of the newspaper job for her. Two daughters were born to them, Ethel Davis Wait (who lived many years in Las Vegas, died in Carson City), Lucy Davis Crowell (who lives in Carson City).

Mrs. Davis' first interest in club work was to help in organizing the Red Cross in Nevada during the Spanish American War. She was the local president as well as having served as Nevada State President for two terms, 1899 and 1900. Nellie joined the Leisure Hour Club and took an active part. She served as president

twice and successfully carried out a project which resulted in the building of the club house. In October 1980, she represented the Leisure Hour Club at a meeting in Reno to form the Nevada Federation of Women's Clubs to be a constituent of the General Federation of Women's Clubs. During the course of the meeting Nellie had to inform them that the Leisure Hour Club had men members too, and that they were unwilling to give them up. (It was decided finally the Leisure Hour Club could become a member with the understanding that the men members were not to vote on Federation affairs, nor were they to be counted for any purpose as members of the club where Federation matters were concerned.) The Federation was formed and Nellie was elected to serve as its first president.

HELEN JANE WISER STEWART
Born 1854

Helen Jane was born in Springfield, Illinois, and moved with her family to Sacramento where she was educated in the public school and Woodland College. Shortly before her 19th birthday she married Archibald Stewart, 20 years her senior. He moved his bride to Nevada and later persuaded Helen that they should temporarily move into the desert wilderness to the Las Vegas Ranch.

Archie was killed in 1884 and Helen was suddenly thrust into the role of directing the operation of the ranch which produced large amounts of fruits and vegetables in addition to the cattle. Her day journal shows the week after his death she sent fifty-five pounds of beef jerky to be sold at 70¢ a pound as well as fruit, corn and wine to the mines and mills in Eldorado Canyon.

Helen took time off away from the ranch to stay with her parents for the birth of her fifth child. She named him Archibald for his father. The other children were Will, Hiram, Eliza and Evaline.

Although the ranch was operating successfully, Helen worried about her children's lack of education. She hired a tutor to come to live at the ranch. Helen had an avid interest in many cultural topics and here was an individual with whom she could share her love of poetry (she collected a scrap book of poetry as well as writing some herself) and he was available to the area for fiddling, singing, and on special occasions for speech making.

The business was expanded and prospered, but after a temporary stay of twenty years, Helen sold the ranch to the railroad. Other people were coming to the area and Will assisted in the establishment of the town of Las Vegas and held various offices of local government. Helen through isolation had long been starved for feminine companionship and now she drained every minute of enjoyment she could from social affairs—she attended frequently and frequently hosted. Her interest in the history of southern Nevada began early and never ceased. She was the first president of the Historical Society in Las Vegas and served on the building committee from Las Vegas to build the permanent home of the Nevada Historical Society. She also joined the Society of Nevada Pioneers. Her collection of early relics was exhibited often and she spoke on early history

many times. She was the author of a chapter in Sam Davis's *History of Nevada*.

Helen was the first woman elected to the School Board and helped establish an Indian School; she was also among the first women to sit on a jury in the county. One of Helen's grandchildren, a namesake, proved to be retarded; the doting grandmother had a special love for this exceptional child and it is exemplified in the naming of a school for retarded children, "Helen J. Stewart School."

Helen cared about people and gave sympathy and understanding to all. When she died, all business closed for the day to honor the town's most prominent pioneer—one who had wrestled with a desert wilderness, making it her home, and who had helped develop the area into the town.

SADIE DOTSON HURST
Born 1857

Sadie Dotson Hurst was born in Iowa where she married Horton Hurst and raised two sons, Dale and Glenn. Upon the death of her husband, Sadie lived with her sons who had interests in various theatrical enterprises in the midwest and then in Reno. By 1918 she had developed a lively interest in club activities and community betterment and filed for a seat in the Nevada legislature in 1918 with her announcement reading "Endorsed by the Club Women of Reno."

Although an ardent prohibitionist, Sadie shunned militancy in other matters and quickly disclaimed association with the somewhat clamorous and controversial suffragettes group. With the dedicated support of the club women, she won election and was seated in January, 1919, the only woman in the legislature, and the first in Nevada. At the capital in Carson City, the local newspaper editor chose to ignore the unusual composition of the Assembly, and saluted "A Splendid Appearing Body of Men."

Sadie worked throughout the 1919 session to attain some progressive goals. She served on the education, federal relations, state institutions, and state prison and insane asylum committees. Notwithstanding these lacklustre appointments, the first Nevada woman legislator introduced and managed several bills. She presented a resolution in petition for national woman suffrage, a bill for registration and licensing of graduate nurses, a proposal to require the wife's consent to the disposal of community property, an act to increase the penalties for the crime of rape and to raise the age of consent, and a bill to prohibit cruelty to animals. All of the proposals reflected current concerns in both state and nation: woman suffrage must have been uppermost in the minds of many voters; Nevada was then the only state that did not require registration of nurses; women then had no prerogatives in the disposal of property jointly owned with their spouses; females had long been used and stigmatized in sex crimes; and the humanitarian spirit of the time suggested that animals should have kinder treatment.

The outcome of Sadie's term inthe legislature was creditable, despite her novice status. The bills she introduced suffered a somewhat better fate than those of many other freshman representatives, and when the legislature was called into Special Session in 1920, Sadie had the distinction of introducing and presiding over the passage of the resolution of ratification of the Nineteenth Amendment.

Stepping out of the traditional and accepted role of women brought Sadie some criticism. Some people recall her personality as somewhat overbearing, but she served gracefully, giving a pattern for other women to follow. The single term apparently accomplished her objectives for she did not seek reelection. She lived in Reno sharing her home at times with sons Dale and Glenn until the family moved to California where the Hurst men continued their theatrical careers. Sadie died in Pasadena at the age of 94 unsung as the Silver State's political pioneer.

DELPHINE ANDERSON SQUIRES
Born 1868

Delphine Anderson Squires was born in Wisconsin but moved to Minnesota where she spent her girlhood and was graduated from high school and Normal School in preparation for her teaching career. She taught in Austin and then the family moved to Seattle so she applied for a position there and was signed to start in the fall. Charles Squires, a childhood classmate, had other plans for her and they were married in Seattle in 1889, establishing their home in southern California. Children of the family were James, Florence, Herbert and Russell.

Elected as first vice president of the California Congress of Mothers (forerunner of the PTA) Delphine held that office when she moved to Las Vegas in 1906 and organized the first branch of the organization in Las Vegas. She became very busy with church, civic and club work and her spacious home became one of the centers of hospitality in the new community—governors, senators and grizzled prospectors in from the hills all were welcomed.

Delphine worked with her husband in publishing and editing the Las Vegas Age, which was started in 1905 as one of the first two newspapers in Las Vegas. The history of Nevada had been a special interest so she engaged in writing her reminiscences and incidents of history for the Las Vegas Age and later the Review-Journal. She had many other interests including painting in oils and water colors. She was a

Gov. Ernest D. Boyle of Nevada signing resolution for ratification of Nineteenth Amendment to Constitution of U.S.—Mrs. Sadie D. Hurst who presented the resolution Speaker of the Assembly D. J. Fitzgerald and group of Suffrage Women Feb. 7, 1920.

UNA REILLY DICKERSON
Born 1881

Una Reilly Dickerson was born in the mining camp of Hamilton, White Pine County, Nevada, where her father was the owner of a general merchandise store and postmaster. Her father's name was James Reilly and her mother's maiden name was Elizabeth Baily.

While still in her teens she taught school in Cherry Creek, Nevada, and later attended business school in Michigan, returning to the state of Nevada to serve as minute clerk for the Nevada State Legislature.

In 1903 she married Denver S. Dickerson, a young miner from the Couer D'Alene, district of Idaho, and the young couple made their home in Ely where Mr. Dickerson was County Recorder, and was also interested in mining. A few years later, in 1906, Denver was elected Lieutenant Governor of the state at the age of thirty-four and the family moved to Carson City. Upon the death of John Sparks, the then Governor of Nevada, in 1908, Denver S. Dickerson became Nevada's youngest Governor.

They had eight children: Harvey, Norinne, June, Donald, Denver, Barbara, Belford and George. All but June and Donald are still alive.

Upon Denver's death in 1925 Una was left with eight children, all minors. She sought and secured the job of law librarian for the Washoe County Law Library, and from February of 1927 until her retirement on October 31, 1956, she served in that capacity. During these years she cared for and educated her children, making a home for them in Reno. In this regard, her accomplishment was recognized when she became the recipient of a well-deserved reward from the Nevada Federation of Women's Clubs when they proposed her and she was selected as Nevada's first "Mother of the Year," in 1945. Upon her death in 1959 an editorial about her referred to her selection and said, "In light of her accomplishments, it is evident no better choice could have been made. Una Reilly Dickerson, daughter of the silver state, was in truth a fine example of all that is epitomized in the word mother."

Norinne has written, "Due to my mother's love and guidance I feel we have all tried to live up to her confidence and faith in us, and I know she was proud of all of us."

Harvey was a three-term Attorney General of Nevada, a former President of the Nevada State Bar Association, and is an attorney in Las

charter member of Eastern Star, also of the Mesquite Club for which she served as president on two occasions. She was president of the Nevada Federation of Women's Clubs and a member of the board of the international organization, General Federation of Women's Clubs. She sponsored the original chapter here of Beta Sigma Phi and became the social sponsor for the later enlarged group of chapters. Young women looked to her for guidance, counsel and help, not only in organizational problems, but also in their personal lives as well.

Many joint tributed were made to "Pop" and "Mom" Squires in their long lives, one follows: "Of no one did Pop and Mom Squires ever speak or write unkindly, for a newpaperman's writing are truly an exemplar of his own character. There was no slander, no villification, no distorted news. Mom and Pop wrote as they lived, and were friends of all. For that they have already gone down in Nevada History."

Vegas. Denver has been Speaker of the Nevada Assembly, Lieutenant Governor of Guam, the United States Information Service Officer in Rangoon, Burma, and a newspaper owner and publisher; presently he is in charge of federal government printing in Washington, D. C. George is a former District Attorney of Clark County and a former President of the Nevada State Bar Association and is an attorney in Las Vegas. Belford has been active in the newspaper business in Reno. All of the children have raised fine families who are following in their grandmother's path of self-reliance, industry, concern for their fellowman, and love of family.

BERTHA BISHOP RONZONE
Born 1885

Bertha Bishop Ronzone was born in Iowa, raised and educated in Fowler, California. At seventeen she met and married a miner, Benjamin R. Ronzone, and in the spring of 1902, Ben took his bride with him to Nome, Alaska.

They had passage on the wooden steamer "Portland" which normally took about two weeks to make the trip; however, as they sailed in sight of the lights of Nome, the ship became trapped in a giant ice floe which was drifting out to sea. They were carried further north into the Bering Straits than any ship had been known to travel. They remained amid the ice for 73 days before finally entering Nome harbor in the bright 2 a.m. sunshine. They were greeted by crowds and a brass band, successful after they had been feared lost.

After a couple of years they returned and settled among the first settlers in the mining camp of Manhattan, Nevada. There were no services available in Manhattan and Bertha started a laundry, doing the work by hand as there was no machinery available for such work. She soon had a crew of nine Paiute Indian squaws working for her to do the washing. Her eldest daughter assisted by collecting and delivering the laundry for the miners.

There was no store there and it was necessary for everyone to travel many miles to buy food and clothing. While she was ill in 1917 she went to recuperate in California and noticed the fine sales on men's socks—just those very small and those very large. She bought them anyway and conceived the idea of purchasing supplies and sending them to her daughter to sell in camp. The socks sold, regardless of fit—if they were too long, they just cut off the toes, since they were in such short supply.

At home Bertha converted one room of her home into a store and went into business on $500 borrowed capital. She bought overalls, underwear, yard goods and notions and although the mining camp was on the decline, her business was successful. She continued to serve the community until the mining camp closed down and then the family located in Tonopah and opened a store known first as Manhattan and later as Ronzone's.

Bertha, soon to be affectionately known as "Mom" to all, was progressive and expanded her business at every opportunity and in several years had stores in three communities, for when it appeared that Boulder Dam would be constructed, she moved to Las Vegas and opened a store there.

They had three children, Amy, Esther and Richard. "Mom" was vitally interested in education, for herself and for her community. She served as a member of the School Board in Tonopah and furthered her own by studying

and graduating from the first year course of the Church of Religious Science receiving a bachelor's degree. Dick served on the Board of Regents for the University, a term in the State Assembly and is currently serving as Clark County Commissioner.

"Mom" Ronzone was named Nevada Mother of the Year in 1959 and her community has said of her: "An outstanding living example of faith, courage, and cheerfulness, all of which comes through the spiritual and moral strength which makes up her character. Her greatest merit is her love of people and she gives freely her affection, kindness and understanding to friends and family alike."

THERESA ALPETCHE LAXALT

Theresa Alpetche Laxalt was born and raised in France and came to the United States shortly after World War I to care for her brother, Michel, who was in ill health. She met and married a sheepherder, Dominique Laxalt, also of the Basque provinces of the Pyrenees.

Both became naturalized citizens. He came a sheep raiser, but in the livestock depression of the 1920's he lost his fortune.

For several years Theresa accompanied her husband while he worked as herder and ranch hand in Nevada and Northern California. Then they moved to Carson City where they undertook a small hotel-restaurant business. Dominique again became a sheep raiser and was away much of the time. Theresa had almost sole responsibility for the hotel. She worked long hours of hard work every day of the week, but the soft voiced Basque woman had dream for the future, and in that small plump body, a will of iron that would make that dream come true.

Her dream was that somehow they could give to all their children a college education; that they might earn their livelihoods with their minds rather than their hands—a dream that they would grow to manhood and womanhood as fine examples of the opportunities for successful careers that America gives those who are willing to work and make the sacrifices necessary.

Friends write that Dominique was bewildered by the insistance of his small, stubborn wife that their children should have college educations, but Theresa prevailed and the time came when Paul, the eldest was enrolled in law school. Following university graduation John and Peter also became lawyers, Robert an author, Marie a school teacher, and Suzanne became a nun in the Holy Family Order. Paul was further to bring honor to his family name as he served as Governor of the state and now represents Nevada in the United States Senate.

It has been said by townspeople and neighbors that Theresa exemplifies to a rare degree the qualities of courage, cheerfulness, patience, affection, understanding and genuine home-making ability; She was always kindly in word and deed, and that this characteristic has been well instilled into the lives of her children; She knew how to raise children. What more can a mother be? Unselfish enough to give up all worldly satisfactions for her children, brave enough to face adversity, capable enough to operate a business in order to provide for her family, and determined enough to instill honesty, ambition, love of family and the love of God into each of them.

MINNIE NICHOLS BLAIR

Born 1886

Minnie Nichols Blair arrived in Nevada as a bride of Ernest W. Blair, a banker of Goldfield. They lived there nine years and then in Tonopah at the time of the "Divide Boom." Following the decline of the camp they moved to Fallon in 1924 where they bought a farm although he continued his banking career. The Farm 'was named the "Atlasta Ranch."

Minnie began raising poultry, at first on a small scale. Finally, her work made the distribution of Fallon turkeys an important business. The Fallon birds were shipped all over the country, and the marketability, fine quality, excellent flavor made Fallon, Nevada, and the Atlasta Ranch significant factors in the state's economy. At the same time Minnie supervised a truck garden and eight hundred laying chickens.

When Minnie retired from the poultry business she could have rested; she did not. Realizing there was a need for a restaurant serving well-prepared economical meals in Fallon, she opened a coffee shop, and with other family members started to serve her own food creations. This led to a new interest, and it was only a short time until Helen Blair Millward

(Minnie's daughter) became known as the "sandwich queen" and had received a national award "Atlasta Good Beef Sandwich."

Minnie's careers are only part of her story. She was always extremely active in civic, charitable and political affairs in every community where she lived. These activities gained her the widest possible acquaintance over her adopted state. At more than 80 years she was still supervising the restaurant in Fallon, and she was named Distinguished Nevadan by the University of Nevada in 1967. Minnie was a cooperative and enthusiastic memoirist for the Oral History Project of the Center for Western North American Studies. Her memoirs are in the special collections at the Universities and contain her reminiscenses about her early days in California and accounts of social, economic, and political affairs of Goldfield and Tonopah; and descriptions of ranch work and other activities in Fallon.

She tells of being a Pen Pal for a fourth grade class in Ohio. Minnie sent postcards of Nevada, magazines and rocks and minerals to them. She wrote to each member individually and still corresponded with three of them while in her 80's. Minnie had three children, Helen, Seward James and Ernest William, Jr.

MARY HILL FULSTONE, M.D.
Born 1892

Mary Hill Fulstone was born in Eureka, Nevada. She moved with her parents to Carson City while still a child. She attended schools in Carson City, graduating with honors from Carson High School.

Intending to study mathematics, she enrolled in the University of California. There, she became interested in medicine and changed her goals. Dr. Fulstone graduated from the University of California Medical School in 1918, one of four women in the class. She interned at Women's and Children's Hospital in San Francisco.

Dr. Fulstone married Fred M. Fulstone the year she finished her medical education and moved with him to Smith Valley, Nevada, where the Fulstones had large ranch holdings. She opened her medical practice in the ranch home, and worked there for several years while at the same time bearing five children and supervising the usual ranch-house activities. The children occasionally assisted in the doctor's office.

As her practice widened, Dr. Fulstone came to be known affectionately to the Smith Valley-

Yerington community as "Dr. Mary." Dr. Mary has officiated at births, deaths, surgical operations, and literally thousands of other medical incidents; she is now (1975) the longest-practicing physician in the state of Nevada. Dr. Mary has probably delivered 4,000 babies in the 55 years she has been a "country doctor."

Because she was acutely aware of the need for improved medical facilities in Lyon County, she spurred the building of the Lyon County Medical Center, and later its upgrading to a certified hospital. In recognition of this effort, the most recent addition to the hospital has been named the "Dr. Mary Wing."

Dr. Mary has not been narrowly devoted to her profession. She served for many years on the Lyon County School Board, and was a forceful advocate for consolidation of the school districts in the area—and effort that improved the quality of education for all children in Lyon County. She has given the same energy to long service on the State Board of Education, where she has been continuously serving for more than ten years.

The Fulstones' three sons entered ranching and allied fields in western Nevada; the daughters, Eleanor and Jeanne (remembered as Nevada's "Toni Twins") operate the Heavenly Valley ski facility at Lake Tahoe—with their husbands as partners.

Dr. Mary's work has received wide recognition. She was Nevada's Mother of the Year in 1950, Nevada's Doctor of the Year in 1961, and was named a Distinguished Nevadan by the University of Nevada in 1964. She is a member of state and county medical societies, and active in civic and educational organizations of Smith Valley and Yerington.

At the age of 83, Dr. Mary Fulstone maintains an active practice. She continued to see patients even when she was herself confined to a hospital bed after surgery. As one of only two doctors resident in her county, she declares that she will probably "practice until I die." The people of Lyon County have reason to hope that her practice continues for many years to come.

MARY AGNES PROWSE ELDRIDGE
Born 1896

"CAN-DO," the pioneer spirit, essence of the American philosophy that won the West and built our society, is still alive and well in Mary Prowse Eldridge. At seventy-nine she is a five-foot, two-inch bundle of energy and zest for living.

An outline of her adult life reads like a western novel, wih a traditional cast of characters, setting, and challenges: a "schoolteacher," a "cowboy," a "homestead," "drought," "hard times," and winning through. . . ."

Her childhood reveals a widowed mother who worked as a tailoress-seamstress to send her daughter through teachers' college—Los Angeles State Normal School.

She came to eastern Nevada in September of 1917, a petite, auburn-haired, newly-graduated schoolteacher; on the Nevada Northern Railway. At Ely she boarded the Osceola-Baker Stage for the journey to the Blackhorse School and her home with its Trustees, Mr. & Mrs. David Eldrige, of English birth.

Her new school was a log cabin. Within two years, she had married the eldest son of the family, her beloved husband George. In addition she had mastered numerous frontier arts and skills: horseback riding, gardening, bottling fruit and vegetables, driving a team, making soap, baking bread, and doing without the amenities of city life. In addition she learned how to milk a cow; although she later advised her daughters to never admit they could, unless they wanted that task assigned to them regularly!

They enjoyed country-style fun; all-night dances in the schoolhouse, fishing trips with everyone packed in the wagon, then cooking their catch over an evening campfire.

She taught school for twenty years, supplementing their ranch income, making it possible for her husband to invest in good livestock and assisting him in meeting the expenses of a growing business. She bore and reared two daughters and a son. Both daughters became school-teachers, married ranchers, and achieved and sustained active community leadership. Her son and his sons remained on the family holdings and pursued the career of cattle ranching with outstanding success.

She continued to share administration of the ranching business; and in spite of a total hip-replacement surgery and cataract removal, she became a volunteer tutor of handicapped children in the community under the RSVP Program. She served on a White Pine County Grand Jury; was named Teacher of the Year in 1969; and Bicentennial Woman of the Year in 1975, with this salutation:

"Indeed, Mary Agnes Eldridge, rancher and teacher, community-serving citizen . . . is a true Bi-Centennial Woman; with respect for, and roots in, the past;—but with face always to the future, and an indominitable zest for participation in the mainstream of life!"

NEW HAMPSHIRE

New Hampshire

Nickname: The Granite State

State Flower: Purple lilac

State Tree: White Birch

State Bird: Purple Finch

Photos

1. Waterville Valley
2. The Old man of the Mountain, Franconia
3. Cog Railroad (White Mountains)
4. Cathedral of the Pines, Rindge
5. Loon Mountain's gondola line
6. Rocky Gorge, Kancamagus Highway
7. N.H. Maine Memorial at Hampton Beach

Committee Members

Co-Chairman—Mrs. Rhea Guild, Gilford
Co-Chairman—Mrs. Elva O. McIntyre, Laconia
Dr. & Mrs. J. Duane Squires, Honorary Members
Alice C. Hanbrick
Meg Geraghty
Betty Trask
Marge Lachance
Caroline P. Stevens
Beatrix Solomon
Phyllis Marriott
Esther Weeks
Fred A. Tilton, Jr.
New Hampshire Historical Society
Laurie Steinsieck

New Hampshire

HANNAH EMERSON DUSTIN
Haverhill, MA   Born 1657

In the days of New Hampshire's early history, women were important yet few acquired fame. The first heroine in the State was Hannah Duston (the early spelling of the name), famous throughout the nation because she possessed courage to kill ten Indians to save her life.

Hannah was born in Haverhill, Massachusetts, in 1657, the daughter of Michael and Hannah Webster Emerson, and lived there until she married Thomas Duston on December 3, 1677.

Thomas and Hannah built a home on the bank of Sawmill Brook, later called Little River. There he started the first brick yard in that town.

They had seven children. On the morning of March 15, 1697, while Hannah was recovering seven days after baby Martha was born, Indians approached the home. Hannah urged Thomas to save the children. He told them to run into the woods toward the garrison house of Onesiphorus Marsh near the bank of the Merrimack River as he mounted his horse to fight the Indians.

The Indians killed the baby and captured Mrs. Duston and Mrs. Mary Neff, her nurse. They were compelled to leave the house which was immediately pillaged. Even though the March wind was cold and the river at flood stage, the Indians, with their captives, paddled up the stream to an island at Penacook, New Hampshire. It is related that, while in camp, Hannah cooked a soup that the Indians consumed heartily and then fell asleep. It is believed that Hannah added to the soup the roots of a plant possessing a sleep-inducing drug.

When the Indians were fast asleep, Hannah and a captive boy killed ten of them with tomahawks, took their scalps, and fled down the river in a canoe to safety in Haverhill, Massachusetts.

Thomas Duston had built a brick home not far from the original home and had taken his seven children there to dwell. Hannah, having returned to safety, joined them and resided there until her husband's death in 1732.

Among the relics of the Dustin Family, displayed in the Museum of the Haverhill Historical Society, is a large piece of white linen, possibly torn from Hannah's petticoat, in which she wrapped the ten scalps to prove that she and teenage Samuel Lennards had in fact killed the Indians.

In Penacook, New Hampshire, a monument stands to honor Hannah Dustin, Woman of Courage. Her remarkable story is shared by both New Hampshire and Haverhill, Massachusetts, where another monument stands, the first in America to be erected to a woman.

MARY BUTLER EASTMAN

Mary Butler Eastman, for whom the Daughters of the American Revolution Chapter is named, was the wife of Lieutenant Ebenezer Eastman, and lived in Gilmanton, New Hampshire, which is now Belmont.

In 1775 Gilmanton, as such, was a struggling frontier of civilization. Life was hard and the people were hardy and independent and imbued with the revolutionary spirit.

Hearing the news of the Battle of Lexington, Lieutenant Ebenezer Eastman, as the leader of a dozen men, left his work in the fields and started for Boston. The women and older men were left to carry on and care for the children.

Lieutenant Eastman and his group reached Charlestown, Massachusetts, in time to help throw up entrenchments at Bunker Hill. They were under the command of Colonel John Stark.

At home in Gilmanton, the remaining men, women and children experienced the hardship of taxation and the depreciation of the Continental currency.

Mary Butler was anxious about the welfare of her husband, Lieutenant Eastman. It was at public worship that the news of the Battle of Bunker Hill was received and she learned that her husband had been slain.

Frantic with grief, she left the meetinghouse and made hasty preparations to leave for Boston. With no real road on which to travel, and on horseback, Mary with her infant in her arms found her way to her father's home in Brentwood forty miles away. There the news of the battle was confirmed, but not the fate of her husband.

Leaving her infant child with a friend, she rode on to Charlestown where she found her husband safe. Her son, Caleb, was also fighting at Bunker Hill with his father, and he too was safe. It was at a later battle in Vermont that Caleb was killed.

In 1837 Mary had survived her beloved husband by forty years. Her gravestone inscription reads, "Mary Eastman, Widow of Lieutenant Eastman."

SUZANNA WILLARD JOHNSON
Born 1730

If you have ever visited Old Fort #4 at Charlestown, New Hampshire, you will be able to picture the following story of Suzanna Johnson, wife of Captain James Johnson.

Captain Johnson and his family lived in a log house at the north end of the river, north of Old Fort #4. At the time of our story, Suzanna was twenty-four years old with three children and was expecting her fourth child.

The settlers of this village became very uneasy over reports of Indians bent upon destruction, but since there were no noticeable signs of trouble, they went about their affairs as usual—farming, hunting, and the usual daily tasks. Although a farming district, Charlestown was within the march of the Colonial Troops, who were pushing back and forth to Canada. It had more the appearance of a military camp than a peaceful farming village by the Connecticut River.

Early on an August morning in 1754, Peter Labaree had come to begin work as a carpenter at the Johnson home. Captain Johnson slipped on his jacket and trousers to let him in, when a terrifying sight greeted him. Indians were outside everywhere. They pushed Labaree into the house. Some of the Johnsons were bound. Suzanna and her three children were left naked. The Indians stole three gowns and gave one of them to Suzanna. At this point they were all ordered on the fearful march to Canada.

As the Indians set the house on fire, an alarm was sounded. In the confusion the group was pushed along by the savages, and Suzanna without shoes and feet bleeding was forced on in this condition. After a march of three miles, the party stopped for breakfast. A riderless horse approached the party but was not shot because Captain Johnson, through sign language, requested its use for his wife.

After a march of seven more miles they reached the river. Before crossing the river, a raft was made for Mrs. Johnson, while the Captain swam in back to push it across. The encampment that night was under the majestic Mt. Ascutney. All captives were bound so as to make any escape impossible.

The captives were aroused at sunrise, and after a watery and tasteless breakfast of hot gruel, the march was renewed. About two hours later Suzanna felt the beginning pangs of childbirth. A brush shelter was made for her and there her baby girl was born. There was joy! Two captives instead of one to sell!

The remainder of that day she was permitted to rest. A litter was made on which to carry the new mother, but the prisoners, having only weak gruel for food, had limited strength and could carry her only for two hours. After a brief rest she was ordered to mount the horse or be left behind.

The next day dragged on with pangs of hunger besieging them. Suzanna's horse was killed and the Indians had a feast. A broth was made for the baby.

Now Suzanna must walk. She was almost hit by a hatchet when she fell during the march. She was saved, however, to continue on this horrendous march. Falling into a beaver pond she nearly lost her baby, only saving her by catching the corner of her blanket. The cruel trek ended at Crown Point, New York, where canoes were provided.

From there, their destination was to St. John's Fort, an arduous journey of four days. Suzanna and the baby were then adopted by the son-in-law of the grand Sachem. The rest of the family were taken to Montreal and sold.

Mrs. Johnson's captivity lasted for four years. She and her baby were sold to a Montreal family. Captain Johnson had been a prisoner and broke his parole, both he and his wife were put in prison.

When Montreal surrendered, Captain Johnson was ransomed and the following summer he joined the forces at Fort Ticonderoga, New York, where he was killed in action.

In 1759 Suzanna came back to Charlestown, returning with the Willards, her parents, who had been captives in Montreal. Suzanna's children, having accepted the culture of their adopted homes, did not even know their mother upon meeting her again.

Here in Charlestown, Suzanna resumed her life. Three years later she married John Hastings and reared a second family, making her the mother of fourteen children in all. She died at the age of eighty leaving thirty-nine grandchildren.

ELSIE CILLEY

"That tea you never shall drink," cried Elsie Cilley and her daughter, Abigail.

For the story behind these words one must turn back to the period of the New Hampshire Land Grant, which was, at that time, a territory in New England, larger in size than some of the principalities of Europe. Elsie Cilley's husband, Captain Joseph Cilley, was the agent for these properties.

Elsie Cilley had the distinction of being the mother of two Revolutionary War soldiers and also the grandmother of two Revolutionary War soldiers. One of her sons, Joseph Cilley, admitted in a letter that he assisted in securing the powder and cannon, etc., that were taken from Fort William and Mary, and in transporting a part of both to Nottingham, where they were stored in a barn for the use of Revolutionary soldiers in New Hampshire.

At the time of the Revolution, Elsie was living with her daughter, Abigail Butler, at Butler's Tavern in Nottingham, New Hampshire. They were both adamant against the tea tax, and often remarked that they were not going to the East Indies for any part of their breakfasts.

One evening, as preparations were being made for dinner, several men arrived at the tavern via horseback. They were warming themselves by the fire, when one said, "I have a packet of tea in my coat-tail pocket, and we will have a cup before we leave. Just then, mother and daughter brought in dinner on a large platter. Upon hearing these words, Elsie's daughter seized the carving knife from the platter, and cut off the man's coat-tails and threw them into the fire saying, "No Tory shall drink tea in my house."

There is an eight stanza poem called "A Tale of Nottingham" about the cutting of the coat-tail. The last stanza is as follows:

> Then quickly she darted forward,
> Her plate of meat she let fall
> And with one deft stroke of the carver,
> Cut coat-tails, pocket and all.
> Then threw them into the blazing fire,
> Before he had time to think
> While she said in a voice triumphant,
> "That tea you never shall drink."

Elsie Cilley lived to be ninety-nine years old. The year before her death, she rode to Pautuckaway Mountain on horseback to design a floral pattern on a quilt for her granddaughter. One is very fortunate to have a quilt or quilt pattern of this patriotic woman.

ELIZABETH PAGE STARK
Dunbarton   **Born 1736**

"Live Free or Die" were historic words uttered in 1809 by the famed husband of Molly Stark, Major General John Stark. In 1945 this motto became the official motto of the State of New Hampshire.

Elizabeth, nicknamed Molly, was the fifth child of Captain Caleb and Elizabeth Merrill Page, born at Dunbarton, New Hampshire, on February 16, 1736.

This section of New Hampshire was still being invaded by Indians, and Molly spent many hours standing sentinel at her father's fort as a look-out for Indians.

The romance of Molly and John Stark was a courtship of a few hours together. There was a time when John was captured by Indians and carried to Canada. Upon his return, February 20, 1758, Major General Stark rode horseback to Molly's home, and not dismounting said; "If you

are ever going to become my wife, Molly, you will have to come with me now." She did not hesitate.

Her first child was Caleb, named after her father. In all, Molly and the General had eleven children.

There are many stories told about Molly. One is that as she and several of her children were dressing one morning, she heard her dogs making an unusual commotion in the woods. Hurrying downstairs she got her gun, climbed a hill and found the dogs had treed a bear. She shot the bear and then sent her sons to get a horse to haul the dead animal home.

During the first part of the Revolutionary War and the occupancy of General Stark at Dorchester Heights, Massachusetts, Molly was directed by her husband to mount guard over West Boston. If General Stark's landing of his troops was opposed, she was to ride into the country to spread the alarm. This was not necessary.

At Bennington, Vermont, in 1777, the famous quote was uttered by General Stark, "There are your enemies, the Red Coats and the Tories. We must beat them tonight or Molly Stark sleeps a widow."

While the General fought at Fort Ticonderoga, New York, a small-pox epidemic plagued the soldiers. Molly sent word to bring the soldiers to her New Hampshire home, which she converted into a hospital. She was nurse and doctor. Not a single case was lost among the twenty patients.

The duties at home were tremendous during the war years. Molly, whose face and deep blue eyes showed great decision, was never at a loss to do her various tasks. She was always able to handle her problems, even when Caleb ran away to join his father at Bunker Hill. Caleb was then the youngest soldier.

The General and Molly were married fifty-six years when Molly, at the age of seventy-eight, died in 1814. The General sat with his head lowered, too weak to follow the procession. He tottered to his room saying, "Goodby, Molly, we sup no more on earth together."

The spirit of Molly Stark lives on in the Molly Stark Daughters of the American Revolution Chapter of Manchester, New Hampshire, organized in 1894; the Molly Stark Hospital in Canton, Ohio, established in the early 1800's; and the Molly Stark Trail from Brattleboro to Bennington, Vermont, as well as in the hearts of her many proud descendants.

DOLLY EMERY COPP

There's far more to the legend of Dolly Copp than a sign hanging over a campground in the White Mountains . . . more, too, than the now-famous golden wedding anniversary story.

Before the fateful day in 1881 when, after fifty years of marriage to Hayes Dodifer Copp, Dolly announced, "Hayes is well enough. But fifty years is long enough for a woman to live with any man", theirs was a story of love and striving in pioneer America.

About 1827 Hayes Copp took off in search of gold in the White Mountains. He found not gold but a savage wilderness . . . one calling for back-breaking labor of felling trees, clearing rubble, and tilling the "black" soil to reap a harvest.

Four years later he returned to Bartlett, New Hampshire to claim Dolly Emery as his bride on November 3, 1831.

Dolly, who has been described as "small in stature, with flaxen hair and light blue eyes that had a flash of keenness . . . and possessed too, with a very glib tongue", joined her husband on a wedding journey back up into the mountains. A sled-type "bridal car" carried their meager possessions and Dolly rode aback a sturdy horse as they headed up to that one-room log cabin Hayes had "rolled-up" near the river in the forest lands of Martin's Location.

There they lived neighborless for some time . . . fighting the bears away from young lambs, the wolves from young cattle, the foxes, raccoons, bobcats and skunks from the poultry and the deer from the ripening grain. The winters were long and intense, the snow was deep and drifting . . . and the summers all too short. But the invincible Copps enlarged their clearing each year and reaped a more ample harvest each fall . . . and the log cabin gave way to a long frame house connected to a roomy barn.

Dolly's energy kept pace with their progress . . . and her daily duties would send today's homemaker into a state of shock.

In the spring, she "set the hens" and raised broods of chickens . . . she helped Hayes shear the sheep, washed and carded the wool and spun it on her loom into cloth or knit it up into socks. In the fall she made hundreds of "tallow dips" and in the spring, the year's supply of soap. By the light of the tallow dips, she knitted and darned or made and mended clothes for the whole family.

Those rows of gnarled decaying trunks on the old Copp farm today were once the proud apple orchard Dolly planted after searching through the woods and along the river bank for the "Johnny Apple Seed" trees that grew everywhere. With constant care and cultivation, the "wildings" responded with yearly harvests of many varieties of apples.

A few years later when the state of New Hampshire contracted with Daniel Pinkham to build a graded wagon road from Jackson to Randolph, the Copp home became a "sort of tavern", although an unlicensed one. Dolly's good food and comfortable beds became famous and the price was right, 25 cents across the board . . . 25 cents for a meal, 25 cents for a bed and 25 cents for feed and care of a horse.

It was then people learned that underneath Dolly's work-roughened exterior lived a woman's love for the refined and beautiful. Her table was laid on a snowy fringed linen cloth, made from flax she had raised, pulled, heckled, spun and woven and set with a silver tea service and delicately ornamented gilt-banded china.

The heavy wooden cradle, painted red and draped with a hand-woven pale blue coverlet, stood as a monument to her motherhood. In it, she rocked four babies . . . Jeremiah, Nathaniel, Sylvia, and Daniel. She raised them through all the trials of pioneer motherhood . . . through poverty and disappointments . . . through joy and love.

As her family grew and life became more prosperous, Dolly's ambition, too, prospered. She realized with the erection of the first of the Glen Houses that "city folks" would be coming her way to see the mountain tops.

Her fame for handicrafts grew . . . nobody wove as many bolts of woolen homespun nor so many yards of linen . . . nobody could match her dyes . . . nor rival her butter, rich cheese, her full-bodied maple syrup or her famous apple butter. She continued to cook, entertain guests and sew gifts . . . and those skillful and eager hands were filled with "tourist" money. Visitors stopped by the Copp Farm for "the only perfect view" of the satanic granite profile, which became popularly known as "Dolly Copp's Imp" . . . and to chat with Dolly and her now-famous family.

Her family grew . . . and eventually the children married and left home. Hayes and Dolly had reached the stage in life where comforts were theirs and it seemed time to quit and enjoy life. Hayes would not leave the mountain he loved . . . so on their fiftieth anniversary date, Dolly made her famous announcement ". . . fifty years is long enough for a woman to live with any man" and they divided their savings of a lifetime and parted with neither ill-will nor argument.

Hayes stayed on the farm until life alone became unbearable and then he returned to his native Stowe, Maine. Dolly spent the rest of her days at the home of her daughter, Mrs. Sylvia Copp Potter in Auburn, Maine . . . but her spirit still lives in the majestic mountains and her memory is immortalized in the now-famous Dolly Copp Campground in the White Mountain National Forest.

JANE MEANS APPLETON PIERCE
Hampton   **Born 1806**

Jane Pierce's quote: "Oh! How I wish he was out of politics", was constantly made during Franklin Pierce's serving as United States Congressman, United States Senator, and finally as President of the United States.

Most women would have been thrilled to stand beside a husband who served his country in such honored roles; but Jane was frail, shy, and did not care about Washington, D. C.

She was torn between her dislike of Washington or being separated from her husband. Their separations were numerous and painful to her. She longed to be with her husband in New Hampshire.

Jane Means Appleton Pierce was born in 1806 at Hampton, New Hampshire, the daughter of Dr. Jessie Appleton, President of Bowdoin Col-

lege. In 1834 she was married to Franklin Pierce.

Let us picture Jane Pierce, frail and shy, a devout South Congregational Church attendant at Concord, New Hampshire; not interested in politics, but intensely devoted to her husband. She had to choose to be with him in spite of his duties in Washington, D. C. or be separated from him because of these duties.

Jane was the wife of the New Hampshire Democratic Party head—a man who was consumed with the burning issues of temperance, slavery, and railroads. She was the wife of a man whose friends were the famous Hawthorne, Longfellow, Jefferson Davis and other outstanding political colleagues. She could not bear the tiresome journeys to Washington, D. C. by coach over rough roads, nor the heat and discomfort of living in the city during the summer months. Living in Washington also meant living in boarding houses until she became First Lady.

Jane fainted away when her husband told her he had been nominated by the Democrats to run for the Presidency.

As to Jane's family life, in spite of her physical frailty she bore three sons; two died early, but her son Bennie lived to see his father nominated for President. Early in January 1853, when the family was returning to Concord, New Hampshire by train, a railroad accident took his life—their third and only living son.

Regardless of the tragedy in her life, Mrs. Pierce assumed all of her duties at the White House, and while she consistently shrank from any public attention, she nevertheless attended receptions and presided at State and private dinners as the occasions arose.

At the end of President Pierce's term of office, the United States was in a prosperous state and looked to a magnificent industrial, agricultural and financial future, but he was not renominated. It was with a great sigh of relief that Jane Pierce left Washington.

The last five years of Jane's life were spent traveling in Europe. Her family hoped that her health would improve but it did not, and she died in 1863 at Andover, Massachusetts.

Jane Means Appleton Pierce may be the only New Hampshire woman to have the honor of being the First Lady of the land. One wishes she had desired this high position or, at least, that she had been happy in it; but we admire and praise her for resolutely accepting and performing her duties to the extent her health permitted.

MARY BAKER EDDY
Bow   Born 1821

To Mary Baker Eddy, born in Bow, New Hampshire, on July 16, 1821, is to be credited the achievement of founding an entirely new religious denomination in our country. This faith is known as Christian Science. Its rise and growth are a remarkable tribute to the unusual woman who began it.

Mary Baker was the youngest of six children. When she was fifteen years of age, her parents moved their family to the town of Tilton, New Hampshire. Here in Tilton, in 1843, when she was twenty-one years old, she was married to George Washington Glover. Her husband died of yellow fever less than a year after their mar-

riage. Three months after his disease their son George was born. Mrs. Glover was so ill that the child was sent to live with his aunt.

During a long period of recuperation, she busied herself with the writing of poetry, much of which was published in New Hampshire newspapers. In 1853 she married for the second time; her husband was a dentist named Dr. Daniel Patterson. In 1861 her son, George, now seventeen years old, enlisted in the Union Army. About the same time, Dr. Patterson went to the fighting front in Virginia to observe military operations there, and was captured by the Confederate Army.

Stricken by all her anxieties, Mrs. Patterson had a prolonged physical relapse, from which she emerged slowly. Upon his release from Confederate custody, Dr. Patterson resumed his dental practice in Lynn, Massachusetts. In February, 1866, following a fall on ice, Mrs. Patterson healed herself by prayer. Out of this experience was born what later became known as Christian Science. In thinking about this recovery, she came firmly to believe that henceforth she would research the Scriptures for insight into the laws of healing as evidenced by the works of Jesus and the Old Testament prophets.

In October, 1873, she divorced Dr. Patterson. Two years later her famous book, *Science and Health*, was first published. It was destined to pass through scores of editions and to be read widely all over the world. In January, 1877, she married for the third time. Her new husband was one of her most loyal followers named Asa Gilbert Eddy. Mr. Eddy died in 1882, and so once again Mary became a widow. In her 1910 edition of *Science and Health*, the author for the first time used the name Mary Baker Eddy, by which she will best be remembered.

The Church of Christ Scientist was formally organized in 1879, and in 1892 the Mother Church in Boston, Massachusetts, was begun. This beautiful building was dedicated on December 30, 1894. In 1908 Mrs. Eddy founded *The Christian Science Monitor*, which has since become one of the most respected newspapers in the United States. Mrs. Eddy's last two years were spent in Chestnut Hill, near Boston. Following her death she was buried in Mount Auburn Cemetery in Cambridge, Massachusetts. Today Mary Baker Eddy is remembered and admired by thousands of people all over the world. Her deep religious convictions as to the power of spiritual healing have brought comfort to multitudes of men and women.

CELIA LAIGHTON THAXTER
Portsmouth   Born 1835

As summer came into its own on June 29, 1835, a baby girl was born to Mr. and Mrs. Thomas B. Laighton in Portsmouth, New Hampshire. They named her Celia—from the Latin, meaning radiant. When Celia was four years old, her father became offended with some of his associates in state politics, and retired to the barren and isolated White Island, one of the Isles of Shoals, ten miles off the coast of Portsmouth. For about ten years he was the keeper of the White Island lighthouse. It was here that this wilderness and beauty of sea, wind, and sky were so impressed upon the mind of his daughter that they became forever part of the very life of Celia Laighton. Bound together with gentle ties, a very close family relationship of mutual dependence developed, due mainly to their isolation. Celia's later love for husband and sons proved as strong as her devotion to her father and mother. All through her short life, if ever family loyalty was divided, allegiance to her parents was the more important.

When her father left the lighthouse, he started a summer hotel on Hog Island, but changed the name to Appledore Island. In the course of the next few decades, the Laighton family entertained a wide variety of notable people, including many authors and artists. At an early age, Celia showed a gift for poetry. Her girlhood was spent in marine surroundings

which coloured the best of the verse she afterwards wrote.

In 1851, at the age of sixteen, Celia married a Boston lawyer by the name of Levi Lincoln Thaxter, who was a devoted student of Robert Browning. They had met for the first time when he came to Appledore to tutor the Laighton children. He was eleven years older than Celia. She and her husband spent part of their time in Boston, Massachusetts, but summers were always spent on Appledore Island where they became the center of a little art colony of their own.

Celia and Levi were soon to have three sons, Karl, John and Roland. When Roland, the youngest, was two years old, Celia's first published poem appeared in the *Atlantic Monthly*. It was called "Landlocked", and expressed homesickness for the sea she loved so much. She was a regional writer, describing the mood and color of the land and the sea she knew, and capturing the spirit of her surroundings. Her poems, mainly in lyrical form, deal with the beacon light, the sea storm, the glint of sails, the sandpiper, the flowers among the rocks in characteristic and sympathetic fidelity. One of the most popular was a poem called "The Sandpiper", about a bird common on the islands. It starts as follows:

> Across the narrow beach we flit,
>   One little sandpiper and I,
> And fast I gather, bit by bit
>   The scattered driftwood bleached and
>   dry.
> The wild waves reach their hands for it,
>   The wild wind raves, the tide runs high,
> As up and down the beach we flit,—
>   One little sandpiper and I.

Celia's son Roland shared with her a love of nature, the sea, and the islands. Celia lived to see him become a well-known cryptogramic botanist, and Professor of Botany at Harvard University in 1891.

At the age of fifty-eight Celia's book of floraculture, "An Island Garden", was published. A few months later, on August 25, 1894, Celia died on Appledore Island amid the surroundings that were so dear to her. The memory of Celia Thaxter still lives on her beloved islands.

Reference: "Sandpiper—The Life and Letters of Celia Thaxter"—written and compiled by Rosamund Thaxter.

SARAH JOSEPHA BUELL HALE
Newport   Born 1788

Can one believe that the supposed author of "Mary Had a Little Lamb" could be a mother who was to play such an instrumental part in shaping the lives of our present day mothers?

In Newport, New Hampshire there is an historical marker dedicated to Sarah Josepha Buell Hale, honoring her for her accomplishments.

A cornerstone for the Bunker Hill Monument was laid in 1825, and though there was much enthusiasm at the time, it did not succeed in raising money for the work yet to be done. Five years later, without funds, the monument was an unfinished eyesore, and almost torn down. Sarah Josepha Hale came to the rescue.

Sarah's father had been an officer in the Revolutionary War, so she asked the gentlemen of the Monument Committee to help raise money for this project. Newspapers throughout the country ridiculed her idea because men had failed in this rather arduous task, how could a woman succeed!

In her first appeal, Sarah raised $3,000. She then sold knitted articles, quilts, beadwork, embroidery, pickles, jams, etc. at a huge bazaar lasting seven days.

The monument, at long last, was finished. When Daniel Webster delivered his second Bunker Hill address he gave little recognition to the ladies' efforts. However, Sarah was not concerned because since her birth in 1788, outside of Newport, New Hampshire, there were few cultural advantages for boys and none at all for girls. Recognition was never expected.

Gordon and Sarah Whittlesey Buell were the parents of this remarkable girl. Sarah was blessed with an intelligent mother who saw to it that her daughter learned Latin, higher mathematics, and mental philosophy. These accomplishments she later put to use by opening a school for girls.

Meanwhile a rising young lawyer, David Hale, moved to Newport. In 1813 Sarah married David. The young lawyer did very well and provided a fine house and a servant to help Sarah with the housework and the care of their two sons.

During her third pregnancy, it was discovered that Sarah had the dreaded disease tuberculosis, which had caused the death of her younger sister.

That autumn David took Sarah in his arms and said, "You are not going to die, I won't let you."

The children were left in Aunt Hannah's care for six weeks while David and Sarah journeyed through the New Hampshire hills. And although the doctor warned them that Sarah would not come back alive, she did—cured by fresh air, wild grapes, and love. Regardless of the cost, grapes were always kept on her table.

The year 1822 was indeed a sad one. David died of pneumonia, and his fifth child was born to Sarah two weeks later. She was shattered by his death, being deprived of his companionship and having five children under ten years of age to care and provide for.

David's Masonic brothers set up Sarah and her sister in the millinery business. Sarah, however, thought of something better—writing a successful novel called "Northwood." Less than a month later in 1827, she was offered the editorship of "Ladies' Magazine," the first magazine published exclusively for women.

At the age of forty, Sarah moved her family to Boston, Massachusetts, and began a career as one of the great editors of the 19th Century. This magazine later joined forces with "Godey's Ladies' Book." Sarah served as the editor until 1877.

What a beautiful and complete woman was Sarah! Through her efforts came reforms and goals, child labor laws, property rights for married women, higher education for women, public health and sanitation codes, playgrounds for children and day nurseries for working mothers. How many of us realize that our celebrating Thanksgiving Day had its origin with Sarah Josepha Hale's prevailing upon President Abraham Lincoln, in 1864, to proclaim Thanksgiving a national holiday—winning for Sarah the title "Mother of Thanksgiving."

New Jersey

T.M.

New Jersey

Nickname: Garden State

State Flower: Violet

State Tree: Red Oak

State Bird: Eastern goldfinch

Photos

1. Barnegat Light

Committee Members

Chairman—Mary Donaldson Haynie,
  Ventnor
Honorary Members
Margaret Mary Haynie Battell, Roselle Park
Jane Matz Driscoll, Collingswood
Brigitte Ruschen Graham, Tuckerton
Bernice Goldblum Goldberg, Ventnor
Margaret Kitchens Minnis, Folsom
Dolores Inemer Mooney, Pleasantville
Elizabeth McCann Pfund, Cresskill
Catherine Droboniku Quinlan, Bringantine
Christine Scavullo Vay, Montclair
Mrs. Jean Featherly Byrne, Princeton
Mrs. Elizabeth B. Myrtetus Cahill, Camden

Credit—Rebecca B. Colesar—N. J. State
  Library

MONUMENT COMMEMORATING THE BATTLE OF
CHESTNUT NECK, N.J. OCTOBER 6, 1778
ERECTED THROUGH THE EFFORTS OF THE GENERAL LAFAYETTE
DAUGHTERS OF THE AMERICAN REVOLUTION

New Jersey

HANNAH OGDEN CALDWELL
Born 1737

When Hannah Ogden Caldwell was ruthlessly and barbarously murdered in her own home by soldiers while protecting her children, the public clamour for revenge rose high. Her father, a Presbyterian minister in Elizabethtown, later served as Chaplain in the American Army and was admired by Washington. A price was set on his head and at times as he preached he had his loaded pistols by the side of his pulpit. Finally in retaliation, his church was burned to the ground in 1780. About this time British troops were advancing and Mr. Caldwell put some possessions and the older children in a baggage wagon and sent them to friends. Feeling that his wife and younger children were safe in the house, he left, but returned to try to persuade her to come with them. Yet he could not believe that a mother, with babies, would be harmed. As he sat on his horse, she brought him a cup of coffee. Seeing the soldiers coming, he took off to join the defense. She in turn, put some valuables in a bucket and lowered it in the well. She retired to her bedroom with her baby. Having nursed the baby and handed it to the nurse, they watched from the window. A lone soldier came up to the window and fired his gun—two bullets entered Mrs. Caldwells breast and she fell dead. The soldiers entered, cut open her dress and rifled her pockets, then destroyed by fire the house and its contents. LaFayette on his last visit to America informed members of the family that he had been with Mr. Caldwell that morning on a hill overlooking the town and with the aid of a spy-glass saw smoke rising but never dreamed that it could be his house. He was sadly wrong. A speaker in the Senate later said "Her children were baptized to piety and patriotism in their mother's blood."

Later another tragedy occurred when Mr. Caldwell, while under a flag of truce went to meet a lady arriving from New York. While handling her luggage, he also was shot dead by a man named Morgan. This man was later tried and executed. A monument stands as stark testimony to this double tragedy. Their children became noted citizens—the eldest son being taken by LaFayette to France—where he was educated and then returned to New York to become a noted editor.

MARGARET HILL MORRIS
Born 1737

One of 12 children, Margaret Hill grew up in Philadelphia and is famous for her "Journal" which contains a running story of the Pre-Revolutionary Days. In 1758 she married William Morris, Jr. a direct descendent who came with William Penn, who was a merchant. She was a dutiful wife, frugality being one of her many virtues. His untimely death in 1766 left her with 4 children (one posthumous) to care for. In time she purchased a house on the "Green Bank" in Burlington, N.J. in 1770. This house was the former residence of William Franklin, the illigitimate son of Benjamin Franklin and the last of the Royal Governors of New Jersey. In financial straits, Mrs. Morris opened a small shop to sell retail medicines. This venture did

not last long. Where physicians were scarce, she often acted as a doctress. Rumor has it she had 30 smallpox cases at one and same time. Later in Philadelphia she showed great courage in dealing with a yellow fever epidemic. She had 6 children including one pair of twins. Her "Journal" was first published in a limited number of 50 copies. It was republished several times—the latest in 1919 by the Friends Historical Society in Philadelphia. Her last years were spent in a sedan chair. A comment on her enlightened views can be observed in one of her written comments in answer to a letter received from a slave boy who worked for her deceased father relative to slavery—"I received as a gift of my dear deceased parent a negro boy; but, how inconsistent with true Christianity is the barbarous custom of keeping in slavery any one of our poor fellow creatures; it has ever been a burden to my mind the thoughts of it, and I have endeavored all in my power to make it an easy servitude—a slavery it shall never be—may the Almighty be graciously pleased to enlighten his mind as well as others. I was greatly affected (on the very day he arrived here) by a memorable sermon of H. Harris, on the duty of parents towards their children and mistresses towards their servants. I endeavour and hope I do discharge mine to those of my household. Lord! grant that they may not be hard-hearted, but that I may be able, with the assistance of thy good spirit, to teach them the way of truth."

LUCY STONE

Born 1818

New Jersey was a major battleground of the suffrage movement and contributed many leaders to its cause. There was one individual who stood out among all of the rest. She was Lucy Stone of Orange. As much as any other person, she helped to give the women of this country equal suffrage rights with men.

Born August 13, 1818 near West Brookfield, Massachusetts, Lucy was a fighter from the beginning. After her brothers were sent to college, she shocked her father by also expressing a desire to go. Upon hearing that he wouldn't give her any financial aid, she became determined to educate herself and proceeded to take various jobs in order to pay for her schooling. Finally in 1847 Lucy was graduated from Oberlin College.

Following her graduation Lucy immediately began to lecture for women's rights. For the next ten years she traveled across the nation, eventually settling in Orange, New Jersey, following her marriage to Henry R. Blackwell in 1857. Although she was a small woman, Lucy was absolutely fearless when debating the merits of women's suffrage. Even her opponents respected her great poise, and angry crowds would often listen to her after howling down every other speaker.

It took a great deal of courage to stand up before a street crowd, mostly male and openly hostile, and speak out for women's rights while being pelted with vegetables. But the suffragettes, determined women that they were, simply collected the vegetables and stood their ground.

By the mid-1860's the women's movement in New Jersey became large enough to be formally organized; so, in 1867, Lucy Stone began the New Jersey Women's Suffrage Association. Two years later in May of 1869, the National Women's Suffrage Association was started with the sole purpose of obtaining the ballot for women through constitutional amendment. A short time later the American Women's Suffrage Association was begun as a second front in the war to gain the vote, and Lucy Stone was named to head it.

Lucy set forth the idea that every woman, because she is a woman, was deprived of all political existence and reduced to the condition of a conquered subject. Taxed without representation and governed without consent, the women's plight was a blot on the sacred partnership of marriage. In order to balance out the unfair laws which governed women's participation in business and the opportunities to own land, Lucy felt that they must have suffrage rights.

After gaining widespread support, Lucy, along with Susan B. Anthony, another well-known suffragette, organized the second women's rights convention in 1850. Held in Worcester, Massachusetts, the meeting was attended by over 1,000 men and women, as opposed to the 1848 conference of only 200 patrons. While it was now obvious that the women's movement was making headway, it was also apparent that their suffrage goals would be difficult to attain.

MARGARET DAVIS FISHER WHITE

Born 1874

Wife of hotelman and former Atlantic City, N.J. mayor C.D. White, mother of sons Josiah and Fisher White and daughters, Bertha Nason, Esther Gilbert and Margaret Haylor. Mrs. White, an avid supporter of the nationally known Miss America Pageant in Atlantic City, was instrumental in organizing the volunteer hostess committee and served as Chairman for more than a decade. From 1928 to 1946 Mrs. White served the State of New Jersey on the volunteer Board of managers of an institution for the profoundley retarded in Woodbine. A cottage residence is dedicated to her memory.

Born in North Adams, Mass. in 1874, she came to the seashore resort with her husband shortly after he graduated from college to enter the hotel business. At the time of her death in 1951, she was an active member, too, in the Woman's Golf Association and a number of Garden Clubs on Absecon Island. Her two sons were associated with their father in the operation of the Marlborough-Blenheim Hotel in Atlantic City. All have been active community volunteers.

VIRGINIA WATSON REEVE
Elizabeth   **Born 1885**

Virginia Watson Reeve, born June 9, 1885, in Elizabeth, daughter of Egbert Perlet and Lillie Hayes Briant Watson. Reuben H. Reeve, Mrs.

Reeve's husband, was a son of Charles and Minnie Reeve. Mrs. Reeve organized in 1930 in Ocean County the Captain Joshua Huddy Chapter of Daughters of the American Revolution of Toms River and served as regent. A charter member of the Ocean County Historical Society and active in the Methodist Church, Mrs. Reeve, was a member of an old and distinguished family of the north of England, Sedgwick 1379.

Mr. and Mrs. Reeve became the parents of the following children:
Fred B., Born September 20, 1908
Evelyn Watson, Born December 27, 1912
Dorothy Virginia, Born April 6, 1914.

Virginia Watson Reeve's children were distinguished New Jersey citizens. Dorothy Virginia was a WAVE during World War 2. Lieutenant Reeve is a member of Pi Beta Phi and Phi Betta Kappa national fraternities, as well as many professional associations. She was at one time in 1953 the only female member of the bar in Ocean County.

ETTA R. SMALL GARRON
Indian Mills   **Born 1887**

Etta R. Small Garron was born in Indian Mills, Burlington County, New Jersey on November 5, 1887. She died on September 12, 1973. Funeral services were held in the United Methodist Church at Indian Mills to which she had membership for 73 years and interment was in Odd Fellows Cemetary at Medford, New Jersey.

One of two daughters of William and Annie Small and a descendent of the John Small family of Old Evesham Township of the 1700's. Etta had one sister, Sadie, who became a teacher. Etta chose to marry Edward M. Garron, who at that time was a tenant farmer. He later had his own farm and also worked on the Burlington County highway department until his death. The Garrons nad nine children. Mr. Garron died in 1954. At the time of her death she had fifteen grandchildren and thirteen great-grandchildren. Late in the 1930's she was approached to board a young boy whose father had died and whose mother was detained in the hospital. This child was the first of twenty-four foster children who have lived with Mrs. Garron. She was the first president of the Indian Mills Parent Teacher Association in 1924 and again in 1933-35. She was a life member of the PTA. In 1935 she painted her own car yellow and thus became Shamong township's first lady bus driver. From 1944 until her retirement in 1962 she drove a bus for the township Board of Education.

Mrs. Garron served as church organist for over fifty years, as well as directed the church choir.

BERTHA ANN STANLEY BUCK
Carmel   Born 1913

Bertha Ann Stanley Buck, fourth child of Bettie and Edward Stanley, was born in Mount Holly, New Jersey, November 4, 1913. She attended Howard High School, Wilmington, Delaware where she graduated with honors for scholastic achievement and exemplary citizenship. She was valedictiorian of her class.

Ann moved to Bridgeton and married William Buck on January 6, 1934. The family lived in Bridgeton for twenty-one years and had six children. In 1955 the Bucks purchased property in Carmel, New Jersey and moved to that community and became active members of the John Wesley Methodist Church. Ann joined the Carmel Volunteer Fire Company Ladies' Auxiliary and was an active member from 1955. All of her

children held responsible positions in their communities. A son, the Honorable Milton A. Buck is a judge in Newark, New Jersey. When her children reached college age, Mrs. Buck went to work at Ancora State Mental Hospital as a psychiatric aide.

MARGARET KITCHENS MINNIS
Born 1921

Mrs. Margaret Kitchens Minnis, was the only child born to Jake and Ruth Kitchens, 54 years ago (1921) in Savannah, Georgia. Her father died when she was fifteen months old. During her youth later in Philadelphia, she was active in community projects, church choir and was a Camp Fire Girl. After completing high school she was accepted at college but in her second year was taken ill and returned home. Her mother died in 1946. During a sad and lonely winter she met George Minnis and married him on November 30, 1946. The Minnis' have three sons: George III age 25; Carlton age 24, and Charles age 19. Margaret and her friend Annabelle Crutchfield were co-founders of the Margaret Ann Day Nursery in 1948, for youngsters between the age of 3-5 years old. Even then Mrs. Minnis recognized the need for services of this nature for working parents who had little or no money. Most of the working mothers at that time did domestic work. Margaret and Ann received no salary. After three years at the center and the birth of two sons, the Minnis family moved to Folsom, New Jersey, where the third son was born.

After moving to Folsom, Margaret discovered that there were no cultural or educational programs for minorities anywhere in the area. She organized a youth club for teenage girls and her husband became involved with programs for the boys. She organized the first Cub Scouts in the community and became a Den Mother. She volunteered as a Nurses aide in the local hospital. When the boys were about 12 years old, the Minnis family decided to share their home with foster children. Many children became part of Margaret's busy life. Margaret organized community action councils to bring social services to South Jersey. She was a Head-Start teacher and Supervisor and was later part of a Migrant Program for Atlantic Human Resources. In 1971, continued her service as area director of the Farmworkers Corporation in Hammonton.

Rick Romarcito

New Mexico

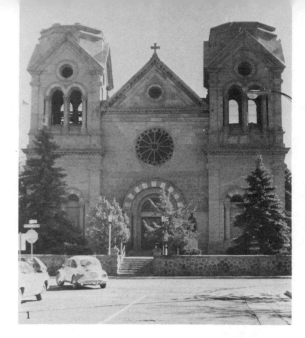

Nickname: The Land of Enchantment

State Flower: Yucca

State Tree: Pinon

State Bird: Road Runner

Photos

1. St. Francis Cathedral, Santa Fe
2. Taos Pueblo
3. Laguna Pueblo
4. Isleta Mission—Isleta
5. Puye Cliff Dwellings

Committee Members

Chairman—Mrs. Ruth Strother
Mrs. Drucilla Summey
Mrs. Lois Printz
Mrs. Dona Henry

Writers

Betty H. Hinton
Mrs. Frances Bear Kyte
Mrs. John C. Rolland
Mrs. Louise C. Rutz
Mrs. Priscilla N. Thompson

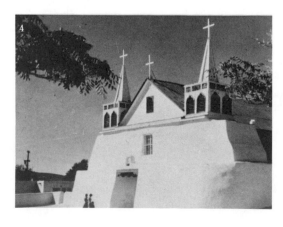

New Mexico

ERNESTINE FRANKE HUNING
Born 1845

The Albuquerque to which Ernestine Franke Huning came as the bride of Franz Huning in 1863 had a population of approximately six hundred consisting of former Mexican citizens who were farmers and traders, and a small gringo society of traders and military personnel. A typical Spanish village, it was centered around a plaza faced by both businesses and homes. The Huning Mercantile, owned by her husband, was on the west side of this square.

Ernestine and Franz met in St. Louis when he returned from a visit to his homeland of Hanover, Germany, after spending sixteen years in New Mexico. She was born in 1845 in Bavaria, and thus had shared a German ancestry. The wagon train that transported Ernestine to her new home also carried her ten canaries, which she refused to leave behind. The treacherous journey took two months, and they were often afraid of attack by Indians.

La Glorieta, her first home, was an old adobe purchased by her husband when he first came to Albuquerque, and was said to be more than a century old. This home now houses Manzano Day School.

Ernestine bore four children: Clara, Lina, Ellie and Arno. Only Clara and Arno grew to adulthood, married and had families of their own. One of Albuquerque's streets is named for her son.

In the spring of 1867 Ernestine's mother and brother were attacked and killed by Indians as they rode with her husband's wagon train enroute to New Mexico for a visit with her. It was several days before she knew of their death.

By 1880 the business had prospered, so the Hunings started the building of a new home, "Castle Huning", which was to take three years to complete. The Castle was a magnificent and imposing mansion. Ernestine's hospitality and prominence brought European grandeur to the dry and dusty little town of Albuquerque.

Ernestine was an industrious woman who cooked, cleaned, sewed, worked in her garden, and cared for her family, often working ten or

twelve hours a day. She was a warm, wonderful woman who had the gift of making people feel welcome, with love for her servants and her friends. Her Thursday afternoon coffees were looked forward to by the dozen English-speaking women in Albuquerque as the social event of the week.

Ernestine was a pioneer woman who worked hard to build a home and raise a family in a new country, and who saw her dreams come true. Before her death in 1923, the railroad had come through, the University was founded, and New Mexico had attained statehood.

GRACE THORPE BEAR

Born 1868

Grace Thrope Bear was born July 18, 1868 in Binghamton, New York, and died April 25, 1940 at Las Vegas, New Mexico, just after attending a banquet meeting of the New Mexico State Federation of Women's Clubs. She had just been awarded a medal for the most outstanding pioneer club woman in the State.

She was the daughter of the Reverend Wallace W. and Julia Austin Thorpe. It was while her father was minister of the Wellington, Kansas Presbyterian Church, that Grace met her husband-to-be, Harvey F. M. Bear. He was superintendent of schools, and Grace was one of his school teachers. They were married in 1893.

In 1902 the Bears with their two children, Frances Armitage and Harvey Robert, moved to the dusty, frontier town of Roswell, New Mexico. There Mr. Bear and his brother-in-law, Charles E. Mason, bought the Roswell Record newspaper. It was the first Democratic daily newspaper in the Territory of New Mexico.

Grace Bear was intensely interested in the affairs of Roswell and the State during the last of the territorial days and the early days of statehood. She immediately became active in local and civic affairs.

In 1905 Harvey Bear died and Grace assumed his interest in The Record, and carried on as Society Editor until her death.

Mrs. Bear joined the Roswell Women's Club in 1902. She served as President of the New Mexico Federation of Women's Clubs from 1923-1925 and as General Director from 1924-1928. The Roswell Women's Club Building stands as a memorial to her. She was founder of the building fund in 1921.

Grace Bear brought Girl Scouting to Roswell while she was President of the New Mexico Federation of Women's Clubs. She remained a member of the Girl Scout Council until her death. She also served on the Salvation Army Advisory Board, and as Chairman of the Chaves County Chapter of the American Red Cross for many years.

Mrs. Bear maintained an active and devoted interest in her church all of her life. She served for nearly twenty years on the Board of Trustees of the Roswell First Presbyterian Church.

One of her finest achievements was her part in securing legislation creating the New Mexico Home and Training School for Mental Defectives at Los Lunas in 1925. The school is now

known as Los Lunas Hospital and Training School. In 1959 she was given an Award of Merit, posthumously, for her services in behalf of mentally retarded children in New Mexico. Her daughter, Frances Bear Kyte, and son, Robert Bear, received this award for her.

JESUSITA ACOSTA PERRAULT

Born 1872

Jesusita Acosta Perrault was born in a villa at Chihuahua, Mexico on January 23, 1872. Her father was Don J. Nepomuceno Acosta. Her mother, Dona Refugito Morales Acosta, was descended from a long line of Spanish Dons. The Villa where Jesusita was born was on an estate granted to the Morales family by Queen Isabella of Spain. However, she lived only the first three months of her life in this atmosphere before her parents moved to Silver City, New Mexico.

Jesusita received her early education at the Academy of Our Lady of Lourdes. When she was eighteen she married Charles May, and was widowed the same year. She then attended Silver City Normal College. After graduation she began a long teaching career in San Lorenzo and San Juan, New Mexico schools. She was the first Spanish-speaking teacher in Grant County. In 1901 she went to visit her family in Chikuahua, Mexico, and stayed to teach for two years.

Over the years, Jesusita made many friends among the politicians, and she became a staunch fighter for good government.

In 1918 Jesusita married Edward Albert Perrault, who was a mining engineer and owned large silver and iron mines near Silver City. They had four daughters—Florence, Dolores, Beatrice and Olivia.

In 1915 Jesusita started a long career of public service as interpreter and translator for the Silver City Selective Service. From 1921-1923 she was Deputy Assessor of Grant County.

Mr. Perault died in 1926, so Jesusita was faced with supporting her four little girls. During 1927-1928 she served as Juvenile Officer for Grant County, but she was to receive even more important posts. In 1929 she was elected Secretary of State under Governor Dillon and served until 1931.

She received a special invitation from the Mexican Government to be present at the inauguration of President Pascual Rubio Diaz.

She was invited to be his guest for two months, but she returned two weeks later after he was wounded by a would-be assassin.

After Mrs. Perrault's term as Secretary of State ended, she went to Albuquerque and started the first U. S. Employment Service in the State, and ran this service until 1933. Later, she wrote "New Mexico Geography" for the American Book Company. She then moved to Santa Fe to teach Spanish at Brownmoor School for three years.

In 1939 she went to live permanently in Taos. With her vast experience in politics, she organized two hundred women, and through their combined efforts, a Republican was elected to office for the first time in many years. She subsequently served as Deputy Assessor, Editor of the Spanish Section of El Taoseno newspaper and City Clerk.

Jesusita Perrault died May 18, 1960 at the age of eighty-eight. All through her long and useful life, she served the people of New Mexico honestly and with faith in its future.

CLEOFAS MARTINEZ JARAMILLO
Born 1877

Cleofas Jaramillo had lived among, and was a part of the early families that settled in New Mexico. She was a descendant of the great Spanish colonizers and a daughter of one of the foremost landowners in the Arroyo Hondo area. Cleofas was born November 1, 1877. Her first schooling was at a small village school. She then attended the convent school in Taos, New Mexico and the Loretto Academy in Santa Fe, New Mexico.

In 1898 Cleofas married Colonel Venceslao Jaramillo. Because of her husband's position, she often entertained New Mexico's most prominent citizens and was a part of New Mexico's early political life. Her husband was a State Senator, was a member of the staff of Governor M. A. Otero during the Territorial period, and was a prominent figure in the development of New Mexico.

Cleofas had three children, two she lost as small children. Her daughter Angelina was tragically murdered when she was a senior in high school. Cleofas was widowed about five years before the death of her daughter, so then she was completely alone.

For many years she watched with a heavy heart the passing of the great Spanish era in New Mexico history, so she decided to record the things she remembered. Her first book was "Spanish Fairy Tales". She then wrote "Shadows of the Past" to preserve the vanishing Spanish folk customs. She also wrote "The Romance of a Little Village Girl", a story of her life, and "New Mexico Spanish Recipes".

In 1935 Mrs. Jaramillo founded La Sociedad Folklorica, a Santa Fe society dedicated to keeping alive the customs and folklore of the area. All meetings were conducted in Spanish and members had to be of Spanish descent. Each year Santa Fe has a Fiesta commemorating the reconquest of the capital by General Diego de Vargas. Because of Mrs. Jaramillo's work, the Fiesta has become an event of great significance, bringing people from all over the country each year. The Folklorica under the guidance of Cleofas, has preserved over fifty old-fashioned gowns dating from 1850 to the 1920's. Each year they present a style show during the Fiesta to show off these gowns.

She exerted great effort to retain and preserve the color and glamour that was once a part of this country. When Cleofas Jaramillo died December 6, 1956 at the age of seventy-nine, she was renowned as one of the states' foremost folklorists.

MARIA MONTOYA MARTINEZ
Santa Fe   **Born 1884**

Maria Montoya Martinez was born about July 1884 at the San Ildefonso Pueblo near Santa Fe, New Mexico, where she still resides today. The daughter of Tomas and Reyes Montoya, Maria was raised like other Indian girls of her times, learning to cook at a fireplace, to clean the mud-floored homes, and to make the pottery for storage and cooking jars and pots. Maria attended the government school at the Pueblo and then spent two years at St. Catherine's Indian School in Santa Fe (1887-1888).

The pueblo language was Tewa and Maria learned to speak English at school and Spanish with her Spanish neighbors.

After school in Santa Fe, Maria received additional lessons from the schoolteacher at the pueblo. While working at the school, she met her husband, Julian Martinez, and married him in 1904. Their honeymoon was spent at the World's Fair in St. Louis, where they sang and danced for the visitors and Maria and the other Indian women made pottery. This was the first of many World Fairs for Maria to participate in. In later years she worked at the San Francisco-Panama-Pacific Exposition in 1915, the Chicago World's Fair in 1933, then on to Washington, D. C., to San Francisco and New York.

Maria had four sons—Adam, Juan, Tony and Felipe. She also raised a sister after her mother died.

Maria's husband, Julian, often assisted archeologists in the summer, digging at old Indian ruins—now part of Bandelier National Monument.

In 1908 Maria started demonstrating pottery-making at the Museum of New Mexico in Santa Fe. What she made could be sold and it was the beginning of pottery-making as a home industry.

It was about 1919 when Julian discovered the method of making black-on-black pottery for which he and Maria became world famous. Maria, always willing to share with others, shared their secret of the black pottery with others in the Pueblo.

Maria has been honored many times. She has been invited to the White House by Presidents Hoover, Roosevelt, Eisenhower and Johnson. Mrs. Lady Bird Johnson has visited Maria at the Pueblo.

Maria has Honorary Doctor Degrees from the University of Colorado, Boulder, Colorado, and New Mexico State University at Las Cruces, New Mexico for her contributions to the art world.

In 1952 she received the French Government's Palmes Academiques Award for outstanding service in art.

Over the years there have been many other awards for this great artist and great lady.

Little did Maria know that she would become a legend when her aunt taught her to make pottery as a child and that through her work her Pueblo as well as her family would become world famous.

Maria to this day retains the customs of the Pueblo and the old ways of the San Ildefonso Indian women.

FRANC JOHNSON NEWCOMB
Born 1887

Franc Johnson Newcomb was a teacher, trading post operator, medicine woman and author. She was born in Jacksonville, Wisconsin in 1887. After finishing high school and a year of teachers training, she taught school in Wisconsin until she accepted a teaching position at Fort Defiance, Arizona in 1912. There she met and married Arthur John Newcomb in 1914.

The Newcombs moved to an isolated trading post near Blue Mesa, New Mexico on the northern part of the Navajo Reservation. Gallup, New Mexico, nearly forty miles away, was their closest source of supplies. This was to be their home for nearly twenty-five years.

It was at this place that Mrs. Newcomb became a trusted friend of the Indians. She was known as Atsay Ashon or medicine woman and often visited remote hogans with a supply of medicines. She was always willing to take in a sick child or adult to help and always had an extra child in her home to care for.

Mrs. Newcomb has a rare photographic memory and artistic talent that made it possible for her to reproduce sand paintings she saw painted in the sand by Navajo medicine men. Reproductive materials were not allowed in the hogans, but the Navajos believe what is in your mind is yours. She was able to reproduce about 600 sand paintings from twenty-seven different sandpainters and medicine men. Many of these sand paintings would have been lost to the Indian people today if she had not recorded them. She often said, "This is my life's greatest contribution." Many of her sand paintings are at the Navajo Ceremonial Art Museum in Santa Fe, New Mexico, which she helped Mary Cabot Wheelwright found.

The Newcombs with their two daughters moved to Albuquerque in 1935. Mrs. Newcomb traveled widely to lecture on Navajo religion and wrote several books on her life among the Indians. Some of her books are "Navajo Neighbors," "Hosteen Klah, a Navajo Medicine Man," "Navajo Omens and Taboos," "Navajo Bird Tales," and "Navajo Folk Tales." "The Shooting

Chant," written with Gladys A. Reichard has just been reprinted.

She won the Woman of the Year Award of the National League of American Pen Women in 1969, and was chosen a "Headliner" by members of Theta Sigma Phi the same year.

While Mrs. Newcomb was President of the Albuquerque Women's Club, the Club expanded Christina Kent Day Nursery, a nursery for low-income families. This was quite an accomplishment in those days. For thirty years the Women's Club supported the nursery until United Community Fund took over.

She also assisted Mrs. Joanna B. Skidmore in the founding of the Visiting Nursing Service in Albuquerque. They started with just one part-time nurse, but the service has flourished over the years.

Mrs. Newcomb died in Albuquerque in 1970, survived by her two daughters, Mrs. Priscilla Thompson and Mrs. Lynette Wilson.

BULA WARD CHARLES

Born 1887

Author, business executive, mother of six, Mrs. Tom (Bula L.) Charles was active in New Mexico for over 65 years. She was born May 14, 1887, the daughter of John R. and Frances Dancy Ward. Her first role was that of mother and housewife, raising a family in the final years of the territory and the rugged days of early statehood.

As her family grew up, she turned to writing, club work and business and achieved success in each. All of her professional work was done under the name of Mrs. Tom Charles, rather than under her given name of Bula, a tribute to her conviction that family ties came first.

Her early years in New Mexico were happy but trying ones. In 1909 the family homesteaded west of Alamogordo and suffered a drouth so great that less than three inches of rain fell in over 12 months. This prompted their move to greener fields, a mountain farm 16 miles from Cloudcroft.

Mrs. Charles did all of her own work, kept a garden, raised chickens, cared for milk from several cows, churned butter, made cheese, baked her own bread, canned, preserved and put away farm produce and meat, made clothes for the family, and even made her own soap.

In 1915, school needs brought the family back to Alamogordo. There, with the children growing up, she joined her husband in the insurance business and she began writing about her beloved southern New Mexico. For over 30 years she wrote for both the El Paso Times and the Associated Press. She wrote for the Albuquerque Journal, the Southwest Stockman Farmer, and other papers and magazines, writing of New Mexico, particularly the Tularosa Basin area. She won awards such as AP Correspondent of the Year, and she recorded history as it happened there.

Taking an active part in club and community work, she served as State President of the New Mexico Federation of Women's Clubs in 1929-1931, was a 50-Year member of the Order of Eastern Star, served on the USO Board, and in 1961, was State Chairman of the New Mexico Christmas Seal Drive.

After the death of her husband in 1943, Mrs. Charles took over as head of the family insurance agency, and in the years that followed she expanded the agency, increased the business and received numerous business awards.

Among 'firsts', she was the first woman to serve as United States Commissioner in her area and filled the post for over two decades, also the first woman on the Board of Directors of Alamogordo Chamber of Commerce. She served for 12 years on the Board of the New Mexico School for the Visually Handicapped.

Her book "Tales of the Tularosa" was published in 1953, and was followed by "More Tales."

In 1959 she received the Zia Award, top honor of the New Mexico Press Women's Association.

There were other honors, all cherished, but the hardest work and she said, the happiest days, were those when she was raising a brood of six in the new and growing State of New Mexico.

Mrs. Charles died on May 11, 1974. She is survived by her six children—Perl, Ralph, Ward, and Ray Charles, Lucile Charles McClernon, Louise Charles Rutz.

JESSIE WIEGAND HOSFORD
Born 1892

Born on a cattle ranch in Nebraska on August 19, 1892, of an English mother and a German father, Jessie Hosford has spent her life helping others. She attended the American Conservatory of Music in Chicago, took her early college work at Iliff School of Theology and received her B.A. and M.A. Degrees at Highlands University in Las Vegas, New Mexico. On April 18, 1917 Jessie married Lisle Hosford. He was Head of the Philosophy Department at Highlands University.

The church and music have run parallel in her life. She began her Sunday School teaching at the age of fourteen and still does substitute work. She was soloist for the Christian Science Church for a period of years, and a member of a quarter which sang Yom Kippur and New Years for thirteen years. She has been director of several church choirs. Today, both the church and music are truly a part of this fine and noble woman.

In the early thirties, the Hosfords chose Las Vegas, New Mexico for their home and consistenty have been active in the affairs of the state. Jessie has served as a Commissioner of Girl Scouts, served on the Las Vegas School Board for eight years, and was secretary of the Las Vegas State Hospital Board for six years.

She is a noteworthy member of the P. E. O. Sisterhood. She is a member of the Federated Women's Club and received the New Mexico Federation of Women's Clubs Award in 1962. She is a leader in their Spiritual Values Group.

Jessie, now known for her successful ventures into the literary world, did not begin her serious writing until her obligations to her husband were completed and her children no longer needed that much of her time. Her first book, "An Awful Name to Live Up To," written after the death of her husband, was voted the best Junior Fiction for 1969-1970, and was given the National Cowboy Hall of Fame and Western Heritage Award. Another book, "You Bet Your Boots I Can," published in 1971 was chosen to be published in England, and at the present time, is in its third printing here in the United States. This year saw completion of another book, and it is currently in the hands of her agent and will be published soon. One of her earlier books was a story of the Carlsbad Caverns and was placed on the textbook list in New Mexico. She also has to her credit many poems and short stories which have been published in various magazines. Many of her poems were inspired by the clear starlit nights, the lofty mountains, the singing streams, and the beautiful desert flowers to be found in the Land of Enchantment—New Mexico.

Not only has Jessie's influence been seen in her two fine sons, Dr. Henry C. Hosford, a physician, and Dr. Phillip L. Hosford, a professor, but she has been an inspiration to many. Truly her life has been one of growing and giving.

PABLITA VELARDE HARDIN
Santa Clara   Born 1918

Christened Tse Tsan (Golden Dawn) in the Tewa language of her people, Pablita Velarde was born in 1918 at the Pueblo of Santa Clara, New Mexico.

During childhood Pablita attended St. Catherine's Mission School at Santa Fe where she first learned to speak English. At seventeen she graduated from Santa Fe Indian School where she studied art under the direction of Dorothy Dunn, pioneer instructor of Indian artists. After graduation Pablita spent two years as assistant art teacher at Santa Clara Day School.

In 1938 the famous naturalist and lecturer, Ernest Thompson Seton and his wife invited Pablita to accompany them on a lecture tour of the United States. This experience was most revealing to the shy, sensitive young Indian girl who had never before journeyed from the northern part of her native New Mexico.

From 1939 to 1941 Pablita was employed by the Government in a CCC project to paint murals for the Museum at Bandelier National Monument in New Mexico. These early paintings are considered to be among some of Pablita's greatest achievements.

While working for the Bureau of Indian Affairs, Albuquerque, she met a young man, Herbert Hardin, and when Pablita was twenty-three, they were married. Pablita preferred to live off the reservation, so the Hardins made their home in Albuquerque. She did not think Indians should remain in close-knit communities.

Through the years Pablita continued to grow as a painter and to gain fame. Her first and most important award was the Grand Prize in the Philbrook Art Center exhibition in Tulsa in 1948. In 1954, Pablita was decorated with the Ordre des Palmes Academiques by the French government.

Many honors have been bestowed upon Pablita by the Gallup Inter-Tribal Indian Ceremonials, Philbrook Art Center, New Mexico State Fair, Santa Fe Indian Market, and New Mexico Arts and Crafts Fair.

After years of preparation, one of Pablita's most significant achievements was the publication in 1960 of her book of tribal legends, "Old Father, the Story Teller," which won an award for the Best Southwestern Book of the Year.

Pablita has appeared in several television productions: "Enchanted Sands," 1964; she was cast as Mary Bluefeather in "Little Bear Died Running," in 1970; and had small parts with Anthony Quinn in TV productions of "Flap" and "The City."

Miss Velarde's paintings are in the permanent collections of the Gilcrease Foundation, Philbrook Art Center, Santa Fe Fine Arts Gallery, the Hall of Ethnology of the Santa Fe Museum, the De Young Museum in San Francisco, the Denver Museum, the Department of the Interior, and in many private collections.

Leading a very active life with her painting, lecturing and writing, Pablita Velarde (Hardin) lives in Albuquerque where her children, Helen and Herbert and their families also reside. She is a member of the Pinon Branch of the National League of American Pen Women; the Gallup Inter-Tribal Indian Ceremonials Association, New Mexico Council of American Indians, and is mentioned in "Who's Who of New Mexico."

FRANCINE IRVING NEFF

Albuquerque   **Born 1925**

Edward and Georga Irving were living in Tampico, Mexico, when they decided their first child about to be born would be a boy, and no doubt, be President of the United States. With this long-range plan in mind, Mrs. Irving crossed the border to Albuquerque, New Mexico to give birth to this child—who was, alas, a girl.

Named Francine, she returned with her mother to Tampico, where her first words were Spanish, and where she established a long enduring love for Spanish-speaking people.

Francine began school in Mountainair, New Mexico, graduating from Mountainair High in 1944. She attended Cottey College, Nevada, Missouri, where she played first violin in the orchestra, was chosen for Phi Theta Kappa, voted Student Scholastic Queen, and graduated first in her class.

Transferring to the University of New Mexico, Francine received a B.A. Degree, with distinction, in 1948. She was a member of Phi Kappa Phi, Mortar Board, Pi Lambda Theta, Sigma Alpha Iota, and Alpha Delta Pi Social Sorority. She has an Honorary Doctor of Humane Letters from Mount Saint Mary College in Newburgh, New York, and an Honorary Doctor of Laws from American International College in Springfield, Massachusetts.

In 1948 she married Edward John Neff, founding partner of Neff and Company, Certified Public Accountants in Albuquerque. Their two children are Mrs. Albert Tomforde, III, Houston, Texas, and Edward Neff, Albuquerque.

Mrs. Neff was active in community work for more than 25 years. She was President of Albuquerque Mortar Board Alumnae, Alpha Delta Pi Alumnae, Albuquerque City Panhellenic Association, Auxiliary to the New Mexico Society of Certified Public Accountants, Camp Fire Girl Leader and a Den Mother, BSA. She is a member of the P.E.O. Sisterhood, National Federation of Business and Professional Women's Clubs, and St. John's Episcopal Cathedral.

In 1964 Mrs. Neff became an active volunteer worker for the Republican Party. She began as a poll worker and State Advisor to New Mexico Teen Age Republican Clubs. In 1967 she became a member of the New Mexico Republican State Central Committee. In 1968 and 1972 she was elected Delegate to the Republican National Convention. She has been a member of the New Mexico Republican State Executive Committee, the Executive Committee Member of the Re-

publican National Committee, and served as the Republican National Committee Woman for New Mexico.

In 1974 she went from volunteer to career status with the appointment of Treasurer of the United States by President Richard M. Nixon. She was sworn in June 21, 1974 as the 35th Treasurer of the United States.

On December 4, 1974, Mrs. Neff received the additional appointment of National Director, United States Savings Bonds Division. She is the first woman, and the first U.S. Treasurer, to become National Director.

She received the 1975 Distinguished Alumnae Citation at Cottey College, and the 1975 Outstanding Alumnae of the Year Award at the Alpha Delta Pi International Sorority's Convention.

New York

"Give me your tired,

your poor..."

Cynthia Moseley

New York

Nickname: The Empire State

State Flower: Rose

State Tree: Sugar Maple

State Bird: Eastern Bluebird

Photos

1. Hell's Gate at Ausable Chasm
2. Fort Ticonderoga Restoration
3. Taughannock Falls
4. Auburn is the home of Wm. H. Seward
5. Old Stone Fort & Museum
6. Elmira College

Committee Members

Chairman—Mrs. W. Stewart Stephens,
  Manlius
Mrs. Walter Moore
Mrs. Charles Moseley
Mrs. Charles Schwartz
Mrs. James V. Connelly
Mrs. Nathan Seagle

New York

MEHITABEL WING PRENDERGAST
Born 1738

Mehitabel Wing was born March 20, 1738 to Quaker parents in Buhman, Dutchess County, New York. She was a noble woman—married to William Prendergast, who was born in Killseny, Ireland, February 2, 1727, and came to Pawling, Dutchess County.

Mehitabel and William Prendergast had fourteen children; eight boys and six girls—

(1) Matthew (married Abigail Aikin) became Justice of Peace of Chautauqua.
(2) Thomas—born September 18, 1758—died 1842, bought acreage at Ripley.
(3) Mary (married William Bemus) became 1st settlers of Bemus Point on Lake Chautauqua. The ferry is operated at this point.
(4) Elizabeth (not married).
(5) James (married Agnes Thompson) settled in Jamestown in 1815. He was elected as First Supervisor and Judge of Court of Common Place in 1814. From 1817-1824 he was Postmaster. He had 2 sons and 1 daughter.
(6) Dr. Jediah (married Dot Mayville.)
(7) Andrew—gave Prendergast Art Gallery and the Library in Jamestown in honor of their son James, who was named after his grandfather (William Prendergast, husband of Mehitabel).
(8) Martin—born April 12, 1769 (married Martha Hunt), Store owner in Mayville.
(9) John Jeffrey.
(10) Susannah (married Oliver Whiteside).
(11) Eleanor—died at age 13.
(12) Martha—not married.
(13) William—Major in War of 1812, became Colonel of Militia.
(14) Minerva—(married Elisha Marvin).

All sons were engaged in politics, law, medicine, or substantial farming. Of their sons, four were Supervisors and three of these became judges and 1 became member of the State Senate.

Chautauqua County's early history is linked closely with a woman whose daring horseback ride nearly two centuries ago, gained the King of England's pardon for her husband sentenced to hang for treason.

That valiant woman of the days when America was just beginning its struggle for political and economic freedom, played a prominent role in the "rent rebellions" along the Hudson River, and later became one of Chautauqua County's pioneer mothers, whose distinguished family shaped history here. Mehitabel Wing Prendergast, mother of James William Prendergast and several other members of their family, lie buried these many years in a small neglected graveyard near Chautauqua, off the Panama Road. It is a tiny part of what was once their 3,000 acre farm, with the waters of Prendergast Creek nearby.

But even before they came here by covered wagon in 1806, these lives had been filled with tragedies and gallantries, penned in books, newspaper articles and historic sketches, with Cavalcade of America once devoting its entire drama to Mehitabel Prendergast, whose horseback ride was claimed to be as noteworthy as Paul Revere's. The source was Carl Carmer's book "The Hudson" with a Chapter on the Prendergasts.

In 1766, when the wealthy manor lords held power in Hudson Valley, William Prendergast rented a few acres from Frederick Philipse, lord of thousands of acres in Westchester and Dutchess Counties, whose huge manor house overlooked the Hudson River at Yonkers.

Prendergast's crops had been poor, and he was behind in his rent. He was disturbed, too, over exacting terms of his lease, providing that he could not will his land to his wife or sons without consent of Frederick Philipse, and that, if after his death that consent was granted, his wife or sons would have to pay the manor lord a third of the value of the farm to keep it, with portion of crops, poultry and labor as yearly payment thereafter. Recalcitrant tenants were sentenced to corporal punishment or imprisonment. Philipse paid the British Crown for his vast estate annual rent of 4 pounds and 12 shillings, the same amount Prendergast was paying yearly for his few acres. Wherever he went, Prendergast spread the story of this injustice.

An army of a hundred were raised, drilled day after day, commanding them to pay honest debts, but not a shilling for rent; they marched against the manor lords, gave a duckling to the Justice who had thrown many into jail—Frantic appeals to Governor Henry Moore to call out militia to suppress the rioters, New York City Council suggested reward of 100 lbs. for apprehending Prendergast leader. Finally 28th Regiment of Grenadiers was ordered from Albany to Poughkeepsie. They took 50 prisoners, but not Prendergast.

Mehitabel had persuaded her husband to give himself to the mercy of the Governor. In her Quaker dress and bonnet, she rode beside her "desperate rebel" husband into the Grenadier's Camp, surrendering to Major Browne. Prendergast was immediately imprisoned on a sloop and taken down the Hudson to New York City. He was brought into crowded Courtroom on August 6, 1766. His 28-year-old wife walked beside him. During the next 24 hours of the Trial, Mehitabel rose to brilliant defense of her husband making every remark that might extenuate his Offense. But the jury came back with the word "guilty," and he was condemned to death by hanging. Mehitabel mounted her horse and rode to Fort George on Manhattan Island to see the Governor, 80 miles away.

With her prettiest dress and bonnet, she begged an audience, strode up and down in front of Governor, he granted a reprieve in the name of His Majesty George III.

What a heroic woman, long will be remembered the Ride of Mrs. Prendergast that saved her husband's life. She was a woman, wife and mother that will long be remembered for her courage, love and devotion to her family, friends and country.

ELIZABETH ANN SETON

Born 1774

Elizabeth Ann was born to the socially prominent Dr. Richard Bayley of New York City and his wife Catherine. She was baptized in the Episcopal Faith in Trinity Church. She was a child during the Revolution and grew into a cultured, beautiful young woman who inherited her mother's charm and vivacity and her father's perceptive mind. Elizabeth played the piano well, danced and sang exquisitely and spoke French fluently.

She married the wealthy young Aristocrat, William Seton, Jr., son of a family of ship-own-

ers with international financial interests. They were devoted to each other and their marriage was blessed with five children.

Elizabeth and a group of affluent young Protestant women formed "The Widows Society," visiting poor widows, bringing food and medicines each day. While she was still in her twenties, her husband met with severe reverses in business and suffered a recurrence of tuberculosis. The Filicchi family, business associates and friends, invited them to Italy to help Will regain his health, but to no avail. He died shortly after their arrival. Elizabeth and her daughter Anna remained as guests of the Filicchis for four months, attending Mass with the family and finding peace and comfort there.

Upon returning home, Elizabeth was faced with two major decisions. The first was the necessity of providing for her family—which led her to try teaching, since she was educated far beyond the women of her time. The second concerned her growing attraction toward the Catholic Faith. Her final decision to become a Catholic cost her the friendship of her spiritual director at Trinity, the Reverend Henry Hobart, and led to other trials as well. Relatives and friends withdrew their children from her school. Forced to give up teaching, she took in boarders to support her family. After many months, Father Simon Bruté, a Baltimore Pastor, urged her to come and start a school in his parish. It prospered immediately and was the beginning of the Parochial School System in the United States. Soon, many young women joined her and the Baltimore clergy suggested that she form a religious community. Elizabeth agreed to do so if she could keep her family with her.

Although the life was difficult, young women of good families continued to join the new order, "The Sisters of Charity," of which she was the first Mother Superior. Elizabeth directed their training and carried on an extensive apostolate of visiting and caring for the poor. During her short lifetime, she established twenty communities, staffing schools, hospitals and child-caring institutions. One group of nuns was sent to her beloved New York to found an orphanage.

An attractive socialite, devoted wife, concerned mother, social worker, courageous widow, inspiring educator, adherent to conscience, despite ostracism, and foundress of a great religious and humanitarian organization whose members now number eight thousand—her's was a life well lived. Elizabeth Seton died quietly on January 4, 1821, surrounded by her beloved nuns and her surviving daughter Catherine, praising the Lord she loved and served so well.

EMMA HART WILLARD
Troy   **Born 1787**

Emma Hart Willard, known as "Pioneer Educator of American Women" herself eager for learning, recognized the injustice and short-sightedness of denying education for girls, and it became her life purpose to free women from ignorance and to widen their horizons.

At age 16 she began teaching, first in her home town, then in Middlebury, Vermont, where she met and married John Willard, a distinguished physician, many years her senior. They had one son and adopted two nieces.

In 1819 she presented her "Plan for Improving Female Education" before the New York State Legislature. It advocated a system of State-supported academies for women. Such academies, she said, would prepare young women better to be wives and mothers (and citizens), train them as competent teachers of the young, and strengthen the social vitality of the Republic. She believed New York would be more receptive than Connecticut to her plan. The citizens of Troy invited the Willards to found a new school in that thriving Hudson

River Commercial center. They accepted gladly.

1821—the Troy Female Seminary opened its doors to 90 young women from seven states. This became the Emma Willard School which is well known today as an outstanding, accredited school for girls. She was a woman to inspire confidence, charming in manner, handsome and vigorous. Not only did she make a most favorable impression on parents, but her pupils idealized her, and were fired with ambition by her enthusiasm.

A member of the Episcopal Church, she was deeply religious, but was very careful not to force her own particular church upon her students, and was firmly resolved that the school should always remain non-sectarian.

One of the first women to write textbooks, she wrote on astronomy, geography, and biology, and was probably the first to provide scholarships for girls and the first educator to train teachers.

She wrote, "We have great need to quicken the process of education to meet the demands of a new age of steam and electricity. We must learn to *value the time* of children."

A book called "Sketches of all Distinguished Women from the Beginning ot A. D. 1850" ranked Mrs. Willard among the distinguished women of the world.

"Probably no other woman in America was as familiar with her country's history, or better informed on current events", concluded Alma Lutz, her biographer.

ELIZABETH CADY STANTON
Johnstown   Born 1815

Elizabeth Cady Stanton was a pioneer advocate of the equality of men and women. A courageous, dedicated, witty, brilliant person who as a young girl was deeply affected by the tragic cases that she listened to in her father's law office. The discriminatory laws under which women lived determined her to work to win equal rights for her sex.

When she grew older, she herself was cruelly hurt to find, upon graduation from the Emma Willard School, that no college in the United States would admit women, and entry into the professions was denied. She studied law with her father, and became interested in temperance and anti-slavery movements.

In 1840 she married Henry Stanton, a well known abolionist, and went with him to the World Anti-Slavery Convention in London. She was shaken to find that the women delegates were not to be seated.

In 1848 she circulated petitions to secure the passage in New York State of a law giving married women property rights.

The mother of seven children, two of them girls, she made sure they had equal rights in their home. All seven children earned college degrees.

In 1851 friendship with Susan B. Anthony proved lasting and rewarding, and their teamwork effective for 40 years. Susan spoke of Elizabeth's home as "well-run", and often took care of the children while Elizabeth did the speaking. Susan managed the business affairs. Elizabeth was the first woman to speak to the State Legislature. She asked for women's right to vote.

With a group of women from 19 states, delegates to the 1st Equal Rights Convention held at Seneca Falls, New York, she formed the National Woman Suffrage Association. Elizabeth was president for two years.

As editor of the "Revolution," a woman's rights newspaper, she proved to be an able writer, also coped with mechanical problems. It was spicy, readable, revolutionary, and last for three years.

She became the most widely known woman speaker in the United States, beginning at age 55 to go on lecture tours. This lasted 12 years and her *topic was family life and the raising of children.*

November 12, 1895, her 80th birthday, was declared Elizabeth Cady Stanton Day in New York City, sponsored by the National Council of Churches. Susan B. Anthony planned the celebration.

1898—her autobiography "Eighty Years and More" was published with the hope that it might inspire others to work toward the same goal of elevating the status of women.

While no organized religion appealed to her, she had over the years worked out her own private system of religious belief. She was firmly convinced that there was some form of life after death.

With Susan B. Anthony and Matilda J. Gage, she compiled "The History of Woman Suffrage."

Eighteen years after her death the 19th Amendment giving women the right to vote was passed.

MATHILDE ROTH SCHECHTER
Born 1859

Mathilde Roth (Schechter) was born in Breslau, Germany December 16, 1859. Her father died just after conducting a Yom Kippur service, when she was very young; and Mathilde had to go to an orphan's home for her education. She was so intellectually superior that she was chosen to attend a seminary for teachers. This was the only profession open to women at that time. And this caused her to become an ardent supporter of equal rights for women in later years. Mathilde took a position in Hungary as a teacher and a few years later went to England to study literature and art.

Later Mathilde went to London to become a tutor to the daughter of the Principal of Jew's College. One day as she was in the College Library, looking for a book to read over The Sabbath, a curly-headed young man offered to help her find one. His name was Solomon Schechter, a very scholarly man already. After making sure that she would keep a Kosher home, so that his parents would be able to visit, he proposed. Solomon and Mathilde were married June 22, 1887 in Jew's College. After they were married, they moved to Cambridge, where her husband was a lecturer in Rabbinic Literature. It was in Cambridge where their three children were born.

In 1903, the Jewish Theological Seminary invited Dr. Schechter to come to the United States to be its president.

Besides helping Professor Schechter, guiding their children and conducting a home that attracted scholars and laymen who had the interest of Judaism at heart, Mrs. Schechter took part in many other activities. During their first years in America, she taught in the Columbia Religious and Industrial School for Jewish girls, which she had founded. She helped compile a book of the most beautiful melodies for the Sabbath and the Holidays, a Hebrew Hymnal.

In 1918, she founded the Women's League for Conservative Judaism, and became its first President. In an address delivered by Mrs. Schechter at the Organization Committee Meeting on January 21, 1918, she stated:

"We wish to serve the cause of Judaism by strengthening the bond of unity among Jewish women and by learning to appreciate everything fine in Jewish life . . . The self-education of Conservative Jewish women is only the first step towards the better education of our children."

Knowing that the Seminary students could do their best work only when they were well fed and housed, she helped bring about the building of the first residence hall for the students and now the newest hall, named for Mathilde Schechter.

Dr. Schechter succumbed of a heart attack in 1915. Then came the days when her only son Frank, who had voluntarily enlisted, was standing in the fighting line on the Western front. It was granted to her to see him return and his presence cheered her and lightened the gloom of her loneliness. In the fall of 1919, she became desperately ill. Through sheer strength of will, she was able to emerge from her sick-bed and continue to live a useful, though less strenuous life devoted to many interests.

A highly cultured and educated woman, Mathilde Schechter kept abreast of the realms of modern life as manifested in Art and Literature. Amid her sorrows, the joy of life never deserted her completely. She could find intense pleasure in looking at the "glorious ocean," in listening to a fine play, in reading a good book or admiring the graces of a pretty child. Her home remained a meeting place for her friends and for lonely and stranded souls. From her conversation, they drew intellectual delight, as well as inspiration and guidance. She entered into the lives of her daughters, who were in foreign lands, through her fascinating correspondence and shared the interests of her son, who was a lawyer of high standing. The self-sacrificing devotion of the latter brightened the last years of her life. She died in Mount Sinai Hospital, New York City on August 27, 1924.

With her went a personality that can never be forgotten, never be replaced.

ANNA MARY ROBERTSON MOSES
"Grandma Moses"
Greenwich   **Born 1860**

Throughout the art world, Grandma Moses is known as "an authentic American primitive." At the age of 12 she left home to work as a hired girl on neighboring farms. Marriage to Thomas Solomon Moses in 1887 took them to Virginia to farm. She sold her own print butter and potato chips, uncommon then. Here they had ten children. In 1905 they returned to New York State and in her words, "left five little graves." 1927—her husband died, her youngest son and his wife took over the farm. Not wanting to be idle, she made worsted pictures until arthritis crippled her hands so she no longer could hold a needle. At 75 she started painting in oils, in earnest. Her works are world famous, having been shown all over the United States, and in Vienna, The Hague, Munich, Salzburg, Berne, and Paris. Her favorite subjects were the green valley lying before her home, skethces of farm and family life as she knew it, and historical themes. She followed current events with lively interest and understanding.

Eight books have been either written or illustrated by her, and seven other books mention her name.

President Truman presented her the Woman's National Press Club Award for her outstanding accomplishments in Art in 1949. President Eisenhower and President Kennedy both commended her for her work. Honorary Doctorates from Russell Sage College, Troy, New York in 1949, and from Moore Institute of Art, Philadelphia in 1951 were awarded. In 1953 she was guest speaker for the Herald Tribune Forum in New York. Edward R. Murrow interviewed her for a telecast "See It Now" series in 1955.

On her 100th birthday and again at 101, Governor Rockefellow proclaimed "Grandma Moses Day" in New York State.

In 1969 a stamp was issued in her honor.

Her works numbered 1,600 and included paintings, tiles, Christmas cards, printed fabric, and plates. Both her works and her life helped our nation appreciate its pioneer heritage and recalled its roots in the countryside and on the frontier. She loved simplicity and beauty. Some of her works are valued at $3,000.

Dr. Otto Kallir, director of the St. Etienne Gallery, New York City in his book "Grandma Moses: American Primitive" says, "Grandma Moses was one of the most inspiring figures of the 20th century. What she expressed in her art are the everlasting sources of vitality from which man draws his strength, courage, and hope. She has shown on image of her country far different from what has come to be regarded as typically American, and the image is truer and more enduring."

ANNA ELEANOR ROOSEVELT
Born 1884

First Lady of The World was the title given by President Truman to Eleanor Roosevelt who became known to millions, and who stood for compassion and hope on every continent of the earth. As New York State governor's wife, United States president's wife, delegate to the United Nations, chairman of the UN Human Rights Commission, as author, humanitarian, she was truly a great mother.

Her mother was Anna Hall Roosevelt and her father was Elliot Roosevelt. Her childhood was filled with unhappiness and loneliness. Her mother died suddenly, when Eleanor was eight, and her father (brother of Theodore Roosevelt) died when she was ten. Elliot, her older brother, died of diptheria as had their mother, and Eleanor with her younger brother, Hall, went to live with Grandmother Hall at Tivoli-on-The-Hudson. She was determined to rise above this unhappy childhood.

She and Franklin Delano Roosevelt, her fifth cousin once removed were married in 1905.

She was well aware that the world outside was a tragic one, but as early as 1917 realized there was something she could do about it. Learning of the deplorable conditions in the Federal Insane Asylum, her insistence finally persuaded the Secretary of the Interior to take action.

By 1919, the Roosevelts had five children; Anna, James, Franklin Jr., John, and Elliot.

As first lady, she largely abandoned the traditional role dedicating her energy and wisdom to the problems of America. She visited labor camps, coal mines, and slums, in order to report the truth of the poverty and conditions to her husband as well as to the nation. Her foremost

goal in public life as First Lady and as humanitarian was universal dignity for all people, world peace and freedom.

After her husband's death in 1945, she had fifteen good years in which she became known to the whole world as someone who cared and could help them. President Truman appointed her to the American delegation to the first meeting of the General Assembly of the United Nations meeting in London in January, 1946. No-one, including herself, was very enthusiastic about her appointment, but later, after working with her, many gave her sincere respect, admiration and confidence.

She travelled widely and was enthusiastically received by the crowds as well as heads of state. Her humility, her effective speeches, and her warm attitude did much to promote the UN and the democratic way.

She was also an author of at least three books; *This is My Story*, 1937, *This I Remember*, 1950, and *On My Own*, 1958. Adlai Stevenson, in his eulogy before the General Assembly of the United Nations on November 9th, 1962 said, "she would rather light a candle than curse the darkness, and her glow has warmed the world."

A new wing added to the Franklin D. Roosevelt Library and Museum has been devoted to Eleanor Roosevelt, and the beautiful Roosevelt mansion at Hyde Park, New York is open to the public. Franklin and Eleanor are buried there in the Rose Garden.

JESSIE WEBSTER PIERCE
Born 1892

Jessie was born in a log cabin on Onondaga Reservation over 80 years ago; she is an able chronicler of the traditions and history of the Onondaga Reservation. She traces her own ancestry as the Chief's daughter, who married Ephraim Webster, the first Syracuse settler, in the late 1790's. Jessie Pierce's own schooling was cut off early. She was needed at home to watch the babies and help with the planting. Indian women are taught to be strong, Jessie says; to bring the wood in, to plant potatoes, throw beans and grow corn.

Jessie Pierce was first married to Raymond Lyons and then Edward Shenendoah and last Andrew Pierce, all of whom have passed away. She is the mother of six children and innumerable grandchildren and great-grandchildren. Her son, Leon Shenandoah, is the Tah-Da-Dah-Ho, that is, the Chief spokesman of the Iroquois Confederacy of Six Nations and she has four grandsons who sit with him as Onondaga Chiefs.

Jessie Pierce has always had a strong devotion to the Longhouse way, its traditions and religion. She is noted in law books as the subject of a landmark Court decision several years ago which upholds Indian exemption from the Sales Tax. Pierce vs New York remains the landmark decision by which all Indians in New York State maintain exemption from sales tax.

In the Longhouse, Jessie Pierce is known as Ga-Yah-Dust Twe, but by all the reservation people she is called "Gram."

Gram has always had a way with selling Indian crafts and her Trading Post has been an established sightseers' stop on Route 11-A since the 1950's. In the past few years, she has almost doubled her wares, adding baked goods, soft drinks and disposable diapers to her stock of Indian Crafts. She hopes to add Indian spoon bread selling once a week at her Trading Post.

Mrs. Pierce has known what it was to have to work—and of attending the three room schoolhouse, of the sicknesses and the smallpox epidemic and the disappointments. She shudders when talk runs to the threat of the land being sold for further non-Indian use—Quote—"We call the land our Mother. Why should we sell it? You don't want to sell your mother."

Jessie Pierce, "still very active," has many plans for the future. She has known ever since she was a young girl that she would live a long

life. She often tells her grandchildren of a dream she had as a child. Belief in dreams is an important aspect of Indian Tradition. In the dream she began to jump with an old clothespole, she jumped higher and higher and felt as if she was flying as high as the house. The dream seemed so real she told her mother about it. Jessie's mother told her that the dream was a sign that she was going to live a long life. "I guess you could say that the dream has come true," says Gram as she sits quietly rocking in her chair.

HELEN HAYES

Born in 1900

Helen Hayes, known at home and abroad for her excellence in fine acting, has starred on stage, screen and television, and has won two Academy Awards during her distinguished career of seventy years.

Born in Washington, D.C., she enjoyed a happy childhood with all her four grandparents taking an active part, and with her companionable parents.

At age five, she made her stage debut in *The Prince Chap* as Prince Charles. She attended parochial schools, travelled, and did an extensive amount of reading, especially biographies.

She was part of The Lew Field's Company in 1910, and at thirteen played in *The Prodigal Husband*.

In her autobiography *On Reflection*, she says, "My father did his small job well and with humility which taught me how to survive success."

Marriage to Charles MacArthur, playwright, was a lasting one of thirty years, and was a satisfying and fulfilling relationship. His father was an evangelist and frowned on the theater. However, he grew to accept and love Helen.

A daughter, Mary, brought much happiness. She became an actress also, and at age nineteen played with her mother in *Good Housekeeping* at Westport, Connecticut. It was there that Mary developed the cold symptoms that proved to be Polio which took her life despite efforts with an iron lung.

A son, James, was adopted while Mary was very young, and the two children had a loving, lasting relationship. Following in Mary's footsteps, Jim became an actor.

Soon after Mary's death, Helen Hayes lost her husband following a lingering illness.

She became interested in and dedicated to the National Foundation to fight Polio. *The Mary MacArthur Fund* was created by the many theater friends and through this a twelve bed respiratory ward was established at Wellsley Center, Boston's Children's Hospital. It proved a training ground for doctors. Much of their work radiated from this center, and finally, Jonas Salk discovered the vaccine which has nearly made Polio a disease of the past.

Many critics consider the role of Queen Victoria in the play *Victoria Regina* (1935) her greatest success. Some of her leading roles were in *What Every Woman Knows, Harriet, The Barretts of Wimpole Street, Twelfth Night, Mary of Scotland, The Glass Menagerie, The Wisteria Trees, A Touch of The Poet, Caesar And Cleopatra*.

Her first Oscar was for her part in her first film, *The Sin of Madelon Claudet* in 1931. Her second was for her part in the movie *Airport* in 1971. She appeared in a N.B.C. television series *The Snoop Sisters*, and in 1975 with her son, James on *Hawaii Five-O*.

In 1955, *The Fulton Theater* in New York was renamed *The Helen Hayes Theater* in her honor.

Also an authoress, she has written several books and articles for *Guideposts* and *The 1974 Yearbook of World Book*.

Now that she is a grandmother to Charles and Mary, she feels three things remain; *Faith, Love* and *Memory*.

CLARE BOOTHE LUCE

Born 1903

Clare Boothe Luce, author, actress, Congresswoman, and ambassador, contributed greatly to women's place in government, and is rightfully named a great mother.

She had no formal education until she was twelve, but was extremely advance in learning as a result of extensive reading and wide travel. She was a very successful scholar.

At age twenty, she married George Brokaw. Their daughter Ann Clare, was born in 1924. George Brokaw died when Ann was quite young.

Clare was editor of *Vanity Fair* (a popular literary magazine of the Twenty's and Thirty's). She was a correspondent for *Life Magazine*, and in 1935, married Henry Robinson Luce, publisher of *Life*, *Time*, and *Fortune* magazines. Her work took her to Europe, The Phillipines, Burma, China, India, and Egypt. She was the first American woman journalist ever to visit the Yellow River area. She met most of the important political leaders.

As a playwright, she wrote many successful Broadway plays, among them, *The Women*.

Her relationship with her daughter, Ann, developed into a friendship, close and warm. They shared an interest in politics. Ann planned to become a diplomat and was enrolled at Stanford University, when at nineteen she was killed in an accident; a crushing heartbreak.

Clare served as Republican Congresswoman from Connecticut for two terms (1943-1947).

In 1946, she became confirmed in the Catholic Church, and wrote a great deal on relgious subjects.

President Eisnehower appointed Clare, Ambassador to Italy in 1953 through 1957. Her husband went with her, running his magazines from Rome. He was strong support to her as he understood the problems in Italy more than anyone.

She received the highest award of the *National Society for Crippled Children and Adults in Texas*.

In Stephen Shadegg's biography, *Clare Boothe Luce*, he states that the Italian Government gave a farewell luncheon for Ambassador Luce and Foreign Minister Gaetano Martino told his guests, "Ambassador Luce was responsible for bringing spiritual, political, and economic unity to Italy." She was given the Grant Cross of The Order of Merit of The Italian republic.

Thirteen difficult assignments were successfully completed before she returned home in 1957.

In 1959 The United States Senate, after a bitter debate, approved her appointment as Ambassador to Brazil. As a result of the political quarrel, Mrs. Luce resigned the Ambassadorship because she felt persuaded that it was no longer possible for her to accomplish the Mission which she felt was so important to Americans.

In 1965 she retired to private life but continued writing, painting, speaking, and keeping informed on National and World affairs.

NORTH CAROLINA

North Carolina

Nickname: Old North State

State Flower: Dogwood

State Bird: Cardinal

Photos

1. North Carolina State Capital at Raleigh
2. Old Well, on campus of the university of N.C. at Chapel Hill (Oldest St. Univ. in the County)
3. Baltimore House, Asheville, N.C.
4. Ashland Plantation House near Henderson
5. Cape Hatteras Lighthouse at Buxton (America's tallest lighthouse)
6. Laurel Mill in the Gold Sand community

Committee Members

Chairman—Mrs. Harriet Pressly, Raleigh
Dr. Gertrude Carraway, New Bern
Dr. Thornton Mitchell, Raleigh
Mrs. Gilbert English, Trinity
Mrs. Mary Chiltoskey, Cherokee
Dr. Eloise Cofer, Raleigh
Mrs. Charles L. Tucker, Jr. Greensboro
Dr. Tom Parramore, Raleigh
Dr. Barbara Parramore, Raleigh
Mrs. Graham Barden, Sr. New Bern
Mildred L. Bingham, Mars Hill

Writers

Mr. H.G. Jones
Mr. Elmer Ottinger
Mr. William O'Shea
Mr. Fred Johnson
Ms. Elizabeth Pfohl Campbell
L. Gette Blythe
N.C. Dept. Indian Affairs, Raleigh
N.C. Dept. Archives & History, Raleigh

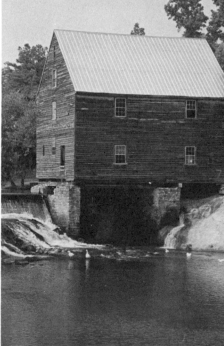

North Carolina

CORNELIA PHILLIPS SPENCER
Born 1825

Cornelia Phillips Spencer was perhaps North Carolina's best known woman of the late nineteenth century. She exercised liberties which few females of her day dared assert, and when a friend called her "the smartest woman in North Carolina," Governor Zebulon B. Vance is said to have added, "And the smartest man too."

For one whose name would become so dear to the South, it seems strange that Cornelia Ann Phillips was born in Harlem, New York, on March 20, 1825. The daughter of James and Judith Vermeule Phillips, she grew up in the shadow of her brothers, Charles and Samuel Field Phillips, both of whom gained fame—the former as a professor and the latter as solicitor general of the United States.

In 1826 the family moved to Chapel Hill where the father joined the faculty of the University of North Carolina. Cornelia was educated by her parents and their neighbors, and she even as a student exhibited talents of literary and artistic merits. Writing became her vehicle of influence; drawing and painting became her means of expression.

In 1855 Cornelia married James Munro Spencer, a young law graduate, and moved with him to Alabama where he entered practice. Their only child, Julia (June) Spencer, was born there in 1859. In 1861, following several years of deteriorating health, the young husband died. Cornelia and her daughter moved back to Chapel Hill.

It was in the years following the loss of her husband and during the tragic Civil War that Cornelia began in earnest her literary career. While her journals and letters constitute the most intimate and expressive of her writings, she also became an author. Her first book, *The Last Ninety Days of the War*, traced the tragic period when the South's hopes faded and defeat became inevitable. Military defeat, however, was not as bitter to Cornelia Spencer as was the misnomer "Reconstruction" during which morality normally associated with government

ceased to control the ambitions of men.

Particularly galling to Cornelia Spencer was the political strangulation of her beloved University of North Carolina which had survived the war but could not survive politicization under the Republican regime. No sooner than it had been closed, the revival of the university became Mrs. Spencer's most consuming interest. Her letters to friends and newspapers were successful, and in 1875 she climbed the steps of South Building to ring the bell announcing the "resurrection" of the university. She decorated the chapel and wrote the hymn for the first convocation.

Mrs. Spencer continued to write for newspapers and magazines, and she authored another book, *First Steps in North Carolina History*, which provided a readable survey of historical events in her adopted state.

Following the death of her husband, Cornelia Spencer found much consolation in the rearing of her only child. She heaped upon June love and affection, but she also held her to account. This strong bond remained unbroken throughout Cornelia's life. Her home was a hospitable meeting place of fertile minds, and June grew up hearing and even participating in the warm and sometimes animated discussions. So active was Cornelia in the affairs of Chapel Hill that she was looked upon as something of a "village arbiter."

In 1894 Mrs. Spencer moved to Cambridge, Massachusetts. She lived the remainder of her life there with June and her husband, Professor James Lee Love. She died March 11, 1908, and was buried in the Chapel Hill Cemetery.

MINA ROSENTHAL WEIL

Born 1859

Mina Weil was a warm, compassionate human being who was able to translate her profound love of family and humanity into personal fulfillment and social betterment and bring a sense of dignity, worth, hope and love to virtually all persons who crossed her orbit.

She was born Mina Rosenthal, daughter of Emil and Eva Oettinger Rosenthal of Raleigh, in 1859. As a girl she lived for a while in Greenville and during the Civil War was sent to Wilson as a "refugee" from Yankee forces. When she was sixteen, Mina was married to Henry Weil in Baltimore. After the marriage, Mina and Henry moved to Goldsboro, where they lived the rest of their lives. Mina and Henry were parents of four children: Leslie, Gertrude, Herman and Janet, distinguished members of a distinguished family. As unostentatious in their charity and attainments as in their Jewish faith, the family assumed quiet leadership in North Carolina in business, agricultural, education and social welfare matters.

Janet remembers such qualities in her mother as love, unselfishness, interest in community affairs, intellectual interests, sympathy and guidance, and maintenance of a high standard of conduct. She says: "Often the Mother who is able to be a close and understanding, loving and inspiring friend, without being obvious about it, is perhaps the more successful Mother." Looking back at Mina Weil's life, Janet says: "Her four children were thoroughly devoted to her. She gave them sympathy yet always maindained standards of conduct."

In a family of many outstanding individuals Mina Weil did much to set the pace and tone for family accomplishments and reputation for

public service. A devoted wife and mother, a superb housekeeper and home planner who presided over meals and household with equal skill, she found time to do "case work" in an era when there were no county welfare departments and no social workers. In the early days she was chairman of the relief committee of the Ladies Benevolent Society and a key member of the board of directors of the Bureau of Social Services. Later the Goldsboro *News-Argus* reported: "The public knew little of her good deeds; of families aided in sickness, of coal sent to the poor, of educational opportunities she opened to young people who were worthy. The story was never told in the public print, she would have blushed had it been. . . ."

Her interests ranged far and wide. As a girl, she had wanted to study medicine. At the beginning of the century, she urged the State Legislature to pass legislation regulating child labor. During the flu epidemic in the last year of World War I, she provided medicine and food to families unable to help themselves and personally organized doctors, nurses and private citizens into service.

Always a pioneer in education, and especially for women, Mina Weil, in 1924, established the Henry Weil Fellowship for Graduate Study at North Carolina College for Women (now the University of North Carolina at Greensboro). In those days fellowships for women were rare, almost without precedent, in southern schools. She served as a trustee of the public schools with dedication and courage. Recognizing the separation of church and state, she filed a minority report opposing religious instruction in the schools.

When Mina Weil died in 1940, a newspaper editorial, entitled "Her Price Is Above Rubies," gave perspective to her life: ". . . Many are the hearts that are sad; the names of those who will miss her are legion. Keen of mind, bright of spirit, incisive and sure in her judgments, sympathetic and helpful in all worthy causes, she made a lasting imprint on this section and its people such as few make. Not one in the crowd but had his own story to tell of how he had been aided by the modest woman who had gone. Pieced together, they reveal a life of rare force."

JANE SIMPSON MCKIMMON

Born 1867

Jane Simpson McKimmon was born of Scotch ancestry in Raleigh, North Carolina, on November 13, 1867. She was brought up in a home filled with an atmosphere of culture and religion. Her education was begun in the Raleigh Public Schools and at sixteen she became the youngest graduate from Peace Institute (now Peace College). She went on to study home economics at Simmons College in Boston.

Jane Simpson married Charles McKimmon of Raleigh in 1886. She spent the first years of her married life taking care of her home, while raising and teaching her four children. As a mother to Charles, Anne, William and Hugh, she was kind, gentle but firm, and an enthusiastic individual. She worked with her children in a very democratic manner, but when that method failed she demanded their attention with her firm voice. Not only was Mrs. McKimmon deeply religious, she was also an artistic person with music being her great love. She sang for many years as a soloist in the choir of Christ Church, where her children were members.

"Miss Jenny" was an excellent cook and many Raleigh kitchens are still using the recipes she was so generous in sharing. Her Sunday dinners are well remembered. The family assembled at the table where the blessing was said and her wonderful broiled chicken and vegetables were served. Background music was always provided by the victrola. Dr. McKimmon spoke to a home demonstration group years later and said, "It is

the getting together that counts. Just what there is to eat is a minor matter."

While the children matured and entered school, she began lecturing in 1908 for the Farmers Institute. This was the beginning of a thirty-eight-year career in State Home Demonstration work by which she strove to improve the living standards of farm women. During this time she served as a founder and as president of the State and National Home Economics Association. Four North Carolina Governors appointed her to boards associated with home economics and farm life. Resuming her education in 1926, she received her B.S. degree and became the first woman to graduate from North Carolina State College, now North Carolina State University. After earning her M.S. degree, she was awarded an honorary Doctor of Laws degree from the University of North Carolina at Chapel Hill.

Her various professional involvements, however, never interfered with her concern for her children and grandchildren to whom she always generously gave of her time. Her grandchildren still remember the delights of a visit to her home where on summer afternoons, in a white dress and a white panama hat with a narrow black band, she seemed to entertain all Raleigh on her front porch. A jar filled with candy from Roysters served as a special treat. The children were always entertained with stories, trips to Capital Square to feed the pigeons and excursions to the market for fresh vegetables; when as an avid golfer she went to the Country Club, they were allowed to caddy for her.

As a organizer Mrs. McKimmon had vision, alertness and efficiency throughout her many years of service. At the same time she never lost her intensely human touch. For what she did for humanity she received world-wide recognition. Very likely, on the other hand, she felt that of greater importance would have been the love and devotion that she richly earned by her service to her family.

CHARLOTTE HORNBUCKLE CHILTOSKEY

Born 1868

The years from 1868 through 1936 were hard years for women in the mountains of the Southern Appalachians, especially on the Qualla Boundary, the home of the Eastern Band of Cherokee Indians, following the "Removal" of the Cherokees to the West, the destructiveness of the Federal laws forbidding native Indian languages in boarding schools and epidemic childhood diseases. It was during these severe times that Charlotte Hornbuckle was born, lived, married Will Chiltoskey, bore ten children and reared to adulthood four, who owed their existence to their mother's use of plants that grew around her home.

Charlotte, with the aid of her kind husband, made every effort to give the best to their children. They had the privileges of a Sunday school nearby, an experience they did not forget. She too imparted the knowledge of her people's idea of the Supreme Being in a way that caused no conflict in the minds of these children. Today many churches in several states display beautifully carved altars, crosses, etc., designed and made by her youngest son, Goingback. Her older son, Watty, was a devout member of his church, conducting Sunday school classes in his native Cherokee language, teaching younger members to sing both English and Cherokee songs.

The Cherokee Indian Boarding School was available to her children through the ninth grade. Her youngest son continued his education in several of the outstanding all-white schools as well as Indian schools, perfecting his skill as a wood-carver, model-maker and teacher. More than thirty years of his work was spent in Federal service. Ute, the oldest son, had an outstanding record of bravery and courage during World War I and two of his sons followed his footsteps during World War II.

A daughter, Amanda Crowe, is the woodcarving teacher at the Cherokee High School and has been for more than twenty years. A son, William, is serving his second four-year term as a commissioner of the Indian Arts and Crafts Board, an appointment made by the Secretary of the Department of the Interior. Watty was the beginner of the woodcarving skill that has passed down to others of the family and has influenced many others. He was also an authority on the Cherokee language. Of her living descendants, one son, one grandson and one granddaughter are retired Civil Service workers and three grandsons may soon join them.

The gathering and preparation of foods was a field in which Charlotte was an expert, passing much of this ability to her children and grandchildren. A book, *Cherokee Cooklore*, contains recipes from three of her descendants. Medicinal plants were well known to her; a recent book, *Cherokee Plants*, is full of such knowledge.

She made cane and oak baskets to use in the home; she was one of the demonstrators of basketmaking at several of the early Cherokee Indian Fairs. Quilts made by her hands warmed the family at night, clothes made by her clothed the family, much of this being done as she tended the food as it cooked on or by the open fire in the stone fireplace. The soap for home use was made by her from the lye from the wood ashes and the surplus fats.

Charlotte, expecting the children to obey her, her husband and all in authority, was happy that her children had learned to speak English in school and still remembered to speak their native Cherokee language. It was this knowledge of Watty and Goingback that made possible the book *Cherokee Words*. Even though Charlotte knew no English, her knowledge of Cherokee lore will live for many years in three books, written in English, in which her strong influence was felt. Although she was born and lived her sixty-eight years in the Cherokee Indian Reservation, her books and many descendants have had a constructive influence on people in other parts of the world, and in a great measure have immortalized her.

MAUDE MOORE LATHAM

Born 1871

Maude Moore Latham was the mother of a courageous son, who gave his life in his country's military service, and a distinguished daughter, who dedicated her life to patriotic achievement. She was an outstanding leader in numerous historical, educational and cultural movements for the betterment of her community, state and nation.

A native of New Bern, she was married there August 10, 1892, to James Edwin Latham, a successful cotton merchant. Twelve years later the couple, accompanied by their two children, moved to Greensboro where they became active in civic affairs. Mr. Latham attained prominence in business and financial enterprises.

For some time Mrs. Latham served on the City Planning and Zoning Board. She was a member of the First Presbyterian Church and a Trustee of the Presbyterian Home for the Aged. The Latham Memorial Hospital at the Eastern Star and Masonic Home was started by her $30,000 gift in her husband's memory. Its reception room was furnished as a memorial to their son, Edward, who died at Fort Thomas, Kentucky, while in the Army during World War I.

A musician, patron of the arts, and collector of fine paintings and antiques, Mrs. Latham traveled extensively, studying music, art and languages. She was a vice president and life member of the North Carolina Art Society and belonged to the North Carolina Folklore Society, State Literary and Historical Association, Carolina Bird Club, Woman's Club and Wednesday Study Club.

Restoration of historic structures especially appealed to her. Her aid was recognized in 1948 when she received one of the first Cannon cups of the North Carolina Society for the Preservation of Antiquities, of which she was a vice president and life member.

Mrs. Latham was a charter member of the National Council for Historic Sites and Buildings, now the National Trust for Historic Preservation. She was on the State Commission to restore Governor Aycock's birthplace and was the first and largest donor toward the purchase of King Charles II's Carolina Charter.

Her gardens were showplaces. She was a member of the Dogwood Garden Club and a life member of the National Council of State Garden Clubs. For notable service she won the 1950 Maslin cup of the Garden Club of North Carolina, for which she acted as treasurer, radio chairman and life member.

With her "million dollar personality," from the age of seven to seventy, she charmed audiences as actress and speaker. She was a tennis player, horsewoman, golfer, bowler, swimmer and dancer. A talented author, she wrote magazine articles and helped compile and finance the 1939 volume of *Old Homes and Gradens of North Carolina.*

Her diversified interests culminated in her desire and determination to rebuild Tryon Palace, North Carolina's Colonial and first State Capitol, in her native town. For this purpose she presented a $125,000 collection of rare English antiques, established two trust funds and bequeathed the residue of her estate to the Tryon Palace Commission, a state agency, which she headed as chairman until her death, being succeeded by her daughter, May Gordon Latham (Mrs. John A.) Kellenberger.

Carrying out her mother's wishes, Mr. and Mrs. Kellenberger devoted their time and means to reconstruct the Palace, furnish it with superb antiques, and surround it with magnificent gardens. Under their inspiring leadership, the Commission bought, restored, furnished and landscaped four nearby lovely old homes. Today the complex stands as a living memorial to Mrs. Latham, whose vision and philanthropy made possible the tourist attraction, educational institution and patriotic shrine as one of North Carolina's greatest assets.

MARY MARTIN SLOOP, M.D.
Born 1873

In 1951 when Mary Martin Sloop, M.D., left her little Crossnore School for underprivileged children in the North Carolina mountains for New York to accept the honors as American Mother of the Year, she wore her only hat, a second-hand one costing two dollars at the school's old clothes store.

But from the moment she and her daughter Emma—Dr. Emma Sloop Fink, also a physician—were settled in the Waldorf by the sponsoring Golden Rule Foundation, the 78-year-old doctor and educator was being observed by a steadily widening audience of blasé urbanites. Reporters and newspaper and magazine feature writers routinely assigned to cover her were writing enthusiastically of her dedicated work in her mountain community and more particularly about her charming simplicity.

Edward C. Aswell, editor of McGraw-Hill, with his associate editor, Ed Kuhn, went to see her and asked her to write her story for his house. He was determined to have her story and she was unyielding. She had no time, and she couldn't write one if she could find the time. Then Aswell took another tack. "But, Mrs. Sloop, if I can get someone to take down your story as you tell it, so that you won't be bothered with any writing chores, would you let us publish it?"

"Oh, that would be fine. I'd like that," she beamed. "Oh, yes, yes." So Mr. Aswell telephoned a writing friend, a professional author—who was living within six miles of her birth-

place but had never seen her—and asked him to consider doing the book. He went to Crossnore, was promptly enamored of her and her storytelling powers, and a three-way agreement was reached. Many taping sessions were held and the manuscript was at length finished and left with her for weeks during which she read not one page; the book was set in type and galley sheets were sent to her, but she professed no time in which to check them. And on March 9, 1953, her eightieth birthday, the book was published.

The book was highly praised, quickly became a best seller, was chosen by one of the nation's largest book clubs, went into twenty American printings and some dozen foreign language translations around the world. But when Mary Martin Sloop, M.D., died January 13, 1962, her *Miracle in the Hills* was still unread—by her.

Over the long years of their unique ministering to the mountain people, Doctors Eustace H. and Mary Martin Sloop were a team; each happily complemented the other. And what they accomplished for the region by pushing long miles out from the little Crossnore campus and for many boys and girls now scattered over the nation and the world, whose successful lives were shaped and given direction by the Sloops, is inestimable. In 1908, the year of their marriage, they had come into the hills from Mecklenburg and Iredell Counties to encounter conditions shockingly primitive. There were no doctors and no schools and the natives, of finest stock but isolated and suspicious of medicine and all "larnin'" and foreigners from the lowlands, had to be won over to the new way before they could be helped. Electricity and even running water were unheard of in the deep coves and the high hills, roads were straggling rough paths, the peoples' diet was hog meat, greens and grease. But the Sloops were determined to change things. And with indomitable courage, hard work, illimitable faith, they did.

"You ask me my philosophy," Mary Martin Sloop said one day to her associate who was helping her with her book. "Work and pray. Yes, and have faith. Not a puny faith that any ill wind might blow away. Seek to emulate the utter and complete faith of the young and beautiful Nazarene. Jesus spoke always of God as the Father. We should know Him too as the loving and all-wise and all-powerful Father. And we should never hesitate to ask Him to help us. He will. Faith is the very cornerstone of Crossnore."

BESSIE WHITTINGTON PFOHL
Born 1881

Mrs. J. Kenneth Pfohl was born Bessie Whittington on July 28, 1881, in East Bend, Yadkin County, North Carolina, and died in Winston-Salem on November 24, 1971. In her lifetime she successfully combined three roles, bringing honor to each: musician, minister's wife and mother.

She began her musical education at a very early age because both of her parents were musical and recognized her talent. Taught by a succession of piano teachers who always "boarded" in her home, she was prepared for entrance to Salem College, Salem, North Carolina, from which she graduated "with distinction" in piano in 1898 and in the academic course in 1899.

Following her graduation from Salem College, she became the music teacher for the Clemmons School of which the Reverend John Kenneth Pfohl, a young Moravian minister, was the principal. On August 21, 1901, they were married and their joint service to the Moravian Church had its beginning. A veritable ministry of music characterized their service, in which were combined Mr. Pfohl's rich baritone voice and Mrs. Pfohl's sympathetic accompaniments.

In 1927 Mrs. Pfohl graduated from Salem College School of Music in pipe organ, and for eighteen of the twenty-six years when her husband was pastor of the Home Moravian Church she was organist and choir director. During this time she organized the first Junior Choir in North Carolina and devoted much thought and effort to the promotion of hymn-study-memory contests among young people. When her husband was made a Bishop of the Moravian Church in 1931, she resigned from her position of organist in order to be of wider service in the religious and musical life of the many Moravian churches within the Southern Province.

When Mrs. Pfohl was installed in November, 1959, as a member of Delta Omicron International Music Fraternity, her citation read: "She has exhibited a dedicated, life-long love of music, has nurtured the musical and cultural life of her family and is a composer and student, particularly in the field of sacred music."

Mrs. Pfohl held many executive positions in organized musical groups at the local, state and national levels. There, again, her greatest contribution was the encouragement of Hymn Study through the National Federation of Music

Clubs. From 1929 to 1960 she held the position of National Chairman of Hymn Study or a related position, either at the national or state level and from 1955 to 1958 she was the National Chaplain.

Mrs. Pfohl was the mother of six children, three daughters and three sons, all of whom were given the benefit of musical training in addition to their academic work. Three of them chose to become professional musicians. Each member of the family played a musical instrument in addition to the piano and a family orchestra was the result. The National Federation of Music Clubs, at its biennial convention in Boston in 1929, presented them with a silver loving cup for the distinction of having been chosen the "Most Musical Family in America."

Bessie Whittington Pfohl would want to be remembered for her three great loves: music, her family and home, and the Christian Church. They were so closely intertwined that she never consciously gave priority to any one of the three.

KATE BURR JOHNSON

Born 1881

Kate Burr Johnson was born in Morganton, North Carolina, February 14, 1881. She was the daughter of Frederick Hill Burr and Lillian Walton Burr. She was a descendant of the Fairfield Branch of the Burr family in America. In 1903 she married Clarence A. Johnson of Raleigh and was the mother of two sons, Clarence A. Johnson, Jr. and Fredrick Burr Johnson.

Mrs. Johnson received her educational training in the public schools of Morganton and attended Queen's College in Charlotte, North Carolina. Because her later work required specialized training, she attended the New York School of Social Work and the University of North Carolina at Chapel Hill.

Mrs. Johnson was a charter member of the Raleigh Woman's Club and later, in 1917, became its president. She was elected president of the North Carolina Federation of Women's Clubs, was a member of the state committee for the sale of Liberty Bonds, and held the office of vice president of the North Carolina Conference for Social Service.

Largely because of her interest in social work, she was appointed in July of 1921 Commissioner of Public Welfare with the recommendation of Governor Morrison. She became the first woman to head a major North Carolina Department and the first woman in the United States to bear the title of Commissioner of Public Welfare for a state. In other capacities of public service, she was an elected member of the American Academy of Political and Social Sciences of the National Probation Association. She was a member of the executive committee of the Child Welfare League of America and chairman of a committee on state and local organizations for the handicapped. In addition, she was a member of the American Association of Social Workers, the National Conference of Juvenile Agencies and the American Prison Association. After her retirement she served on the Prison Advisory Commission in North Carolina under Governor Kerr Scott.

Kate Burr Johnson's greatest satisfaction probably came from helping to improve the prison conditions for the state; she was instrumental in helping to eliminate cruelty to prisoners on chain gangs in North Carolina. While Commissioner, she was involved in important changes in the law and the formation of new and needed institutions.

In 1930 Mrs. Johnson was asked to become Superintendent for New Jersey's State Home for Girls. During her nineteen-year tenure in Trenton, New Jersey, she administered the home for delinquents and developed a state-wide program of classification for and among women prisoners of the State of New Jersey. In 1948 Mrs. Johnson retired and returned to Raleigh.

In 1951 she was awarded the honorary degree of Doctor of Humane Letters by the Woman's College of the University of North Carolina. In 1954 she was the recipient of the North Carolina Distinguished Service Award for Women presented annually by the Chi Omega Sorority.

Kate Burr Johnson died August 22, 1968, and was buried in Oakwood Cemetery in Raleigh, North Carolina.

MARGARET HOOD CALDWELL

Rural life in North Carolina has made tremendous progress in the past five decades, and Margaret Hood Caldwell, wife of veteran agricultural leader Harry B. Caldwell, has been a part of every movement for the betterment of agriculture and rural life during this period.

Prior to the 1930's, rural electrification and telephones were practically non-existent; rural roads were impassable in much of the fall and winter season; soil erosion was taking its toll and programs to promote conservation of natural resources did not exist; one-room, one-teacher schools dotted the country side; and health facilities and doctors were needed in rural areas across the state.

In view of these needs, Margaret Caldwell's indefatigable spirit led her on to work for bet-

ter conditions so that rural communities of the state might have many of the advantages of urban life. Her efforts have borne fruit as she has articulated the needs and concerns of rural people to the members of Congress, the General Assembly and governmental agencies.

Her interest in rural youth has been manifested in various ways: as Director of North Carolina and National Grange Juvenile Grange activities; as advisor on Maternal and Child Welfare in the U. S. Department of Labor when Frances Perkins was Secretary of Labor and as a member of the first White House Conference on Children in a Democracy when Franklin Roosevelt was President of the United States; and as a member of the United Forces for Education. In North Carolina she has served on many college boards of trustees. She has established the Margaret H. Caldwell Scholarship at North Carolina State University and has been a strong supporter of youth activities in the Grange and in the church. She has been the State Master of the North Carolina Grange for fourteen years—the only woman elected to this position.

Aside from her participation in many activities to improve North Carolina's economy, tax structure, public education and particularly its rural life, she has been involved in programs that are world-wide in scope such as being a member of the United Nations Conference and delegate to the International Federation of Agricultural Producers in Rome, Dublin, London and the United States.

Mrs. Caldwell is also a mother and homemaker. She has two sons, Harry, Jr. and Robert, both of whom are taking their place in business and community affairs. She is devoted to her three lovely granddaughters, Catherine, Janet and Elizabeth.

All of the Caldwells are members of Greensboro's First Baptist Church where Mrs. Caldwell is teacher of the Devotion Bible Class, the largest class in the church, being designated as the "Caring Class" by the Southern Baptist Convention. She has been on the Finance, Missions and the Pulpit committees of the church and was the first woman to be selected speaker on Laymen's Day by the church.

Mrs. Caldwell has received many honors from Presidents and Governors. The University of North Carolina at Greensboro awarded her an Honorary Doctor of Laws Degree in 1957; she was named "Woman of the Year" in 1945 by the *Progressive Farmer*. She received the State

Farmer Degree from Future Farmers of America and was named State Honorary Member of Delta Kappa Gamma in 1974.

Mrs. Caldwell believes that all people should be involved in church, family life and public affairs. "The future well-being of the nation," she says, "is largely dependent upon the high quality of our homes and the progressive attitudes of our people."

MOLLIE HUSTON LEE

Born 1907

Mollie Huston Lee, a wife, a mother and a career woman. Few people are able to combine three roles and perform each with love and enthusiasm. Mollie Lee has proven to be the type of person to combine all three roles successfully.

She was born in Columbus, Ohio, on January 18, 1907. She received her undergraduate degree from Howard University and the B.L.S. from the Columbia University School of Library Science where she was the first Afro-American to receive a scholarship. She was married to the late Dr. James S. Lee, Sr. who was head of the Biology Department at North Carolina Central

University. She is the proud mother of one son, James S. Lee, Jr., a graduate of North Carolina State University, a farmer and radio director.

Mollie was constantly involved in activities that could assist her in providing wholesome activities for her son's continued growth. She was president of the Durham Chapter of Jack and Jill of America for two years and was Mid-Atlantic Regional Director for eight years. During that time she planned regional meetings with programs geared to interest youth and mothers. The purposes of the organization reflect Mollie's philosophy concerning parents and children. They are:

1. To aid in the development of a fully integrated child along the educational, emotional, physical, recreational, religious and social lines.
2. To aid mothers in learning more about their children by careful study.

From the beginning of her library career in 1930 as librarian at Shaw University and the thirty-seven years as public librarian in the City of Raleigh, she made every effort to sponsor programs which would give mothers information on family living and child care. Mollie was responsible for some of the country's most celebrated Black authors of children's literature coming to Raleigh. Such authors as Langston Hughes, Arna Bontemps and Jesse Jackson came for little remuneration, just to participate in the special presentations for children and to share Mollie's enthusiasm.

Mollie Huston Lee was a successful career woman as well as a successful mother. Her career includes a long string of "firsts" and honors. She was the first Black to receive a scholarship to the Columbia University School of Library Science. On the state level she was the first Black public library supervisor and first supervisor of the Delta Public Library in Louis-

burg, North Carolina. She was also the Governor's appointee on the State Library Board and the first Black woman elected "Tar Heel of the Week."

In addition to a string of "firsts" Mollie was responsible for establishing the Richard B. Harrison Library and guided it through three decades. Within this time Mollie established one of the finest Black Collections of Literature that exist in the southeast. The selection of children's books in this collection is outstanding. Mollie wanted Blacks to know about and be proud of their heritage.

Love for her family as well as the community, a desire to share and care, productive planning and an understanding family enabled Mollie Huston Lee to succeed as a wife, mother and career woman.

North Dakota

North Dakota

Nickname: Sioux State

State Flower: Wild prairie Rose

State Bird: Western meadowlark

Photos

1. Harvesting
2. Badlands scene
3. Stock raising
4. Fishing & picnicing on Lake Sakakawea
5. State Capital with Fairbanks Statue of pioneers
6. Rodeo competition
7. State of Sakakawea
8. Peace Garden

Committee Members

Chairman—Mrs. Earl Bucklin, Mandan
Mrs. H.W. Case, Bismarck
Mrs. V.C. Swenson, Mandan
Mrs. H.B. Uden, Mandan
Mrs. Blanche Vande Walle, Bismarck
Russ Hanson
"Bill" Leingang, Bismarck

Writers

Hazel Eastman
Mrs. Deborah Hertz
Mrs. M.B. McGuigan
Glenn J. Frutti
Ruth Lunney Jocobsen
Mrs. Harold Jensen, Sr.
Mrs. Dave M. Robinson
Mildred S. Werlesberger
Mrs. Ella Rorentzen
Rev. H.W. Case

North Dakota

LINDA W. SLAUGHTER

Born 1843

Linda Warfel Slaughter has been referred to as "unquestionably the outstanding woman of Dakota in the 1870's and 1880's." She was at once mother, homemaker, professional writer, amateur painter, school teacher and superintendent, church worker and postmistress. Through her writing she left a legacy of history on life in pioneer Dakota which is treasured, not only as authentic, but as the only recorded history of an early frontier area.

Educated beyond the usual for her time and from a comfortable background—she met the challenge of frontier life, so alien to her beginnings, with her usual enthusiasm.

She was born in Cadiz, Ohio, February 1843 to General Charles and Mary (Boyd) Warfel. Upon graduation from Oberlin College she went south for a missionary society to work among the freedmen. Here she met Dr. Benjamin F. Slaughter, a surgeon with the Kentucky Mounted Infantry, whom she married at Cadiz on August 20, 1868.

In 1871 he was ordered to Fort Rice, Dakota Territory; and later to Camp Hancock where the infant town that grew around it developed into Bismarck, N. Dak. Later, rather than be transferred, Dr. Slaughter resigned his commission and became a citizen of the town.

Linda Slaughter was the first postmistress; started the first Sunday School, and worked diligently for every denomination which attempted to establish a church there.

She started a school which, when a county was organized in 1873, became the nucleus of the public schools and she was then appointed County Superintendent of Schools. In 1877 she was appointed Department Superintendent of Institutions for Dakota Territory.

Before marriage her books, *Summerings in the South* and *Freedmen of the South*, plus some girlhood poems "Early Efforts", had been published. From the frontier she wrote articles for papers in New York, Chicago, and St. Paul. In 1874 she wrote for the Burleigh County Pioneers Association, a pamphlet "The New North-

west" containing descriptions of the area. (This is now listed in Rare Books.) In addition to many sketches, she also wrote "The Amazonian Corps" and "Leaves from Northwestern History."

In 1889 Mrs. Slaughter organized "The Ladies Historical Society" from which the present day North Dakota State Historical Society evolved.

She was a charter member of the Daughters of the American Revolution, and active in the Women's Christian Temperance Union—being press superintendent of the latter in territorial days.

In the 1880's she spent many active winters in Washington, D. C. She was Vice-president of the National Press Association of that city and State Vice-president of the National Women's Suffrage Association.

In 1895 she was admitted to practice before the Bureau of Pensions, by the Law Division of the Department of Interior.

In later years she homesteaded, taught a country school, and established a postoffice at Slaughter, N. Dak.

She raised three daughters—her only son, born at Fort Rice, died shortly after birth.

Dr. Slaughter died in 1896 at age 54, and she was fifteen years a widow. Her own death occurred in 1911 after six years of suffering from a disease, not definitely diagnosed but which led from crutches, to wheel-chair, to bedridden.

SUSAN WEBB HALL

Born 1850

Susan Webb Hall was born June 11, 1850 daughter of Mr. and Mrs. Samuel Hall of Weymouth, Massachusetts where she grew up and was educated.

At twenty-seven she heard the call to adventure by becoming a foreign Missionary to the Indians in the West. She remained for eight years in Nebraska.

In the meantime Charles Hall, also a foreign Missionary, while transporting Indian children to Mission schools, met Susan Webb. They were married in 1886. They picked up eight-year-old Robert and six-year-old Hannah, children of Charles' former marriage, and arrived at Ft. Berthold on July 4, 1886.

Susan tells in her own words of the arrival at Ft. Berthold: "We approached Ft. Berthold on a steamboat on the Missouri River. We had boarded at Bismarck. The vastness and loneliness of the rolling prairies was appaling. The coming of the steamboat was a great event and everybody met there—representatives from the Agency, Indians in their blankets and the children."

Charles and Susan started a school for Indian children in their home but the parents came instead. They represented three tribes: the Mandan, Hidatsa, Arikara. These later became the Three Affiliated Tribes.

The Halls told the Indians, "If you come five days, then on Friday you eat." They were given small gifts of food and told about God's love. Susan made calls with her husband to their homes in the village.

In 1890 when the Indians began moving out on their government allotments, the Halls traveled many miles to keep in touch with them in their prairie homes.

By 1891 Evan and Deborah had been added to the Hall family. The four children grew to love Indian brothers and sisters as the Mother did.

The Mission Home was the center where workers came for refreshment of mind and body. It had the atmosphere of a strong and deep Christ-like love.

In 1897 the Mission Home was moved to Elbowoods. The Indians had carefully taken down the Mission house and rebuilt it at Elbowoods where the Agency had been established. Soon a second generation boarding school was begun at the request of the parents who had gone to the first school. Native leaders carried on the church work.

Several Indian women lived in the Hall home from time to time and became leaders among their own people.

Susan said: "There are two things I'd hoped to do, to help the women become better Christians, and tell the young men that Christianity is real." An Indian woman replied, "You have given your life for us." *'Ho Was-tay'* translated *'Good News'* was the name the Indians gave the Protestant Church.

In 1925-26 the Memorial Church at Elbowoods, N. Dak. was finished and dedicated in Susan Webb Hall's honor. It stands on the prairie 15 miles south of Parshall, N. Dak. near the cemetary where are the graves of many of the Ft. Berthold Reservation dear ones.

Susan passed away November 20, 1922.

ANNA D. DERSHEIMER KINDRED
Born 1856

"Political Activist" and "Woman's Liberation-ist" would have been strange terms to Anna Dersheimer, who came to Dakota Territory to homestead in 1883; but this pioneer lady would have been in the thick of the battle for social reform and equal rights if she were living to-day.

The daughter of Peter Dersheimer and Laura Woodbridge was born in Clarks Summit, Pennsylvania, December 15, 1856 and was educated at the Wyoming Seminary in Pennsylvania. Her forbears on both sides of her family were active in the Revolutionary War.

Traveling to Lisbon, Dakota Territory with a friend, she secured a horse and buggy and went 22 miles to Sargent County to settle. The prospect of living alone in a claim shanty soon lost its appeal for the young teacher and she returned to Lisbon. She secured a position as teacher in a one-room school located where Enderlin is today. Each day Anna waded the Maple River to get to her school from her boarding home. The buffalo had been driven from the prairie by this time in 1884 but there were many buffalo horns which the children collected and brought to school. These were sent back East at the end of the year to be used commercially. Ducks and geese were plentiful in the area as were wild flowers.

On one occasion she kept three children in a plowed field all night to protect them from a dreaded prairie fire.

Anna met F. E. Kindred in the bank in Lisbon where she cashed her salary check. They were married in 1888 and resided in Richland County. (John Miller, the first Governor of N. Dakota was a neighbor and member of her Sunday School class.) They moved to Traill County in 1890 and later to Fargo.

In 1913 when the women began to fight for the right to vote, Mrs. Kindred traveled throughout the state accompanying the leader of the group, Mrs. E. M. Darrow. Mrs. Charles Amidon and Jeannette Rankin, who later became the first U.S. Congresswoman, also joined them.

A group of concerned citizens in Fargo conducted a social survey in 1915. Health and sanitation problems were great for the city of 2,878 homes. The city was pressed to appoint health inspectors (no pay). Mrs. Kindred was one of those inspectors. Her reports on the sanitary conditions and the abundance of rats in business places caused such a commotion that a reporter from the Fargo Forum accompanied her on inspection trips. Her reports were verified and the city fathers were pressured into starting a systematic kitchen garbage collection.

Mrs. Kindred was a charter member of Fargo's first Community Club, a group that studied civic questions. She was also a member of the Fine Arts Club founded in 1911, the New Era Club, and the Daughter's of the American Revolution.

The Fargo Forum featured her as an outstanding Pioneer Mother in 1931.

She died May 15, 1937.

ANNA R. MILLER BURKHART
Born 1868

Anna R. Miller Burkhart, daughter of Joel and Katie Miller of Elkhart, Indiana was born July 4, 1868. She married Samuel W. Burkhart of Elkhart on December 31, 1887. Ten children were born to them.

Her husband Samuel was a member of an ad hoc committee in 1893 which came to North Dakota through promotion by the Northern Railroad to study the possibility of settling and helping to develop the land. The Burkharts and three children then came to North Dakota with an immigrant group in 1894.

Anna's home was given to hospitality, always

ready to provide shelter and food to those in need, especially at the Church District Conference time, and the Fall Festivals held in the "Mother Church" at Zion, N. Dak. The church was known as "Mother Church" because most of the congregations of Dunkards (German Baptist Brethren) in North Dakota, Eastern Montana, and Canada were an outgrowth of this congregation. Many people came many miles with horses and buggies for transportation. These needed places to stay as often the dirt roads became impassable and the weather inclement.

Sister Burkhart made the bonnets and prayer veils for all the women and girls who were members of the church and she also had on hand dozens of veils when extras were needed.

Anna was a midwife from the age of eighteen years and served in that work for practically every home in the community. At times when the conditions in the homes of expectant mothers was unfavorable she took the mother into her own home for delivery of the baby and care until the baby was at least 10 days old.

In pioneer days there were no hospitals, undertakers, or a demand for embalming so she sometimes was called on to prepare bodies for burial.

When the 1918 influenza epidemic struck, she was the first to become ill. The doctor would not name it as such because there were no known cases closer than Minneapolis, Minnesota. But it was not long until other homes in North Dakota had members who became ill. Since she had recovered from the flu she was not afraid to go in and help in any way needed. She often went to homes where there was death and took over responsibility for helping. When her own children were sick she still went to other homes in the day time leaving Father Burkhart to care for those at home. When she came home at night she would care for the duties of the home.

Being a Deacon's wife she was always on hand to help in church activities. She was one of the first women to organize a Ladies Aid to make clothing and bedding for the needy. But in such a busy life her family and home were never neglected.

Mother Burkhart died in December, 1947, at the age of 79 leaving a legacy of good deeds for others to emulate. The years have passed since her death and many people still stop at the home of her daughter, Mrs. Katie Louck, in Cando, to find from Anna Burkhart's diary the date of their birth to serve as confirmation for a Birth Certificate.

JESSIE MAE WENCK LUNNEY
Born 1870

Jessie Mae Wenck Lunney was born in Watsontown, Penn. in 1870, daughter of Mr. and Mrs. Wenck. She became an orphan at the age of thirteen and lived with relatives in Harrisburg until her uncle, D. M. Holmes, who was an early pioneer of Grand Forks, persuaded her to come to North Dakota. She arrived in 1889.

A summer school session at the University of North Dakota and a few months at Mayville Normal enabled her to get a teacher's certificate and she taught in many rural schools in the county. One time she had the experience of looking out the school house window and seeing a group of about twenty Indians dressed in native costume coming toward the school. She was alarmed but was happy when they passed by without paying any attention to the school.

Her career as a teacher ended when she married James Lunney who had a homestead. They had four children.

She knew nothing of country life except what she had learned while teaching. It was a big change for her but she had determination. She always raised a big garden, canned and pickled the produce, sewed for the family, and cooked for several hired men who were required to do the farm work as those were the days of horse power. Yet she found time for many extra ac-

tivities. During World War I, she was township chairman of the knitting and sewing classes of the Red Cross.

She always took an interest in school affairs and served as clerk for many years. She spent the small salary she received as clerk to buy books for the school library. She organized a Reading Circle for the girls in the neighborhood. During the summer vacations many of the neighborhood girls walked three or more miles to attend this Reading Circle.

Washing dishes was an enjoyable event. While the children took turns washing dishes Mother would wipe them and quote poetry.

In 1904 a postal route from Larimore to Fergus took in Moraine Township and Jessie became postmistress at Moraine Post Office which was one room of Lunney's home. This continued for about ten years when a rural route was established.

Jessie also found time to write for the weekly paper and each week "Moraine News" appeared in "The Larimore Pioneer." She also wrote special features.

Sunday was Church Day and every Sunday when the weather was suitable the family drove the twelve miles to Larimore in a spring wagon, surrey, or sleigh to attend services.

She insisted that her two daughters board and room in town and attend high school and also continue their education to obtain teacher's certificates.

Jessie received neither praise nor fame and yet like many other mothers, each in her own way, she did contribute to the culture, industry, and religion of a needy country. She died in 1961.

MARY MCNAMARA NEVENS
Born 1872

Mary McNamara Nevens was born in Limerick, Ireland, February 1, 1872, the daughter of Mr. and Mrs. John McNamara. She spent her early life in Ireland and attended the National Model School for Girls in Limerick. A thirst for education brought her alone at the age of 15 to Dakota Territory to an uncle's homestead in Pembina County in June 1887. She completed her grade school in Ireland but she attended the log school to gain knowledge in civics, American history, and the American system of money.

She got her teacher's degree at the University of Valparaiso, Indiana and taught successfully for 12 years before marriage and one year following. She married Wm. Nevens January 6, 1902.

At the age of 87 she wrote by longhand her own 13 page biography. She related how she milked two cows before leaving for school and again in the evening. She remembered seeing a band of Indians in Red River carts passing the school. The men sat in the carts and the squaws and children followed walking. Her uncle built a sod house and plastered it with a mixture of water, mud, and lime. Later he built a log house.

Her biography states: "It is wonderful to note, true goodness and self-sacrifice is never beaten, not even by death itself. None of those people had much wealth at that time, but possessed strength, skill, a mighty faith, and a mind to work. The original pioneers were a courageous people and weathered many difficult years. The example and influence of those pioneers has been kept alive long after they are gone."

During the early years, her uncle broadcast grain by hand carrying the seed in a sheet. When threshing time came the farmers exchanged work with each other and the women did the cooking each trying to outdo the other. Dried fruits from the store and dried berries from local woods were used. There was no canning as jars were not yet available.

Her biography goes on: "In memory I recall the kitchen stove, the wood box to be filled each night, the kerosene lamps, laundry tub and washboard, coal stove in the parlor, center table with ball-fringed cloth, family album, spinning wheel, corn-husk or straw filled mattresses, patch-work quilt, dash churn, medicine shelf containing plenty of goose oil, sulphor, and molasses—the spelling bees; box socials, trips to town on Saturday afternoons in buggy, cutter, or bob sled with sleigh bells jingling. Friends and neighbors met and chatted in store or street. All these things are fast becoming a legend and although they bring nostalgic memories, we would not wish them back. I am thankful I have lived to see a better life than we ever dreamed."

In 1961 Mrs. Nevens was the recipient of the Dakota Territory Centennial Award signed by Governor William Guy and other dignitaries.

Her four daughters followed her footsteps and became teachers. One entered a religious profession and is employed in India.

Mrs. Nevens died in August of 1965.

PAULINE SHOEMAKER CROWLEY
Born 1879

Pauline Shoemaker Crowley was a liberated woman two generations before the phrase was invented. At age 90 she told a granddaughter, "Do lots of interesting things while you are young so you have interesting thoughts when you are old." She had lived her advice.

She was born in 1879 of Holland Dutch ancestry, the second of three girls of Andrew and Susannah Shoemaker in the little village of Shoemakers, Penn. beside the Delaware River. After graduating from the East Stroudsburg Normal School in 1897 with recommendations that proclaimed her very proficient in Greek and Latin, she taught school in that area for several years.

Her cousin had gone west, and he secured a teaching position for her at Mandan High School where she was principal three years from 1901 to 1904. She had ridden side saddle in Pennsylvania but in the rugged west she switched to riding astride—with a trooper from Fort Lincoln and many times on the Ralph Ward ranch on the Fort Berthold Reservation west of Garrison. In 1910 she participated in their week-long horse roundup. To do so she had to get a note from Dr. LaRose that for health reasons she needed a vacation.

She taught one year in Sheridan, California arriving when the cracks from the San Francisco earthquake were still visible. The following summer she spent a couple of months with a

young couple following their sheep camp over the Sierra Nevada mountains. But she longed for North Dakota and returned to Bismarck where she taught in the Will School.

She thought she had done almost everything else in the West so in 1911 she filed on a homestead north of Hebron along the Knife River. Here four neighbor children were students in her claim shack for several years. The desks were set outside over the weekend. In 1914 she married a neighboring rancher Matt Crowley and moved to Elm Creek in Mercer County. They had three daughters.

Although 15 miles out in the country she was interested in civic affairs. Rural school teachers often lived at the ranch. Later she joined Daughters of the American Revolution and participated in Church groups.

Her husband was one of the early members of the Independent Voters Association which was organized in opposition to the takeover of the Republican Party by the Non-Partisan League. She also participated in political activities and helped elect her husband to the state legislature as representative in 1911. They also helped elect a Democrat John Moses as Governor.

When the oldest daughter started high school, she and the girls moved into a brick house in Hebron which had been acquired earlier with this need in mind. Here she started the Hebron Study Club and was president again 30 years later.

In 1937 she was chosen by Governor Moses as the first woman member when the newly created Board of Higher Education was formed.

She died at the age of 91 in 1960.

LAURA NELSON PLUMMER
Born 1880

Laura Nelson Plummer was born of emigrant parents, Mr. and Mrs. John Wilhelm Nelson in Republic, Michigan, October 27, 1880 and moved with them to Dakota Territory in 1885 traveling by train, ox team and wagon. They spent one winter in Grand Harbor and homesteaded at Leeds in 1886. From this pioneer home, a sod house before the frame building was built, she entered the first local one-room school in 1889, coping with the others with the scarcity of texts and desks. Two years later she became "printer's devil" and baby sitter for the town's newspaper editor and wife, Mr. and Mrs. A. J. Garver. She learned to set type in the printers stick, transfer it to the galley and print the paper so well that when Mr. Garver was detained in 1893, she, at thirteen years, published the paper alone, even printing a requested Pound Notice.

Later she went to Arvilla to attend high school, earning her way at a home, but quit to work at the Wm. Plummer Company General Store in Minnewaukan, North Dakota where she worked for five years. She saved enough money to attend the University of North Dakota Normal School for a summer and taught a school near her home for their three months' term. She turned down an offer to return, to marry Clarence F. Plummer of the Wm. Plummer Company on May 10, 1903. Six children were born to this union.

Mrs. Plummer continued her education by wide reading and by taking advantage of courses offered in the community including the Devils Lake Chautaugua. She was very creative—painting in oil and water colors, enjoying crafts of seed and shell work, gardening and writing poetry. Her poems were published in papers and anthologies: *Dakota Farmer, Prairie Wings, New Jersey Country Bard, North Dakota Singing, Paetar, Poets on Parade,* and *Harrisons.*

An active member of the Minnewaukan Presbyterian Church, she served as trustee, Sunday School teacher, Christian Endeavor leader, Women's Association officer, Presbyterial Young People's secretary, Missionary Society officer, and was a member and officer of the Women's Christian Temperance Union, Golden Leaf Chapter, Order of the Eastern Star, Degree of Honor, and was a charter member and officer of the federated club Timely Topics. Later she

joined the Lake Region Pioneer Daughters. She was active in community projects until her age and a fall in 1966 handicapped her somewhat. She died after nearly three years of invalidism on August 20, 1970, survived by four children, five grandchildren, and three great-grandchildren. Her influence on her family and community was always highly inspirational and her gift of friendship extended to the many young people who roomed in her home or were friends of her children.

CLARA NELSON HERSETH
Born 1884

Early in life Clara Lydia Nelson embraced a philosophy of love, learning, and serving others. Clara was born March 12, 1884 to Nels and Eleana Nelson. The family migrated to Dakota Territory. Clara was overjoyed when her father purchased an organ for her 13th birthday. She took lessons and served as church organist. Clara attended Concordia College until the death of her mother.

In 1905 she married Nels Herseth at Milton where Nels operated a meat market. Two years later they loaded a few pieces of furniture, her organ, oxen, chickens, and a cow on an emigrant car and headed for a homestead in western North Dakota near a settlement called "Hobo Kingdom" which became the village of

Battle View. Their sod shanty on the prairie was a favorite with other homesteaders especially bachelors who came for Clara's Scandinavian hospitality including baking, laundering, mending, and Clara's organ playing.

Clara and a neighbor Hannah Johnson, drove twenty miles to White Earth for supplies and mail. Threat of prairie fires and rebellious oxen made the long trip memorable. The journey home seemed shorter as they avidly read the "White Earth Weekly." They chuckled over the gossip column trying to identify "unusual characters" by their escapades. The papers were saved to cover shanty walls.

Meanwhile Clara and Nels impatiently waited for the arrival of the first child. Seven girls and one boy followed in rapid succession completing their family. They built a frame house which soon bulged at the seams. Besides cooking, baking, washing, canning, and gardening, Clara took care of an invalid sister until her death and cared for her sister's two motherless children. A nephew came from Norway and stayed two years. Later Uncle Sandy and Uncle John lived with them for many years. There were times when the children had their differences, Mother had her own way of quelling the chaos, even using the "proverbial rod" on all to get the culprit.

Sewing was a never ending job, someone always needing clothes. Printed flour sacks were saved for petticoats, bibs, and dish towels.

Recreation originated in the home. Long winter evenings were enjoyed by reading, singing, games, and pulling taffy. Every family awaited the 4th of July picnic and Christmas programs.

The Herseths were members of Bethel Lutheran Church where Mrs. Herseth served as church organist, choir director, and Sunday School superintendent. It took patience for a busy mother to give music lessons to family and community.

In her early forties Clara was stricken with multiple sclerosis leaving her right side paralyzed confining her to a wheel chair. She spent hours crocheting tablecloths and other articles for her beloved church with a specially designed hook. Friends and neighbors who stopped to chat with the cheerful invalid came away spiritually refreshed as they observed her Christian faith and selfless love. Her husband remained a friend, good father, and faithful companion until his death in 1945. Mrs. Herseth continued to be a source of comfort and inspiration. She died in 1947.

INA BEAUCHAMP HALL

Born 1905

Ina Beauchamp Hall, daughter of Peter Beauchamp and Adeline Powell, was born on Berthold Reservation March 4, 1905. Ina was a delicate child and even though she suffered a stroke while in high school, she graduated. She was the first person of Indian blood to graduate from a public school.

She taught school until her marriage to Edward Hall. After her marriage she managed a ranch with her husband while raising nine children.

To help with expenses, she accepted a "temporary" teaching position. She improved this school, organized the first 4-H Club and the first Parent Teachers Association, and made the school a center for community activities. At the age of 41, she started to attend summer sessions at a teacher's college. Seven years later, after much hard work, and difficulty, including the death of her husband, and the loss of her home, she secured her teaching certificate.

Continuing to teach, she became a school principal of an all-white school and initiated many improvements and advancements for the benefit of the pupils. She next accepted an appointment with the North Dakota State Extension Service as extension agent for her reservation. In this capacity, she started thirteen 4-H Clubs, four Home-Makers Clubs, and four Community Development Clubs. She raised the money to establish a community center and worked to obtain better housing for the reservation Indians.

It would be difficult to list all of the wonderful service rendered by Mrs. Hall in her lifetime. She served three terms on the North Dakota Commission on Adult Education, organized and wrote the curriculum for the first arts and crafts training schools which served as models for other reservations, and started the annual reservation fair, and numerous other activities.

Somehow, she was able to buy another home and to send all nine of her children to college. She was a pillar of strength in times of sorrow and need, and a friend to Indian and non-Indian alike. No doubt she was the outstanding leader at Ft. Berthold.

She was North Dakota Mother in 1966.

Ohio

Nickname: Buckeye State

State Flower: Scarlet Carnation

State Tree: Ohio Buckeye

State Bird: Cardinal

Photos

1. Replica of Charles Goodyear's 1839 "laboratory"
2. Hocking Valley Scenic Railway
3. Original Mormon Temple at Kirtland
4. German-American Festival, Tdedo
5. Stan Hywet House & Gardens, Akron
6. Hocking Hills State Park Dining Lodge
7. Roadside rest area on 1-71
8. Wileswood Country Store, Huron
9. Sea World of Ohio, Aurora

Committee Members

Mrs. Robert J. Wherry, Columbus

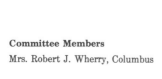

Ohio

MARY SHERIDAN

Born 1810

A bit of fate destined Mary and John Sheridan to be persuaded to leave Baileborough County, Ireland. Their coming helped shape the destiny of America. Mary's brother had been in a fight and had left Ireland to escape the hands of the law. After months the Sheridans had a letter to the effect that if Mary, her husband, and two children would come to America that a job awaited him on the Erie Canal at Albany. They responded and came to Boston in 1831.

The family could not afford Cabin fare and were herded together on the ship with many others. Cholera broke out and their only daughter, Rose, died and was buried at sea.

From Boston they went by stagecoach and hired wagon to Albany, New York. John and Mary's brother, Jimmy Minaugh, constructed a log cabin for the family. In March, 1831, Phillip Sheridan was born, later to become one of the Civil War heroes. In 1833, the family moved to Somerset in Perry County, Ohio. John was hired to work on the new National Pike that would join the West to the East. The Maysville Pike ran from Zanesville, Ohio to Maysville, Kentucky (people were ferried across the Ohio River). This road was considered a main artery of travel for many years.

Mary insisted on living in the country where she could teach the boys about gardening and where she could cook for her husband and others building the pike. Their cabin was owned by General Richey.

When she had left Ireland, Mary could neither read nor write, but anxious to learn she took a teacher in to board and became an avid reader and read the world's best literature. Determined that their sons would be good scholars, she made them study. They moved back to Somerset, Ohio, so the boys could get training at a school located in the Village. However, poverty overtook them through bad investments and the boys had to get jobs. Mary insisted that Phillip study books when not working at the Village store. She hoped he would become a priest, but Phillip was anxious to have an appointment to West Point. He studied history, political maneuvers of the statesmen of his time and military achievements of Napoleon. He had met and talked with Sherman, newly graduated from West Point.

Later, Phillip inquired about getting an appointment. His opportunity came when General Richey's appointed scholar failed his examinations. The world is aware of the splendid victories later made by General Phillip Sheridan; and, that he was made General of the United States Army; and, that his mission to Europe brought him great honor.

Colonel John and Pvt. Michael Sheridan both fought on the Northern side during the Civil War. Mary lived to see all return. All had merited honors during the war.

Mary Sheridan was a dominant, courageous, and fearless mother. Her sons inherited these qualities. The family liked to recall how Mary fearlessly wrestled a pig to get Michael's hand out of the pig's mouth.

MARGARET GREY SOLOMON
Wyandot County   **Born 1815**

In what is now Wyandot County, a daughter was born to an influential Wyandot Chief in the year of 1816. She was named Margaret.

When Margaret was seven years old, the first Industrial Arts School was opened in Upper Sandusky. She was the very first pupil enrolled. She learned the spinning and carding of flax and wool and learned how to sew. She learned how to read and write which at the time was most unusual for an Indian child.

In the old Wyandot Mission, Margaret was taught to appreciate the principles of Christianity and she became very religious. The mission school had its beginning through James H. Findley, a leading Methodist Missionary to the Wyandots. Margaret was dedicated to Christianity and although a woman she became the first of her tribe to teach the gospel of peace and goodwill to her people.

Margaret was eighteen years old when she married Chief Solomon and brought a new worker into the field of Christianity. She persuaded her husband to study about Christ and he, Chief Solomon, became a fully ordained minister. The Chief and Margaret Solomon had eight babies but none survived infancy. Thus, Margaret sad and disappointed with the loss of her own family, decided that she would administer to all the children of her race. She worked hard and became known from the center of the State of Ohio to Lake Erie. She was known to red man and the white man alike and was admired by both and became known to all as "Mother Solomon."

In the early 1840's, the Wyandots were ordered by "the Great White Father" in Washington to leave their "happy hunting grounds" and to go westward beyond the Mississippi River and even beyond the mountains. Many Indians had studied Christianity, had accepted the white man's religion, and the brotherly love that had been taught was shattered. The Wyandots were angry and no one more angry than Chief Solomon. However, Margaret persuaded the Chief and others to accept the situation and they did. In 1843, the Wyandots moved by wagon train and settled in Kansas.

Mother Solomon treasured old memories of her home in Ohio, the place where all of her children were buried. After her husband's death, she sent a written message to Washington and pleaded that she be allowed to return to her homeland. The request was granted. It was a great homecoming for Margaret Solomon. The Mission Church at Upper Sandusky was restored in 1889. At its dedication, all listened intently to Mother Solomon chant the native songs of her tribe.

Mother Solomon lived near Hayman's Mill in a frame cabin. On August 17, 1890, she passed away. Her ashes rest in the old Mission Cemetery close to those of tribal chiefs and others who called her "Mother Solomon."

MIRIAM PIERCE WILLIAMSON
Wilmington   **Born 1822**

Miriam Pierce Williamson was born in Wilmington, Ohio, in 1822, to Mr. and Mrs. Richard Pierce, both Quakers who had come to Wilmington in 1813. Her father, an abolitionist, was an editor of the newspaper, Advocate for Peace.

At eighteen years of age, Miriam was married to a Virginian, Dr. Francis Williamson, a graduate of the Rush Medical College at Philadelphia. Their first home was in Wilmington, but later they moved to Waynesville, Ohio.

Miriam gave birth to six children and family needs were urgent. She and Francis agreed that material things could come later. However, Miriam was soon earning a bit.

This young mother had a magnetic personality and a real ability to heal others. Miriam was a brilliant woman with great physical and mental endurance. She decided to study medicine by reading her husband's medical books. Under his guidance and supervision Miriam was soon practicing as a professional doctor. People were skeptical and considered her a female oddity. However, it did not take long before people respected this energetic woman and sought her to heal them. She was a tremendous success. In later life, Miriam became the sole support of her family. She was highly honored by the whole community.

Her death came suddenly in 1890, and the Waynesville Press printed the following news item:

"After having been absent on professional duty most the late spring and summer, Dr. Miriam Williamson was summoned here a few weeks ago on account of sickness in her own family. Then her ministrations being no longer necessary, she came one day of last week, to her home in this place, for a little rest and preparation before leaving on the following Monday for Richmond, where sick ones anxiously awaited her coming. Last Saturday forenoon she was out in town attending to affairs of the household, and in the afternoon she was at home, entertaining friends and sewing, and apparently in her usual health. But at four o'clock 'the silver cord was loosed, the golden bowl was broken', and her spirit, freed from its tenement of clay, had soared away to the realms of beatific rest."

Miriam, an early Ohio mother and resolute person found that she had freedom to do what she determined to do. She served humanity, practicing medicine, and healing the sick long before licensing of doctors was thought about.

LUCY WEBB HAYES
Chillicothe   Born 1831

Lucy Webb was the youngest child and only daughter among three children born to Dr. James and Maria Cook Webb. Lucy was born on August 28, 1831, in Chillicothe, Ohio. When Lucy was two years old, there was a cholera epidemic that caused the death of her father. At ten years of age, the family moved to Delaware, Ohio, where she and her brothers would attend Ohio Wesleyan University. Here, in this famous college town, she met her husband to be, Rutherford B. Hayes, a practicing lawyer in Lower Sandusky (Fremont), Ohio. He fell in love with 'her beauty, genuine warmth, and her sincerity, but never fully appreciated her capabilities. Hayes' mother approved of Lucy for her son.

In 1848, the Webb family moved to Cincinnati and Lucy attended and graduated from the Cincinnati Wesleyan Women's College.

She and Rutherford B. Hayes were married on December 31, 1852. Three of eight children born to them died in infancy.

Lucy was a courageous woman and a tactful and popular one, displaying an almost perfect type wife for an ambitious husband, who as a young lawyer was swiftly rising in the political field. He became City Solicitor of Cincinnati from 1858-1861. During the Civil War years,

Lucy would visit her soldier husband between campaigns and when he was severely wounded at South Mountain, Maryland, she went to care for him until he recovered. Hayes became a Congressman following the war and Lucy was the perfect hostess while in Washington. She became First Lady of Ohio during the three terms when Hayes was Governor 1868-1872, 1876-1877.

She became First Lady of the nation when her husband became President. She was the first wife of a President to hold a college degree. From 1877-1881, the Hayes family tried to serve as a model family for the nation. Smoking was forbidden, no alcoholic drinks were served, no dances were held at The White House. Neither lawn parties nor card parties were allowed. Daily prayers and hymn singing were the rule for all the household. She was often called "Lemonade Lucy" but she did not seem to mind. She herself was not a prohibionist, but she upheld her husband's ideas while he was President. She was so hospitable and well liked that it has been said that she rivaled Dolly Madison's popularity. As the President's wife she was very happy, enjoying both official and personal private life while acting as the nation's hostess. She was a great help to our nineteenth President of the United States as he sought to create harmony in the country following the reconstruction period of the Civil War.

After living in Washington Lucy found happiness at her home in Spiegel Grove, Fremont, Ohio. She was known to love people and all the majesty of nature. She died on June 25, 1889, and is buried beside her husband on a knoll in Spiegel Grove.

MATTIE MCCLELLAN BROWN
Born 1838

Mattie was the daughter of Jane and David McClellan and although born in Baltimore, Maryland, in 1838, her parents moved to Ohio in 1840.

At the age of twenty, Mattie was married to Rev. W. Kennedy Brown in 1858. Dr. Brown was head of the Cincinnati Wesleyan College so it was only natural that Mattie's dynamic personality would influence and inspire students to become better thinkers. Later, Mattie became Vice-President of the College.

Mattie Brown was a Cincinnati lecturer, educator, and reformer. So brilliant were her lectures that a committee from Greensburg, Pennsylvania, introduced her as a lecturer on National topics in Music Hall, Philadelphia, in the winter of 1864.

She was a Temperance Leader and identified with the order of Good Templars for her unique work. She was the only woman lecturer to speak out on the public platform in Ohio. She upheld women's equal position in all professional and business life. Her official duties, correspondence, decisions, plans for work, and promotional ability were clearly explained in conversation, by letter or when speaking to individuals or to groups.

In 1869, she agreed to enter into the Prohibition Party Movement provided that it should stand for women's full suffrage. She cooperated in all areas, held offices, promoted conventions, spoke, wrote, and lectured until 1896, when the Prohibitionists adopted a single plank. Mattie was finished with the organization and walked out.

Mattie was a mother to three sons and three daughters. They were Orson Graff Brown, Richard McClellan Brown, Klem Thaw Brown, and Wessie Brown Robertson, Charme Brown Shippen, and Marie Brown Shanks.

Mattie was an organizer and an originator of clubs with school mothers. She started the fresh air movement in Cincinnati in 1888.

She is credited as being the organizer of the first women's state temperance association (at Columbus, Ohio in 1874), and that she inaugurated the National W.C.T.U. at Chautauqua, N.Y., in November, 1874.

She became internationally known after representing the Good Templars of Ohio at the London Convention in 1873. She visited in many provinces while abroad and lectured frequently. Another time she was a delegate for the Prohibition Party and attended the international convention at Berne, Switzerland. This speech was widely publicized. All the leading newspapers spoke highly of Mattie Brown. In England, The Glasglow, Liverpool, Edinburgh, and London papers spoke most flatteringly of Mattie McClellan Brown. One paper said, "One who speaks sincerely deserves much praise."

Her service and achievements in life would be hard for any woman to attain at any time or in any age. She was granted the unusual Literary Degrees from Pennsylvania colleges in 1882-Ph.D., 1883-LLD.

REBECCA DAVIS RICKOFF
Cincinnati

Rebecca Davis Rickoff was the daughter of Professor Monroe Davis of Cincinnati, Ohio. She was valedictorian of her high school class. At twenty-one years old she began a teaching career. This lasted for a two year period only. Rebecca fell in love with the Superintendent of the Cincinnati Public Schools. They were married.

According to the custom most people would have expected that Rebecca would give up outside interests and become a devoted wife. Married teachers were frowned upon and not allowed in many systems. Married women teachers were occasionally allowed to teach if the family was in dire circumstances due to ill health or death of a husband. Girls getting married secretly were fired when the marriage was revealed. Although Rebecca did not continue to teach in the school system she, as a born educator, was determined to accomplish more than her household duties. Rebecca gave birth to one daughter. And, in spite of a mother's home and family responsibilities she found time to write and publish educational articles. Many times she found time to lecture on these articles. She spoke out furiously in both lectures and articles on the vital issues of the day (educational issues). Because of her educational insight and principles in the field of Education she was asked, and she accepted the role as the leading speaker for the National Educational Association. Later, she did all in her power to establish the first kindergarten in Cleveland, Ohio. She invited Elizabeth Peabody to come and lecture on this new development in education.

Rebecca's husband became Superintendent of the Cleveland Public Schools. This was a help to Rebecca. She and her husband became equally distinguished in Cincinnati and Cleveland.

In 1873, Mrs. Rickoff edited leaflets for supplementary reading. Soon afterwards, she and Professor Rickoff collaborated with Dr. William T. Harris, editing the famous "Appleton Readers."

Rebecca was active in organizations. She was a member of the Women's Congress when the first meeting was held in Cleveland. Her leadership brought her the distinction of being President of the Young Women's Christian Association; also, of being chosen as President of the American Social Science Association. However, Rebecca's chief interest remained in the educational field and she kept abreast of new methods of learning. Her involvements in organizations and her ability to present a woman's viewpoint on important issues of the time helped lay a pathway for women leaders who are heard in America and over the world today.

On an extensive tour in Europe, Rebecca took the time to study the English "Education Act." She and her daughter were both presented at court—to Queen Victoria. Rebecca was endowed with a brilliant mind, with great energy and determination to expose her views and ideas.

Her charming personality was no hindrance when working to influence leaders and educators.

OTELIA KATHERINE COMPTON
Born 1859

Otelia Katherine Compton (Mrs. Elias Compton) believed people should be healthy, alert, and interested in current events. To keep fit she swam daily. An article in Scientific Monthly described her thinking as nimble as any logician's and her reading "ardent as any scholar's."

Otelia's husband was Dr. Elias Compton, who was Dean of Wooster College where he taught Philosophy for forty-one years. Their three sons and a daughter hold over thirty-one college degrees and use up much space in Who's Who in America.

Earl T. Compton, eldest and distinguished physicist, was best known as President of Massachusetts Institute of Technology. Arthur was a professor at the University of Chicago and won the Nobel Prize for Physics. The third son, Wilson, became President of the State College of Washington. Mary, the Compton's only daughter (Mrs. Herbert C. Rice), was a Presbyterian Missionary and Principal of Christian College, Allahabad, India.

When Dr. Elias Compton was asked about the secret of rearing children so successfully, he replied, "Their mother." Son Wilson said that his mother depended on the Bible, soap, and castor oil. Otelia denied that she had any special formula, but all knew that she believed a religious background for her family was most important.

Otelia wrote, "The tragedy of American life is that the home is becoming incidental at a time when it is needed as never before. Parents forget that neither school nor the world can reform the finished product of a bad home. They forget that their children are their first responsibility." As a mother, Otelia took her responsibility seriously but was a cheerful and happy person who made home a place that her family loved. She often remarked, "Motherhood has its own career. Nothing is superior to it. Motherhood is a woman's greatest privilege and a challenge." She would be shocked to hear how some people have felt about children and motherhood in the nineteen hundred and seventies. Otelia is gone but not forgotten.

Her ideas of motherhood are still remembered and treasured in the hearts of many. Otelia said, "There is a kind of heredity that is all-important, the heredity of training. A child isn't likely to learn good habits from his parents unless the parents learned them from their parents. It is handed down from generation to generation."

Elias made about fourteen hundred dollars a year and Otelia spent his income with care. Each child had duties and learned the importance of saving part of all earnings. Children's chores were so arranged that nothing interfered with school work or with recreation needed to develop healthy bodies.

At the age of seventy-four, "for achievement as a wife and mother of the Comptons (educators and scientists) Otelia was awarded a Doctor of Law Degree by Western College, where she had earned her B.A. in 1886. For this achievement, The Golden Rule Foundation (American Mothers grew out of this organization) selected Otelia as American Mother of 1939 in New York City. This was a national honor and Ohio was proud of their first Mother of the Year. (American Mothers Committee, Inc. has been selecting representative mothers of ideal motherhood annually since 1935.)

Otelia died at the age of eighty-five, but her ideals and great principles live on in her descendants.

MARTHA KINNEY COOPER
Born 1874

Martha Kinney Cooper was the fourth child of Major and Mrs. Joel F. Kinney and although born in 1874, in New Port, Kentucky, the family moved across the Ohio River to Cincinnati, Ohio, where Martha received her schooling.

In 1897, Myers Y. Cooper and Martha were married. Mr. Cooper came from Louisville, Ohio, where he had known farm life, but he wanted to start his own real estate business in Cincinnati. Two children, Raymond and Martha, were born to the Coopers.

Martha was a loving mother and a concerned parent not only for her own children but, due to wide interest in cultural things, she had the welfare of many in her heart. She was a religious and patriotic person and did her part by being active in the Women's Clubs: Cincinnati Women's Club, Three Arts Club, Musicians of America. The National League of American Pen Women made her an honorary member.

Culture was important to Martha and she had many friends with like interests. One friend was the delightful poet, B. Y. Williams, mother of our present Director of Ohioana Library, Mrs. Bernice Williams Foley, a most dedicated and hard worker.

In 1929, Martha's husband became Governor of Ohio and they moved into the Governor's Mansion at 1234 East Broad St. It was while living here that Martha Kinney Cooper decided to make a collection of the works of Ohio Writers, to be housed in the Mansion, and thus give honor and recognition to authors of the State of Ohio.

She sought help from all directions. Thirty men and women, distinguished in many areas of activity were invited to participate. Among these was Mrs. Depew Head, Field Representative of the Ohio State Library. Later she became Executive Director of the Ohioana Library. An enthusiastic Martha invited her interested group to the Mansion where plans were formulated for building our Ohioana Library of great distinction. Clara Keck Heflebower, who would later become National President of the American Federation of Pen Women, proposed the beautiful name "Ohioana Library."

Even after the Coopers returned to Cincinnati to "The Pines," an 1827 farmhouse that had been turned into a gracious homestead, Martha Kinney Cooper's main interest was to support the new library. She taught herself typing and spent hours building the files on all obtainable data about early authors.

Their last years were spent at "The Pines" with their loved ones. Martha, Mrs. Kinney Cooper, passed away in 1964. The Library gains more and more recognition and lives on as a great tribute to her dedication.

MARY MOORE DABNEY THOMSON
Born 1887

Mary Dabney Thomson was the daughter of Dr. and Mrs. Charles W. Dabney and was born in the year of 1887. Her father was the President of the University of Tennessee. From childhood Mary felt at home on a college campus and had an inborn desire to study books. Later on, Dr. Dabney became President of Cincinnati's Municipal University in the beautiful State of Ohio. So, Mary grew more familiar with the role of a college president and recognized the value of an educational institution.

The family went to Europe before Mary had finished college and while vacationing Mary found time to widen her educational experience. She studied French, horseback riding, and the feminine art of designing millinery. The more exposed Mary was to any knowledge enriching her life, the happier she became.

On their return from Europe numerous parties were given to welcome them home. At one party, Mary met Alexander Thomson, a student of history, chemistry, physics, economics, and art. With two people having such broad and varied interests they enjoyed each other's company and were married. Alexander's background was helpful in his labor management relations and he became most successful in business. After considering many tracts of land they settled in Indiana farming country. Mary knew that the sturdy, independent, hard working farmers would be excellent examples for her family through direct association.

Mary was an active participant in women's activities of this rural community.

Four sons were graduated from Yale. The boys said that their mother taught them by "example" and not by "lecture." She had faith in them and expected them to live up to that faith.

In 1940, Mary, now widowed, was offered the Presidency of Western College for Women at Oxford, Ohio. She accepted and became almost a mother to three hundred new daughters.

Her Presidency of the Cincinnati Young Women's Christian Association led to an appointment on the National Board of the organization. Ten years later she was honored as an ideal mother for her contribution to education of American youth. She was ever active in her community and church. She was on the Women's Symphony Committee of Cincinnati and was also on the Community Chest Board.

Mary Dabney Thomson is still living in her own home in Cincinnati, Ohio.

FLORENCE ZWICK
Maximo   **Born 1894**

Florence Zwick was born on June 28, in Stark County, Maximo, Ohio, in the year 1894. She was educated at Kent Normal School and taught four years. She married Herman Zwick, owner of a general store.

Florence is the mother of eleven. A niece, orphaned at fourteen came to live in the Zwick home. So Florence was truly a mother to a dozen children. A devout Catholic, Florence believed in Christian guidance, discipline, organization and much love for her family. As a helpmate she never failed her husband and thoroughly learned the art of managing a business skillfully. She and Herman were both leaders in the community and the church.

Thirty-two years ago Florence was left a widow with seven children still at home. She continued the business and made dreams that she and Herman had talked about come true. In 1956, Florence opened a beautiful new store in Louisville, Ohio and another in 1965 between Canton and Massillon. While running a successful business she also reared a successful family. Florence believes that daily mass, faith in God, hard work and maintaining a sense of humor through the years have brought happiness and success to her and her loving family. Florence planted seeds of love in her children and future generations will continue harvesting church and community leaders.

Florence says that life is for the living and she has been a source of inspiration and stimulation to widows.

Florence has belonged and held offices in most of the civic and church organizations (state and national) in her community. Organizations that have benefited by her leadership are; the Columbus Woman's Club, St. Annes Rosary Altar Society, American Legion Auxiliary Society, Louisville's Woman's Club, Circle of Mercy, Canton's Woman's Club and National Council of Catholic Women. Florence promoted UNICEF, FISH and WISC. She frequently staged and narrated fashion shows to benefit organizations. She organized a Day Center in Canton, Ohio. She studied and taught Theology in the Catholic Church School and wrote and published articles in the National Catholic Magazine.

Having helped to organize Constitution Day, she has always sponsored a candidate for the Queen's Contest.

Florence has excellent rapport with all who participate in any enterprise, and brings people into cohesive working units. She enjoys serving on educational committees and public affairs committees. She has dignity, is gracious, energetic, scrupulous, impartial, fair, has perserverence and is considerate with love for people.

JESSIE KING CAVE

Born 1897

Jessie King Cave was born in Hancock County. She graduated from Ada High School, Ada, Ohio. Her next move was to Columbus, Ohio where she attended Ohio State University and graduated as a Home Economic's major.

As an assistant dietitian she worked at Jefferson Hospital, in Philadelphia, Pennsylvania for one year and then spent two years as the head dietitian at Grant Hospital in Columbus, Ohio. She did post-graduate work at Wittenberg University in Springfield, Ohio. While there she was a substitute teacher and taught home economics for one year in Dayton, Ohio.

In 1921 she helped found the Ohio Dietetics Association in Columbus, Ohio.

She married Ray Cave, a pharmacist for Grant Hospital, in 1925. She is the mother of Richard King Cave who is married and lives in Canton, Ohio.

She and her husband had pride in their community and donated spruce trees to the Westgate and Glenwood recreation centers for shade and beautification.

After her husband passed away she honored him by setting up a memorial at Grant Hospital to help support the Chaplaincy of the institution.

Jessie holds a fifty year membership at Hoge Memorial Presbyterian Church. She helped to organize the Junior High Department, has taught Sunday School and has held the office of

President for the Ladies Aid Society, Missionary Society, Columbus Presbyterial Society and formerly was Vice-president of the Ohio Synodical Society.

She is a past member of the Advisory Committee of Westminster Terrace, a Presbyterian Home for the elderly. She is the past president and life-member of Church Women United of Columbus and at present serves as historian.

She has served on the board and is a life-member of The Young Womens' Christian Association.

She is a member of Womens' Christian Temperance Union, Ohioana Library, Alumnae Club of Ohio State University at Columbus, Ohio and is a life-member of the O S U alumnae Association. She is a member of the Hilltop Community Council and has served on advisory boards for the Westgate Recreation Center. She is a charter member of the Highland Garden Club and serves as historian.

Jessie's hobbies are tatting, knitting, and playing hymns on her piano when she is not working. She collects vases from all parts of the world. The smallest is but one inch high. She is always on call to give shuts some special joy. She has given many persons transportation to meetings.

JERRIE FREDRITZ MOCK

Born 1925

Jerrie Mock was born to Mr. and Mrs. Timothy Fredritz on November 22, 1925. Her grandfather was Raymond Wright of Detroit, Michigan. Jerrie and her husband, Russell, are the proud parents of two sons, Gary and Roger, and one daughter, Valerie Ann. They have two grandchildren.

Jerrie Mock, although petite, is a courageous bundle of energy and must have been born to compete and set records in the aviation field. She recaptured the Amelia Earhart record flying from Russia. She has set nine United States speed records and nine world speed records (1969) in a single engine Cessna plane (nicknamed Three-Eight Charlie). She was the first woman to fly solo around the world, and the

first woman to fly a single engine airplane across the world's largest ocean. She has received many awards for her expert flying. The plane flown around the world was actually spoken of as The Spirit of Columbus. Bexley, a suburb of Columbus, and Columbus both claim Jerrie Mock.

When she was getting ready for the world trip, her family helped her to pack the plane and her sons and husband kept telling her what to do and not to do. It was twenty-nine days before they saw her again. Jerrie said that all the news people, photographers, and dignitaries caused her some tension. When ready to fly from Lane Airport, she thought, "What lies ahead, beyond this airport? And she thought of the great oceans, jungles, deserts, mountains, and. . . ." Then all at once she knew that she was going to find out for her tiny plane, fully readied and carrying two extra large tanks of gas on the inside of the plane (passenger seats had been removed), and looking like a brand new air bird (plane was eleven years old but conditioned like a new one) was eager to get into the air.

She climbed into the plane, fastened down anything that she could, turned on the autopilot and looked at the Jet Navigation Chart, prepared by Captain Art Weiner of the United States Air Force. It was funny but on the map Bermuda looked real close. Seven thousand five

hundred feet in the air she heard the Tower Controller say, "Well, I guess that's the last we'll hear from her . . ." "For only a month Jerrie hoped."

On her return, the Governor issued a proclamation and designated a Jerrie Mock Day. A world of congratulations were in line but the happiest moments were those when the family was once again around her with love that only a close-knit family can understand.

In nineteen seventy, Jerrie became an author of "Three-Eight Charlie" Around the World Trip, published by Lippincot.

The Mock home is filled with Jerrie's mementos, curios, and antiques from around the world. Jerrie uses her possessions and frequently dresses in some native costume.

Significant "Firsts" belonging to Jerrie Mock are:

First woman to fly solo around the world

First woman to fly U.S.–Africa via North Atlantic

First woman to fly the Pacific single-engine

First woman to fly the Pacific West to East

First woman to fly both the Atlantic and Pacific

First woman to fly the Pacific both directions

Jerrie is still in the process of writing a cookbook of famous recipes collected from places around the world.

LILLIAN DIEBOLD POLING
Canton   **Born 1880**

FOUR SCORE YEARS AND ONE! And all but her young childhood years have been dedicated to the service of humanity. Lillian Diebold was born May 7, 1880, in Canton, Ohio, and educated in the schools of that city. She received her Certificate of Teaching in Home Economics from the University of Ohio in Columbus. At a very early age her interest was centered upon the home and the great need for improving the living conditions of the underprivileged. In Canton, Ohio, with this thought uppermost in her mind, she became chairman of an Americanization committee, organized a nursery during the flu epidemic of World War I, and, as a teacher of home economics in a school district with fourteen nationalities, she founded the

"Little Nell House." Here young girls were given instruction in home-making and boys were taught worthwhile trades—they helped build the "Little Nell House."

As this indomitable young woman went about her teaching the need for adequate meals for little ones drew her attention. She pioneered in the middle west for the program of serving milk to underprivileged children in the public schools. But it was to all humanity that she was devoted. From the neglected and the undernourished children to young girls and boys in need of counseling and direction and then to the older forgotten mothers—shut-ins in hospitals and institutions, no longer remembered by their families, with few pleasures in their daily lives—these were another concern of Lillian Poling.

In Philadelphia she collaborated with Mrs. Katherine Strawbridge and founded the organization known as "Flowers for the Flowerless," bringing beauty and a ray of sunshine into the hearts of thousands. And God lives closely in the heart of this devout woman. Also in Philadelphia she founded the Religion in Life Group, bringing together Catholic, Protestant, and Jewish women for the purpose of interfaith understanding.

Now for nearly a decade she has been president of the American Mothers Committee. To her determination to develop and strengthen the moral and spiritual foundation of the homes of America goes the major credit for the basic program of the Committee—Family Life Institutes and Counselor Motherhood Services, reaching young mothers with pre-school-age children, helping them with the problems of their new lives and in the rearing of their children—the future of America.

At the age of 81, this remarkable woman, in addition to her duties as the wife of one of the world's most prominent ministers and editors, Dr. Daniel A. Poling, sustained a daily schedule of activities that would tax the stamina of a thirty-year-old. Mrs. Poling's chief interests and activities always centered in the church. She has organized and conducted prayer groups, taught Sunday School classes and for several years served as president of the international and interdenominational Woman's Board of Home Missions.

In 1955, Mrs. Poling was awarded the Medallion of Honor of the Women's International Exposition as a Woman of Achievement for that year.

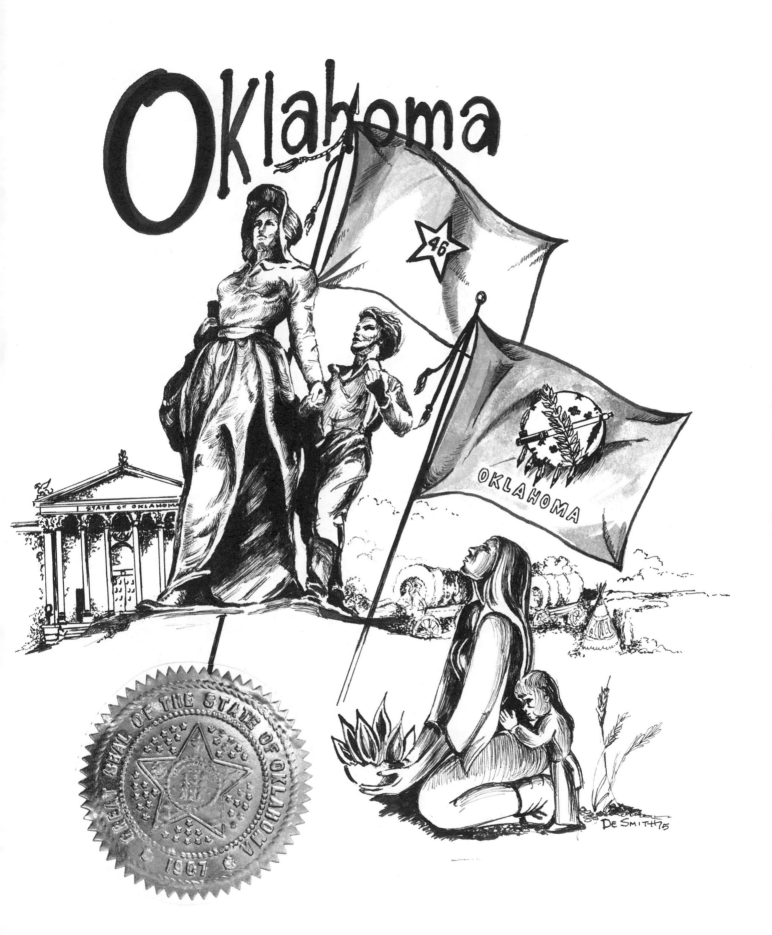

Oklahoma

Nickname: The Sooner State

State Flower: Mistletoe

State Tree: Redbud

State Bird: Scissor-tailed flycatcher

Photos

1. American Indian Exposition, Anadarko
2. Cherokee Indian Village near Tahlequah
3. Restored Fort Gibson Stockade
4. 89'er Statue
5. Tulsa—Oil Capital of the World
6. Quartz Mountain State Park
7. Futuristic Monorail—State Fair
8. National Finals Rodeo

Committee Members

Chairman—Mrs. Fred Zahn, Oklahoma City
D.E. Smith—artist

Oklahoma

ANNE ELIZA WORCESTER ROBERTSON

Born 1820

Born in 1820, Anne Eliza Worcester was to begin a life totally involved with mission work, first through her parents as Cherokee Missionaries, then later when she became a teacher and linguist at the Creek Tullahasse Mission near the present day town of Muskogee, Oklahoma.

As the oldest daughter of Samuel Austin and Ann Worcester, she learned early to respect the intellectual life. She was born at Brainerd Mission for the Eastern Cherokees in Georgia and became resolved as a young girl that Indian tribes should hear of the Gospel through their own language. At fifteen she excelled in Greek and Latin at St. Johnsbury Academy in Vermont little knowing then that the classic languages which she loved would set the stage for her later being recognized as an outstanding scholar of almost thirty years work with the Creek language. In 1846 she left her studies and was accepted by the American Board of Commissioners for Foreign Missions as a teacher at her father's Park Hill Mission station near present day Tahlequah, Oklahoma. There she readily saw the need to communicate with the Indians in Creek.

Her stay at Park Hill was short because she was swept away in 1850 by her new husband, Reverend William Schenck Robertson to a home in the Creek Nation. Except for a short period during the Civil War, Tullahassee Mission was to be where she lived and worked for the next thirty-five years. Hers was a strenuous life of teaching six hours, care for more than one hundred students and a large staff, regular household duties and, in time, care for her own four children. During the period from 1851 to 1860 their children, Ann Augusta, Mary Alice, Grace Leeds and Samuel Worcester were born. The three girls were later equally devoted to mission work, whereas Samuel Worcester went on to teach in the public school system. Mary Alice later served as United States Supervisor for Creek Schools and was the first woman elected to represent the state of Oklahoma in Congress.

Anne Eliza Robertson's dedicated position at the mission certainly influenced her children's decisions for teaching careers.

Soon after arriving at Tullahassee Mission she was busy with learning Creek words. Her great linguistic ability plus sheer devotion to the endeavor of giving the Bible to the Indians enabled her to complete the awesome task of translating the New Testament, as well as articles, hymns, vocabulary studies and other publications into the Creek language. Mrs. Robertson did much work with the Smithsonian Institute concerning the language of the Indians at the mission. The New Testament was published in 1887 and was through the fifth printing by the time she died in 1905. During the period from 1860 to 1889 she produced an English and Creek vocabulary. She was the first American woman on whom the honorary degree of doctor of philosophy was bestowed; this was conferred by Wooster University for superior attainments in the field of linguists. Anne Eliza Worcester Robertson as a woman who managed with the understanding and help from her husband and children, to do what she set out to accomplish.

SARAH WATIE

Born 1820

The Civil War tested the endurance of countless women whether their sympathies were with the Union or Confederate armies. Such was the case of Sarah Caroline Bell Watie. Having been married in 1843 to Stand Watie, a man of undisputed prominence both as a colonel and brigadier general in the southern forces and also as Principal Chief of the Southern Cherokees, Sarah Watie was to know only too well the anxieties which would accompany her union to a man of his eminence at such a controversial time.

Sarah Caroline Bell was born in 1820 in the Old Cherokee Nation east of the Mississippi River. After removal of the Cherokees in 1838 to the Cherokee Nation West, Sarah met and married Stand Watie. The first several years of their marriage was during a time of much upheaval in the newly moved Cherokee Nation until a degree of peace and quietude was achieved by 1846. At this time the Watie's first son Saladin was born, the first of three sons and two daughters.

By 1860 tension in the Cherokee Nation was building as it was in all of the nation, tension which crescendo was the Civil War. Sarah Watie fled with her children and other Confederate Indian families to refugee camps in the Chickasaw and Choctaw nations and in Texas; Mrs. Watie chose Texas where relatives would be living. Saladin Watie, fifteen years old at this time, was made a captain and remained with his father until the war's end. Sarah lived in Rusk County, Texas at the beginning of the war with four of her children: Cumiskey, Watica, Minnie, and Jacqueline. The lines of communication were such that she would go for months without hearing from her husband; pencils became impossible to get and her letters were soon written on torn ledger sheets for lack of paper. Conditions became so deplorable that some Confederate regulars were used for the task of gathering cotton to send to Mexico to be made into fabric for clothes, a plan which was not successful. Sarah was desperate for cards to comb cotton for weaving clothes for her family and others. Her health along with other refugee's was broken by the adverse conditions and anxieties met each day. Schooling for the children was all but non-existent; nevertheless, Sarah exposed them to what was available. Torn by the desire to be with her husband and oldest son, she implored them to let her travel to war-torn areas to see them. Stand Watie went to great measures to secure supplies for them, but nothing lasted very long when so many people were in need. Sarah spent the duration of the war with relatives in Lamar County, Texas, eager for reunion with her family.

At the war's end Sarah and the four children after rejoining Stand and Saladin commenced to gather their scattered belongings and settle in Webbers Falls in present-day eastern Oklahoma. Sorrow was not long in coming though, Saladin died at the age of twenty-one in 1868 following Cumiskey's death in 1863.

Despite their bereavement, Sarah Watie was determined that the remaining children should have an opportunity for an education. As this was of prime concern, no sacrifice was too great, and the children were sent away to schools. Their hopes for their children were shattered

when Watica became ill and suddenly died in 1869. Having been schooled in misfortune and disappointment, Sarah met this with the same courage as before. This courage was again tested within a short time with the passing of Stand Watie and her two daughters. Alone, Sarah Watie in 1874 moved to a cabin hidden deep in a glen about six miles west of present-day Grove, Oklahoma. It was the kind of place where she had hoped to live with her family one day. Here she lived out the rest of her days, dying seven years after her daughters.

NARCISSA CHISHOLM OWEN
Born 1831

Born in 1831 in a log cabin in an area known then as Arkansas Territory, Narcissa Chisholm was one of three children born to Melinda Horton and Thomas Chisholm. Shortly thereafter, the family moved to Webbers Falls in the Cherokee Nation which is present-day Oklahoma. Her mother was a descendent of Samuel Horton of Philadelphia and her father was the son of John D. Chisholm of Scotch descent. He spoke and lived with the Cherokees and was considered a man of note in the Cherokee Nation West.

Narcissa until the age of twelve was reared in the area of Webbers Falls. At this time she made the journey to Evansville, Indiana where she decided to live and go to school. Her interest lay in the area of teaching, and she was eager to study in the music field. After several years of education, she taught vocal and instrumental music and decided to move to Fayetteville, Arkansas. In Fayetteville she secured a teaching job at Mrs. Sawyer's School. Her decision to leave this job and move to Jonesborough, Tennessee had much to do with shaping her exciting life for it was in Jonesborough that she met and married Robert Latham Owen I who at that time was civil engineer of the East Tennessee and Virginia Railroad and later its president. The marriage was performed by the eminent Methodist missionary and educator, David Sullins at the house of the chief justice of Tennessee. Narcissa was teaching at the time at the female seminary presided over by Sullins. Narcissa and Robert began their married life together there in Arkansas.

They were the parents of two children, William Otway Owen and Robert L. Owen. Through the dedicated energy of the parents, Robert was to become one of best known political leaders from the state of Oklahoma in the national political arena. The talented, ambitious Narcissa along with her husband believed that a first-class education was of prime concern, so off he went at an early age to a school in Baltimore. His college years were spent at Washington and Lee University where he received honors. During the time that he was away at the university his father died, and hard times followed close behind his death. Robert and William Owen decided that their future might be more promising if they returned to Indian Territory with Mrs. Owen. The move was made in 1879 and proved to a particularly good one for the Owen family as their wealth had been depleted not long after the death of Mr. Owen. Here Narcissa could be with relatives and Robert could pursue opportunities which would, in time, advance him to the forefront of state and national politics. He was appointed United States Indian Agent for the Five Civilized Tribes under Grover Cleveland resigning that position in 1889. As a lawyer, he served as secretary of the first Bar Association in Indian Territory. After Oklahoma statehood, he served two terms as a United States Senator. He was often referred to as Oklahoma's first citizen. Robert L. Owen's exciting, active life gave evidence of Narcissa's gentle, yet determined design for promising careers for her sons.

AUGUSTA J. C. METCALF

Born 1871

Alternately wielding a watercolor brush delicately and wrestling thirty acres of bottomland into control was all in a day's work to Oklahoma's western artist, Augusta Metcalf. Born in Kansas in 1871 to parents from Pennsylvania, Augusta moved to No Man's Land in 1886 which is the Panhandle of Oklahoma. They lived in a dugout before a sod house became their home in a land where the turbulent summers and cutting winters were a sure test for survival. If her mother was afraid of this venture to the West, Augusta was not aware of it and in turn developed the spirited attitude manifest in pioneer families and desperado alike who bore the disappointments of the unyielding elements and earth of that particular region, No Man's Land or Neutral Strip as it was also called.

After a final move with her family to a claim on the Washita River by then known as Beaver County, Oklahoma, she began what would be a long and vigorous life in this location. She and her family got right down to the business of erecting a picket house which would only service them until a stone house could be made. During this time she experienced the excitement of soldiers camped near her house enroute to Camp Supply and the thrill of carrying mail on horseback to neighbors from the tiny post office. Augusta learned to ride a horse early and began to herd cattle on what was then free range. Riding was one of the real pleasures which lasted throughout her life. Riding side saddle was considered the appropriate way for a girl or woman to ride at that time.

Her days were filled with tasks which might seem today to be particularly tedious or difficult, yet this is the stuff of which her deft strokes with a pen or brush would later make come alive to those who have seen her paintings. Augusta, having been married at the age of twenty-four in 1905 not long after her father's death carried on alone after 1908 caring for her son Howard, two and one-half years old and her failing mother. She had the arduous task of farming twenty-five acres of row crops and thirty acres of bottomland with the added burden of caring for cattle. She bore the work and hardship alone until her mother died in 1917. Her mother had been a guiding influence in her life and, having been a teacher in Pennsylvania, had schooled Augusta well and strengthened her delight in drawing. It was during these years that Augusta illustrated some of her mother's writings published in educational journals in the East. She also began sending some of her paintings to well known people; a miniature painting was sent to Thomas A. Edison which he greatly admired and so stated in a letter to Augusta in 1912. Later, numerous paintings were done for President Theodore Roosevelt and his friend Roger D. Williams of Lexington, Kentucky. Mr. Williams later recommended her work highly in a written statement in a popular sports magazine of that time.

His laudatory statement is only one of hundreds in the years since this country began to sample her work. Only a person as closely involved in the scenes which she depicted in her paintings could make them come alive as she has done. Scenes of riding the range, country weddings, shoeing horses, bleak but beautiful hills, cowboys bedding down for the night—all this is but a mere sample of the history in art that she has given us. This is the saga of the settlement of the American West as Augusta Metcalf saw it, and it rings visually as true as anything written on such an adventure.

RUBY HIBLER HALL
Eufaula   **Born 1912**

Ruby Hibler Hall was born Feb. 27, 1912 in Eufaula, Okla. the daughter of Rev. L.G. and Beatrice Hibler. She married Ira Hall July 2, 1930. Ruby and Ira have made notable contributions to their community, Okla. City., state and nation. They are the parents of 6 fine children— 4 girls & 2 boys. One son, a full time employee of Honeywell in Palo Alto, Calif., is also studying for his Doctorate in Economics at Stanford Univ. The other son is President of his Consultant Firm in Washington, D.C. Their daughter Janice is with the American Manpower Training program in Boston, Mass. Daughter Jessilyn Ann White is Director of OEO for Honeywell in St. Petersburg, Florida. Daughter Carol A.

Hardeman is working on her Doctorate at Okla. Univ. in Human Relations. Daughter Iris M. Bruce is with the Okla. State Dept. of Ed. in the counseling and guidance service.

While being a very busy mother Ruby has continually pursued working in her field of education and community service. She is presently serving on the State Bd. of Regents for Higher Education and is one of a national committee of five representatives of minority groups in State Bds. of Higher Education. She taught English in the Okla. City public schools and served as Title One coordinator for the public schools. She is a speech pathologist. She has been active in the Alpha Kappa Alpha Sorority; works closely with Jack & Jill Mothers; Urban League; League of Women Voters; is a national officer of the Speech & Hearing Ass; is presently National Historian of National Colored Federated Clubs of America and is a candidate for National President of this organization.

She and her husband are working diligently to strengthen the family unit. She is beginning publication of a national magazine to be called FAMILORE, a project in which her entire family will be involved. Her husband is writing a book on the family and marriage. He has just retired as a school administrator having served as Principle of both Elementary and High Schools and Associate Director of 97 Black State High schools.

They are the proud grandparents of three— two girls and a boy. Truly Ruby Hall is a great American mother serving her family and country with love and dignity.

Oregon

Nickname: Beaver State

State Flower: Oregon Grape

State Tree: Douglas fir

State Bird: Western meadowlark

Photos

1. Succor Creek
2. Capital Building in Salem
3. Vista House—Crow Point State Park
4. Multnomah Falls
5. Lost Lake & Mt. Hood
6. Heceta Head Lighthouse
7. Hiking trails in Ecola State Park
8. Portland's Internation Rose Test Gardens
9. Here Lived "Father of Oregon", Dr. John McLoughlin

Committee Members

Chairman—Mrs. Hazel McCracken, Corvallis
Valerie Nichols & Mary Nichols
Cora Kuhlman
Mrs. Celia Steward
Victor & Nita Birdseye
Emily Logan
Esther Pangborn
Charlene Edwards
Steve Sinovic
Rollie Ralston Smith
Dr. Kenneth Holmes—Prof. of History—
  Oregon College of Education, Monmouth,
  Ore.

Writers

Bertha Holt

Oregon

MARGUERITE WADIN McLOUGHLIN

On the very fringe of the advancing American frontier there was one kind of woman who played a significant role in our history who has often been neglected or forgotten by subsequent generations: that is the Indian or part-Indian part-white wife of the frontiersman. There was always an area beyond the farmer's frontier where lonely men sallied forth to trap and to trade, and they went without women from back home. It was these men who took mates "according to the manner of the country," marrying them Indian style as they contacted the tribes in the vast West. It all began with the earliest Indian-white contacts during colonial times and continued all the way to the Pacific shore. "Squaw man" was a term of disdain applied to such persons, but thousands of modern Americans can trace their genealogical tree to such a union several generations back.

Such a wife was Marguerite Wadin McLoughlin, the partner of the giant fur trader John McLoughlin, Hudson's Bay Company gentleman, and for many years virtual ruler of the vast Oregon Country of our Pacific Northwest. He is now called the "Father of Oregon," and his statue stands surrounded by green lawn in the Capitol grounds at Salem. He had met Marguerite Wadin, daughter of a Swiss trader, Jean Etienne Wadin, and a Cree Indian woman, and they had begun to live together, probably in 1811, in the Great Lakes area of modern Canada. Marguerite was the widow of Alexander McKay, another fur trader who had suffered a violent death on the Pacific Coast. She was somewhat older than John McLoughlin, is thought to have been born about 1780 in central Canada.

When John McLoughlin build the great fur emporium of the West at Fort Vancouver (site of present Vancouver, Washington, and now being rebuilt by the National Park Service), his wife was with him, and she remained at his side until McLoughlin died, an American citizen, in the new Territory of Oregon in September, 1857. She lived another two years and five months and experienced a "most peaceful death" in February, 1860, in Oregon City, Oregon. Their common law marriage had been given legitimacy by the Catholic missionary Father Francis Norbert Blanchet, later Bishop of Oregon, at Vancouver on November 19, 1842. Marguerite was unable to sign her own name, placing her "X" on the document. There were four children: John, Elisabeth, Eloisa, and David.

Marguerite McLoughlin was the lady of the fort through all the years her husband was in charge. One biographer tells us that "the deference that McLoughlin showed his wife in public was the envy of all American wives, who lost no time in citing him to their husbands as an example worthy of emulation." Her calm, stable disposition was often a counterbalance to his fiery temper. It was said that she would sit and sedately sew as he ranted and raged, and all the while she talked quietly in measured tones until the rage subsided.

When the two went forth on horseback to survey the settlements, she rode a magnificent horse, which, according to a contemporary, was decked out with silver trappings and strings of small bells upon the bridle reins. The same observer wrote, "Dressed in brilliant colors, she wore a smile which might cause to blush and hang its head the broadest, warmest and most fragrant sunflower. By her side rode the lord, the king of the Columbia, and every inch a king, attended by a train of trappers, under a chief trader, each upon his best behavior."

Such a person was the first "First Lady of Oregon," who reigned for twenty years in quiet dignity, inheritor of the blood of the Old World and the New World, and transmitting the highest qualities of both cultures to generations to follow.

MELINDA MILLER APPLEGATE

At the side of the men who blazed the trails and built the homes in early frontier Oregon were strong, courageous women. These are a few incidents taken from the crowded life of Melinda Miller Applegate, devoted wife of Charles, eldest of the three Applegate brothers who, with their families, were leaders in the "Great Migration" of 1843. All were well suited to the rigors of a two-thousand mile trek, which would include the first successful passage of wagons beyond Ft. Hall (Idaho). The wagon train was composed of one-thousand people, one-hundred-twenty-five wagons and several thousand head of loose stock. Soon after leaving Independence, Missouri, the train divided into two sections—those with livestock forming the famous "Cow Column", with Jesse Applegate as Captain, ably assisted by his brothers, Charles and Lindsay.

Melinda was thirty-one years old at this time and despite the responsibilities of caring for her eight children, found time each evening to write an account of the day's activities. Whenever possible, she and her daughters would gather fresh greens along the trail to supplement their meals. Dr. Marcus Whitman, the famed missionary, who had joined the wagon train at the Platte river, told her she had done more for the health of the train than anyone else.

In November, upon reaching The Dalles (Oregon), rafts were constructed to float the wagons downstream on the Columbia River. Two of Melinda's nine-year-old nephews were drowned and her own son left injured, but alive, when a raft overturned during the dangerous passage. A few weeks after this experience, Melinda gave birth to a healthy son. In later years, the tragedy at The Dalles, was one factor in the determination of the Applegates to seek out a southern route into Oregon for the benefit of later immigrants.

Settling eventually in a beautiful valley, near what is now Yoncalla, Oregon, Charles and Melinda built a lovely home, completed in 1856. Even though Melinda was by then the mother of fifteen children, her home was the center of hospitality for neighbors—both Indians and whites. Travelers were welcomed and provided for, whether they stayed a few days or several months. Like Melinda, the Indian women had babies almost every year so that real friendships developed as the mothers visited. The Indian women admired the beautiful patchwork

quilts, and with Melinda's assistance, mastered the art of making them.

Education was an essential to this family, and children as young as four were taught to read, write and "cipher". The first school house was built of logs, on the Applegate homestead. A library was ordered from New York and shipped around the Horn.

In her span of seventy-five years, Melinda exemplified the best qualities of humanity, as by her quiet example she instilled in her family the qualities of consideration and compassion for others.

The Applegate House still stands today, a spacious two-story structure framed by graceful black walnut trees that are themselves well over one-hundred years old.

"The bravest battles that are ever fought;
  Do you ask me where and when?
In the annals of History you will find them not;
  They were fought by the Mothers of Men."
(Adapted from "The Bravest Battle" by Joaquin Miller)

TABITHA MOFFATT BROWN
Courage Undaunted

Tabitha Moffatt Brown arrived in Oregon at the age of 66—a widow, weary and starving. Clutched in her hand was but six cents to establish herself in this new land. Crippled since childhood, she walked with the aid of a cane but her courage never faltered in the long nine months' trek that took the lives of several members of her family and demolished most of the wagons in her train.

Mrs. Brown's son, Orus, preceded her to Oregon and he persuaded his mother to join a wagon train going west.

With few exceptions, the journey was pleasant and uneventful until they were within 800 miles of Oregon City. At this point they met a man who declared he could guide the train through the short cut Applegate Trail.

Many were the trials and misfortunes that dogged the emigrants on this cut-off trail. Deserts without grass or water laid a heavy toll on their cattle. The high mountains made wrecks of their wagons. Indian attacks left emigrants sick, weary, and dying. The Indians stole Grandma Brown's prized mare.

After long, devastating experiences the remaining group reached the Umpqua Valley.

Friendly Indians from the Jason Lee mission heard of Mrs. Brown's plight and carried word to her son, Orus, who set out in haste to rescue the party. With painstaking travel, they reached the valley.

Enroute to her new home, Mrs. Brown described her journey and her precious needles:

"In the gloomy stillness of the night, footsteps of horses were heard rushing toward our tents. Directly a Halloo! It was the well-known voices of Orus Brown and Uncle John Pringle. Who can realize the joy? Orus, by his persuasive perseverance, encouraged us to move in an effort to reach the settlement.

On Christmas day, at 2:00 p.m., I entered the house of a Methodist minister, the first house I had set my foot in for nine months.

For two or three weeks of my journey down the Willamette, I had felt something in the end of my glove finger, which I supposed to be a button. On examination at my new home in Salem, I found it to be a six-and-a-quarter cent piece. This was the whole of my cash capital to commence business in Oregon.

With it I purchased three needles. I traded off some of my old clothes to the squaws for buckskins and worked the leather into gloves for the Oregon ladies and gentlemen which cleared me upwards of $30."

While there, Mrs. Brown heard of the suffering and death of emigrants on the plains. Many children were left orphans to be cared for by strangers.

Mrs. Brown persuaded Reverend Harvey Clark to establish a home to receive all poor children. He donated 200 acres of land as a foundation fund and Grandma Brown agreed to work a year without remuneration.

To this orphange came children who lost parents on the trip west. Enrollment began at 14 but soon reached 40. The building later became the Tualatan Academy, then a charter was granted for a university, to be called Pacific University. Today, a thriving, modern university is a blessing to Oregon.

A simple epitaph on an old grave stone in a Salem cemetary sheds little light on the life of courageous Tabitha Brown.

Oregon education would be poor indeed, had Tabitha Brown not been counted among her illustrious teachers.

CLARISSA STEIN BIRDSEYE
Born 1834

"I was one of the first white women to come through the Cow Creek Canyon, and I was scared to death."

"Indians?"

"No, not Indians, although we could see smoke from their teepees. It was the guns those soldiers carried. No matter where I rode, some gun was pointed straight at my head!"

"Why were the soldiers there, Granmother?"

"Protection, Child. You see, your grandfather and I were newly married and were on our way from Portland to our home in Southern Oregon. But let me start at the beginning. I was born in Wellsburgh, Virginia, October 20, 1834. I had two brothers and three sisters. Our lives centered around the church, as did most others in our town. When I was old enough, I was sent to a girl's academy to learn to be a lady. No, no cooking or house-keeping. We had Negroes for that. Father was a saddle and harness maker, and would come home from the shop to tell us exciting stories some of his customers related about their experiences on the trail to The Ore-

gon Country. The tales were exciting, but we did not really believe most of them.

"When I was seventeen, tragedy struck in the form of an epidemic of scarlet fever. Most of the young children in Wellsburgh died of it. I guess the three of us older children were not as susceptible, but the little sisters, and our younger brother were among the victims. Saddened by the tragedy, and at the same time fascinated by stories of the Oregon Country, Father and Mother were soon preparing to join a wagon train and head west. Only Jane knew that I had no intention of accompanying the family, for I was in love, and planned to marry Wesley Hobbs. Wes and I had discussed the matter, and decided that the simplest way would be for me to say nothing, simply go with my family to Independence, Missouri where the wagon trains were made up. Wesley would meet us there, we would be married and return to Wellsburgh. But it was not to be. A heart broken and humiliated girl went along with her family to Oregon, sure that she had been jilted. Several years and four children later, I was to learn that the delay had been unavoidable. I consoled myself by naming my infant son *Wesley*. Your grandfather called him Jack, which I guess is not hard to understand.

"The trip west with its dust, fatigue, boredom and other problems is the kind of thing you have read about, though our train had few encounters with Indians.

"Within a year after our arrival at The Dalles on the great Columbia River, I met and married your grandfather, David Nelson Birdseye. He was a trader and packer from Jacksonville in the southern part of the territory, where gold mining was making many people rich. We spent our honeymoon in Portland, and went on horseback to Jacksonville where his store would offer for sale goods he had purchased from emigrants off The Trail, as well as staples purchased in Portland. Soldiers accompanied us to protect us not only from Indians, but from thieves who sometimes waylaid travelers as they came through the mountain passes.

"After a few months in Jacksonville, I decided I would be happier living on the Donation Land Claim which your grandfather had taken up. It was located some twentyfive miles to the north on the beautiful Rogue River. Our home was a one room cabin. It had dirt floors and a fire-place instead of a stove, but your grandfather had kept it neat and clean. In place of glass windows, oiled paper was tacked over the openings to let in light. One day I was cooking over the fire-place when I heard the paper tear. I turned to see the head of an Indian emerge through the hole, his beady eyes staring at me through the torn paper. As I stood frozen with fear, he opened the door and strode in followed by four companions. They stood for a few moments before the fire, then produced a pipe which they passed from one to the other, and finally to me. I was too frightened not to take my puff, after which they left as they had entered. As soon as I could collect my wits, I ran as fast as I could to where David and the men were building fence.

"That shows they are friendly," said your grandfather. "You handled it just right, Clary."

"All Indians in our valley were not to remain friendly, however, and after some extreme cruelties on the part of some white men, it was necessary to build a fort on our property where people from miles around would come at night for protection.

"The day finally came, however, when a treaty was signed, the Indians were gone, and it was safe to build the fine home we had planned. Before the house-warming, I unpacked the beautiful dishes and vases I had kept safe since we had left our home in Virginia.

"My home and my garden were sources of great pride and pleasure for me. I seemed to have the ability to make things grow. In fact the huge grape vine near the back gate came from a whip I once used to encourage old Prince to bring me home from Jacksonville!

"Five children were born to us. James, the eldest, was born while we still lived in the cabin. Your grandfather was a kind and loving husband and father, though the name of Wesley Hobbs would forever stand between us. Men in those days often left their families for a time, and returned, picking up where they left off, or trying to. I'll always remember the time he left for town, asking if there was anything I needed. It was spring, and I reminded him that we had not yet bought our seed corn. When he returned nearly three years later, he had it—twenty pounds of seed corn! He said only that stories of silver mines in Montana had lured him there.

"So you see, life was not easy, but one could not deny that it was interesting."

RHODA QUICK JOHNSON

Born 1844

Aunt Rhoda Johnson was born Rhoda Quick March 23, 1844, the daughter of James and Martha Ann Quick. She spent her early years in Peoria, Illinois.

The Quicks left for Oregon in 1851. They reached Kanesville, now Council Bluffs, Iowa, where they had to spend the winter since their oxen were stolen and they had no means to replace them. Reequipped, they set out for Oregon in the spring of 1852, arriving in the Willamette Valley on September 14, 1852.

In the summer of 1853, James Quick made a trip over the coast range to what was then Yamhill County to locate his claim. Later that year, in October, 1853, he moved his family to his 640-acre donation claim near Tillamook Landing.

In addition to Rhoda and her family, the trip was made by Cad Eller, Al White and Bob Higgenbothem. There were no roads and the route followed Indian and game trails, going by way of Grand Ronde, the Salmon River, past the cape and Sandlake to the mouth of the Tillamook River. From the mouth of the river they were rowed to Tillamook Landing by the Indians. From there they walked to John Tripps homestead.

At the time of their arrival, the only settlers in that area were the families of Eldridge Trask and Nathan Dougherty and six single men—Joe Champion, the first settler; John Tripp, Henry Haynes, Warren Vaughn, Peter Morgan, and Sam Howard.

The Quicks settled into their homestead next to that of Eldridge Trask. There wasn't much in the way of equipment they were able to bring with them, and that first winter they had to live off the country. The settlers made all their own furniture and the women cooked in the fireplace.

Rhoda recalls, "We children went barefoot all year round. When I turned out early on a frosty winter morning to do the milking and other chores, my feet would get so cold I would make the cows lying on the ground get up so I could stand where they had been to warm my feet. That first winter we lived on milk and butter, deer and other game. There wasn't a dust of flour, and strangely enough, we didn't seem to miss it. Mr. Trask had a shop for his tools near his house, and every night his children, me and my brothers and sisters would go out into the tool house and by the light of a tallow dip or a whale oil lamp, we would study the school books Mr. Trask had. The first sure-enough teacher we had was Mrs. Esther Lyman. She taught in the Dougherty house, and I was one of her pupils."

On January 3, 1861, Rhoda married William Johnson. William and Rhoda had seven children—Lewis, Henrietta, Ed, Jessie, Eva, Tom and Lottie. During her 90th birthday celebration, Rhoda helped to organize the Tillamook County Pioneer Association.

After an eventful life, Rhoda Johnson passed away at her home near Tillamook December 18, 1939, a true Pioneer.

ELIZABETH ROE CLOUD

Portland

Elizabeth Bender Roe Cloud, half Chippewa and born on a Minnesota Indian Reservation was selected American Mother of 1950. Her husband, Henry Roe Cloud, was a full-blooded Winnebago. The contribution of this couple to American life has been outstanding.

There must have been something special about Elizabeth Bender's Reservation home. Her brother, "Chief" Bender will long be remembered as the all-time great pitcher for the Philadelphia Athletics. When Elizabeth was ready for college she traveled all the way to Virginia to attend the well-known Hampton Institute. Then the challenge of Florence Nightingale took her to Philadelphia where she studied nursing at Hahneman Hospital. Years later she had the opportunity for further study in Wichita and Kansas Universities. Elizabeth was destined to enter one of the needy areas of American life, that of the American Indians. She was nurse, teacher, writer, lecturer, and of course wife and mother and took seriously all the tasks that came her way with innate good humor.

She was proud of the young man she had married—wasn't Henry the first Indian ever to graduate from Yale? He had such patience and such splendid ideals. When he finished at Auburn Theological Seminary he was ordained to the ministry.

The couple later opened a high school and a boarding home for Indian children known as the American Indian Institute. Besides four daughters of their own Henry and Elizabeth considered themselves as parents of the large family of children at their school, advising, encouraging and understanding their adolescent problems. In 1930 Henry left this Presbyterian school to take up responsibilities with the United States Indian Service, where his training and first-hand knowledge proved to be most useful. The Indian Reorganization Act under which Indian Americans are helped to improve their status was largely his responsibility. In all his work Elizabeth was alongside to help and encourage. Someone said of her, "Her work reflected a deep abiding faith in the final solution of long-range problems."

Elizabeth urged her daughters to get a variety of experiences, sent them to college in different parts of the country. Marion, the eldest, was the first Indian to graduate from Wellsley. All four had to work while they were in college.

Ann and Ramona at Vassar, Lillian at Stanford University.

Elizabeth's own example was an illustration of her concern with helping others. When there was a nursing shortage at Ordnance Depot Hospital, she served as a volunteer night nurse. During the war she even helped to harvest, driving a truck to gather in the pea crops. She has organized clubs for Indian women and got them to participate in Grange activities. One of her projects in Oregon has been the encouragement of Indian arts and crafts among the women of the reservation.

This remarkable woman with her accomplishments, her great "aliveness," since her husband's death has continued to work to improve conditions for Indian women and children. Already the Mother of four charming and successful daughters (a son died at age 3), she had enlarged her family to take in an entire people, a people whose treatment has been a blot on the conscience of America. Elizabeth Bender Roe Cloud is a distinguished All-American Mother.

* * *

"Mother is the name of God on the lips and in the hearts of little children."—THACKERAY

CARRIE B. HERVIN

I first met Carrie B. Hervin in 1947 when she came to Corvallis, a university town, to help a group of women organize a local League of Women Voters. We were greatly impressed with her dynamic personality and her creative leadership which was to guide us through our provisional period. I think that all of us admired her spiritual and intellectual integrity and that we were aware that here was an individual whose spiritual, social and political beliefs were in harmony so that she was a person at peace with herself and the world.

The name of Carrie B. Hervin, widow of Israel E. Hervin, formerly the manager of the Metropolitan Life Insurance Co., appears in *Who's Who of American Women* with a long list of distinguished credits. Only with great energy and efficiency can an individual accomplish so much while making her family her first priority. As her daughter says ". . . she is sensitive, loving, deeply concerned about all people, but especially devoted to her children, grandchildren, and now great-grandchildren. . . . From the time her children were born, through the years when she willingly baby-sat her grandchildren she has been an inspiration to them and they have returned her boundless love."

In Portland, the city of Mrs. Hervin's birth, she has continued to play an active roll in community affairs. A patron of the Arts, a member of the Executive Committee for both the Community Chest and United Fund where she also served on the budget committee, a board member of the Council of Social Agencies, a founding member of the World Affairs Council of Oregon, Mrs. Hervin also dedicated herself to religious service. She has served as President of the Portland chapter of Hadassah and as a Board Member of Temple Beth Israel Sisterhood.

The League of Women Voters continued to be one of her biggest interests and Carrie Hervin referred to it as a "continuing school for training in citizenship." During World II she was President of the Portland League, the largest group in Oregon. Despite the many other important demands on women's time during the war, she greatly expanded the membership. It was during her terms of office she developed the neighborhood units where members met to study and discuss the issues of local, state and national government. The concept proved so successful, discussion units were adopted by the Leagues throughout the country.

Because of her reputation as an organizer and as an individual with a good background in foreign affairs, Carrie Hervin was elected to the State Board of Oregon. She acted as advisor to new and established Leagues and helped in the development of leadership. The next step was

election to the National Board of the U.S. League. Again, her field was organization of new State Leagues and advisor to Board Members. She was appointed as the first observer from the League to the United Nations.

Her expertise in government and International Relations made great demands on her as a speaker to other organizations throughout the state of Oregon. Carrie Hervin's reputation led to appointments by Mayor Dorothy Lee of Portland to: The Mayor's Committee for the Reorganization of City Government; by various Governors of Oregon to the Governor's Committee for Children and Youth; Governor's Committee for the Aging; Governor's Committee for Study of Consolidation and Location of T. B. Hospitals.

Surely the greatest gift parents give to a community is their children, and what they do with their lives reflects the love and care of those parents. Israel and Carrie Hervin succeeded well for we have Jason A. Hervin, married to the former Marie Easterly, President of Hervin Co., manufacturers of pet foods. He has served as a member of the Board of Directors of Associated Products based in New York, as a member and officer of various business related clubs and associations. Jason Hervin also finds time for civic service for he is active in United Good Neighbors and is President of Southwest Hills Residential League. He and his wife have a daughter, Mia, a graduate of Whittier College, who lives in Salem and is the secretary for Medical Malpractice Task Force.

There is the daughter, Barbara H. Schwab, married to Judge Herbert M. Schwab, Chief Judge of Oregon's Court of Appeals. She has served as a Board Member and officer of the Portland League of Women Voters; World Affairs Council; Oregon Symphony Board; Young Audiences Board, Reed College Board for Alumni Assn.; Perry Center Board; Boys and

Girls Aid Society Board; Advisory Council to the President of the University of Oregon Health Sciences Center and member of the Executive Committee.

The Schwabs have one son practising law in San Francisco, a son who is a resident in surgery at U. of California Medical Center in San Francisco, a daughter, married to a U.S. Navy Lieutenant, who is a librarian in Maryland.

Carrie B. Hervin, devoted wife, dedicated mother, has given of her own beautiful self to her community, her state, her nation. To those of us who worked with her, a great inspiration, an elder statesman.

DOROTHY LAWSON McCALL

Dorothy Lawson McCall has led many lives through her careers of author, lecturer, volunteer worker, rancher, senior citizens' activist and almost gubernatorial candidate. It's a life that has seen many contrasts from her early years as the pampered daughter of a millionaire to her current activism.

An unqualified success at whatever she has undertaken, she has found most fulfillment as a mother. "Behind every successful mother is an understanding man," she says with conviction. "The cooperation of a wife and husband is the foundation of a happy homelife."

She sees this cooperation as extending into child care, "It's only good common sense. Children need both of their parents." Even today it is obvious that her marriage with the late Hal McCall exemplified this kind of "teamwork" and she makes frequent use of the words "us" and "we."

Originally from Massachusetts, Hal and Dorothy McCall came to Oregon after their marriage in 1910. Her millionaire father, Thomas W. Lawson ("The Copper King"), presented them with a wedding gift of 640 acres of undeveloped land in Central Oregon and Mrs. McCall vividly describes the era in her first book, "Ranch Under the Rimrock."

It was a huge jump from Boston's culture to the Central Oregon frontier for the eastern educated McCalls. Their goal to make the ranch a successful business took years of hard work and it was there that the five McCall children grew up. Tom, a two-term governor, is probably the best known of these children. A popular chief executive, he brought an innovative and exciting brand of leadership to Oregon. Under McCall, Oregon became an inspiration to the entire country in the areas of environment, land use planning and energy self-sufficiency. The other four children, Henry Jr. (Harry), Dorothy Jr. (Bebs), Sam and Jean have likewise pursued successful and varied careers in business, academia and community service.

Hal McCall died in 1947 and Mrs. McCall came to Portland where she did a great deal of volunteer work with the Division of Vocational Rehabilitation, Retired Senior Volunteer Program and "wherever people needed help."

Like son Tom, Mrs. McCall has always had a lively interest in the political scene. At the age of 85 she composed a letter to the editor of the Oregonian to announce: "Now that 1973 has drifted away into limbo, I have come to the conclusion that I should run for governor."

The firestorm that followed that announcement was incredible. NBC and CBS sent out crews to interview the sprightly, plain-spoken octogenarian. Editorial writers were enchanted and a columnist for a large city daily remarked, "Maybe it's time little old ladies ran the country."

One of the many issues raised during her "campaign" was the way that able-bodied men and women are "forced from active lives and careers at an arbitrary age when everyone's contribution to society is deeply needed." Although not a candidate in the traditional sense, she nevertheless heightened citizen awareness to problems of the elderly.

Now in her eighty-seventh year, she is cur-

rently at work on her third book which is to be a collection of historical recipes. Her zest for living and her interest in people around her show no signs of abating. Perhaps a letter to a local newspaper from one of her admiring fans sums up Mrs. McCall's attitude best: "Go to it, Gallant Lady! Make a mark for age and wisdom and courage. This world needs a reminder that years alone don't put a person on the shelf."

BERTHA HOLT

Born 1904

I am grateful to the Lord for many blessings. He gave me life and love from wonderful Christian parents, in 1904 in Des Moines, Iowa. He blessed me with health from good food and exercise from working in our big garden, and with joy in accomplishment from hard work. He allowed me to receive a Bachelor's Degree in Science from the State University of Iowa, and to become a registered nurse. He brought Harry Holt, a South Dakota farmer into my home, when he escorted a carload of pigs to Iowa, and chose this man of God to be my husband.

I thank Him, too, for giving us those happy years together as we struggled with adverse weather and elements to raise grain on hundreds of acres of gently rolling prairie. I enjoyed shovelling seed wheat into pails and handing them down to Harry from the truck, to fill his grain drill, or squirting grease from a grease gun into those 103 nipples on the combine, at 4 A.M. To hear the golden grain rattle into the tank as the combine crawled along the field and to smell the dust from the thresher was a joyful experience. I thank the Lord for the four children born to us there, and for the severe drought of the 1930's which sent us and all our friends to the west coast.

I am grateful for the lumber business my husband established at Creswell, Oregon for which I kept books and cared for two more daughters who were born during that time.

Looking back, I can rejoice in the severe heart attack and crippling effects on my husband, which drew us both closer than ever to the Lord, on Whom we learned to surrender our desires, ambitions, and problems.

I praise the Lord for opening our hearts to the call from Korea, where war had caused unspeakable tragedy in lives of children orphaned or abandoned by the backwash of conflict. He led us to adopt eight parentless babies home

from Korea. I was grateful our six natural children were willing and able to help with the work, and that we had a big house to meet the needs.

The change in our lives was not only the never ending work, the additional correspondence, being interviewed by newsmen, TV appearances, and having many visitors, but there was a change in our hearts, a longing to do God's will, not ours, and an urgent desire to help others in need..

We had rescued eight children but thousands more needed parents. We received hundreds of letters weekly from couples wanting children. Within four months, the Holt Adoption Program was established through which over nineteen thousand orphans have found the joy of being loved, wanted, and needed in homes in every continent on the globe.

My most joyful experience is when I personally place a child into the outstretched arms of his parents. God's plan for him has been accomplished when he and parents meet.

Because of this work, I have made approximately thirty-three round trips overseas and travelled extensively in Europe and this country. I have been honored many times for what the Lord has allowed us to do. In America I became Oregon's and the National Mother in 1966. Two sororities made me honorary International member, and I was titled twice "Woman of the Year," also "Woman of the World" and "Samaritan of the Year." The Lord allowed me to visit with four Presidents of countries, two vice Presidents, and with many senators and celebrities. In Korea I was given many honors by mayors and governors, and was awarded the honorary degree of Doctor of Letters by Chung Ang University, and was presented two very top honors by President Park Chung Hee at his home. These citations and honors were given in appreciation for helping helpless children, but I feel the glory belongs to the Lord through Whom it was done.

This is the most exciting and rewarding experience anyone can have and I thank God that He allowed me to have a little part in it.

JUDGE MERCEDES F. DEIZ

Born 1917

Ask The Honorable Judge Mercedes F. Deiz about her achievements and she wants to talk about her children, 32-year-old Bill, a television news reporter and actor in Santa Monica, California; her daughter, Karen, 23, like Bill a college graduate, currently working for the Housing Authority of Portland; and her youngest son, Gilbert, 22, a news photographer working for KGW-TV, Portland, Oregon.

Judge Deiz is proud too of her husband, Carl H. Deiz, a budget analyst for the Bonneville Power Administration, "without whose supportive help over all of these years none of my own abilities could have been developed."

Now a Portland, Oregon resident (she's been in Oregon since 1948) Judge Deiz was born in New York City, December 13, 1917. Portland, Oregon is now her home.

Judge Deiz was elected to the office of Circuit Court Judge (Domestic Relations! Department in 1973 for a six-year term. She is the only black woman ever to serve as a Circuit Court Judge in Oregon. For several years prior to ascending to the Circuit Court bench, 1970-1972, Judge Deiz was a District Court Judge in Multnomah County. From 1968 to 1970 she was employed as a hearing officer for the Oregon Workman's Compensation Board.

Judge Deiz practiced law, primarily as a trial lawyer in Portland from 1960 through 1967.

She worked as a legal secretary while attending law school. She received her J.D. Degree from Northwestern College of Law in 1959. From 1949 through 1953 she served as a law library assistant for the Bonneville Power Administration.

Judge Deiz was recognized as a Woman of Accomplishment in 1969 as the "First Black ever elected to remunerative office in the State of Oregon" service.

Much of Judge Deiz' off-duty time is devoted to activities related to her profession. She is currently serving on the Governor's Commission on Judicial Reform and on the Oregon State Bar Committee on Public Service and Information. She was a former secretary-treasurer of the Multnomah County Bar Association, a former chairman of the Minor Courts Committee and has been a lecturer for the Family Law Seminar. She has been chairman of the Status Offenses Committee of the National Council of Juvenile Court Judges and is on the faculty of the National College of Juvenile Judges.

A life-long civil rights advocate, Judge Deiz is chairman of the State Advisory Committee to the U.S. Civil Rights Commission and is an active member of the National Association for the Advancement of Colored People and the Urban League.

Judge Deiz is a member of St. Phillips Episcopal Church. Her service activities include participation in the Family Counselling Service and membership on the Endowments Committee of the State Scholarship Commission and the National Committee for the Support of Public Schools.

Professional Women's League, PHI DELTA GAMMA and Queens Bdnch are among her organizational interests. In addition she has in the past been Chairman of the Metropolitan Youth Commission, a member of the Metropolitan Study Commission, Portland Community College Council, the Race and Education Committee of Portland School District No. 1 and the Board of Directors of Good Samaritan Hospital and the Oregon Mental Health Association.

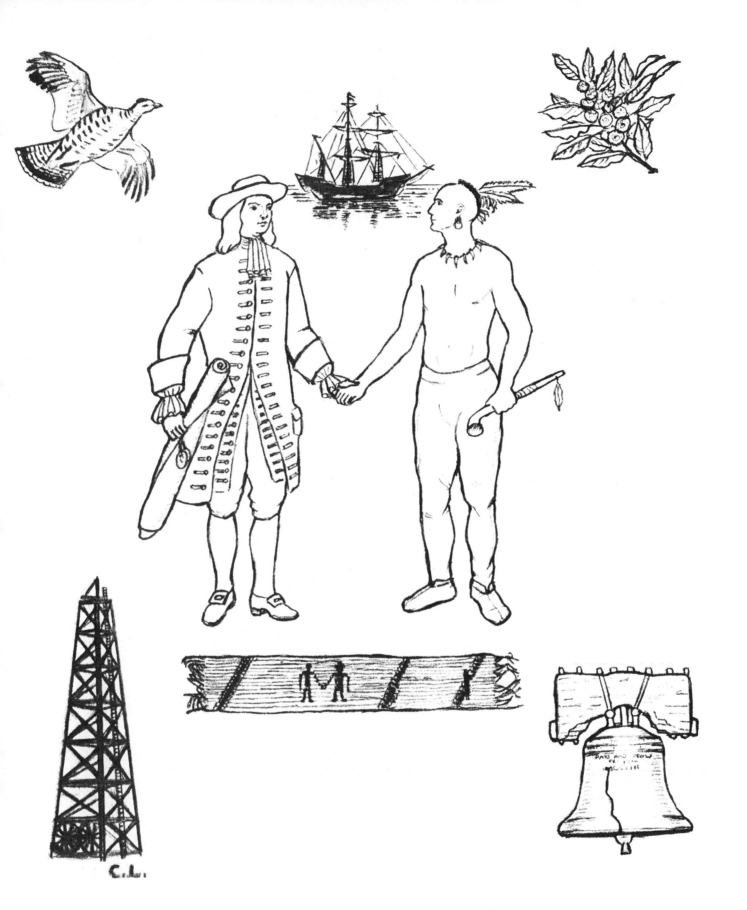

Pennsylvania

Pennsylvania

Nickname: Keystone State

State Flower: Mountain laurel

State Tree: Eastern Hemlock

State Bird: Ruffed grouse

Photos

1. Gruber Wagon Works
2. Valley Forge State Park

Committee Members

Chairman—Mrs. Lynmar Brock, Newtown
  Square
Mrs. Howard C. Paul
Mrs. Enos H. Horst
Mrs. Charles B. Barclay
Mrs. Margaret H. Bacon
Mrs. Gordon Parker
Mrs. Dorothea W. Sitley
Maris Darlington (Sarah P. Brock)
Mrs. Donald A. Kidder
Mrs. Douglass Burdick
Katherine R. Sturgis, M.D.

Writers

Elizabeth Ann Flynn
Jane Levis Carter
Lynmar Brock, Jr.
Bernadette Walkovic
Robert Looney, Free Library Of Phila.
Carl Lindborg—Artist

Pennsylvania

MARGARET COCHRAN CORBIN
Franklin County **Born 1751**

Margaret Cochran Corbin was born Franklin County, Pennsylvania, near Rocky Spring Church, November 12, 1751. Her father Robert Cochran was killed by Indians 1756 and his wife taken captive. Margaret and her brother were fortunately absent from home visiting an uncle. He sheltered the orphans. Margaret married 1772—John Corbin a Virginian. When the Revolution broke out he enlisted in the first company of Pennsylvania artillery. In the pay list and muster rolls he is listed among the matrosses. In 1776 John Corbin was an outwork defender at Fort Washington accompanied by his wife. In the attack occured the incident which has placed Margaret Corbin's name upon the tablets of fame in American History.

John manned a gun in the hillside battery attacked by the Hessians where the battle raged hardest and longest. The Hessians succeeded in securing this position. In the midst of the battle Corbin, stopped by a ball, fell dead at his wife's feet. Instantly she stepped into his place and worked the gun with redoubled skill and vigor, fighting bravely until she sank to the earth pierced by three grapeshot in the shoulder. Although terribly wounded she recovered but was disabled for life. A soldier's half pay and the value of the soldier's suit of clothes annually were voted her by the Continental Congress while John Jay presided. The British took over 2000 American Prisoners among them Molly Corbin. It is believed that her bravery excited sufficient sympathy to cause her parole in the custody of General Greene. She was brought to Philadelphia and her injuries treated there.

Her name was on the Corps of Invalids payroll from August 1780 to June 1781. She was paid $33.30. A year later Molly was in a deplorable condition with the use of only one arm. In General Knox's papers a notation said that Mrs. Margaret Corbin has not drawn any liquor with the rations allowed her since the first of January 1782. William Price, Commissary and Military Stores, wrote, "I have procured a place for Capt. Molly till next spring if she should live so long, at 12 shillings per week."

Margaret Corbin died 1800 and was buried at Highland Falls, New York, her grave never marked except by a cedar tree. March 26, 1926, the New York DAR State Regent, Committee of members, historians and officials from West Point went to her grave, opened it and placed the bones in a suitable casket. With fitting ceremony they reinterred her in the West Point Military Cemetery. A granite monument erected by the DAR was dedicated. A bronze plaque showing a figure in relief of a woman firing a cannon, reads in part "In Memory of Margaret Corbin, a heroine of the Revolution, known as Captain Molly, 1751-1800. In appreciation of her deeds for the cause of Liberty and that her heroism may not be forgotten—Another marker was erected by Franklin County Chapter, DAR near her birth place. Many members of the Rocky Spring Chapter, Daughters of the American Colonists, participated also.

BETSY ROSS
Philadelphia **Born 1752**

Betsy Ross, maker of the first flag, is a name familiar to everyone. Some say the story is legend but documentation presents a ring of truth.

Elizabeth Griscom Ross Ashburn Claypoole, was born in Philadelphia of Quaker parentage January 1, 1752. A young woman of charming personality she was much admired for her sparkling blue eyes, light brown hair and trim figure. When 21 she married John Ross, upholsterer, whose father was an Episcopal Minister. They were married "out of meeting" at Huggs Tavern in what is now Camden, New Jersey. Betsy adopted her husband's trade which she continued as a widow after his tragic death, January 21, 1776. The widow Ross married Joseph Ashburn at Gloria Dei (Old Swedes) Church, Philadelphia—June 15, 1777. They had two daughters. Ashburn, prisoner of war, died in Mill Prison, England, March 3, 1782. John Claypoole brought the sorrowful message to Betsy. In time she married him at Christ Church—May 8, 1783—five daughters were born—Zillah Ashburn and Harriet Claypoole died but Clarissa, Susanna, Rachael and Jane Claypoole and Eliza Ashburn grew to maturity. John Claypoole died 1817 and Betsy died January 30, 1836. Both were buried in the Free Quaker burial ground removed later to Mr. Moriah Cemetery.

From the time of her first marriage until her retirement, because of loss of sight, ten years before her death, Betsy conducted an active business in her flag and upholstery shop. The shop, moved to large quarters on Second Street, was profitable during the Revolutionary War and thereafter.

In 1870, 34 years after Betsy's death the story generally told was confirmed by separate affidavits sworn to by Rachael Fletcher, who refers to her mother as Elizabeth Claypoole; by Sophia B. Hildebrandt, a granddaughter and by Margaret Boggs, a niece who for many years aided Betsy in her business.

The story places the time of the meeting of Mrs. Ross with the Committee of Congress as June 1776 for documentation crediting with Betsy Ross as suggesting using the five point star as part of our national emblem. A folded paper pattern of the star found 1922 in Samuel Wetherill's safe. It had remained unopened for over a century. In faded ink on the pattern was Mrs. C. Wilson (Clarissa Claypoole, Betsy's daughter). He was the Claypoole's contemporary when they lived on the north side of Mulberry (Arch) Street between third and Bread Street. Documented is the fact that to support herself she was making flags in 1777. Millions have believed the story. In 1892, 1,052,270 Americans

contributed towards establishing the flag house on Arch Street, Philadelphia, as a national shrine. Betsy Ross conducted herself with distinction throughout a long, difficult and eventful life. She was resourceful, creative, talented and a loyal patriot who actively supported the cause of freedom. As a working mother she supported and reared her family. She was loved and admired by all who knew her. Betsy Ross was truly a mother of achievement in American History.

LUCRETIA MOTT
Philadelphia   **Born 1793**

The American Woman Suffrage Association at its 1880 meeting, Worcester, Massachusetts, passed a resolution:

"This convention presents its greetings to its venerable early leader and friend, Lucretia Mott, whose life in its rounded perfection as wife, mother, preacher and reformer is the prophesy of the future of woman."

To many nineteenth century women, Lucretia Mott was a model, combining a deep love of home and family with an active public life. Born Lucretia Coffin, Nantucket Island 1793, educated at Nine Partners School near Poughkeepsie, New York, Lucretia came to Phila-

delphia in 1810. She married James Mott 1811, and devoted her life, until her death 1880, to public affairs in Philadelphia and the nation.

As a Quaker minister she had a liberalizing impact not only on the Hicksite branch, Society of Friends, but also on the whole development of free religious inquiry. She founded the Philadelphia Female Antislavery Society and was a leader in the American Convention of Antislavery Women. The American Antislavery Society sent her to London 1840 as representative at a World Antislavery Convention. The convention refused to seat her because she was a woman. This incensed Elizabeth Cady Stanton, present as a young bride, and led Lucretia and Elizabeth together to plan the 1848 Seneca Falls Convention, the birth of the women's rights movement in this country. From that day onward, Lucretia was a source of inspiration and encouragement to the women who led the fight.

Lucretia Mott helped develop three institutions providing women with higher education, Female Medical College of Pennsylvania, Female School of Design (Moore College of Art) and Swarthmore College. She helped women doctors establish practice against enormous public prejudice. She helped found a society providing opportunity for poor women to earn a living by needlecraft. After the Civil War she gave motherly support and encouragement to the women who went South to teach school and provide material aid to the newly freed slaves.

Lucretia helped found three pacifist societies. She practiced nonviolence, boycotted slave products, disobeyed unjust laws, confronted hostile mobs with only the power of moral force and went directly to those in authority, including the President, to demand peaceful policies.

All these things were achieved by a woman scarcely five feet tall, weighing less than 100 pounds. Lucretia not only raised her own five children, but took an active hand with her grandchildren and great grandchildren and many relatives. Her Philadelphia home was headquarters for visiting friends, reformers, and intellectuals. It was not unusual for her to have twenty or thirty for dinner, night after night, and though she had some help, she generally did most of the baking herself. Whenever she had a free moment to sit down her hands were busy with knitting or unravelling rags for carpets. One of her secrets seemed to be that she drew strength from her ability to love and give. "How lucky we are to have so many to care for" she once wrote her sister.

HARRIET LANE JOHNSTON
Lancaster   **Born 1830**

James Buchanan, the only bachelor President of the United States, chose his vivacious 27 year old niece, Harriet Lane, as his First Lady. Her good manners and insistence upon the social amenities curbed the growing political animosities and greatly aided her hard pressed uncle in maintaining channels of responsible communication between temperamental partisans of North and South.

Born in Mercersburg, Pennsylvania 1830 Harriet was the youngest of four Lane children. Her mother died 1837 and her father two years later. Relatives cared for the elder children but Harriet insisted that her uncle "Nunc", become her guardian. Buchanan accepted the responsibility gladly but not lightly. She moved into his Lancaster home under the care of his housekeeper, Miss Hetty Parker. Although deeply engrossed in public affairs she soon became the center of his personal and family life.

He supervised her education at private schools. Later he introduced her to fashionable circles "in the best manner." She joined him in London, where he was Minister to the Court of St. James. Queen Victoria gave "dear Miss

Lane" the rank of Ambassador's wife. Harriet was a strikingly beautiful girl with masses of fair hair and deep blue eyes. Her captivating mixture of spontaneity and poise won her many admiring suitors and enlivened social gatherings.

While the years of Buchanan's Presidency stand out as the apex of Harriet Lane's public career, they marked only the beginning of her durable work. In 1866 she married Henry Elliott Johnston, a Baltimore banker, and had two sons (James Buchanan Johnston and Henry Elliot Johnston). For 20 years Harriet gave up social activities to devote herself almost entirely to her family. They usually summered at Wheatland, which came to her after her uncle's death 1868.

Between 1881 and 1884 Harriet lost her two children through rheumatic fever and also her husband. She sold Wheatland and moved from Baltimore to Washington. Harriet determined to create a medical institute to study and treat children's diseases. In 1883 she inaugurated plans for the Harriet Lane Home as a long-residence children's hospital with surroundings congenial to young patients—an idea then unique in medical practice. In 1893 Johns Hopkins University made the home the pediatrics sections of the new school of medicine. The agreement provided that it should admit children of all nationalities, races and creeds, and specialize in pediatric training for doctors and nurses. This bequest, a landmark in medical history, established the first pediatrics medical center in the nation.

Harriet gave major impetus to establishing a National Fine Arts Collection in Washington. She willed her personal collection to the private Corcoran Art Gallery until Congress founded a National Gallery where her paintings could be transferred. Now the National Gallery has a major collection of world art treasures, government-owned, which provide inspiration and instruction for all.

Few women in the literature of real life present such a story so dramatic, so poignant and so productive as that of Harriet Lane. She became "queen" of a republic and from the depths of personal tragedy she built visions of a restored public appreciation for the character and work of her beloved uncle, a better world for children and enhanced respect for the fine arts. Before her death in 1903, by foresight and careful planning, she brought all these public-spirited hopes to fruition.

MAYBELLE K. PRICE
Philadelphia **Born 1887**

Mrs. Walter Price was, indeed, a woman of achievement!

In 1919, she was concerned about the soldiers that were blinded during World War I and their rehabilitation in the ways and means to become self-supporting and in helping their morale. As a dedicated Red Cross volunteer, Mrs. Price helped to organize and develop the Braille Department of the Southeastern Pennsylvania Chapter of the American Red Cross in 1921 in Philadelphia.

At that time, many people did not know the meaning of Braille so the first task was to educate the public. In 1923, the first class in Braille Transcribing was started and soon developed a group of qualified braillists in building up a library of textbooks for the blind students to complete college educations and to pioneer innumerable things which have now become standard practice. Then, Braille became a national activity of the American Red Cross and Chapters all over the country called upon Mrs. Price for guidance in getting started.

After twenty-three years of service in Red Cross, Mrs. Price founded the Volunteers Service for the Blind with her dedicated volunteers who were conscious of the great need that existed for the civilian blind too. At the same time, the Library of Congress took over their library of brailled material which they had accomplished in distributing libraries to all 50 states of the Union and placed 550,000 brailled books in these libraries.

During World War II, the need for student materials became acute and Mrs. Price suggested to the State Prison Superintendents that they allow them to teach the prisoners to transcribe books for the blind with proper care and exactness which resulted in many prisons throughout the United States becoming active in transcribing braille. Still another step was taken in 1950, when Mrs. Price learned about some recording machines and from then on, the volunteers did every book possible on these machines. This idea spread like wildfire across the country and a wonderful world of knowledge and reading was opened up to our blind population.

As the Founder and Honorary President until her death, of her independent organization of the Volunteers Service for the Blind, Mrs. Price pioneered by inventing a guide device whereby a sightless person can write a check in longhand and for series of playing cards and Braille cards to assist in using dial telephones, writing portfolio and a published monthly children's magazine, with the transcription of music, the invention of a new process for making manuscript for duplication (which spread over the United States and to India), and even the social services of finding false teeth and false eyes for the Blind. Finally, an entirely new aid to the blind was the complete production of text books on phonograph records and Mrs. Price with her workers produced about 3,200 of them in 1950. Now they are world-wide in scope.

Maybelle Price, born 1887, Philadelphia, died April 7, 1973, leaving Walter, Jr., a granddaughter, and Mabelle (Mrs. Carl S. Brandt). Helen died previously.

Is this not a work rarely equalled by one woman?

PEARL S. BUCK
Perkasie   Born 1892

She sat patiently in the hotel lobby, unassuming yet dignified and authoritative, with a hat of unknown vintage on her thick graying straight hair. Looking at her luminous eyes the whole world seemed mirrored within. They were sad and contemplative but keen, observing, warm and friendly when she greeted someone. Pearl S. Buck, Nobel Award winner in Literature 1938, Pulitzer Prize 1932, was receiving the Gimbel Award in Philadelphia that day. She had come from her home in Perkasie, Bucks County, to be honored again, not only as a famous author, but for her service to humanity.

Founder of "Welcome House" she wished to start the Pearl S. Buck Foundation for care of Amerasian children in their own countries with headquarters in the City of Brotherly Love. The monetary award that day made this dream possible.

Her knowledge of conditions for the unwanted in the Far East, where she had lived for many years and which formed a background for several of her books and articles, instigated the work of "Welcome House." Her influence as a world leader plus her enthusiasm and ability to inspire others with compassion for these outcasts brought about a world-wide change and opportunity for them. Lecturing became an ad-

junct to writing but she spent many hours at her desk in her country home in Pennsylvania with her facile pen.

Pearl Sydenstricker Buck, born Hillsboro, West Virginia, June 26th, 1892 was the daughter of Absolom and Carolina (Stulting) Sydenstricker, Presbyterian missionaries in Chinkiang, China. A.B. Randolph Macon Women's College, M.A. Cornell University and Yale; Litt D West Virginia University, LID Howard University, St. Laurence University, married John Lossing Buck May 13, 1917. They had Carol and Janice.

She was educated in Shanghai and taught in Nanking 1921-1931. "The Good Earth" 1931, her best known novel, depicted the struggle of a Chinese peasant and his wife for land and security. Divorced 1934, she married Richard J. Walsh, her publisher, and adopted many children. Many articles, short stories and the autobiographical, "The Bridge for Passing," followed. Fiction was written under the pen name John Sedges. She received many honors and Pearl Buck's death at the age of 83 in Danby, Vermont 1973 her summer home, left a lifetime of dedicated and courageous work to alleviate social inequities and hopefully bring peace and happiness through better world understanding.

CATHERINE DRINKER BOWEN
Haverford

"Do you mind if I don't stand while I talk?" asked Catherine Drinker Bowen, historian, biographer. She smiled slightly as she seated her tall straight body into a chair on the platform in Germantown, a section of Philadelphia. One watched her strong, angular face, serious and intense. Her forceful and interesting personality asserted itself as she spoke. Incidents in the countless hours spent in historical research, amusing and dramatic, fascinated the audience. Much research had to be done before her twelve books could be written. Determination, thoroughness and accuracy of details, all on file cards, resulted in bringing historical background and character into her come-alive subjects.

Catherine Drinker Bowen was born in Haverford, Pennsylvania, January 1, 1897, daughter of Dr. Henry S. and Aimee (Beaux) Drinker. Her father was long-time president of LeHigh University. She married Ezra Bowen, economics

professor Lafayette College. They had two children, Catherine Drinker (Mrs. George N. Prince, Seattle and Ezra, Editor Life Time Books, and four grandchildren. They were divorced and he died in 1945. July 1, 1939 she married Dr. Thomas McKean Downs, Philadelphia surgeon who died 1960.

An intellectual home atmosphere combined with her intense interest in music lead her to study at Peabody Institute of Music and Institute Museum of Art, now Moore College of Art. Cecilia Beaux, famous artist, was her aunt. Her first book, "Beloved Friend", biography of Tchaikowski 1937, with Barbara von Meck and "Free Artist", Anton Rubenstein, combined her love of music and writing. Kitty Bowen was an accomplished violinist and joined a group of chamber music enthusiasts at her brother's home in Merion each Sunday night. Practicing every day was her therapy from writing.

"Yankee from Olympus" 1939, Justice Oliver Wendell Holmes and "John Adams and the American Revolution", a Truman favorite 1950 were popular. Six years were spent to write "The Lion and the Throne", a biography of Sir Edward Coke, Elizabethan jurist. This won a National Book award and the Phillips prize American Philosophical Society. Many law students are required to read it.

Although she never went to college twelve honorary degrees were conferred on this eminent historian, as well as being elected Phi Beta Kappa.

Her former research produced "Francis Bacon", (Coke's great rival) The Temper of a Man. Her greatest contribution to American literature is "Miracle at Philadelphia" 1966. Here the reader is a part of the stormy, brilliant sessions where the Constitution of the United States was born. This dramatic moment in history, May to September 1787, is seen through the eyes and words of the participants.

Kitty Bowen's last book, "The Most Dangerous Man in America, Scenes from the Life of Benjamin Franklin" is more fragmented in extent due to terminal cancer which cut her work short November 1, 1973. Yet this illuminating and absorbing collection of essays presents fitting climax to a literary life of an outstanding American historian, a Distinguished Daughter of Pennsylvania.

MARGARET MEAD
Philadelphia   **Born 1901**

Dr. Margaret Mead is a world renowned anthropologist whose volcanic-like eruptions of ideas, opinions, controversial theories belie her traditional grandmother looks. But when she talks or writes her many faceted personality

emotes with outstanding attention. There is never a dull moment when one comes in contact with this dynamic woman, sparkling, witty, interesting—leaving one breathless with her knowledge of human beings. Dr. Mead is curator Ethnology, American Museum Natural History, New York. She was born in Philadelphia December 16, 1901, daughter of Edward Sherwood and Emily (Fogg) Mead. She grew up in a family where everyone was an individual. It was expected that one could understand what was being discussed and take part in the conversation. The family as an integral and essential unit in any culture led her to 50 years of intensive study of living primitive societies.

Always desiring to be an anthropologist she had the opportunity in 1925 to do field work in the Far East, particularly Admirality Islands, Samoa, Bali and New Guinea. Living with and writing about these people brought newer insight about human beings whose only difference is in their culture. This resulted in a book "Coming of Age in Samoa" in 1928. She believed the continuity of life through knowledge gained of grandparents through oneself to grandchildren is an entity of time each person needs, to become a full human being in the present. Margaret Mead, who kept her own name through three marriages, first married 9th month 1923 Luther Cressman, Theological Seminary Student; second marriage, Reo Fortune and third, Gregory Bateson, fellow Anthropologists. Told that she could never have children it was a great joy to her that Mary Catherine Bateson (married J. Barke Kassarjian. Granddaughter, Sevanne Margaret born March 1969) was born December 8, 1939 when Margaret was 38. She was a pioneer in advocating babies to be with mothers in a hospital room, to be fed when need arises and not on a schedule and bathed at the convenience of the mother.

Her popular "Male & Female" was published 1949 and "Keep Your Powder Dry", 1942, are among many from her prolific pen. "Anthropologists and What They Do", 1965 plus "Blackberry Winter", an autobiography are later. Her numerous books depict relationships between Psychology and Cultural change in societies. Any subject dealing with people interests this active, vibrant woman who finds time to serve on boards of many national organizations and societies as well as editing, contributing articles and lecturing. Her honors are legion but no one deserves them more than this distinguished mother.

KATHARINE BOUCOT STURGIS
Haverford   Born 1903

Katharine Boucot Sturgis was born September 6, 1903, daughter of Morris and Hannah (Rottenberg) Rosenbaum. She married Joseph R. Boucot March 23, 1944 (died May 5, 1962) during her first premedical year, University of Pennsylvania. After being out of college thirteen years, she matriculated at Pennsylvania State University when her children were ten and seven. In her senior year at Woman's Medical College of Pennsylvania, she developed tuberculosis. After two years in sanatoria, she completed her senior year half-time, receiving her M.D. in 1942.

Turning a handicap into an asset, she specialized in lung disease, training at Detroit's Herman Kiefer Hospital. Convinced that early detection would reduce the rate of new tuberculosis infection, she returned to Philadelphia 1945, invited by the Philadelphia Tuberculosis Association to direct their mass chest x-ray survey program. By 1947 she also directed Philadelphia's municipal chest x-ray surveys. Among her clinical appointments were Visiting Chief, Division of Chest Disease, Philadelphia

General Hospital, the Veteran's Hospital and the Barton Memorial and White Haven Division of Jefferson Hospital.

Her major research involved tuberculosis among diabetics and the detection of curable lung cancer. She was appointed Professor and Chairman of Preventive Medicine and Clinical Professor of Medicine at her alma mater in 1952. She received her Master's degree in Public Health from John Hopkins and was board certified in Preventive Medicine in 1954.

She has been a relentless crusader against smoking, occupational carcinogens, and air pollutants. Among her numerous "first woman" offices are presidencies of the Philadelphia County Medical Society, College of Physicians of Philadelphia, Eastern Section of the American Trudeau Society and American College of Preventive Medicine, as well as Philadelphia Tuberculosis Association and Delaware Valley Citizens' Council for Clean Air.

From 1960 through 1970, she was Chief Editor of the American Medical Association's Archives of Environmental Health, the first woman chief editor of a major United States medical journal. She is the author of more than 100 articles on pulmonary disease.

Dr. Sturgis received three honorary degrees—from Keuka College, Beaver College, and Woman's Medical College—and numerous honors such as Distinguished Daughter of Pennsylvania, Penn State Woman of the Year, Gimbel Award, Trudeau Medal National Tuberculosis Association, Strittmatter Award Philadelphia County Medical Society and the Distinguished Service Medal American College of Preventive Medicine. She was the first woman member of the Council of the National Institute of Environmental Health Sciences and currently serves on the Health Advisory Committee of the Federal Environmental Protection Agency.

Her life combines happily a demanding professional career with motherhood. Her son, Arthur James Boucot, Ph.D. is Professor of Geology at Oregon State University and her daughter, Nancy Boucot Cummings, M.D. (Mrs. Milton Curtis Cummings, Jr.) is Associate Director for Kidney, Urologic and Blood Disease, National Institute of Arthritis, Metabolism and Digestive Diseases. Dr. Boucot married Dr. Samuel Booth Sturgis, November 18, 1964. Dr. Sturgis believes that her studies when her children were small encouraged their scholarliness. She thinks her children's examples provide a stimulating milieu for her seven grandchildren.

Ruth Patrick
Philadelphia

Any one seeing Ruth Patrick for the first time would place her as a gracious homemaker or volunteer worker more than as a famous scientist who delights in wading and sampling water and aquatic life in many rivers and streams throughout the world. Her love of biology engendered by her father when she was a child in Kansas City, Missouri, became her lifetime profession. Dr. Ruth Patrick, Department of Biology Professor, University of Pennsylvania, is founder and outspoken chairman of a 70-man department of limnology at the 158 year old Academy of Natural Sciences in Philadelphia. As a limnologist, diatom, systematist and environmentalist—her work has taken her to over 700 rivers and water ways at home and abroad. She was the first to diagnose the health of a stream by measuring the diversity of plants and animal species that grow in it. For this she was recently elected to the prestigous National Academy of Sciences—one of only 9 living women out of 870 members and 12 ladies in the Academy's history.

In June 1975 she was awarded the Dr. of Science degree from Swarthmore College for her work concerning the need for fresh water and the industrial needs for society. Dr. Patrick told the graduates that the energy problem is crippling the economy of Europe and pollution is an international as well as a national problem. She urged people to save energy and to learn how to better use, not abuse, our natural resources and how to produce quality food at less energy cost. "We must eliminate waste and reuse materials".

W. B. Hart, a water pollution pioneer, urged Ruth Patrick to apply herself to solving society's problems. He raised $65,000 from Pennsylvania's Chamber of Commerce and donated it to the state which then gave Dr. Patrick the job of How Pollution Effected Pennsylvania's Rivers. This survey was held in the Connestoga Basin Farm Lands near Lancaster. Michael Bandler's article in the Smithsonian states "Any changes in kind of aquatic species and in relative sizes of a aquatic population gives a warning sign. She developed a system which shows by a type of shift what kind of pollution is entering the stream."

Ruth Patrick born Topeka, Kansas, daughter of Frank and Myrtle (Jetmore) Patrick, married Dr. Charles Hodge IV, July 10, 1931. They have

one son, Charles Hodge V. She earned a B.S. degree Coker College 1929 and a M.S. University of Virginia 1931, PhD 1934.

She is the recipient and naming of many U.S. and International Honors in the World among them distinguished daughter of Pennsylvania. The enjoyment of her home and family plus her time consuming scientific work make for a strenuous but happy, interesting life for this energetic mother. Her advice, of which she is an exponent, is "to build constructive relationships with others since the growing world population makes it more important today to work harmoniously."

PUERTO RICO

Institute of
Puerto Rican Culture

Puerto Rico

Photos

1. La Fortaleza
2. Porta Coeli
3. El Morro (1539)
4. Casa Blanca (1523)

Puerto Rico

LOLA RODRIGUEZ DE TIO
San German   **Born 1853**

Surely the most outstanding Puerto Rican mother of her time, Lola Rodriguez de Tio was prominent as poet, politician and mother. It is difficult to write a short biography of her, because her many interesting anecdotes and achievements are enough to fill a book. One of the most beautiful books written about her is *Lola de America* by Carmen Leila Cuevas.

Lola's parents were the distinguished magistrate Sebastian Rodriguez de Astudillo and his wife Carmen Ponce de Leon, a descendant of the great explorer and first Governor of Puerto Rico, Juan Ponce de Leon.

Because Lola was an avid, extremely intelligent girl, her own father took charge of her education. She refused to go to a conventional school because she had no patience to learn in the class-room. Her determined temperament surfaced in all her important decisions. Once, while strolling through the streets with her sister Aurora, she saw a handsome youth, just arrived from Spain. "You see that man?" she said to her sister. "Well, he is going to be my husband some day". Of course, Aurora was shocked, but had to laugh. What an idea!

At twenty, Lola was married to the man she had chosen, Bonocio Tio Segarra, a man of liberal ideas, who proved to be her perfect counterpart. The couple had two daughters, Patria, and Mercedes who died at age three. Patria inherited the lyrical temperament and intellectual unrest of her mother, who guided and inspired her.

Mrs. Tio's political views made great impact on the island. She wanted independence from Spain for Puerto Rico. In 1887 there were a lot of political persecutions in Puerto Rico. Under the governorship of General Romualdo Palacios, a group of Puerto Rican patriots were taken prisoners and locked in the cells of "El Morro Fort". With her usual determination, Mrs Tio acted immediately. She wrote a forceful letter to the Ministry of Justice in Spain, on behalf of the rebels. The letter made such a favorable impression in court, that the prisoners were released. This is a unique case in the annals of Puerto Rican history. In the archives of Lola's daughter, Patria, there is an historic document addressed to Mrs. Tio, signed by all the patriots released. In it they express, in a very special manner, their gratitude to Lola, whom they called "our guardian angel".

Twice, Lola and Bonocio were exiled. They went to Venezuela, and later to Cuba, where the couple established their residence. As expatriates, Lola and Bonocio made a common cause for Cuba's independence. At the same time, and by way of her pen, Lola defended independence for Puerto Rico. In one of her most famous and beautiful poems, she used the simile that Cuba and Puerto Rico were the two wings of a bird, receiving flowers and bullets in the same heart. History can hardly condemn Lola for making Cuba her second country. There she was the object of countless honors. Because she was a cosmopolitan soul, she was celebrated everywhere: Venezuela, Paris, Madrid and New York, paid her homage.

Lola's poems are among the most beautiful and patriotic of Puerto Rican literature. Some of her poetry books are: *Mis Cantares* (My Songs), *Claros y Nieblas* (Light and Mist), and *Mi Libro de Cuba* (My Book of Cuba).

During her visits to Puerto Rico, Lola was always acclaimed by all. In her last visit she was given a reception at the Puerto Rican Atheneum, where many eminent participants, such as Luis Muñoz Rivera, Jose de Diego and Ferdinand R. Cestero, were present.

Doña Lola Rodriguez de Tio died and was buried in Havana, Cuba.

ANA ROQUE DE DUPREY
Aguadilla   **Born 1853**

Regarded by many as the first Puerto Rican liberated woman, Ana Roque started the movement for women's suffrage in 1917, founding the first feminist organization, "Puerto Rico Feminine League".

Ana's mother, Cristina Geigel, died when Ana was four. She remained in the care of her father, Ricardo Roque, and her grandmother, Ana Maria Sapia, a veteran teacher. Both provided Ana with an American education, instilling in her the love of freedom. In her autobiography she says: "My father and grandmother taught me that education was the most important thing in life. I learned to read at age three-and-a-half and used to sleep with my books". When she went to school, although the tuition was only $1.50, her father paid $10.00 because he wanted his daughter to learn in two years what others learned in six. She mastered French and English.

At thirteen Ana started her own school, and wrote a Universal Geography, which was used as a text book for many years in the island's schools.

At nineteen, Ana married Luis E. Duprey, of French ancestry, and went to live at his estate, where she studied biology, geography, meteorology, philosophy and astronomy. In her spare time she praticed the piano. She was teacher of her children, Borinquen, Hortencia, America, and Luis Enrique.

In 1878 Mrs. Duprey went to live at San Juan, where intellectuals and scientists used to gather at her home to discuss astronomy and watch the heavens through her telescope. In 1885 Ana began to study for her bachelor's degree in liberal arts. She held many teaching positions and wrote several text books in grammar and geography. She also edited five newspapers, among them, "The Women's Herald". She wrote thirty-two novels and was the first lady to be a member of the prestigious Puerto Rican Atheneum.

As a scientist her name went beyond the limits of her island. The French Astronomic Society made her honorary member. She wrote *Botany in the West Indies* in both English and Spanish. It received many prizes, but remained unpublished because the cost of publication was to high. The University of Puerto Rico granted her the title of Doctor in Literature Honoris Causa.

When Mrs. Duprey was almost eighty, women were granted the right to vote. Friends carried her to the polls, but as she was not registered, the chief advocate of women's suffrage could not cast her vote. She never knew of this irony because they made her vote through an affidavit, which was not valid, since she had not been registered.

ROSARIO ANDRACA DE TIMOTHEE
San Juan   **Born 1873**

This eminent educator excelled in cultural, social and religious affairs. Born in San Juan, her parents were Eugenio Andraca and Lorenza Cotray. Because she was the oldest of a large family, Rosario had to assume great responsibilities when her father died, so she was deprived of childhood diversions. In the evenings, she used to sew and embroider by the light of an oil lamp, while her friends played. In spite of this, she strove to become an educated and prominent person. At sixteen, she qualified with honors to teach elementary school. She was listed in "The Official Gazette" in 1889, as the youngest of the most distinguised teachers.

Rosario married Pedro Carlos Timothee, teacher, journalist, pharmacist and lawyer. They had three children, Pedro, who died as a child, Carlos Eugenio, dead too, and Rafael, a prominent physician.

Mrs. Timothee resumed her education while teaching; in that way, she obtained the title of high school teacher and later studied pharmacy. She and her husband established a private school. When the change of sovereignty for Puerto Rico, the United States Government found in Mrs. Timothee a teacher fully capable of teaching the new English courses.

Being a fervent admirer of Abraham Lincoln, Rosario worked toward erecting a marble statue of the great emancipator at Lincoln School, where she was principal. Rosario herself started the collection of funds with $1,000.00 from her savings.

Mrs. Timothee edited the educational magazine "El Hogar" (The Home). She was co-founder and prominent member of the Puerto Rico Teachers Association.

In 1945, when Rosario retired from her teaching career, she received a public homage at Lincoln School, where three generations of students surrounded her. From then on, Doña Rosario dedicated herself to religion. On the day of her death, her house in San Juan, where she had lived since her marriage, was visited by hundreds of friends.

CARMEN SANABIA DE FIGUEROA
Aguadilla   Born 1882

Many musicians have passed through the tutorship of Carmen Sanabia de Figueroa, her own children being the most famous.

Carmen's father was Jose Sanabia and her mother was Inocencia Ellinger, of Dutch descent. At eight she was the pupil of Jose Lequerique, Professor Castañer and Ana Otero. When her father died, Carmen started her career as piano teacher to help support the family. In 1903 she married Jesus Figueroa and went to live in San Sebastian, where her husband was Director of the Municipal Band. In 1909 the family moved to San Juan. Their children are: Pepito, Narciso, Guillermo, Rafael, Carmelina, Leonor, Angelina and Kachiro, all musicians. The five sons form the internationally renowned Figueroa Quintet.

Mrs. Figueroa worked in many public schools as music teacher, in addition to having private students. Her home was the site for the preparation of many musical programs, and her advice was often sought. Carmen sent her children to further their musical education in Spain and France, while she worked. She preferred to remain in the shadow, while her progeny were conquering fame.

Because Mrs. Figueroa was a devout Chris-

tian, she was grateful to God and tried to reciprocate by helping the needy. In 1950 she was named San Juan's first Mother of the Year, a well deserved honor to a great mother, woman and artist.

Music is a way of life with Mrs. Figueroa's descendants. At this writing, her grandchildren, Ivonne and Guillermo Jr. are opening their way to fame, too. Carmen could have said, like the mother of the Gracchus Brothers: "My jewels are my children".

MARIA CADILLA DE MARTINEZ
Arecibo   **Born 1886**

For her intellectual, artistic, social and civic works, Maria Cadilla has a prominent position in Puerto Rican history. This remarkable woman was educator, poet, essayist, historian, lecturer and painter.

Maria's parents were Armindo Cadilla, from Spain and Catalina Colon, from Hatillo, Puerto Rico. The Cadilla family has been privileged in yielding many prominent personalities to the Puerto Rican culture. Maria had a thorough education, begining in the private schools of the island and culminating at the Central University of Madrid, where she received her Doctorate in Philosophy and Letters with concentration in Hispanic studies. She learned to paint with famous Puerto Rican painter Francisco Oller.

At seventeen Maria was married to Julio Tomas Martinez, an architect and painter. From this union several children were born, but only two of them reached adulthood, Tomasita and Marita.

During her life Doctor Cadilla de Martinez received countless honors. Some of them as follows:

1. Seven gold and silver medals in elementary school.

2. First prize, gold medal and diploma, given by the Society Writers and Artists of Puerto Rico for her story "El Tesoro de Don Alonso" (Don Alonso's Treasure).

3. First prize, gold medal and diploma, for her oil painting "El Rio de mi Pueblo" (My Town's River, given by the Puerto Rico Atheneum.

4. "La Societe Academique d'Historie Internationale" of France gave her a gold medal and honorary membership for her work "Ethnography of Puerto Rico".

5. The American International Academy awarded her their Honor Insignia.

As an historian, Maria was given merits by, among others, The Order of San Luis Rey of France, The Indian Andrha Research University, The Society Folkloric of Mexico and America Group of Mexico.

Among Doctor Cadilla's best literary works we find: *Cuentos de Lillian* (Tales of Lillian), *Cazadora en el Alba* (Huntress at Dawn), *Raices de mi Tierra* (Roots of my Homeland), *Poesia Popular de Puerto Rico* (Folk Songs of Puerto Rico) and *Cancinones Infantiles de Puerto Rico* (Children's Songs of Puerto Rico).

In Doctor Cadilla's poems there is a sense of wonder for all the things in Nature. "La Rosa" (The Rose), "Vespertina" (Vesper) and "Torre de Marfil" (Ivory Tower) are regarded as the best of her poetic output.

Dr. Maria Cadilla's civic life was notable too. She participated actively in feminist movements, and was a member of several women's associations.

ISABEL ALONSO DE MIER
Vega Baja   **Born 1886**

A dedicated Puerto Rican writer and civic leader, Mrs. Mier has a distinguished place in the history of the island. Her parents were Alfonso Perez and Juanita Aragones, both of Spanish origin.

Isabel attended primary and secondary school in Vega Baja, and was pupil of Puerto Rican writer Manuel Fernandez Juncos. Then she went to Spain and studied under the tutorship of Jose Ortega Y Gasset and Tomas Navarro Tomas.

Isabel married Mariano Mier, of Spanish ancestry. They had two sons and a daughter, Gonzalo, Mariano, and Isabel Maria. When her husband died, she concentrated on the education of her children.

As a writer, Mrs. Mier collaborated with local newspapers "El Imparcial" and "El Mundo," and the magazine Puerto Rico "Ilustrado." Along with Marian Wolf, she wrote *A Guide to Puerto Rico*, for the benefit of tourists. A splendid civic worker, Isabel was an active member of: Catholic Daughters of America, Women's Civic Club, Salesian Ladies, Society for the Blind and Orphan Children's Shelter.

Among the many awards she received are: Pontifical Decoration "Pro Ecclesia et Pontifice" in 1950, Woman of the Year 1963 of San Juan, Grandmother of the Year 1963 (Catholic Daughters America) and the Outstanding Member Medal (Women's Civic Club of Puerto Rico). In 1930, Governor Theodore Roosevelt named her member of the Committee to Preserve Historic Places. She worked hard toward the restoration of Cristo Chapel in San Juan, a National Monument, said to be the smallest in the world.

Mrs. Mier certainly stands as an individual who has touched many lives, and because of it, has made them richer in thinking and doing.

MARIA MARTINEZ DE PEREZ ALMIROTY
Ponce   **Born 1889**

María Martinez de Perez Almiroty lives very quietly at La Egida, a home for the elders of the Puerto Rico Teacher's Association. She is a cheerful little woman of 86. Despite her old age, Mrs. Perez has an amazingly clear mind. Only her body is aging.

Doña María's parents were Carmelo Martinez, a lawyer, and Elvira Acosta. She was educated in Ana Roque de Duprey's private school. In 1912 María wedded Federico Perez Almiroty.

They had two children: Federico, a lawyer, and Blanca, secretary.

Mrs. Perez Almiroty was a school teacher for nine years. Then she entered politics and civic work. She fought for greater participation of women in government matters.

Doña María was elected vice president of the Liberal Party, and was also member of the Municipal Assembly of Río Piedras. In 1936 she became the first woman Senator of the Puerto Rican Legislature.

As a civic leader, Mrs. Perez Almiroty was co-founder and first president of the Women's Civic Club, one of the most prestigious organizations of Puerto Rico. The Girl Scouts Council of Puerto Rico was formed under the leadership of this noted lady. María reorganized the Children's Home and worked for the construction of The Girls' Home, for homeless girls.

When the American Cancer League was established in Puerto Rico, Mrs. Perez Almiroty acted as first secretary, then treasurer, and later vice president. She is still active in the League as honorary president. In 1965 she was elected Woman of the Year.

To sum up, Mrs. Perez Almiroty's whole life has been a series of distinguished services to the community.

MARTA ROBERT DE ROMEU
Mayaguez   **Born 1890**

An eminent physician and civic worker, Dr. Robert was also involved in politics. The doctor lives alone and quietly in a residential section in Condado. She is perfectly capable of taking care of herself at 85. She is quite nimble, alert, and still drives her own car.

Dr. Robert's parents were Adolfo Robert and Agripina Besosa. She married Francisco Romeu, a businessman. The couple had two daughters: Hilda, and Nora, who died with her little daughter in a plane crash.

As a girl, Marta was a pupil of Ana Roque de Duprey. In 1914 she obtained her doctorate in medicine and surgery at Tuft Medical College, in Boston. Then she returned to Puerto Rico and worked in San Aurelio Hospital and Perea Clinic in Mayaguez. In 1918 Dr. Robert was Head of the Gynecology Department at the Mayaguez Polyclinic. Later she went to work at New York Post Graduate Hospital. There the

doctor joined the Social Suffragist League, of which she was president.

Keeping on her medical career, Dr. Robert returned to Puerto Rico, and occupied the positions of Medical Director and Obstetrician in the Maternity and Children's Hospital in San Juan, and Medical Director of the Division of Maternity and Children of the Dept. of Health.

On her political side, Dr. Robert was appointed National Committeewoman in charge of Puerto Rico's qualifications for Federal funds. She also worked extensively on behalf of women's suffrage, attending public hearings on island affairs in the United States Congress. Dr. Robert was delegate for Puerto Rico of the Republican Party in the U. S. A.

The doctor has a sharp memory regarding past activities. On her medical side we quote her significant remark, "I put an end to midwifery in Puerto Rico!"

JOSEFINA BARCELO DE ROMERO
Fajardo   **Born 1901**

Josefina Barcelo de Romero is one of the most distinguished political figures of Puerto Rico. She is the daughter of Puerto Rican patriot Antonio R. Barcelo and Josefina Bird. Josefina was educated in the College of the Sacred Heart of San Juan and Kentwood, Albany.

At seventeen, Josefina married engineer and lawyer Antonio Romero; they had three children: Gloria Maria, Calixto, and Carlos, who is the mayor of San Juan. Besides, they were foster parents of their nephew Antonio Barcelo. Sharing her father's interest in the political, social and economic welfare of the island, Mrs. Romero took an active part in the political cam-

paigns of Don Antonio, who was president of the Liberal Party.

When women in Puerto Rico were granted the right to vote in 1932, Mrs. Romero participated actively in the inscriptions. In the early years of women's suffrage, men were reluctant to let their wives get inscribed. Doña Josefina made a habit of going by car to the remotest corners of the island to fetch women for the inscriptions. Her role became increasingly important, as she won the respect and confidence of the men. She was expecting her third child during that period.

She was elected president of her party in 1944, becoming the first Latin American woman to hold such a post. Her political career influenced her son in his successful bid for the mayorship of San Juan. She remembers, "As a small child, my son Carlos went along with me in my trips throughout the island. He was absorbed in all my activities, and was deeply interested in all he saw around him.

Doña Josefina is an active member of many organizations, among them: Women's Civic Club, Puerto Rico Chapter of the United Nations Organization, Volunteer Corps of the Rio Piedras Municipal Hospital and Our Lady of Lourdes Congregation.

She is still in politics as delegate to the conventions of the New Progressive Party, of which her son Carlos is president.

ANA G. MENDEZ
Aguada   **Born 1908**

Mrs. Ana G. Mendez is one of Puerto Rico's V.I.P.'s. She is a beautiful woman with a very sweet smile. Her chief concern is education, but she has also been intensely active in civic, social, and charitable affairs.

Ana came from a large family. Her parents were Francisco Gonzalez Monge of Mayaguez, and Ana Cofresí, of Cabo Rojo. At sixteen, Ana married José Mendez, a businessman from Vega Baja. The couple had three children: Dora, Grecia, and José. With the help of her husband and her mother, Ana continued her education.

After finishing her bachelor's degree in commercial education, Ana enrolled in New York University and obtained her Master in Arts. She took a job as teacher, but wasn't content with just that; she had to do more. Her great

didactic anxiety made her venture into a new project. With the help of two colleagues, Mrs. Mendez established a new private high school. That meant hard work; and proved to be harder than Ana had anticipated, because she had only $1500 and nineteen students to begin with. But she never relented. That was the beginning of what is now a concern of millions of dollars and service to ten thousand students. Mrs. Mendez got involved in the personal problems of her students, in a genuine desire to help them. Similarly, and quoting her daughter, "Despite all her work, our mother is always there when we need her."

Mrs. Mendez achievements in higher education have filled a necessity in the educational problems of Puerto Rico. The Ana G. Mendez Educational Foundations, all fully accredited, consist of:

> The Puerto Rico Junior College (First junior college in the island)
> Puerto Rico Junior College Foundation
> University of Turabo
> The Ana G. Mendez Educational Foundation

Mrs. Mendez has undertaken responsibilities that would have scared many other women. Her "curriculum vitae" is unbelievable. Because her deeds fill pages, and the list of honors granted her are equally lengthy, we must obviate them for this purpose. We will only mention that she was granted the title of Doctor in Humanities, Honoris Causa, by the Catholic University.

Of course, Ana wasn't infallible, and she probably made mistakes and corrected them. But, we quote her, "I always put my Creator ahead. My faith in God and Humanity has never dwindled."

RHODE ISLAND

Rhode Island

Nickname: Little Rhody

State Flower: Violet

State Tree: Maple

State Bird: R.I. Red

Photos

1. First Baptist Church (1775)
2. Old Court and State House (Prov.)
3. Tour Synagogue, Newport
4. Statue of Roger Williams
5. City Hall, Prov.
6. State House, Prov.
7. John Brown's 2nd home (1780)

Committee Members

Co-Chairman—Mrs. H. Wells French, Middletown

Co-Chairman—Mrs. William Gardner, Warwick

Mrs. Louis B. Cappuccio, Watch Hill
Mrs. Frank E. Greene, Providence
Mr. Avery T. Waterman, Jr., Greenville
Mrs. Edmund A. Sayer, Wakefield
Mrs. Harry Guny, Providence
Mrs. Lucille L. Jewell, Providence
Mrs. William D. Wiley, Providence
Mr. Kevin O'Neil, Warwick
Mrs. William H. Gardner, Jr.
Mrs. Richard F. Sprague

Rhode Island

CATHERINE LITTLEFIELD GREENE
Block Island   **Born 1724**

Catherine Littlefield Greene, wife of Nathanael Greene and patron of Eli Whitney in his development of the cotton gin, was born in New Shoreham, Rhode Island, on Block Island, to John and Phebe Littlefield. Her father represented Block Island in the colonial assembly from 1747 to the Revolution.

Not too much is known of the childhood of Catherine, but it is presumed she attended the town school and the Baptist meetinghouse.

Through her distinguished family connections, she acquired a knowledge of Rhode Island society beyond Block Island. An aunt, Catherine Greene, whose husband became the second governor of the state, was a close friend of Benjamin Franklin. It was at William and Catherine Greene's house in Warwick, Rhode Island, that Catherine Littlefield, on July 20, 1774, was married to Nathanael Greene of Coventry, Rhode Island. He was General Washington's most trusted officer.

Catherine came to command the affectionate respect of the great men of her day for her courage and charm. General Washington took note of her at Valley Forge in the grim winter of 1777-78. She had followed her husband to share the hardships of those bitter months with the men upon whose fortitude the success of the Revolution depended.

Catherine's gallantry of spirit in the face of danger and acute discomfort won her Washington's grateful admiration.

In the autumn of 1785, following the war, the family settled on Mulberry Grove plantation on the Savannah River, which was given to them by Georgia, in recognition of General Greene's services.

Nine months later, at the age of forty-three, Nathanael Greene died, leaving a young widow with five small children.

Entrusting the management of the plantation to Phineas Miller, the children's tutor, she returned every summer to Newport, already very much a center of Rhode Island society.

On her journey homeward from Newport in the fall of 1792, a traveling companion was Eli Whitney, newly graduated from Yale, whom Phineas Miller had secured as a tutor for a South Carolina family. His teaching plans collapsed, but he stayed on at Mulberry Grove, absorbed in a mechanical project suggested by his hostess. Struck by his ingenuity, Catherine Greene had persuaded him to turn his talents to devising a machine that could rapidly strip the tenacious seeds from short-staple cotton and thus make it a profitable crop to raise.

There seems to be no basis for the legend which later credited her with contributing one of the basic principles of the design, but it was her confidence in him which encouraged Whitney to work for six months behind locked doors in a basement room of the plantation house.

In April, 1793, Whitney announced that he had completed a working model of an engine of "gin".

Descriptions of the main features of the gin had leaked out. As it was simple to build, copies began to appear in Georgia before Whitney (his patent secured in March 1794 and a partnership formed with Phineas Miller) could manufacture half a dozen gins. The prolonged struggle to establish the partners' rights early, threatened the firm with bankruptcy. Catherine Greene, in 1795, enabled it to continue by committing her entire resources to the effort.

The following year, on June 28, she and Miller were married. The expensive lawsuits forced the sale of Mulberry Grove in 1800 and removal of the family to Dungeness, another plantation on the Greene estate.

Miller succumbed to fever and died in 1803, worn out at thirty-nine. By 1807, Whitney had established title to his invention, but his patent expired in that year, ending any real hope of financial return. Catherine Greene Miller died in 1814, at age fifty-nine. Her perception of Whitney's gifts had opened the door to a new era for the South.

ELIZABETH BUFFUM CHACE
Valley Falls   Born 1806

Elizabeth Buffum Chace, anti-slavery and woman suffrage leader, was born in Providence, Rhode Island, December 9, 1806, to Arnold and Rebecca Buffum. She came from a long line of Quakers, and was reared in that tradition in Smithfield, where her father was a farmer and hat manufacturer. At seventeen, she settled in Fall River, Massachusetts, after her marriage in June 1828 to Samuel Buffington Chace, the son of a Fall River cotton manufacturer. Their first five children all died in childhood, and in her bereavement, Elizabeth turned to anti-slavery work which had long been part of a family tradition. Her grandfather had sheltered fugitive slaves and her father was a founder (1832) and first president of the New England Anti-Slavery Society. She began as vice president of the Fall River Female Anti-Slavery Society which she helped form in 1835. In 1840, she moved her home and activities to Valley Falls, Rhode Island, where she devoted years of effort to the organizational side of anti-slavery. The Chace home also became a station on the Underground Railway for fugitive slaves on their way to Canada.

Between 1843 and 1852, Mrs. Chace had five more children and her endeavors were limited to what she could accomplish at home. An active feminist, Mrs. Chace co-organized a Rhode Island woman suffrage association, of which she was president for thirty-nine years. In 1869, she joined and ardently supported the Woman Suffrage Association and primarily worked on the state level tending to organizational affairs and appearing before the legislature. In 1887, she spent substantially and worked persistently for a woman suffrage amendment but it was defeated. She resigned from the Rhode Island Women's Club because of its refusal to admit a Negro applicant. In 1883, she began agitating for the admission of women to Brown University and lived to see the establishment of a women's college affiliate with Brown in 1897.

Interested in prison reform, Mrs. Chace successfully pressed to have women serve on a penal board and was named to an advisory "Board of Lady Visitors" by the legislature. Stating that the board lacked power and influence, she resigned six years later. Striving to remove orphans from reform schools, she helped secure the establishment of the Rhode Island Home and School for Dependent Children in 1884.

With old age limiting her activities, she held committee meetings in her bedroom, wrote articles for periodicals, and, in 1891, published *Anti-Slavery Reminiscences*. When well over eighty, she took up watercolors, and, during one of her periodic ill-turns, anxious inquirers were informed she was giving painting lessons to her nurse.

An indefatigable worker, a moving speaker, and a constant office-holder, Elizabeth Buffum Chace came to command widespread respect. She died of "old age" and lung congestion in Central Falls shortly after her ninety-third birthday. A Free Religious Association co-worker conducted the funeral; burial was in Swan Point Cemetery in Providence.

MARTHA CROSS BABCOCK
Westerly   Born 1814

Martha C. Babcock was born October 2, 1814, in Westerly, Rhode Island, the youngest daughter of John and Mary Cross. She attended school at the Plainfield Academy, Plainfield, Connecticut; Friends School, Providence, Rhode Island; and completed her education in the City of New York. Shortly after, she married Edward W. Babcock on November 27, 1833. She continued to live in Westerly until she died.

Mrs. Babcock was prominent among the founders of the Episcopal Church in Westerly. She was a tireless worker in all the church departments but most especially in the Sunday School. She organized an infant class which increased from a membership of seven or eight to two hundred.

Martha Babcock was a true friend of the poor, helping to supply their needs and encouraging the parents to send their children to Sunday School. Her task was not easy, and she overcame many trials although she was discouraged often. The steadfastness of her character was remarkable. Nothing seemed to divert her from her purpose. Undaunted, she pursued her Christian endeavors as one in love with her work, showing forth her beautiful Christian consecration. Through her many charitable deeds, she became known to many and was loved and respected by all who knew her.

After her husband's death in 1857, she found her estate embarrassed by a large debt, which, after eight years of self-denial and economy, she paid to the last penny.

When the war broke out, Mrs. Babcock was one of the first to volunteer and encourage others to work for the relief of the soldiers.

She was very public-spirited and engaged in every good work for the benefit of the country. She was especially interested in education for day laborers and used her influence in establishing and maintaining an evening school.

She was a strong advocate of the present graded high school system and worked very hard to secure this system of graded schools for the children of Westerly. For this reason, her son established a Memorial Fund in her honor to be given to three students annually who shall present the best three essays on one or two subjects, previously announced to the school by the principal.

Her one son, Edward W. Babcock, took orders and became an Episcopal clergyman. Her death in Providence, April 27, 1873, was quiet and peaceful. Her body was brought to Westerly where she is buried in River Bend Cemetery. She was mourned by all the community.

IDA SILVERMAN
Providence   **Born 1882**

Ida Silverman, a leader in the founding of Israel, was born on October 31, 1882, in Kovno, Lithuania. When eight months old, she came to America, and from the time she was 10 years old, she made her home in Providence. At eighteen she married Archibald Silverman, a Providence jewelry manufacturer and civic leader, without whose encouragement, as she often expressed in public, she never would have been able to accomplish so much. They had three sons and one daughter, and, although her early married years found her busy with her family, both she and her husband were active in dozens of charities. She was Jewish Mother of the Year in 1951 and Rhode Island Mother of the Year in 1954. Rhode Island College awarded her an honorary Doctor of Education in 1954 and Bryant College a Doctor of Humanities in 1959.

Her life work mainly, however, was helping to establish the state of Israel, for which she was awarded the "Silver Medal" in 1964 as the woman who had done most for the upbuilding of Israel. In the course of her activities, she logged 600,000 miles of air travel having visited what was to become the Jewish state 20 times prior to its founding, all the countries in Europe and South America, the West Indies, Panama, Mexico, Dutch Guana, Australia and New Zealand. She was received by Presidents, Prime Ministers, Ambassadors, Cardinals, Archbishops, Governors, and Lord Mayors, in practically every country she visited.

Limitation of space prohibits the listing of all her many honors and activities; however, to mention a few: Mrs. Silverman was founder and later president of the Ladies' Auxiliary of the Jewish Orphanage of Rhode Island; organized the Providence chapter of Hadassah in 1924; organized the Israel Synagogue Building Fund, organized and became president of Friends of Butler Hospital in 1955 and later prevented the sale of Butler Hospital which today is the Butler Mental Health Center in Providence; was Chairman of the first campaign in 1956 of Rhode Island Mental Health Association; was only woman delegate in 1927 to the Conference on Jewish Minority Rights in Zurich, Switzerland; was only woman vice president of the National Zionist Organization of America, and also vice president of the American Jewish Congress and the Hebrew University Hospital Building Fund.

Over the years, Mrs. Silverman spent months at a time in Israel. She established a 70-acre mixed fruit farm and became chairman of a water development company in the Valley of Jezreel. In 1946, she was a founder and became a member of the board of a company that built the Sharon Hotel in Herzilia. A forest nearby, the Ida Silverman Forest, was named in her honor.

Having lost her husband in 1966, Mrs. Silverman decided in 1971, at the age of 89, to leave her family and friends in Providence to take up residence in Israel, saying at one time, "I want to go home. I'm going to be buried there. I couldn't die anywhere else." She had her wish. At the age of 91, Ida Silverman died in Israel and was buried in a cemetery at the Mount of Olives outside Jerusalem, where many notable persons lie in rest.

LUCILLE PUTNAM LEONARD
Providence   **Born 1895**

Although Lucille Putnam Leonard was born in 1895 in the little western Massachusetts town of New Salem, she married a Rhode Islander, Newton Peckham Leonard, in 1918, and has since been a resident of this state. She is the only daughter of Willard and Myra (Tenney) Putnam. Her father was a gentleman farmer, Probate County judge and school committee chairman in New Salem. Lucille went to school in New Salem, graduated from Mount Holyoke College in 1916, and later did a year of graduate study at Simmons College in Boston.

It was in Rhode Island, however, where she became involved in church and civic work as her two daughters were growing up. She also did substitute teaching in the schools of Providence and surrounding communities—in those days married women were not allowed full time teaching positions.

Her career in civic activities might be said to have begun in the Parent Teacher Association in which she has held all offices on the local and state level. She also served as the National PTA president from 1952-1955. While in that capacity she represented the United States in Italy for seven weeks in the "Friend-to-Friend Program for Giving"; was on Governor Stassen's Advisory Board on Foreign Affairs; and was also chairman of the Advisory Committee for Young Workers appointed by the United States Department of Labor.

Her first civic involvement other than the PTA pertained to school committee elections and working for "open" school committee hearings. The Mayor of Providence appointed her to the Advisory Committee on City Recreation. Later she was appointed by Governor McGrath to the Commission to study public welfare insti-

tutions. McGrath's successor, Governor Roberts, appointed her to the Public Assistance Commission, a committee established by the legislature, where she worked during the terms of five different governors. From 1955-1960, she was chairman of the Child Welfare Committee and continues to serve on this committee at the present time. She is also still serving on the Advisory Committee for the Rhode Island School for the Deaf having been appointed by Governor DelSesto. She has served on the state and national level for both the Girl and Boy Scouts of America.

Bryant College and the University of Rhode Island presented her with the honorary degree of Doctor of Humanities and Rhode Island College gave her an honorary doctorate of Education.

The Rhode Island PTA honored Lucille with a "This Is Your Day" affair, and presented her with many gifts for her years of devotion. Lucille's family and many friends are amazed at her vitality, her wit, her many activities and hobbies, and the realization that, at age 80 plus, she is now teaching parliamentary law and acts as a moderator and adviser for various organizations. Lucille Putnam Leonard, Rhode Island Mother of the Year in 1955, is truly a remarkable woman.

MARY GLASCOW PEEK CONGDON
Arcadia   Born 1898

This gentle lady with a kindly and endearing personality is the daughter of a Sachem of the Narragansett Tribe of Indians whose English name was Glascow. Her mother was Wahenna (Hannah) of the Wamponages whose genealogy, recorded on Cape Cod, goes back to 1741.

Princess Red Wing—Mary Glascow Peek Congdon—was born in Connecticut on March 21, 1898. Her family moved to Harrisville, Rhode Island when she was five years old, where she attended the public schools, graduating from Burriville High School, Pascoag, Rhode Island in 1910 as class valedictorian. Then she entered Friends School for Teachers in Pennsylvania; taught in Voorhees Institute, Aiken, South Carolina, for one year but returned north for health reasons and entered the Industrial Art School in New York City. The course included study in the Indians' Art Section of the American Museum. Due to this training, for a short time, she painted art objects in New York for the Gorham Manufacturing Company in Providence. Her art work brought her to the attention of many outstanding people who recognized

her other gifts of understanding, compassion, knowledge and insights into the American Indian with the result that she became a member and later vice president of the World Government Association with headquarters in New York City. Later she was chosen for membership in the Speakers Research Committee of the United Nations and numbers among her friendships prominent world leaders like the late Eleanor Roosevelt and Madam Pandit.

However, her home base has long been Rhode Island. Her first husband was a Tama Indian named Peek. Their two children were Walter Peek, a teacher in Chamberlain High School in Tampa, Florida and Susan Peek, Mrs. Earl Miller of Warwick, R. I. Her second marriage, in 1937, was to a Mohigan Indian Chief, White Oak—Daniel Congdon, in a 300-year-old Indian marriage ceremony, held in the Narragansett Hotel, Providence where eighty Indian guests and many prominent citizens gathered for the venison dinner. Her adopted son, Thomas Sanders, is half Indian and is professor of English and Indian literature in South Florida University. He and son Walter Peek have compiled AMERICAN INDIAN LITERATURE published in Glencoe in California in 1973—an anthology of literature gathered from North, Central and South American Indian writings. Her godson, John David Fadden, a Mohawk of St. Regis Reservation in New York is an art teacher in the Saranac Lake Schools and also the artist on the largest Indian newspaper ARKESASNEE.

Princess Redwing has given freely of herself to serving others: twenty-eight summers in children's camps; director of State Girl Scout and Camp Fire Girls boards; speaker for religious and civic groups; and now curator of the Tomaquag Indian Museum located in the tiny and picturesque village of Arcadia at "Dovecrest" where she lives with Mr. and Mrs. Ferris Dove, who operate a fine restaurant and an authorized Indian Trading Post.

Currently Princess Redwing is a member of Rhode Island Bicentennial Committee.

In June of 1975, the University of Rhode Island honored her with the degree "Doctor of Human Affairs" and on October 14, 1975, the Chariho Business and Professional Women's club named her "Woman of the Year".

Princess Redwing looks much younger than her years. She does not believe in looking back to "the good old days" but rather to keeping fit and mentally active and, in her words, "alive to what's ahead."

OLIVE FUCIER THOMAS WILEY
Warwick   Born 1902

Olive Fucier Thomas was born in Warwick, Rhode Island July 12, 1902, the second daughter and third child of Daniel W. and Emily (Pinder) Thomas. She attended the Norwood Grammar School and was graduated from Cranston High School.

On January 14, 1925, she was married to William D. Wiley and became the mother of six children, all of whom are college graduates and have distinguished themselves in their chosen fields.

As a young woman, Olive became a Girl Scout leader and later, as her daughters and sons became scouts, she served as Den Mother and on various committees of Girl Scout organizations. With her husband, she attended the Metropolitan Bible School in Wisconsin for two years. With her children in school, she became active in P.T.A. organizations, and at one time was a member of four different P.T.A. units. In 1956 she was elected as the first president of the newly formed P.T.A. at the Warwick Veterans Memorial High School, subsequently receiving a Life Membership from that unit. Olive even followed her children in college by participating in the Patrons' Association at the University of Rhode Island, the parent organization there, one of whose functions was to help sponsor the Christian Association.

Community service has been a hallmark of Mrs. Wiley's life. For thirty-five years she has been active as a Board member of the Providence Shelter for Colored Children, and at one time conducted clothing centers for this agency, distributing clothing to needy families with children. She has served in many capacities on the Board of Managers of the Home for Aged Colored Women, now Bannister House, and for five terms was elected president of the Board. She was a member of the Development Committee for the building of the new Bannister House in Providence and is presently a member of the Board and of the Admissions Committee of the agency, a 160-bed health care facility.

Her other community activities through the years included membership on the Warwick Advisory Committe for Urban Renewal; the Governor's Committee for Children and Youth; treasurer of the Women's Intergroup Committee (WIC's); and a member of the Children's Services Advisory Committee of the R. I. Division of Social Welfare.

She has been and continues to be an active member of the Urban League of Rhode Island, the Providence N.A.A.C.P., the John Hope Settlement House; budget panels for the United Way, and others. As president of the Mount Hope Day Care Center, she spearheaded the drive which resulted in obtaining and refurbishing the present facilities of the center on Hope Street in Providence.

During the years, Mrs. Wiley has been called upon and responded as a neighborhood leader in solicitations for the Cancer Society, the Heart Fund and other drives; participated in the World Day of Prayer and other church observances. She is an active member and officer of the First Church of the Nazarene in Providence and also supports the missionary work of the Metropolitan Church Association.

In 1963, Mrs. Wiley was chosen as Mother of the Year by the Irreproachable Beneficial Association, an organization of black men which annually honors outstanding black citizens. Then, in 1965, she was named Rhode Island Mother of the Year by the Rhode Island State Mothers' Association of the American Mothers' Committee, Inc.

This year, Mr. and Mrs. Wiley celebrated their 50th wedding anniversary. Mrs. Wiley continues active in many projects. Recently she represented Rhode Island, upon appointment by Governor Philip Noel, at the dedication of a statue in Washington, D. C. honoring Mrs. Mary McLeod Bethune. Every week she visits the folks at Bannister House and conducts a devotional service in the chapel there for all who will attend, besides serving as a volunteer in occupational therapy. In addition to all of the above, she is on the Executive Board of the Providence Christian Women's Club.

FLORENCE KERINS MURRAY
Newport   Born 1916

Judge Florence Kerins Murray was born in Newport, Rhode Island on October 21, 1916, to Mr. and Mrs. John X. Kerins. She is married to Paul F. Murray, also a lawyer, with whom she practiced law under the firm name of Murray & Murray from 1942 to 1956. They have one child, Paul F. Murray, Jr.

She received her A.B. from Syracuse University and her LL.B. from Boston University. In 1972 she completed a graduate course at National College of the Judiciary. From 1971-1974, Judge Murray was the Staff and Faculty Adviser of the National College of State Trial Judges in Reno, Nevada. She is also a member of Kappa Beta Pi and Alpha Chi Omega.

In July of 1942, Judge Murray enlisted in the Women's Army Corp, was commissioned a second lieutenant September 1942, promoted to captain December 1942, to major in September 1943 and to lieutenant colonel January 1945, serving four-and-one-half years in all. She was awarded the Army Commendation Certificate and Ribbon, and the Legion of Merit.

From 1948 to 1956 she served in the Rhode Island Senate. She has been chairman of the Special Legislation Committee, a member of the Newport School Committee from 1948 to 1957, serving as chairman from 1951-1957. Judge Murray also has been a member of the various Governor's advisory committees such as: Social Welfare, Revision of Election Laws, Alcoholic, Mental Health and Family Court.

On the national level, she was a member of the 1950 White House Conference on Youth and Children, a member of the 1952 Annual Assay Commission, and a member of the Civil and Political Rights Committee of the President's Commission on Status of Women. Appointed by the Secretary of Defense, she served from 1952-1958 as a member of the National Defense Advisory Committee on Women in the Service.

Judge Murray has been admitted to the Rhode Island Bar, the Massachusetts Bar, Federal District Court, the United States Supreme Court, the U. S. Tax Court and the U. S. Court of Military Appeals.

She has received so many honors and awards that it would be impossible to enumerate them in this allotted space. However, what might be considered the climax of a brilliant career came in 1956 when she was appointed Associate Justice of the Rhode Island Superior Court.

Wife, mother, lawyer, judge, government and civic leader, Florence Kerins Murray is indeed a woman for all seasons.

MARGARET F. O'CONNOR ACKROYD
Providence

Mrs. Frederick S. (Margaret F.) Ackroyd, like her parents, Mr. and Mrs. William H. O'Connor, was born in Rhode Island. In a life crammed with citations, two stand out: she was a successful advocate of women's rights a generation ago, and she was named by the Providence Journal "Man" of the year in 1970.

As a specialist in women's affairs for the U. S. Department of Labor, Bureau of International Labor Affairs, she viewed women's activities in Japan, Korea, Thailand, Philippines, Saigon and Iran. She was consultant on minimum wages in Turkey and on employment standards for women in three Latin American countries.

A 1929 graduate of the University of Rhode Island—her husband was in the class of 1930—she later was awarded an honorary doctorate in public administration. The accompanying citation defines her achievements, "Starting your career at a time when it was unusual for a woman to add responsibilities of a job to those of a wife and mother of two sons, you proved what is now generally accepted, that a woman's profession, far from endangering her family life, may actually enrich it as well as the community she serves." She did graduate work in economics at Brown and Syracuse Universities.

Her two sons are Dr. Frederick W. Ackroyd, chief of surgery at Mt. Auburn Hospital, Cambridge, Massachusetts, and James A. Ackroyd, a teacher and coach in Providence schools. There are seven grandchildren.

Among her countless distinctions are election to Rhode Island Hall of Fame, the Stitely Award by American Society of Public Administration, Women of Achievement Award by R. I. Federation of Business and Professional Women, Beta Gamma Sigma by the Honors Society for Economics and Business Administration and Honorary membership, presidency of National Consumers' League from 1969 to 1974, R. I. Permanent Governor's Commission on Status of Women, membership on Study Committee on Protective Legislation of President Kennedy's National Commission on Status of Women.

She is past president of Providence American Association of University Women, a member of the liaison committee of the A.A.U.W.–International Federation of University Women, and an adviser of University of Rhode Island Continuing Education and the American Association of Public Administration.

She was chief of the Rhode Island Department of Labor, Division of Women and Children and Commissioner of Minimum Wage from 1940 until her retirement in 1970. She was executive vice-chairman of R. I. Governor's Advisory Committee on Status of Women from 1968 until 1971.

Since her retirement Mrs. Ackroyd has served as consultant to the Bureau of International Affairs, U. S. Department of Labor, as Coordinator, Women's Program-Worldwide. She works with the State Department, Office of Labor Affairs, and with the Women's Bureau, Department of Labor, in arranging international assistance programs.

She has been an expert adviser on labor standards and women's programs to labor ministries in developing countries and has represented the State Department of Labor at Geneva, Switzerland, at the United Nations Commission on Status of Women.

ROSE BUTLER BROWNE
Providence

Dr. Rose Amanda Butler Browne was born in Boston, Massachusetts, in what she calls in her book LOVE MY CHILDREN, the slums of South Boston. She was the eldest daughter and the third of seven children of Frances (Lindsey) and John Robinson Butler.

In her own words again, "My family had absolutely no status symbols, for in those days before the start of the century, poverty was still an accepted way of life." This lowly entry did not deter her, for all her life she was "armed to the teeth with security and self assurance," an inheritance from a loving family.

Early in Rose's life her family moved to Newport, Rhode Island, where she attended the public schools. After high school, she enrolled in what was then Rhode Island Normal School and was graduated with honors. Years later she returned to her alma mater, now Rhode Island College, to receive an honorary Doctor of Education degree. But between her Normal School diploma and the honorary doctorate, Rose, now Mrs. Emmett T. Browne, wife of the Reverend

Mr. Browne, a Baptist minister, had earned a Bachelor of Education degree from the University of Rhode Island, a Master of Education from Rhode Island College and a Doctor of Education from Harvard University—the first black woman to earn such a degree from Harvard.

Mrs. Browne's first teaching position was at Virginia State College in Petersburg. Eventually, she became chairman of the Psychology Department there. Later, when her husband assumed a pastorate in West Virginia, she became head of The Department of Psychology at West Virginia State College. Other positions included head of the Department of Education at Bluefield State College, professor of Education and chairman of the Department at North Carolina Central University, and director of the Happy Hours Child Care Center of the Mt. Vernon Baptist Church, Durham, North Carolina.

Eleven years after their marriage, a son, Emmett T., Jr. was born to Reverend and Mrs. Browne. He is now serving in the U. S. Air Force, having spent some time in Vietnam. Mrs. Browne has always had "her children" living in her home, as she helped countless young people in and through school. Indeed, while she was a student at the Normal School, she subsidized a home in Providence, with her mother, where black girls from Newport and elsewhere who wished to attend college in Providence could live without encountering the housing discrimination so prevalent at the time.

Wherever she has lived, Dr. Browne has been active in community and religious affairs. In North Carolina, she was appointed by Governor Terry Sanford to the Governor's Commission to Study the Needs of the Mentally Retarded and received the Diamond Watch Award at North Carolina Central University for outstanding service as a teacher, leader, and scholar. In 1969, Rhode Island College dedicated a 156-unit residence hall for women on the campus as the Rose Butler Browne Residence Hall.

Upon the death of her husband in 1971, Dr. Browne returned to spend her retirement years with her sisters in Rhode Island. She continues active, however, as a member of the Board of Directors of the R. I. College Foundation, the R. I. Committee for the Bicentennial, and many others. She is chairman of the Validation Committee for the State of R. I. Fund of Renewal of the American Baptist/Progressive National Baptist Convention. This year she was an official delegate to the Baptist World Alliance in Stockholm, Sweden.

One of her most noteworthy contributions was the work for her doctorate at Harvard and the demonstration project in connection with it to increase the reading capabilities of underprivileged, especially black children. This project is detailed in Dr. Browne's autobiography, LOVE MY CHILDREN, a version of which has been published in French and is used in teacher-training institutions in South East Asia, in Frenchspeaking African countries, and in the Carribbean.

South Carolina

South Carolina

Nickname: Palmetto State

State Flower: Carolina jessamine

State Tree: Cabbage palmetto

State Bird: Carolina wren

Photos

1. Cherokee Foothills Highway
2. Table Rock
3. Golf & Beach Club
4. Gulf & Outdoor playground
5. Fort Sumter
6. Myrtle Beach
7. Lake Murray near Columbia
8. Middleton Place Gardens & Plantation Stableyards

Committee Members

Chairman—Mrs. James Cuttino, Jr. Sumter
Honorary Chairman—Mrs. Irving F. Belser

South Carolina

JANE BLACK THOMAS
Born 1720

Jane Thomas of Pennsylvania, married John and they came South to the Spartanburg area just prior to the American Revolution. Here in the Fair Forest section they established their home and had 9 children.

Col. John Thomas, Jane's husband organized the Spartan Regiment for fighting the British in the area, and over the up country. During his many campaigns, Jane stayed at home, one of her main duties being to guard the ammunition of Gen. Thomas Sumter's forces which were hidden in her attic.

Jane's husband and two sons were captured by the British and imprisoned in the fort at Ninety-six, some 60 miles from her home. Jane made the long trip to visit her husband and sons in prison on a cold and rainy day. But shortly after her arrival she overheard char women talking of an ambush planned on her son's regiment camped at Cedar Springs. Jane made a hasty visit in Ninety-Six and rode straight through the countryside to warn of the ambush. She arrived in time, and British forces found the Americans ready for them when they arrived. Jane was credited with having saved the regiment from capture and defeat.

ELIZA LUCAS PINCKNEY
Born 1723

Eliza's contribution to the Carolina colony centers on her interest in agriculture. The Lucas family were English, Eliza's father serving military service on Antigua Island, when the family came to Charleston seeking the good health of Mrs. Lucas. Col. Lucas returned to his military duties and Eliza took charge of the Carolina plantation. She was fascinated by the growing season of her new home and experimented with many seeds she had brought with her from the Indies. Her success with indigo, ginger and cotton vastly expanded the colonist's wealth of export.

Eliza became the second wife of Chief Justice Charles Pinckney. She had been educated in London and further continued her studies in America by reading law, and studying agriculture.

Eliza had three children, one, Charles Cotesworth Pinckney, who signed the Constitution as a delegate from South Carolina.

REBECCA BREWTON MOTTE
Born 1738

Between Charleston and Camden, along the Congaree River, Fort Motte was built as another protection for the surrounding settlers. Rebecca, native to the area, married Mr. Motte and shortly afterwards built a large home near the site of the fort. Following the fall of Camden to Tarleton, Francis Marion, the Swamp Fox, retreated to Fort Motte where Rebecca offered her home as refuge. She moved to a cottage near by and from there fed and tended the wounded returning from Camden. She gave her whole efforts to the care of the troops of the Swamp Fox. One of Rebecca's daughters had married Gen. Thomas Pinckney, who returned from Camden. His wounds were dressed by his wife who upon completion of her deed promptly fainted, but she had saved her husband's life.

Farleton's plans to attack Fort Motte became known through the network of continental spies. To keep the supplies from falling into the British hands, the necessity arose to burn Rebecca's home. Marion reluctantly approached Rebecca and apologized that the house would have to be burned. Rebecca watched as bows and flamable materials were prepared. Just before the first shot was made, Rebecca came forward with her own bow and burning arrow and asked that hers be the first to strike her home.

Rebecca had six children and following her husband's early death, she continued his farming enterprise, clearing all debts, and leaving her name honored among heroines of South Carolina.

ELIZABETH MATHEWES HEYWARD

Elizabeth was the daughter of Governor John Mathewes. She grew up in Charleston in the throes of the pre-revolution skirmishes. Elizabeth married Thomas Heyward, signer of the Declaration of Independence. He had been quite active in the rebellion of the colonists and was captured by the British during the siege of Charleston. He was pardoned but later imprisoned and sent to St. Augustine.

Elizabeth remained in her Charleston home during the English occupation smuggling all information and materials she could to the American forces. On the occasion of the British victory at Gilford a general illumination of all homes was commanded. Elizabeth refused by completely darkening her home and even upon threat of imprisonment in the dreaded Provost did not light one candle. Again, a general illumination was commanded on the anniversary of the English occupation of Charleston. And, again Elizabeth refused. This time, she was threatened with the burning of her home. Given until midnight to light her windows, Elizabeth stated she would not honor those who held her husband prisoner. Her home was saved by an intervening English officer and is today open as a museum.

DORCAS NELSON RICHARDSON
Born 1741

Dorcas Nelson was born on the south side of the Santee River. Her family owned Nelson's Ferry which crossed the river and led on to Stateburg and Camden. When Dorcas married Col. Richard Richardson, she didn't have to go far to her new home—just across the river and a few miles west. Here Dorcas gave birth to 10 children, and watched them grow in character and take their places in South Carolina history as leaders of the state. There are seven governors among her descendants.

During the Revolution, life was no easier for Dorcas than for her contemporaries of the back country. Her home, in all its elegance was taken over by Tarleton as his headquarters. During Tarleton's stay, Dorcas' husband was captured and imprisoned in Charleston, but he managed to escape and returned to his home. He hid in the swamp near the house and came to call his swamp home John's Island. Here, Dorcas sent food to him everyday by trusted servants and often managed to visit him, taking the children with her. Richardson was never found in his swamp home and later returned to his family. On one occasion, his young daughter was sitting on the lap of Tarleton who asked where her father was. The child said "John's Island", but the general only laughed saying John's Island was on the coast, no where near.

Dorcas lived to be 93 years old.

SARA REEVE GIBBES
Born 1746

Sara Reeve was born on Johns Island on a plantation along the Stono River. She married Robert Gibbes of Charleston but returned to her home when Mr. Gibbes became an invalid of gout and was confined to a wheel chair for the remainder of his life. It fell Sara's lot to manage Mr. Gibbes' extensive estate and businesses. Sara had 8 children of her own and 7 orphaned children of her husband's sister. She also adopted 2 other orphans and the care of 17 children were added to her responsibilities.

Situated in the path of the approaching British, Sara's household kept constant vigil. The expected moment came in the middle of the night. Warned of the coming peril, Sara quickly and quietly woke her family and ordered them to dress while she clothed her invalid husband. The British arrived, stunned to find they were expected. They encamped on the Gibbes' grounds, confining the family to a small apartment. Sara went about her business of feeding and caring for the intruders, gathering all information she could for the American forces. The family remained on the plantation until they learned the American forces planned to attack the British there. She then slipped her family to a neighboring plantation only to find one of her 17 charges had been left behind. Secretly returning to the home, the boy was rescued and later became a general in military service.

Sara continued her efforts on behalf of the colonists through all of the Revolution and reared all of her children to become proud Americans.

REBECCA CALHOUN PICKENS
Born 1746

Rebecca Calhoun was born in the Long Canes of Ninety Six District. As a young girl, the Calhoun family was attacked by the warring Cherokee Indians, and only a few survived the massacre that followed. Rebecca, in her teens, hid in the woods with other members of the family who managed to escape death until rescued. Because of all the Indian troubles around the area, Andrew Pickens, known for his tactics with the Indians, came to Long Cane, and met Rebecca. Here they were married in 1765, and had 9 children.

Rebecca, too, had the responsibilities of the home during her husband's campaigns of the Revolution, and the care and safety of her children. Her troubles did not end with the Revolution, though, as her husband still loved the back country. And, Rebecca was moved with her family to Hopewell in the Pendleton District. General Pickens figured in all of the treaties and compromises with the Indians in the country's move west. The Indians greatly respected Pickens, but often the family left their home and moved into the block house near by. The Indians passed by the Pickens home many times, but one night, Rebecca was awakened by much noise and saw her home being burned. She escaped into the woods, but the next day, her youngest child broke out with chicken pox and died, and she had to nurse others to keep them alive.

The Pickens made their permanent home at Tamassee some miles west, and saw one son become lieutenant governor of the state and one a governor.

ELIZABETH MARTIN

Elizabeth Martin had nine children, 7 sons who she sent to war for the colonist's cause. She parted with her sons, telling them, "Fight for your country! Fight till death, if you must, but never let your country be dishonored. Were I a man I would go with you."

During the absence of the men in Elizabeth's life, two of her daughters in law lived with her. They did all they could to harrass the British in and around their home. On one occasion, they learned of dispatches that were being sent to the British forces. The ladies dressed in men's clothes and hid along the road, until the couriers came by. With fear, but determination, they stopped the couriers, took the dispatches, and sent the men on paroled. The following day when the couriers returned they stopped at the house, and here they were fed by the ladies, never knowing they were the ladies who had taken their dispatches.

Some time later, Elizabeth was questioned about her sons fighting for the American forces. "You have enough of them," said the officer. "I wish I had 50!" was Elizabeth's retort.

MARTHA BRATTON

Martha married a colonel of the York District.

In 1839, Martha was honored by toast: "Honor and gratitude to the woman and heroine who proved herself so faithful a wife—so firm a friend of liberty!" So was spoken of Martha on her contribution during the first check of the British after the fall of Charleston.

Martha's husband had taken part in the fight again the British in the countryside in and around Kings Mountain. Trying to locate her husband, the British confined Martha and questioned her at length. Martha refused to give the information of her husband and the forces with him. No threat to her could make her divulge her secrets. Finally a gun was pointed at her, yet Martha still refused. Just as she was to be shot, the second in command came forth to save her life. Later this same man was captured by the American forces. He asked for Martha, and she, upon seeing him, spoke in his behalf and saved his life.

One of the most interesting episodes in Martha's fight was in her efforts to protect the supplies sent up to the troops by John Rutledge. To keep them out of the enemy's hands, Martha made a powder trail to the stock pile, and stood at its beginning. When the British forces arrived to capture the supplies Martha lit the powder which ran to the supplies and burned them.

SOUTH DAKOTA

Land of
Infinite Variety

South Dakota

Nickname: The Coyote State

State Flower: American pasqueflower

State Tree: Black Hills Spruce

State Bird: Ring-necked pheasant

Photos

1. Ingalis Home
2. Laura Ingalls Wilder
3. Surveyor's House
4. "The Prairie is my Garden" by Harvey Dunn
5. "After School" by Harvey Dunn

Committee Members

Chairman—Mrs. Cora Stavig, Sioux Falls

South Dakota

MARGARET WYLIE MELLETTE
Born 1843

South Dakota can be proud of their "First Lady"—because she was South Dakota's *first* "First Lady".

Margaret Wylie was born August 6, 1843 in Bloomington, Indiana. Her father was Prof. Theophilia Wylie at the University of Indiana and was also pastor of the Reformed Presbyterian Church. The Wylie home is now owned and preserved by the University of Indiana in Bloomington.

"Maggie", as her family and friends called her, attended the Bloomington public schools and the Academy. She continued her education at Glendale Female College near Cincinnati.

When Arthur Mellette came to enroll at the University of Indiana, his brother, Jim, introduced him to Maggie. He was a year older than Maggie. In May, 1866, they were married. Four sons were born to the Mellettes: Wylie, Charles, Andton, and Richard. Some records mention one daughter, but a granddaughter of the Mellettes (Mrs. George Ide, now living in California) says that her grandmother often said she wished her grandfather could have known her, because he always wanted a little girl.

The Mellettes lived in Muncie about ten years after their marriage. Arthur was a lawyer, at one time district attorney, and served for a time in the state legislature.

The nursing of a "tuberculous" brother caused the Mellettes to move west to a "health resort" and to settle in Springfield, Dakota Territory, in 1878.

There Arthur became register in the U. S. Land Office, which moved to Watertown in 1880. He served in public offices and was appointed governor of Dakota Territory. Nine years later, when South Dakota attained statehood in 1889, he was declared the first governor by acclamation. Therefore Mrs. Mellette was the *first* "First Lady of South Dakota".

Mrs. Mellette was active in the First Congregational Church of Watertown, serving as president of the Ladies Aid Society and Auxiliary (1882-83), during which time the Society purchased a small second-hand cabinet organ, raising funds in part by having a strawberry festival. The church choir practiced at their home.

She did exquisite needlework, beadwork, and china painting. Her diary documents her longing to have further education which could help her draw and paint.

She had a great interest in Indians and was a friend to them. When the front door of the house was left open, she might find a group of Indians sitting on the floor around her Chickering square piano, the first in Watertown, which the Indians thought magic. One would strike a note and all would listen, then another would strike a note, and so on.

The Mellette home, with its exquisite furnishings, is preserved as a Museum for Watertown and South Dakota.

In 1938, Margaret died at the age of 95. She is interred beside her husband in Mt. Hope Cemetery, Watertown.

BETSY DALAGER
Born 1852

Symbolic of the contribution of a host of unnamed pioneer mothers to the creation and development of our state is the story of Betsy Dalager. An historical marker in Day County (n.e. S. D.) tells her story. As a widow with five children and her widowed mother, she emigrated in 1884 by oxdrawn wagon from Minnesota to South Dakota, a journey that took two weeks. Prairie fires were not uncommon, strong winds often carrying them for miles. In 1886, Betsy and her mother, Guri, realizing they were in the path of one, rushed to the barn to save the livestock, only to be trapped there themselves. The barn became Guri's funeral pyre. Betsy, her clothes aflame, ran out and jumped into the shallow well. The children, who had run to plowed ground, helped their mother out, after the earth had cooled. She lived through a long battle with burns and later rheumatism, which

left her a cripple. For 36 years, this slight figure in a wheel chair was the symbol of the indomitable spirit which had brought her to this frontier country.

Despite the fact that she spent 36 years in a wheelchair, Betsy proved her claim, raised her five children, was a steadfast member of her church and an active participant in community affairs until her death in 1922. We are tracing only one branch of the family. Julia Dalager, a deeply spiritual woman, who married Chil H. Chilson in 1904. To this union were born Herman, Borghild, Esther and Clara.

Herman, president of a store for 40 years and president of the National Merchants Association; listed in Who's Who in the Midwest, Who's Who in Finance and Industry, Dictionary of International Biography; served on five different state boards; president of the S. D. Ornithologistic Union; served on the Board of Regents of Augustana College for 19 years. He is the only non-Minnesotan ever to be elected to the Executive Council of the Minnesota Historical Society in its 149 years.

He and his wife, Agnes, have two children. Charles, continuing as president of his father's store was the recipient of the Distinguished

Service award. He and Virginia have two children: Carol and David. Joan, a former teacher and organist, married Jim Iverson, awarded the 1963 N.C.A.A. national Coach of the Year. Their children; Nancy and Paul.

Borghild, married to Edward Peters, a banker and mayor of Webster. Her artistic home shows her creative talents. They have two sons: Edward, a Sioux Falls physician, admitted to A.O.A., an honorary medical fraternity, and Charlotte have two children: Edward and Susan. John, a law partner in Hartford, Connecticut, travels to many countries, using his expertise in international law. He and Charlotte have three children: Douglas, Julie and Mark.

Esther, a former Dean of Women at Augustana Academy, is a charter member and dedicated teacher of Bethany Fellowship College and Missionary School (Minneapolis), which has over 100 mission centers abroad.

Clara; Chairman, Speech Department, Augustana College, is the wife of J. Earl Lee, a distinguished music educator and Music Department Chairman. Clara served as national committee woman for the Republican party. She is the recipient of numerous state and national honors. Her students are imbued with her enthusiasm and zeal for educational excellence. She is a much sought after speaker throughout the midwest.

How fortunate for the state of South Dakota and our country that Betsy's life was saved in that devastating prairie fire!

IDA MARIE LARSEN TUVE

Born 1872

Ida Larsen Tuve was a substantial contributor to liberal education for young South Dakotans in the late pioneer days.

She was born in 1872 in Ridgeway, Iowa to her parents, Lauritz Henrik Gudmund Larsen and Marie Christopherson. After attending the Ridgeway Public Schools from 1878 to 1888, her interest in music determined her going to the Northwestern University Conservatory of Music where she graduated. She taught piano in her home town of Ridgeway before being invited to come to Augustana College at Canton, South Dakota, in 1892. Here she was head of the Music Department, teaching both voice and piano, and serving as organist at the Canton Lutheran church until 1901. In 1893 she became Mrs. Tuve.

Augustana grew rapidly, but the college was a close-knit family, and the Tuve home was the center for many college affairs. Educational and professional visitors to Augustana, Lutheran pastors and church leaders, invariably had an early invitation to stay at the Tuves.

Canton became a center for many cultural, educational and religious activities and Ida Tuve was an enthusiastic participant and leader. Concerts, lectures, study clubs, Chautauqua, Boy Scouts, church conventions and school competitions, all could count on her support. Many times she was hostess to the planning committees and her home became the group headquarters. Ida Tuve was community minded, and determined that the women should participate.

The name Tuve has a great deal of meaning for people in South Dakota. It is a name to be respected and has been honored by Augustana College (now in Sioux Falls) as a name for one of its buildings. When the four children of the Tuve family have all made enviable records and received so many degrees and honors that space will not permit enumerating them, we can assume they have gone far.

Ida Tuve's three sons and one daughter followed their parents in education. Rosemond became an international authority and teacher in the field of Medieval English literature, with special recognition from Princeton, Harvard, and Oxford Universities. She was the recipient of many honorary doctorates and awards. At Oxford, some dons do not encourage their students to hear the lecturers who come, because they feel if their work is superior, it will be published. However, when Rosemond Tuve came to Oxford, the dons recommended very strongly that *she* should be heard!

Richard, the youngest, became a research chemist at the Naval Research Laboratory, responsible for several inventions and instruction in their use. George, the eldest, became an engineering educator, author, editor, and research scientist. Merle became a research physicist. He was a principal in the earliest radar discoveries, was in charge of the development of the proximity fuse, and a recognized authority in radio astronomy. He received many degrees and honors including the Order of the British Empire.

Ida Tuve's parental discipline was strict, her personal accomplishments many, but her greatest joy was in the accomplishments of her four children.

SISSEL CATHERINE FINSETH BOE
Born 1874

It will be one hundred and two years on September 22, 1976 since Sissel was born to the Honorable and Mrs. A. K. Finseth at Kenyon, Minnesota and who later was destined to become an outstanding and influential lady in South Dakota.

She was graduated from the Winona, Minnesota State Teachers College after which she became a teacher at Little Falls and Marshall, Minnesota. Later she was made Dean of Women and instructor at the Lutheran Normal School in Sioux Falls, S. D.

In 1900 Miss Finseth was married to the Rev. N. Boe, pastor of the St. Olaf Lutheran Church in Sioux Falls (1893-1904) and later pastor of the Nidaros congregation at Baltic, S. D. (1904-1917). In 1917 the Rev. Boe was elected the first president or bishop of the South Dakota district of the Norwegian Lutheran Church, which is not the American Lutheran Church.

Mrs. Boe contributed much to aid her husband in his ministry by acting as organist and director of choirs and choral groups. She organized the Women's Missionary Federation of South Dakota and became its first president in 1919.

In 1959 she was honored by this organization for her contribution to women's work in the church for forty-three years.

Mrs. Boe was always interested in educational and cultural activities. She was an active member and, for many years, historian of the History Club in Sioux Falls. Wherever she went and whatever she did, her influence was felt. She was an able speaker and active up to the end of her life. Remembered as a woman of poise and dignity, she possessed great leadership ability, but she was never too busy to be the gracious hostess, as well as a devoted mother of four daughters and one son.

As a mother she influenced her children by helping them to see, hear, and read the best of what life has to offer. She gave them their first piano lessons; she encouraged them to work for higher degrees so that they in turn could make their contributions to society. Today, Dagny, Karen and Lois (Mrs. Francis Hyslop) have retired from active careers in higher education in New York City, Wisconsin and Pennsylvania. Borghild is still active in social work in Beloit, Wisconsin. Nils A. Boe, an attorney, served South Dakota as legislator. Speaker of the House, and Lieutenant Governor for a number of terms. Later he was elected Governor for two terms. At present he is Chief Judge of the U. S. Customs Court located in New York City.

Mrs. Boe, whose life spanned an era from the horse and buggy days to that of the greatest technological achievements, was a woman of courage and vision. She was an inspiration to her family as well as to the many people whose lives she touched.

LORENA KING FAIRBANK
Sioux Falls   **Born 1874**

On July 4, 1975, Lorena King Fairbank observed her one hundred and first birthday, a truly momentous anniversary! This gracious, spirited and independent lady, until 1944 a resident of Sioux Falls, South Dakota, now lives alone with the help of two maids, in her unique Georgetown-Washington, D. C. residence that she addresses as "The Hidden House in Ivy Lane"—a one-time coach house tucked away from confusion—and intrusion. It has been the pattern of her life to share her wisdom and her intellectual and cultural pursuits whth all who meet her as casual callers or invited guests.

In 1903, she graduated from the University of Chicago where she had been a student of speech and literature. When she returned to South Dakota, she was inspired to stimulate an interest in self improvement in the Arts. To this end she gave private lessons in dramatic reading and public readings in verse and drama. Soon she gave her attention to the Drama League and to the Civic Theatre. To this day her main interest lies not in the past but in the present and the future.

Lorena King was born July 4, 1874, at Hampton, Iowa, where her father, a Quaker and a Republican, was an eminent lawyer. She was seven years old when her father moved his family to Chamberlain, South Dakota, a townsite on the Missouri River, of which he was prime founder. Here she prepared for college by attending the Academy at the University of South Dakota at Vermillion. At 15 she was ready to enter college, but the depression of the 1890's and her mother's frail health prevented her entrance for eight years. After a year at Armour Institute of Technology, she entered the University of Chicago in 1899 and graduated in 1903, having specialized in speech and literature.

She was 15 when Dakota Territory, in 1889, was divided into two states and, with her father, resented the fact that women had not received the right to vote. She became an ardent suffragette and marched in parades in Washington and New York. In 1904 she became a member of the American Association of Collegiate Alumnae, the organization which later became the American Association of University Women. In 1923 she organized several branches in South Dakota, one of them being in Sioux Falls. When these branches were combined into the South Dakota State Division, she became its first president in 1926. In 1968 she was honored by the South Dakota State Division's establishment of an endowed fellowship which bears her name and which now provides an annual doctoral fellowship administered by A.A.U.W.

But it is her home life that is most endearing, inspirational and worthy of emulation. A quiet, stately woman, devoted to the family; presiding with grace as hostess to groups of friends at unusual and charming garden parties, song recitals, ballet, and dramatic readings of verse and literature. Here the featured entertainment was always—not the cup of tea alone—but the presentation to the audience of her renowned and capable artist friends, whose art she desired to share with her many guests. Her husband, Arthur Boyce Fairbank was until 1936, the year of his death, a distinguished lawyer in South Dakota. Their only child, John King Fairbank, the eminent authority and expert on China, is chairman of Harvard University's Council on East Asia Studies. His wife, Wilma, is an artist and archeologist. They have two daughters.

GUNDA JACOBSON LAWRENCE
Born 1876

Both Carl and Gunda's parents were from Norway. Gunda's father had been skillful in Norway, building a noted church altarpiece, but Gunda was born in a sod hut in South Dakota before her father could build a proper house. Carl Lawrence taught in Canton, S. D. high school where Gunda also taught. She was also an enrapt member of Carl's Bible Class. Carl proposed to this girl—pretty, fair, though 5 years his junior. Determined that he should never regret his marriage to a country girl, Gunda was also determined to be a good mother. They were devout members of the Lu-

theran Church. They had two sons—Ernest and John.

The book "An American Genius" by Herbert Childs is the story of Ernest's life. The boys grew up in Canton—coincidentally, across the street from the famous Tuve family. (Merle Tuve became an internationally known scientist as well). The two boys, Ernest and Merle, great pals, rigged up "monkey wireless" as they called it, sending messages to each other—startling the neighbors. Engrossed in electricity, they spent every spare moment experimenting and later turned to wireless telegraphy. They remained life long friends.

Carl Lawrence was called the LaFollette of South Dakota. When he was elected Superintendent of Public Instruction, the family moved to Pierre, where he served for two terms. They moved back to Canton but later moved to Springfield and Aberdeen, where he became President of two of the state's colleges.

Ernest attended the U. of Chicago and received his Ph.D. from Yale. Gunda was not surprised that their son went on to be a Professor of Physics at the U. of California when he was only 29 years old. She said "Ernest was born grown up" which became a family cliché.

His work at the U. of California absorbed the rest of his life. Here he developed the famous cyclatron. The name of Ernest Lawrence was becoming known in the world of science. He was urged to join the Harvard faculty but instead, through the years, he made his Radiation Laboratory at Berkeley a mecca for physicists from every continent. He received the Nobel prize in 1939 when he was 38 years old.

John, who graduated from Harvard Medical School, later taught at Yale Medical School, then joined Ernest at the U. of California, working on neutron radiation, and the medical application of the cyclatron. John also received broad recognition.

When Ernest Lawrence died (age 57), President Eisenhower said that, in a real sense, Ernest Lawrence had given his life for his country. On the Berkeley campus, the new Lawrence Hall of Science, devoted to developing improved methods of science education, stands as a fitting memorial to Ernest Lawrence. The Laboratory has become a mecca for scientists the world over.

His mother's saying "Ernest was born grown up" was not far from the truth. She encouraged him, believed in him, and had the right to be proud of him.

MADGE MERCER ERSKINE
Sturgis   **Born 1882**

Mrs. Erskine's parents were both natives of Wood County, Ohio. In 1882, her father, Tom Mercer, filed a claim on land in Sully County, South Dakota. Madge was born at Mitchellville, Iowa, in 1882 and was six months old when she came with her mother and two year old brother, Roscoe, via rail to Blunt, S. D. in the spring of 1883, arriving midst a Dakota blizzard. Upon graduating from Pierre High School, she passed her examination in the spring of 1900 (17½ years old) and with her teacher's certificate began teaching, first at Harrold and then at Sturgis. In 1907 she married Rev. Carroll Erskine. He was the beloved pastor of the First Presbyterian Church at Sturgis, S. D. from 1906 to 1953, except when he served as a Navy Chaplain. Her one surviving son, Bayard of Knoxville, Tennessee, retired after 37 years of service with TVA, as assistant to the Engineering Design Director.

The sons of Madge Erskine have always had admiration and fond memories of this very capable and versatile lady. Briefly, she was receptionist and hostess at the Manse; Bible scholar and Sunday School teacher, counsellor to many girls; janitor for the church plant, including the washing and ironing of the choir robes and preparing the quarterly communion table; a guiding hand and consultant on many church activities and functions as dramatic productions, bazaars, church dinners, banquets, wedding parties, etc.; and as an avocation she sewed for three men and for many years cut and made their suits, shirts, pajamas, etc., along with related washing and ironing of their clothes. These duties were accomplished only by 16 or 18 hour days, 7 days a week. She was a capable speaker and writer, the ghost writer and editor for many letters and newspaper articles that were typewritten by my father.

Throughout her life, Mrs. Erskine had a willingness and commitment to being a child of God and servant of mankind. Through prayer, study of the Bible, and dedication, "she stretched forward" toward the high calling of Jesus Christ, personally and in her relationships with others. Her life was characterized by devotion to her family, unfailing and steadfast loyalty to the teachings of Jesus Christ, deep convictions on moral and spiritual issues, and a genuine appreciation of others. To people in need of spiritual as well as physical things, she

opened her heart and resources to share the basics of life as food, clothing, as well as the scriptures. Throughout her life, whether in periods of depression or prosperity, my mother consistently disciplined herself in time, industry and thrift so that she might more ably and efficiently serve her family, her church, and her community.

This mother once said, "The two hardest things for me in life were, first, to give up my husband and second to sell my home. But I am determined in my new situation in the State Veterans Home at Hot Springs, that I will never complain, and that I will always be grateful to God and others for my good fortune." During her long stay in the Home and final weeks of serious illness and pain, she never broke this pledge. She died in 1973.

ANNA BERTIA HUSEBOE LARSON
Lennox   **Born 1883**

Mrs. Lewis Larson (nee Anna Bertia Huseboe), wife, mother, homemaker, was born on a farm near Lennox, South Dakota, April 29, 1883. She came to Sioux Falls at the age of six, and except for two years has lived there since. Her mother died when Anna was only eleven, leaving her to help care for two younger brothers. She attended school in Sioux Falls and Augustana College in Canton, South Dakota.

On September 9, 1903 she married Lewis Larson (1878-1950) who at that time operated a general store in Sioux Falls. In 1906 he became city auditor, and later served as secretary to Senator Coe I. Crawford in Washington, D. C. While there in 1911 he began the study of law. His parents had the theory that a lawyer must necessarily be a slippery sort of fellow, so out of deference to them his law study had been delayed. His career proved to be a contradiction to their theory.

Two years later he returned to Sioux Falls to practice and to serve the public in many areas. In 1919 he became Juvenile Court Judge—a position he held until his death in 1950, attaining outstanding success in helping to restore many a young person to wholesome activities. His theory was that the first step in correcting delinquent children is getting them to tell the truth, with Reform School as the last resort.

A tribute to the Judge speaks of him as a "modest, gentle person who moved about with a minimum of ostentation, who in his 30 years as Judge was an earnest and thorough student of Juvenile law—was fearless and independent in his decisions; severe but always kind".

His areas of service seem limitless: his church, Young People's work, Sunday School Superintendent for 25 years, local church council and boards, National Church Council 26 years, Local and State Welfare, Y.M.C.A. local boards, Boys Work Committee 20 years, National Council & Executive Board 13 years. His influence was felt in all worthwhile activities, in the growing city as long as he lived.

The Larsons became parents of five children, one daughter and four sons. All attended public schools and all five were graduated from Augustana College, Sioux Falls, and went on to graduate schools.

Mrs. Larson was chosen South Dakota State Mother in 1951. She was for years active in the women's work of the church.

Her interest in music was a strong factor in their family life. All the children were taught to play musical instruments. Even to this day their family gatherings feature song fests and instrumental music.

Her children:

Marguerite—Mrs. Marcus Hogue, homemaker, teacher of music, piano and organ, organist.

Palmer K.—Lawyer, also choir director, Y.M.C.A. board member, served on the National board.

Dr. L. Arthur—Rhodes Scholar, lawyer, taught at Cornell, Ithaca, N. Y., Pittsburgh U., presently Professor of Law, Duke University, author, advisor to President Eisenhower, Director of U.S. Information Agency, music composer.

Dr. Donald—taught Political Science, Miami University, Coral Gables, Florida. Had an early TV program. Deceased.

Richard—Pastor—taught Bible at U. of South Dakota. Parish pastor, Casper, Wyoming, Madison, Wisconsin.

FRANCES STILES LAMONT
Aberdeen Rapid City   **Born 1914**

From a career as journalist, to homemaker, mother of four, with dynamic involvement in community and state volunteer service, to a "second career" as state senator after her children were grown and her husband, of 35 years, had died of a heart attack, typifies the wide range of activity for Frances "Peg" Lamont of Aberdeen, a life long South Dakotan.

Her husband, Bill, a Harvard graduate and a talented artist, encouraged Peg's volunteer work. Both his family and hers considered community service a joy and obligation.

Peg, an only child, was born in Rapid City, S. D. in 1914. Her father was elected Senator at age 27, the youngest on record. In 1933 her father became president of the First National Bank in Aberdeen. Peg graduated with highest

honors from High School and in journalism from the U. of Wisconsin, where she was active on many boards, and received the Wisconsin legislative award for graduate study, earning an M.A. in political Science in 1936.

Their son, William, and his wife, Tara, are both architects (degrees from Harvard and Columbia) in Washington, D. C. Nancy is completing her Ph.D. in Comparative Education at the U. of Wisconsin. Peggy (Mrs. Greg Lauver) an M.A. in Art History, is a doctor's wife and directs a museum at Rochester, Minnesota. Fred is a senior at the U. of S.D.

Peg was honored in 1974 as South Dakota Mother of the Year and in New York in May was awarded the American Mothers Association citation for civic responsibility. She announced her candidacy for State Senate and became the first woman elected to the post from her district. Her new career bloomed with appointments: in 1975 to the Joint Appropriations Committee and the Health and Welfare Committee. Bills she sponsored in the field of health, child care, and education passed. She was appointed to the U. of S.D. Health Service Advisory Council; named to the Advisory Council for the S.D. School for the Deaf; assigned to Interim Study Committees on Special Education and Learning Disability, the Nursing Home Policy Committee and assigned to the 12 state Midwest Legislative Conference.

An Episcopalian, Peg was active in her church. A lifelong Republican, she held many precinct and regional assignments. She was active in Little Theater, Red Cross, Girl Scouts, P.T.A., League of Women Voters and many other groups.

In A.A.U.W. Peg served as state president, on national committees, elected to the National A.A.U.W. Educational Foundation (1970-1975) and was National Chairman of the Women Author Project in 1975. Credited with starting the Mental Health Chapter and 10 county Mental Health centers, she was elected to the National Mental Health Board (1956-1960).

In the field of Aging, Peg was appointed by five Governors. In 1959 to the S. D. Commission on Aging; in 1961 the White House Conference on Aging; for 9 years as chairman of the S. D. Advisory Council on Aging to the chairmanship for the S. D. delegation to the White House Conference in 1971. She was host to the Educational TV series on the elderly in S. D.

Honors in addition to "Mother of the Year" include "Aberdeen First Lady", S. D. Diplomatic Ambassador", "U. of Wisconsin Alumni Distinguished Service Award" (1975) and many others.

VIRGINIA DRIVING HAWK SNEVE
Flandreau   **Born 1933**

Virginia Driving Hawk was born in 1933 on the Rosebud Sioux Indian Reservation, S.D., to Rose Ross and the Rev. James H. Driving Hawk, priest in the Episcopal Indian Mission. She attended school on the Rosebud Reservation and graduated from St. Mary's Episcopal High School for Indian Girls. She attended South Dakota State University, Brookings, receiving a Bachelor of Science degree in 1954. In 1955 she married Vance M. Sneve. They have three children, Shirley Kay, Paul, and Alan. They lived in Pierre and Rapid City, S. D. and later Cedar Rapids, Iowa, where Virginia took courses in expository writing at Iowa State College. She began free lancing with short stories and nonfiction articles about American Indians.

Mrs. Sneve called this time (when rejection slips and returned manuscripts made her hate to see the mailman) as "her character and skill-building period". "The rejections taught me humility and perseverance, but most important during this discouraging time, I was learning how to write." In 1964 the Sneves moved back to South Dakota where both were employed at the Bureau of Indian Affairs, Indian H.S., Flandreau, S. D. Virginia taught English, speech, and drama and served as a guidance counselor at the school from 1965-1970. She received her Master of Education Degree in 1969.

In 1971 her book JIMMY YELLOW HAWK was the winner of the American Indian category in the contest of Minority Books for children. Holiday House, New York, published the book and also HIGH ELK'S TREASURE, 1972; WHEN THUNDERS SPOKE, 1974; BETRAYED, 1974; THE CHICHI HOOHOO BOGEY MAN, 1975. In 1975 BOYS LIFE published her short story, "The Medicine Bag", which will also be included in Scott Foresman's 9th grade literature book. In 1972 Mrs. Sneve edited SOUTH DAKOTA GEOGRAPHIC NAMES for Brevet Press, which also published THE DAKOTA'S HERITAGE and THEY LED A NATION. In 1975-76 she will edit and compile the history of the Episcopal Church in South Dakota. She serves on the Bishop's Standing Committee and as a consultant editor for Brevet Press and as an Indian consultant and writer for KESD Public Television in South Dakota.

Mrs. Sneve lectures and participates in seminary and symposiums on Indian history and contemporary affairs. In June 1973 Mrs. Sneve was one of the featured juvenile authors at the Fort Hays Kansas State College Children's Literature Conference. In July, she was an instructor at Black Hills State College, conducting a children's literature workshop. Mrs. Sneve is an enrolled member of the Rosebud Sioux tribe and served on the United Sioux Tribes Cultural Arts Board of Directors in 1972-73. Awarded the 1974 Distinguished Alumnus Award from South Dakota State University, she is a member of the University's Advisory Council. In 1975 she was named Woman of Achievement by the National Federation of Press Women. She says, "I hope my writing can re-educate non-Indians into realizing that the American Indians are asking only that the wrongs of the past be righted and that we be recognized as having the same feelings and needs common to all people."

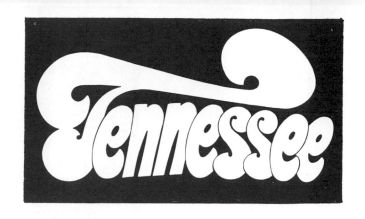

In an East Tennessee valley near Maryville, the Sam Houston School-house stands in a quiet cove, sheltered by oak, maple, and sycamore trees. It is the oldest original schoolhouse in Tennessee,

Tennessee

Nickname: Volunteer State

State Flower: Iris

State Bird: Mockingbird

Photos

1. Marble Springs, home of first governor of Tenn.
2. Tenn. State Capitol, Nashville
3. The Stately home of Andrew Jackson
4. Fort Nashburough
5. Belle Meade Mansion, Nashville

Committee Members

Chairman—Mrs. S. Haskins Ridens, New Bern

Mrs. Bradley Currey, Lookout Mountain

Tennessee

SARAH GEORGE DOUGLASS
of Sumner County   Born 1711

Sarah (George) Douglass born 1711 was the wife of Colonel Edward Douglass had seen her husband, seven sons and two sons-in-law fight during the Revolution and all came home safely. All she could hear from the men folk was the new land "west" the government was giving the soldiers for their loyalty. Several of their friends had gone on to the deepest wilderness on the Cumberland River and brought back glowing reports of the vast and luscious greenlands. The only problem was troublesome Indians. Then Sarah's children began to leave for the new lands, even her daughters and their husbands. Elmore Douglass was the first one to go out and see the new country and return to get the rest of the family. Sarah Douglass wanted to be near her family and in her declining years, having been married 45 years, she left for the wilderness country with her husband, Col. Edward Douglass.

Sarah Douglass had spent many hours making sure her children were well educated. Her husband insisted, too, that his children be educated but probably better educated than most people were in those days. Col. Douglass was a lawyer though he never practiced law. What good would all the education in Latin and Greek do these children when they went to the wilderness? Sarah's heart was heavy but she saw other families of culture, the Seviers, the Donelsons, the Robertsons, the Bledsoes, the Neelys and others leave for this new promise of a new country. Sarah was to face the most difficult days of her life during the winter of 1778-79 as she and her family began their journey to the Cumberland settlement.

It was the coldest winter on record and this gentle lady began to know what frontier life would be like. But in the Cumberland settlement Elmore Douglass and Ezekiel Douglass were already making their place in the life of that constantly threatened community. Their education was needed in this wilderness to help set up some sort of government and in 1788 the commissioners of Sumner County met at the home of Elmore Douglass. At this time there were no settlements at Chicago, Indianapolis, Memphis, Knoxville, or Cincinnati. Detroit was a small fort and most of the rest of the western country was Indian territory. Davidson and Sumner Counties were deep into the wilderness with unfriendly Indians on all sides, completely cut off from the outside for any help of any kind.

Sarah's eldest son, John, was killed by the Indians after he had volunteered in 1778 as an express to Blackmore's station thirty miles away. His horse returned to Bledsoe's bespattered with blood. A search party found Douglass' body, and they buried it in a sinkhole.

History was written that the sons and daughters as well as Sarah's husband, Col. Edward Douglass, from 1785 until they all died contributed to the cultural, political, and spirutal life of Sumner County, Tennessee. Their children were: John Douglass who was killed by the Indians, William Douglass who married Peggy Stroud, Elizabeth Douglass who married William Cage, Elmore Douglass who married Betsey Blakemore, Ezekiel Douglass, who married May Gibson, Sally Douglass who married Thomas Blakemore, Edward Douglass, Jr. married Elizabeth Howard, Reuben Douglass married Elizabeth Edwards and James Douglass married Catherine Collier.

SALLY RIDLEY BUCHANAN
Holston East   Born 1750

Fighting Indians was a way of life for Sally Ridley, daughter of Colonel Daniel Ridley. She spent most of her life in a picketed fort or within running distance of one.

Although her father fought in the Revolution it was in the midst of this war that Col. Ridley took his family and pushed west to what was known as the Holston Country or better known now as East Tennessee. This was about 1779-1780. That winter was considered to be the worst winter on record. Sally was still a young child but she was familiar with hunger, cold, discomforts and the ever constant threat of the Indians. By 1790 the Holston Country was considered more peaceful than it had been for years but Colonel Ridley was not to stay in that area much longer. No one knows why the early frontiersman left a comparatively safe and settled community to face the hardships of the developing wilderness but many families were making settlements on the Cumberland River in Davidson County and Sumner County along the river. It was one of the most dangerous spots of all the new settlements as the Indians spoke peace but killed, scalped, and tortured the white families as they moved westward.

Sally's husband, Major John Buchanan had been among the first settlers of the Cumberland. The Buchanan family had pushed on to the Cumberland area when the Ridleys stopped at the Holston Country. Major Buchanan had been married before and lost his wife, Mary Kennedy in childbirth. The baby lived and in this wild and difficult country a man needed a wife. Sally Ridley married Major Buchanan, and history proved her to be the ideal wife for Major Buchanan. She was strong, healthy, knew the ways of frontier life and understood the role a wife played in the life of a man who was a leader.

Buchanan's Station was well known along the route westward. It was built to protect not only the Buchanan family but the settlers in the nearby area, as well as travelers to and from the well established communities and state capitols of North Carolina and Virginia from the raiding Indians. At best, life in such a fort was disagreeable, overcrowded, hot, filled with the cattle and personal belongings of the protected families, as well as slaves, newborn babies and even the tools for farming the land.

On September 30, 1792 Sally Ridley Buchanan's contributions toward saving the fort from attack by the Indians made a deep impression on historians since that time. Long ago the Tennessee Historical Commission set up a marker bearing the date and only the name of "Mrs. Buchanan". The bronze marker may be seen in Davidson County, Tennessee near where Elm Hill crosses Mill Creek, a tributary of Cumberland River.

Four hundred of the finest warriors of the Creek and Chickamauga Indian tribes had come to destroy Buchanan's and only seventeen white men were in the fort to protect it. It was a bloody battle but Sally's courage, knowledge of the ways of Indians, her bravery at the risk of her own life was long to be remembered and honored. Sally Buchanan's first baby was born only eleven days after the famous Siege of Buchanans. So, Sally risked not only her life but the life of her unborn baby as well, on that memorable day.

LOUISE SEVIER GIDDINGS CURREY

Born 1903

Born in Chattanooga, Tennessee, in 1903, Mrs. Louise Sevier Giddings Currey is still a resident of that state. She now lives in Lookout Mountain. Both her family and the family of her husband are deeprooted in the history of Tennessee having come from Virginia and North Carolina with the first pioneers who attempted to cross the mountains. Their thirty-three years of married life have been dedicated, and continue to be dedicated, to their home and children, their church and community and in extraordinary measure to "doing for the least of these . . ."

Mrs. Currey is the mother of six children and foster mother of hundreds of wards of the Hamilton County Juvenile Court. When her four older children reached school age, for health reasons they could not attend regular schools. They required protective care at home. Mrs. Currey taught these four children herself for several years until they were able to take their places with other children in the local schools. Their scholastic standing was found to be of the highest quality. Her children are a monument to her training, direction and devotion: Louise Sevier Currey Collins, 32, graduated from Sweet Briar College cum laude in International Relations. She is now an analyst in the Department of Defense in Washington, D.C. Bradley Norton Currey, Jr., 30, is a scholarship graduate of Princeton University, having worked through the four years to cover his additional expense. He graduated from Woodrow Wilson School of Government and International Affairs with commendation and is now Vice-President of the Atlanta Trust Company of Georgia, Atlanta, Georgia. Frederick Giddings Currey, age 28, graduated in three years from the University of Chattanooga with a B.S. in Business and Economics. He is with the Equitable Securities Corporation, Houston, Texas. Henry Douglas Currey, 24, is a student at the University of Houston, Texas, and will be graduated in June,

1976 with a B.S. in Economics and Mathetmatics. Robert Brownlee Currey, 21, enlisted for three years in the U.S. Army. He plans to attend college upon completion of his service with the Armored Division at Fort Lewis, Washington. Elizabeth Norton Currey, 17, is an honor student at Girls' Preparatory School, and president of the senior class. She will be graduated in June and plans to attend college.

Louise Currey is the indefatigable champion of all neglected children, regardless of race or religion. She has worked tirelessly through the years for the improvement of the conditions and the system in the juvenile courts. To her labors are attributed the abolishment of the whipping post in the State of Georgia and the separation of dependent and neglected children from delinquents held by the courts in her own state. She is ready at all times to give these young people her personal time, her guidance and her loving understanding. She has worked for and succeeded in getting better housing quarters for these children.

Her interest in children covers wide horizons. She has, through her efforts, achieved the modernization of the Lookout Mountain School, resulting in higher standards for its graduates.

Her energies, assisted by every member of her family, are currently directed toward a residential treatment center for mentally and emotionally disturbed children, and for the establishment of a "home" for juveniles returning from vocational training schools that they may have a decent place to live while finding their independent places in the community.

The entire life of this outstanding mother is devoted not only to her own children but to all children. She has raised hundreds of thousands of dollars for medical, educational, legal and welfare projects of major and vital need, including the erection of a modern Juvenile Court Center at a cost of $300,000, and the equipment and direction of a playground for negro children.

She has worked selflessly as a member and as an officer of many important organizations including: the PTA, the School Board of Lookout Mountain, Hamilton County Committee for Crippled Children and Adults, the YWCA, the Juvenile Court Commission, the Council of Community Forces, National Board of Probation and Parole. And culture and art also hold her interest. She is a member of the Garden Club, the Chattanooga Symphony Assoc., the Art Assoc., and the Opera Assoc. of Chattanooga and the Chattanooga Little Theatre. The manifold work of this remarkable mother embraces many and varied fields. In 1966 she was elected American Mother of the Year.

JOSEPHINE WAINMAN BURSON
Memphis

Josephine Wainman Burson was born in Memphis and educated in the public schools and Memphis State University. She is a member of Baron Hirsch, Beth Sholom Synagogues.

Her civic achievements are many: Commissioner Tennessee Department Employment Security-1967-71; Member Governor's Cabinet; Governor's Commission Status of Women, 1967-71; Chairman Tennessee Savings Bond Committee, 1967-69; Vice-President Interstate Conference Employment Security Administrators, 1968-70; Trustee Memphis State University Foundation; Vice-Chairman Advisory Committee Women and Girls Employment Enabling Service; Vice-President Women in Cable Communications, 1973-74; Judicial Selection Committee, 1974; Past President Hadassah, Memphis, 1947-48.

She received the 1969 Humanitarian Award from B'nai B'rith. She was a deligate, five international Congresses Jerusalem Delegate, World Conference Soviet Jewry, Brussels, 1971. In 1975, she was made National Mother of the Year.

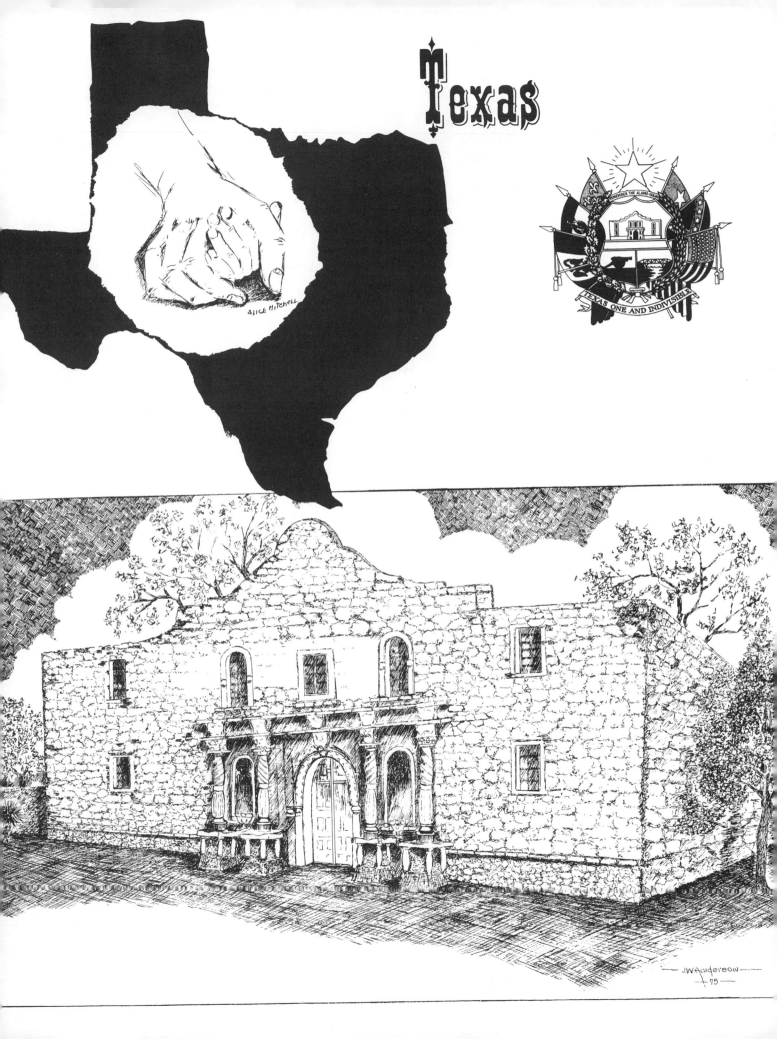

Texas

ALICE Mitchell

TEXAS ONE AND INDIVISIBLE

J.W.Anderson
75

Texts

Nickname: The Lone Star State

State Flower: Bluebonnet

State Tree: Pecan

State Bird: Mockingbird

Photos

1. San Jacinto Monument & State Park
2. The Pecos River
3. Waxahachie's courthouse "Texas Morrish"
4. The Abul Kalam Azad
5. Windmill & cattle on the high plains near Canyon

Committee Members

Chairman—Mrs. R.E. Wendland
J.W. Anderson—artist
Alice Mitchell—artist
Miss Katharine Burchard
Mrs. Melvin B. Barrow, Brazoria
Mrs. John L. Dodson, Jr. Del Rio
Mrs. Bob Hart, Driftwood
Mrs. Gladys Hogan, Brenham
Mrs. R.G. LeTourneau, Longview
Mrs. Donald E. Redmond, Austin
Mrs. Karl E. Wallace, Fort Worth
Mrs. Kenneth L. Wickett, Fort Worth
Mrs. Lee Griffin
Katherine Burchard
Sandra Gazalez Devereaux
Minnie Gilbert
Gladys S. Hogan
Mrs. Freeman E. Perkins
Dr. E.C. Rowand, Jr.
Nels E. Stjerstrom
Mrs. Kenneth L. Wickett

Texas

DONA ROSA MARIA HINOJOSA DE BALLI

Born 1755

Doña Rosa Maria Hinojosa de Balli was Texas' first cattle queen, though she never made her home on a ranch. Today, nine generations later, she has many descendants on both sides of the lower Rio Grande, a surprising number of whom live on segments of original family land grants. Her courage, sagacity and generosity are revealed in voluminous legal and family records and through local legends.

Rosa grew up in Old Reynosa, Mexico, where her father, Captain Juan José Hinojosa, was "alcalde." Born in 1759 or 1760 in nearby Camargo, she was the sixth child of Captain Hinojose and Dna. Maria Antonia Ynes Benavides. Both parents were of the Spanish nobility. The first colonists built their villas on the south bank but their herds soon spread across the river onto land still held by the Spanish Crown. The cowboy, symbol of the Southwest, originated on the Texas Rio Grande.

More pasture land was needed and on July 4, 1776, Rosa's husband, Captain Rosé Maria Balli, and her father began proceedings to acquire title to the La Feria and Llano Grande land grants. Captain Balli died just before the grants were finally approved in 1790. Under Spanish law, a widow inherited her husband's full authority. Doña Rosa was left with three minor sons and an estate heavily encumbered by debt.

She had the La Feria grant perfected in her name and subsequently obtained several other large grants in the names of her sons and a brother, Vicente Hinojosa. The town of La Feria, Texas, takes its name from the La Feria grant, where the Balli family maintained ranch headquarters and a chapel. Together, the family held title to about one-third of the present Lower Rio Grande Valley. Like the true Spanish matriarch she was, Doña Rosa exercised unquestioned authority over their little kingdom, keeping meticulous records of what was due each son and herself. In her later years, Nicolás, whom she fondly referred to as "My son, the priest," assisted her. A secular priest, he later

was granted Padre Island, which is named for him.

But for her warmth and generosity and piety, Doña Rosa's memory would not still be cherished, for her ranch empire crumbled shortly after her death in 1801. Her eldest son, Captain Juan José Balli II, then "alcalde" in Reynosa, was imprisoned by Spanish colonial authorities on charges that were never fully disclosed. He died in prison within a year, but not before his brothers had expended enormous sums in his defense, postponing division of the family estate. Soon José Maria II died and it took the Padre twenty years to pay off the last indebtedness, thereby saving the inheritance of Chico's children, Doña Rosa's only grandchildren.

During her lifetime, neighboring ranchers often sought her advice and borrowed her farming tools. Abstract records note that the Fernandez brothers, owners of an adjoining grant, kept their papers and valuables in Doña Hinojosa's strong box. Various deed records refer to her "rancherias" as identifying landmarks. Her name as godmother appears on scores of christenings in Our Lady of Guadalupe Church in Reynosa Vieja.

The matriarch's lengthy will provided for rewards to servants, including cancellation of outstanding debts owed by her majordomo and several foremen. It was her custom to lend a few sheep or other livestock to ranch workers, permitting them to repay her from the increase. Her "jewelries" went to the family chapel at Santa Maria.

NATHANELLA SODERGREN BERLING

Born 1885

Mrs. Nathanella (Nellie) Sodergren Berling and husband, John Edward Berling, are natives of Sweden. They were adult and living in New York when they met and married in 1905. Later they came to Texas and settled in Houston in the early twenties, where they were at the time of his death, in 1950. Mrs. Berling continues to make her home there.

Nellie was born to Johan and Margaret Elizabeth Boberg Sodergren January 8, 1885, in Faron (Gotland) Sweden. The father was in charge of a government school on this island, and the mother taught in it. Religious education was stressed there, so Nellie studied the Bible and Catechism along with her other studies, which doubtless accounts for the fact that her life was devoted to church work. She was baptised, confirmed and married in Lutheran churches, the state church of Sweden, but in Houston they joined the Second Presbyterian Church, in which both served faithfully many years. However, Mrs. Berling worked in all churches; her own and especially in a small Lutheran church near-by; thus she contributed much to ecumenical and inter-racial work in Houston. Her social

work for underpriviledged has been outstanding. For example, during the great Depression, while she was president of the United Council of Church Women, she was determined to get milk for the poor of the city. It was discovered that several dairies ran their skimmed milk down the drain, and her request for the milk was granted. Through the help of Houston's Mayor and all the churches in the area, milk cans and trucks were procured, six distribution centers were established at churches, and five hundred gallons of milk were provided daily to those in need. Her Christian Service Board also secured jobs such as yard hands or as watchmen, for the unemployed. Women chauffeured people to hospitals and clinics, collected used clothing, made innumerable layettes, and took foods where needed. They collected and sent tons of clothing to war-torn areas—in particular, sent three thousand pounds of clothing, plus medicines on the ship "Texas Friendship for Korea".

She served on Houston Church Women, the Young Women's Christian Association, Veteran Hospital Volunteer workers, and Red Cross Boards, and in numerous ways has passed on to others the benefits of her heritage: basic concepts of character and dignity, and humility with gratitude for every blessing. She has attended many worldwide fact-finding missions . . . all of which increased her interest in Laubach's literacy program and neighborhood projects, returning to report and act. Her home, being near the Medical Center, three universities and vocational school, became a focal point for many meetings resulting in opportunities to serve.

Mrs. Berling has three devoted children: James Paul Berling, Grace Selma Vandewater, and Mary Frances Mullin, who live respectively in Houston, Schenectady, N.Y. and Cocoa Beach, Florida. There are nine grandchildren, each following in footsteps of parents and grandparents, in attaining noble characteristics as well as university degrees with scholastic distinction in music, engineering and science.

Since she was named Texas Mother of 1965, Mrs. Berling received an injury to her eyes bringing on increasing blindness. As a result, she chose to retire to Holly Hall, a home which she was active in building during her active years. There she lives happily, with frequent visits from friends and family. Her life's work still continues, as one of inspiration, meaning, and significance.

ANNA EMMA JAHN BIESELE
Born 1888

When Mrs. Anna Emma Jahn Biesele was nominated for Texas Mother of 1964, to which honor she was named, University of Texas friends and associates of her and her husband, Dr. Rudolph Leopold Biesele, a Professor of History for many years at the University of Texas, literally poured love into their mail. The gist of these letters seemed to be to proclaim her an ideal mother. One of these letters read thus: "Some mothers may have travelled more, some will have made more public addresses, even maybe had more spectacular careers. But Mrs. Biesele to me represents the all too often unrecognized mother—the one who makes her choice to give her life and energies to making a happy, enduring home. Before the days of vitamins in a bottle, she studied the dietary needs of children and saw to it that such needs for healthy minds and bodies were met. She also attended to spiritual needs and shared with all of her family a love of beauty. There were flowers in the home, even when money was scarce. Unable to attend college in her youth, she read and studied along with her children and husband as they advanced toward higher degrees. She has never stopped learning and encouraging her family to push on to attain whatever they might seek to attain. If all Americans had had a mother as wise, as understanding, as diligent, as content to stay happily with the high calling of rearing a good family, we could probably dispense with jails and certainly there would be less of pettiness and pretense. Mrs. Biesele has inculcated the virtues of loyalty to family, church and country, acceptance of civic responsibility, and qualities of pride in achievement and advancing in areas of knowledge. The carrying over of these traits in the grandchildren, who have reached the age of responsibility, indicates that the influence of grandmother is still at work.

Mrs. Biesele has a right to be proud of her family heritage. The family into which she was born in 1888 in New Braunfels, Texas, set an example of shouldering civic responsibilities and her father served as mayor of New Braunfels for several years. She and her husband enjoyed and drew strength from their religious and church life, giving regularly and generously of time and money. In recent years they helped to organize and expand a new Presbyterian Church in Austin. Dr. Biesele worked hard, ably assisted by his wife, in securing his Ph.D. degree. In the face of economic odds, all five of their children achieved marked records: two of their sons were high school Valedictorians, Doctors of Philosophy, and university professors; three of their children made Phi Beta Kappa, and the fourth made Tau Beta Pi, honorary engineering fraternity. Three sons are listed in *American Men of Science* and one in *Who's Who in America*. Their daughter has aided her husband in his writing of books on the use of computers in business. Their daughters-in-law are active workers for moral and civic improvement in their communities. Their 16 grandchildren and several great-grandchildren are following the same pattern. Someone has said, "No other family could equal the Bieseles' for their nearness to each other, scholarly achievements, and mutual pride in each other's successes." What greater testimony to the worthiness of a mother than that her children do her honor?

PEARLE OWENS GILLIS

Born 1888

When a couple of very modest means with no famous ancestors and no education beyond high school produce a family of highly educated, creative children, all of them competent musicians, we are interested to know the secret. American Mother of 1949, Pearle Owens Gillis of Ft. Worth, Texas, and her husband Earl, are such a couple. Pearle was a quiet little person, described as the "cook apron type" but she had six children whose influence in missions, literature, and music are felt from Argentina to New York and Texas. Three sons hold earned doctor's degrees.

Pearle Gillis' life was devoted to her family and to her church, Polytechnic Baptist, around which the family life revolved. Though there was very little money when the children were small, Pearle still determined that each would have a musical education. Everybody pitched in to help. The children had paper routes, ran errands, mowed lawns, did chores for the neighbors. The friendly rivalry in the family, the feeling of esprit de corps, that each one must uphold the family honor, was recognized by all who came in contact with them.

Earl Gillis was a Post Office employee. In the evening he liked to relax with his fiddle. As the children learned a little about music, they played with him. It was not long before they had a rather good ensemble for more than family enjoyment. The religious and musical atmosphere of the home is reflected in the later activities of all the children. Dr. Carroll Gillis received his Doctor of Theology degree from the Southwestern Baptist Theological Seminary, is an author, teacher, musician and has served as a missionary in Argentina. Don's doctorate is in music from Texas Christian University. He is a composer, writer, teacher, and worked as production manager at NBC. Dr. Everett received his Ph.D. from the University of Texas and is an author, poet, scholar, and professor. Eileen Gillis Plemons is a musician and teacher. Evelyn Gillis Gray a musician and Management Specialist; and Lewis Dean Gillis a composer, arranger, and teacher.

There were other young people in the Gillis home, too. In addition to her own flock of six, Pearle adopted eight boys who needed assistance in order that they might complete their education. While attending to their material needs: cooking, washing, ironing and sewing for them, Pearle guided and inspired them to greater effort as she did her own children. One of these boys became a director of a symphony orchestra and a professor of musicology.

As one of her children said, "It was not, however, for any single accomplishment by any of us that our mother was chosen to be the American Mother of 1949, rather, it was because the helping hands of our parents reached out to give a chance to many others that this honor came. Our home was never empty, no one was ever alone. The Gillis house seemed to be a place which always welcomed others to be a part of the family."

Perhaps it was her devotion to Christ, or maybe the aesthetic and moral training of music that was the secret in her life as she went about doing good. Anyway, it seems to have been a pretty good combination; and Pearle Owens Gillis, born in Somerset, Kentucky, educated in Cameron, Missouri, through her children, has given beauty and music, and goodness to the world.

I love to think of her like a blessed candle,
　Burning through life's long night,
Quietly useful, simple, gentle, tender—
　And always giving light.
　　　　　　　　　Lee Shippey

ARABELLA OWENS BRINDLEY
Elgin   **Born 1892**

Arabella Owens Brindley, religious and civic leader, story teller, and philanthropist, was born and reared in Elgin, Texas, March 4, 1892, to William and Mary C. Owens. She graduated from Kidd-Key College in Sherman, Texas, with a major in speech.

Dr. G. V. Brindley, Sr., brought her to Temple as a bride in 1913 where she has been active in all phases of community life. She has served as president of the City Federation of Women's Clubs; of the Bell County, District, and Texas Medical Auxiliaries; the Woman's Study Club; the Domestic Science Club; and the United Daughters of the Confederacy.

In 1951 she was selected as the outstanding woman in Temple by the Jr. Chamber of Commerce. In 1954 she was selected as outstanding woman of the 4th District of the Texas Federation of Women's Clubs. In 1956 she was chosen as the Texas Mother of the Year by the American Mothers Committee in Texas.

She is a life member of the Board of The Temple Public Library after having served on it for 40 years. She was instrumental in obtaining the old post office building to house the library in 1964.

Mrs. Brindley says that her greatest satisfaction in life has come from her 40 years of church school work with the young people in her Baptist church, and from her volunteer work in the Temple hospitals. Her husband took her with him to visit many of his patients who needed cheering up.

Upon the death of her husband, Mrs. Brindley sponsored the G. V. Brindley surgical lectureships at Scott and White Hospital, which are not only for the medical profession but for all interested persons.

She continues to be a source of inspiration to her friends and community, and is acclaimed as one of the most beloved women in Temple. She has continued her talent as a fascinating story teller, giving pleasure through the years to the Rotary Club and other organizations, especially at Christmas time. In 1974, at age 82, she told the Christmas story nine times to groups of children and adults.

She has three sons, all doctors, seven living grandchildren and eight great grand children.

RAMONA RODRIGUES GONZALEZ
El Paso   **Born 1907**

In 1974, *El Quinto Sol*, an outstanding Chicano magazine published at Berkeley, featured Chicano women writers. Among these was Ramona González. Her family was delighted by this honor, which one could say culminated her many struggles in life.

She was born Ramona Rodrigues on January 6, 1907, in El Paso, Texas. The desert, arid environment must have been a challenge to her from childhood. This challenge, which faced many women in this area, was to play an important role in her later life, making her strong in the midst of adversity. She is outstanding in that being Mexican-American she accomplished much for her time and place. She was graduated from El Paso High School in 1923. She had the ability and desire to go to college but she was discouraged by friends and the economy. This dream of hers, although never accomplished, was harbored instead for her own children. Among her other dreams was the secret desire to be a writer; even more remote than the desire to go to college.

She married Manuel González on September 21, 1930, in El Paso, Texas. Even during those meager and difficult depression days, she was not discouraged about starting a college fund for her four children. She had a personal wish to work, but her duty for family and home won. Instead, she and her husband set up a small restaurant with their home in the back. Rapidly her fame around the barrio grew. Neighbors complimented with, "I'd give anything for Ramoncita's tamales." "Have you tasted her soup?" Eventually the restaurant became González Grocery, a well-known landmark in the area. Not only does the family have its fondest memories there, but countless families recall events and happenings at "la tiendita," now razed to make way for a freeway.

She and her husband helped numerous people in El Paso and Juárez with clothes and food. It was not uncommon for them to "adopt" families near starvation in Juárez. When she was not occupied with this, she crocheted and sewed for the family and the ladies' auxiliary of the Mormon Church. When her husband developed an ulcer, she rapidly became an expert on nutrition. To this day she seldom opens a can or a prepackaged food. The family seldom lived alone. There were cousins, aunts and uncles, and friends, who always had a home there. A brother's close friend came for a week and stayed for a year. Yet, she was never heard to complain. She managed the family, relatives, and the grocery store.

In 1958 she developed breast cancer, which sent waves of terror over her family. However, it was through her courage that we found strength in those difficult days. Yet, she and her husband saw to it that their children graduated from college: Dr. Norma G. Hernández, Dean of Education at the University of Texas at El Paso; Manuel González, Jr., engineer; Ismael González, pharmacist and Mrs. Sandra G. Devereaux, teacher.

During recent years, widowed and her children gone, she does not weep and wring her hands. At the time her last daughter married, "el movimiento Chicano" was starting in Texas. Emphasis was on Mexican-American food, music, dance and literature. Literature! Her dream back in the '30's. Could she? Recalling the good things of barrio life, she started to write. She now unearthed memories that had lain buried over fifty years. Rich, natural stories came forth. Some were sad, others comical. They all depicted the many characteristics of Chicano life. She has written articles for the El Paso Herald Post and is presently compiling a collection of Chicano sayings for publication.

Why should Ramona González be a Bicentennial mother? She represents the best of two traditions: Mexican and American.

EVELYN PETERSON LETOURNEAU

Born 1900

Mrs. Robert G. LeTourneau, nee Evelyn Peterson, was born in Santa Rosa, California, in November 1900. Her parents, father Scandinavian and mother English, were middle class people, deeply religious, industrious, and extremely hospitable. She had one sister and three brothers, she being the eldest. She married Robert G. LeTourneau in 1917. He became a world famous inventor and designer of heavy duty earth moving equipment and huge off-shore oil drilling platforms.

Because of her husband's work as a manufacturer and contractor, she moved a great deal living in California, Illinois, Georgia, Mississippi and in Texas for many years. Often her lot was to live in tents, steel and concrete buildings, and, at one time, even in a converted railroad box car. Through all of this, she proved herself capable, cooperative, and ready to support him in order to assist him in making a success of his business. He died June 1, 1969. Mrs. Le-Tourneau is the mother of five, grandmother of nineteen, and great-grandmother of seven. All four of her sons are following in their father's footsteps, both as businessmen and witnessing Christians. Richard, the oldest son, is president of LeTourneau College, Longview, Texas, and vice-president of the LeTourneau Foundation. Ben and Ted are also associated with the college in management. Roy is president of the Le-Tourneau Foundation and a businessman in Orlando, Florida. The daughter, Mrs. Gus (Louise) Dick, is a homemaker in Moline, Illinois, where her husband is an executive in manufacturing.

In 1946 when the LeTourneaus moved to Longview, Texas, to build another manufacturing plant, Mrs. LeTourneau saw an opportunity to realize her dream of establishing a non-denominational Christian college. LeTourneau College is a fully accredited college of engineering, technology and the liberal arts and has over 700 students enrolled.

Working with young people did not begin in Longview. As a teenager she taught and transported thirty youngsters to Sunday School in a trailer. She founded a Bible Camp for young people in Winona Lake, Indiana, and operated it from 1938 to 1948. For two years, in Toccoa, Georgia, she taught a class in religion for a total of six hundred young people. This was followed by the establishment of ranches for disadvantaged boys at Little Rock, Arkansas, and Lindale and Longview, Texas.

Mrs. LeTourneau has received many honors and awards. In 1969 she was the Texas and National Mother of the Year. She continues to travel and to speak to people in all parts of the country and in all circumstances of life. She says her purpose is to encourage them to face all situations with a "will to win," drawing upon unrealized resources of mind and body, but above all to recognize the courage and strength that comes through faith in God and commitment to His purposes. She has filled speaking engagements for church groups, civic organizations, school assemblies, and parent-teacher groups, women's clubs and meetings on behalf of the Young Mothers Council Service. She has appeared in various parts of the country from the west to the east and from Canada to the southern part of the United States from 1969 to 1975. She has devoted about two-thirds of her time to her speaking ministry.

She now spends more time at her home in Longview, Texas. Her home is adjacent to the college, providing close contact with the students and greater participation in the college activities. Her interest will always be in helping young people find a rewarding life. She still enjoys being called "Mom" by the nearly seven thousand who have attended the school which she and her husband founded.

MARY LOUISE MORRIS ROWAND
Born 1918

It is hard to put Mary Louise Rowand on paper: editors across the country struggle to describe who she is and what she does to people. Ruth Weber, N. Y. editor of *Churchwoman* writes, "This peregrinating preacher has become one of the most heralded speakers to traverse the country. It's her warm but forthright style, her creative idea-spinning, her homespun parables, and her deep faith that endear her so totally to audiences of whatever denomination!"

How to sum up a life so full and vibrant? I have often said, "Mary Louise is jealous for God!" She was born Sept. 1, 1918, one of eight children, to D. Harry and Dora Morris in Fairmont, West Va. She is married to Dr. E. C. Rowand, pastor of the Central Christian Church, Dallas. They have two children, Diane, married to Johnny Simons, and Edward III.

Mary Louise wants everybody to be loving, missional, joyful, involved, committed. She will not settle for lesser goals. By keeping her mind stretched with continuous reading, her heart and soul warmed by prayer, her body dedicated to serving others in need, and her faith undergirded with the sense of joyful duty, somehow she manages to pack into every day at least two days of living. She goes where she is needed, beginning in her home: hers is a family that LIKES each other, and enjoys being together, from camping-tenting vacations all over the U. S. for the four of them, to the day-by-day experiences in their home, involving school, community, and the 1400 members of their "wider Church family." The way this mother took this mixture of the difficult and the dear, living and teaching that the Church is to redeem and transform, overcoming the pitfalls so plentiful in a parsonage, because the tasks are so magnificent—giving tender-loving-care in abundance and the secret ingredient of genuine

fun, produced the good life. Ed and Diane are grown and out in the world, happy, healthy, emotionally stable, tender, caring; both creative artists, who show forth in their lives the compassionate, active personal involvement their mother had. Her spirit of encouragement, hope, and joy are a vital part of a daughter who now helps produce, direct, and create adult and children's drama at Casa Mañana Theater in Ft. Worth, and a musician son who is playing and singing his way into a fulfilling and worthwhile life style, serving others.

The church is her next great love, where she has "mothered" countless hundreds, not only her local congregations, but the church universal. In recent days, her main contribution to community, state, and nation is not only her power to put into words WHO we are, WHY we are, and WHAT we are, as children of God, but more: that she herself not only knows the words, but has lived a life to match. It is the reason she is one of the most in-demand speakers in the country, standing in front of literally thousands of people in giant assemblies or intimate workshops.

Mary Louise is a fully ordained minister of the Christian Church, is a Trustee of T.C.U., and serves as liason between the student body and the Board. She has been selected annually since 1965 as one of the top ten news-shapers in the Dallas area, named the most valuable woman in the field of religion in her city, and one of the most valuable women in civic affairs by the Young Women's Christian Association. In 1974 the mayor declared a "Mary Louise Rowand Day" in the city of Dallas. Her executive positions through the years are too numerous to list, but she is presently the Deputy Vice President of Church Women United in the U.S.A., heading millions of women here and across the world.

How she manages to divide herself up into so many pieces, yet retain her own inner peace and direction, might be an impossibility to some, but just be part of the joy of living for Mary Louise.

LUCILLE BISHOP SMITH
Crockett   Born 1892

Mrs. Lucille Bishop Smith, a resident of Ft. Worth, Texas, was born September 5, 1892, in Crockett, Texas, to Mary Jackson and Jessie Bishop. She received her public school education in Crockett and attended Wiley, Samuel Houston, Prairie View A&M, and Colorado State College.

Throughout her long and notable career as teacher and business leader, Mrs. Smith received many honors and awards for outstanding service to humanity through education, civic affairs, social and welfare agencies, religious organizations, character building activities and leadership training. Through research and experimentation, she developed and published many original ideas in the culinary arts.

She developed the first Hot Roll Mix in the United States; set up the first Commercial Foods and Technology Department at the college level with an apprenticeship training program at Prairie View A&M College; published a cook book, "Lucille's Treasure Chest of Fine Foods," and at 82, founded and became president of her family corporation, "Lucille B. Smith's Fine Foods, Incorporated."

Outstanding recognitions and awards include Service to Youth Award, YMCA, 1970; member of the Governor's Commission on the Status of Women, 1969; honored with "Lucille B. Smith Day," proclaimed by the city of Ft. Worth, April 28, 1966, for 50 years service to ALL humanity; and twice honored as MERIT MOTHER OF TEXAS, 1969 and 1970.

Also she has received laureate citations and awards for outstanding service from Eta Phi Beta, 1967; Campfire Girls, 1966; Beta Tau Lamba, 1966; Epsilon Pi Tau, Inc., 1962; Zeta Phi Beta, 1953; T. L. Holley Service Award in Industrial Education, 1966; KNOK AM-FM Citizens Award, 1962; Woman of the Year, Federated Women's Clubs, 1961; School of Industrial Education and Technology Award, 1959; and Prairie View A&M College "Distinguished Partner in Progress Award," 1966.

She is a member of St. Andrew United Methodist Church, the United Negro College Fund, NAACP, NRTA, holds life membership in the PTA, YWCA, the Fort Worth Chamber of Commerce, and is listed in WHO'S WHO.

During a period of over 50 years of dedicated service, Mrs. Smith and her late husband, U. S. Smith, whom she married in 1912, reared and educated their three children to live lives of leadership and usefulness. They and her eight grandchildren all have graduate degrees from leading colleges and universities of the nation. She has thirteen great-grandchildren.

Her son, Armstead B. Smith, is Director of Manpower Development, Ft. Worth. His wife, Goldie, is Homemaking Consultant with the Agriculture Extension Agency. Her daughter, Gladys Smith Hogan, is secretary of the School Board, Brenham; former supervisor of schools, and member of the State Board of Examiners, TEA. Her son, Ulysses S. Smith, Jr., is coordinator of Public School Band Music, Detroit. His wife, Elnora, is secretary-treasurer, Home Federal Savings and Loan Association, in Detroit.

Though opportunities were limited, and tasks very difficult, Mrs. Smith kept faith in God, her fellowman, and the causes for which she saw the need; and with her determination and dedication, her efforts were always crowned with success.

Utah

Nickname: Beehive State

State Flower: Sego lily

State Tree: Blue Spruce

State Bird: Calif. gull

Photos

1. Kennicott Copper—Bingham Canyon
2. Temple Block—Salt Lake
3. Seagull Monument—Temple square
4. Bryce Canyon

Committee Members

Chairman—Mrs. Miner
Odessa Cullimore
Lois Dohl
Lucille Smith

Utah

EMMELINE B. WOODWARD WELLS
Salt Lake City   **Born 1828**

Emmeline Blanche Woodward was born February 29, 1828 at Petersham, Massachusetts to David Woodward and Deiadama Hare. Her people came from England. Her early life was characterized by adversity and her dauntless courage and determination to rise above it. When she was just sixteen years of age, her husband's family apostatized from the Latter Day Saints Church and moved from Nauvoo, leaving the young wife alone, far from her Massachusetts home. Her young son died in that year and she lived with Bishop Newel K. Whitney, whom she married the following year. She migrated with his family to the Salt Lake Valley. When her second daughter was only five weeks old, Bishop Whitney died.

Emmeline began to teach school as she had done before in Massachusetts and Nauvoo and Winter Quarters. In two years she met and

married Daniel H. Wells and spent the rest of her life in security and three more daughters were born to her.

As her children grew older Mrs. Wells spent more and more time in public service pursuits. She was editor of *The Woman's Exponent*, first published in 1872. She was editor and publisher in 1877.

In 1876 Mrs. Wells was given a mission call by Brigham Young of directing the gathering and storing of wheat, which was turned over to the Government in 1918. President Woodrow Wilson called upon Mrs. Wells to thank her for wheat given at the beginning of the war.

In 1910 she became the General president of the Relief Society of the Latter Day Saints Church and served until 1921. In 1879 she attended the National Suffrage Convention in Washington and in 1882 was a member of the Constitutional Convention.

Throughout her life she took delight and comfort in her excellent literary work, both poetry and prose, which remains today as a memorial to her industry and artistry.

She died April 25, 1921 in Salt Lake City, Utah.

DR. ELLIS REYNOLDS SHIPP
Salt Lake City   **Born 1847**

"There is the picture of our outstanding woman of the last hundred years," wrote a noted Doctor, "and I believe it will be another hundred years before Utah produces another woman whose service to mankind exceeds that which she has rendered." Dr. Ralph T. Richards wrote of her, Dr. Ellis Shipp, "Unquestionably the outstanding woman of her time. . . . The West owes her a debt of gratitude."

One other quote sums up why Dr. Shipp is listed here among the great women of Utah: "She won the enduring love of a whole people. She never lost the spirit of her calling, keeping alive the vision of a pioneer, seeking constantly new adventure in her profession and exploring every avenue to progress.

Ellis Reynolds was born January 20, 1847, in the Iowa wastelands, Davis County, where her parents William Fletcher Reynolds and Anna Hawley were encamped at a logging site. After her mother's death she lived with her Hawley grandparents near Mt. Pleasant and later was invited to live with the President Brigham Young family for ten months.

She married Milford Bard Shipp, Sr., in 1866. He had had two previous wives. When she had four sons, she decided to study medicine in the Philadelphia Women's Medical College. She returned home for a brief visit when she became pregnant again, but she would not give up her dream of becoming a doctor.

Upon the completion of her training, she taught nursing and traveled from Canada to Mexico teaching obstetrics. She also traveled from Colorado to Nevada in the same work teaching women to care for themselves. Beginning in 1878, she became a staff member of The Deseret Hospital; founder of her own school of obstetrics, which she promoted for 59 years. This was her greatest contribution to the welfare of the women of the West.

Dr. Shipp published many articles in the *Utah Sanitarian* and the *Woman's Exponent* relating to health, medicine, and the feeding of children.

She was a co-editor of a pioneer medical journal; she was a delegate to the National Council of Women in Washington, D.C., and President of the Utah Women's Press Club.

In 1938, at the age of 91, Dr. Ellis R. Shipp was elected to Utah's Hall of Famous Women. She had been an intimate acquaintance of Susan B. Anthony, Elizabeth C. Stanton, and Clara Barton in her time.

Dr. Shipp was the devoted mother of nine children, five of whom lived to make names for themselves. One son was an M.D. and the other son an LLD. Her three daughters studied music; one at Ann Arbor, one received an M.A. from Columbia, and one did study at the University of Utah.

Devoted to the Latter Day Saint church all of her life, Dr. Shipp was for many years a member of the General Board of the Relief Society. She attended over 5000 maternity cases and has been presented numerous honors, including medals of her alma mater, the Women's Medical College of Philadelphia and Washington, D.C. Medical Society. She died January 31, 1939 at the age of 92 in Salt Lake City, Utah.

(Material gleaned from The Early Autobiography and Diary of Ellis Reynolds Shipp, M.D. by Deseret News Press 1962.)

SUSA YOUNG GATES
Salt Lake City   Born 1856

One of the great women of her generation, Susa Young Gates was noted for her organizing genius and leadership ability, and her versatile and voluminous accomplishments. As prolific writer, public speaker, administrator, teacher, musician, suffragist, genealogist, traveler, originator, she lived a multi-faceted life. But she cherished most her role as wife and mother of 13 children, five of whom lived to maturity. She had two children by her first husband, Dr. Alma B. Dunford, dentist, and eleven by her second husband, Jacob F. Gates. Only five of her children lived to maturity and some were premature births.

Susa Young was born March 18, 1856, to President Brigham Young and Lucy Bigelow in the historic Lion House in Salt Lake City. She was said to be more like her great pioneer leader-father than any of his other children, growing up under his eyes and influence and remaining close to him always.

She attended the University of Utah and later graduated from the Brigham Young University. She studied at Harvard in the summer of 1892.

Of her five living children, the oldest was Leah Dunford Widtsoe, lecturer and author and wife of college president, Dr. John A. Widtsoe; another daughter was Lucy Gates Bowen, international grand opera and concert singer, a prima donna in the Berlin Royal Opera House for several years. Brigham Cecil Gates, oldest son, was a graduate of the Schrwenk Conservatory of Berlin, Germany, being an outstanding musician and composer. He was director of the Latter Day Saints McCune School of Music, and conductor of the famous Mormon Tabernacle Choir. Another son, Harvey H. Gates was a successful author and scenario writer. Franklin Y. Gates was a chemistry and physics professor of Brigham Young University, chief engineer of the Federal Radio Commission, Washington, D.C. and in charge of research during transition from silent to talking movies for Warner Brothers.

Mrs. Gates wrote nine books, including the first Mormon novel by a Mormon and a major biography of her father, Brigham Young. Also active in politics and women's organizations she helped organize the National Household Economics Organization, served as a delegate and speaker to five Congresses of the International Council of Women, and was the Utah organizer of Daughters of the American Revolution, Daughters of the Utah Pioneers and National Women's Press.

She attended several Republican National Conventions, served as an officer of the Relief Society and the Young Ladies Mutual Improvement Association, and was a member of the Board of Regents of Brigham Young University and Utah State Agricultural College. In Utah she entertained such prominent American women as Ella Wheeler Wilcox, May Wright Sewall, Clara Barton, and Susan B. Anthony; carried on correspondence with Tolstoy, William Dean Howells, and other literary figures; published several woman suffrage pamphlets. Twenty-two pages are required just to list her writings. She worked in the Salt Lake Temple and wrote the first Mormon genealogical treatises.

Her father's advice she always followed. His words that follow embody her philosophy of motherhood:

"Daughter, use all your gifts to build up righteousness in the earth. Never use them to acquire name or fame. Never rob your home, nor your children. If you were to become the greatest woman in this world, and your name should be known in every land and clime, and you would fail in your duty as wife and mother, you would wake up on the morning of the first resurrection and find you had failed in everything; but anything you can do after you have satisfied the claims of husband and family will redound to your own honor and to the glory of God."

She died May 27, 1933 at age 77 in Salt Lake City, Utah.

ALICE MERRILL HORNE
Fillmore   **Born 1868**

Alice Merrill Horne was born in a log cabin in Fillmore, Utah on January 2, 1868. She was the daughter of Clarence and Bathsheba Smith Merrill. Alice studied at the University of Deseret and was the valedictorian at her commencement in 1887.

As a young wife and mother, she was elected to the third Utah State Legislature. She introduced a bill for two hundred education scholarships for four years each to be awarded annually. Eight thousand young teachers became recipients. As a member of the legislature she was the chairman of the committee that obtained a land-grant to establish the University of Utah and selected the site for the University—scenic spot in the eastern foothills overlooking the Salt Lake Valley.

At the closing session of the legislature in 1899, Alice introduced a bill for art. It passed unanimously. Thus, Utah had the first state-art institute in the United States. For many years the permanent state art collection was called "The State Alice Art Collection" in her honor.

In 1904 she was selected by the United States to attend the International Council of Women in Germany, where she delivered two addresses—"My Experiences in the Legislature," and "What Utah is Doing in Art."

Her picture, surrounded by her family, appeared on the front page of *Progress*, the newspaper of the National American Woman Suffrage Association, July 1909, with the caption under her picture:

> Mrs. Alice Merrill Horne of Salt Lake City and her family. When Mrs. Horne was in the Utah Legislature she introduced a bill to create an art institute.

Alice was the first secretary and the second president of Daughters of the Utah Pioneers.

She was the wife of George Henry Horne and the mother of six children—three boys and three girls. Two of her sons are medical doctors—Dr. Lyman M. Horne, gynecologist and obstetrician, who has delivered thousands of babies in the State of Utah, and Dr. Albert Merrill Horne, a prominent radiologist in Midland, Texas. A third son died in infancy. Mrs. Horne's eldest daughter, Mary, became the wife of an influential rancher in Craig, Colorado. Her second daughter, Virginia, has pursued an art and music career and has sung in the famed Tabernacle Choir. Her third daughter, Zorah, is known throughout Utah as a concert pianist and is the wife of a distinguished Utah trial judge.

Alice served as a member of the Relief Society General Board for her Church for fourteen years. In this capacity she wrote a handbook on art entitled, *Devotees and Their Shrines* that was used as an art and architecture text from 1914-1916.

A tireless worker, Alice set up hundreds of permanent and traveling art exhibits throughout the State of Utah. She was fondly called Mama Horne by the Utah artists. She was awarded the Utah Federation of Women's Clubs Medal for public service and the Academy of Western Culture Medal for her work in art.

She died in Salt Lake City Oct. 1, 1948.

AMY BROWN LYMAN

Born 1872

Born February 7, 1872, at Pleasant Grove, Utah, she was the daughter of John Brown and Margaret Zimmerman Brown.

She married Dr. Richard R. Lyman, September 9, 1896, in Salt Lake City, Utah. She was the mother of Wendell Brown Lyman and Mrs. Alexander Schreiner.

STUDENT AND TEACHER

A graduate of the Normal School of Brigham Young Academy, 1890.

Taught at Brigham Young Academy and then at Salt Lake Elementary School.

Attended the following universities and organizations: University of Utah, University of Chicago, Cornell University, Hull House, founded by Jane Addams, and the University of Denver.

SOCIAL WORKER, LEGISLATOR and CHURCH WORKER

She participated in social work and several humanitarian organizations from 1917 to 1942. She served on many public and private boards, including the State Committee of Social Services. It was through her leadership that the Latter Day Saints Church initiated and adopted social work philosophies and procedures.

From 1923-1924, Mrs. Lyman served in the Utah State House of Representatives. As chairman of the Public Welfare Committee of the House she introduced and successfully led the passage of the Federal Sheppard-Towner Act which, "promoted the welfare and hygiene of infancy and maternity." As vice chairman of the Education Committee she promoted a measure which empowered the University of Utah and the Utah State Agricultural faculty members to procure old-age annuities.

Mrs. Lyman served from October 1909 to April 1945 on the general board of the Relief Society of the Church of Jesus Christ of Latter-day Saints. From 1940-1945, she served as general president of the same organization. During that time she worked on the modernization of their record-keeping system, various national women's councils and the *Relief Society Magazine*. She also organized and directed the Social Service Department within the Relief Society. This included its employment bureau, child-placing agency, social work training programs, and extensive health and nurse-training courses.

A LEADER AMONG WOMEN'S LEADERS

Represented the Relief Society at fourteen sessions of the National Council of Women and attended two international congresses of women.

She was honored by election to executive offices in the National Council of Women. She served in various capacities for ten years.

PUBLICATIONS

In Retrospect, 1943. Autobiography of Amy Brown Lyman.

Lighter of Lamps. 1947. Biography of Alice Louise Reynolds.

LIST of SPECIAL HONORS

1924–Election to Pi Gamma Mu, Social Science Honor Society of America, which has the purpose of advancing the scientific study of social problems.

1931–Establishment of Amy Brown Lyman

Relief Society Loan and Scholarship Fund by the Relief Society.

1937–Honored by Brigham Young University which bestowed its "Distinguished Alumnus Award, presented as an expression of esteem for meritorious achievement which has brought honor and distinction to her Alma Mater and inspiration to her alumni."

Elected an honorary member of the American Association of Mental Deficiency.

1943–Elected by Salt Lake City Council of Women to its Hall of Fame.

1954–Received Honorary Life Membership Award by the Utah State Conference of Social Work for outstanding contributions in the field of social work.

Listed in *Who's Who in America*.

Listed in *Who's Who Among American Women*.

She died December 5, 1959, in Salt Lake City.

OLIVE WOOLEY BURT
Salt Lake City   Born 1894

Olive W. Burt was born May 26, 1894 in Ann Arbor, Michigan, the daughter of Jed Foss Wooley, Sr. and Agnes Forsyth Wooley. Three years later, the family returned to Salt Lake City, where Mrs. Burt has since lived. In 1922 she married Clinton R. Burt, and had three children; Eda Forsyth (Mrs. Winton R.) Boyd; Beverly Anne (Mrs. Burt E.) Nichols, and Clinton Robin. She has four grandchildren.

Mrs. Burt has been teacher, newspaper woman, world traveler and author. She taught in elementary and high schools in Utah, Wyoming and Pennsylvania; college courses at University of Utah; adult classes for Brigham Young University. For eighteen years she was on the Salt Lake Tribune, and for ten years on the Deseret News. Her work included writing, editing and conducting various youth activities. She originated The Tribune School News and Views column, and organized its Knighthood of Youth in which at one time sixteen thousand children were active.

Mrs. Burt has sold one adult and more than fifty children's books. Also, for adults: ten plays, 49 stories, 5 serials, 335 articles, 121 poems; for children: 19 plays, 15 short stories, 9 serials, 73 articles, 157 poems. More than a million copies of her books have been sold world-wide; they

have been translated into German, Marathi, Italian, Japanese, Korean, Thai, Burmese, Dutch, Arabic and Braille.

Mrs. Burt appears in Women's Who's Who in America, Who's Who in the West, Contemporary Authors, Foremost Women in Communications, as well as all other notable collections. She received the Boys' Clubs of America Award, 1955; Mystery Writers of America *Edgar*, 1959; National Federation of Press Women "Woman of Achievement" Award, 1964; Sigma Delta Chi "Service to Journalism" Award, 1965; Delta Kappa Gamma "Service to Education" Award, 1967; "Olive Burt Day", Indianapolis, 1963; made "Fellow", Utah Historical Society; Utah Folklore Society; Utah Poetry Society; Honorary Member League of Utah Writers, 1970—life member.

Mrs. Burt is also a member of National League of Am. Pen Women, National Federation of Press Women, Mystery Writers of America; Western Writers of America, Utah Press Women, Utah Historical Society, Utah Folklore Society, Utah Poetry Society.

BELLE SMITH SPAFFORD
Salt Lake City   Born 1895

Belle (Marion Isabell) Smith Spafford, is richly endowed with driving executive and leadership abilities, with intelligence, wisdom, keen insight, sound judgment, a quick wit, and a deep and abiding faith.

She was born in Salt Lake City, October 8, 1895, the seventh child of John G. and Hester Sims Smith. Following Normal School, she continued her education at the Brigham Young University where she later became a special instructor in remedial work for retarded children. In 1921 she married Willis Earl Spafford and bore him two children, a son and a daughter.

Mrs. Spafford was called to the General Board of Relief Society of the Latter Day Saints Church, in 1935, and for seven years served as editor of "The Relief Society Magazine." She was chosen Second Counselor by Amy Brown Lyman, in 1942 and on April 6, 1945, she was called to be General President where she served for thirty years. Under her direction the Relief Society Building was built, a long cherished dream of women of the Latter Day Saints church to have a building of their own.

Recognition and honors have come to Mrs. Spafford for her outstanding service to her

Church and the Nation. The Brigham Young University awarded her the Alumni Distinguished Service Award in 1951, and in 1956, an honorary Doctor of Humanities degree. In 1959, she was given a Citation of Appreciation by the Crusade for Freedom. She served on the 1961 White House Conference on Aging, and for many years has served on the Board and held executive positions on the National Association for Practical Nurse Education and Service. She continued to hold office in the National Council of Women of the United States and the American Mothers, Inc.

She is the author of several excellent books about women's role. She is in great demand as a lecturer and advisor.

REVA BECK BOSONE
American Fork   **Born 1895**

Reva Beck Bosone spent forty years in public office in the Postal Service, in Congress, as a judge, and as a teacher in Utah. She was appointed a judicial officer of the U.S. Postal Office Department in 1961. She was Utah's first woman Congresswoman and she was re-elected for a second term in 1948.

Mrs. Bosone served as a state legislator before becoming a judge. She was a jurist in Utah courts and on Capitol Hill. For twelve years, from 1936-1949 she was a Salt Lake City Court judge and helped rehabilitate alcoholics.

Mrs. Bosone was the first woman judge in the State of Utah and she served brilliantly.

Mrs. Eleanor Roosevelt, a friend of Mrs. Bosone, spoke of Mrs. Bosone as refreshingly outspoken.

Mrs. Bosone was a native of American Fork and she taught in High School in Ogden and at the University of Utah.

After her forty years of government service, Mrs. Bosone retired to live with her daughter, Mrs. Arthur Couch, and has lived in northern Virginia and in Kansas City, Kansas.

A forthright jurist, capable and brilliant, Mrs. Bosone is greatly respected in the State of Utah. In 1974, Mrs. Bosone was the speaker at Commencement at Westminster College. She advised the graduates, "Do right and fear not." That seemed to be her own philosophical guide.

Reva Beck was born April 2, 1895 in American Fork, Utah, to Christian Mathias Beck and Zelpha Ann Chipman (Beck). At 80 years of age she now lives quietly with her daughter in Lawrence, Kansas. Her husband Joseph Bosone died in 1973.

DR. VIRGINIA CUTLER
Park City   **Born 1905**

Dr. Virginia Cutler is just concluding her service in a nationwide Major Appliance Consumer Action Panel which she has directed since its inception in April, 1970. This appointment is the latest milestone in a near half-century career during which she has gained worldwide recognition in the field of family economics and housing.

She was born in Park City, Utah, December 17, 1905 to Robert and Mary Jensen Farrer. She was married to the late Ralph Garr Cutler, is the mother of two sons, Robert, a research analyst, deceased and Ralph Garr, plastic surgeon, and she has eight grandchildren.

Dr. Cutler received her BS degree from the University of Utah in 1926 and also studied at Stanford University where she obtained an MA degree in 1937, at Vassar College, at the University of Pennsylvania's Wharton School, and at Cornell University, where she received her Ph.D. degree in 1946.

She began her teaching career in high schools in Utah in 1926 and taught in California schools from 1936 to 1938 before taking a position as Colusa (Calif.) home demonstration agent for the University of California. She held this post until 1944.

From 1946 to 1954 Dr. Cutler served as professor and head of the home economics department at the University of Utah, leaving to become a technician in home economics education for the U.S. International Cooperation Administration. In this assignment she served two years in the field of home economics teacher training in Bangkok, Thailand, and five years in Jakarta, Indonesia.

In 1961 Dr. Cutler accepted the position of dean of the College of Family Living at Brigham Young University.

Recipient of a Fulbright professorship award in 1966, she took a three-year leave of absence to establish a department of home science at the University of Ghana in West Africa. She served as professor and head of the department. On her return to the United States she became Brigham Young University's first distinguished professor, and served as head of the Family Economics and Home Management Department for two years.

Dr. Cutler is a life member of the American Home Economics Association and of the American Association of University Women. She was the AAUW Woman of the Year for Utah in 1966 and State Mother of the Year and National Merit Mother in 1972. She was a delegate to the World Forum of Women in Brussels and the recipient of Brigham Young's Distinguished Service Award, both in 1962. She has also received distinguished service awards from the University of Utah and Cornell University. She is a member of numerous professional, honorary and alumnae organizations, including Sigma Xi, Phi Kappa Phi, and Omicron Nu.

Her most recent distinctions were: (1) being chosen by students of Brigham Young University for the outstanding Womanhood Award in 1974 and (2) being invited to serve on the President's White House Council for Consumer Affairs 1972-74, and (3) receiving three national awards on behalf of the Major Appliance Consumer Action Panel.

IVY BAKER PRIEST
Kimberly   Born 1905

Ivy Baker was born September 7, 1905, in Kimberly, Utah, to O.D. and Clara Fernley Baker. She was the oldest of seven children. The family moved to Bingham, Utah, shortly after her birth.

Mrs. Priest took extension courses from the University of Utah following high school. She had to leave college in her freshman year to support the family when her father became ill.

Mrs. Priest worked for the telephone company, various department stores and also taught evening classes in American history and citizenship. She was married to Roy F. Priest, a wholesale furniture salesman, in 1935. Her husband died in 1959. In 1961 she married Sidney Stevens, a Beverly Hills real estate man; he died in 1972. She had her name legally changed to Priest when she ran for California treasurer in 1966.

Mrs. Ivy Baker Priest served as United States Treasurer during the Eisenhower administration. She was an active Republican all her life, being so encouraged by her mother. She served many positions in the party and was a leader in the movement that brought about the first minimum wage law for women of Utah. She was the second woman U.S. treasurer in the nation's history. She served from 1953 to 1960 and her signature appeared on $62.8 billion in paper currency.

She was elected California's first woman treasurer in 1965. She served with the Ronald Reagan administration until 1974 when she declined to run for a third term because of ill health.

She considered among her greatest accomplishments the establishment of the California Treasurer's Office as the sole salesman of California bonds. She reported that the Pooled Money Investment Board she headed earned the state $350 million.

In 1952 she was assistant to the Chairman of the Republican National Committee. In 1950 she ran unsuccessfully for Congress. She was defeated by another woman, the Democratic incumbent, Representative Reva Beck Bosone.

Mrs. Priest was named one of 20 most outstanding women of this century by the Women's Newspaper Editors and Publishers Association and was former director of the National Safety Council. She took a great interest in helping handicapped children. She was the National Chairman of the 1957 Easter Seals

Campaign. She worked extensively in the Red Cross.

Mrs. Priest died June 23, 1975 in Santa Monica, California of cancer. She was 69. Her only son, Roy Baker Priest, was killed in 1971 at the age of 28 in a boating accident. She was survived by two daughters, Patricia Priest Jensen of Tarzana, California, and Nancy A. Valenzuela of Long Beach, California, four grandchildren and six brothers and sisters.

Vermont

Vermont

Nickname: Green Mountain State

State Flower: Red Clover

State Tree: Sugar Maple

State Bird: Hermit thrush

Photos

1. Gathering Sap
2. Granite Quarries, Granitville
3. Nat'l Life Ins. Co. of Vermont, Montpelier
4. Coolidge Birthplace, Plymouth
5. Stone Village
6. Ski Slopes Mt. Mansfield
7. Monument to the Battle of Bennington

Committee Members

Chairman—Mrs. Charlotte L. Gage, Montpelier
Mrs. Dorothy Shea, Honorary Chairman, Former Senator
Mrs. Marian Campbell, Montpelier
Mrs. Georgiana Bottamini, Montpelier
Mrs. Margaret Holt, Montpelier
Mrs. Stella Gage, Montpelier
Leonard Cetrangelo—artist

Writers

Charlotte L. Gage
Stella C. Gage
Margaret Holt
Dorothy M. Lewis
Allie P. Lourie
Margaret Nye

Vermont

ANN STORY

Born 1742

Scattered across the United States live many descendents of Ann and Amos Story—a pioneer family of Vermont. As did so many in the year 1774, they decided to push inland seeking a place of freedom in which to live.

Leaving his wife and four of the children in Connecticut, Amos and the oldest son, Solomon, aged 13, set off to establish a new homestead. He chose an area near Salisbury, Vermont where that first winter they completed a sturdy log house. When spring arrived, they began to clear a field to be planted in wheat and other necessary foods.

Sudden disaster came when a huge Vermont sugar maple fell the wrong way killing Amos instantly. Traveling miles to the nearest habitation, where Middlebury now stands, the boy enlisted the aid of Mr. Benjamin Stanley and his two sons who carried the body back to their home for decent burial. Only then did Solomon set out to carry the sad news to his mother in Connecticut who was anxiously awaiting their return.

Though grief stricken over her husband's death, she was determined to fulfill the plans and dreams they had shared for a new home in the hills and forests of Vermont. So, disposing of much of their household goods, this thirty-three year old mother was able to purchase a pack horse and head north with her three sons, Solomon, Samuel and Ephraim and daughters Hannah and Susanna.

Clearing land for needed crops, chopping wood for the fire, hunting game—the many chores of a pioneer—were capably handled by this mother and her youngsters. However, Ann's purpose was more than mere survival in the new home. Freedom, independence and self-government were the goals she desired for the children and the country, and she was prepared to defend these ideals. This devotion became well known to her fellow compatriots. When other isolated families learned that the British had enlisted the help of Indians to raid these scattered settlements, they fled to safety in South-

ern Vermont. Ann had become a respected advisor to the Green Mountain Boys and assured them she would not abandon her home and would continue to support their activities. This determination cost them their house.

Warned by the children, who kept constant watch, that an Indian War Party was approaching, Ann and her brood loaded a canoe with needed household goods and food. The Otter Creek was at flood stage so they could cross the creek and float among the dense woods completely hidden. From this vantage point they watched the burning of their home.

Undaunted by this new disaster, they set to work replacing the log cabin their father had built with one made of poles—all that they were able to handle. Assured of a careful sentry system by day, it was imperative to find a safe place at night. Ingeniously, they fashioned a cave under large tree roots along the creek edge which the canoe could glide into and leave no trace.

And so, this outpost became a valuable communications center for the back woodsmen intent on preserving their independence. A monument to the courage and perserverance of this woman stands on the site of the original cabin. It reads:

ANN STORY
IN GRATEFUL MEMORY OF HER
SERVICE IN THE STRUGGLE OF THE
GREEN MOUNTAIN BOYS
FOR INDEPENDENCE

EMMA HART WILLARD

Born 1787

The year was 1819 and the document "An address to the Public; Particularly to the Members of the Legislature of New York, Proposing a Plan for Improving Female Education." Warm approval was given by John Adams, James Monroe, and Thomas Jefferson to the author, a pioneer in equal education for women, Emma Hart Willard.

The daughter of Samuel and Lydia (Hinsdale) Hart, she was the sixteenth of her father's seventeen children. His liberal views influenced her disregard of the accepted view that a girl should train herself for a life of intellectual inferiority. At age twelve, she was teaching herself geometry, an unheard of activity. Taking advantage of the educational opportunities in various academies, she had gained enough experience by the age of twenty to be appointed preceptress of a female academy in Middlebury, Vermont—fertile ground for the young educationalist.

Middlebury College was founded in 1800, and at the same time the townspeople provided for girls by starting one of the first schools in the country built especially for girls—this was the institution Emma Hart was asked to direct in 1807.

A gentleman, Dr. John Willard, who served as U.S. Marshal (1801-1811) supported these liberal ideas and shared Emma's ambitions, so they joined forces by marrying on August 10, 1809.

Their only son, John Hart Willard, was born in 1810.

Ill fortune in the nature of financial reverses for her husband brought Emma the opportunity which led to her success as an educator, for in 1814 she opened a school in her home—"The Middlebury Female Seminary." Denied admittance to classes or exams at Middlebury College, she pursued her interest in the "non-ornamental" subjects, teaching them to herself so she could pass on such knowledge to her students.

Encouraged by her success in Middlebury, she recognized a greater opportunity was available in New York State, which led to the historic proposal made to that legislature. Though it failed she still moved to Waterford, N.Y., there opening an academy. When Troy, N.Y. raised taxation for the support of female academies, this lady moved there to open a school in 1821. Before the first Normal School was founded in the U.S., her seminary had turned out 200 teachers.

Emma Willard died at Troy in 1870 in her 84th year. The Troy Female Seminary was in 1895 renamed the Emma Willard School.

CLARINA HOWARD NICHOLS

Born 1810

Bloomers and knitting needles represent symbolically the life and personality of one woman who ardently and vocally supported the nineteenth century woman's rights movement in Vermont and across the continent. Clarina Howard Nichols and her daughter Birsha often appeared clad in the knee length skirt and turkish pantaloons adopted by the suffragettes, and when traveling or sitting quietly in a meeting, hands knitting busily, Clarina was feminine, but rebellious over the unwarranted restrictions placed upon her sex.

Surrounded by a family actively engaged in the growth of Townshend, Vermont, it is little wonder that youthful Clarina was given all the education available including the district school and a private school where the teacher was an Amerst graduate. Grandfather Levi Hayward (original name was later changed to Howard) emigrated from Mendon, Massassachusetts in 1775 settling in Townshend. Here Clarina was born, daughter of Chapin and Birsha (Smith) Howard on January 25, 1810.

Two years after her graduation from school Clarina married John Carpenter in 1830. The young couple moved to Herkimer, New York. While there three children were born, daughter Birsha C. and two sons named Chapin Howard and Aurelious O. In addition the busy mother also founded a Young Ladies Seminary. For unknown reasons she returned to Townshend in 1839.

This marked the beginning of her life-long dedication to the struggle for women's rights as in 1840 she began writing for the "Windham County Democrat" published in Brattleboro. Her views were shared by the paper's publisher so it is not surprising that, following a divorce from Mr. Carpenter, she married George W. Nichols March 6, 1843. Their only son, George, was born in 1844.

As her husband suffered poor health, she assumed greater responsbilities at the newspaper. Her management and introduction of new features greatly increased circulation, but her editorials and articles plunged her into full-scale participation in the woman's rights movement. Following one such series, the support of legislators enabled passage of measures in 1847 granting married women the right to inherit, own and bequeath property, followed in 1849 by five by-laws allowing women to hold joint property deeds with their husbands and giving wives the right to insure their spouse's lives.

Though her greatest interest lay in the legal disabilities of women, she became involved in the political rights arena when she appeared before the Vermont legislature to urge passage of a measure which would allow women to vote in district school meetings. The measure failed, but Clarina had achieved a milestone for she was the first woman privileged to address the Vermont legislature.

Asked to speak at many meetings she was continually traveling to Massachusetts, New Hampshire, New York and Pennsylvania, always a serene figure busily knitting. But Mrs. Nichols felt that the West might provide more fertile ground for her crusade as it seemed more difficult to repeal unjust laws in older states than to assure just laws in the younger ones. In her private life, she also hoped a change in climate might improve her husband's health and open up new vistas for her children, so in the spring of 1855 the family journeyed westward, Ottawa, Kansas the destination. Mr. Nichols lived only a

few months dying in August of that year.

Once again Clarina pressed her campaign for women's rights, an active lobbyist at the Kansas constitutional convention in 1859, she was the only woman to attend given a chair next to the Chaplain, her knitting ever present. The efforts were rewarded for, included in the Wyandotte constitution were equal education rights for women in state schools, voting privileges for women in all local school matters and equal rights of mothers to custody of their children.

Before she retired in 1871 to the home of her son George in California, Mrs. Nichols worked with Suasn B. Anthony in the unsuccessful attempt to pass woman suffrage in Kansas in 1867.

In her 75th year Clarina Howard Nichols died in Potter Valley, California where she had continued writing until ill health stilled her crusade for woman's place in the sun.

JULIA C. DORR

Born 1825

A warm, loving and moral woman and mother, Julia C. Dorr was one of the most well known poets of her time, ranking high in the regard of her contemporaries. Classed with the Concord group of artists, she formed lasting friendships with many renown poets of the time including Emerson, Longfellow and Whittier.

Julia Dorr was not Vermont born, but is thought of as a Vermonter. Though born in Charleston, South Carolina in February 1825, the daughter of William Young Ripley and Zulma Caroline Thomas, she spent a good share of her childhood in Middlebury, Vermont where her father farmed, and all but ten years of her married life in Rutland where her father had been a pioneer in the marble industry and her husband, Seneca M. Dorr, was a prominent state legislator. She and her husband and their five children founded their home, "the Maples" on the banks of the Otter Creek in Rutland. Here Mrs. Dorr herself helped to plant and to tend the lovely gardens of flowers and trees from which the house received its name.

Though she was a famous poet, Mrs. Dorr was not a woman who allowed her creative work to keep her from her family. She was wife and mother first, highly aware of the needs of her

husband and children, and her work desk was always accessible to them. Her works, in fact, had never been published up to the time of her marriage. Then her husband, an understanding and encouraging man, brought her first novel to New York in search of a publisher and also arranged for publication of her poems. By all accounts, her work improved steadily as her marriage flourished.

She was acitve not only in the world of letters—she gave much of her time to community interests. Among her most notable achievements must be listed the founding of the Rutland Free Library, one of the first of its kind in Vermont. She was for 33 years the president of the "Fortnightly," the literary society of her church. She was also active in the movement for women's interests.

Poetry was Mrs. Dorr's favorite and most famous vehicle and her sonnets the most acclaimed of her works. Her poems are of life's beauty and of her own love of life. She possessed a spontaneity that made everyone comfortable with her. She was gifted with a creative well-balanced mind and a feeling heart. These God-given gifts are evident in all her writings.

Julia Dorr's poems speak often of Vermont, its outstanding beauty and history. Her poems of the "Vermont Volunteer" eloquently display the sentiments of Vermont's men and women about their war volunteers and those lost in the

war. The State would often request her to commemorate any special event. Her ode "Vermont" was especially written for the centennial celebration at Bennington in 1877. It is perfectly fitting, then, that still 100 years later during the celebration of America's bicentennial, that she be honored as one of Vermont's most beloved poets and mothers.

MYRA COLBY BRADWELL

Born 1831

Among the many losses in the Chicago fire of 1871 were records of the "Chicago Legal News". Only the subscription book was saved by Bessie, the thirteen year old daughter of Myra Colby Bradwell, the publication's editorial publisher. Three days later, on schedule, from Milwaukee, Wisconsin, Mrs. Bradwell printed the "Chicago Legal News" with an appeal to lawyers to help in replacing the destroyed libraries of the Chicago lawyers, among them her husband's probate library, one of the West's most complete.

This forceful and energetic mother was born in quiet Manchester, Vermont on February 12, 1831, the daughter of early Boston Settlers, Eben and Abigail Hurd (Willey) Colby. The family moved westward, first to Portage, New York and later to Elgin, Illinois where Myra completed her education at the Ladies' Seminary. When James Bolesworth Bradwell proposed, the Colbys were not happy, but permitted the marriage of their daughter on May 18, 1852. Their objections were mainly concerned with the financial insecurity of their new son-in-law who was only an aspiring law student.

Establishing their home in Memphis, Tennessee, they soon opened a private school. James continued his law studies and Myra began studying law under her husband's tutelage. Shortly after their first child, Myra, was born in 1854, the family moved to Chicago and her husband was, in 1855, admitted to the bar. Six years later he was elected county judge of Cook County and in the years that followed became an important force in Illinois law and politics.

Meanwhile their daughter Myra had died in 1861 but three other children had been born— Thomas (1856), Bessie (1858) and James (1862), who died two years later. Bessie was the heroine who saved the precious subscription list. Both surviving children became lawyers. Bessie, among other distinctions, was the pioneering chairwoman of the American Association of University Women's Committee for graduate fellowships.

In 1868, Mrs. Bradwell began her long career as the publisher of the "Chicago Legal News". Simultaneously, the husband and wife team started a printing, binding and publishing firm "The Chicago Legal News Company". In her editorial columns, Myra shaped much of the opinions of the legal profession in the Midwest for 25 years. Active in the Illinois suffrage movement, she influenced passage of laws that involved the right of married women to their own earnings and widows to an interest in their husbands estate in all instances.

In 1890 at the age of 59, she made her second application for admission to the bar, having been denied entrance in 1869 by the State Supreme Court on the grounds that she was a woman. Two years later she was admitted to practice before the supreme Court of the United States.

Successful in lobbying for Chicago as the site for the World's Columbian Exposition, she lived to see it become a reality, but died the following winter at sixty-two. The Illinois State Bar Association wrote in tribute to Myra Bradwell: "No more powerful and convincing argument in favor of the admission of women to a participation in the administration of government was ever made than can be found in her character, conduct and achievements."

CARRIE BURNHAM KILGORE
Born 1838

In 1908 the first balloon ascension of the Philadelphia Aeronautical Recreation Society carried one woman passenger, Mrs. Carrie Burnham Kilgore, aged 70. In 1909, Mrs. Kilgore died after an eventful career as a crusader and mother.

Carrie Burnham was born in 1838, third child of James and Eliza Burnham in the quiet community of Craftsbury, Vermont. Losing her mother when she was three and her father at twelve, Carrie was left in the custody of guardians who thought education for girls as non-essential. None-the-less, at age fifteen she began teaching school. With various earnings she continued her education at Craftsbury Academy and Newbury, Vt. Seminary. However, over work and poor health brought on an attack of typhoid fever. When she recovered, she went to

live with an older sister in Wisconsin and continued her teaching career there.

As she was particularly interested in physiology, she came in 1863 to New York City to enter in the first class of women admitted to the Bellevue Hospital Clinics Hygeio-Therapeutic College. Becoming increasingly aware of inequities under which women lived, she began in 1865 to read law informally with Damon Young Kilgore whom she later married February 22, 1876. They had two daughters, Carrie born in 1877 and Fanny born in 1880. Though devoted to her family, she continued her struggle to obtain the right to practice law. After ten years of constant battle, she was admitted in 1881 to the University of Pennsylvania Law School and when she graduated in 1883, she was the first woman to attain this honor.

Mrs. Kilgore's career in law progressed from admittance to the Orphan's Court in Philadelphia (1883) to the State Supreme Court (1885) to the Supreme Court of the United States in 1890. When her husband died in 1888 she took over his practice which comfortably supported herself and her daughters. Upon her death in 1909, Carrie Burnham Kilgore was laid to rest in the peaceful cemetary at Craftsbury, Vermont.

MILDRED MARIE LUCAS AUSTIN
Born 1874

Born May 16, 1874, in Burlington, Vermont Mildred Marie Lucas Austin was the daughter of Mr. and Mrs. Fenton Smith Lucas. Her family moved to St. Albans, Vermont, and it was there that she met Warren R. Austin, a student at the University of Vermont, who she married. He was later elected United States Senator and subsequently became the first U.S. Ambassador to the United Nations.

Mrs. Austin became interested in Girl Scouts and worked with them for years. As a National Advisory Committee member, she spent many hours as hostess entertaining visiting foreign Girl Guides and Ambassadors at the Girl Scout "Little House" in Washington. When she and her husband went to New York while he served at the United Nations, Mrs. Austin continued her Scout activities. After her return to Burlington she entertained National Girl Scout visitors, and maintained a special interest in the Vermont Girl Scout camping program.

Her life was filled with people of the world. It

was her duty to sit next to the Russian André Gromyko in their days at the United Nations. Traveling abroad every year she dined often at the Paris home of the Duke and Duchess of Windsor. The Austins were good friends of President and Mrs. Herbert Hoover. Occasionally, Mrs. Austin and Mrs. Hoover spent afternoons knitting together.

In Washington, Mrs. Austin was a member of the Senate Ladies Club, the Congressional Club, Washington Chapter of the American Red Cross and A.W.U.S.

During their offical life at the United Nations, she lived in the Waldorf Astoria in New York City. When entertaining in the Waldorf, she frequently used geraniums for decoration instead of lavish floral arrangements. They made a big hit with the guests who were used to the more pretentious bouquets.

While in New York City Mrs. Austin was a member of the Advisory Council and Board of Managers of the New York Botanical Gardens, the Advisory Council of the Girl Scouts of America, the Public Libary Association, the New York Committee for Foreign Members of the National Colonial Dames, the Republican Club and Colony Club.

On her return to Burlington, Mrs. Austin joined the Garden Club, served on the Lake Champlain Committee, belonged to the Historical Society and the Colonial Dames and was an honorary member of the Klifa Club and attended the First Congregational Church.

Her husband died December 25, 1963. Mrs. Austin lived to be 98 years of age. She had two sons Warren R. Austin Jr. and Colonel Edward Austin both of Burlington, six grandchildren and eighteen great grandchildren.

FLORENCE RICHARDSON WALLACE

Born 1875

The day came when the last of the seven children was graduated from college, and the mission was accomplished. The children of James Wallace, farmer and churchman, who never could go to college, had all made it. It was the great labor and steadfast devotion of his wife, Florence Richardson Wallace, which made the dream come true, for he had died in the flu epidemic of 1918 when the oldest child was only 15.

Florence Richardson was born on a hill farm in East Washington, Vermont, youngest child of

Robert and Rosetta Dexter Richardson, in 1875. Her formal education was completed with one year at Concord, N.H. High School. When she was twenty-one she went to work on the Wallace farm on Blush Hill in Waterbury, Vermont. Soon she married the young farmer there, and accepted the role of farmer's wife and daughter-in-law in residence.

Some seven years later their first child was born and in the next seven years she had six other children. The rearing of them and the care of her husband's father and mother through their final years were tasks she shared with him. When he died the purpose and pattern of their family life was well established— that included faith in God and loyalty to the Church, zeal for an eduation, and a high regard for life on a farm.

Using her husband's life insurance to pay off the mortgage on the farm, Florence Wallace accepted the task of running it as the way of life for her family, conducting family worship as her husband had every morning. Somehow the endless labors were accomplished and the difficulties surmounted. As an example, for years they planted an extra field of sweet corn which when sold to the local cannery assured payment of taxes.

One or two of the boys with their mother ran the farm while the others went to high school and later to college. Her large farm kitchen was a bakery, cannery, laundry and chapel. She made nearly all of her children's clothes by the light of a kerosene lamp working far into the night. The same kitchen was a study hall and a social room where everyone was always welcome.

When she turned over the farm to her son Keith she chose not to live with any of her children, but served as a housekeeper for farm families in Connecticut and Ohio. She visited her children and grandchildren scattered as they were in a half dozen states. Her death came in the home of one of her sons at the age of seventy.

Her children entered many fields: Leilia is a minister's wife; Robert, crippled by polio since his early twenties, is a successful office manager; William is a lifelong pastor of the Methodist Church; George, a leader in the environmental movement, has been a Professor of Ornithology at Michigan State University; Keith, while running the farm, also has served as President of the Vermont Farm Bureau; Avelyn is a postal worker in New York State; Alice is Professor of Bible at Texas Wesleyan College.

"Strength and dignity are her garments. Her children rise up and call her blessed." Prov. 31

GRACE GOODHUE COOLIDGE
Born 1879

Of the First Ladies to preside in the White House, Grace Coolidge was one of the most beloved for her diplomacy, her quiet sense of humor, her warm response to people everywhere.

Born in Burlington, Vermont on January 3, 1879, Grace was the only child of Captain Andrew Goodhue, a mechanical engineer, and Lemire Barrett Goodhue. She graduated from Burlington High School and the University of Vermont. She was a strong force in her class and one of the organizers of the Vermont Chapter of Pi Beta Phi Sorority. After college, in the fall of 1902, she enrolled in the Institute Training School of the Clarke Institute for the Deaf in Northampton, Massachusetts. She taught first in the primary and then in the intermediate school. As a result, the school became one of her major causes and she did much in her later years to raise funds for the school and extend the scope of work for the deaf in general.

In the fall of 1905 she was married in the family home in Burlington, to Calvin Coolidge, a young lawyer from Northampton, Massachusetts. The couple began married life together in Northampton and it was here that their two sons, John and Calvin, were born. She believed that she was marrying a country lawyer. She

and Calvin Coolidge were exact opposites, yet she never underestimated the depth and continuity of his devotion, and she was a vital part of his life, his happiness and his success.

Grace Coolidge was part of his rise from Mayor of Northampton to State Senator, from Lieutenant Governor of Massachusetts to Governor, from the Vice-Presidency of the United States on to the Presidency upon the death of Warren Harding. Her tact and intuition, her own disciplined approach to life, her radiance of spirit that was catching made her popular wherever they went.

The death of their second son, Calvin, while they were in the White House, was a great tragedy. He was a student at Mercersbury Academy. In 1934 the students dedicated their year book to Grace Coolidge with the following inscription: "The boys of the Mercersburg Academy most respectfully dedicate the annual book of the school to Grace Coolidge—a Mercersburg mother and Regent, a graduate of the University of Vermont, recipient of the highest honoary degrees in American academic life, trusted counsellor of many noble enterprises, in simple, private life or exalted public station always the same genuine gentle, gracious spirit. 'She openth her mouth with wisdom and in her tongue is the law of kindness'."

Coolidge served the better part of two terms in the White House. They then returned to Northampton where he died on January 5, 1933. She continued her many humanitarian interests, such as working for the deaf, helping to raise funds to bring refugee children from Germany to this country during the war and being active in Red Cross work.

Her son John, an industrialist, his wife and two daughters were one of the great joys of her life. She died in Northampton on July 8, 1957 at the age of 78. Her son continues her interest in her husband's birthplace in Plymouth where the homestead and its contents, at her request, were turned over to the State of Vermont shortly after her death. It is now under the jurisdiction of the Vermont Historic Sites Commission and run as the Coolidge Memorial Center.

DOROTHY CANFIELD FISHER
Born 1879

There could be no greater evidence of the profound influence of early environment and parental example than that in the life of Vermont's beloved citizen, Dorothy Canfield Fisher. Though born in Kansas, educated in the Midwest, it was her deep-seated roots in the Green Mountain State that bought her to the little town of Arlington, near the ancestral home of Grandfather Canfield, to witness her extraordinary career as author, educator, and humanitarian. Her father, James Canfield, a noted educator, had a deep concern for his daughter's education. Her mother, Flavia, though born in Wisconsin, had New England forebears. Her interests, outside of household duties, lay in the field of art and civic affairs. Such background brought outstanding leaders to the Canfield home impressing Dolly, as she was then called, with the world outside. Being musically inclined, she studied violin and while in Ohio, played with string quartets.

In the course of these early years, her father went abroad occasionally. When Dolly graduated from Ohio State, it was quite natural that she too should have the stimulus of further education in such institutions as the University of Paris, a summer at the British Museum in London, and finally in Hanover to study German. Back in New York after two years she took her Doctor's Degree in Philology at Columbia and with her knowledge of four languages, she was ready to start a teaching career.

About that same time, a football player named Robert Fisher, who had become her ardent admirer, took his degree at Columbia and entered law School. He later abandoned this career in favor of the literary field. On May 9, 1907 John and Dorothy were married and moved to an old house on the Canfield property in Arlington, Vermont with a combined wealth of $7,000!

After a year of adjustments and literary achievements, they took a trip to France. Upon their return, their first child, Sally, was born in 1909. With the publication of her first novel, in serial form, by Everybody's Magazine, Dorothy decided to go to Rome for several winter months, a fortuitous choice, as she was asked to meet and interview Madame Montessori, innovator of a new pedagogical system. This contact was the beginning of decades of writing and teaching.

Dorothy Canfield Fisher

A great joy was added to the family living under the shadow of Redwood Mountain when a son James was born, named for Dorothy's father. Husband John was elected to the State Legislature and so the couple rented a house in Montpelier for the terms. In 1933 their Sally and John Paul Scott were married ultimately providing Dorothy and John with four grandchildren. Jimmy, too, a student at Harvard, had fallen in love, later to be married, but he became a war casualty in the Phillipines, dying there in 1945.

In the years that passed there was a plethora of books—24 novels, non-fiction and Vermont Traditions in 1953—and royalty checks but more significantly numerous degrees and honors. She served on the "Book of the Month Club", lectured, traveled and pioneered her philosophy of life. As they aged together, she remarked to a friend, "The old shell of the body seems to become a little harder to inhabit." During the later years, she suffered increasing deafness and a stroke; John survived a heart attack. But her golden spirit was creative, thoughtful and pioneering to the end. Today two simple marble stones mark the graves of Dorothy and Robert Fisher in the cemetary of St. James Church in Arlington. They died only one year apart.

The Editorial Board of The Book of the Month Club wrote, in part,

"A confirmed Vermonter, she was also a cosmopolitan in both space and time . . . Her death leaves our country poorer. Her life enriched it."

VIRGINIA

Virginia

Nickname: Old Dominion

State Flower: Flowering Dogwood

State Bird: Cardinal

Photos

1. Monticello
2. Pres. Woodrow Wilson's birthplace
3. Scotchtown
4. Confederate Capital
5. John Marshall's Home
6. Original Virginias' capital
7. Stratford Hall
8. Yorkstown Freedom Monument

Committee Members

Chairman—Mrs. H.E. Glave
Mrs. Louis Spilman
Mrs. T. Ray Jarrett
Mrs. Curtis L. Pulliam
Mrs. E.H. Wright, Artist

Virginia

POCAHONTAS

Born 1595

The young Virginia colony, established at Jamestown by the London Company of England, owed much in its early years to the Indian maiden, Pocahontas. Pocahontas was the daughter of the powerful Chief Powhatan, whose tribe was part of the Algonquin Indians.

She first came into prominence in July, 1607, when the leader of the Jamestown colony, Captain John Smith, was captured by Powhatan's warriors. Smith was ordered to be executed by a beating with clubs. At the time of the execution, Pocahontas, a girl of twelve or thirteen, rushed forward, took Smith's head in her arms, and asked that he be spared. As this was a custom of the Indians, the story has considerable merit as to its authenticity.

Pocahontas is credited with saving Smith's life a second time in 1608, when Powhatan invited Smith to be his guest. The warriors were to seize Smith while dining. Pocahontas warned Smith of the plan and he was able to escape.

In 1613, Pocahontas again appeared on the scene of the English colony. She was enticed on board an English ship and taken to Jamestown as a hostage. She was sent to a new inland town of Henrico. Here she was converted to Christianity and took the name of Rebecca. Pocahontas was the first Indian to be converted by the English.

Within the Jamestown colony, tobacco had become an important commodity. John Rolfe, a young planter, was involved in the development of new varieties of tobacco. John Rolfe also became interested in the young maiden, Pocahontas. Governor Dale of Virginia, saw the political value of such a union and gave his consent to the marriage. Chief Powhatan also consented to the union.

Pocahontas and John Rolfe were married in the church at Jamestown on April 15, 1614. The marriage signaled the beginning of almost uninterrupted peace between the Virginia colonists and the Indians.

In 1616, Pocahontas, John Rolfe and their young son, Thomas, sailed to England. They re-

mained there for about ten months. Pocahontas was known as the "Lady Rebecca" and was a sensation in London society. Even though she had been raised in the Virginia wilderness, she conducted herself with poise and dignity. Lady Rebecca was charmed by English life, but left it to return to Virginia. As the ship was leaving England, she became ill, perhaps with smallpox, and died. Pocahontas was buried near St. George's Church, Gravesend, England. Thomas Rolfe came to Virginia as a young man and married a Virginia girl. Many families can trace their origins to this marriage and thus to the Indian girl who was important on both sides of the Atlantic.

Pocahontas left her mark on the history of her time. Her regal, yet unspoiled dignity was an important factor in the relationship between the Indians and the English colonists. Her aid in saving the Virginia colony remains an important part in the development of America.

MARY BALL WASHINGTON
Born 1708

Her famous son, George, was not born in a hovel, as is sometimes reported. It was probably a house that had four rooms on the first floor. Her husband, Augustine Washington, was called Gus.

Mary was the only child of an elderly father and his second wife. His children by his first wife did not approve of his marriage, so he supposedly gave them their portion of his estate before he died. Mary is presumed to have been born at Epping Forest, and grew up midst much wrangling with her half-brothers and sisters, for Mary was quite young at his death.

Her mother died when Mary was twelve. Very little is known about her later girlhood years, but much of the time was spent with a guardian.

Mary was never described as a beauty, being of large angular frame. She did not mature into a graceful adult. Augustine Washington is presumed to have met and married Mary in England while she was visiting one of her step-brothers. She was twenty-three at the time of her marriage, which is a rather advanced age for a single lady in this time. Augustine was a recent widower with two young children to raise and surely must have taken this into consideration. He was seventeen years Mary's senior.

Augustine brought Mary directly to his home near the Potomac River. The house is no longer standing where George was born. Mary had four more children, three sons and a daughter.

After several moves, Gus finally settled at Mount Vernon in Virginia. George was eleven and Mary was thirty-five when her husband died. The responsibility of rearing her growing family and operating a plantation fell upon her shoulders.

She ruled her growing family with authority and commanded respect at all times. It is said that George's determination and demanding of the respect of his men during the Revolutionary War eminated from Mary's characteristics.

Mary was not illiterate and managed the plantation very efficiently.

George almost became a sailor, but at his mother's pleadings and tears he did not go to sea, and learned to become a surveyor, and later a soldier.

Mary had a keen financial sense regarding business and money, and she became quite

grasping in money matters. In fact, she was portrayed as being miserly in her transactions.

As George became more involved in the coming war, he saw less and less of his mother. Although he and his mother did not always see eye to eye, they are said to have been much alike in temperament and ambition.

When the Revolutionary War became more eminent, George persuaded his mother to leave the farm and move into Fredericksburg in a cottage near her daughter.

Mary died at the age of 83, of what has since been determined as cancer.

JANE RANDOLPH JEFFERSON
Born 1720

While Jane Randolph's family can trace their pedigree back into England and Scotland—little can be found out about Jane. It is supposed Jefferson wrote very little about her, as he wrote very little about his wife, because of his reticence in revealing any personal feelings.

Jane was the daughter of Isham Randolph and Jane Rogers. Isham met Jane while in England on mercantile interests. Their first daughter, Jane was born in the London Parish of Shadwell.

Peter Jefferson, not much of an aristrocrat by the Randolph standards, was nevertheless an aggressive and enterprising young man. He courted and married Jane when she was nineteen. Although largely self-educated, he was a competent surveyor and acquired large tracts of land.

After the birth of two daughters Peter moved to a westerly tract of land five miles west of Charlottesville. He named the farm Shadwell, after his wife's birthplace in England. Thomas Jefferson was born there in 1743. Not long after his birth, the family moved to a gracious James River plantation where Peter was guardian of a friend's children and estate after the friend's death. Tom had the advantages of tutoring and more ingratiating surroundings than at Shadwell. During this time Tom's mother had several daughters and one more son, who has been described as a simpleton. Tom's father died in 1757, and Tom and his mother returned to Shadwell.

He married and took his bride to Monticello, who lived only ten years after their marriage. Jane stayed at Shadwell until it burned. It is reported that a neighbor remarked that Jane had tried four times to burn it down, and had finally succeeded. Jane remained on the farm, living in some outbuildings that escaped burning, with her younger children, until her death. She is said to have been very irratic in her later years.

It is not thought that Jefferson had brought her to Monticello until Jane died of a stroke. She is buried in the family cemetary at Monticello.

ELIZABETH BASSETT HARRISON
Born 1730

Again we have a President whose mother's life is an enigma. Elizabeth Bassett was born on a plantation owned by Colonel William Bassett, possibly around 1730. She is said to have married Benjamin Harrison of Berkeley, a neighboring plantation.

It is presumed her girlhood years were in early tide-water elegance, although nothing remains of the home in which she was reared.

After marriage, at sixteen, she gave birth to seven children, William Henry Harrison being the last. Her husband served uninterruptedly in Virginia's House of Burgesses until he went to Philadelphia, where in due course he signed the Declaration of Independence. He was also a mi-

litia Colonel, and Governor of Virginia from 1781 to 1784. Surely, Elizabeth was familiar to being a guest and a hostess in the elegant houses of both Richmond and Williamsburg.

William Henry Harrison was advised to find a profession other than that of a planter, since his elder brother would inherit the planation. He was a student at the University of Pennsylvania until he quit to join the Army and fight the Indians out in the Northwest Territory.

The publicity used about him, when he was running on the Whig Party, as a Presidential candidate, was to portray him as a rough and ready backs-woodsman. He actually had settled in the Ohio Valley and had a Country Estate on the Ohio River.

His mother, who died at sixty-two, never lived to see her son inaugurated. Since Mr. Harrison was sixth-eight at the time of his election, and having stood in a drizzle during the inauguration, he caught pneumonia and died within a month after taking office.

NELLIE CONWAY MADISON
Born 1731

Born Nelly Conway at Port Conway, Virginia, Nelly was the daughter of a tobacco warehouse owner. In later years historians changed her name from Nelly to Eleanor, but she remained Nelly to herself during her ninety-eight years. Possibly the friction between black and white caused the name to be held in low esteem.

The Madisons had come from humble beginnings, but Nelly's father-in-law had much ambition, and started to buy acreage for a plantation at Orange, Virginia. He called his home Montpelier and Nelly's husband eventually had a plantation of over 4000 acres.

Nelly had twelve children and as the family grew they required more spacious quarters than the original wooden house that they were living in in Montpelier. The new dwelling was never more than a comfortable home until Nelly's son remodeled it when he became President.

James was the oldest child. It is presumed that Nelly had the average education that females received in those early days. Certainly she had taught her children to read, for James was sent to study at Princeton. Nelly is portrayed as a busy plantation wife and mother.

References are made of her writing James of some shirts she was fashioning to send to him.

At the age of sixty-eight her husband died and James, with his wife Dolly, became the owners of Montpelier. Dolly and Nelly were great friends and during the years of the Presidency the hordes of guests that visited Montpelier always spoke lovingly of Nelly. An apartment within the mansion was made for her, and she received guests there.

Nelly suffered from chronic malaria, but apparently was able to keep it under control with medication. A year before her death a guest in the house described her as having no pain or sickness, and other than a slight deafness, was able to read and knit. Her face was not as wrinkled as her son's who was twenty years her junior.

ELIZA JONES MONROE

Born 174?

The date of Eliza Jones Monroe's birth is almost as hazy as to the lack of information as to where she was born. She presumably was raised in Westmoreland County and her ancestors were from Wales. The Jones family was not affluent, for her father was described as an "undertaker in architecture." No more description as to what this might indicate.

As Eliza married into the Monroe family, it is not thought to have been a notable event. Spence Monroe, her husband, was a farmer and a joiner. A word used in place of carpenter.

The most notable Jones ancestor was a brother of Elizas, who was a judge and later a member of Congress. James Monroe, Eliza's son, always wrote more of his uncle than of his mother. Upon the uncle's death he left his estate to be divided among the children of his late sisters, "allowing my nephew James Monroe the first choice."

The farm to which Spence Monroe took Eliza, his bride, is marked in Westmoreland County. The home is no longer standing, and the soil analysis of the property indicates it was of very poor quality for farming.

James Monroe was the eldest of five children. His mother must have taught the fundamentals of an education, for he went to William and Mary at sixteen. Perhaps, between his mother and his uncle, were instilled within him the desire to be educated.

The date of her death is also a mystery.

SARAH STROTHER TAYLOR

Born 1760

Sarah Strother was born of influential parents and her father ran a large plantation west of Fredericksburg. She was educated by tutors imported from Europe for the Strother children, which was most unusual for the times.

At eighteen, Sarah married "Old Zack's" father, who must have taken some time off from the Revolutionary War to court and marry Sarah. She had a total of nine children, Zachary being third in line. His father was Richard Taylor.

After the Revolutionary War, Richard had no inheritance to return to, so he decided to take his growing family to a land grant bonus due him from the war. He scouted into new territory, which soon became Kentucky, and returned to take his gentle wife and family down the Wilderness Trail.

Eventually Sarah Taylor had a gracious and comfortable plantation near Louisville, but in the early years, the going was rough. She must have had plenty of stamina along with her gentleness, for in the beginning she had a log cabin, the same as other pioneering women.

She tried to keep a vestige of civilization along with the hard daily work. She insisted her children all learn to read and she tutored them in all the three Rs.

Sarah Taylor died in 1822 before her son became President of the United States.

MARY ARMISTEAD TYLER

Born 1761

Little is known of Mary Armistead, for all of the family records were destroyed during the Civil War. She was the daughter of a prominent planter and married at the age of sixteen. Her husband was a prominent lawyer and later a judge. He served three successive terms (now an impossibility) as Governor of Virginia. It is felt that Mary had been educated in the true Virginia gentlewoman style of her day. Certainly she entertained in the Governor's mansion.

Her sixth child and the second son, was named after her father, John T. Tyler. He desired more fame than his illustrious father. However, when he ran for office the second term, as President of the United States, he was too ardent a states-righter for the North to admire.

ANNE HILL CARTER LEE

Born 1773

Anne Hill Carter grew up on Shirley Plantation on the James River in Virginia. Her childhood was one of strong family and community ties. She was a Carter, and her family had been forerunners in the growth of Virginia. She was Anne Hill Carter Lee, mother of General Robert E. Lee, and four other children.

In 1793, when she was only nineteen years old, she married one of the heroes of the Revolution, Henry ("Light Horse Harry") Lee, seventeen years her senior. A storybook plantation girl, she was to know quite a different life after her marriage—a life of constant indebtedness, a philandering husband who twice went to debtor's prison, and continual loneliness and uncertainty.

Light Horse Harry was three times Governor of Virginia, served in the state General Assembly, and was elected to one term in the Congress. But he dreamed of easy wealth and was forever speculating in risky land deals. He was away from home months at a time, and Anne was left quite alone to cope with running the neglected Lee Plantation, Stratford, rearing her own five children plus two stepchildren. She was frequently forced to sell furniture, land, and horses to satisfy her husband's debt collectors.

Because she was not accustomed to being alone, she often packed up her family and went to her childhood home for long visits. Her first two children were born at Shirley, and she spent the last seven months of her pregnancy with Robert E. Lee there.

Although she raised the children in love and respect for their father, she was determined from the beginning to teach and instill in them other values and morals, those of the Carter family. The Carters believed that the discharge of one's duties, to the best of one's ability, was one's primary moral obligation. This included duty to one's family, one's church, and one's community.

These things Anne taught children, in addition to their daily academic lessens. She taught them patience, self-control, self-denial, and frugality.

Through it all, she was never too serious or downhearted to laugh, and never too busy to neglect the little things that mean so much to small children.

Anne Carter Lee was the dominant figure in the life of all her children, but we see her dominance particularly in her youngest son, Robert. In 1809, when Robert was only two years old, his father was jailed for thirteen months, because he owed so much money. Then in 1812 Henry Lee was badly maimed in a political riot. The following year he left by himself for the Barbados Islands to recover his health, leaving Anne with five children between the ages of two and fifteen. This was the last time Anne or the children ever saw Henry, for he died in 1818 in South Carolina.

Robert's sense of duty was monumental. All his life *duty* determined his actions: First, duty to his studies at West Point, to the care of his mother during her years of ill health, to his country in the service of the United States Army. Although he did not believe in secession, it was duty to his native state of Virginia which led him to resign from the United States Army and take over the leadership of the Army of Northern Virginia. There· followed his sense of devotion and duty to his soldiers, to Jefferson Davis (even when Lee felt Davis was in error), to his wife and children.

General Robert E. Lee was not born with these qualities. He came into this world with the *potential*, but it was his mother, Anne Carter Lee, who nurtured and developed the potential to a reality. In so doing she gave to this country a great man, a writer, a great military tactician, a great father and husband—a hero in the old-fashioned sense of the word. Here-in lies Anne Hill Carter Lee's greatness.

JESSIE WOODROW WILSON

Born 1826

Although born in Carlisle, England in 1826, Jessie Woodrow's parents migrated to the United States when Jessie was just nine years old. She was one of four children—two girls, Marion and Jessie—and two boys, Woodrow, born in Staunton, Virginia, and then Joseph R.

Five weeks after landing in New York in February, 1836, Jessie's mother died. As the eldest of the two daughters, Jessie no doubt helped with the responsibility of running the household for her father. This may have accounted for the seriousness of her personality.

The family settled in Chillicothe, Ohio, where they resided until 1849. Jessie was a student at the Steubenville Female Academy when she met Joseph R. Wilson, a brilliant young minister, a native of that city, who was teaching there at the Male Academy. They were married June 7, 1849, by her father, the Reverend Thomas Woodrow.

Living for a short time in Chartier, Pennsylvania, the young couple soon moved to Hampden-Sydney, Virginia, where Joseph assumed a post on the faculty of Hampden-Sydney College there. Here it was that two girls were born to them, first Marion and then Annie.

In 1854, Dr. Wilson accepted a call to the First Presbyterian Church in Staunton, Virginia. And here it was that the Reverend and Mrs. Wilson's first son was born, December 28, 1856, a son destined to be the 28th President of the United States. Their second son and their last child, Joseph R. Junior, was born eleven years later.

Woodrow was a delicate child. He was not entered in school until he was nine years old. His mother, Jessie, watched over his every need and desire until his marriage. A dear and close relationship developed between Woodrow and his mother and he later wrote his wife that the

"best in womanhood came to him through his mother's apron strings."

When Woodrow met and subsequently married Ellen Louise Axcon, Woodrow's mother expressed complete happiness and said: "She is exactly the one I would choose for him", and she welcomed "Ellie Lou" with equal love and warmth as that accorded previously only to her beloved family.

Although she enjoyed playing the harpsichord and the guitar, which she did beautifully, nevertheless she remained shy and extremely serious throughout her life. She was most capable of handling her duties as a minister's wife and was a completely devoted mother, giving love, warmth and a sense of security to every member of her family. In fact, she was primarily a homemaker, devoted wife and understanding mother.

Jessie's cookbook shows notations of favorite dishes of each member of her family. She was well educated, sensible and in every way a positive influence on her famous son.

In 1888, shortly after his mother had passed away, Woodrow wrote to his father: "I bless God for my noble, strong and saintly mother."

MAGGIE LENA WALKER

Born 1867

Maggie Lena Draper Walker was born in Richmond, the daughter of a house slave. At the time of her birth, her mother was a cook in the household of a wealthy Richmond spinster.

Mrs. Walker attended school in Richmond and entered Richmond's Armstrong Normal School (high school), graduating at the age of sixteen. After graduation, Maggie became a teacher in the Lancaster Schools. While teaching, she was a part-time student in accounting and salesmanship. She also held a part-time job, working for the Woman's Union, an insurance company. This relationship advanced her interest in the United Order of St. Luke—a mutual self-help organization which she had joined at the age of fourteen. Due to her interest and leadership qualities, she became secretary to a Council of the Order and was a delegate to a national convention.

In 1886, Maggie married Armstead Walker, a man several years her senior. He was associated with her father in the contracting and construc-

tion business in Richmond. As a young wife and mother of two sons, she still was active in the affairs of the United Order of St. Luke.

As she advanced in office, she noted the organization was in dire financial straits. When she was elected Grand Secretary, an office she held until her death, she inaugurated many new ideas to help her people. Feeling the need for greater activity and service for the people of her race, she implemented the founding of a savings bank, chartered and managed by the people of the Order of St. Luke. This opened up employment for black women, who previously were relegated to domestic roles.

Mrs. Walker established a black newspaper for news of her race; she founded a factory to increase employment for black workers; she concurred in the establishment of a department store with merchandise catering to blacks. This was the only failure, to which Maggie Walker commented, "Our race has much to learn, both as salesmen and purchasers."

Her most outstanding success was the establishment of the St. Luke Penny Savings Bank, of which she was made president. She was the first woman president of a bank, and one of the first black bank presidents.

Each member of the Order of St. Luke was urged to buy shares on small monthly payments if necessary, and to establish an account in the bank, even if the account was very small.

In the next decade, Mrs. Walker founded and was president of the Richmond Council of Colored Women; led a drive to raise money for Virginia Independent school for colored girls; raised money for the black TB sanitorium; promoted the establishment of a black community center; for better health care for blacks and served on various boards of civic institutions.

During this period she had several personal tragedies and became a cripple due to a knee injury. Her husband was killed and a son was involved in his death.

The merger, in the 1920's, of two black banks in Richmond changed the name of the merging banks to the Consolidated Bank and Trust Company, and Mrs. Walker became chairman of the board and retained that title until her death in 1934.

The Horatio Alger style in which Mrs. Walker rose from poverty to affluence is a source of inspiration to all young Americans, and is especially an inspiration to young people of minority and ethnic groups.

Washington

Washington

Nickname: Evergreen State

State Flower: Coast rhododendron

State Bird: American Goldfinch

Photos

1. Courtyard of Pacific Science Center
2. Teton Ridge
3. Lower Falls of Yellowstone River
4. Devils tower National Monument
5. Capitol Building in Olympia
6. Big Horn Mountains

Committee Members

Chairman—Mrs. Edna C. Kaslinsey
Ms. Mary Price
Mrs. Thelma Fullner

Writers

Carol Brownfield
Grace Bryhildsen
Tina Morgan
Theda Cline Peterson
Chloe Sutton
Edna Whitney
Sherri Zirker

Washington

MINERVA JANE MAYO CLINE
Born 1847

Mrs. William Cline was one of the first mothers to settle in Sidney, the name of which was changed to Port Orchard in 1893. She was known to everyone as "Aunt Jane", and was so kind and helpful to so many: caring for the sick, assisting in the births of babies, and even helping dress, and prepare the dead for burial. She was always ready to serve.

Minerva Jane Mayo Cline was born in Pike County, Illinois, February 21, 1847, and married William Cline, a civil war soldier, December 24, 1865, when she was 18.

Their children, Robert and John, were born in Illinois. John lived only 3 months. The family moved to Nebraska in 1869, where Rachel and George were born. Then they went to Kansas, where Levi, Mary Ellen, Sarah, and Emma arrived.

The Clines were farmers, and after several years of drought decided to travel west, where it was reported to be thriving. With their seven children, one a tiny baby, and several other families, they set out in covered wagons, following the "Oregon Trail" to Portland, Oregon. Then it was on to Olympia, Washington, where they boarded the steamship "Messenger", which took them to Kitsap County, landing them on the beach, at high tide, at Harper. The cattle and horses were pushed overboard to swim ashore.

With all their belongings, they walked the beach to Colby, fording Curley Creek. Then, in the dark hours of night, they walked several miles to their homestead at Long Lake.

It was January, 1884, when they arrived to join her husband Billie's five brothers, one sister, and their families.

In 1886, they all decided to move to Sidney (Port Orchard) where things were prospering.

Jasper Scott built the first hotel in 1887, but wasn't well, so the Clines purchased, enlarged, and operated it, until it burned in 1892. It was "Aunt Jane" who prepared the meals, the bread and pasteries, and took care of the rooms, all the time caring for her seven children.

In 1900, the Brick Hotel that Judge Yakey owned was not doing well, so, once again, "Aunt Jane" was asked to help this hotel prosper.

The Clines were charter members of the Christian Church, first meeting in their homes, then building the Church, June 1888. Aunt Jane did many things to help the church grow. She made the bread and wine for the weekly communion for many years, taught classes in Sunday School, and worked for the ladies aid.

After her daughter-in-law died, she cared for their three children, and raised them as her own.

Such a woman surely deserved her reputation as a wonderful person and a builder of the community.

MARY JANE ODELL SUTTON
Born 1860

Mary Jane Sutton was born Mary Jane Odell, daughter of Simeon and Rachel Odell, July 7, 1860, in Vernon County, Missouri. She was the second child of twelve eventually born to this couple.

Mary Jane had some recollections of the Civil War, being about five years old when it closed. She could remember when her father came home from service in the Union Army. She could also remember when her grandfather Odell was shot by the "Bushwhackers" and his body left lying in the road. The women had to bury "Grandfather"—as no man dared show his face—it was near the end of the Civil War and tension was strong in Missouri.

Mary Jane also remembered that when her father was away in the Army, her mother hitched up the horses, loaded the family possessions and her two little daughters into the family wagon, and drove north to her parents' home in Ray County. It was no longer safe in Vernon County for those with "Northern Sympathy."

After the Civil War, the Missouri school system was a shambles. One of Mary Jane's great regrets was that she had had such poor opportunity for an education. She had a good mind, and when of "high-school age", she served in a home having a good library. She read the writings of Sir Walter Scott—a truly liberal education. This was typical of her life—to take advantage of her opportunities.

In the spring of 1884, Mary Jane went to Ray County (Missouri) to visit an aunt. There she met *William Sutton*, a native of Ray County, whom she married in September, 1884.

The Suttons' first home—was on the Sutton farm, near Orrick, Ray County, Missouri—where they lived for four years, and their first child, Colleen Chloe, was born.

In the fall of 1887, William and Mary sold out, and in March, 1888, moved to Los Angeles, California, where they lived for about six months. Then, they took passage on the old "S.S. Umatilla" and arrived in Seattle the last of August, 1888.

In November, 1888, they moved again—on the *S.S. Leif Erickson* to the newly-plotted town of Sidney (now Port Orchard), about sixteen miles west of Seattle. Here William and Mary bought an acre of land—on which they built—and where they lived the rest of their lives.

On January 22, 1893, the couple's second child was born, in the midst of the worst "Depression" the country has ever known. He was named "Jesse William Sutton" grew up in Port Orchard, married and is now a grandfather—a credit to his parents and his native city.

During the "Depression" Mr. William Sutton went to Alaska, found work, and saved his family. During his absence, Mary Jane worked at whatever she could find to do, and helped along.

By 1900, the Puget Sound Navy Yard had opened up. William Sutton found employment there. After that, life was eased for the family.

Mary Jane never ceased to work. As long as she lived, she worked to help her children and then her grandchildren.

William Sutton, her husband, died rather suddenly in 1940, and for the next twenty-two years Mary Jane lived with her daughter, Chloe, in the home her husband had provided.

Mary Jane died on her "Wedding Day," September 15, 1962, in her 102nd year of age, and was buried beside the husband of her youth in the Port Orchard Cemetery.

GINA PEDERSEN

The following account, told by Gina Pederson, demonstrates the spirit and character which helped establish the state of Washington.

"About the middle of September, 1893, my brother and I left Seattle for Neah Bay. Here we were to meet Captain Lonsdale and my husband, Captain Sander Pederson, in the sloop Alert that was to take us to Lake Ozette or rather to Sandy Point on the ocean beach.

We stayed at the hotel on the Indian Reservation at Neah Bay for three days because it was very stormy. We tried one day to get out but had to turn back, as it was blowing too hard to get around Cape Flattery. We decided to walk the beach to Ozette River. However, there was no place to stay there so we started for Lake Ozette and came to the Ozette post office where Mr. Palmquist was postmaster at the time. We were very tired after walking all day (about 23 miles) but Mr. Palmquist and his sister made us very comfortable and we stayed there overnight.

The next day we left in a canoe to go to the southwest corner of the lake where our home was to be. During the summer we had a log cabin built but there were no windows or doors in it. The windows were on the sloop Alert so we had to wait until she arrived before putting them in. About half-way between Ozette and Swan lived a family named Bakke, where we stayed a week. By that time the boat was in and my husband and some other men began packing over the trail from Sandy Point in to the lake, about 2 miles. Packing meant carrying things on their backs as there were no horses or roads.

We got our windows and our cook stove in the most necessary things and began house-keeping. The cabin was 14 feet by 18 feet. It was divided into two rooms. One was 12 by 14 feet and the other smaller room was to be a grocery store.

The stock in the store was all packed in from the beach and at the lake was taken in canoes. Capt. Pedersen did most of the packing as Capt. Lonsdale made trips to Seattle to bring in supplies. For about three years we had this store. It was the only one at the lake and only groceries were sold.

In 1894 the Swan post office was established

and I was appointed postmistress and served until 1899. The mail came in once a week from Ozette post office.

We lived for about two years in the one room but built on two more rooms at the end of that time. The lumber for the rooms came from one cedar log which was split into shakes. We had the front door for the house brought in from Seattle and we were very proud of our door. The door of the store was split from a log and most of our furniture was made from the material at hand. No one had anything better so we were all satisfied.

There were quite a few people living at Ozette at this time. Most of them were single men living on their claims. There were also a few families but as there were no roads there was not much travelling.

After we had the post office more people came to Swan for their mail. There was not very much mail but it helped us keep in touch with the outside world.

Our cabin was up about 30 feet from the lake. In the winter the lake rose so high that we all had to build on high land. We bought our first cow after having been there nearly a year. Up to that time we lived on canned milk. We did not raise anything on the land the first year, as it had to be cleared and everything done by hand. The trail between the ocean beach and the lake was made by a few settlers going together and donating their work. After we had lived there for about two years we were able to have a garden and we had plenty of milk, so everything went along well.

Our daughter, Esther, was born at Swan the first year we lived there and was nearly five years old when we left. She very seldom saw any other children, as the people were living so far apart. There were no doctors out there so we were all thankful if we could keep well.

I had had a toothache for a long time when we heard of a man on the ocean beach who had a pair of forceps. We walked to the mining camp at the beach. The dental chair was a nail keg and it was placed close to a creek where we could get water if it was needed. It was not very easy but I got relief from the toothache.

We were away only three weeks, in six years, from the place. I had to go to Seattle to see a doctor. We came home from Seattle on a small sailing schooner, the trip requiring a whole week.

By 1897 or 1898 most of the people had left their homes and gone away, as there was no way to make a living. If we were able to raise anything on the land we could not sell anything. On April 1, 1899 we left Ozette Lake and it took two days to walk to Clallam Bay where we took a boat to Seattle.

In 1935 I next saw Ozette Lake and it only took an hour and a half to go by automobile from Clallam to the lake, so times have certainly changed."

ERNESTINE EDITH MILLAY
Born 1896

"When I see a face brighten up with new confidence or get a letter from someone I helped, that is all the reward I need."

Thus Ernestine Edith Millay (Mrs. A. K.), veteran teacher of twenty-four years, sums up the recognition she has received for a lifetime of dedication to others.

Mrs. Millay started teaching in a country school in La Crosse, Washington, in 1914, when eighteen-years-old. Later, in 1921, she received her Bachelor's degree from Washington State College at Pullman, Washington.

Her formal teaching included secondary school classes and eight years as visiting teacher in Moses Lake, Washington. Her informal teaching covers thousands of hours of private tutoring, helping intelligent non-readers and problem readers. She has given hundreds of all ages a chance for a better life by improving their reading capacity.

Now, at 79, she still has private students. Since retiring in 1962, she accepts no pay for tutoring services, but works, she says, because she loves it and wants to help others.

Mrs. Millay discovered early in her career that the most important key to success is restoring a student's self-image and self-confidence. "I do this," she says, "by having confidence in him."

When Mrs. Millay came to Moses Lake in 1949, she was challenged by five intelligent seventh-graders who could not read. In searching for a method to help them, she discovered the Fernald Reading Method, then being used in a clinic school at the University of California at Los Angeles.

Mrs. Millay adopted this method for the five students with great success. She became so enthusiastic about it that in 1953 she went to UCLA where she took, observed, and taught classes.

She incorporated the Fernald Method into her visiting teaching program and in junior high

classes at Ephrata, Washington, the last three years she taught.

The Fernald Method works on the precept that non-readers cannot learn through sight and hearing only, but need to use their hands. Children are taught to trace words written in large script, saying them as they trace. They write something each day and are helped with words they don't know or cannot spell.

The written stories are typed and students read them. Words they don't know are listed and they repeat the tracing process.

After retirement, Mrs. Millay wrote and published two booklets, *Help Your Child Read* and *Steps to Better Reading*, as guides for parents of troubled readers. She has dispensed these at cost or free-of-charge, so others could teach, thereby widening the extent of her work.

In 1968, Mrs. Millay left her retirement to help young men who could not read at Columbia Basin Job Corps Center in Moses Lake. Teachers using standard remedial methods were having no success. Mrs. Millay, with her two-pronged method of inspiring confidence and applying the Fernald system, had remarkable success. She continued this work until, at seventy-five, she retired the second time.

Born in Kansas in 1896, Mrs. Millay came to Washington when six years old and grew up on a farm in Whitman County. She took time off from her teaching to have five children, devoting a number of years exclusively to their rearing.

She and her husband live in Moses Lake and now have sixteen grandchildren and four great-grandchildren.

EDNA CATHERN KARLINSEY
Tacoma   1908

Edna Cathern Karlinsey was born in Granite, Utah, October 1, 1908, and grew up on an irrigated farm in Wyoming. Soon after her high school graduation, her mother died of pneumonia, and she became housekeeper for her father and five brothers and one sister.

Two years later, her father remarried, leaving her free to attend college and teach school.

In 1934, she married Kurt Karlinsey and raised a family of seven, six boys and one girl. During World War Two, they moved to Tacoma, Washington, so he could work in the shipyards.

When the last child entered kindergarten, she returned to teaching, and taught nineteen years in Washington elementary schools. She retired in 1972.

Besides teaching and raising her family, she was always busy in her church. She taught her first Sunday School class when 12-years-old, and has held some position in church most of the time since, including teacher, inservice leader, and president in Primary, the children's organization of the Church of Jesus Christ of Latter-day Saints. In the Mutual Improvement Association, for the teenagers, she was speech and drama director, attendance secretary, inservice leader, and president. In the women's organization, she has been class leader, visiting teacher, and for the last three years, president. Among other things, this includes helping to administer the church welfare program.

In the community, she has helped also. She has held offices in Pre-School and P.T.A.

While working with the Primary organization, she helped organize eleven different Cub Scout packs.

For many years she has marched to collect money for muscular dystrophy, Heart Association, cancer and arthritis. Her neighbors knew her, and have been quite generous.

In 1969, she was chosen Mother of the Year by the Washington State Mothers Committee. Since then, she has been treasurer for two years, president for one, and is presently vice president of this organization.

Six of her children are married, and there are twenty-three grandchildren.

MARY TOOZE PRICE
                                                    Born 1915

Mary Price was born May 19, 1915, in a small town in Ohio. She was the sixth daughter of Michael and Mary Tooze, and their only child born in the United States, her parents and five sisters having been born in the British Isles.

Mary Elizabeth Tooze Price was raised, educated, and finally married her high school sweetheart in the small town of East Sparta, Ohio. Mary and Albert lived in Ohio till 1944. During this time, they were blessed with two daughters and a son. Mary was active in her church, P.T.A., and was a Girl Scout Leader. She also completed her course in practical nursing, and assisted the doctors in the area with obstetric cases at home, and anywhere else she was needed.

The Price family left Ohio and moved to Washington state in 1944. Again Mary became active in her community. She was very busy in her church, taught Sunday School, was active in the women's groups, visited the ill and shut-ins, and collected clothing for the needy families.

As her children became interested in the youth activities, she was a Campfire Leader for ten years, and was a Den Mother in Cub Scouts for eleven years. She helped to train other Den Mothers for which she received the Golden Acorn Award for her services to youth.

In 1946, when her second son was a year old, there was a great need for foster homes, especially for babies. Her love of children and nursing experience prompted her and her husband, Al, to open their home to foster children. Their

first foster child was a newborn who had Cerebral Palsy, from a birth injury. This opened new horizons for Mary. From taking her foster baby, Butch, to Children's Orthopedic Hospital in Seattle for treatment, she became very interested in nursing and helping handicapped children.

She has been called "Mom" by several hundred foster children, about fifty percent of whom have been handicapped. She has cared for infants with just about every birth defect. There have been some failures, as some of the babies were terminal when Mom Price (as she is called by most of her friends) took them into her home. As Mary says, "some sadness, but much more happiness to see these children improve, and many achieve their full potential." More than a dozen have been placed in adoptive homes.

Mary was named "Woman of Achievement" in 1967 for Kitsap County. She is still active in her church, does volunteer work for a school for the handicapped, and is on the Board of Directors of two Junior Rodeo Associations.

Her favorite scripture is "As you did it to one of the least of these . . . you did it to me." Mom and Dad Price are the parents of seven, two by adoption, and grandparents of fourteen grandchildren. She was Washington State Mother of the Year for 1975.

BERNICE GOURLEY

The lives of over 500 children have been changed, some drastically, but always for the better, because of Mrs. Bernice Gourley. Herself the mother of five children, she still found time on her hands around 1946 when she and her family lived in Graham, Washington.

Mr. Gourley did heavy construction work and blacktopping, and would be gone long hours from home. It was then she decided to care for foster children. After submitting her application, but before being approved as foster parents, the Gourleys' home, living conditions, their backgrounds, and other factors had to be thoroughly checked.

The first foster child was a 14-month-old boy, who was like a little animal when the Gourleys received him. He had been in nine different foster homes and felt very rejected and suspicious of everyone around him. He lived with them for five years before he was satisfactorily adopted into another family. When he left, he secretly took one of his "truck-driving Daddy's" slippers and a glove. Twenty years later, Mrs. Gourley found out where and why that slipper had disappeared.

This was the beginning of over two decades of selfless devotion to children to whom the world had not been kind.

The problem of transportation between Graham and Tacoma, where they had to go for checkups and medical service, helped them decide to move to Tacoma in 1948.

For about the first five years of caring for foster children, the Gourleys' own five children were at home. Bernice says, "My children helped raise the foster children." She is pleased that the foster care was a family affair and that her children have always been interested in the other children and still today, if possible, come over to see any new child placed in the home.

She is proud that none of her charges have ever looked like underprivileged children. She has always seen that they were dressed attractively even though they usually arrive at her home with only the clothes they are wearing or simply wrapped in a blanket and a diaper. They estimate that they have spent well over $10,000 of their own funds on the care of foster children.

When a new child comes into her home, she begins to make a record book for him. Information in the book covers many items such as shots the child has received, type of food he

eats, and many other things, including pictures that would be helpful to the new mother when the child is adopted.

She has cared for many children who have been ill, some not expected to live, but with love, constant care, and prayer, the Gourleys have never had a foster child die. They have served as an interim or emergency receiving home for the children too young to be kept at the county detention home. They request infants preferably.

Bernice Gourley has also raised a fine family of her own. No matter how much care the foster children required, Bernice's own children have never lacked for love and affection. Her own children are now married and all live within the county. There are 19 grandchildren, 15 step grandchildren, and 22 step great-grandchildren.

Besides the tribulations and joys of raising a family, there has also been heartache. They lost a son, Calvin, in the Korean war.

Bernice is a faithful member of her church, The Church of Jesus Christ of Latter-day Saints. She was a Primary teacher for a long time, and is now a substitute teacher working with children from 3 to 14 years old. She is a member and visiting teacher in the church Relief Society.

She is on the Pierce County Advisory Board for foster home emergency care and belongs to the Washington State Foster Parents Association.

Surely the world is a better place because of Bernice and Ralph Gourley, and for the hundreds of children whose feet they have helped set on the right path.

LORA WILKINS MAGNUSSON

The lovely Latin lady was dying with a strange blood disease. Who met her at the airport, brought her to her home, sat her down to peeling peaches and talking girl-talk, took her to blood specialists while in town, then sent her home again making arrangements for her to come again? Who nursed her dying mother for two years, carrying her bodily from room to room as needed, feeding and caring for her until her passing—at the same time caring for children whose mothers were working? Who cared for a destitute family, befriending them and giving them what they needed during the trying time the father was in prison? Who would take care of the service-men during the war (World War II and the Korean War), inviting sometimes as many as 25 home because one couldn't leave a buddy? They would bring sleeping bags and cover the floor of her home on weekends, just to escape the barracks, if only for a night or two.

Lora Wilkins Magnusson must have been born to a life of service—for there isn't a day that goes by in which she isn't giving something of the above. She has survived several floods, has nursed her family through serious illnesses, accidents, even open-heart surgery—her medicine being chiefly that of truly caring.

While living in Bellevue, Mrs. Magnusson helped establish the first geneology library. Being an avid geneologist herself, she helped many trace their family lines. Moving then to Spokane, she helped establish a Special Interest Group that provided counciling for divorcees, widows and widowers. Her basement became a home away from home where they were invited to just watch T.V., play games, or relax. Many "parents-without-partners" found help through her and her husband, who was Deputy Director of Federal Housing Administration. She personally went to many of their homes and helped them re-decorate on a penny, learn to sew, quilt, can, and otherwise save money and live well. She has never accepted any remuneration for her services. Many sick and otherwise afflicted have received loaves of homemade bread and fruits and vegetables from her garden. One mother was taught by her how to care for her children in order for her to have them restored to her again.

Her children are now following in her footsteps and bring honor to her through striving to live good lives. They have received such honors

as: (1) Outstanding Teacher of the Year (Bette), (2) Outstanding Young Women of the Year (Sherri, Bette, Faye) (3) Washington All American Family of the Year (Ron Zirker family, daughter Sherri) (4) Washington Young Mother and National Honor Mother (Sherri). Their professions include Melvin, a licensed electrician; Ron Doxey, a dentist; Ron Zirker, a school psychologist and farmer; Paul Hudspeth, contractor and builder; Bette, a school teacher; Faye, a secretary; Sherri, a nursery school teacher; and Bob, staff member of the Performing Arts Dept. of Expo' '74.

Mrs. Magnusson was honored as one of Washington's Mothers of the Year. The saying that "God couldn't be everywhere and so He sent us Mothers" is the best way to describe the influence Mrs. Magnusson has been upon all who knew her!

PEARL WALL ZIRKER

Day after day, the men and boys bent their backs to the wind, chopping out the sagebrush, clearing away the heavy rocks, turning and overturning the dry barren soil, coaxing the sifting earth to accept a few seeds and hold them long enough to sprout. Hot and dusty, they would come into their homes, only to find them full of the dust they just left. The women would have to set the table turning the plates upside down, for the dust would whirl and fly, sifting into every nook and corner. It was said that it could sift right through the window panes.

Dust storms became so bad that in order to drive through it, one had to open the car door and squint to find the white line so it could be followed. This, of course, made driving perilous—but, worse than that, was the discouragement the farmers felt after they had planted the seed. The wind would tear through the fields which had recently been loosened and aired, and would blow their entire crop away. Many times, the farmers would have to replant as many as four or five times. Some didn't replant at all, but took a loss and left.

Then there were those pesky jack-rabbits! They apparently grew tired of whatever diet they had enjoyed before the farmers moved in, so farmers generously prepared a banquet of wheat for them. On one occasion, those hungry, ornery jack-rabbits cleared off forty acres of wheat, clean as a whistle. As more and more settlers moved in, however, the rabbits began moving out. It must have disturbed eating time when they looked up more and more into the barrels of shotguns held by a very firm, determined farmer repeating, "Stay off, it's mine!"

This wasn't the year 1852, as one might suppose. It was one hundred years later—and the families that moved into what was called the Columbia Basin Reclamation Project were truly modern-day pioneers.

Pearl Wall Zirker left her comfortable home in Utah, and all that was dear and familiar, to follow her husband to this strange, untamed land of "promise." She had faith in the vision of

her husband, John Eugene Zirker, who could see a brighter future for his sons and daughter. He knew that the land was fertile, and would begin to yield with the proper care. She saw that the air was clean and fresh, the community young and unpolluted with the vices and crime of better-established cities. So she courageously stood by him while her husband and sons battled the elements and the soil until the time it answered with the abundance of which it was capable.

Today, both of her sons are well-to-do farmers, managing their fields in such a way as to send their sons and daughters to college—all of whom have been the valedictorians, student-body Presidents, and graduates of universities of high caliber. They too can look back on having completed their master's degrees and they are serving as a principal of a high school and as a school psychologist. The daughter also graduated and taught several years and has raised fine, upstanding citizens. Her progenitors down to the third generation are living upon this land, tamed at John and Pearl's expense, amidst hundreds of fruit and pine trees, lush, yielding fields, operating modern dust-free equipment, and raising fine, unspoiled children who are achieving great things, unhampered by drugs and the normal temptations of youth.

And so we salute her courage to follow her husband, and stand by him during the first years of disappointment and trial, for she did not live long enough to see the fruits of her labors. She passed away June 10, 1961, following the marriage of her last son and the birth of his first child, content at least to see each child launched toward a successful life.

JOSEPHINE HASBROOK HOFFMAN

"Josephine Hoffman, THIS IS YOUR LIFE!" The Toastmistress Club in Moses Lake, Washington, surprised Mrs. Hoffman by honoring her for twenty years of outstanding and dedicated service in their organization. She had presented numerous workshops on voice projection and related topics throughout the state of Washington and the region, which includes Oregon, Idaho, and Utah. Many of the women she had trained and have since trained have won first place in many state and regional competitions and have been recognized internationally. She was re-

cently honored as Toastmistress, Council Woman of the Year, and was awarded the regional "Rolling Along Award" for the one who has contributed the most throughout the year.

She is known for her unceasing search for improvement in any given project or person. Always the teacher and mentor, she garners the deepest love and respect from her students, for they have discovered that listening to her and following her counsel has brought them great success. She loves people, and seems to have an innate sense of how to help them reach their unique individual potential. As they arrive at the heights she envisions for them, she becomes their favorite for life—and she has received testimonials year after year that attest to this fact.

Considering the fact that she was headed for a promising singing career on the concert stage, one wonders at the chain of events that endeared her to so many—especially when it is known that she was widowed twice and suffered irreparable damage to her singing voice.

In 1941, she moved to Vancouver, Washington, and began teaching recreational singing to some 3000 children in overcrowded classrooms—while parents went to work in the shipyards during World War II. For five years she cared, and prepared them for stage shows to sell United States Savings Bonds. She taught them all the virtues of cleanliness and kindliness as well.

Through the years, she worked five years as Women's Editor for the "Daily Herald", ten years as a Field Office Assistant in the Red Cross and was on hand to assist during the terrible airplane crash where 187 men were killed. She worked many years with the Job Corps teaching an appreciation for the beautiful, providing them with experience in gracious living, and endeavoring to instill within each person a sense of dignity and self-worth. It was said of her, "Her ability to establish rapport with the races is unlimited." Indeed, she helped train O.C. Smith, the famous singing star who made famous the song "God Didn't Make Little Green Apples"—and spent two years, partly without financial remuneration, working with the Mexican migrants at the day care center.

Her incredible ability to bring out a person's sterling qualities and her indomitable belief that ANYTHING is possible if the right steps are followed, rules are obeyed, and a teachable attitude is developed led her to the Pageant Arena where for twenty years she has groomed and prepared, shaped, and developed countless hopefuls for the crown. She never encouraged a spirit of competition *among* the girls—rather, she encouraged each girl to find her OWN strengths and build on them. Thus, each girl became a "winner" under her tutelage—for each emerged poised and strengthened *within*—knowing she was true to her own individuality.

In fact, that is Josephine Hoffman's most outstanding attribute: her ability to care enough about an individual that he or she becomes the canvas in the hands of a loving artist. She paints the good she sees so vividly. The individual takes on the beautiful hues as his or her own—then the transformation is astounding. The success she has brought into the lives of so many is phenomenal—creating a bond between mentor and student that is indissoluable.

MARGE (MARJORIE) LEWIS OWEN

With relatives on each side during the Civil War, and a member of her family in every war, including a brother and a husband who were both injured in World War II, it's a wonder that Marge Owen didn't come to this earth just a-fighting! As it was, she was born in Salt Lake City, Utah, to Karl and May Cox Lewis in a house that formerly belonged to Brigham Young's wife, Esther. Always, there was a

fierce pride in her country—and she fought along side her husband to tame the land enough to live on it. Yes—this valiant lady was a homesteader on a 640 acre ranch and every spring she helped take a pack string of mules and rode horses into the homestead where they built a 10 x 12 cabin to live in.

She helped fence the place and rode for the family cattle. For fun, she ran wild horses, sometimes catching and breaking one to sell to the United States Cavalry. She carried water from a spring and burned sagebrush in the stove. She ground her own flour, killed venison for meat, and always kept the bean pot on for hungry lineriders who would come to visit and stay all year!

Marge became a mother to a daughter and a son, Sharon and Joseph. When times changed and money was scarce she would play a game with her children. She had them jump on their piggy-banks and offered a balloon to the one who broke his first so they could have enough money for supper.

But, one must remember that this was the Marge who had worked her way through business college, completing the sixteen-month course in nine—the Marge who was editor of the school annual, winner of letters in baseball, volleyball, basketball and even football. It was Marge who was elected student-body president—the first in the history of the school—a golf and bowling champion.

It was also Marge who nursed her husband, Sam, after his injury in World War II. She saw him in and out of hospitals for years. It is the same Marge whose dream it was to attend college and study journalism. The dream at the time was impossible due to the great depression, but she did manage some correspondence courses and worked for a while as Sports Editor for a newspaper. It was her move to Warden, Washington, that finally gave her an opportunity to put her talents to use.

She began working for the "Warden Register," the community newspaper, and after several years she bought it. Working almost single-handedly, she has managed to keep a town together through it. There isn't a function or a game in town that she doesn't attend. The write-ups she gives are rememberances for anyone's scrapbook. She leaves the heavy news, the horror-stories, the war stories, and the like for another media. Her stories concentrate on the lives of the people—particularly the young—and the GOOD they are doing. Servicemen and students living away from home love them and even relatives living away keep up on everyone in town through the paper. It is truly a community newspaper, containing the history of the lives of the inhabitants in great depth.

Perhaps this quality earned her the SIGMA DELTA CHI EXCELLENCE in JOURNALISM AWARD in 1969 for Washington State. Whatever it was the professionals saw, they liked it. The Cougars of Warden High saw something they liked. They saw her face at every game—and their pictures and great coverage in every edition. They presented her with a plaque which read: To Marge Owens, Cougar Booster Extraordinary for her undying support and devotion. (Anyone attending a game with Marge knows she makes more noise than an entire rooting section, and only the brave and stalwart sit next to her due to the unconscious trampling of the foe she gives to whoever is within hearing distance.) This kind of enthusiasm does not go unnoticed or unloved. Warden calls her their own town "booster" EXTRA-ORDINARE!

SHIRLEY HAFT AGRANOFF

Picture two families of Russian Jews—each escaping from Russia during the Bolshevik Revolution where so many Jews were slaughtered—each with their sights on America, where "streets are paved with gold," one arriving via London, England—the other through Asia and Europe—eventually to settle in the "land of the free," one in Chicago, one in Seattle. By a quirk of fate, a newspaper ad, a chance meeting on the street—the son meets the daughter and two of a kind eventually marry—creating one of Washington's finest and strongest families!

Shirley Haft, already a fine pianist, married the famed Gregor Agranoff, a noted violinist and violin maker who was raised and tutored in the same home as celloist, Gregor Piatagorsky. A graduate of the Moscow Conservatory of Music, Gregor Agranoff concertized all over Europe at the age of nine. Upon his escape from Russia, he began teaching violin at the University of Washington. Thinking to study in the East, he stopped at Chicago where he became a teacher of hundreds of students. Marrying Shirley gave him an accompanist for both himself and his students. During the crash of 1929, they moved out west where they worked together with the Hollywood Baby Orchestra. Under his tutelage, many of these small children were playing difficult numbers such as the Mendelssohn Concerto. Shirley accompanied them as they performed at numerous events.

An illness in the family brought the Agranoffs to Washington where Mr. Agranoff's father had established the Louis Hotel. Within three months his father died. Being loyal to his family, the Agranoffs stayed to care for his mother. In 1938, they bought the hotel and stayed to become a pillar of strength to the community of Soap Lake.

Mrs. Agranoff then began to wear many hats: first, wife and companion to her talented husband; second, mother to three children; third, as organizer of the first P.T.A. in Soap Lake and subsequently its president for a time; fourth, a member of the Eastern Star, where she became Worthy Matron and Deputy and Grand Representative of South Dakota for the State of Washington; and fifth, hostess of The Louis Hotel.

It was as hostess of the hotel that many of her sterling qualities began to emerge. The Great Depression was still taking its toll throughout the country, and many a family, or men looking for work, stopped there for lodging, with little or nothing to give in return. She never turned anyone away. Many offered their services to help out at the hotel. Some simply needed sustenance and help and she could not refuse it.

When World War II began, and Larson AFB and Ephrata AFB were established, she met the planes and gathered up the privates and generals alike and brought them "home" to her kitchen. Many that she befriended left for battle and never returned. Others still send Christmas cards of love and endearment.

Between preparing lunch and dinner, she was found on the streets selling United States Savings Bonds. Her greatest help during these busy years were her devoted children. They have since grown and moved—but each has stayed in the State of Washington to become a pillar in his and her own right. Julian Agranoff is Grant County Planner, Director; Efrem Agranoff is a successful lawyer in Everett, Washington; and Miriam is a teacher-evaluator at the University of Washington.

Both Mr. and Mrs. Agranoff have truly found the "streets paved with gold" as their families envisioned they would; for, to them, their ability to help mankind, raise a close-knit and loving family, and reside in a comfortable home where every need is taken care of by their children and their ability to provide for themselves due to their talents and excellent health is the "gold that does not lose its value;" for it has bought the happiness and contentment they so richly deserve!

West Virginia

West Virginia

Nickname: Panhandle State

State Flower: Rosebay rhododendron

State Tree: Sugar Maple

State Bird: Cardinal

Committee Members

Chairman—Mrs. E. Forrest Jones,
Charleston

West Virginia

ANNA MARIE (REEVES) JARVIS
Born 1836

Anna Reeves Jarvis might be called the mother of Mother's Day. Born in 1836 in Culpepper County, Virginia, she moved to Philippi in 1848 when she was twelve years old. She married Granville E. Jarvis and had eleven children.

Prior to the War Between The States, Mrs. Jarvis started an organization which she called Mother's Day Work Clubs, organizations of women who did charitable work in their local communities, including providing home remedy medicines for the indigent inspecting milk for the children, making available nursing services and providing sanitary instruction services, sponsoring as much as possible women to care for families in which tubercular mothers existed.

The importance of the good works of this mother at this time cannot be overemphasized. When the war began in this section of West Virginia where Mrs. Jarvis lived, soldiers were being sent to both sides. She got her members of these organizations together and had them to swear that good will would be foremost and in fact the only thought in their work was for the soldiers of both sides. When soldiers occupied the town, Mrs. Jarvis and the members of her clubs provided nursing services for sick soldiers, many of whom had Typhoid Fever which was a dreaded disease.

After the War Between The States, Mrs. Jarvis organized her "Mothers Friendship Days". These were friendly meetings of former soldiers and sympathizers of both the Union and the Confederacy—designed to bind up the wounds caused by the late conflict. They were highly successful and effective.

A Philippi attorney later said "It was a wonderful sight to see the boys in blue and the boys in gray meet, shake hands and say, "God Bless you brother, let us be good neighbors and friends."

While living, Mrs. Jarvis was often heard to say, "I hope someone will sometime establish a Memorial Mother's Day for mothers living and dead". Mrs. Jarvis died in 1905.

It was the work of her daughter, Anna, a spinster, at the time of Mrs. Jarvis' death who began a campaign to bring about the institution of Mother's Day. She worked unceasingly at the task, holding meetings, talking to every available influential person of her mother's idea, writing letters by day and night.

In 1907, she and her friends held a private Mother's Day service at Andrews Church on the anniversary of Mrs. Jarvis' death. It was the following year, however, that Mother's Day began to be celebrated in earnest on a wide scale.

On May 10, 1908, a fully prepared program was held at the Andrews Church under the direction of Miss Jarvis and Church School Superintendent L.L. Loar. The printed program for the occasion carried the following: "The second Sabbath of May is Mother's Day, a day for loyal sons and daughters to especially honor their mothers".

A resolution was adopted that morning by the congregation to making the second Sunday of May each year as Mother's Day and the historic Andrews Church became the Mother Church of Mother's Day.

DR. SUSAN DEW HOFF

Born 1842

Dr. Susan Dew Hoff was born in Keyser, West Virginia, November 24, 1842. She practiced Medicine for forty years. Susan Dew was reared in a medical environment. In that day, doctors were few and far between in the country. The roads were hard to get over, there were no telephones and patients suffering from broken bones, sores, wounds or other illnesses were often brought to the doctor's office. Doctors had to rely on their own resourcefulness. There were no other doctors near.

Susan Dew was not more than 8 years old when she began to help her father, a country doctor. She would run errands for him, holding bandages, handing him his instruments—learning by doing. She was a constant companion of her father. He explained every situation in detail to her, lectured her on every subject. He took her with him on his calls and afterwards talked over the case with her. She said "I do not think any graduate of any medical school had as many lectures as I did."

In 1869, she was married to James D. Hoff and for a number of years her time and energies were given to her four children and her husband. After her father's death, his patrons, knowing her familiarity with medicine came to her for advice but it was against the law for her to practice even when she felt perfectly competent to do so. She had inherited her father's medical library and she had access to the library of her brother, a doctor in Salem.

When she confided in her husband that she might study up and take the State Board exam, he said "you can't do it Susan" and her brother teased her when she told him her intentions. He advised her, however, to take just one branch of medicine such as Midwifry if she wanted to. She said, "I'll show you whether I can or not". She took the exam and passed. It took a day and a half. It was both oral and written. The exam was held in Wheeling, West Virginia. Dr. E. C. Myers, president of the State Board of Health said in congratulating her: "You are the first and only woman who has ever come before the Board and you have passed one of the best exams of anyone who has ever been before the Board".

Dr. Hoff, after receiving her certificate, continued to take her father's old patrons. She looked after all who came to her. "I went day or night" she said, "good roads or bad, rain or shine to black or white, rich or poor".

For the first ten years of her practice, she rode horseback. I always had a good horse and could get off or on any place in the road. She said, doctors have lots of temptations; when people asked me to do certain things, I gave them lectures instead of medicines.

Dr. Hoff charged five dollars for a confinement case during the first fifteen years of her practicing. "I gave all my time to rearing my family and practicing medicine."

Dr. Hoff, now eighty-six, has the same indomitable, pioneer spirit that caused her to overcome almost unbelievable obstacles, to success in her chosen work at an age when most women of her time already considered themselves aged. She is active. Her mind is clear and keen with a good sense of humor. In less than four months recently she pieced and put together four quilts.

In 1907, Dr. Hoff was honored by the Governor of West Virginia as the official delegate to represent West Virginia at the Convention for the Prevention of Tuberculosis held in Atlantic City, New Jersey. She went and remained on to attend the American Medical Association which immediately followed.

Dr. Hoff was one of the pioneers of her sex in a difficult field and the way of the pioneer is always hard. Dr. Hoff votes on every election. "Oh, I am ashamed for the women who do not vote" she says. She had four children. Miss Lucy Hoff is a trained nurse with whom she makes her home.

SAMANTHA JANE (ATKESON) MORGAN

Born 1843

Samantha Jane (Atkeson) Morgan, artist, housewife and mother, was born Jan. 27, 1843, in a log house on the north bank of the Kanawah River about two miles west of Buffalo, the oldest town in what is now Putnam County, W. Va.

She was descended from Atkesons who came to America from Armagh County, Ireland. Her grandfather, John Atkeson, was married in Greenbrier County to Mary Donnally, daughter of Col. Andrew Donnally of Indian wars fame.

Her father, Thomas Atkeson, was born in Greenbrier County in 1804. He bought a 400-acre farm in the heart of the Kanawha Valley near Buffalo in 1835. There he spent the remainder of his life.

Thomas Atkeson was married in 1836 to Virginia Harris Brown, daughter of a Kanawha Valley settler. He and his growing family lived in the log house, where Samantha Jane was born, until 1854. Then they moved into a new, 13-room brick residence about a half mile from the river. The residence and its spacious lawn became known as Lawnvale.

Samantha Jane was one of nine children. Her brother, William Oscar, later became a congressman from Missouri. A second brother, Clarence, became a doctor in Alabama. A third, Thomas C., became president of Morris Harvey College and later dean of the school of agriculture at West Virginia University. Thomas C. was the father of Mary Meek Atkeson Moore, well known writer of rural life stories.

As a child, Samantha Jane had early impressions of steamboats plying the river and stagecoaches rumbling along the road in front of Lawnvale.

During the Civil War, there was a skirmish of Union troops and Confederate cavalrymen near the gate to the Atkeson yard. In one of her earliest artistic efforts, she painted the little battle scene from memory.

Soon after the war she studied under fine artists in Cincinnati. Thus began a lifetime career of painting of portraits, wildlife and landscapes, with special emphasis on flowers, fruits and tall birds.

In 1870 she completed what is regarded as her masterpiece. This is a picture of a French girl in Indian costume, shown in a moment of hesitation when given the choice between re-

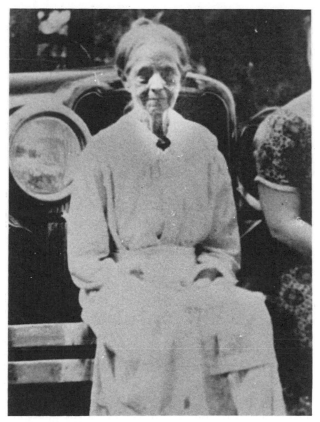

turning to her people or remaining with Indians who reared her.

On Oct. 12, 1875, Miss Atkeson was married to a farmer named John Morgan. His family, which came from the Shenandoah Valley of Virginia in 1846, lived about 15 miles upstream on another farm.

Four sons were born to the couple. John (1876-1947) became a mechanic and ferryboat operator; Thomas (1878-1946), a photographer; Rembrandt (1880-1964), a veterinarian and farmer; and Albert Sidney (1883-1973), a taxidermist and owner of Morgan's Museum, a collection of mounted animals and relics.

At the large Morgan home on a knoll overlooking the wide river bottoms opposite the town of Poca, the artist continued her painting in a studio with special windows to permit entry of northern light.

She developed the technique of providing painted backgrounds for mounted animals. Many of her paintings are of birds or other animals killed by her sons. One of her live subjects was "Fox," a red stallion trained by Rembrandt to do tricks.

Painting was a consuming interest almost to the very end of her life. She left an unfinished landscape scene on canvas when she died of a stroke March 31, 1926, at the age of 83.

CAROLINE SOUTHWORTH BENEDUM

Born 1869

The Southworth family was English and seems to have been originally of Norman-French extraction. Caroline Southworth was born of the union of Daniel Southworth and Elizabeth Smith in what is now Bridgeport, West Virginia. After her mother's death and the remarriage of her father, she made her home with an uncle, John Smith, in Bridgeport. When Caroline became Emanual Benedum's second wife in 1860, she assumed a position of local eminence and wide community responsibilities. She was a tall, fair-haired woman with a natural dignity, religious and practical. In the deeper sense she was beautiful, her rather serious attitude toward life only enhancing her charm. Emanuel and Caroline began their life together, not long before the War Between the States burst upon the nation, in the small community of Bridgeport which represented a simple culture based upon well-considered standards of personal conduct, upon firm religious faith, upon a co-operative spirit and the habit of hard work. Caroline bore children all through the decade following their marriage. In 1862 a daughter had arrived—Ella May. Clora Cornelia, born early in 1865, followed; then Kate Elizabeth, who died in infancy. The first son of Emanuel's second marriage, Charles Yantis, joined the family in 1867. On July 16, 1869, Michael Late Benedum was born. One more daughter, Sophie, came in 1871, when Michael was still toddling about in the dresses that boys of that era wore during their first few years.

Caroline Southworth Benedum had the look of being able to discharge the management of the family. She was a tall woman, taller than her husband. At the time of her marriage, she weighed 128 pounds, and seems to have been both strong and capable. And in practice, she not only attended to her own household, but acted as a nurse when there was illness in the neighborhood. "Rich or poor, you'd find mother there helping," said Michael Benedum years later. "She was straight as an arrow, and had the type of carriage you would turn around and look at." Caroline Benedum was devout and her sterness apparently sprang from her determination that her children should be properly trained and instructed. Every Wednesday night she made sure that they went to prayer meeting at the Methodist Church. "On Sunday morning," Michael Benedum remembered, "she saw that we went to Sunday School and stayed for the sermon." That was mother's job and we had better not play truant, either. The Sundays were quite long in those days." But the family atmosphere was in no way grim. Caroline was a wonderful cook, and the table was always a good one. There were candy pulls in the winter, and as the children grew older, dancing. An organ and piano provided music for that and for group singing in which everybody joined. There was talk—Emanuel's forte, and the children were often read to in the evenings. There were plenty of books in the house. The Benedum household was a busy one. Five was the usual rising hour. Caroline and her daughters spun wool from their own sheep to make clothing for the family, as well as quilts for the beds and rugs for the floors.

As the years went on, the home and the family in Bridgeport preserved much of the atmosphere Mike had known as a boy. Emanuel Benedum still presided over the house and Caroline Benedum still ran it. Caroline Southworth Benedum died on September 19, 1900. To her youngest son, Michael, this was the breaking of the first link of a family chain that had bound him closely to his home where from earliest childhood his mother had been the center of the household and an ever-present source of spiritual strength and reliance.

IDELL BINGMAN RANDOLPH

Born 1876

Idell Bingman Randolph was born in Salem, West Virginia, October 10, 1876. She was the Mother of United States Senator Jennings Randolph. She was married to Ernest Randolph born in 1868 and died in 1931. She graduated from Salem College, Harrison County West Virginia. She married her college classmate and was married in the college chapel by the President of Salem College. Idell and Ernest Randolph had three children, Jennings, Ernest and Ernestine. Idell, with her father, in 1896 rode to the college chapel in a horse drawn carriage in a champagne colored gown of silk that was lined, boned, and stayed made with expert needlework. Every seam was finished expertly. The gown is now in the Harrison County Historical Museum in Clarksburg, West Virginia. Every-

one in the village of Salem was invited to the wedding, for almost everyone in Salem was a Randolph or a Davis.

Endowed with a sense of service and duty as a young lady, Idell had a charming and outgoing personality. Relating well to people, a commendable characteristic her son Jennings displayed all through life. Her daughter Ernestine Randolph Car was more then a gleam in Idell's eyes. Idell's son Jennings described his mother as "a wonderful woman". She made a deep impact on his life. "She created a home of peace, security and love for all of us". Idell lived with her son Jennings until her death June 18, 1953, after her husband died. Her son described her, "as one of the unapplauded molders of men." Faithfully rearing her children with a sense of service and duty of country and to their fellowmen and to the community, school and church. She lived to see her son Jennings become one of West Virginia's most beloved statemen and best informed on vital issues. He served in the United States Congress in the House of Representatives, and elected to the United States Senate and re-elected in 1972.

A special tribute was made in the Halls of Congress by Congressman Randolph in tribute to his Mother. The speech was recorded in the Congressional Record, May 11, 1933. Calling her the immortal builder of heroes and describing her love as the greatest love of all.

KATE ELSTON STONE

Kate Elston Stone was one of the first women delegates to the General Conferences of the Methodist-Episcopal church, this distinction being shared with Miss Frances Willard—world outstanding missionary, mother, founder of a girls school, teacher, lecturer. Miss Kate, as she was known, was born in West Virginia, served as secretary-treasurer of the Women's Foreign Missionary Society. She had a zeal for and her service in mission work was so fruitful, it was her privilege to dispense between three and four million dollars accumulated throughout the world, while serving as Secretary-Treasurer of the Foreign Mission Society. She made a tour of the world, visiting all the mission field of her great church. Twice she visited South American fields. It was not Mrs. Stone's brilliant mind or her adaptability to every circumstance that endeared her to hosts of people throughout the world so much as the personal touch she imparted to all with whom she came in contact. She had a genius for friendship.

The daughter of Dr. and Mrs. Stone was born in America. Miss Kate herself was a native of

Wheeling where she frequently came back to visit. Her daughter is married to Rev. A. H. Wilson. They live in New Rochelle, New York. One of "Miss Kate's" big projects in social service while living in Bombay, India was that of cleaning up the docks, it was a renewal project clearing out of sections adjoining the docks. At the rescue mission, a derelict was heard to say, "when Mrs. Stone gets her eye on a feller, he just has to be good for the time being."

Fifty years were spent in contact with peoples all over the world through her foreign mission work and world travels to see conditions she reviewed in their reports to her.

Miss Kate had the knack of always making her hats and clothes becoming to her and in addressing a group in Brooklyn, a woman after the meeting rushed up to her and exclaimed, "Oh, Mrs. Stone, you are the best dressed missionary we have ever seen." She refuted the idea of some people that missionaries are not well dressed and that brainy women are not practical or domestic.

Her's was an outstanding life, her interest undiminished of which she had gladly given herself. Her last official act was with Bishop William Oldham to purchase land in a suburb of Buenos Aires, Argentina for a school for girls in which she was deeply interested.

In 1930, while in Florida, she passed away. Here was a life full of years of labor for mankind.

CAROLINE STULTING SYDENSTRICKER

Born 1892

Caroline Stulting Sydenstricker was the mother of Pearl S. Buck, Nobel Prize and Pulitzer Prize winner of literature was a Presbyterian missionary to China. She was quick in mind and strong of heart with courage. From Utrecht, Holland, her father and grandfather came in search of religious freedom and settled in Western Virginia.

Throughout all her growing years, her daughter Pearl was aware that her mother's real life remained in her own house across the sea which was in America. She made homes in China that were exquisite in taste. She was of a gay disposition, fastidiously neat and clean.

Her mother's house became more than the house in which Pearl Buck was born. It became the symbol of security and peace in a world

where there was neither security nor peace, Pearl Buck once said.

Pearl Buck's mother, a remarkable woman had taught Pearl both to sew and cook, feeling that knowledge was power and that whatever Pearl's station in life, these accomplishments would not be amiss.

Pearl Buck wrote, "I am sure there are just as many stupid men as women. I saw in my mother's case a brilliant woman who suffered from the false conception that my mother's mind was inferior because of being a woman and this hurt her".

The Sydenstrickers had returned from China to Hillsboro, West Virginia (Pocahontas County) in 1892 where their famous daughter Pearl was born in her mother's house on June 26. They returned later to China where Pearl grew up. There were seven children, only three lived to maturity.

Every summer Pearl and her mother would go up the Yangtze River to spend several weeks on Kuling Mountain. This trip was tedious and meant two days and a night of wretched accommodations on a river steamer, a night in the city of Kukiang in the Rest House then a weary joint in a sedan chair across the plain and up the mountains.

But richly rewarded for all this effort for there the spot is especially beautiful. The cottages are almost lost in the dense foliage as they cling to the side of the mountain. The sunsets are gorgeous.

The family, mother, father and Pearl spent the summer before Pearl entered Randolph Macon College in Switzerland by the blue waters of Lake Lucerne overshadowed by the majestic Alps.

At the age of 64 years, Caroline Stulting Sydenstricker passed away and was buried in China. Her daughter, Pearl, had cared for her in a dedicated way for 3½ years prior to her passing.

ANNA LATHAM BARNETTE

Anna Latham Barnette, world famous, prize winning sculpturess was born in Grafton. She was the daughter of General George Robert Latham, one of the founders of West Virginia and a United States Congressman. She began sculpting at the age of 57 after her only son, Frank, was killed in a World War I battle in France. She studied at the Maryland Institute of Art in Baltimore and soon learned she had an exceptional feeling for line design and form in sculpting. Many of her subjects she sculptured were famous West Virginians or forms of "typical" West Virginia Mountain people. Some were named The Mountain Madonna, The Moonshiner, The Woman at the Churn. She used clay mixtures which were dug from the earth near her home.

She wrote a book "Handcraft of the Southern Mountains." Her sculptures were likened to the fine German and Swiss craftmenship of centuries ago. Her originality was so evident; it was often mentioned by knowledgeable craftspeople. It gave the impression of magolica as an individual and distinct effort on the contemporary sense.

She was completely original in her objects created. Mrs. Barnette won a gold medal from the Maryland Institute of Art which was the most coveted of all their awards. She won first prize at the Pittsburgh Exhibition, where her ranking made West Virginia second among the 48 states; she gave exhibitions at White Sulphur Springs and at the New York World's Fair in 1939 where her work attracted special attention by observers from all over the world.

Mrs. Barnette died in 1948 in Buckhannon where she had lived much of her life. Her figurines have become museum and collectors pieces and are sought after everywhere.

LOUISE MCNEILL

Miss McNeill, West Virginia's most eminent poet, was born on a farm near Marlinton, West Virginia. In private life, Miss McNeill is Mrs. Roger Waterman Pease. The superb qualities of her poetry have brought honors to her and to her State more than to any contemporary poet.

Miss McNeill was born and grew up in Pocahontas County. Her family has called her birthplace home since pre-revolutionary days. As a young girl, she was a pupil at the two-room school where her father was a teacher.

Miss McNeill studied at Concord College with a major in English and later received her Master's in English from Miami University in Ohio, choosing to go further, she studied at West Virginia University where she later was awarded her doctorate in history. Her doctoral dissertation *Kanawha and the Old South* has been published by the West Virginia University press in Morgantown and is used throughout the schools of West Virginia as a text book. An early work of hers and perhaps her most famous, is a collection of poems in 1939 with a forward written by Stephen Vincent Benet called *Gauley Mountain.*

These poems are historical and trace the lives of some West Virginia families. Pioneer life played a great role in her writings.

In 1947, *Time Is Our House* became her second volume of poetry. This collection was printed as a winning book by the Bread Loaf Writer's Conference.

Just recently her book of poems *Paradox Hill from Appalachia to Lunar Shore* was published by West Virginia University Foundation, Inc. In this, pioneer life again plays a great role, also the projection of the questionable future is included in her poems. Miss McNeill writes in the regular conventional verse form. She thinks that the beauty of poetry lies in content and meaningfulness rather than just form. She sees poetry as being an asset to the spirit and to society. Miss McNeill has strong feelings about her heritage, her West Virginia homeland. Her ability to transfer these feelings into beautiful poetic rhythms is what makes her poetry so unusual. Her works are well known to the editors and publishers of such respected national literary publications as Saturday Review and Atlantic Monthly both of which have published her poems. She has also been a writer for the Ladies Home Journal, Saturday Evening Post, Harper's and Good Housekeeping as well as a number of other magazines.

Miss McNeill has taught at Concord College, West Virginia University, Potomac State College, Pocahontas County public schools and Fairmont College.

Miss McNeill is married to Roger Pease whom she met at a writer's conference in Middlebury, Vermont. Mrs. Pease is a former instructor at West Virginia University. The Peases have one son, Douglas, a graduate of the University of Connecticut.

IVA DEAN COOK

Iva Dean Cook was named West Virginia Educator of the year by the State Association of Retarded Children in 1974. She was State Coordinator of Special Education Instructional Materials. She was designated Outstanding Teacher of the year by the West Virginia University Graduate Center.

Mrs. Cook, a mother, enrolled at Marshall University to keep herself occupied after her youngest child entered the first grade in 1958. At Marshall she received one of the first two federal scholarships for graduate work because of her high academic standing. The scholarships were for work in special education. She later assisted in establishing Fairfield School in Huntington for retarded children. She wrote a book entitled Occupational Notebook for Teachers of Retarded Students. The book is based on knowledge which she gained while at Fairfield, the first for mentally retarded high school in the United States.

In 1970 she was selected and hired to organize the Statewide Special Education Instructional Materials Center, located at the College of Graduate Studies located at West Virginia State College's Campus. At the time she was hired there were only two pilot programs on teaching materials for retarded students in the United States.

Within three years the number had grown tremendously with 14 Regional Centers and 500 Associate Centers. The one in West Virginia being an affiliate of the regional center at the University of Kentucky.

Mrs. Cook and her husband had two daughters one of whom Pam, was married to Roger Childers only eight days when he was killed in the Marshall University plane crash. The Cooks lived in Huntington but later moved to Scott Depot, Putnam County, West Virginia. Mrs. Cook has been recognized widely for her sensitivity and deep understanding of the retarded child both in oral and written situations.

W I S C O N S I N

Wisconsin
Mothers of Achievement
1776 · 1976

WOODRUFF

JUNEAU CO.

KOHLER

PORTAGE

MADISON WATERTOWN

MILWAUKEE

JANESVILLE

"Honor to woman! To her it is given
To garden the earth with the roses of heaven."

Wisconsin

Nickname: Badger State

State Flower: Butterfly violet

State Tree: Sugar Maple

State Bird: Robin

Photos

1. St. Mary's Church, Jefferson
2. Milwaukee
3. Boulder River—Superior National Forest

Committee Members

Chairman—Mrs. Velma Hamilton Madison
Mrs. Leslie Ness
Mrs. Conrad Elvehjem
Mrs. David Frank
Mrs. Eldon Russell
Mrs. Harry Hamilton
Miss Elaine Zweifel

Wisc. Women's Axilary of the State
  Historical Society

Wisconsin

MARGARETHE MEYER SCHURZ
Watertown   **Born 1832**

Margarethe Meyer Schurz, founder of the first kindergarten in America, was born in Hamburg, Germany, on August 12, 1832. While still in Germany, Margarethe came under the influence of August Froebel who, through his book on Mother Plays and Nursery Songs, advanced the notion that the "primary educative forces were to be found in the home and in the methods, tunes, and accents which German mothers used to bring up their children." It was he who opened up a children's school in Thuringia in 1840, calling it a kindergarten because he "envisioned the school as a garden in which each child was nurtured like a flower by deft and shielding hands." When Froebel was invited to Hamburg, Margarethe's family were among the patrons of the new school. She studied under his tutelage and became a kindergarten enthusiast in her mid-teens.

Migrating from Germany to England to help in the first kindergarten in London, Margarethe met and married Carl Schurz, whose family were among the first settlers of Watertown, Wisconsin. The couple left London shortly after their marriage and, following a brief sojourn in Pennsylvania, went to Watertown to be united with other members of the Schurz family.

After the family was settled, Margarethe applied kindergarten techniques of songs, games, and equipment to the play of her little daughter, Agatha, and her nieces and nephews. Other mothers became interested in the use of organized and guided play. In December of 1856 Mrs. Schurz took over an old building and opened the first school of its kind in America.

This first kindergarten did not last long. Its immediate influence was probably slight. More significant is the fact that Margarethe Schurz converted Elizabeth Peabody to the kindergarten cause. In 1859 they were both house guests in the home of a mutual friend in Boston. The behavior of the little Schurz boy was so unusual that Miss Peabody noted it. Mrs. Schurz explained that it was the natural outcome of kindergarten training. She related the story of

Froebel. As a result, Miss Peabody became the founder of the first English-speaking kindergarten.

After this meeting with Miss Peabody, Margarethe is not heard of again in connection with the kindergarten movement. She devoted herself almost entirely to her family.

Mrs. Schurz was a beautiful and charming woman. Throughout her married life she was a confidant and genuine inspiration to her noted husband, who served as a U. S. Senator and Secretary of the Interior. She was appreciated by her family and acquaintances in many places. Here in Wisconsin we claim her as one of us and remember her as the founder of the first kingergarten in the United States.

Four children were born to Margarethe and Carl Schurz, two sons and two daughters. She died in March 1876 at the age of 43.

VINNIE REAM HOXIE
Madison   **Born 1847**

Vinnie Ream Hoxie, internationally famed for her sculpture, began life in a log cabin in the frontier town of Madison, Wisconsin, in 1847, the first white girl born there. Her father, Robert Lee Ream, with his wife, Lavinia, had come to the tiny settlement as a U.S. surveyor. In these primitive surroundings, where Indians were her friends and companions, Vinnie developed her vivacious personality and her many talents. Her father encouraged one of her early interests, music, when he bought a guitar for her from an itinerant salesman. She taught herself to play it and then taught others who had also bought guitars.

When she was ten, her father's work took the family to Columbia, Missouri. She and her sister attended the Academy of Christian College where they received their formal education. Vinnie excelled in art and music. She made many acquaintances there who became lifelong friends.

In 1861, the family moved to Washington, D.C., where the 14-year-old Vinnie found a completely different and exciting world. The family lived in a boarding house and met many interesting politicians. Vinnie took a job in the post-office and found time to help in the hospitals where she did practical nursing, entertained with music, and wrote letters for the men.

On Vinnie's first day in Washington, she saw the solitary President walking down the street. From then on her "dearest ambition" was to do a sculpture of the head of Abraham Lincoln. Miraculously, she achieved this ambition.

Through the efforts of her Congressman friend from Missouri, Mr. James Rollins, she became, at 16, a student of Clark Mills, the foremost sculptor of the time. It was also through Rollins that President Lincoln learned of Vinnie's ambition and agreed to pose for her. For five months Abraham Lincoln spent half an hour a day with her, while Vinnie, as she said, "sat in her corner and worked to preserve in marble the sorrow and compassion that were so much a part of his great sense of justice." On April 14, 1865, Lincoln had his last sitting. The clay model was almost completed and he was pleased with it. That night he was assassinated.

After his death Vinnie was urged to apply for the commission to do a statue of the martyred President, whom she had come to know so well. Congress awarded the task to her. This acclaim brought sudden fame to the young girl. Her studio, where she worked on the model, became a tourist attraction and a gathering place for important Washingtonians.

After her model had been approved, she and her parents went to Europe to choose the marble. In Europe this tiny unassuming girl of 19 captivated several people. In Italy she did a bust of the great Antonelli, and she played the harp for Franz Liszt who wrote a piece of music in her honor. But her special task was to find the marble. She finally chose the marble of Carrara. When her finished statue was unveiled in a public ceremony in the Capitol, it was acclaimed a success.

Vinnie continued her work as a sculptor and did busts of Custer, Grant, Admiral Farragut, and many others.

When she was 37, she married Lt. Richard Hoxie of the U.S. Engineers. They were devoted to one another and she gave up her career at his request. She and her husband, who became a Brigadier General, led an interesting life. After the birth of their son, Vinnie was never strong. Her husband provided her with a beautiful studio where she pursued her music and her artistic interests. She had great pleasure and satisfaction working with children, especially blind children, teaching them to model clay.

Vinnie died on November 20, 1914, in Washington. She was buried in Arlington National Cemetery where her model of Sappho marks her grave.

CARRIE JACOBS-BOND
Janesville   **Born 1862**

Carrie Jacobs-Bond is remembered all over the world for her songs. She was born in Janesville, Wisconsin, on August 11, 1862, the only child of Dr. and Mrs. Hannibal Cyrus Jacobs, both natives of Vermont. A boulder on West Court Street in Janesville marks her birthplace, the site of her grandfather's house.

After her father's death in 1870, the family moved into her grandfather's hotel, the Davis House, where Carrie spent hours at the piano. She came from a musical family; John Howard Payne, writer of "Home Sweet Home" was her grandfather's first cousin. At 18, she married Edward J. Smith, a men's clothing salesman in Janesville, but divorced in 1888. They had one son, Frederick Jacobs Smith, to whom she was very devoted. She remarried when she was 27 to Dr. Frank Lewis Bond, a widower with whom she lived happily in Iron River, Michigan, until he died in 1894 after a tragic accident. Left with her 8-year-old son to support, she moved back to Janesville and began writing songs and painting china to supplement her income.

"Seven Songs—as unpretentious as a wild rose" was published by her own firm, The Bond Shop—Carrie Jacobs-Bond and Son. Although her son had left school at 18, he graduated as a civil engineer after taking evening and correspondence courses, and worked for the Burlington Railroad for three years. Her most popular songs were *I Love You Truly, Just A 'Wearyn' For You,* and *The End of a Perfect Day,* written in 1910. It was at that time that she moved to Hollywood, California, where she lived for more than 30 years. She wrote over 115 songs and became financially successful, receiving numerous honors. Sorrow and tragedy confronted her in 1929 when her son committed suicide because he was becoming blind. At the age of 84, Carrie Jacobs-Bond died on December 26, 1946, and is buried at Forest Lawn Memorial Court of Honor in California.

BELLE CASE LAFOLLETTE
Summit   **Born 1859**

Belle Case was born in the village of Summit, Juneau County, on April 21, 1859, the daughter of Arson and Mary Case. She was richly endowed with talent and possessed outstanding qualities of leadership; yet was a woman of simple manners and broad sympathies.

In her undergraduate days at the University of Wisconsin, which she entered at sixteen, she was an outstanding student. She received her law degree in 1885, the first woman to receive such a degree from the University of Wisconsin Law School and the first woman to be admitted to the Wisconsin Bar.

Her marriage to Robert M. LaFollette in 1881 was the beginning of a political family which provided continuous leadership in Wisconsin for over fifty years. A third generation member is presently serving in the State Capitol. As wife and mother of three (two sons and a daughter), Belle Case LaFollette was a remarkable example of the woman who inspired and advised her family without sacrificing her own responsibility to the greater society.

She was an ardent suffragist and pacifist. She was not merely a suffragist in theory; she was

active in the cause for women's rights long before the vote was won. She was a pioneer in every aspect of the movement, applying her principles to her own life. When the great crusade for equal rights was successful in 1921, she was among the first to realize that it would take more than the ballot to change and improve society. Education on the use of the ballot, the duty of the voter, and the social problems facing women became the new challenge. The newly created League of Women Voters was designed to meet the challenge, and Belle LaFollette became a part of the organization. In 1930, her name was placed on a bronze memorial plaque in the Washington office of the League as one of fifteen most active women in obtaining ratification of suffrage in Wisconsin. Her pacifism was reflected in her affiliation with organizations such as the Women's International League for Peace and Freedom.

Mrs. LaFollette was an early advocate of rights for the newly liberated blacks in this country. As early as 1885, when her husband was a first term Congressman, she observed the conditions of the black people in Washington. In the same year, she made a trip through the South and witnessed the dehumanizing and inequitable treatment of Negroes. Her reaction was a sympathetic interest toward, and espousal of, the cause of human rights, which continued throughout her life.

It is well known that Belle Case LaFollette could have had the senatorship upon the death of her husband in 1925, but she refused it. She wanted her sons, Robert and Phillip, to have the opportunity to carry forward their father's political doctrines.

Her greatness as a woman and as a citizen is best summarized in the following: "To change the bitter conditions under which the majority of the human race supported life was her chief preoccupation."

ZONA GALE BREESE
Portage   **Born 1874**

Zona Gale was a Wisconsin daughter who reached the heights of literary success in the 1920's and 1930's by winning praise in every branch of literature: the short story, novel, drama, poetry, essays, and biography.

The only child of Charles and Elizabeth Gale, she was born in Portage, Wisconsin, on August

26, 1874. She was a bright, imaginative girl who lived in a dream world of romance. In early childhood she began putting her thoughts into the written word as a fulfillment of creative expression. Her first "book", written when she was seven, was a story printed on sheets of brown paper sewn together and illustrated with her own drawings.

Miss Gale graduated from the University of Wisconsin in 1895 with a major in English. During her university years she won prizes and awards for poems, and her first fiction was sold to the *Evening Wisconsin* for $3.00. She was one of the first women reporters in Milwaukee. Her first job assignment was with the *Evening Wisconsin* although she transferred early to the *Milwaukee Journal*.

While she made her living as a reporter, she was determined to succeed in fiction writing. She wrote volumes of unsaleable fiction in off-hours. One Spring, after joining the staff of the *New York World*, she conceived an idea while walking through Central Park—an idea which generated 40 stories that sold immediately. Thus encouraged, she resolved to concentrate on what people thought, felt, and talked about. She wrote 83 tales entitled *Friendship Village*, which were "delicate vignettes" of small town, homey experiences of ordinary people whom she remembered from her childhood. These stories endeared her to a large reading public and made her one of the most widely known American writers of her generation.

Zona Gale returned to Wisconsin in 1912 and spent the rest of her writing career in Portage among the people she loved.

Back in Wisconsin, she threw herself into many causes. She worked for Senator Robert M. LaFollette, lectured for the suffragist movement, and became an ardent pacifist. She was a member of the University of Wisconsin Board of Regents and Board of Visitors. She helped many students in need of financial assistance to finish at the university.

In 1928 she married William L. Breese, a Portage banker and industrialist. Each of them had an adopted daughter to whom Zona Gale devoted herself for the next ten years.

Before she could finish her autobiography, Zona Gale died on December 27, 1938. She was buried in Portage where her name lives in loving memory.

WILHELMINE DIEFENTHAELER LABUDDE
Milwaukee   **Born 1880**

"Mrs. Conservation" was the affectionate nickname given to Wilhelmine Diefenthaeler LaBudde, early champion of Wisconsin's natural environment. Her concern for lakes and streams, her promotion of reforestation and preservation of virgin timberlands, and her opposition to the indiscriminate use of insecticides are a few of the areas of accomplishments which merited national, state, and local recognition for Mrs. LaBudde long before the present interest in ecology.

Wilhelmine Diefenthaeler was born on October 1, 1880, near Elkhart Lake, Wisconsin, where her father was Justice of the Peace and a real estate broker. She graduated from Grafton Hall in Fond du Lac and later studied to become a concert singer. In 1907, she married Edward LaBudde who established a Feed and Grain Company in Milwaukee. Their three children, two daughters and a son, were born there.

Mrs. LaBudde began her work in conservation as chairman of conservation for the Milwaukee County Federation of Women's clubs in the 1920's and for a decade worked indefatigably for the protection of the environment. During this period, she started an educational program in cooperation with city and county schools. She assisted in reviving Arbor Day celebrations and setting up bird sanctuaries. She led con-

servationists in obtaining passage of a state statute requiring the teaching of conservation in all Wisconsin schools.

Mrs. LaBudde worked also for the establishment of school forests so that school children and members of 4-H Clubs could participate in reforestation projects. She inspired massive tree planting in Milwaukee County.

Important fish and game laws were passed in Wisconsin in 1938. Mrs. LaBudde had a voice in making recommendations to the Conservation Department as a member of a 71-county advisory committee. As early as 1935, she had secured public support in defense of owls and hawks, kingfishers, and snapping turtles from the hands of gun clubsmen. The John LeFeber Medal was presented to her by the Wisconsin Humane Society for her efforts to save porcupines from extinction.

Other causes included work to protect Indian lands, work to restore the Horicon Marsh, and work to protect rivers.

She died in Milwaukee in 1955.

MINNETTA LITTLEWOOD HASTINGS
Madison   **Born 1884**

Minnetta Hastings possessed great energy, intelligence, and compassion, which she demonstrated in home and community, and in educational, civic, and religious organizations. She became nationally known as president of the National Congress of Parents and Teachers, 1943-46. Earlier she had been active in the Wisconsin Congress and served as president, 1933-37. Her theme throughout her presidency was "All children are our children." She was chosen

as educational consultant to the United States delegation to the United Nations charter meeting in San Francisco in 1945 and carried to that conference her ideas of the importance of eliminating illiteracy and establishing worldwide child services. As consultant to the UN, she helped in the formation of UNESCO and UNICEF, hoping to help children everywhere and stimulate education worldwide. She carried news from this conference to the PTA in Hawaii.

Minnetta met William A. Hastings in high school and soon married him. He was a businessman associated with the Madison Ray-O-Vac Company. They had two sons, Donald W. and W. Harold Hastings. While active as mother and homemaker, she went to the nearby University of Wisconsin and earned both a B.A. and a Master's degree. She and her son Donald received their degrees at the same commencement in 1927. Waynesburg College in Pennsylvania granted her an honorary doctorate.

Her own community asked her to chair a newly formed Committee on Aging. This was a new frontier for Madison, but she accepted the challenge of exploring this field and served as an enthusiastic chairman from 1949 to 1959. Minnetta was a tireless church worker and served as director of the Presbyterian Student Foundation for 25 years, at the same time maintaining a keen interest in the Wisconsin Historical Society, the P.E.O. Sisterhood, the Woman's Club, and the Community Welfare Council.

The PTA of Wisconsin set up a scholarship in 1953 to encourage competent teachers and to assist promising students who wish to become teachers.

Still an active participant of all good things in the Madison community at the age of 78, she died May 24, 1962, of injuries received in an automobile accident.

Minnetta Hastings gave a lifetime of public service, maintained her home, her family, each of whom had very successful careers, and still continued her own growth through education and experience. She showed love toward people everywhere, young or old. Physically tall, she said her mother told her to "stand tall" and so she did, but with sincere humility.

DOROTHY REED MENDENHALL
Madison   Born 1875

Dr. Dorothy Reed Mendenhall's name in this volume of American Mothers is especially appropriate, for it was her pioneering which made childbearing a safer and happier experience for mothers everywhere. Her own unhappy experience at the time of the birth of her first child, a daughter, Margaret, who died within 24 hours of birth, aroused her indignation at the poor medical treatment afforded a mother and her new-born child. She dedicated her life to improving maternal care and establishing good health programs for infants and children.

Dorothy Reed, the daughter of William and Grace Kimball Reed, was born in 1875 in Columbus, Ohio, where she lived until her father's death. Mrs. Reed moved Dorothy and her brother and sister back to the family home in Talcottsville, New York. Dorothy, who was privately tutored in America and in Europe, began her formal education in 1918 when she entered Smith College.

During her stay there she applied for entrance into a new school of medicine opening in Baltimore, in spite of her family's disapproval of a medical career for a woman. Johns Hopkins approved her application. After receiving her B.A. degree from Smith in 1895, she entered the Medical School. Even though male students and some professors resented females in the medical profession, she and one other woman persisted in spite of discouraging experiences. In 1900 Dorothy Reed was one of 43 medical school graduates in the fourth class to graduate from Johns Hopkins. She received a fellowship to do research on Hodgkins disease and in her studies identified the human cell necessary for the diagnosis of the disease. It was named the "Dorothy Reed" cell.

She left Hopkins to accept a six-month residency at the New York Infirmary for Women

and Children, and then went to Babies Hospital in New York from 1903 to 1906.

That year she married Charles Mendenhall, who took her to Madison, Wisconsin, where he was a professor of physics at the University of Wisconsin. After a harrowing experience at the time of the birth and death of her first child, an experience she felt was due to medical ineptitude, she gave birth to three healthy boys. Two of them are living and prominent today: Thomas Corwin Mendenhall II, who assumed the presidency of Smith College in 1959, and John Talcott Mendenhall, professor of Surgery at the University of Wisconsin Medical School.

While Dr. Mendenhall carried on her role as mother and faculty wife in her lovely home, she became active in the field of medicine. She travelled, lectured, and wrote for the Extension Service of the University of Wisconsin, College of Agriculture, the U.S. Department of Agriculture, the American Red Cross, and especially, the United States Children's Bureau, which she served for more than 20 years. She pioneered in establishing "Well-Baby" and Pre-School Clinics and a program of pre-natal care for the state. Her reports on child care statistics and procedures in Scandinavia, where she studied for the U.S. Children's Bureau, were instrumental in improving child care in the United States. Her vigorous pursuit of the development of sound principles in the care and understanding of children and mothers revolutionized pre-natal and infant care and childbirth practices in America.

After the death of her husband, Dorothy Reed Mendenhall continued her busy career as mother, grandmother, homemaker, doctor, scientist, and medical pioneer in Madison. Late in her life she moved to Chester, Connecticut, where she died at the age of 89.

THE HONORABLE GOLDA MEIR
Born 1898

From relative obscurity, this great woman emerged to the world scene in the short space of a few decades. Her broad knowledge, her strong convictions, her courage, her consummate skill in highly charged political affairs and her innate motherliness led the nations of the world to applaud her forthright stance. She was born in Kiev, Russia, and later lived in Pinsk. She was brought up in the traditional Jewish faith. She recalls the endless tea drinking—many guests in their house and singing for hours. Faithfully they kept the Sabbath and all Jewish festivals and feast days. Because of hard financial times, her father gathered enough money to go to America to find work and where he lived alone for three years. In her recently published autobiography she tells of the daily struggles and fears because of their Jewish faith. It was in 1905 that the father, having secured a job in Milwaukee, began preparation for the family reunion. Escaping was not easy but she recalls stops in Vienna and Antwerp, then 14 days living in a dark cabin with 4 others and being treated like cattle. Arriving in Milwaukee the father bought them all new American clothes and entered the children in school. Despite her regular job requirements she was made the Valedictorian of her class at the age of 14. Her parents were so against her entering High School that she ran away to Denver to be with her now married sister. She claims that her sister Sheyna, 11 years her senior, had a profound influence on her life. They talked for hours about the problems of the Jews. Here she met a man whom she grew to love, Morris Meyerson. She was called back to Milwaukee by illness of her mother. She was recovering slowly when war came and their home was full of activity by the local Jews who were enlisting and going off to war. There she first met Ben-Zvi who was to become Israel's 2nd President and later the famous David Ben-Gurion. She began to learn of the sufferings of the Jews in Palestine. Gradually, her mind and heart were made up—she *must* go to Palestine to live and join the Labor Zionist movement. Her lover, Morris, finally agreed to marry her and go to Israel also—following the Balfour Declaration in 1917 which established Palestine as a National Home for Jews. Since the war was in progress they delayed departure—until 1920. At last, she was leaving her adopted homeland. Later she would visit it often in years to come.

After a disastrous long trip by ship and train they arrived in Tel Aviv, the first provisional capital of the Jewish State. Housing units were being built, agriculture was expanding everywhere and new patterns of government established. At times 1,000 immigrants were arriving daily to be settled in cities and villages and be absorbed in a new pattern of modern civilization. Raising funds by the millions, particularly in the U.S.A., was a critical necessity. Golda Meir's personal life was of relative unimportance—much as she loved each of her several homes. Time came when she felt she must establish her headquarters in Jerusalem.

During her fabulous life (she lived in utmost simplicity) she held audiences with Presidents and Royalty around the world, always evoking admiration for her modesty and her astuteness. Years of internal confusion and strife plagued her new country. In due time, Madame Meir found herself Prime Minister and formed her first Cabinet. In the summer of 1956 she was confronted by the first of the terrorist activities—a challenge—one that was to haunt her to Munich and beyond.

The slow but meritorious rise of this great woman cannot be delineated in this limited resume. Surely as she walked side by side with the undauntable Ben Gurion, her vision, her patriotism grew and her faith strengthened in the destiny of Israel.

One of her spectacular distinctions was her ambassadorship to Russia in 1948. Only Madame Vajaya Pandit held that post representing a major country. She arrived in time to witness the funeral of Zhdanov, one of Stalin's closest associates. It somewhat overshadowed this remarkable event of her appearance in the land of her birth. She began to observe the cooling attitude toward the Jewish element. She attended the Great Synagogue where she received an ovation. But her stay had many confrontations that finally forced her return to her country.

Tension was rising in the Middle East and the harassment of Jews was escalating in many areas of the European and the Mediterranean

countries. The lack of money was a constant source of worry since Israel was in the throes of building a homeland, a costly enterprise.

To adequately cover the Meir history would almost parallel the checkered existence of Israel itself, the war, the refugee problem, the world wide Jewish heroism and dilemmas. Here however, we are concerned with the story of one of the world's great women. She has constantly grown in stature and has won the respect and admiration of the world—a woman Prime Minister among so many great men! To carry the burden of such a complex and explosive assignment would have daunted most heads of state. She proved a rock of stability to her political friends and foes—truly monumental in grandeur!

In the midst of these overwhelming situations, the love of her family was always uppermost in her heart. To be required to give of her life to her country interfered with her warm family home life to a heartbreaking degree.

In recognition of this aspect of her life and in deep respect for her signal achievements and devotion to her country, her family and her Jewish faith the American Mothers Committee, Inc., presented their World Decade Award on May 6, 1974. It was carried by special telephone lines over 7,000 miles and amplified to a waiting audience of 1,000 persons in the Grand Ballroom of the Waldorf Astoria in New York City. At the close of this telephonic event, the audience rose and gave a resounding salute to this great mother-stateswoman.

The citation reads:

Golda Meir, Founding Mother of the State of Israel, world-renowned stateswoman who has devoted her full spirit to the quest for international understanding so that the children of all lands might live in peace and amity; who, in the public schools of the United States learned to cherish the American concepts of democratic freedom and independence; and who, reared in the tradition of her faith, was early embued with the vision of social justice of the Hebrew prophets—ideals she sought to fulfill for her people and mankind; who, as a young pioneer, tilled the fields of Palestine so that barren soil might bloom; who, as her country's first Minister of Labor, built homes for survivors of the cruelest oppression history has recorded; who, as Foreign Minister, created ties of friendship not only with powerful nations but strove to cooperate with the new, struggling countries of Africa and Asia; and who, finally, as Prime Minister, never despaired of the search for peace but steadfastly held high the goal of fruitful collaboration with all the peoples of the Middle East. Having herself known both the joy of creative labor and the anguish of sterile war, she has never stopped striving for conditions in which all young lives—Israeli and Arab, Jew, Christian and Moslem—would flourish in dignity and well-being.

For her great work for peace, the American Mothers Committee, Inc., representing 50 states, the District of Columbia, and Puerto Rico, is proud to confer on Golda Meir the citation of World Mother of the Decade.

RUTH DEYOUNG KOHLER
Kohler

Ruth DeYoung Kohler became a beloved citizen of this state through her marriage into a prominent Wisconsin family. Daughter of a Chief Justice of the Illinois Supreme Court, she was an honors graduate of Smith College where she was elected to Phi Beta Kappa. Before her marriage, she was Woman's Editor of the *Chicago Tribune*.

During her association with the *Chicago Tribune*, she helped cover the political conventions of 1932, 1936, and 1940. After her marriage, she conducted a weekly radio program "Women

World Wide" over the Mutual Broadcasting System.

Throughout her marriage, Mrs. Kohler's time and interest were primarily concerned with home and family. The Kohlers had three children: Herbert V. Jr., Ruth DeYoung II, and Frederic Cornell.

Mrs. Kohler believed in the benefits of travel, and planned family trips to places in the United States, Europe, South America, Canada, and Mexico. She closely observed the educational development of her children and used all available sources to increase their interest in literature and the arts.

Ruth DeYoung Kohler's achievements were outstanding. She was the founder and first president of Women's Auxiliary of the State Historical Society. She organized the Kohler Women's Club and was a director of the general Federation of Women's Clubs. In the Women's Club sponsorship of Girl Scouts of Kohler, she served for nine years as commissioner of the Kohler Girl Scout Council. In 1931 the famous Austrian-style edifice known as the Waelderhaus, built by Mrs. Kohler in memory of her father, was dedicated as Girl Scout Lodge.

When Wisconsin observed its centennial in 1948, Ruth Kohler was chairman of the committee on Wisconsin women. This committee traced Wisconsin family life for the past century with a series of twelve rooms, beginning

with the wigwam of an Indian family and continuing through a modern living room. She sincerely believed that "each of us is a trustee of the past."

Many honors were bestowed upon Mrs. Kohler. She was a trustee of Lawrence College and the Layton School of Art. She was a member of the National Layman's and Laywomen's Committee of the National Council of Churches, and vice-president of the state conference of the American Association of University Women.

Fellow members of the Kohler Women's Club paid her this tribute: "We who know her gracious personality, her active mind, her vital faith, and her outreaching qualities have something we can treasure but scarcely can put into words. What she was exceeded all the things she did."

KATE PELHAM NEWCOMB
Woodruff

Kate Pelham Newcomb was born in Kansas and educated in New York, but left her indelible mark in the Lakeland district of northern Wisconsin.

There were not many doctors in Rice Creek, Wisconsin, in the early 1920's. Thus, when one of the two doctors serving the Lakeland area discovered that there was an obstetrician there who was not practicing medicine, he immediately pressed her into service. In her words, "Before the ink was dry on my license, my telephone began to ring at all hours of the day and night."

Thus Dr. Kate—Angel on Snowshoes—mother and devoted wife, began a thirty-year labor of love to a whole area of our state. Patients flocked to her and often she had to drive a hundred miles a day to make house calls on back roads and used snowshoes to visit homes which could not be reached by car. Her husband contrived a "snowmobile" to transport her over roads not cleared by snowplows.

The Newcombs' son, Thomas, was born in 1926, and they later adopted a daughter, Eldorah.

Kate Newcomb not only cared for the sick, she also worked tirelessly as a health officer to improve drinking water and the milk supply. She sent samples of water and milk to state laboratories and posted the reports. She established camp health and infirmary systems which took care of the health of children and laid the foundation for a strong preventive medicine attitude among campers in our lake country.

Her dream was a hospital for the lakes area. Friends began a drive which later mushroomed into a project which gained national publicity. After a television appearance on "This is Your Life", more then $100,000 came in pennies, nickels, dollars, and checks for larger amounts from all over the U.S. The Lakeland Memorial Hospital became a reality.

Dr. Kate continued her rounds as country doctor with her tasks made easier by the modern new hospital. She hoped a young doctor "willing to undergo the rigors of country practice" would join her.

Before she found such a person, Dr. Kate broke her hip and died in surgery on May 30, 1956. She brought service and dedication to the obscure communities of northern Wisconsin, and the "beloved, grayhaired doctor" of the north woods captured the hearts of the nation.

WYOMING

Wyoming

Nickname: The Equality State

State Flower: Indian paintbrush

State Bird: Meadow lark

Committee Members

Chairman—Mrs. W. Eliot Hitchcock,
  Laramie
Mrs. Otto Lembcke, Laramie
Mrs. James Oxley, Fort Collins
Dr. Don Fronk, Fort Collins
Mrs. Hugh Lake (Minnie), Fort Collins
Erma Sundby Wilson
May N. Ballinger
Susan Riske
Sally H. Mackey
Vandi Moore
V. G. Bales
Rebecca T. Northen
Carolyn Charkey

Wyoming

ESTHER HOBART MCQUIGG MORRIS

Born 1814

To Esther Morris, the women of Wyoming owe a debt of gratitude, not to be forgotten in this or coming generations. She has rightfully been called the "Mother of Women Suffrage", and the First Justice of the Peace in the world.

Esther Hobart McQuigg was born in New York State in the year 1814. She married a surveyor, Artemus Slack, who soon died leaving her with a son, Edward Archibald. She moved to Illinois, where she married John Morris, by whom she had twin sons, Robert C. and Edward. In 1868 John Morris took his two sons and Edward Slack to South Pass City, Wyoming. Mrs. Morris joined her family there in 1869.

A most authentic and interesting account of the enactment of the "Female Suffrage Law" is found in "How Suffrage Came to Wyoming" written by Dr. Grace Raymond Hebard of the University of Wyoming and published in November, 1920. Quoting from the above authority the statement made by Capt. H. G. Nickerson of Lander, Wyoming, a one time resident of South Pass, and contained in an affidavit made by him and in the official files of Wyoming in which he says "To Esther Morris due the credit and honor of advocating and originating women suffrage in the United States. At the first election held at South Pass, (then in Carter County, Wyoming), on the 2nd day of September, 1869, Colonel William H. Bright, democrat, and myself, republican, were candidates for the first Territorial Legislature. A few days before election, Mrs. Morris gave a tea party at her residence at which there were present about forty ladies and gentlemen. Col. Bright and myself being invited for a purpose, for while seated at the table, Mrs. Morris arose and stated the object of the meeting. She said, 'There are present two opposing candidates for the first legislature of our new territory, one of whom is sure to be elected, and we desire here and now to receive from them a public pledge that whichever one is elected will introduce and work for the passage of an act conferring upon the women of our

new territory, the right of suffrage.'

"Of course we both pledged ourselves as requested and received the applause of all present. Col. Bright, true to his promise, introduced the bill and it became a law."

"As a result of this foresight, our husbands, fathers, brothers, and sons have always been accustomed to the company of our women at the polls, to their taking in matters of public interest in their several communities."

In addition to being the mother of Women Suffrage, Esther Morris occupies another distinctive and unique position in the official life of Wyoming. On February 14, 1870, she was appointed Justice of the Peace at South Pass City, which was in the central part of the state near the Oregon Trail, her name being suggested by Judge John W. Kingham, of the District. Acting Governor, Edward M. Lee issued her commission. This was the first time in the history of the world that any women had held judicial office. This position she held till the first day of November, 1870, having tried 70 cases during her administration, and none of which, when taken to a higher court, were ever reversed.

That she retained her poise and mental faculties to a remarkable degree is evidenced by the fact that in 1894, when past 80 years of age, she was elected a delegate to the National Republican Convention held in Cleveland on June 19th of that year and that she attended the same. It was on this occasion that the Chicago Tribune and many eastern papers gave interesting accounts of her activities on behalf of woman suffrage and of her having served as a Justice of the Peace.

On Statehood day she made the speech for the women of the state and at which meeting the women presented the state with the state flag.

When Miss Susan B. Anthony visited the state in the early 90's, Mrs. Morris presided at the public meeting given in her honor. The affair was a notable one, being attended by the State Officials and men and women prominent in public life.

Upon the death of Mrs. Morris in 1902, one of her sons published an eulogy, from which is quoted the following: "Her quest for truth in this world is ended. Her mission in life has been fulfilled. The work she did for the elevation of womankind will be told in the years to come, when the purpose will be better understood."

MARGARET BURNETT SIMPSON
Born 1874

Margaret Louise Burnett was born January 24, 1874 to Fincelious and Eliza Burnett. Because of the hostilities of unfriendly Indians, the women, children and elderly who lived on the Wind River Indian Reservation were evacuated to Salt Lake City to ensure their safety. That is where Margaret was born. When hostilities ended, the Burnett family returned to Lander near Fort Washakie where Margaret's father was a U. S. Government agronomist.

Margaret received her elementary education in Lander schools and the equivalent of High School in Ursula Convent in San Antonia, Texas while living with her grandparents. On returning home at age seventeen, she volunteered to teach at St. Stephen's Mission on the Arapahoe Indian Reservation, a position she held for four years. She learned their language and translated books into Arapahoe texts for the children.

While teaching here, she met her future husband, William Simpson, who came to Wyoming on a cattle drive in 1884 with his father. Assisted by Father Scullen, Margaret helped him complete his education, including Latin, enabling him to be admitted to the bar.

William and Margaret were married in an Episcopalian Church in Fort Collins, Colorado on October 18, 1893. During their marriage they lived in Lander and Jackson where William operated the first store. Later they lived in Meeteetse, Thermopolis and Cody where he practiced law. Three children were born to this union, Virginia, Glenn and Milward.

Margaret Simpson's lifetime achievements were many. Besides caring devotedly and protectively for her own three children and her dynamic husband, she was instrumental in organizing the first Episcopal Churches in Lander and Meeteetse; working tirelessly to acquire the furnishings for the new Episcopal Church in Cody; working actively in acolyte; having St. Margaret's Guild named for her; being a charter member of the order of Eastern Star of the Lander and Meeteetse chapters, surviving other members of the original Buffalo Bill Museum Association, acting as President of Wyoming War Mothers during World War I and being lauded by President Wilson for her tireless nursing efforts during the "flu" epidemic of 1917.

A source of great pride to her were the accomplishments of her son, Milward, who served as President of the Board of Trustees of the University of Wyoming from 1943-1955, the State Legislature in 1926, Governor of Wyoming 1954-1960, U. S. Senate from 1962-1966, and as a practicing attorney in Thermopolis and Cody. He and his wife, Lorna, were the parents of two sons, Peter, Assistant to the President of Casper College and Alan, Lawyer, ten years a legislator and Speaker of the House of Representatives 1974-1975.

On her hundredth birthday, family and friends, among them children from St. Stephen's Mission, gathered to honor "Nanny" Simpson at the home of her grandson, Alan.

Margaret passed away quietly at her home on March 10, 1974 having been preceded in death by her husband, a son and daughter. Her living son's tribute to his Mother - - - "she was a saint on earth".

NELLIE TAYLOE ROSS

Born 1876

Nellie Tayloe Ross was born in St. Joseph, Missouri, November 29, 1876. Her elementary education was received in private and public schools and after graduation from High School was supplemented considerably by study under special instructors, including a two year course in kindergarten training school from which she graduated in Omaha, Nebraska. She did not long pursue teaching, however, because of frail health.

It was while visiting her fathers relatives in Tennessee that she met William B. Ross, a young lawyer just admitted to the Bar, and son of Ambrose Ross, an attorney of Dover, Tennessee, and his wife who was a Miss Gray. In the year 1901 William Bradford Ross moved to Wyoming and engaged in the practice of the law, his marriage to Miss Tayloe occurring in 1902. They were the parents of four children, twin sons George Tayloe and James Amtrose, born in 1903. Alfred Duff, who died at the age of ten months and William Bradford, born in 1912.

Late in September of the year 1924, Wyoming watched with anxiety the outcome of a sudden and serious illness of Governor William Bradford Ross, who had been elected two years before for a four-year term. His death on October 2nd filled the people of the state with grief,

for he was a man who had won the love and respect of the citizens by his sterling qualities of public and private virtue.

At this time, Mrs. Ross was fairly well known throughout the state where she had lived for more than twenty years; through those contacts she had made at the State Capitol, among her friends and neighbors, and as wife of Governor William B. Ross during the 21 months in which he had held the office. Being a true helpmate to her husband, she had frequently accompanied her husband on his campaign tours of the state in previous years and in this manner her charm of personality and her gifts of intellect and understanding had become known to a comparatively large circle as well as to the personal friends and political associates of herself and her husband. It was this knowledge that she had been intimately acquainted with all of his public plans and purposes that inspired them to urge her upon the people of the state as the logical person to finish his term of office.

Immediately the question uppermost in the minds of the public was "Who will be his successor?"

On November 4, 1924 when Wyoming elected a woman governor, Wyoming preserved the

record of being known, not only as the first suffrage state, but also as the first state in which a woman was actually invested with the powers and duties of the governship.

Nellie Tayloe Ross was inaugurated on January 5, 1925. In her brief opening message to the legislature, she explained at the outset that she had been aided in preparing her message by extensive notes assembled by her husband for the message that he had planned to deliver. With pride she reported that during her husband's administration, the valuation of railroads for tax purposes had been increased by eleven million dollars and that the total state taxes had been reduced. She urged the legislature to continue shifting the tax burden from small property holders to large ones. Recalling a coal-mine disaster at Kemmerer in which one hundred persons had died on August 14, 1923, she asked for improved safety regulations. She called for increased state investment in farm loans to aid depressed agriculture. She repeated her husband's complaint that Wyoming had not kept pace with progressive states in restricting work hours for women, and she recommended ratification of the Child Labor Amendment, which had been submitted to the states by the United States Congress. She proposed the enactment of a statute that would make it as great a crime to buy liquor as to sell it.

Contemplating the awesome fact that 35 of the state's 120 banks had failed in the past year, Mrs. Ross asked for a "sound banking law" and "some form of a guaranty provision."

The legislature adopted new coal-mine safety regulations, passed a new banking code, and enlarged the farm-loan fund. Also, a child-labor law barring employment of children under sixteen in hazardous occcupations was adopted.

Nellie Tayloe Ross's term of office expired on January 3, 1927. She had proved to be a good governor who gave the state a respectable, dignified, and economical administration. Intelligent, tactful, and gracious, she became a competent administrator and effective public speaker.

Her work for the Democratic national committee subsequently brought her appointment as director of the United States Mint, in which capacity she served for twenty years (1933-1953). Still vivacious and charming, living in retirement in Washington, D.C., she exclaimed in 1964 with obvious sincerity: "I am very grateful for all that the wonderful people of Wyoming have done for me."

EVELYN CORTHELL HILL

Born 1886

Evelyn Corthell Hill spent the eighty-eight years of her life involved in one facet or another of motherhood supported by her artistic talents. First, there were the four generations of family she had mothered in the traditional role by helping to sketch individual lives. Then there was her work as a country school teacher, newspaper editor and public servant through which she helped raise the City of Laramie and picture its destiny. Her motherhood also included numerous Wyoming and Rocky Mountain landscapes to which she gave birth on canvas.

Evelyn was born in Laramie, Wyoming, the eldest of seven children, to Nellis E. Corthell, a well-known Wyoming Lawyer, and Elinor Quackenbush Corthell on May 4, 1886.

Married in 1911 to John A. Hill, a professor who became Dean of the College of Agriculture at the University of Wyoming and later, acting President of that institution, the couple homesteaded west of Laramie. Evelyn gave birth to four boys and a girl.

Following her graduation from Wellesley College, Evelyn helped educate future citizens of Albany County when she taught in two country schools. From 1909 to 1911 she was general manager and editor of the *Laramie Boomerang*, the daily newspaper. She was instrumental in bringing the city manager form of government to Laramie and served for two terms on the City Council. Evelyn lobbied for mineral severance tax in the State Legislature twenty years before it was adopted. She helped found the Laramie League of Women Voters, Great Decisions discussion groups and was active in the Laramie Women's Club, local historical society and Democratic Party.

When she received the "Community Service Award" in 1958 from the Laramie Daily Boomerang and the Laramie Lions Club, she was lauded for "her participation in all areas—public service and interest in welfare and destiny of the community."

Evelyn Hill attained stature as an artist for her paintings of the Laramie Plains and scenes of the Rocky Mountains, many of which have been exhibited in galleries across the nation. Completing over 1,000 paintings and drawings, some belong to art patrons throughout the country and one of her works was featured in a French art magazine. She studied at the Art Student League in New York City and at the Chicago Art Institute; some of her later teachers include Illya Bolotowsky, Daniel Garber and Boardman Robinson.

Evelyn Corthell Hill's impact has been that of a bi-centennial mother because her concern for her family, friends, city and state is a lasting one illustrated in her grandchild's tribute: "Once finished, she never hesitated to brighten our colors or heighten our mountains as her lectures always stressed the need for intellectual growth."

HELEN BISHOP DUNNEWALD
Born 1891

Her children shall rise up and call her blessed—in China and Nigeria, in Taiwan and Japan, in Malaysia and Norway, in South Africa, Korea, Palestine and Austria, and, of course, in America.

Helen Bishop Dunnewald, after rearing her own two children, reached out to include young people coming to the University of Wyoming from around the world. Parents from many nations have accepted their children's absence more readily because she has been a mother by proxy.

Designated Wyoming's Mother of the Year in 1969, Helen Dunnewald richly deserves contin-

uing honor because of her interest in, and love for, the youth of the world. Foreign students attending the University of Wyoming become immediately a part of the growing Dunnewald family. They are not only entertained in groups in her home, but are also given individual attention, and the smallest problem for them becomes important to her. Each year many return to visit the home where they found encouragement, understanding and warm affection in a strange land.

Helen Dunnewald's interest in young people—in *all* people—is not surprising when one knows that her family before her reached out to help others as missionaries in Hawaii. Her first job was evidence of her interest in others; she became, in 1915, a hostess in a housing unit for Johns Hopkins students. Next, she taught in Connecticut at what is now Storrs University, before volunteering to go overseas as a canteen girl for the Y.W.C.A. in 1918.

Born October 26, 1891, in Oakland, California, and educated at Pacific University in Oregon, she decided to return to the west coast after the war, and accepted a teaching job in her home town. Greener pastures beckoned, however, in 1920, and she became director of Helen Newberry women's residence hall in Ann Arbor, Michigan. Five years later she became Dean of Women at the University of Wyoming.

She was married in 1928 to Professor T. J. Dunnewald, of the University of Wyoming. They had a son, John, and a daughter, Ann, and had forty-six happy and exciting years together before her husband's death in 1974.

While creating a loving home atmosphere for her family, Helen Dunnewald also found time for civic activities, serving on the boards of Ivinson Hall School for Girls and the Cathedral Home for Children, both in Laramie; assuming responsibility to her church and federated woman's club; helping organize clubs for Spanish American and Black women in the community, and working with the United Fund. Her creative mind found many productive and happy activities to occupy youngsters, and she worked alongside them in projects destined to help them become good citizens.

At 84, this warmly human woman is still alert to the needs of those around her. She cherishes memories of visits to the homes in many countries of the students she has mothered, and her postman brings her letters almost daily from faraway places where her "Adopted" children live. Truly, because of her love for them, they call her blessed.

ALICE HARDIE STEVENS

Born 1900

Editor Alice Stevens began her Bicentennial Edition of the *Laramie Daily Boomerang* with the Declaration of Independence, "This country's most famous document."

The July 12, 1975 publication, her final gift to the community she served as a journalist, historian and civic leader over 50 years, contains accurate historical articles by the editor and many Albany County residents. Additionally, it reflects Mrs. Stevens' life of immeasureable devotion to family, friends, and country.

She and her husband, Professor Emeritus Wilmer E. Stevens, reared four daughters: Jean Davies, Janet Thigpen, Joan Howard and Jere Tulk. All received degrees from their parents' school, the University of Wyoming. They all came for the Stevens' golden wedding anniversary in 1973.

Alice Louise Hardie was born in Pennsylvania and came to Laramie, Wyoming with her family in 1918 as an 18-year-old with unforgettable blue eyes that sparkled with the enthusiasm she kept throughout her 75 years.

Her 30-year career in journalism, which began when she was a college-newspaper editor, brought 21 top honors to the Boomerang in 1953-55 through Wyoming Press Women's competitions and the Alberta Hilands non-fiction award. Yet Alice Stevens never spoke of the achievements that inspired her colleagues, who cannot forget the guidance she offered on request in a soft voice filled with wisdom, kindness and patience.

While her children were young, Mrs. Stevens served as a non-salaried publicist for Laramie's Woman's Club, Public Health Nurses, Community Chest, Neighborhood Center Salvation Army, Cancer Fund, USO, Council of Women's Organizations and American Association of University Women.

As LWC president during World War II, she headed war-bond drives and was a member of the USO board. She also helped to found a local league of Women Voters.

The charter member of the Laramie Plains Museum Association assisted with the establishment of the first local museum in City Hall's basement and led a fund drive to preserve the last building at Fort Sanders that is now a community center.

She publicized the annual Foreign Relations Seminar at UW, where she taught speech and journalism part time, and was advisor to Tri Delta sorority.

She accompanied Professor Stevens on a 1958 sabbatical leave to study United Nations' parlimentary procedure and sent reports to the Boomerang. The national UN Association presented her its Distinguished Service Award after she promoted the nationwide observance of UN Day.

A second Distinguished Service Award came from the Lions Club and the Boomerang in 1965.

As a member of the Centennial Committee, she spearheaded the campaign to acquire the historic Ivinson mansion as a permanent museum. An auxiliary building, named in her honor, is used as a community center.

The Laramie Plains Bicentennial Committee member felt she must honor her commitment to edit a commemorative publication and did not tell anyone she was ill. After her special edition was published, she entered Colorado General Hospital for treatment of a rare and fatal blood disease and never knew the bicentennial effort would receive Wyoming State Historical Society's highest award.

REBECCA TYSON NORTHEN
Born 1910

In those precious, hectic years when she was raising her children, Rebecca Northen began growing orchids. Today, while *her* children are raising children, she continues to grow orchids.

It's a bit different these days, however, for she now shares her orchid knowledge with people the world over. Considered by many the world's foremost authority on orchids, she now travels thousands of miles annually to speak to orchid growers around the globe.

Her interest in the exotic plants was sparked by the section on orchids in a horticultural encyclopedia acquired early during her marriage to H. T. Northen, a botany professor at the University of Wyoming. She ordered a flask of 100 seedlings; was erroneously sent 1,000, and soon had orchid plants growing in every room. Later, she and her husband assembled their own greenhouses, and in the insuing years has grown over 100 species, has written three books on orchids and is now doing one on species for Prentice-Hall. She has collaborated with her husband on three other books, *The Secret of the Green Thumb*, *Greenhouse Gardening*, and *Ingenious Kingdom, The Remarkable World of*

Plants. Her first book, *Home Orchid Growing*, widely considered the best book available on orchid culture, has gone into three editions, while her *Orchids as House Plants* has recently been revised for publication by Dover Publications.

She has spoken at several World Orchid Congresses, among them those held in Australia in 1969, Colombia in 1972, and Germany, 1975, and was guest speaker at the South African Orchid Conference at Durban in 1973. She will speak at the Philadelphia Bicentennial meeting in March, 1976. Many times she has given talks at the Western, Mid-America and Eastern Orchid Congresses, and she makes several tours a year to speak to orchid societies. For five years she has been a trustee of the American Orchid Society.

A special joy and great source of information for her has been collecting orchids in their native habitats. She has gathered them in the wilds of Mexico, Central and South America, Jamaica and South Africa.

She has given unselfishly of herself to others interested in growing orchids, spending many hours with, or corresponding with them. Her warm personality and infectious enthusiasm for the exotic plants have endeared her to orchid lovers around the world.

Dr. Northen, her husband and former chairman of the University of Wyoming's Botany Department, is now retired. Their children are Dr. Philip T. Northen, teaching at California

State College at Sonoma; Tom, a Laramie, Wyoming business man, and Betty, wife of Dr. R. B. Lyons, who is in charge of funds for medical training, Region 10 of the U. S. Department of Health, Education and Welfare. The Northens have seven grandchildren. Rebecca has seen many fruitful years since her birth in Detroit, Michigan, August 24, 1910.

VANDI MOORE

Born 1912

Vandi Moore is known all over Wyoming. She and her husband, Horace, came to Laramie from Nebraska forty years ago, Horace to work for the Union Pacific Railroad, and Vandi to raise their children, Jerrold and Ginny, and to enter upon a varied career.

She nurtured a gift for writing by studying journalism and speech at the University of Wyoming. Her first news story, about the blizzard of 1949, was published in the *Laramie Daily Boomerang* and gained her a position on its staff. She worked successively for the newspaper (and still contributes articles), for radio station KOWB, and for *Laramie Life*, and as secretary in various University offices and the Laramie Chamber of Commerce.

Since then she has become a successful free lance writer, with articles published in the *Denver Post* EMPIRE MAGAZINE, in Wyoming, and many national magazines. She writes fiction as well and has sold stories for young and old. She was the first president of the recently organized Wyoming Writers Association.

After serving on the Albany County Red Cross board, she was, for fifteen years, director of public relations for the Wyoming Division of the American Cancer Society, traveling all over the West and to national meetings in New York.

Vandi is deeply involved in church affairs. She has served on the boards of the National Council of American Baptist Women and the state board of the Wyoming Baptist Convention. From 1972-1974 she served on the board of the Colorado Baptist Home Association, which has jurisdiction over four nursing and two senior citizens homes, and is presently a member of the Laramie Baptist Service Corporation which is planning a home for retired persons.

Vandi and Horace have a special interest in young people. As directors of the American Baptist Student Activities at the University for two and a half years, they lived in the Student Center, counseled the young people, and were substitute parents for many.

During World War II they "adopted" six soldiers from Fort Warren, having them at their home for weekends. During the Army Special Training Program, they "adopted" several of those young men. The fondness these men acquired for the Moores continues today, and they often come back to visit.

Vandi and Horace also have a special feeling for the Indians of the state. Vandi has twice attended and written about the All American Indian Days at Sheridan. They have entertained in their home groups of Indian students.

Their children, now married, have a boy and two girls each. Jerrold is Director of Regional Planning for the state of New Hampshire. Ginny's husband, T. Terrence Phllips, does research for Columbia Gas Company.

Nine years ago the Moores moved to a community in the Laramie River Valley at the foot of the Rocky Mountains, quite a distance from Crandall, Georgia, where she was born May 1, 1912. Vandi has become story teller for the "Big Valley", relating both its colorful pioneer history and its present-day happenings. Her articles reveal both the close-knit life of the Valley, and the warmth of her own personality.

MARGARET OHLER HILL

Combining two careers has become commonplace for American women, many of whom have successfully raised a family while holding down a job. Combining three careers is a little less usual, and few women add a fourth dimension to their busy lives.

Margaret Hill, homemaker-mother, teacher and author, is now carrying a speaking schedule as well, complementing the careers and making a contribution to her community and state.

Arriving in Laramie in 1945 with her husband, Bob, and two young daughters, she had seven years of teaching behind her and had already published articles in juvenile and educational magazines. Taking in stride the addition of another daughter and a son when twins were born to her while she was completing her bachelor's degree requirements, she began writing teen-age novels. When the twins reached high school, their mother was obtaining her master's degree from the University of Wyoming while counselling on a provisional certificate at Laramie High School. She has now been a counsellor for eleven years, at the same school.

Meanwhile, she has published six teen-age novels, "Goal in the Sky," "Hostess in the Sky," "Senior Hostess," "Really, Miss Hillsboro!", "The Extra Special Room," and "Time to Quit Running." Literally hundreds of articles have appeared under her by-line in such magazines as *Parents, National P.T.A. Magazine, Grade Teacher, My Baby, The Writer* and *Writer's Digest*; four Public Affairs Pamphlets have been published by the Public Affairs Committee of New York City: "Drug Use and Abuse," "School Counselling," "Parents and Teen-agers," and "Getting the Retarded Child ready for School."

Because of the retardation of her youngest daughter, she has made indepth study of retarded children, enabling her to write and speak from personal experience and knowledge of a subject close to many parents.

Her expertise in the fields of writing and counselling have led to the fourth dimension of her career, speaking throughout the state of Wyoming and elsewhere on her two fields, as well as on the subject of retarded children.

Unwilling to rest on her laurels, Margaret Hill keeps up on modern trends in counselling and writing through the organizations to which she belongs: National Press Women, Wyoming Press Women, National Writers' Club, Society of Children's Book Writers, National Education

Association, Wyoming Education Association, Albany County Education Association, Wyoming Writers, Laramie Writers' Group, American and Wyoming Personnel and Guidance Associations, National Association of Retarded Citizens, and the Albany County Association for Retarded Children.

Her children are: Geraldine (Mrs. Bill) Butterfield, Kathleen (Mrs. Russ) Carpenter, Ton Hill and Christine Hill.

THYRA GODFREY THOMSON
Born 1916

Thyra Godfrey Thomson has lived the fulfilled life that many women dream of. She is serving her third term as Wyoming's Secretary of State, is the devoted mother of three handsome and successful sons, a proud new grandmother and attentive daughter. She has successfully managed a political career and close family life simultaneously.

As the seventh child and only daughter of James and Rose Godfrey, Thyra entered the world in Florence, Colorado on July 30, 1916 with a need to compete successfully in a "man's world." She has done so.

A graduate of Cheyenne High School and a cum laude graduate of the University of Wyoming, Thyra married Keith Thomson and worked as a secretary while he attended law school. The couple then moved to Cheyenne and Thyra began her "nest building years."

In 1954, Keith Thomson was elected to Wyoming's lone congressional seat and the couple moved to Washington, D.C. with their three young sons. For six years Thyra assisted with his career and was a homemaker and mother. She kept up her personal goals by taking graduate courses and writing a newspaper column.

Just one month following his election to the U.S. Senate in 1960, Keith Thomson died of a heart attack. Thyra returned to Cheyenne with her 16, 13 and 8-year-old sons to build a new life for the family.

In November of 1962 she was overwhelmingly elected to the post of Secretary of State. She has been re-elected three times, each time proving the top vote-getter in the state. She is always in great demand as a speaker and has written several newspaper and magazine articles over the years.

In spite of her busy schedule, she managed to provide a very secure home for her sons. The quality of the time she spent with them is demonstrated in the accomplishments of the boys and the close relationship they all still have with their mother.

Bill Thomson, his wife, Toni, and their young son, Keith Dean, make their home in Cheyenne where Bill practices law. Bruce will graduate from UW in December, after several years as a professional actor, and K. C. is in business in Cheyenne. Thyra also has her mother, Rose Godrey in Cheyenne to watch with pride her daughter's accomplishments as the state's highest woman official.

For many years, Thyra Thomson was the nation's highest elected woman statehouse official. She has been honored by many outstanding groups. Alpha Delta Kappa, women educator's honorary named her International Woman of Distinction. The University of Wyoming named her a Distinguished Alumni. Wyoming Press Women named her their Woman of Achievement. She has been tapped by many honorary societies.

During her tenure as Secretary of State for Wyoming, the office has greatly improved the quality of it's service to the people. She saw to it that the election code was revised and saw the Uniform Securities Act become law.

Thyra Thomson is what the women's liberation movement wants to see. She is a woman who values the quality of life; saw to it that she was prepared with an education to fulfill her career goals; married the man of her dreams; raised a family; truly managed to combine all the facets of true womanhood successfully into a life of fullfillment.

Supplemental List

When the Bicentennial project of the American Mothers Committee was started it was planned to issue a small booklet in each state to feature 30 historic mothers. As can be noted in the Foreword, it became evident that the hundreds of stories would be of national interest. However, to publish 1500 stories would make a book of unmanageable size and prohibitive cost. Therefore on the advice of several distinguished editors we reduced the number of mothers to be featured to approximately 10, and to list the names of others that were submitted on a Supplemental List. This in no way reflects on their merits and the editors are proud to honor them. Space would not permit delineations of their fields of interest or achievements.

Several State Committees urged the inclusion of the names of their State Bicentennial Chairmen. However to be fair to all, the editors regretted that the established policy precluded it. Their names appear on the montage pages preceding each State Chapter.

ALABAMA
Mrs. David Vess, Birmingham
Beatrice H. Morrison, Greensboro
Evelyn Walker Robertson, Fayette
Willodean Cooner Claunch, Jasper
Willie C. Bragg, Jr., Fayette
Sara W. Simpson, Berry
Emily Cranford Tubbs, Walker County
Bertha Strickler

ARIZONA
Winona M. Barbour, Brookban
Ellen Brophy
Nellis T. Bush, 1889
Louie Gaze Dennett, 1887
Isabell Selmes Greenway
Susan Janet Smith Jarvis
Edith Olive Kitt, 1878
Sarah Elizabeth Ferrin Lines
Elizabeth Seargent Oldaker
Etta Julia Vaughn Oliver, 1876
Vernettie O. Ivy
Juanita Mae Reger
Margaret Wheeler Ross, 1867
Harriet B. DuBois Vickers, 1852
Rhoda Jane Perkins Wakefield
Mattie L. Williams
Minnie Guenther

ARKANSAS
Ann Rector Conway, 1770, Walnut Hill
    Plantation
Carry Nation, 1846, Eureka Springs
Mary Elliot Ashley, 1865, Little Rock
Marcello Morgan Pearce, 1868, Magnolia
Susie Newton Pryor, 1900, Camden
Megnon Ross Haden, 1898, Greenbriar
Ann Sharpe Holmann, Little Rock
Ruth Myers Lincoln, 1897, Van Buren
Betty Gene Fowler Sparks, Little Rock
Ola Pearce Davis, Magnolia
Cora Essex, Stuttgart
Thelma Carter, Green Forest
Catherine Dees Hidy, Little Rock

Dorothy Cheyne, 1898, Fort Smith
Marguertie Rice, Little Rock
Willie May Gazort, Little Rock
Jetta Ford Sink, Newport
Judge Bernice Lichty Kizer, Fort Smith
Margaret Hickey Letzig, Little Rock
Willie Oates, Little Rock
Willie Maude Tucker, Little Rock
Vera Kilpatrick, Texarkana
Elizabeth Fulton Wright, 1824, Little Rock
Ruth Tate, Camden
Beatrice Lucinda Davis Keith, 1882, Benton
    County
Eleanor Sellors Berry, 1915, Bayou Meto Dewitt
Mollie Thatcher Mashaw, 1886, Lewisville
Margaret West Wynn, Fordyce
Tishie King Teague, 1875, Little Rock
Eloise Weir, Little Rock
Mrs. C. A. Dawson, Marked Tree
Mrs. C. W. Strickland, Arkadelphia
Ruth Donnell Anderson, North Little Rock
Nell Wallace Couch, 1886, Magnolia
Ruth Wooley Andress, Marysville
Nettie Hicks Kilgore, 1867, Magnolia
Mildred Farley Bass, Little Rock

CALIFORNIA
Kate Douglas Smith Wiggins
Frances Xavier Cabrini
Mrs. Herond N. Sheranian
Mrs. Elena Zelayeta
Mrs. Velma Hooper McCall
Mrs. Meta Weir Bruce
Mrs. Annetta Vincent Wood
Mrs. Dale Evans Rogers
Mrs. Dorothy Johnson Paul Bacon
Mrs. Phoebe E. Ashe Smith
Mrs. Vera Calder Stratford
Mrs. Gwendoln H. Brown
Mrs. Lucy Guild Toberman
Mrs. Jennie Hope Chapman Fitt
Mrs. Harriett Bulpitt Randall Campbell, M.D.
Mrs. Josephine Guerra Massimini
Mrs. Sybil Brandt
Mrs. Ida Cummings Mayer

California Continued
Mrs. Delmar Daves
Mrs. Ettie Lee
Mrs. Marian Van Waters
Mrs. Ellen Beach Yow

COLORADO
Lou Ethel Hunter Gardner, Boulder
Mrs. Valentine B. Fischer, Boulder

DISTRICT OF COLUMBIA
Mrs. Jouett Shouse
Mrs. Esther Peterson
Mrs. Katharine M. Graham
Abegal Adams
Dolly Madison
Emily Edson Briggs
Frances Hodgson Burnett
Kate Fields
Margaret Baird Smith
Madeline Vitter Dahlgren

FLORIDA
Mrs. Charlotte Friedland, Melbourne
Mrs. Lassie Goodbread Black, Lake City
Mrs. Albert Golden, Milton
Mrs. Robert H. Chenault, Vero Beach
Mrs. J. H. Fulcher, Eau Gallie
Mrs. Clint Byrom, Milton
Mrs. Sam I. Merritt, Tallahasee
Sophie Mae Mitchell, Sebring
Louise M. Taylor, Cocoa Beach
Dolly Mae Rose, Tampa
Agnes Granberry Chalker, Orange Park
Mrs. Ann Robinson
Alma Lee Roy, Indian River County

GEORGIA
Elizabeth Grisham Brown, 1826, Atlanta
Marion Peel Calhoun, 1886, Atlanta
Nellie Boyce David, 1895, Columbus
Edith Lester Harbin, 1876, Rome
Corra White Harris, 1869, Cartersville
Nancy Hart, 1735, Wilkes County
Nina McClure Head, 1885, Dahlonega
Sara Porter Hillhouse, 1763, Washington
Coretta Scott King, 1927, Atlanta
Mary Musgrove Bosomworth, Yamacraw
Martha McDonald Moore, 1884, Atlanta
Ida Allen Prather, 1885, Atlanta
Sue Brown Sterne, 1881, Atlanta
Sexta Eavenson Strickland, 1868, Atlanta
Charlotte de Bernier Taylor, 1806, Savannah

IDAHO
Mary Belknap Forney, 1865, Moscow
Lesley Williams Benoit, 1895, Twin Falls
Alice Taylor Walters, Boise
Tina Bellinie, Twin Falls
Gretch Kunigk Fraser, 1919, Sun Valley

ILLINOIS
Fredrika Guernsey Akerly, 1898, Milford
Mary Irish Alvey, 1912, Lincoln
Ella Owsley Brainard, 1840, Lincoln
Maude Kearney Browning, 1909, Benton
Maria Simpson Clingman, 1809, Cedarville
Aribel Hume Dennis, 1831, Chambersburg
Louella Carver Dirksen, 1899, Pekin
Elizabeth Smith Duncan, 1808, Jacksonville
Eva Jane Harper Follmer, 1904, Urbana
Barthena Hill Garrison, 1812, Coles County
Ann Armstrong Keys, 1845, Beason
Dr. Felicia Dorothy Koch, 1908, Granite City
Sarah Bush Lincoln, 1788, Coles County
Caroline Chamberlain Lutz, 1844, Lincoln
Hononegah Mack, 1798, Rockton
Gertrude Ross Reid, 1916, Carlinville
Mayme Force Stine, 1883, St. Elmo
Emma Scott Tucker, 1916, Freeport
Norma Hoblit Woods, 1889, Lincoln

IOWA
Mary Frances Huntress, 1871
Elizabeth Noyes Wharton, 1856
Carrie Roberts, 1888
Hazel T. Nelson, 1903
Lena Nelson Tow
Mrs. Alice Mae Keiley, 1891
Mary E. Cook, 1817
Emily Mackel Hughes, 1887
Honors Harrington Murphy Ambrose, 1856
Ruth Lowry Kunkel, 1881
May Poindexter Cooney, 1875
Grace Fitzgerald West, Sheldon, Iowa
Mary Plimpton Francis and Mame Paddock, 1856
Mary S. Kerlee, 1856
Isabel White Brenner, 1882
Harriet Peck Fenn Sanders, Birthplace,
    Tallmadge, Ohio, 1834
Ida Louise Dahms Hafferman, 1891
Lucinda Ann Chapman Belshaw, 1866
Nelly Sinclair Maclay, 1866, Scotland
Margretta Bohrnsen Luthje, 1875
Millie Skaw (Millie Mae Metcalf), 1885
Frankie Dillon McDonald, 1884
Marie Cahil Cooney, 1845
Hertha Lohse Lund
Virginia Belle Baker Hansen
Katherine Grant, Birthplace, Hungary
Mrs. John Willard, Sr.
Mamie Doud Eisenhower, Honorary President,
    American Mothers Committee (See Foreward
    Dedication)
Lou Henry Hoover (Mrs. Herbert) (See California
    Mothers)
Bess Streeter Aldrich (See Nebraska Mothers)
Laura Ingalls Wilder (See Nebraska Mothers)
Ida B. Wise, Nat. President WCTU
Annie Savery Callanan
Honor Willsie Morrow, Editor Delineator
    Magazines
Susan Glaopell, Author & Playwright
Alice Van Wert Murray, Farm Bureau Leader,
    1965 Iowa Mother

Iowa Continued

Mrs. Max Mayer, Early Des Moines council women who perfected Iowa Highway Patrol organization. One of 4 in Iowa's first Hall of Fame.

Ethel Lewis Collesteu (Mrs. C.C.), Noted Leader and President Iowa P.T.A., 1937-39

Helen LeBaron Hilton, Dean of Home Economics Department, Iowa State University

Mrs. Henry Wallace, Mother of Henry Wallace, Secretary of Agriculture, Wife of founder of Wallace's Farmer

Ruth Suckow, Noted Author

Beatrice Blackmer Gould, Editor Ladies Home Journal

Martha Duncan, Radio commentator, I.S.U., Ames

Ann Landers, Abigail Van Buren, Twin sisters, syndicated columns of advice

Mrs. Percy Lainson, National president American Legion Auxiliary, 1954-55

Mrs. Thomas F. Sullivan, Mother of the 5 Sullivan brothers who died on the Battleship Iowa in World War 2

Mildred Pelzer, Painter

KENTUCKY

Iva Grace Solomon Peters, Trenton
Margaret Price Sheehan, Danville
Eliza R. Cooksey, Ashland
Nannie Peace Booth, Walbins Creek
Mrs. Margie Helm, Bowling Green

MAINE

Martha Ballad, Augusta
Susanna Curtis Cony, Fort Western
Mae Craig, Gur Gannett Newspapers
Rev. Hilda Ives, Portland
Lucy Knox, Thomaston
Zilpha Wardsworth Longfellow, Portland
Sarah Emery Merrill, Andover
Rebecca Gould Sewall Webster, Gardiner
Silva Stanislaus, Lincoln
Harriet Beacher Stowe, Brunswick
Sarah Payson Willis (Fanny Fern), Portland

MARYLAND

Florence A. Rogers

MICHIGAN

Mary Austin Wallace, 1835, Calhoun City
Cornelia Blanche Groefsema Kennedy, 1923, Detroit
Alice Follett (Mrs. Edwin F.) Uhl, 1884, Grand Rapids
Dorothy (Mrs. Stanley S.) Kresge, 1901, Detroit
Lucille (Mrs. Guy A.) Hemenger, 1906, Algonac
Berenice (Mrs. Stanley T.) Lowe, Battle Creek
Veda B. (Mrs. Harry W.) Anderson, 1919, Ann Arbor
Helen Wallback (Mrs. William) Milliken, 1922
Madame Antoine de la Mothe Cadillac, 1660, Detroit

Mrs. John Johnston, 1781, Michilimackinac
Lucinda Hinsdale (Mrs. L. H.) Stone, 1814, Kalamazoo
Deborah Crane (Mrs. Richard R.) Harkness, 1823, Adrian
Laura Blancher Smith (Aunt Laura) Haviland, 1823, Raisin Valley
Diana (Mrs. Lewis) Piper, 1823, Eaton Rapids
Mary Anne Bryant (Mrs. Perry) Mayo, 1825, Marshall Township
Lizzie Merrill (Mrs. Thomas) Palmer, 1837, Detroit
Mary E. Green, M.D., 1843, Charlotte
Emma Nichols Wanty, M.D., 1851, Grand Rapids
Dora D. Martin, 1854, Paw-Paw

MINNESOTA

Celia Elizabeth Dunnell Leavitt, 1840, Minneapolis
Lucille Kahnke Miller, Sr., 1922, Janesville
Agnes Carson Hopkins Ponds, 1825, Bloomington
Caroline Krell Probst, 1901, Wilmont
Marie Sonander Rice, 1886, Minneapolis
Edwina Hurlbut Ryan, Sr., 1888, St. Paul
Lily Elizabeth Sahlstrom Samuelson, 1886, Wayzata
Eva Creighton Vinton, 1891, Minneapolis
Ethel Ross Weld, 1898, St. Paul
Goldie Kenner Wolfe, 1913, Duluth

MISSOURI

Panthea Grant Boone Boggs, 1801, Jefferson City
Ida Martha Doerr Bond, 1880, Perryville
Rebecca Bryan Boone, 1775, Mexico
Sacajawea Charbonneau, 1784, St. Louis
Madam Marie Therese Bourgeois Chouteau, 1733, St. Louis
Caroline Reed Drew, 1882, Columbia
Myrtle Page Fillmore, 1845, Kansas City
Jessie Benton Fremont, 1824, St. Louis
Julia Dent Grant, 1826, St. Louis
Phoebe Apperson Hearst, 1842, Salem
Elizabeth Craig McBride, Paris
Eleanor Fry McGee, 1793, Kansas City
Mary Frances Paxton Penney, 1842, Hamilton
Mary Whitney Phelps, 1812, Springfield
Martha Head Price, 1810, Chariton
Edna Burt Quigley, 1875, Centralia
Betsy Shelby, 1842, Lexington
Mary Easton Sibley, 1793, St. Charles
Elizabeth (Bess) Virginia Wallace Truman, 1885, Independence
Mary Harmon Weeks, 1851, Kansas City

MONTANA

Mrs. John Willard
Nellie Sinclair Maclay
Maria Cahill Cooney
Mame Paddock
Mary Plimpton Frances
Mary S. Kerles
Lena Towe
Emily Mackel Hughes

Montana Continued
Harriet Pack Fenn Sanders
Ida Louis Dahma Hafferman
Lucinda Ann Chapman Belshaw
Alice Mae Keiley
Margaret (Margretta) Bohrnsen Luthje
Millie Skaw
Frankie Dillon McDonald
Mary E. Cook
Hazel T. Nelson
Mary Frances Huntress
Honors Harrington Murphy Ambrose
Elizabeth Noyes Wharton
Ruth Lowry Kunkel
Hertha Lohse Lund (Mrs. Geo. N.)
May Poindexter Cooney
Virginia Belle Baker
Katherine Grant
Mary Fox Howe
Grace Fitzgerald West
Mrs. A. F. Longeway
Nannie T. Alderson

NEBRASKA

Bess Furman Armstrong
Anne Linger Campbell
Barbara Myers Cobb
Nellie Throop Magee
Elizabeth Newell Marti
Eliza Wilcox Merrill
Mary Doland Mullen
Mrs. Keith Neville
Dr. Hettie Kersey Painter
Dr. Susan LaFlesche Picotte
Julia Ann Pollard Sheldon
Grace McCance Snyder
Dr. Olga Sadilik Stastny
Hazel Struble Stebbins
Mrs. C. K. Struble
Johanna Schmefel Stuefer
Melva McFarland Swedburg
Virginia Yapp Trotter
Esther Carter Griswold-Warner
Elizabeth Lemen Weritz

NEW HAMPSHIRE

Mrs. J. Duane Squires
Mrs. Mary Greely
Mrs. Frank S. Streeter
Mrs. Lafell Dickinson
Mrs. Alpha Harriman
Mrs. Hilda Brungot
Mrs. Eileen Foley
Mrs. Charles McDuffee
Mrs. Elizabeth Webster
Ocean Born Mary
Mrs. Alan Shepherd
Sarah Countess Rumford
Eunice Cole (Goody)
Martha Wentworth
Mrs. J. Randolph Coolidge
Mrs. Mary Dobson
Mrs. Martha Jackson Pendexter
Mrs. Harriet Foule Smith
Mrs. Judith Webster Shannon

NEW JERSEY

Anne Morrow Lindberg
Mary Donaldson Haynie, Atlantic City

NEW MEXICO

Ethel Tyler Huning, 1893, Los Lunas
Beatrice Enos Ortiz, 1868, Santa Fe
Filomena Jojola deBaca, 1892, Albuquerque
Willie Gilpin Woodburn, 1894, Clovis
Effie Jones Collins, 1887, Albuquerque
Ida Franklin Mauk, 1878, Portales
Ada May Rea, 1883, Portales
Theresa Lovato Tabet, 1912, Belen
Elizabeth Drinkard Sims, 1892, Eunice
Lula E. Anderson, 1906, Albuquerque

NEW YORK

Ruth Stafford Peale (Mrs. Norman Vincent)
Rilda Bee Cliburn
Georgiana Farr Sibley

NORTH CAROLINA

Rachel Caldwell, 1742, N. C.
Jane Gray Logan, 1747, Iredell County
Mary (Polly) Jonesleech Speight, 1765, New Bern
Eliza Jane Lord de Rosset, 1812, Wilmington
Addie Worth Bagley Daniels, 1869, Raleigh
Inglis Fletcher, 1879, Alton
Foy Johnson Farmer, 1887, Scotland County
Pearl Lee Moore, 1899, Wake County
Norma Connell Berryhill, 1902, Warren County
Nancy Winbon Chase, 1903, Wayne County
Vera Lowry, 1915, Robeson County
Margaret Harper, 1917, Southport
Fannie Bickett, 1870, Henderson
Gladys Tillett, Morganton
Sallie Southall Cotton, 1847, North Car.
Beulah Vernon Apperson, Davie County
Mary Mendenhall Hobbs, 1852, Guilford County
Lyde M. Merrick, 1890, Durham
Mary Bayard Clarke, 1830
Guion Griffis Johnson, 1900, Folfe City, Texas

NORTH DAKOTA

Addie Mae Mccollum Claflin, 1863, Mandan
Martine Sivertson Enget, 1876, Powers Lake
Rachel S. Morgart Halfpenny, 1863, Devils Lake
Emma Calhoun Hall, 1850, Ft. Berthold
Mrs. Ronnaug Halvorson, 1881, Bonetraill
Ida Attalia Hurnsdon Ims, 1859, Sims
Martha Glew Jones, St. Thomas
Gertie Steine Larson, 1878, Hettinger
Marie Gielstad Hange, 1881
Rosa R. Maxwell, 1875, Garrison
Anna Bergetta Nilsen Nelson, 1861, Lork
Elsie Powell, 1870, Devils Lake
Alvida Jackson Sheard, 1882, Cathay
Eva Etta Miller Smeltzer, 1865, Cando
Mrs. Mollie Stevens, 1875, Hettinger
Margaret Hargrave Veitch, 1864, Williston
Mrs. Betsey Sondrall Walla, 1866, Arnegard
Clara Alice Bigler Wagemann, 1876, Cando
Almyra Graves Wood, 1856, Crary
Bridget O'Connell Walters, 1873, Williston

OKLAHOMA

Mrs. Hattie Lee Herd Cooper

PENNSYLVANIA

Harriet Lane
Lydia Darragh
Mrs. Thomas Potter
Mrs. Efrem Zimbalist
Mrs. John Wintersteen
Ann Hawkes Hutton
Princess Grace of Monaco
Dr. Emily H. Mudd

PUERTO RICO

Alejandrina Benitez de Arce de Gautier, 1814-
    1879, Mayaguez
Josefa Campiz Carlo de Delgado, 1830-1901, Cabo
    Rojo
Isaura Arnau de Ruiz Gandia, 1844-   , Santurce
Pilar Defillo Amiguet de Casals, 1853-1931,
    Mayaguez
Trinidad Padilla de Sanz, 1864-1957, Vega Baja
Amina Tio de Malaret, 1865-1939, San German
Carmen Bozello Guzman de Huyke, XIX Cent.,
    Arroyo
Consuelo Vicil de Pales Matos, 1872-1946,
    Guayama
Ana Dolores Perez, Marchand Dr. M.SC., 1886-
    , Utuado
Josefa Arena de Armstrong, 1887-   , Anasco
Patria Rodriguez Martinez de Rivera, 1890-1925,
    Utuado
Dolores M. Pinero de Diaz, Dr. M.Sc., 1895-1975,
    Carolina
Maria Luisa Fernandez de Mateo, 1896-   ,
    Mayaguez
Juana Rodriguez Mundo, 1900-1975, Loiza
Carmen Leila Cuevas, 1912-   , San German

SOUTH CAROLINA

Mary Roper Coker

SOUTH DAKOTA

Cora Hjertaas Staving, 1900, Sioux Falls
Lillian Calvert Lushbough, 1904, Sturgis
Virginia Cotton Stoltz, 1913, Watertown
Mathilda O'Connor Geppert, 1887, Vermillian
Janet Herring Dewitt, 1926, Sioux Falls
Marian Jean Randall Nickelson, 1926, Belle
    Fourche
Mrs. Claude Van Nuys, 1880, Rapid City
Mrs. Joseph Parmsley (Melina), 1887, Ipswich
Mrs. Benjamin Evans (Esther), 1888, Verdon
Mrs. Hans Sorenson (Alvilda), 1901, Brookings
Mrs. I. D. Weeks (Virginia), 1902, Vermillion
Mrs. Joe Oyan (Ethel), 1907, Sioux Falls
Mrs. Harvey Ross (Agnes), 1910, Flandreau
Mrs. Carolyn McGibney (Carolyn), 1913, Spearfish
Mrs. D. L. Hersrud (Judy), 1917, Black Hawk
Mrs. T. H. Satler (Isabel), 1918, Yankton
Mrs. Laura Ingalls Wilder, 1867, DeSmet
Mrs. Meda McCullen, 1877, Miller
Mrs. Kate Markham, 1885
Mrs. L. A. Pierson (Edith), 1901, Sioux Falls
Mrs. Irene Trotzig, Ipswich
Mrs. Dorothy Delicate, Lead (Homestake Mine)
Mrs. Robert Lusk (Jeanette), Huron
Mrs. Edna Grubl, Meade County

TENNESSEE

Mrs. Leo R. Burson
Florence (Flo) Rogers, Dyersburg

TEXAS

Mrs. Nora Wendland, Texas Chairman
Mollie Kirkland Bailey, 1844, Houston
Louzelle Rose Barclay, 1881, Temple
Janey Slaughter Briscoe, 1923, Austin
Idanell Brill Connally, 1919, Houston
Pearl Terrell Daniel, 1882, Temple
Elida Garcia de Falcon, 1879, Rio Grande City
Thelma Rawls Fletcher, 1905, Salado
Norma Elizabeth Rhodes Gabler, 1923, Longview
Sarah Ann Stinson Hogg, 1855, Austin
Margaret Lea Houston, 1819, Independence
Margaret Lois Killingsworth Jackson, Longview
Eliza Griffin Johnston, 1821, China Grove
Bobbie Davis Jones, 1914, Galveston
Lucy Ann Thornton Kidd-Key, 1839, Sherman
Henrietta Chamberlin King, 1832, Kingsville
Jane Herbert Wilkinson Long, 1798, Richmond
Mary Helvey Newman, 1872, Dallas
Viola Kellum Redmond, 1905, Austin
Beth Sewell Snow, 1902, Harlingen
Crystelle Robert Wickett, 1909, Ft. Worth

VERMONT

Ellen Ortensa Peck Bailey, 1847, East Montpelier

UTAH

Mrs. Glen Walker Wallace, Salt Lake
Lavinia Fugal, 1879, Pleasant Grove
Lorena Chipman Fletcher, 1888, American Fork
Stella Harris Oaks, Provo
Romania Penrose, Salt Lake City
Ramona Cannon, Salt Lake City
Wilma Boyle Bunker, Salt Lake City
Cucretia Jane Miles Evans, Salt Lake City
Phyllis McGinley
Florence Jepperson Madsen, Provo
Alberta Henry
Martha Hughes Cannon
Lucy Beth Cardon Rampton
Kate B. Carter
Caroline Eyring Miner
Lucile Dimond Smith
Eva Stewart Ashton
Emma Cornelia Sorenson Lund
Ruth May Fox, Salt Lake City
Juanita Brooks, Salt Lake City

WYOMING

Mrs. Carl Willford, 1881, Saratoga
Mrs. Mae Mickelson, 1903, Big Piney
Mrs. Clara Calista Deloney Mills, 1872, Evanston
Mrs. George (Nan) Driscoll Kuntzman
Mrs. Laura (Peggy) Williams, 1903, Sheridan

ACKNOWLEDGEMENTS

The American Mothers Committee, Inc. expresses its deep gratitude to the hundreds of persons, to companies and institutions that have made it possible to publish this unusual volume as its contribution to the Bicentennial Year of 1976.

    The Charles E. Tuttle Co. Publisher, Rutland, Vermont
    The Rumford Press, Concord, New Hampshire
    The Colonial Press, Clinton, Massachusetts
    The Mohawk Pulp and Paper Co., New York

For financial support ranging from gifts of $15,000 to $100.00 without which it would have been impossible to carry out the project:
    Florists Transworld Delivery, Major Grant, $15,000–1974-1976, Michigan
    The Joe and Emily Lowe Foundation, Mrs. David Fogelson, New York
    The F.R. Foundation, Dr. & Mrs. Frank Stanton, New York
    The J.C. Penney Foundation, Mrs. J.C. Penney, New York
    The Abel Foundation, Miss Alice Abel, Nebraska
    Sperry and Hutchinson Co., Mrs. Elaine Pitts, New York
    The Mohawk Pulp and Paper Co., Mr. Charles Liessler, New York
    Mr. & Mrs. Russell S. Marriott, Md. and N.H.
    Mrs. Charles Schwartz, New York
    Mrs. Edwin G. Lewis, New Hampshire
    Bicentennial Committee (Mothers Committee) New Hampshire
    Bicentennial Committee (Mothers Committee) Nebraska
    Mr. & Mrs. S. Haskins Ridens, Tennessee
    Mr. & Mrs. Isaac Stewart

ADDITIONAL CONTRIBUTORS

    Mrs. Sherman Drawdy, Georgia
    Miss Margaret Gage, California
    Mrs. Olga F. Engdahl, Nebraska
    Dr. Alton Ochsner, La.
    Mrs. G. Stanley McAllister, New York
    Mrs. T.C. Lozier, Mo.
    Mrs. Sarah Brock, Pennsylvania
    Mrs. A.E. Dohrenwend, New York
    Mrs. Anthony E. Botts, Illinois
    Mrs. Herrold N. Sheranian, California
    Mr. & Mrs. Eugene Scott, Louisianna.
    Mrs. Virginia McDonald, Connecticut
    Mrs. Charles Woods, Illinois
    Mrs. Mary Filser Lohr, New York
    Mrs. Belle Spafford, Utah
    Mr. & Mrs. Clarence W. Hall, Florida
    Mrs. Betty Levinson, Illinois
    Mrs. Katherine Tedeschi, Massachusetts
    Mr. & Mrs. W. Howard Green, Pennsylvania
    The Gold Seal Co. North Dakota
    Mr. & Mrs. Kemmons Wilson, Tennessee
    Mrs. Fred Zahn, Oklahoma
    Mr. Dallas Sherman, N.Y.

For services beyond the call of duty:
SPECIAL TRIBUTE TO:

Dr. J. Duane Squires, Vice Chairman, American Revolution Bicentennial Administration, Historian for the State of New Hampshire

The Honorable Lindy Boggs, La., Member of the House of Representatives on the American Revolution Bicentennial Administration

John W. Warner, Administrator American Revolution Bicentennial Administration

Mr. William Butler—Deputy Assistant Administrator, ARBA

Mr. Sydney Eiges, Communications, ARBA

Mr. Louis Raskin, Program Liaison Officer—ARBA

Mr. Robert O'Brien, Senior Editor, Readers Digest

Mr. Charles Liessler, President, Mohawk Pulp and Paper Co., New York, N.Y.

The Rev. Dr. Edward Elson, Chaplain of the U.S. Senate

Mr. Mitchell Backon, Vice President, Rumford Press, Concord, N.H.

Mr. Charles Meunier, Mrs. Vicki Carter, Rumford Press, Concord, N.H.

Mr. Donald Berg, Manager, The Charles E. Tuttle Co. Rutland, Vt. (Publisher)

Mr. Fred Mitchell, Colonial Press, Clinton, Mass.

Mrs. Dorothy M. Lewis, Chairman—Bicentennial Committee

Mrs. Russell S. Marriott, Vice Chairman—Bicentennial Committee

Mrs. Lynmar Brock, Consultant—Bicentennial Committee

AND

Members of the Bicentennial Honorary Committee:

Mrs. Mamie Doud Eisenhower, Chairman

Mr. Robert O'Brien, Editor, Reader's Digest

Dr. J. Duane Squires, New Hampshire Historian

Honorable John D. Vanderhoof, Former Governor, Colorado

Dr. G. Roy Fugal (retired), General Electric Company

Mrs. J.C. Penney, Member, Advisory Council

Mrs. Dale Evans Rogers, Hollywood

Mrs. Stanley S. Kresge, Advisory Council, Michigan

Mrs. Clark Gable, Hollywood

Mrs. Belle Spafford, Advisory Council, Utah

Dr. Norman Vincent Peale, New York

Mr. S. Haskins Ridens, Advisory Council, Tenn.

Mrs. Denny Griswold, Publisher, Public Relations News, International, New York

Mrs. Harper Sibley, Advisory Council, New York

Mrs. Oswald B. Lord, Advisory Council, New York

Mrs. Sherman Drawdy, Past President, American Mothers Committee, Inc. Georgia

Mrs. R.G. LeTourneau, Past President, American Mothers Committee, Inc., Texas

Mrs. Kemmons Wilson, 1970 National Mother, Tenn.

The Rev. Terence J. Finlay, D.D., New York

Dr. Carl A. Berntsen, Advisory Council, New York

The Hon. Lindy Boggs (La.) Member of Congress

Lady Malcolm Douglass-Hamilton, Advisory Council, New York

Mr. Lowell Thomas—New York

Honorable John Glenn, Jr., Ohio

Mr. Garry Moore, New York

Mr. Dallas Sherman, Advisory Council, New York

Mr. Billy Casper, Utah

Mr. Edward Weeks, Editor Emeritus, Atlantic Monthly Press, Mass.

Mr. Don Flowers, President, Florist's Transworld Delivery, Michigan & Maryland

National Executive Bicentennial Committee
American Mothers Committee, Inc.

Mrs. Dorothy Lewis, N.H.
National Chairman

Dr. J. Duane Squires, N.H.
Vice Chairman, ARBA
Washington

Mrs. Russell S. Marriott, MD.
Vice Chairman

Mr. Dan Flowers, MICH.
President,
Florists' Transworld Delivery

Mrs. Lynmar Brock, PA.
Consultant

Mrs. Mary Filser Lohr, NY
President,
American Mothers Committee,
Inc. Ex-Officio

The publication of *"Mothers of Achievement in American History 1776-1976"* is a dream come true. Through the initial grant of $15,000 from the Florist Transworld Delivery, the American Mothers Committee dared to embark on such a prodigious task. For many years this public spirited colorful industry has worked closely with the American Mothers Committee. It was a natural for them to pay tribute to Motherhood, past and present. The American Mothers Committee, Inc. expresses deep gratitude for their faith and interest. Because of this tangible cooperation, other donors added contributions in varying amounts to make possible the printing of this volume.

STATE MOTHERS 1935-1975

This book has been compiled by the American Mothers Committee, Inc. of New York, N.Y. The following list includes the names of National mothers elected annually 1935-1975 by jury, by state. An asterisk marks the names of the national "American Mothers of the Year". A bronze Honor Roll listing the national mothers is displayed in the south lounge of the Waldorf Astoria New York, N.Y. It was dedicated by Mrs. Mamie Doud Eisenhower.

ALABAMA

Mrs. Mary Warren Christ Butler, *Huntsville*..........1975

Mrs. Willielary Shute Stewart, *Fayette*..........1974

Mrs. Geraldine Graves Jordan, *Tuscaloosa* 1973

Mrs. Annie Elsie Zimmerman Graham, *Courtland* 1972

Mrs. Constance Trinque Desaulniers, *Talladega* 1971

Mrs. Catherine Ashmore Whitehead, *Oxford* 1970

Mrs. Maye Jackson Price, *Newton*..........1969

Mrs. Carrie Newton Wright, *Berry* 1968

Mrs. Sara Reeves Allen, *Troy* 1967

Mrs. Emily Price Holmes, *Letohatchie*.1966

Mrs. Emma Payne Flowers, *Ozark* 1965

Mrs. Virginia Machey Jordan, *Centre*..1964

Mrs. Johnnie Butler Norton, *Selma* 1963

*Mrs. Mary Celesta Johnson Weatherly, *Fort Payne*..........1962

Mrs. Frances Rockwell Vail Clark, *Bessemer*..........1961

Mrs. Carrie Dobson De Bardeleben, *Lowndesboro*..........1960

Mrs. Eulalia Ruth Vess, *Birmingham*..1959

Mrs. Mary B. Coleman, *Eutaw*..........1958

Mrs. Mary Davis Henry, *Anniston*........1957

Mrs. Elizabeth Chew Anderton, *Birmingham*..........1956

Mrs. Martha V. Barker, *Boaz*..........1955

Mrs. I. D. Nolen, *Alexander City*..........1954

Mrs. Annie Whitehurst Jordan, *Birmingham*..........1953

Mrs. Lillian Hart Folsom, *Uniontown*..1952

Mrs. Walter B. Merrill, *Heflin*..........1951

Mrs. R. K. Jones, *Pepperell*..........1950

Mrs. Mae Goodyear Green, *Montgomery* 1949

Mrs. Lela Bell Morgan Simmons, *Andalusia*..........1948

Mrs. J. Hereford, *Gurley* 1946

Mrs. Archie Barr, *Birmingham*..........1943

ALASKA

Mrs. Ruth Evangelin Towner, *Kenai*....1975

Mrs. Mable Reynolds Rasmussen, *Fairbanks*..........1974

Mrs. Ruth Elizabeth Banks Regan, *Fairbanks*..........1973

Mrs. Margaret I. Haggland, *Fairbanks*..........1972

Mrs. Mary Kevin Gilson, *Valdez*..........1971

Mrs. Ann Lou Cramer, *Ketchikan*........1970

Mrs. Edrel Annette Kelly Coleman, *Ft. Wainwright*..........1969

Mrs. Mildred Hotch Sparks, *Haines*....1968

Mrs. Louise Argetsiner, *Juneau*..........1967

Mrs. Elizabeth Sheldon Hakkinen, *Haines* 1966

Mrs. Paul V. Clumpner, *Detroit, Mich.* 1955

Mrs. Henry H. Chapman, *Sitka* 1954

Mrs. Delia Hamilton Watson, *Mountain View*..........1953

Mrs. Carol Beery Davis, *Juneau*..........1952

Mrs. Michael J. Walsh, *Nome*..........1951

Mrs. Edward Arthur Hering, *Fairbanks*..........1950

ARIZONA

Mrs. Mary Frances Pinkard Kelly, *Tucson* 1975

Mrs. Mildred Boyer Jarvis, *Mesa*..........1974

Mrs. Evelina Ranaud Sprietsma, *Phoenix*..........1973

Mrs. Cora Elizabeth Thorp, *Bisbee*........1972

Mrs. Fran Vail Luther, *Phoenix*..........1971

Mrs. Vera Irene Pratt Dingman, *Mesa*1970

Mrs. Eleanor Britton Davey, *Phoenix*...1969

Mrs. Lois Martineau Kartchner, *St. David*..........1968

*Mrs. Minnie Knoop Guenther, *White River*..........1967

Mrs. Vida Driggs Brinton, *Mesa*..........1966

Mrs. Dorothy M. Van Dyke, *Phoenix*....1965

Mrs. Flossie Wills Barnes, *Casa Grande*..........1963

Mrs. Hazel Bendure Johnson, *Wilcox*..1959

Mrs. John Purdy, *Winslow*..........1958

Mrs. Sophronia Brown Sherwood, *Mesa*..........1957

Mrs. Dorothy M. B. Cross, *Phoenix*.......1956

Mrs. Nellie Miller Ritter, *Kirkland*......1955

Mrs. Alvan W. Fenn, *Benson* 1954

Mrs. Emma Mae Browne Hewette, *Tempe*..........1953

Mrs. Mary Otis Blake, *Chandler*..........1952

Mrs. E. S. Edmonson, *Nogales*..........1951

Mrs. E. Payne Palmer, Sr., *Phoenix*......1947

ARKANSAS

Mrs. Mildred Farley Walker Bass, *Little Rock*..........1975

Mrs. Ruth Donnell Anderson, *North Little Rock*..........1974

Mrs. Margaret Lucille West Wynne, *Fordyce*..........1973

Mrs. Anne Sharpe Garrett Holmann, *Little Rock*..........1972

Mrs. Vera McCoy Kilpatrick, *Texarkana*..........1971

Mrs. Dorothy Mace Cheyne, *Fort Smith*..........1970

Mrs. Jetta Ford Sink, *Newport*..........1969

Mrs. Marguerite English Rice, *Little Rock*..........1968

Mrs. Mae Hargis Flanders, *Little Rock*..........1967

Mrs. Mary Catherine Williamson Wyrick, *Magnolia*..........1966

Mrs. Catherine D. Hidy, *Little Rock*.....1965

Mrs. Cora Baker Essex, *Stuttgart* 1964

Mrs. Thelma O'Dell Carter, *Mountain Home*..........1963

Mrs. Agnes Ball Gray, *Little Rock* 1962

Mrs. Carolyn Myers Lincoln, *Little Rock*..........1961

Mrs. Venita Pearcy Bennett, *El Dorado* 1960

Mrs. Eloise Field Weir, *Little Rock* 1959

Mrs. Ola Pearce Davis, *Magnolia*..........1958

Mrs. Virgie Waskom Dawson, *Marked Tree*..........1957

Mrs. Daisy Paschal McCollum, *Emerson*..........1956

Mrs. Katherine Wilson Hyatt, *Monticello*..........1955

Mrs. Mary Davis Woodward, *Magnolia*..........1954

Mrs. Willie May McIntosh Cazort, *Little Rock*..........1953

Mrs. Alice Harris Walker, *Forest City*.1952

Mrs. Owen O. Axley, *Warren* 1951

Mrs. T. J. Raney, *Little Rock*..........1950

Mrs. James R. Echols, *Monticello*..........1949

Mrs. Agnes Wynne Twitty, *Fordyce*.....1948

Mrs. David D. Terry, *Little Rock*..........1947

Mrs. Roberta Fulbright, *Fayetteville*....1946

Mrs. John W. Rhea, *Waldo* 1945

CALIFORNIA

Mrs. Josephine Guerra Massimini, *North Hollywood*..........1975

Mrs. Harriett Bulpitt Randall Campbell, *Glendale* 1974

Mrs. Jennie Hope Chapman Fitt, *Concord*..........1973

Mrs. Lucy Guild Toberman, *Los Angeles* 1972

Mrs. Gwendolyn H. Brown, *Los Angeles*..........1971

Mrs. Vera Calder Stratford, *Los Angeles*..........1970

Mrs. Phoebe E. Ashe, *Sherman Oaks*...1969

Mrs. Dorothy Johnson Paul Bacon, *Hollywood*..........1968

Mrs. Dale Evans Rogers, *Beverly Hills* 1967

Mrs. Annetta Vincent Wood, *Oakland*.1966

Mrs. Meta Weir Bruce, *San Diego*..........1965

Mrs. Velma Hooper McCall, *Palm Desert*..........1964

Mrs. Elena Zelayeta, *San Francisco*.....1963

Mrs. Marie Gutke Sheranian, *Beverly Hills* 1962

Mrs. Edmond F. Ducomun, *San Marino*..........1961

*Mrs. Emerald Barman Arbogast, *Los Angeles* 1960

Mrs. Lillian Harris Mathias, *Tulare*.....1959

Mrs. Ruth Hannaford Weed, *Coachella*..........1958

Mrs. Margaret Edna McMillan, *Palm Springs* 1957

Mrs. Mary Neagle Ragen, *San Diego* ...1956

Mrs. Ruby Berkeley Goodwin,
Los Angeles 1955

Mrs. E. Llewellyn Overholt, Sr.,
Los Angeles 1954

Mrs. Margaret Rose Murray,
San Francisco 1953

Mrs. Jessie Munro Reiner,
Santa Barbara 1952

Mrs. Walter A. Rubner, *Van Nuys* 1951

Mrs. Jesse Hays Baird, *San Anselmo* ...1950

Mrs. Mary Catherine Fletcher,
San Diego 1949

Mrs. Ralph M. Pederson, *Stockton* 1948

Mrs. Allen Irvine Forkner, *Stockton* 1947

Dr. Aurelia Reinhardt, *Burlingame* 1946

Mrs. Albert T. Quon, *Los Angeles* 1945

Mrs. John A. Pritchard, *Burbank* 1944

Mrs. Nora W. Edmundson,
Santa Monica 1943

*Mrs. Frances Eleanor Smith,
Claremont 1936

COLORADO

Mrs. Dorothea Cole Ferrill, *Pueblo* 1975

Mrs. Jane Toth, *Westminster* 1974

Mrs. Eleanor Carlson Flanders,
Longmont 1973

Mrs. Mildred Ellenberger Reyher,
Wiley 1972

Mrs. Electra Wilson, *Colorado Springs* 1971

Mrs. Blanche Mowry Rucker, *Norwood* 1970

Mrs. Dorothy Jean Fisher Wayt,
Cortez 1969

Mrs. Aurelia Childs Anderson,
Longmont 1968

Mrs. Margaret Yager Talbott,
Palisade 1967

Mrs. Edna Botsford Hollis, *Denver* 1966

Mrs. Minnie Hauser Lake,
Fort Collins 1965

Mrs. Julia Hickman Retherford,
Denver 1964

Mrs. Lou Ethel Gardner, *Boulder* 1963

Mrs. Philistia Sebree Huiatt, *Florence.*1962

Mrs. Gertrude Spencer Kiteley,
Longmont 1961

Mrs. Mabel V. Skogsberg Walter,
Loveland 1960

Mrs. Leah Silverberg Eisen, *Denver* 1959

Mrs. Bert Mathias, *Monte Vista* 1958

Mrs. Grace Curtis Trevithick, *Pueblo* 1957

Mrs. Inez Remy Scott, *Fort Collins* 1956

Mrs. Martin Clark Kistler, *Loveland* 1955

Dr. Portia M. McKnight Lubchenco,
Sterling 1954

Mrs. Bernice McDermott Schuster,
Denver 1953

Mrs. Bernice Christensen Crowther,
Sanford 1952

Mrs. Odd C. Pfeiffdr, *Durango* 1951

Mrs. E. B. Davis, *Fort Lupton* 1950

Mrs. Max Berueffy, *Boulder* 1949

Mrs. Mary Ann M. Morrison, *Greeley* ...1948

Mrs. William H. Mott, *Denver* 1947

Mrs. Herbert David Ulmer, *Denver* 1946

Mrs. Leon E. Lavington, *Denver* 1945

Mrs. John Shafroth, *Denver* 1944

CONNECTICUT

Mrs. Elizabeth Gombos Turrell,
Fairfield 1975

Mrs. Marion Odell Foote, *Hebron* 1974

Mrs. Margaret Fagan Casey, *Milford* ..1973

Mrs. Harriet Chaikind Weinerman,
Hartford 1972

Mrs. Eleanor Phillips Hutt, *Milford* 1971

Mrs. Doris Galloway Cassidy,
Stamford 1970

Mrs. Evelyn McIntyre Conley,
Stratford 1969

Mrs. Helen B. Andrew Ewen, *Orange.*.1968

Mrs. Elizabeth Beers Gold,
West Cornwall 1967

Mrs. Helen Seger Burr,
Brookfield Center 1966

Mrs. Marjorie Mueller Freer,
West Hartford 1965

Mrs. Franchon Hartman Title,
West Hartford 1964

Mrs. Idella May Hill Clark, *Seymour* ...1963

Mrs. Dorothy Spellman Hutton,
Somers 1962

Mrs. Julia McElhiney Halsey,
Bridgeport 1961

Mrs. Sylvia Knox Bingham, *Salem* 1960

Mrs. Jane Ware Hoyt, *Stamford* 1959

Mrs. Anna S. Weinerman,
West Hartford 1958

Mrs. Edith Girven Sicilian, *Pawcatuck* 1957

Mrs. Mary Connolly Lee, *New Haven* ..1955

Mrs. Julius Levinson, *Stamford* 1954

Mrs. Rachael Clark Neumann,
New Britain 1953

Mrs. Sarah L. Fleming, *New Haven* 1952

Mrs. Douglas O. Burnham, *Watertown* 1951

Mrs. H. Edward James, *Rocky Hill* 1950

Mrs. Allen Latham, *Norwich Town* 1945

Mrs. Carlton Blanchard, *Norwich* 1944

DELAWARE

Mrs. Pearl Murray Townsend,
Frankford 1975

Mrs. Doris Townsend Lewis, *Dover* 1974

Mrs. Regina Swartz Mitten, *Dover* 1973

Mrs. Lillian Alice Jasa Milbury, *Dover* 1972

Mrs. Sadie Cathcart Conly,
23 W. Reamer Avenue 1971

Mrs. Majorie Willoughby Speakman,
Smyrna 1970

Mrs. Marie Marguerite Romig
Huntington, *Wilmington* 1969

Mrs. Florence F. Yackle Kershaw,
Newark 1968

Mrs. Elizabeth H. Stewart,
New Castle 1967

Mrs. Helen I. O'Roarke Tierney,
Newark 1966

Mrs. Catherine T. Freeman, *Lewes* 1965

Mrs. Anna Margaret Moffet O'Neill,
Smyrna 1964

Mrs. Emily Anna Lewis, *Seaford* 1963

Mrs. Vera Gilbride Davis, *Dover* 1962

Mrs. Anna Matthews Aydelotte,
Delmar 1961

Mrs. Bessie Ellegood Mayer, *Dover* 1960

Mrs. Hannah Dodd Thompson,
Rehoboth Beach 1959

Mrs. Aline Noren Ehinger, *Dover* 1958

Mrs. Delema Ashton Wilson Isaacs, Sr.,
Lincoln 1957

Mrs. Margaret C. Seitz, *Wilmington* 1956

Mrs. Esther Rabin Zurkow, *Dover* 1955

Mrs. Edgar J. Boggs, *Cheswold* 1954

Mrs. Fannie Donoho Stein, *Seaford* 1953

Mrs. Elizabeth Smallcross, *Odessa* 1952

Mrs. W. Mattie Brown, *Wyoming* 1951

Mrs. Jonathan Willis, *Milford* 1950

DISTRICT OF COLULBIA

Mrs. Genevieve Novella Johnson,
Washington 1975

*Mrs. Phyllis Brown Marriott,
Kinsington 1974

Mrs. Erma L. Steiger Patterson,
Washington 1973

Mrs. Josephine La Venia Isenbecker,
Alexandria 1972

Mrs. Marian Powell Anderson,
Washington 1971

Mrs. Etta Weaver Richwine,
Washington 1970

Mrs. Vida May Savage Thomas,
Washington 1969

Mrs. Sara Schilling Bartges,
Washington 1968

Mrs. Alicia V. Davison, *Washington* 1967

Mrs. Helen Louise Chitteck Elson,
Washington 1966

Mrs. Mary Johnson Benson,
Kensington, Md. 1965

Mrs. Herminia Haynes Aiken,
Chevy Chase 1964

Mrs. Nellie Butler Deane, *Washington* 1963

Mrs. Stella Kopulos, *Washington* 1962

Mrs. Thelma Mae Watson Hastings,
Washington 1961

Mrs. Myrtle Cheney Murdock,
Washington 1960

Mrs. Mabel Kramer Eberhardt,
Washington 1959

Mrs. Jessie Barnes Sudduth,
Washington 1958

Mrs. Sarah Pratt Atwood, *Washington* 1957

Mrs. Madeline Juneau Maloney,
Washington 1956

Mrs. Jean Cummings Collingwood,
Washington 1955

Mrs. Clardnce T. Nelson, *Washington* ..1954

Mrs. Marie Louise Chesley,
Washington 1953

Mrs. J. M. Dawson, *Washington* 1952

Mrs. Lou Porter Woodruff,
Washington 1951

Mrs. George O. Bullock, *Washington* 1950

Mrs. Mary McLeod Bethune,
Washington 1949

FLORIDA

Mrs. Lyda Thomas Bethea DuBose,
Lakeland 1975

Mrs. Jewell Wells Golden, *Milton*..........1974

Mrs. Dolly Blosser Rose, *Tampa*............1973

Mrs. Harriett Anna Grimm Lightfoot,
Lakeland 1972

Mrs. Nell Gattis Byrom, *Milton* *1971*

Mrs. Evelyn Greene Blum,
West Palm Beach 1970

Mrs. Anita Stuart Miller Spurlock,
Milton..1969

Mrs. Helen Moore Torrance, *Orlando*...1968

Mrs. Mary Mills Silber,
Satellite Beach 1967

Mrs. Edna Sims Green, *Ocala* 1966

Mrs. J. Hillis Miller, *Gainesville* 1965

Mrs. Grace Rowell Fisher, *Tallahassee* 1964

Mrs. Viola Olive Kissling, *Jacksonville* 1963

Mrs. May Howard Austin McEachern,
Miami..1962

Mrs. Lassie Goodbread Black,
Lake City..1961

Mrs. Najibah Katibah David, *Tampa*...1960

Mrs. Joe Boute Bryan Weaver,
Kissimee..1959

Mrs. Emily Murray Vance,
Coral Gables..1958

Mrs. Roberta Broadhurst Bennett,
Jacksonville..1957

Mrs. Sarah Scarborough Davis Lewis,
Tallahassee..1956

Mrs. Mary Agnes Granberry Chalker,
Orange Park 1953

Mrs. Wilma Ray Fisher Rogers,
Winter Park..1952

Mrs. George V. Tillman, *Lake Wales* ...1951

Mrs. E. Harold Johnson, *Orlando* 1949

Mrs. Frederick H. Baggott,
Panama City 1945

Mrs. Edna Giles, *Umatilla* 1944

Mrs. M.A. Coleman, *Panama City*.........1943

GEORGIA

Mrs. Bernice Ivey Minter, *Elberton* 1975

Mrs. Lucile Almand Lanford,
Stone Mountain 1974

Mrs. Sarah Goode Irvin Bullock,
Eastman..1973

Mrs. Evelyn Patrick Randolph,
Winder 1972

Mrs. Cornelia Turner Thornton,
Cordele 1971

Mrs. Essie Lee Cook Mathis, *Decatur*..1970

Mrs. Mary Monk Whatley, *Reynolds*.....1969

Mrs. Elizabeth Barksdale Johnson,
Washington..1968

Mrs. Margaret T. Cochran......................1967

Mrs. Fairy Hester Drawdy, *Augusta*....1966

Mrs. Ross M. Hoffman, *Albany* 1965

Mrs. Margaret Kapps Francisco,
Columbus 1964

Mrs. Louise Carmichael Cabaniss,
Maxeys..1963

Mrs. Lena Addis Kay, *Bryon* 1962

Mrs. Gene DuBose Barksdale Thomas,
Washington 1961

Mrs. Kathleen Acree Whiting, *Albany* 1960

Mrs. May Belle McGarity, *Dallas* 1959

Mrs. Ira F. McMinn, *Toccoa*....................1958

Mrs. Winifred Smith Maxwell,
Lexington..1957

Mrs. Ruth Bowers Wilder, *Waleska*......1956

Mrs. Kate Strickland Harman,
Carrollton 1955

*Mrs. Love McDuffie Tolbert, *Columbus* 1954

Mrs. Frances Virginia Glover,
Newman..1953

Mrs. Necie Woodall Collins, *Acworth* ...1952

Mrs. Eugene Talmadge, *McRae*..............1951

Mrs. Richard Brevard Russell, *Winder* 1950

Mrs. James F. Whitehead, *Athens* 1949

Mrs. Madolon Moore Hardy, *Augusta*..1948

Mrs. James C. Malone, *Atlanta*..............1947

Mrs. C. Stewart Colley, *Grantville*........1945

*Mrs. Lucy Keen Johnson, *Gainesville*...1935

HAWAII

Mrs. Hannah Kapaskam Kuka Keolanui,
Honolulu 1975

Mrs. Amy L.K. Wung Richardson,
Honolulu 1974

Mrs. Zena Mossman Schuman,
Honolulu 1973

Mrs. Ellen B. Fullard-Leo, *Honolulu* 1972

Mrs. Annie Asam Kanahele, *Honolulu*.1971

Mrs. Eureka Bernice Ryan Forbes,
Honolulu 1970

Mrs. Martha Poepoe Hohu, *Honolulu*...1969

Mrs. John A. Burns 1963

Mrs. Emma Kalcionamoku Ai Hausten,
Honolulu 1959

Mrs. Sophie Judd Cooke, *Honolulu*........1957

Mrs. Myrtle Johnson Schattenburg,
Honolulu 1956

Mrs. C. C. Cortezan, *Kauai*....................1954

Mrs. Edith Alvord Willey, *Paia* 1951

Mrs. Edgar J. Walker, *Maui* 1950

IDAHO

Mrs. Alice Maynard Yensen, *Parma* 1975

Mrs. Ella Kangas Eld, *Donnelly* 1974

Mrs. Mary Jabrosky McClusky,
Twin Falls..1973

Mrs. Lola Gamble Clyde, *Moscow* 1972

Mrs. Helen Irene Doud Henderson,
Filer..1971

Mrs. Minnie Edgecombe Keim Odle,
Nampa..1970

Mrs. Jean Wentworth Higer, *Emmett* .1969

Mrs. Lena Nash Rice, *Hill City* 1968

Mrs. Christina B. Petersen,
Twin Falls 1967

Mrs. Imogene Ashmore Unzicker,
Buhl..1966

Mrs. Dorcas T. Riley, *Nampa* 1965

Mrs. Alta Sisler Howard, *Emmett*........1964

Mrs. Emily Hancock Smith,
Idaho Falls..1963

Mrs. May Willard Fodrea, *Boise* 1962

Mrs. Helen Margaret Hinden Wilson,
Payette..1961

Mrs. Frances Wilson Renner,
Lewiston..1960

Mrs. Susannah Catherine Boyd,
Nampa..1959

Mrs. Marion B. Kerby, *Cascade*..............1958

Mrs. Sigrid Maria Smith, *Twin Falls* ..1957

Mrs. Hannah Hagebak Hoff,
Horseshoe Bend..1956

Mrs. Laura Jean Albright, *Juliaetta* 1955

Mrs. Howard J. Maughan, *Preston*........1954

Mrs. Esther Carter Packard, *Boise*........1953

Mrs. Marian Orean Langdon,
Twin Falls 1952

Mrs. Violet Butler, *American Falls*......1951

Mrs. Alfred Budge, Sr., *Boise*................1950

Mrs. Robert L. Brainard, *Wardner*.......1949

Mrs. Anna Marie Oslund, *Troy*..............1948

Mrs. Francis Ernest Millay, *Lewiston* ..1947

ILLINOIS

Mrs. Esther B. Drinkard Grover,
Chicago..1975

Mrs. Eugenia Mott Hass, *Champaign*..1974

Mrs. Mary Irish Alvey, *Lincoln*..............1973

Mrs. Josephine Leonard Lund,
Gibson City..1972

Mrs. Maude LaVerne Kearney Browning,
Benton..1971

Mrs. Emma Elizabeth Scott Tucker,
Freeport 1970

Mrs. Gertrude Weiss Bohlmann,
Milford 1969

Mrs. Marie Laun Johnson White,
Greenview..1968

Mrs. Mary L. St. Peter, *Gilman*..............1967

Dr. Felcia Dorothy Koch,
Granite City..1966

Mrs. Bertha Boehning Nicholas,
Springfield..1965

Mrs. Frances Brent Killey, *Mommouth* 1964

Mrs. Fredrika Gurnsey Akerly,
Milford 1963

Mrs. Alice Selleck Wright, *Onarga* 1962

Mrs. Eva Jane Harper Follmer,
Forrest..1961

Mrs. Ruth Gebhardt Firth, *Galesburg*..1960

Mrs. Sarah Wallace Self Smith,
Oakdale 1959

Mrs. Emma C. Fulkerson, *Carbondale*..1958

Mrs. Cassie Cross Reeves, *Weldon*........1957

Mrs. Addie Crouse Carroll, *Greenville*..1956

Mrs. Charles Herbert Woods, *Lincoln*..1955

Mrs. George H. Moseley, *Metropolis*.....1954

*Mrs. Ethlyn Wisegarver Bott,
Belleville 1953

Mrs. Grace Selby Smith, *Ozark .z*.............1952

Mrs. Lucille Winbigler, *Monmouth*........1951

Mrs. John E. Kemp, *Kewanee* 1950

*Mrs. F. William Fischer, *Chicago*...........1949

Mrs. Etta Belle Olwin, *Robinson*............1948

*Mrs. Helen Gartside Hines,
Springfield 1947

Mrs. Harvey S. Smith, *East St. Louis* ..1947

Mrs. Herbert Waldo Hines,
Billings, Montana 1946

Mrs. F. W. Thompson, *Chicago*...............1945

617

INDIANA

Mrs. Rose Stair Goodman, *New Paris* .1975

Mrs. Nell Prall Souers, *Garrett* 1974

Mrs. Martha Lee Kasler, *Indianapolis*.1973

Mrs. Caroline Godley O'Dell,
Indianapolis..1972

Mrs. Marian Wood Adair, *Fort Wayne*1971

Mrs. Norma Deluse Barton,
Indianapolis..1970

Mrs. Esther Creighton, *Warsaw* 1969

Mrs. Lucia Smith McClure,
Martinsville..1968

Mrs. Eva Elizabeth Wickes, *Dayton*......1967

Mrs. Martha Pauline Morton Graves,
Princeton..1966

Mrs. Margaret Stephenson Moore,
Indianapolis..1965

Mrs. Frances May Hunt, *Indianapolis*.1964

Mrs. Marie Cutshall Hand, *Akron*........1963

Mrs. Lillian Matthews Robbins,
Indianapolis..1962

Mrs. Helen Coblentz Smith, *Warsaw*...1961

Mrs. Pearl Haddix Risher,
Indianapolis..1960

Mrs. Frances Sheller Smith, *Milford* 1959

Mrs. Sarah Thayer, *Hope*.........................1958

Mrs. Elizabeth C. H. Blizard,
Logansport..1957

Mrs. Martha Mallery McMahon,
Noblesville..1956

Mrs. Lucy B. Young, *West Lafayette*....1955

Mrs. D. E. Lybrook, *Young America* 1954

Mrs. Blanche E. Kemmer, *Lafayette*.....1953

Mrs. Pearl Miller White, *New Albany* .1952

Mrs. Fred J. Marxson, *Lafayette*...........1951

Mrs. Edward Harrington, *Hazleton*.......1950

Mrs. Fred W. Dierdorf,
West Terre Haute.......................................1949

Mrs. Nelle Rhodes Ham, *Paoli*...............1948

Mrs. W. W. Reedy, *Zionville*...................1947

Mrs. David Williams, *East Chicago*.......1946

Mrs. William E. Ochiltree,
Connersville...1945

Mrs. Sophie Willer, *Indianapolis* 1944

Mrs. Irene Gerard, *North Webster* 1943

IOWA

Mrs. Jean Elaine Hardie Willis, *Perry*1975

Mrs. Louise Koonce Lyon, *Clinton*........1974

Mrs. Betty Rugen Schutter, *Algona*......1973

Mrs. Lucille E. Bonnett Mitchem,
Marshalltown 1972

Mrs. Margaret Ruth McCollum,
Des Moines 1971

Mrs. Mildred Thornton Fry, *Corydon* ...1970

Mrs. Edith Rose Murphy Sackett,
Spencer...1969

Mrs. Helen Elizabeth Wendel Thompson,
Des Moines..1968

Mrs. Virginia Price Bedell,
Spirit Lake...1967

Mrs. Betty Barry Berrie, *Dubuque*........1966

Mrs. Alice Anderson Van Wert,
Hampton...1965

Mrs. Hilda Graubart Weingart,
Des Moines...1964

Mrs. Adaline Lincoln Lush, *Ames*..........1963

Mrs. Louise Hast Becker, *Waverly* 1962

Mrs. Faylesta Harriett Bybeck,
Bettendorf..1961

Mrs. Esther Youel Armstrong,
Cedar Rapids 1960

Mrs. Mary Ingram McFarlin,
Montezuma...1959

Mrs. Prudence E. Clark, *Mason City* 1958

Mrs. Irma Keene Roadman, *Dike*..........1957

Mrs. Ruth Heydon Lampe, *Iowa City* ..1956

Mrs. Everett O. Fenton, *Des Moines*.....1955

Mrs. Martin H. Driftmier,
Shenandoah 1954

Mrs. Lilly May Riggs, *Ames*...................1953

Mrs. Charles S. Hickman, *Centerville*...1952

Mrs. Eugene T. Hubbard, *Iowa City*.....1951

Mrs. Raymond Sayre, *Ackworth*.............1950

Mrs. Nelly Schippers Dykstra,
Orange City...1949

Mrs. Hiram Cole Houghton, *Red Oak* ..1948

*Mrs. Janette Stevenson Murray,
Cedar Rapids 1947

Mrs. A. L. Wood, Sr., *Sioux City*............1945

Mrs. E. E. Coffey, *Iowa City*...................1944

Mrs. John I. Mather, *Ames* 1943

KANSAS

Mrs. Kathleen Marie Schnoor Garwood,
Hays..1975

Mrs. Betty Sawhill Nagel,
Valley Center 1974

Mrs. Truly E. Fosbrink Yust, *Wichita*.1973

Mrs. Velma Adeline Base Klotz,
Wichita 1972

Mrs. Ruth Jane Knostman, *Wamego* 1971

Mrs. Carolyn Goetz Willcoxon,
Junction City 1970

Mrs. Lillian Grace Parker Pierce,
Marion..1969

Mrs. Elva Cole Overman, *Longton*.........1968

Mrs. Mary Williamson Webb,
Independence..1967

Mrs. Mildred Mullett Marrs,
Arkansas City..1966

Mrs. Mamie Alexander Boyd,
Mankato 1965

Mrs. Esther Melvina Schuman,
Neodesha 1964

Mrs. Esther Hiebert Ebel, *Hillsboro*.....1963

Mrs. Lida Goldie Moore Hattan,
Wichita 1962

Mrs. Alice MacDonald Wynne, *Hays*....1961

Mrs. Jessie Mae Hershey Rymph,
Wichita 1960

Mrs. Irene Henderson Kelley, *Atwood* .1959

Mrs. Victor Haffich, *Garden City*...........1958

Mrs. Harriet Sack Taylor, *Norton* 1957

Mrs. Irene Frantz Bittinger,
McPherson 1956

Mrs. Ollie E. K. Knoche, *Stafford*...........1955

Mrs. Charles A. Mahin, *Wichita* 1954

Mrs. Mary Cobb Payne, *Manhattan* 1953

Mrs. Nellie Kuska, *Colby*.........................1952

Mrs. G. W. Corporon, *Arcadia*................1951

Mrs. Ralph F. Lamar, *Topeka* 1950

Mrs. William Edgar Clayton,
Independence..1949

Mrs. Jessie Fisher Maier,
Arkansas City..1948

Mrs. Albert Ensign Hastings,
Coffeyville..1947

Mrs. Sheffield Ingalls, *Atchison*............1946

Mrs. D. J. Eisenhower, *Abilene*...............1945

Mrs. W. A. Smiley, *Junction City* 1944

Mrs. Martha L. Miller,............................1941

KENTUCKY

Mrs. Constance Lillman Litzanberger,
Elizabethtown 1975

Mrs. Ruth Flowers Bryant, *Westwood*..1974

Mrs. Mabel Bradbury Hite,
Jeffersontown 1973

Mrs. Anne Priest Baker, *Madisonville*.1972

Mrs. Mannie Peace Booth, *Wallins*.......1971

Mrs. Lula Marie Brown Barton,
Corbin...1970

Mrs. Laura Esther Sparrow Moorman,
Glen Dean..1969

Mrs. Minnie Benton Peterson Swinford,
Cynthiana...1968

Mrs. Zelma Benton Aton, *Louisville*.....1967

Mrs. Elizabeth Elliott Mayo, *Morehead*1966

Mrs. Grace S. Peters, *Trenton* 1965

Mrs. Omeda Hadden Terry, *Jackson* 1964

Mrs. Beulah Morgan Smith,
Bowling Green 1963

Mrs. Lucile Hicks Kirksey, *Paducah*.....1962

Mrs. Dorothy Skinner Stovall,
Hazel Green...1961

Mrs. Minnie Jones Moore, *Mallie*.........1960

Mrs. Mary Loula Graham Beavers,
Hopkinsville...1959

Mrs. Elizabeth W. Holliday, *Jackson*...1958

Mrs. Gena Finch Hilliard, *Clinton*.........1957

Mrs. Helen Dryden Neill, *Russellville*..1956

Mrs. Benis Carnes, *Wilmore*...................1955

Mrs. Nelson B. Rue, *Bowling Green*......1954

Mrs. Lillian Brewer Spragens,
Lebanon 1953

Mrs. Helen Chadwick Gartrell, Sr.,
Ashland 1952

Mrs. John G. Worth, *Lexington* 1951

Mrs. William V. Sudduth, *Winchester*..1950

Mrs. Lottie Forbes Rue, *Harrodsburg* .1949

Mrs. Elizabeth H. H. Posey,
Henderson...1948

Mrs. C. C. Howard, *Glasgow* 1947

Mrs. William Hardy Rousman,
Mayfield..1946

*Mrs. Emma Clarissa Clement,
Louisville 1946

Mrs. Richard O. Moberly, *Richmond*.....1945

Mrs. Percy Kendall Holmes,
Lexington 1944

Mrs. Matthew C. Darnell, *Frankfort*....1943

*Mrs. Dena Shelby Diehl, *Danville*..........1941

LOUISIANA

Mrs. Grace Winifred Malven Patterson,
Shreveport..1975

618

Mrs. Eleonora Gordon O'Keefe,
  New Orleans..1974
Mrs. Ozet Perot DeBlieux, *Bastrop*.......1973
Mrs. Myrtle Killmer Hill, *Crowley* 1972
Mrs. Elaine Faust Hislop,
  West Monroe..1971
Mrs. Dorothy King Scott,
  West Monroe..1970
Mrs. Blanche Alwood Chauvin,
  Ferriday..1969
Mrs. Ruth Gillispie Lancaster,
  Ferriday..1968
Mrs. Martha De Rouen, *Bell City*..........1967
Mrs. Cornelia Lane Pauche, Sr.,
  Lake Charles 1966
Mrs. Isabel Ochsner, *New Orleans*........1965
Mrs. Frances Anderson Riehl,
  Lafayette...1957
Mrs. Laurence Dupre Pavy, *Opelousas*.1956
Mrs. Pearl Jarnagin Watson,
  Lake Charles 1955
Mrs. Cornelia Power Staples,
  Opelousas 1954
Mrs. Anna Hopkins, Givens, *Lafayette* 1953
Mrs. Lenna Petty Jenkins, *Mansfield*...1952
Mrs. Malcolm S. Dougherty, *Jackson*....1951
Mrs. Carruth Jones, *Baton Rouge* 1950
Mrs. Charles W. Lyman, *Crowley*..........1949
Mrs. Leola Belle Nixon, *Monroe*............1948
Mrs. Richard Stagg Parrott, Sr.,
  Eunice...1947
Mrs. Reeva L. Font, *New Orleans*.........1945

MAINE
Mrs. Pricilla Smiley McKallip,
  Winslow 1975
Mrs. Louise Dube Blake, *Falmouth* 1974
Mrs. Lillian N. Judkins Abbott,
  Buckfield 1973
Mrs. Lois M. Shepard, *Gardiner* 1972
Mrs. Carmen E. Hallee, *Waterville*.......1971
Mrs. Doris Stanley Greenwood,
  Sebattus..1970
Mrs. Eleanor Theresa Foster Hill,
  Bath...1969
Mrs. Nellie Louise Benson Gould,
  Dixmont 1968
Mrs. Ruth E.T. Rines, *Gardiner*.............1967
Mrs. Grace Blanchard Brown,
  Vasselboro..1966
Mrs. Ethel R. Tibbetts Cobb, *Saco* 1965
Mrs. Lora Yeaton Hilton, *Anson* 1964
Mrs. Esther B. Doliber, *Augusta*............1963
Mrs. Edna Steen Cianchette, *Pittsfield* 1962
Mrs. Mary Slattery Perham,
  West Paris 1961
Mrs. Maisie Townsend Lee, *Augusta* ...1960
Mrs. Chessel A. Bryant Davis,
  South Montville.......................................1959
Mrs. Eleanor Kelley Dineen, *Gardiner*1958
Mrs. Nellie Rose Bull, *Presque Isle* 1957
Mrs. B. Ruth Couture, *Waterville*..........1955
Mrs. James W. Skehan, *Houlton* 1954
Mrs. Annie Florence Kenoyer,
  Weeks Mills..1953
*Mrs. Toy Len Goon, *Portland* 1952

Mrs. Chauncey Wentworth, *Augusta*....1951
Mrs. David A. Dickson, *Portland* 1950
Mrs. Earle L. Bridges, *West Pembroke* 1947
Mrs. Etta W. Robinson,
  South Portland...1946
Mrs. George W. Akeley, *Presque Isle* ...1945

MARYLAND
Mrs. Barbara Butts Dunn,
  Chevy Chase...1975
Judge Mary T. McQuillan O'Hara,
  Hyattsville..1974
Mrs. Esta Hyre Fox, *Lutherville* 1973
Dr. Ruth Elizabeth Derouin Burke,
  Chevy Chase...1972
Mrs. Anna Zahn Rice, *Hyattsville* 1971
Mrs. Neola Waldron Bolinger,
  Waldorf...1970
Mrs. Sibyl Peaslee Hall Moon,
  Annapolis 1969
Mrs. Mildred Garland Finlon,
  Chesapeake Beach 1968
Mrs. Thelma M. Bigelow, *Chestertown*.1967
Mrs. Elsie M. Lloyd Randolph, *Elkton*.1966
Mrs. Agnes M. Hicks, *Towson* 1965
Mrs. Caroline Reisler McGill,
  Thurmont 1964
Mrs. Lucille Schwartz Oosterhous,
  Tacoma Park 1963
Mrs. Grace Baird Cohen, *Oxon Hill* 1962
Mrs. Sadie Baker Ayd, *Baltimore*..........1961
Mrs. Elizabeth Bowling Cook,
  Baltimore..1960
Mrs. Allene L. Moreland, *Lothian* 1959
Mrs. John Howard Hopkins, *Laurel* 1958
Mrs. Lucy Virginia Barnsley,
  Gaethersburg 1957
Mrs. Mary Agnes Guy, *Clements* 1956
Mrs. Helen Klein Taylor, *Salisbury*......1955
Mrs. Albert I. Love, *Cambridge* 1954
Mrs. Cora Chapin Perry, *Cumberland*..1953
Mrs. Mary Hancock Gregory,
  Fredrick..1952
Mrs. Namoi G. Peabody, *Chevy Chase* .1951
Mrs. Rebekah B. Stonebraker,
  Hagerstown 1950
Mrs. H. Ross Coppage, *Baltimore*..........1949
Mrs. Cecil Ward Smith, *Cumberland*....1948

MASSACHUSETTS
Mrs. Nellie Tung-Yng Shih, *Boston*.......1975
Mrs. Melnea Jones Cass, *Roxbury* 1974
Mrs. Elizabeth Parker Hartl,
  Dorchester..1973
Mrs. Vera Chapman Shaw,
  Newton Centre 1972
Mrs. Carol Adams Schmidt, *Worcester*.1971
Mrs. Helene Mary Greenwood Regonetti,
  Plymouth...1970
Mrs. Phyllis Griesbach Garrand,
  Turners Falls...1969
Mrs. Edna Cookson Sinclair,
  Greenfield...1968
Mrs. Anna E. Morrissey, *Westfield* 1967
Mrs. Virginia Burns Parkhurst,
  Newton Center 1966

Mrs. Anne Campbell Stark, *Detroit* 1953
Mrs. Charles F. Kuhn, *West Pontiac* 1952
Mrs. Ambrose W. Crusoe, *Detroit*..........1951
Mrs. Henry Ford, *Dearborn*....................1950
Mrs. Leola Staples Loughrin, *Cadillac*.1949
Mrs. Lina Thornton Marshall,
  Benton Harbor 1948
Mrs. George D. Ninger, *Marshall*..........1947
Mrs. Olive B. Rockwell, *Three Rivers*...1946
Mrs. Perry Hayden, *Tecumseh*................1945

MINNESOTA
Mrs. Gladys Kjedahl Severson,
  Nerstrand..1975
Mrs. Dorothy Jeanette Schemmel Willette,
  Winnebago..1974
Mrs. Ruth Youngdahl Nelson,
  Minneapolis 1973
Mrs. Adeline Heyer Ballenthin,
  Faribault...1972
Mrs. Jonette Elise Rafshol Rotto,
  Fergus Falls...1971
Mrs. Isantha Powrie LeVander,
  St. Paul 1970
Mrs. Ruth Gebert Nelson, *Cushing* 1969
Mrs. Stella Marion Kroll, *St. Paul*.........1968
Mrs. Clarette S. Emmons, *Albert Lea* ..1967
Mrs. Melva Joyce Myland Sulerud,
  Halsted 1966
Mrs. Ida Eleanor Saetre,
  Henning (Otter Trail Co.)....................1965
Mrs. Haxel Bolin Solhaug, *Hopkins*......1964
Mrs. Anna Williams Bucher Fowler,
  Duluth 1963
Mrs. Norma Newstrom Larson,
  Cambridge..1962
Mrs. Stella F. Wallace, *Minneapolis* 1961
Mrs. Irene Malgaard Hauser,
  So. Minneapolis.......................................1960
Mrs. George B. Palmer, *Minneapolis*....1959
Mrs. William K. Evans, *Austin*..............1958
Mrs. Marie Elizabeth Norstad,
  Minneapolis 1957
Mrs. Adele Von Rohr Heise, *Winona*...1956
Mrs. Louise W. Fraser,
  South Minneapolis 1955
Mrs. Carlye M. Scott, *Minneapolis*........1954
Mrs. Roy H. Good, *Minneapolis* 1953
Mrs. William C. Wood, *Mankato*............1950
Mrs. Edwin H. Kopplin, *Litchfield*.........1949
Mrs. Manley L. Posseen, *Minneapolis*..1947
Mrs. Robert James Rock, *St. Paul*.........1946
Mrs. William R. Bagley, *Duluth* 1945
Mrs. Ethel Bliss Baker, *Minneapolis* 1944
Mrs. Nellie H. Olds, *Duluth*....................1943
Mrs. Edith Graham Mayo, *Rochester* 1940

MISSISSIPPI
Mrs. Frances Dale Pillow, *Greenwood* ..1975
Mrs. Hazel Martin Howell, *Canton* 1974
Mrs. Wardie Mae Cossitt Newcomb,
  Blue Mountain...1973
Mrs. Jessie Day Allred, *Collins* 1972
Mrs. Pernecie Stroud Knight,
  Mt. Olive...1971

Mrs. Ellen Polson Krohn,
Great Barrington.....................................1965

Mrs. Helen Feng Chen,
South Lancaster.................................1964

Mrs. Sarah Redans Shedd, *Boston* 1963

Mrs. Dorothy Southwick Day,
Worcester...1962

Mrs. Hassie Towler Grigsby, *Norwell* ..1961

Mrs. Reta Slack Larsen, *Arlington* 1960

*Hon. Jennie Loitman Barron,
Brookline..1959

Mrs. Katherine Sabino Tedeschi,
Rockland 1958

Mrs. Jennie Valerie Clapp,
Framingham 1957

Mrs. Elsie Lapham Jones, *Barnstable*..1956

Mrs. C. Noble Lapworth, *Stoughton* 1955

Mrs. Lawrence C. Jasper, *Rockland* 1954

Mrs. Kate Elizabeth Farrington,
Cambridge 1953

Mrs. Madeline Kountze Dugger Kelly,
West Medford 1952

Mrs. Thomas W. Prince, *Brockton*.......1951

Mrs. George C. Proctor, *Winthrop* 1950

Mrs. Ethel Piper Avery, *Malden*............1949

Mrs. Genevieve Pfeiffer Taylor,
Boston..1948

Mrs. James Warren Sever, *Cambridge* 1947

Mrs. James Gordon Gilkey,
Springfield...1946

Mrs. Harold R. Keller, *Newtonville* 1945

Mrs. Thomas H. Murray, *Brockton*........1944

Mrs. Thomas Small, *Chestnut Hill* 1943

MICHIGAN

Mrs. Gertrude Radatz Gromer,
Grand Rapids 1975

Mrs. Ruth Porth Wier, *Harper Woods* .1974

Mrs. Eula Constock Abby, *Lake Orion*.1973

Mrs. Ninabelle Saunders Ray, *Jackson* 1972

Mrs. Jenna V. Laug Browning,
Grand Rapids 1971

Mrs. Alice Mae Hall Abel,
Cedar Springs...................................1970

Mrs. Myrtle Ruth Oxender,
Constantine 1969

Mrs. Reba Farrell Schroeder, *Grawn* ...1968

Mrs. Mary Ellen Stier, *Richmond*..........1967

Mrs. Ethel Bahel Pregitzer, *Onaway*....1966

Mrs. Elizabeth A. Frier, *Cadillac* 1965

Mrs. Ruth Featherly Hunsberger,
Traverse City.....................................1964

Mrs. Eleanor McManus Tupper,
Southgate 1963

Mrs. Elizabeth Kruempel McGuire,
Royal Oak 1962

Mrs. Ivy Florence Brooma Payton,
Lansing 1961

Mrs. Fern Briggs Gearhart, *Charlotte*..1960

Mrs. Beulah H. S. Bayley,
Battle Creek......................................1959

Mrs. Mattie Baker McFall, *Detroit*........1958

Mrs. Gertrude Rassner Miller, *Detroit*.1957

*Mrs. Jane Maxwell Pritchard, *Detroit*..1956

Mrs. Bruce Bailey, *Detroit* 1955

Mrs. Fred Wurtsmith, *Detroit* 1954

Mrs. Kathryn Elizabeth Tennis Ballard,
Vicksburg 1970

Mrs. Ruth H. Ferguson Eckhardt,
State College...................................1969

Mrs. Effie McDonald Perry,
Philadelphia......................................1968

Mrs. Doris Lang Hardin, *Jackson*..........1967

Mrs. Marion Opol Shake Dees,
Jackson...1966

Mrs. Evelyn Taylor Majure, *Utica* 1965

Mrs. Martha Louise Edgar Kurts,
Jackson...1964

Mrs. Marie Violette M. Arceneaux,
Bay Street Louis 1963

Mrs. Annie Ray Weathers, *Greenville*..1962

Mrs. Dorothy Cunningham Vinzant,
Vicksburg..1960

Mrs. Grace Beasley O'Keefe, *Jackson* ..1958

Mrs. Evelyn Miller Evans, *Vicksburg*...1957

Mrs. Ella Walker Williams, *Corinth* 1956

Mrs. Mary B. P. Bagley, *Jackson*..........1955

Mrs. Vernon B. Hathorn, *Jackson* 1954

Mrs. May Hall Buchanan,
Blue Mountain................................1953

Mrs. Eva B. Denman, *Charleston*..........1952

Mrs. J. F. Campbell, *Jackson* 1951

Mrs. R. C. Eley, *Moss Point*....................1950

Mrs. C. C. McDonald, *Bay St. Louis* 1945

MISSOURI

Mrs. Dorothy Frost Shull, *Carthage*......1975

Mrs. Mary Lou Wideboor Lederer,
Warrensburg 1974

Mrs. Doris Martin Bradley, *Lexington* .1973

Mrs. Ruth LaTuille Matthews,
Kansas City..1972

Dr. Wanda Hollingsworth Walker,
Maryville 1971

Mrs. Augusta Marie Zimmerman
Higginbotham, *Albany*........................1970

Mrs. Laura Jean Stephens Mathews,
Rothville..1969

Mrs. Mary Grace Hird Suchland,
House Springs...................................1968

Mrs. Gertrude L. Volk, *Florissant*........1967

Mrs. Victoria K. Cervantes, *St. Louis* ..1966

Mrs. Grace B. Weigle, *Fulton*................1965

Mrs. Ethel Edwards Harrington,
Atlanta..1964

Mrs. Helen Hardy Myers, *Webb City* ...1963

Mrs. Edna Lee Jordon Hebert, *Fulton* 1962

Mrs. Evelyn Weeks Duncan,
Kansas City.......................................1961

Mrs. Louise Howreth Lippitt,
Meadville 1960

Mrs. Blanche Mallary Binns, *Liberty*....1959

Mrs. James Blair, Sr., *Jefferson City* 1958

Mrs. Euna Grace Reger Humphreys,
Galt...1957

Mrs. Ella Belt Ensminger, *Hickman* 1956

Mrs. Ruth Kelso Renfrow,
Arlington, Va.....................................1955

Mrs. Fred J. Schuster, *Pilot Grove* 1954

Mrs. Maude Hall Jones, *Moberly*............1953

Mrs. Rupert L. Rinehart, *Kirksville* 1951

Mrs. May Kennedy McCord,
Springfield..1950

Dr. Emma Arabella Thompson,
Columbia...1949

Mrs. Laura White Clemmer, *St. Louis*.1948

Mrs. F. W. Stamper, *Moberly*.................1947

Mrs. Martha Truman, *Independence* 1946

Mrs. George W. Diemer, *Kansas City* .1945

Mrs. Paul A. Johnston, *Kansas City*.....1944

Mrs. J. W. Fifields, *Kansas City*...........1943

MONTANA

Mrs. Maxine Foxall Mc Dede,
Fort Benton 1975

Mrs. Evelyn Evans Richardson,
Laurel..1974

Mrs. Saralda Nathe, *Redstone* 1973

Mrs. Sarah Helen Ring Harvey,
Bozeman..1972

Mrs. Leona Elizabeth Bronson Scoles,
Baker...1971

Mrs. Martha Haar Huber, *Glendive* 1970

Mrs. Gladys Alpha Yost Wohler,
Billings..1969

Mrs. Emily Colgate Robinson,
Miles City...1968

Mrs. Edna H. Tucker, *Lolo* 1967

Mrs. Katherine H. Lenington,
Fort Benton 1966

Mrs. Bessie Meyst Heiken, *Billings*......1965

Mrs. Lucille Burt Middleton, *Butte*.......1964

Mrs. Nellie Broderick Sanderson,
Billings..1963

Mrs. Evelyn Grace Stevens Moore,
Sidney 1962

Mrs. Jean McAuliffe Walterskirschen,
Missoula..1961

Mrs. Elizabeth Davey Lochrie, *Butte*....1960

Mrs. Laura Mae Brainard, *Bozeman*.....1959

Mrs. Mildred Miller Blevins, *Chenook*...1958

Mrs. Lydia Freier Rieger, *Plevna*..........1957

Mrs. Cora Belle Trask, *Deer Lodge*........1956

Mrs. Lillian Lund Peterson, *Kalispell*..1955

Mrs. Ambrose Cheyney, *Stanford* 1954

Mrs. Jean Maris Rhodes, *Havre*............1953

Mrs. Jennie Elfriede Bridenhaugh,
Billings..1952

Mrs. Fanny Cory Cooney,
Stanwood, Washington..........................1951

Mrs. Lewis Gutherie, *Reedpoint* 1950

Mrs. Charles S. Baldwin, *Kalispell*........1949

Mrs. Maude Minar Schmidt,
Fort Benton 1948

Mrs. Elmer David Gallagher,
Claremont..1947

Mrs. J. J. Hagan, *Glasgow*......................1945

NEBRASKA

Mrs. Dorothy Inez Gaeth, *Fremont*.......1975

Mrs. Hazel Struble Stebbins, *Lincoln*...1974

Mrs. Eleanor Vail Enersen, *Lincoln*......1973

Mrs. Ruth Randel Smith, *Auburn*.........1972

Mrs. Amy Leonard Nuernberger,
Wakefield 1971

Mrs. Lucille Keller Dorwart, *Sidney* 1970

Mrs. Ruth Anna Courtright Kennedy,
Brownville 1969

Mrs. Ellen Nolting Spangler, *Omaha* ...1968

Mrs. Catherine L. Elliott, *Scottsbluff* 1967

Mrs. Helen Jorgensen Adams, *Brady* ..1966

Mrs. Miriam A. Worlock, *Kearney* 1965

Mrs. Ella Herink Reichmuth, *Leigh* 1964

*Mrs. Olga Pearson Engdahl, *Omaha* ...1963

Mrs. Helen McCormick Pitstick,
Nebraska City 1962

Mrs. Marie Burchess Gray, *Hastings* ...1961

Mrs. Mabel Dow Thompson, *Lincoln* 1960

Mrs. Margaret Keifer McLafferty,
Lincoln 1959

Mrs. Martha de Fresse, *Freemont* 1958

*Mrs. Hazel Hempel Abel, *Lincoln* 1957

Mrs. Carmen Garcia, *Scottsbluff* 1956

Mrs. M. E. Crosby, *North Platte* 1955

Mrs. A. B. Newell, *Grand Island* 1954

Rev. Charlotte Briggs Dillon, *Ponca* 1953

Mrs. Maude H. Weaver, *Falls City* 1952

Mrs. W. Max Gentry, *Gering* 1951

Mrs. Walter Kiechel, *Tecumseh* 1950

Mrs. Herbert Brownell, *Lincoln* 1949

Mrs. E. J. Loutzenheiser, *Gothenburg* ...1948

Mrs. Leslie David Spence, *Beatrice* 1947

Mrs. Robert G. Simmons, *Lincoln* 1946

Mrs. J. M. Harding, *Omaha* 1945

Mrs. Henry Vincent Parle, *Omaha* 1944

*Mrs. Harriette Flora Gray, *Omaha* 1937

NEVADA

Mrs. Helen Ruth Early, *Las Vegas* 1975

Mrs. Elizabeth Y. Lenz, *Reno* 1974

Mrs. Virginia Ann Rasmussen Zobrist,
Las Vegas 1973

Mrs. Meryl Dunn Jones, *Las Vegas* 1972

Mrs. Vilda Bulloch Ronnow, *Reno* 1971

Mrs. Mary Bethana Hamphill Lowman,
Las Vegas 1970

Mrs. Jessie Lam Stewart, *Las Vegas* ...1969

Mrs. Theresa A. Laxalt, *Carson City* ...1967

Mrs. Gladys K. Dula, *Las Vegas* 1965

Mrs. Emma Le Vera Williams Calvert,
Caliente 1964

Mrs. Amy Thompson Gulling, *Reno* 1963

Mrs. C. C. Taylor, *Reno* 1958

Mrs. Catherine Thiel Gianella, *Reno* 1957

Mrs. James Peckham, *Reno* 1956

Mrs. Harriet Keep Arentz, *Reno* 1955

Mrs. Julia Ann Walther, *Fort Halleck* .1953

Mrs. Agnes Gregory, *Elko* 1951

Mrs. Fred M. Fulstone, *Smith* 1950

Mrs. James S. Jensen, *Reno* 1949

Mrs. Benjamin R. Ronzone, *Las Vegas* 1948

Mrs. Joseph L. Collins, *Ely* 1947

Mrs. Daisy Holcombe Burke, *Reno* 1946

Mrs. Una R. Dickerson, *Reno* 1945

NEW HAMPSHIRE

Mrs. Catherine Tuttle Squires,
New London 1975

Mrs. Marie von Bergen Tolander,
Henniker 1974

Mrs. Lena Florence Fowler Young,
Suncook 1973

Mrs. Lillian C. Siebneicher, *Concord* 1972

Mrs. Dorothy Cunningham Thompson,
Etna 1971

Mrs. May Barnes Holmes, *Alstead* 1970

Mrs. Dorothy Sheldon McGettingan,
Wilton 1969

Mrs. Doris Phelps Bean, *Warner* 1968

Mrs. Rhea Coleman Guild, *Laconia* 1967

Mrs. Iphigenia Ghikas Copadis,
Manchester 1966

Mrs. Kathleen Kelly Mullen,
East Concord 1965

Mrs. Sarah Lipinsky Bresnick,
Manchester 1964

Mrs. Ida Louise Ockerblod Dudley,
Hanover 1963

Mrs. Laura Harrington Dole,
Peterborough 1962

Mrs. Rena Payne Osborne, *Pittsfield* 1961

Mrs. Margaret N. Healy, *Concord* 1960

Mrs. Martha A. Huntress Long,
Kingston 1959

Mrs. Arthur Olson, *Keene* 1958

Mrs. G. Monte Chesley, *Lyme Center* ...1957

Mrs. Dorothy Lutie Knox, *Concord* 1956

Mrs. Chester W. Doe, *Northwood* 1955

Mrs. Benjamin Goodman,
Baker's Crossing 1954

Mrs. Louise May Carlisle, *Jefferson* 1953

Mrs. John W. Crawford, *Tilton* 1952

Mrs. Arthur Chickering, *Pembroke* 1951

Mrs. Earl Ramsey, *Milton* 1950

Mrs. Rachel White Adams, *Lincoln* 1948

Mrs. Lillian Foss Cooper, *Rochester* 1946

Mrs. Albert W. Fortier, *Chocorua* 1945

Mrs. Fred Cumings, *Troy* 1944

NEW JERSEY

Mrs. Margaret Kitchens Minnis,
Folson 1975

Mrs. Bertha Ann Stanley Buck,
Millville 1974

Mrs. Mary Yoder Howe, *Linwood* 1973

Mrs. Etta R. Small Garron,
Indian Mills 1972

Mrs. Mary Donaldson Haynie,
Ventnor 1971

Mrs. Gladys Damon Rader,
Ocean Grove 1970

Mrs. Dolores Galler Cooper,
Atlantic City 1969

Mrs. Julie Denison Lerke, *Whitehouse* 1968

Mrs. Olive Bond Polk, *Roselle* 1967

Mrs. Helen Jackson Kranenburg,
Tenafly 1966

Mrs. Mabel Jackson Robinson,
Madison 1965

Mrs. Mary Virginia Rupp Gaffney,
Ventnor 1964

Mrs. Edna Alexander Seely,
Eatontown 1963

Mrs. Beatrice Augusta Larson Johnson,
Nutley 1962

Mrs. Priva Konovitz Kohn, *Trenton* 1961

Mrs. Ruth Parlin Sanborn, *Glen Ridge* 1960

Mrs. Lena Tomasson Jannuzi, *Nutley* ..1959

Mrs. Mary Starr Mecum, *Salem* 1958

Dr. Lillian Moller Gilbreth,
Upper Montclair 1957

Mrs. Helen Lee Johnson,
Atlantic City 1956

Mrs. Robert Crane, *Pittstown* 1955

Mrs. Charlotte Douglas Wiss,
Morristown 1954

Mrs. Margaret Stevenson Mountsier,
Nutley 1953

Mrs. Elizabeth Middleton Maddock,
Trenton 1952

Mrs. William H. Hayford, *Paterson* 1951

Mrs. Richard E. Shope,
New York City 1950

Mrs. Alfred Robie Driscoll,
Haddonfield 1949

Mrs. Irene Mason Harper,
Moga, Punjab, India 1948

Mrs. Gabriel d'Eustachio,
Perth Amboy 1947

Mrs. Arthur David Thaeler, *Arlington* .1946

NEW MEXICO

Mrs. Harriet Heneveld Kempers,
Albuquerque 1975

Mrs. Lois Garber Crum, *Aztec* 1974

Mrs. Dona Burgard Henry,
Albuquerque 1973

Mrs. Addie Ratliff Money, *Portales* 1972

Mrs. Ruth Balfour Strother,
Albuquerque 1971

Mrs. Stella Sanchez Gallegos, *Belen* 1970

Mrs. Theresa Louato Tabet, *Belen* 1969

Mrs. Kay Curley Bennett, *Gallup* 1968

Mrs. Maren S. Hargrove, *Farmington* .1967

Mrs. Frances Ravenel Shipman,
Santa Fe 1966

Mrs. Lucy McCauley McMullen,
Silver City 1965

Mrs. Molly Price, *Santa Rosa* 1963

Mrs. Lucille Lamp Johnson, *Clovis* 1958

Mrs. Florence Gascoigne Goddard,
Mesilla Park 1956

Mrs. Joe B. Hill, *Albuquerque* 1954

Mrs. Lillian R. Herring Russell,
Roswell 1953

Mrs. Fred Luchs, *Los Alamos* 1952

Mrs. Floyd Santisteven, *Santa Fe* 1951

Mrs. Clinton H. S. Koch, *Albuquerque* .1950

Mrs. Mary Katherine Seery, *Belen* 1948

Mrs. J. L. Evett, *Albuquerque* 1947

Mrs. Byard D. Boyce, *Albuquerque* 1946

Mrs. Loren Allen Malcolm, *Koehler* 1945

NEW YORK

Mrs. Gertrude Botsford Moseley,
De Ruyter 1975

Mrs. Mary Kuzawsi Lazarek, *Oswego* 1974

Mrs. Esther Forbes Twentyman,
Homer 1973

Mrs. Doris Montague Huntley Walsh,
Syracuse 1972

Mrs. Mary Mulherin Crowe, *Eden* 1971

Mrs. Palma Isadora Hanson Goodwin,
Guilford..1970

Mrs. Catherine Littler Stephens,
Manlius...1969

Mrs. Lucile Leonard LeSourd,
Gaithersburg (New York City)...........1968

Mrs. Gladys Houx Rusk,
New York, N.Y.......................................1967

Mrs. Adele Katzenstein Ginzberg,
New York City...1966

Mrs. Kathryn Sisson Phillips,
New York City...1965

Mrs. Alma Hopkins Kitchell, (Yoder)
Larchmont..1964

Mrs. Ruth Stafford Peale,
New York City...1963

Mrs. Stella Katsorhis Spanakos,
Brooklyn...1962

Mrs. Louise Heath Leber,
Hastings-on-Hudson...............................1961

Mrs. Irene Dady Moore, *Cazenovia* 1960

Mrs. Constance Mott-Smith Falconer,
Burnt Hill..1959

Mrs. Helen Reed Anderson, *Westbury*.1958

Mrs. Margie Lee Smith Johnson,
Middleburgh..1957

Mrs. Hattie Barringer Personeus,
Suffern...1956

Mrs. John Herbert Mears,
Garden City...1955

Mrs. Russell J. Cooper, *Buffalo*..............1954

Mrs. Agnes Louise Grant, *Redfield*........1953

Mrs. Kathryn Grace Dwyer Coffee,
Albany..1952

Mrs. Bernard Gordon, *New York City*.1950

Mrs. Thomas Donachie, *Yonkers*............1949

Mrs. Martha Ackerman Lewis,
New York City...1948

Mrs. Harry T. Welty, *Yonkers*................1947

Mrs. Arthur Glenn Milks, *Cattaraugus*1946

Mrs. Murray B. Smith, *Bemus Point* 1945

*Mrs. Georgiana Farr Sibley, *Rochester* 1945

Mrs. T. Q. Donaldson, *New York City*..1944

Mrs. Ella Gorman Stanton,
New York City 1943

NORTH CAROLINA
Mrs. Josephine Stuart Lacaster,
Raleigh 1975

Mrs. Ruth Cook Phillips, *Pinnacle*.........1974

Mrs. Beatrice Laughton Phillips,
Morehead City..1973

*Mrs. Esther Hunt Moore, *Hickory*.........1972

Mrs. Eula Birch Amaker, *High Point*...1971

Mrs. Elizabeth Purnell Rand, *Garner* ..1970

Mrs. Rosa Currie Croom, *Maxton* 1969

Mrs. Emma Johnson Allison, *Sylva*.......1968

Mrs. Jeannette P. Simpson,
Jacksonville...1967

Mrs. Mary Lee Swann McMillan,
Raleigh 1966

Mrs. Sarah R. Haworth, *High Point* 1965

Mrs. Annie Maude Davis Bunn,
Raleigh 1964

Mrs. Mary Elizabeth Hunt Henley,
Chapel Hill..1963

Mrs. Grace Morris White Stephenson,
Pendleton 1962

Mrs. Odessa Arnette Memory,
Wagram 1961

Mrs. Eva Doris Taylor Fernald,
Wilson..1960

Mrs. Edith Moore Hall, *Cullowhee*........1959

Mrs. Eunice H. Wagoner, *Gibsonville*...1958

Mrs. Anna Barrow Gordon, Sr., *Spray*.1957

Mrs. Mary Kerr Spencer,
Winston Salem...1956

Mrs. Arthur Dixon Cashwell,
Hope Mills 1955

Mrs. Thomas J. Lassiter, *Smithfield* 1954

Mrs. Nelle Haynes Gregory, *Halifax*....1953

Mrs. Virginia Edgerton Simms,
Raleigh 1952

Dr. Mary T. Martin Sloop, *Crossnore*......1951

Mrs. Edgar F. McCulloch,
Elizabethtown 1950

Mrs. Harriet Byrne Pressley, *Raleigh*..1948

Mrs. Karl Bishopric, *Spray* 1947

Mrs. Robert Russell, *Asheville*...............1946

Mrs. P. P. McCain, *Southern Pines* 1945

Mrs. Walter P. Sprunt, *Wilmington* 1943

*Mrs. Elizabeth Vize Berry, *Greensboro*.1942

NORTH DAKOTA
Mrs. Hazel Wickman Brennan, *Rolette* 1975

Mrs. Margaret Luella Taylor Bubach,
Litchville..1974

Mrs. Mabel Ryan Torkelson, *Crosby* 1973

Mrs. Ella Overby Stedje, *Hettinger* 1972

Mrs. Eileen Clark Eggl, *Cando*...............1971

Mrs. Delia Dubs Paddock, *Minot* 1970

Mrs. Thelma Bell, *Ellendale* 1969

*Mrs. Elizabeth Grossman Bodine,
Velva..1968

Mrs. Julia M. Stevens, *Fargo* 1967

Mrs. Ina Beauchamp Hall, *Parshall*......1966

Mrs. Thelma Hyde Klingensmith,
Mandan..1965

Mrs. Berthelda Ballantine Facey,
Larimore..1964

Mrs. Margaret O'Connor, *St. Thomas*...1963

Mrs. Anne Sofia Bucklin, *Mandan*.........1962

Mrs. Ella Oksness Lorentzen,
Powers Lake 1961

Mrs. Blanche Neimeir Nienas,
Thompson...1960

Mrs. Hedvig Clausen Svore, *Bismarck* 1959

Mrs. Margaret K. Breuer, *Emmet* 1958

Mrs. Dora Swanson Erickson,
Watford City...1957

Mrs. Eva Voris Case, *Bismarck* 1956

Mrs. Gussty Jennette Fossum,
Maxbass...1955

Mrs. J. Way Huey, *Jamestown*...............1954

Mrs. Delia M. C. Coghlan, *St. John*.......1953

*Mrs. Theo C. Torgerson, *Washburn*......1952

*Mrs. Saunders J. Sanders, *Fargo*...........1951

Mrs. Clara T. G. Bechtle, *Valley City*..1950

Mrs. Josephine M. Paulson Lierboe,
Turtle Lake...1949

Mrs. A. M. Powell, *Devils Lake* 1948

Mrs. Peter Langseth, *Wahpeton*............1947

Mrs. Stephen H. Hoag, *Harwood* 1946

Mrs. M. E. Code, *Lisbon*...........................1945

OHIO
Mrs. Norma Hatfield Timberlake,
Toronto 1975

Mrs. Florence Gulling Zwick,
Louisville 1974

—None— 1973

Mrs. Katherine Sinclair Minor,
Steubenville 1972

Mrs. Caroline Boyer Harrison,
Columbus 1971

Mrs. Viola L. Armstrong, *Wapakoneta*1970

Mrs. Louise Cinthy Stone Stokes,
Shaker Heights 1969

Mrs. Mary F. Leader, *Deshler*...............1967

Mrs. Dorothy Nichol Dolby,
Cincinnati 1966

Mrs. Elizabeth Hazlett Buchanan,
New Philadelphia.....................................1965

Mrs. Ruth Mougey Worrell, *Columbus*.1964

Mrs. Rebecca Battelle Taylor, *Lima* 1963

*Mrs. Clara Sproat Glenn,
New Concord 1962

Mrs. Helene Louise Garmhausen
LeMaster, *Sidney*....................................1961

Mrs. Geneva Steiner Dilley, *Athens*......1960

Mrs. Maria Vallas Spirtos, *Campbell* 1958

Mrs. Bertha Cordell Hull,
Yellow Springs...1956

Mrs. Clara Margaret Bode,
New Knoxville 1955

Mrs. Basil Pavlatos, *Springfield* 1954

Mrs. Ruby Clark Brown, *Sidney*............1953

Mrs. Lillian G. Meyer, *Elyria*.................1952

Mrs. Bertram John Swinnerton,
Lancaster...1951

Mrs. William F. Marting, *Ironton* 1950

Mrs. Leo W. Schmidt, *Cleveland* 1949

Mrs. Helen Gibbons Lotspeich,
Cincinnati 1948

Mrs. John L. Miller, *Cambridge* 1947

Mrs. Joy Seth Hurd, *Cleveland*...............1946

Mrs. Harold H. Burton, *Cleveland*........1945

Mrs. Blanche Taylor Lightburn,
Cresline 1944

*Mrs. Mary Dabney Thomson, *Oxford*....1943

*Mrs. Otelia Katherine Compton,
Wooster 1939

OKLAHOMA
Mrs. Helen Bafferty Paul Sutton,
Oklahoma City 1975

Mrs. Ruth Gardner Gooden,
Kingfisher 1974

Mrs. Gladys Smith Ellis Balyeat,
Oklahoma City 1973

Mrs. Mary Virginia Dunlap Godlove,
Lawton 1972

*Mrs. Betty Anthony Zahn,
Oklahoma City 1971

Mrs. Zuma Velma Rogers Myers,
Frederick 1970

Mrs. Golda Langham Brown,
Duncan 1969

Mrs. Margaret Vessels Love,
Oklahoma City 1968

Mrs. Ann W. Knappen, *Tulsa* 1967

Mrs. Beatrice L. Johnson, *Chickasha*....1966

Mrs. Blanche T. Primrose, *Norman* 1965

Mrs. Hattie Lee Herd Cooper,
Shawnee...1964

Mrs. Johnnie Bishop Chisholm,
Springfield..1963

Mrs. Eleanor Naylor Caughron,
Oklahoma City 1962

Mrs. Merle Frances Newby Buttram,
Oklahoma City 1961

Mrs. Margaret Russell Black, *Lawton*..1960

Mrs. Gertrude Gindling Harlow,
Oklahoma City 1959

Mrs. Ruby Seal Rizley, *Oklahoma City*1958

Mrs. Gladys Lednecky Berney,
Oklahoma City 1957

Mrs. Maud Lorton Myers, *Tulsa* 1956

Mrs. Lutie Mauldin Anthony,
Oklahoma City 1955

Mrs. Clyde M. Becker, *Chickasha* 1954

Mrs. Alma Curry Keys,
Oklahoma City 1953

Mrs. Laura Bell Parks, *Oklahoma City*1952

Mrs. Virgil Browne, *Oklahoma City* 1951

Mrs. John Frank Martin,
Oklahoma City 1950

Mrs. E. P. McMahon, *Lawton* 1949

Mrs. Minnie Lee Barrow, *Okemah* 1948

Mrs. Etta Louise T. Grimm,
Oklahoma City 1947

Mrs. Tom B. Ferguson, *Watonga*...........1946

Mrs. A. H. Holloman, *Frederick* 1945

Mrs. W. S. Kerr, *Oklahoma City*............1944

Mrs. Henry G. Bennett, *Stillwater*........1943

OREGON

Mrs. Esther Trusty Pangborn,
Bay City 1975

Mrs. Mary Sheehy Heriza, *Baker* 1974

Mrs. Letha Ward Wakeman,
McMinnville...1973

Mrs. Catherine Moritz Lyon, *Salem* 1972

Mrs. Virginia Heacock Helm,
Portland 1971

Mrs. Leah Koch Sauer, *Portland*............1970

Mrs. Grace B. Allison, *McMinnville*......1969

Mrs. Anne Kennedy Smith, *St. Paul* 1968

Mrs. Celia S. Steward, *Corvallis* 1967

*Mrs. Bertha Marion Holt, *Creswell* 1966

Mrs. Vivian Dobson Patterson,
St. Helens...1965

Mrs. Alice Godsey Harris, *Enterprise*..1964

Mrs. Lillian Linklater England,
Springfield...1963

Mrs. Bertha Herring Kirsch, *Maupin*..1962

Mrs. Ethel Paulus Odell, *Gresham* 1961

Mrs. Hazel Palmer McCracken,
Corvallis...1960

Mrs. Marie Myers Bosworth, *Medford*..1959

Mrs. Ruth C. Foster, *Nyssa* 1958

Mrs. Elsie Argeletia S. Reynolds,
Portland 1957

Mrs. Ann Josephine Dunham,
Lakeview..1956

Mrs. Florence Naomi Brinks, *Portland*1955

Mrs. William Kletzer, *Portland* 1954

Mrs. Vera Houston Moser, *Corvallis* 1953

Mrs. Frankie Cauthorn McIntyre,
Pendleton 1952

Mrs. H. S. Bolinger, *Hood River* 1951

*Mrs. Elizabeth Roe Cloud, *Portland*......1950

Mrs. Robert E. Taylor, *Eugene* 1949

Mrs. Maude Rast Kidder, *Roseburg*.......1948

Mrs. J. Roscoe Lee, *Baker*......................1947

Mrs. Howard Oliver Mansfield,
Freewater 1946

Mrs. George H. Hyslop, *Corvallis*..........1945

PENNSYLVANIA

Mrs. Helen Kochanowski Wilson,
Aliquippa..1975

Mrs. Catharine Snyder Wink,
Shillington...1974

Mrs. Louise Glinkerman Jordan,
Clarion 1973

Mrs. Sarah Pratt Brock,
Newtown Square....................................1972

Mrs. Margaret Dumont Paul,
Pittsburgh...1971

Mrs. Irene Kumitis Soponis,
Minersville..1970

Mrs. Rose Margaret Dudenhoeffer Wright,
Greensburg..1969

Mrs. Marjorie Gahring Snelling,
Allentown..1968

Mrs. Catherine B. Bauer, *St. Mary's*....1967

Mrs. Mary Kiskadden Kerr, *Oil City*....1966

Mrs. Rhea K. Spatz, *Pittsburgh*.............1965

Mrs. Miriam L. Tice Karsnitz,
Meyerstown 1964

Mrs. Sarah Carahan Henry,
Brooksville..1963

Mrs. Louise Graham Brown,
Pittsburgh...1962

Dr. Emily Hartshore Mudd, *Haverford*1961

Mrs. Edna Phillips Rosenbaum,
Philadelphia..1960

Mrs. Mary Hill Norton, *Gouldsboro*.......1959

Mrs. Samuel Perry, *Newcastle* 1958

Mrs. Kathryn Louise Moseley,
Pittsburgh...1957

Mrs. Anna Elizabeth Pugh, *Wayne*.......1956

Mrs. Lulu Hall Pratt, *Coatesville* 1955

Mrs. William J. Heydrick,
Philadelphia..1954

Mrs. Flora Belle Waugaman,
Blairsville..1953

Mrs. Mary Barton Luckie,
Swarthmore...1952

Mrs. Henry L. Mollenauer,
Eighty Four 1951

Mrs. W. H. Harmon, *Grove City* 1950

Mrs. Samuel Witmer, *Hanover*...............1949

Mrs. Emma Campbell Cocklin,
Dillsburg..1948

Mrs. Ralph H. Bergstresser,
Selinsgrove..1947

Mrs. Allan W. Wallis, *Philadelphia* 1946

Mrs. Daniel A. Poling, *Germantown*.....1945

*Mrs. Harriet Duff Phillips, *Pittsburgh*.1944

Mrs. Jacob R. Miller, *Bellwood*..............1944

PUERTO RICO

Mrs. Judith Acevedo Ufret,
San German 1975

Mrs. Julia Morcado de Gonzalez,
Rio Piedras 1974

Mrs. Rosa Martinez de Aponte, *Ponce*..1973

Mrs. Delia Mendez De Hernandez,
San Lorenzo 1972

Mrs. Altagracia H. de Bonilla
El Paraiso, *Rio Piedras*........................1971

Mrs. Rafaela Ortiz de Colon, *Caguas* ...1970

Mrs. Antonia Carattini de Vega,
Ponce...1969

Mrs. Paquita Barreto de Rodriquez,
Rio Piedras 1968

Mrs. Justa A. de Borges, *San Lorenzo*.1967

Mrs. Elisa Arce De Adorno, *Arecibo*.....1966

Mrs. Julia Fernandez Rivera de Colon,
Cidra..1965

Mrs. Dolores Figueroa V.D.A. Feliciano,
Vega Alta 1964

Mrs. Tomasita Pabón de Martinez,
Lajas 1963

Mrs. Matilda M. Berrocal,
Puerto Nuevo 1962

Mrs. Amparo Gonzalez de Carrasquillo,
Guayama 1961

Mrs. Josefa Costa Sanabria de Guzman,
Humacao..1960

Mrs. Vereranda Badillo Vda. de
Fernandez, *Aquadilla* 1959

Mrs. Flora Torres De San Miguel,
Ciales 1958

Mrs. Julia Marin de Villafane,
Mayaguez 1957

Sra. Nelida Costas de Caro,
Rio Piedras 1956

Mrs. Luist Davila de Ronda,
Cubao Rojo..1955

Mrs. Rufina Castilla de Lozada,
Las Piedras 1954

Mrs. Dona Arminda Reyes Vda. de Iguina,
Arecibo...1953

Mrs. Isidora Aponte Bunker,
Ria Piedras 1952

Mrs. Maria Anselmi de Monserrate,
Rio Piedras 1951

Mrs. Blas Vda. de Silva, *Hato Rey* 1950

RHODE ISLAND

Mrs. Eva Grant Thurston, *Warwich*.....1975

Mrs. Lillian Thistle Gardner,
Warwick 1974

Mrs. Mildred Barnett Hanley,
Pawtucket..1973

Mrs. Lillian Caroline Turco Cappuccio,
Watch Hill 1972

Mrs. Mary Grace DiMaio Barbieri,
Providence 1971

Mrs. Ethel T. Gildes, *Pawtucket*............1970

Mrs. Louise Helen Gizzarelli,
Providence 1969

Mrs. Louise Avery Favorite, *Rumford*.1968

Mrs. Margaret M. Monroe, *Providence*.1967

Mrs. Ella May E. Greene, *Providence*...1966

Mrs. Olive T. Wiley, *Warwick* 1965

Mrs. Ruth Baun Sayer, *Providence* 1964

Mrs. Ruth J. Skoog, *Rumford* 1963

Mrs. Helen Speck Burrows, *Cranston*...1962

Mrs. Lois Loizeaux Hunt, *Cranston*......1961

Mrs. Mae Morris Ltye, *Providence* 1960

Mrs. Margaret Doublas Reese Langdon,
Providence 1959

Mrs. Louvan A. Lockwood, *Lakewood*...1958

Mrs. Anna Louise Angell French,
Newport......................................1957

Mrs. Frances Louise Crowell,
Central Falls................................1956

Mrs. Lucille Putnam Leonard,
Providence 1955

Mrs. Archibald Silverman, *Providence*..1954

Mrs. Mabel Louise Maynard, *Westerly* 1953

Mrs. Lena Ashe Whitford, *Wyoming*....1952

Mrs. Vernon W. Cooke, *Pawtucket*........1951

Mrs. Leonard B. Colt, *Little Compton*..1950

Mrs. Harold R. Shippee, *Pawtucket* 1949

Mrs. George E. Bennett, *Cranston*........1947

SOUTH CAROLINA

Mrs. Phyllis Hollingsworth Smith,
Easley 1975

Mrs. Martha Lorena Cloninger Durham,
Landrum 1974

Mrs. Bertha Elizabeth Keisler Rikard,
Lexington 1973

Mrs. Jessie Matheson Blackwell,
Bennettsville 1972

Mrs. Louise Eargle Seastrunk,
Columbia 1971

Mrs. Winnie Ruth O'Dell Looper,
Greenwood 1970

Mrs. Emma Jane Varn Risher,
Bamberg......................................1969

Mrs. Clarice Townsend Wilson,
Greenville 1968

Mrs. Sara Bye McEachern, *Columbia*...1967

Mrs. Mary Catherine McNab Whitaker,
Williston 1966

Mrs. Margaret B. Poole, *Clemson* 1965

Mrs. Mattie Elizabeth Ratteree West,
Camden 1964

Mrs. Wilhelmina Weldon Porcher, Jr.,
Charleston 1963

Mrs. Mary Hough Swearingen,
Columbia......................................1962

Mrs. Hessie Thomson Morrah,
Greenville 1961

Mrs. Clara Gooding McMillan, *Ulmers*.1960

Mrs. Lucile Howell Sims, *Orangeburg*..1959

*Mrs. May Roper Coker, *Hartsville* 1958

Mrs. Rosalie Cliatt Rayle, *Sumter*........1957

Mrs. Esther Garrison Latimer,
West Columbia..............................1956

Mrs. Marion E. Carter, *Elliott* 1955

Mrs. Luther E. Gatlin, Sr., *Newberry*....1954

Mrs. Sarah Jane Guess, *Denmark* 1953

Mrs. Mary Briggs Baskin, *Bishopville*..1952

Mrs. Lottie Coyner Muller,
Blythewood....................................1951

Mrs. E. P. Kennedy, *Aiken* 1950

Mrs. Blanche Mobley Creech,
Spartanburg 1949

Mrs. Constance Furman Herbert,
Sumter..1948

Mrs. John William Thurmond,
Edgefield 1947

Mrs. Andrew J. Evans, *Dillon*................1946

Mrs. A. C. Holler, *Ridge Spring*............1945

Mrs. Annie Hudgens Dunlap,
Mountville 1944

Mrs. P. Frank Price, *Florence*................1943

Mrs. Joseph D. Arthur, Sr., *Union*........1942

SOUTH DAKOTA

Mrs. Marian Jean Randall Nickelson,
Belle Fourche..............................1975

Mrs. Frances "Peg" Lamont,
Aberdeen 1974

Mrs. Inez Dunker Knickrehm, *Verdon*.1973

Mrs. Ruby Frances Judy Johnston
Hersrud, *Black Hawk* 1972

Mrs. Minnie Homuth Lundquist,
Erwin..1971

Mrs. Alice Carolyn Morrison McGibney,
Spearfish 1970

Mrs. Edna Lass Mundt, *Mobridge*..........1969

Mrs. Naomi Eddy Knudsen, *Rosholt* 1968

Mrs. Barbara S. Graff, *Clark*................1967

Mrs. Grace L. Sherwood Monroe,
Sioux Falls..................................1966

Mrs. Virginia Lee Cotton Stoltz,
Watertown....................................1965

*Mrs. Cora Stavig, *Sioux Falls* 1964

Mrs. Lillian Calvert Lushbough,
Sturgis..1963

Mrs. Virginia Shawkey Weeks,
Vermillion 1962

Mrs. Grace Parry Nelson,
Rural Stickney..............................1961

Mrs. Nella B. McGregor, *Pierre* 1960

Mrs. Lena Kemnitz, *Aberdeen* 1959

Mrs. Frencys M. Naslund, *Faith*............1958

Mrs. Alvilda Myre Sorenson,
Brookings......................................1957

Mrs. Ida B. Alseth, *Lake Preston*............1956

Mrs. H. J. Peterson, *Bryant*....................1955

Mrs. Walter Hellmann, *Millboro* 1954

Mrs. Kate Sabin Nachtigal, *Platte*.........1953

Mrs. Harriet C. Meagham Horning,
Watertown....................................1952

Mrs. Lewis Larson, *Sioux Falls*..............1951

Mrs. John N. Melin, *Aberdeen*................1950

Mrs. Flora Radcliffe Harmon,
Springfield....................................1949

Mrs. Gertrude Lenz, *Conde* 1948

Mrs. John L. Pyle, *Huron* 1947

Mrs. William Gregory Lacey,
Sioux Falls..................................1946

Mrs. H. A. McKee, *Mitchell* 1945

Mrs. Mathilda Geppert, *Vermillion*.......1944

Mrs. Blanche McNickle, *Doland*..............1943

TENNESSEE

Mrs. Josephine Wainman Burson,
Memphis..1975

Mrs. Grace Stanton Webb, *Athens* 1974

Mrs. Marie Burke Moore, *Memphis*.......1973

Mrs. Doris Hickman Jarrett,
Lexington......................................1972

Mrs. Irene Whitehead Miller,
Johnson City................................1971

*Mrs. Dorothy Lee Wilson, *Memphis*......1970

Mrs. Elizabeth Moss Brown,
Dyersburg....................................1969

Mrs. Barnette Mildred Evans Mills,
Oak Ridge 1968

Mrs. James M. Campbell, *Memphis* 1967

Mrs. Corinne Calhoun Bailey,
Clarksville....................................1966

Mrs. Jean H. Edgar, *Athens*....................1965

Mrs. Ada Hawley Rogers,
Johnson City................................1964

Mrs. Anna Louise Ward Henry, Sr.,
Pulaski 1963

Mrs. Christina Elizabeth Phillips
Forrester, *Watertown*....................1962

*Mrs. Louise Sevier Giddings Currey,
Lookout Mountain..........................1961

Mrs. Leah Carter Knox, *Nashville*........1960

Mrs. Mary Merrill Emilich Shadow,
Decatur..1959

Mrs. Myrtle Ferguson Christenberry,
Knoxville......................................1958

Mrs. Annie Bass Wiley, *Halls*................1957

Mrs. Louise Malone Ross,
Germantown 1956

Mrs. Novella Ramsey Burks, *Columbia*1955

Mrs. Fred T. Fowler, *Somerville* 1954

Mrs. Maybelle Good Clement, *Dickson* 1953

Mrs. Lillian Neblett Scott, *Memphis* 1952

Mrs. Elmore M. Godfrey, Jr.,
Fountain City................................1951

Mrs. Willard M. McCallum, *Henderson*1950

Mrs. Charles Clifton Rogers,
Dyersburg....................................1949

Mrs. Iona Elizabeth Householder,
Knoxville......................................1948

Mrs. Newman Brandon, Jr., *Nashville*.1947

Mrs. John L. Wade, *Johnson City*..........1946

Mrs. E. A. Andrews, *Signal Mountain*.1945

Mrs. Walter M. White, *Nashville*..........1944

Mrs. Frank S. Osborne, *Columbia*..........1943

TEXAS

Mrs. Camille Shield Wallace,
Fort Worth....................................1975

Mrs. Madie Ellen McElveen Barrow,
Brazoria..1974

Mrs. Viola Kellum Redmond, *Austin*...1973

Mrs. Margaret Lois Killingsworth Jackson,
Longview......................................1972

Mrs. Lois Ann Evins Lien, *Lewisville*..1971

Mrs. Bobbie Davis Jones, *Galveston*......1970

*Mrs. Evelyn Peterson LeTourneau,
Longview......................................1969

Mrs. Mary L. Chesnut Fisher,
Kerrville 1968

Mrs. Betty B. Dodson, *Del Rio* 1967

Mrs. Nora Lee Wendland, *Temple*.........1966

Mrs. Nathanella S. Berling, *Houston* 1965

Mrs. Anna Emma Jahn Biesele,
Austin..1964

Mrs. Jennie Dysart Holcomb,
Wellington..1963

Mrs. Janet Baines Brockett, *Arlington*1961

Mrs. Lucy Rede Franco, *Presidio*...........1960

Mrs. Linnie B. Bowmer, *Temple*...........1959

Mrs. Jessie D. Boardman, *Amarillo*......1958

Mrs. Arabella Owens Brindley,
Temple...1956

Mrs. W. C. Schutts, *Fort Worth*.............1955

Mrs. Rolla C. Vestal, *Whitewright*........1954

Mrs. S. E. Tucker, *Wortham*...................1953

Mrs. W. M. Blake, *Lubbock*.....................1952

Mrs. M. L. Ramey, *Denton*......................1951

Mrs. Preston H. Dial, *San Antonio*.......1950

*Mrs. Pearle Owens Gillis, *Fort Worth*..1949

Mrs. Lavinia Parker McDaniel,
Abilene..1948

Mrs. George T. Jester, *Corsicana*..........1947

Mrs. Ella Stevens Watson, *Hillsboro*....1946

Mrs. M. S. Dockum, *Corsicana*...............1945

*Mrs. Grace Noll Crowell, *Dallas*............1938

UTAH

Mrs. Elva Acklam Stark,
Salt Lake City..1975

Mrs. Florence Todd Britsch, *Orem*........1974

Mrs. Caroline Eyring Miner,
Salt Lake City..1973

Dr. Virginia F. Cutler, *Provo*.................1972

Mrs. Cecil Mann Fisher, *Orderville*.......1971

Mrs. Alta Estella Cutler Rust, *Vernal*.1970

Mrs. Elizabeth Peterson McKay,
Ogden..1969

Mrs. Kathleen Smith Farnsworth,
Beaver...1968

Mrs. Marian G. Nielson, *Blanding*........1967

Mrs. Irene Thompson Fletcher, *Logan*.1966

*Mrs. Lorena Chipman Fletcher, *Provo*.1965

Mrs. Lurena E. Warnick,
Pleasant Grove.......................................1964

Mrs. Ora Nelson Anderson,
Brigham City..1963

Mrs. Ethel Dimond Smith, *Murray*......1962

Mrs. Nettie Jane Barber Wilcox,
Kaysville...1961

Mrs. Grace Watkins Senderegger,
Midway..1960

Mrs. Eva Leona Hansen Carlson,
Richmond...1959

Mrs. Elsie Richards Kohler, *Midway*....1958

Mrs. Genevieve Raine Curtis,
Salt Lake City..1957

Mrs. Luella Adams Dalton, *Parowan*...1956

*Mrs. Lavina Christensen Fugal,
Pleasant Grove.......................................1955

Mrs. David O. McKay, *Salt Lake City*.1954

Mrs. Luella Wakefield Washburn,
Salt Lake City..1953

Mrs. Cora Lindsay Bennion,
Salt Lake City..1952

Mrs. John C. Swenson, *Provo*.................1951

Mrs. James H. Linford, *Logan*...............1950

Mrs. Roland A. Madsen,
Brigham City..1949

Mrs. Mina Murdock Broadbent,
Salt Lake City..1948

Mrs. Wilfred W. Richards, *Logan*..........1947

Mrs. H. Ray Pond, *Richmond*.................1946

VERMONT

Mrs. Helen Hersey Dick, *Springfield*....1975

Mrs. Earlene Mildred Dalysympe Fitch,
Wilmington..1974

Mrs. Katheryn N. McKenzie Haugsrud,
Arlington...1973

Mrs. Georgina Manfirni Bottamini,
Barre...1972

Mrs. Irene R. McCormack, *Rutland*......1971

Mrs. Madge Taylor Hamilton,
West Brattleboro....................................1970

Mrs. Allie May Peck Lourie, *Rupert*....1969

Mrs. Phyllis Ovitt Dudley,
East Montpelier.....................................1968

Mrs. Mary B. Maynard, *Wilmington*....1967

Mrs. Margaret Bruce Nye, *Milton*.........1966

Mrs. Sophie F. Cassin, *Rutland*.............1965

Mrs. Helen R. Merriam, *Lyndonville*....1963

Mrs. Eileen Calvin McGinley,
North Springfield..................................1961

Mrs. Martha McCain Bucklin, *Rutland*1959

Mrs. Grace Merithew Crossman, *Ira*....1956

Mrs. Ellen Bailey Goodell,
Wells River...1955

Mrs. Clarence P. Cowles, *Burlington*....1954

Mrs. Fanny Hurlburt Bicknell,
Jerico Center..1953

Mrs. Mary Barry Branon, *Fairfield*......1952

Mrs. Thomas S. Brown,
South Burlington...................................1951

Mrs. Martin J. Paulsen, *Danville*..........1950

Mrs. Prudence Stickney Mayo,
Northfield...1949

Mrs. Margaret Veronica Condon,
Pittsford...1948

Mrs. Edward L. Rowe, *Peacham*...........1947

Mrs. Floyd B. Jenks, *Cleveland, Ohio*...1946

Mrs. Severus Westin, *Proctor*................1945

Mrs. William H. Wills, *Bennington*.......1944

Mrs. Inez M. Bryan, *Montpelier*...........1942

VIRGINIA

Mrs. Corria Ann Ball Ellis Ratliff,
Grundy...1975

Mrs. Mary Frances Warden Lambert,
Richmond...1974

Mrs. Anna Beahm Mow, *Roanoke*.........1973

Mrs. Mary Katherine Houchins Puliam,
Blacksburg..1972

Mrs. Lovona Millard Glave, *Ashland*....1971

Mrs. Marion Louise Stevens Gearreald,
Norfolk..1970

Mrs. Winifred Cabel Skinnell Davis,
Rocky Mount...1969

Mrs. Catherine Jane Mason Swezey,
Waynesboro...1968

Mrs. Epsie Baldwin Vale, *Farmville*......1967

Mrs. Katherine Kirk Bain, *Crozet*.........1966

Mrs. Nolie D. Lee, *DeWitt*.....................1965

Mrs. Helen McHenry Holliday Holt,
Staunton..1964

Mrs. Saluda Bugg Evans, *Forksville*.....1963

Mrs. Ellen Bell Magill, *Blacksburg*.......1962

Mrs. Virginia Quarles Jarrett,
Richmond...1961

Mrs. Mila Lillian Reynolds Sibold,
Newport...1960

Mrs. Eula Lee Kennedy Long,
Roanoke...1959

Mrs. Norman C. Bailey, *Orange*............1958

Mrs. Anne Page Johns, *Richmond*.........1957

Mrs. Leona Edwards Trippeer,
Roanoke...1956

Mrs. Elizabeth Phelps Rucker, *Moneta*.1955

Mrs. James S. Higgins, *Hopewell*...........1954

Mrs. Leah Sykes Young, *Courtland*......1953

Mrs. Louisa Gilmer Edmunds, *Halifax*1952

Mrs. John Titus Glick, *Bridgewater*......1951

Mrs. Henry Clay Graybeal, *Radford*.....1950

Mrs. Louis Spilman, *Waynesboro*...........1949

Mrs. Mary Whitworth Calcott, *Norfolk*1948

Mrs. Robert Bird Jennings, *Roanoke*....1947

Mrs. John L. Fairly, *Richmond*...............1946

Mrs. Thomas W. Smith, *Richmond*........1945

Mrs. L. Irving Thomas, *Richmond*.........1944

WASHINGTON

Mrs. Mary Elizabeth Tooze Price,
Port Orchard..1975

Mrs. Lora Wilkins Magnusson,
Spokane...1974

Mrs. Suncion Buyson Dela-Cruz,
Seattle...*1973*

Mrs. Eva Jordan Miller, *Port Angeles*..1972

Mrs. Grace Ireme Montgomery,
Banton City...1971

Mrs. Victoria A. Freeman, *Longview*....1970

Mrs. Edna Cathern Dickson Karlinsey,
Tacoma..1969

Mrs. Alice Bush Leonard, *Concrete*.......1968

Mrs. Thelma C.M. Fullner, *Everson*......1967

Mrs. Alice Pearl Brain, *Thorp*...............1966

Mrs. Joyce S. Cheeka, *Olympia*..............1965

Mrs. Mary Ann Campbell Bigelow,
Olympia...1964

Mrs. Xerpha McCulloch Gaines,
Pullman...1963

Mrs. Victoria T. Ott, *Irby*.......................1962

Mrs. Maude Kimball Butler,
Cathlamet...1961

Mrs. Rose Wetherell Nelson, *St. Johns* 1960

Mrs. Bertha M. Tollefson, *Tacoma*........1959

Mrs. Blanche M. Allen, *Spokane*............1958

Mrs. Anna Mae McGrath Martin,
Walla Walla..1957

Mrs. Frances Swayze, *Tacoma*...............1956

Mrs. Hilda O. Leak, *Kelso*......................1955

Mrs. Benjamin David Morrison,
Puyallup..1954

Mrs. Marie Agnes Page, *Spokane*..........1953

Mrs. John L. Hill, *Longview*..................1952

Mrs. Floyd L. Perry, *Pasco*....................1951

Mrs. J. D. McCannon, *Spokane*..............1946

Mrs. George Buchan, *Seattle*..................1944

WEST VIRGINIA

Mrs. Ruth Stephenson Norman,
Charleston...1975

Mrs. Ruth Mansberger Shearer,
  Philippi 1974

Mrs. Eleanor Lee Gay Chandler,
  Charleston 1973

Mrs. Edith Naismith Barbar,
  Charlestown 1972

Mrs. Rose Mary Howard, *Charleston*....1971

Mrs. Allie Gay Murphy Steorts, *Clay*...1970

Mrs. Gladys Marie Adkins Dodson,
  Charleston 1969

Mrs. Pauline Dunfee Douthant,
  Huntington...1968

Mrs. Evelyn H. Smith, *Huntington*.......1967

Mrs. Virginia Robertson Tompkins,
  Charleston 1966

Mrs. Edna McGuire Keith, *Spencer*.......1965

Mrs. Mary Lucille Ferrick Kiessling,
  Huntington......................................y....1964

Mrs. Blanche Ballard, *Fayetteville*.........1963

Mrs. Grace Bengel Sullivan, *Pennsboro*1962

Mrs. Mary Dunkle Ruddle, *Franklin* ...1961

Mrs. Emma Marjorie Jerry Welden,
  Morgantown 1960

Mrs. Marguerite Johnson White,
  Bridgeport 1959

Mrs. Elsie C. Baber, *Morgantown*..........1958

Mrs. Mabel Turley Sims,
  Pence Springs......................................1957

Mrs. Lily Samples Shafer, *Clendenin*...1956

Mrs. Marie McClune Lewis,
  Moundsville 1955

Mrs. Antoinette Tiano Colombo,
  Nutter Fort..1954

Mrs. Florence Hanlin Johnston,
  Wierton..1953

Mrs. Ersula Williams S. Halterman,
  Moorefield..1952

Mrs. Alex R. Thompson, *Alderson*.........1951

Mrs. Rufina Dunbar, *Gauley Bridge* 1950

Mrs. F. H. Brown, *Summersville* 1949

Mrs. Lennie Crim J. Myers, *Philippi* ...1948

Mrs. Ernest D. Conaway, *Morgantown* 1947

WISCONSIN

Mrs. Jessie Hill McCanse, *Madison*.......1975

Mrs. Velma Bell Hamilton, *Alma*..........1974

Mrs. Bernita Doebbert Ness, *Alma*.......1973

Mrs. Bernice Elizabeth McCorkel,
  Superior 1972

Mrs. Elaine Meyer Marquardt,
  Tigerton 1971

Mrs. Alice Bigley Snow, *Clintonville*....1970

Mrs. Marren Bruhn Henry, *Baraboo*.....1969

Mrs. Mareta Kahlenberg, *Two Rivers*..1968

Mrs. Constance W. Elvehjem,
  Madison..1967

Mrs. Dorothy Amanda Wallace Branham,
  Rice Lake...1966

Mrs. Julia T. Jacobson, *Hixton* 1965

Mrs. Josephine Sullivan Nixon,
  Ontario...1964

Mrs. Anna Dahl Iverson, *Mt. Harab*.....1963

Mrs. Victoria Sobezyk Baclawski,
  Superior 1962

Mrs. Bess Marie Anderson Spees,
  Oshkosh..1961

Mrs. Katherine Warren Sutherland,
  Milwaukee..1960

Mrs. Clarence A. Muth, *Wauwatosa*......1959

Mrs. Emma Caroline Walter, *Phillips*..1957

Mrs. Attabelle Jane Harris,
  River Falls...1953

Mrs. Metta Iren Tremper, *Kenosha* 1952

Mrs. Woods Dreyfus, *Milwaukee* 1951

Mrs. Harry Spence, *Milwaukee*...............1950

Mrs. Charles E. Van Hecke,
  Stevens Point 1947

Mrs. Carl Bong, *Poplar* 1946

Mrs. J. W. Boren, *Marinette* 1945

WYOMING
  —None— 1975

Mrs. Hazel Huff Wiley, *Manderson*.......1974

Mrs. Rosaline Leola Fair Hefele,
  Douglas...1973

Mrs. Elizabeth Winninger Hirchcock,
  Laramie 1972

Mrs. Veoma McArthur Stahle, *Basin*...1971

Mrs. Andja Raicevich, *Cody*....................1970

Mrs. Helen Bishop Dunnewald,
  Laramie 1969

Mrs. Annemarie Lembcke, *Laramie*.....1968

Mrs. Beulah Grace Meier, *Kemmerer*...1967

Mrs. Mary Bevan Berry, *Cheyenne*........1966

Mrs. Carrie J. Murdock, *Pinedale* 1965

Mrs. Mary Elizabeth Ford, *Laramie*.....1964

Mrs. Jennie Clark Powell, *Saratoga*......1963

Mrs. Mary Forbes Coffey Thomson,
  New Castle 1962

Mrs. Lois Hall Lamb, *Casper*.................1961

Mrs. Grace Stevenson Fillerup, *Lovell*..1960

Mrs. Jean Willard Brooks Lathrop,
  Casper..1959

Mrs. Phoebe E. Stout, *Casper* 1958

Mrs. Mary Estella Brown Harmon,
  Afton 1956

Mrs. Tandy Brown, *Cheyenne* 1954

Mrs. Marie Swanson Lofgren,
  Sheridan 1953

Mrs. Elvira Sostrom Peck, *Riverton*......1952

Mrs. Alvah F. Brubaker, *Glenrock*.........1951

Mrs. Lloyd Taggart, Sr., *Cody*................1950

Mrs. Frank Howard, *Wheatland* 1945

Mrs. Annabelle Hufsmith, *Casper*.........1944

Indicates American Mother of the Year

Bibliography

Arizona

Special Credits at Bank
Burt Firemann, History Dept., Arizona State University

Colorado

Western History Dept.
The Denver Public Library
The Colorado State Historical Society
Mr. Ralph Taylor, Historian

District of Columbia

National Council of Negro Women
The Columbia Historical Society
"Famous Virginians"

Idaho

References and authorities
Sacajawea, by Grace Raymond Hebard, University of Wyoming, Lewis and Clark Journals, *Idaho Yesterdays*, Vol. 2, No. 2, 1958; *The Idaho Story*, Vol. 2, by Poets and Writer's Guild.

Kansas

Dwight D. Eisenhower Library
The Menninger Foundation
Kansas State Historical Society
Resources
White's Mother Pushed for Civil Rights, by Edna Sherman, *Topeka Capitol Journal*, February 1, 1970.
Autobiography, by William Allen White, The Macmillan Company, 1946.
Condensed from *Papers of Clarina I. H. Nicols*, edited by Joseph G. Gambone, *Kansas Historical Society Quarterly*, Volumes 56, 57.
Notable American Women, Belknap Press, Harvard University, 1971.

Maine

Mothers of Maine, by Helen C. Beedy, Portland, Thurston Print, 1895.
Notable American Women, 1607-1950, Vol. II, by Mary Hoxie Jones, Cambridge, Mass., Belknap Press of Harvard University, 1971.
A Procession of Friends, Quakers in America, by Daisy Newman, Garden City, New York, Doubleday & Company, Inc., 1972.
Helen C. Beedy, Portland, Thurston Print, 1895.
Notable American Women, 1607-1950, Vol. III, by Richard D. Birdsall, Cambridge, Mass., Belknap Press of Harvard University, 1971.
The Maine Book, by Henry E. Dunnack, Augusta, Maine, 1920.
Historic Churches and Homes of Maine, Maine Writers Research Club, Portland, Falmouth Book House, 1937.

Maryland

Side-lights on Maryland History, with Sketches of Early Maryland Families, by Hester Dorsey Richardson, Cambridge, Md., Tidewater Publishers, 1967, p. 44.
Ibid. p. 23.
Richardson, pp. 23-67.
The Lords Baltimore, by Nan Hayden Agle and Frances Atchinson Bacon, New York, Holt, Rinehart, and Winston, 1962.
My Maryland, by Beta Kaessmann, Baltimore, Md., Maryland Historical Society, 1955.
Princess Mary of Maryland, by Nan Hayden Agle, New York, Charles Scribner's, 1956.

Massachusetts

Letter and Familiar Letters, by Abigail Adams.
Builders of New England, by Shirley Barker, Dodd, Mead and Co., 1965.
Profiles and Portraits of American Presidents and Their Wives, by Margaret Bassett.
Portraits of American Women, by Gamaliel Bradford, Houghton-Mifflin Co., 1917.

Girls Who Became Famous, by Thomas Y. Crowell, 1886.
Mothers of America, by Elizabeth Logan Davis.
Times to Remember, by Rose Kennedy.
Eleanor L. Shea, Womens' Editor, *Transcript-Telegram*.
Women 1770 to Present, Radcliff-Harvard Press, 1950.
Newspapers and family biographical sketches.
Personal interviews and letters with telephone calls and photographs from contemporary family members.
Encyclopedia Britannica
Who's Who 1960

Michigan

Michigan Women in the Civil War, Michigan Civil War Centennial Observance Commission, 1965.
Courage Was the Fashion, by Alice Tarbell Crathern, Wayne University Press, 1953.
Women of the War, by Frank Moore, S.S. Scranton & Company, 1867.
Michigan Women, by Georgiady, Romano & Lusk, Franklin Pub., Milwaukee, Wis., 1970.
The Believer, by Clancy and Davies, Coward-McCann, Inc., New York, 1960.
Michigan, by Willis F. Dunbar, Eerdmans Publishing Company, 1965.
History of the City of Grand Rapids, by Baxter, Munsell & Company, 1891.
Leaves From Our Lives, Women's Press Club of Michigan, 1891.
Geography in the Grades, by Etta Wilson, Department of Public Instruction, 1898.
Nurse and Spy in the Union Army, by S. Emma Edmonds, W. S. Williams & Co., Hartford, Conn., 1865.
Lucinda Hinsdale Stone, by Belle McArthur Perry, Blinn Publishing Company, 1902.
A Woman's Life Work, by Haviland, S. B. Shaw Publisher, 1881.
One Woman's Work for Farm Women, by Jennie Buell, Thomas Todd, Boston, 1908.
The Story of Grand Rapids, by Z. Z. Lydens, Kregel Publications, 1966.

Minnesota

Wright County Journal

Waverly Press

American Red Cross Volunteer Publication, St. Paul Area Chapter

Personal Interview

Whipple-Wright and Allied Families, by Charles H. Whipple, Commercial Printing House, Los Angeles, 1917.

Fifty Years of Church Work in the Diocese of Minnesota, by The Rev. George C. Tanner, D.D., St. Paul, 1909.

Saint Mary's Hall 1866-1966, by Mary Stevenson Thomas, Faribault, 1966.

The Faribault Democrat, July 18, 1890.

Who's Who, Minnesota Women 1924, p. 307.

Minnesota Posten, Oct. 27, 1950 and Mar. 23, 1961.

Republican Daily Eagle, Red Wing, Mar. 15, 1961.

West Central Daily Tribune, Willmar, Mar. 18, 1961.

Stageberg Family Bible.

Ole Williamson Family, a private family history.

The Friend, June 1947.

Minnesota State Medical Association

University of North Dakota Alumni Review

Various local newspaper articles, unidentified

Grand Forks Herald

Autobiography of Lena Hetteen Olson, oldest daughter of Mör Hetteen, now in Harriet Olson's memoirs.

Memoirs of Sylvia Hetteen Lisell from accounts told her by her mother Lydia Hetteen, third daughter of Mör Hetteen.

Social Studies for Minnesota Schools, by Vannest, Smith, Lindquist, Clark, Seventh Year. C. 1936.

The North Land: A History of Roseau County.

Picture from Sylvia Hetten Lisell of Mör and Far Hëtteen.

In behalf of the Roseau County Historical Society

Verona (Stubbs) Devney—Bibliography.

Her Idea Grew and Grew, by John G. Hubbell.

How One Woman Shook Up Church Work, by Richard C. Davids, Farm Journal, June, 1968.

Operation H.O.P.E. Newsletters

Northfield Sews and Ecumenical Seam, pp. 83-84, Catholic Digest, May, 1967.

Readers Digest

The History of Redwood County, Minnesota, compiled by Franklyn Curtiss-Wedge, Vol. II, Chicago, H.C. Cooper, Jr. & Co., 1916, pp. 910-911.

Who's Who in Minnesota, Minnesota Editorial Association, 1941, Minneapolis, pp. 464-465.

Redwood, Story of a County, by W.E. Webb and J.I. Swedberg, Redwood County Board of Commissioners, 1964.

St. Paul Pioneer Press, special article, Jan. 21, 1954. Obituary, Jan. 28, 1956.

Additional Resource: Collection of letters in the possession of Dr. B.F. Fuller, Jr.

Floral Homes: or First Years of Minnesota, by Harriet E. Bishop, New York, 1857.

History of St. Paul and Vicinity, Vol. I, by Henry A. Castle, Chicago, 1912.

Fifty Years in the Northwest, by W. H. C. Folsom, St. Paul, 1888.

Dakota Land or The Beauty of St. Paul, by Colonel Hankins, New York, 1868.

Indian Chiefs of Southern Minnesota, by Thomas Hughes, Mankato, 1927.

Minnesota Historical Society Collections, Vol. 4, History of the City of St. Paul and the County of Ramsey.

Minnesota Historical Society Collections, Vol. 14 and 17.

Minnesota Historical Society *Scrapbooks*, Vol. 80, 9, 12 and 15.

Minnesota History, Vol. 14, 1933, pp. 86-87.

Minnesota History, Vol. 38, No. 3, Sept. 1962, p. 131.

Old Rail Fence Corners, by Lucy Leavenworth Morris, Austin, 1914.

Indian Legends of Minnesota Lakes, by T. M. Newson, Minneapolis, 1881.

Pen Pictures of St. Paul, Minnesota, by T. M. Newson, St. Paul, 1886.

Thrilling Scenes Among the Indians, by T. M. Newson, Chicago, 1884.

Mss Reminisceness of Thomas A. Robertson, 1918. Manuscript Dept., M. H. S.

St. Paul *Daily Press*, March 28, 1873 and May 1, 1873.

St. Paul *Daily Press*, March 8, 1868.

St. Paul *Minnesota Pioneer*, March 13 and 20, 1850.

Taopi's letter to H. B. Whipple, Feb. 3, 1869, Manuscript Dept., M. H. S.

The Literary Northwest, January, 1893, Vol. II, No. 4, St. Paul, D. D. Merrill.

Mss Transactions of the Trial of Shakopee and Medicine Bottle. Manuscript Dept., M. H. S.

U. S. Indian Office Records. Census of Fort Snelling in 1862. Manuscript Dept., M. H. S.

Journal of the Rev. S. D. Hinnan, Missionary to the Santee Sioux Indians and Taopi, by H. B. Whipple, Philadelphia, 1869.

Mss. H. B. Whipple Papers, Manuscript Dept., M. H. S.

History of Dakota County, by J. Fletcher Williams, Minneapolis, 1881.

Minneapolis Journal April 2, 1907, Obituary.

Three Score Years and Ten, by Charlotte Ouisconsin Van Cleve, Minneapolis, Harrison and Smith, 1888, p. 78.

Three Score Years and Ten, by Van Cleve.

Minneapolis Journal, April 2, 1907.

The Van Cleve Family, by Horatio P. Van Cleve, New York, privately published, 1959, Van Cleve family tree, p. 6; *History of Hennepin County and the City of Minnespolis*, by George E. Warner, Minneapolis, North Star Publishing Company, 1881, p. 649.

The Van Cleve Family, by H. P. Van Cleve, pp. 38, 39.

See Horatio Phillips Van Cleve and Family Papers in Minnesota Historical Society.

Three Score Years and Ten, by Van Cleve.

Minneapolis Journal, April 2, 1907.

Undated letters [1880s] of Charlotte O. Van Cleve in Van Cleve Papers.

Presidential address of Charlotte O. Van Cleve, undated [188?], in Van Cleve Papers.

Presidential address.

Three Score Years and Ten, by Van Cleve, p. 89, on slavery; p. 57, on Indians; and *History of Hennepin County*, by Warner, p. 650, on suffrage.

Minneapolis Journal, April 2, 1907, Obituary; *The Van Family*, by H. P. Van Cleve, pp. 42, 43, Deafness and blindness.

See, for example, diary, 1904, Van Cleve Papers.

Minnesota, Its Story and Biography, by Henry A. Castle, Chicago and New York, Lewis Publishing Company, 1915.

Sketch of General and Mrs. H. P. Van Cleve Pioneers of the Northwest, by Clara Peabody Crocker, Minneapolis, no publisher, 1920. In Horatio P. Van Cleve and Family Papers.

Charlotte Ouisconsin Clark: A True Pioneer Woman of the Northwest, by Ona B. Earll, in *Wisconsin Magazine*, September 1926, pp. 13, 19.

Encyclopedia of Biography of Minnesota, History of Minnesota, by Charles E. Flandreau, Vol. 1, Chicago, New Century Publishing and Engraving Company, 1900.

Fifty Years in the Northwest, by W. H. C. Folsom, St. Paul, Pioneer Press Company, 1888.

Who's Who Among Minnesota Women, Mary Dillon Foster, compiler and publisher, St. Paul, 1924.

Helena Herald, August 18, 1869.

Minneapolis Journal, April 2, 1907, Obituary.
Minneapolis Tribune, April 5, 1907, Obituary.
St. Paul Dispatch, April 2, 1907, Obituary.
St. Paul Pioneer Press, April 5, 1907, Obituary.
Minnesota Biographies 1655-1912, Collections of the Minnesota Historical Society, by Upham, Warren and Rose B. Dunlap, Vol. XIV, St. Paul, Minnesota Historical Society, 1912.
Three Score Years and Ten, by Charlotte O. Van Cleve, Minneapolis, Harrison and Smith, 1888.
Van Cleve, Horatio Phillips and Family, Papers. Manuscripts collection in Minnesota Historical Society, St. Paul.
The Van Cleve Family, by Horatio P. Van Cleve, New York, privately published, 1959.
History of Hennepin County and the City of Minneapolis, by George E. Warner, Minneapolis, North Star Publishing Company, 1881.

New Hampshire

Stories of New Hampshire, by Eva Speare.
Franklin Pierce, by Roy Franklin Nichols.
New Hampshire Folk Tales, by Mrs. Moody and Mrs. Guy Speare.
The World Book Encyclopedia
The Connecticut and the Valley of the Connecticut, by Edwin M. Bacon.
Whatever Happened to the Cradle, by Ashley Montague.
The Laconia Evening Citizen
Dr. J. Duane Squires, State Historian

New Jersey

State Library, Trenton
Mrs. Rebecca, Colestar

New Mexico

Excerpts from: *Maria, The Potter of San Ildefonso*, by Alice Marriott; *Indian Women*, by Lela and Rufus Waltrip.
Shadows of the Past, by Cleofas M. Jaramillo.
Romance of a Little Village Girl, by Cleofas M. Jaramillo.
Allow Me To Present 18 Ladies and Gentlemen and Taos, New Mexico, by Rebecca Salsbury James.
Trader on the Santa Fe Trail, Lina Fergusson Browne, ed., Calvin Horn Publisher, Inc., Albuquerque, N. M., 1973.
These Were the Valiant, by Ann Nolan Clark, Calvin Horn Publisher, Inc., Albuquerque, N. M. 1969.
Home in the West, by Harvey Fergusson, Duell, Sloan and Pearce, New York, 1944.

North Dakota

State Historical Society

Pennsylvania

Carlos R. Allen, Jr., Professor of History, Widener College, Chester, Penna. 19013.
Mrs. John Carl Foster, Jr., State Regent, Penna. State Society, Daughters of American Colonists, Wyndham Drive, York, Penna. 17403.
Jerry William Frost, Librarian, Friends Historical Library, Swarthmore College, Swarthmore, Panna. 19081.
Reed Harris, President Emeritus, Freedoms Foundation Consultant, The Brookings Institute, 34 S. High Street, West Chester, Pa. 19380.
Mrs. James John, Member, Pennsylvania Historical and Museum Commission, Harrisburg, Pennsylvania 17105.
Mrs. Howard C. Paul, State President, American Mothers Committee, Inc., 10 Crestmont Drive, Pittsburgh, Penna. 15220.
Miss Jane A. Rittenhouse, Associate Librarian, Friends Historical Library, Swarthmore College, Swarthmore, Penna. 19081.

Mrs. H. Everett Sanford, Past President, Pennsylvania Federation of Women's Clubs, 1514 Maple Avenue, Verona, Penna. 15147.
Mrs. F. Karl Witherow, Past President, Republican Women of Pennsylvania, 348 Arbor Way, State College, Penna. 16801.

Puerto Rico

Mujeres de Puerto Rico, by Angela Negrón Muñoz.
Igualdad de Derechos y Oportunidades de la Mujer en P. R.
Lola de America, by Carmen Leila Cuevas.
Hombres y Mujeres de Puerto Rico, by Carlos M. Carreras.
P. R. Living, Special Bicentennial Edition, Tourist Dept.
Comisión de Derechos Civiles, Commonwealth of Puerto Rico.
University of Puerto Rico Library
University of Puerto Rico Library, Mayaguez Branch.
Institute of Puerto Rican Culture, San Juan, P. R.
Arts and Sciences Academy, San Juan, P. R.
El Mundo newspaper library
San Juan Star newspaper, April 18, 1975.
El Mundo newspaper, October 25, 1975, October 29, 1975, November 5, 1946.
San Juan City Hall, Public Relations Dept.
Centro Cultural José de Diego, Aguadilla, P. R.
Ana G. Mendez, by Dr. Antonio Guindulain.

Vermont

Vermont Historical Society
Vermont Historical Library

Wisconsin

Wisconsin Women's Auxiliary of the State Historical Society

**Not all states
furnished a
Bibliography.**

Index of Mothers

632